PRENTICE-HALL SERIES IN ACCOUNTING

Charles T. Horngren, Editor

AUDITING: AN INTEGRATED APPROACH, 2/E
Arens/Loebbecke

FINANCIAL ACCOUNTING: PRINCIPLES AND ISSUES, 2/E
Granof

FINANCIAL STATEMENT ANALYSIS
Foster

INTRODUCTION TO MANAGEMENT ACCOUNTING, 4/E
Horngren

COST ACCOUNTING, 4/E
Horngren

CPA PROBLEMS & APPROACHES TO SOLUTIONS, 5/E VOLUMES I & II
Horngren/Leer

A NEW INTRODUCTION TO FINANCIAL ACCOUNTING, 2/E
May/Mueller/Williams

AUDITING PRINCIPLES, 4/E
Stettler

BUDGETING, 4/E
Welsch

DICTIONARY FOR ACCOUNTANTS, 5/E
Kohler

2nd
edition

AUDITING:
AN
INTEGRATED
APPROACH

Alvin A. Arens, Ph.D., C.P.A.
Price Waterhouse Auditing Professor
Michigan State University

James K. Loebbecke, C.P.A.
Partner
Touche Ross & Co.

Prentice-Hall, Inc., Englewood Cliffs, New Jersey 07632

Library of Congress Cataloging in Publication Data

ARENS, ALVIN A
   Auditing, an integrated approach.

   (Prentice-Hall series in accounting)
   Includes index.
   1. Auditing.   I. Loebbecke, James K., joint author.
II. Title.
HF5667.A69 1980   657′.45   79-28407
ISBN   0-13-051656-2

Editorial/production supervision
   and interior design by Ann Marie McCarthy
Cover design by Wanda Lubelska Design
Manufacturing buyer: Edmund W. Leone

This book contains quotations and adaptations from publications copyrighted
in all years from 1951 through 1978 and © 1979 by the American Institute of
Certified Public Accountants, Inc. Such passages have been reprinted or adapted
with permission of the American Institute of Certified Public Accountants.

Printed in the United States of America

10 9 8 7 6 5 4 3 2

PRENTICE-HALL INTERNATIONAL, INC., *London*
PRENTICE-HALL OF AUSTRALIA PTY. LIMITED, *Sydney*
PRENTICE-HALL OF CANADA, LTD., *Toronto*
PRENTICE-HALL OF INDIA PRIVATE LIMITED, *New Delhi*
PRENTICE-HALL OF JAPAN, INC., *Tokyo*
PRENTICE-HALL OF SOUTHEAST ASIA PTE. LTD., *Singapore*
WHITEHALL BOOKS LIMITED, *Wellington, New Zealand*

CONTENTS

v

3

LEGAL LIABILITY   *77*

4

AUDIT EVIDENCE AND DOCUMENTATION   *109*

5

AUDITOR'S RESPONSIBILITIES AND DECISION PROCESS   *139*

6

UNDERSTANDING THE CLIENT'S BUSINESS AND PLANNING THE ENGAGEMENT   *173*

7

THE STUDY AND EVALUATION OF INTERNAL CONTROL *211*

Objectives.   Divide the System into Transaction Cycles.
Define Detailed Internal Control Objectives.   Elements of Internal Control.
Overview of Audit Process.   Review of the System.   Preliminary Evaluation.
Summary.

8

NATURE OF AUDIT TESTS *256*

Types of Audit Tests.   A Framework—Tests of Transactions.
A Framework—Direct Tests of Financial Balances.
Integration of the Different Parts of the Audit.

9

AUDIT OF THE SALES AND COLLECTION CYCLE *279*

Overview.   Nature of the Sales and Collection Cycle.
Internal Controls and Audit Tests for Sales.
Audit Procedures for Processing of Sales Returns and Allowances.
Internal Controls and Audit Tests for Cash Receipts.
Audit Procedures for Charging Off and Recording Uncollectible Accounts.
Effect of the Results of Tests of Transactions on the Remainder of the Audit.
Appendix A Case Illustration.

10

DETERMINING SAMPLE SIZE USING ATTRIBUTES SAMPLING, AND SELECTING THE ITEMS FOR TESTING *324*

The Nature of the Problem.   Judgmental Sampling.   Random Selection.
Attributes Sampling.   Nature of Attributes Estimates.
Appendix B Case Illustration.

11

COMPLETING THE TESTS IN THE SALES AND COLLECTION CYCLE—ACCOUNTS RECEIVABLE *369*

Review of the Tests of the System.   Direct Tests of Financial Balances.
Confirmation of Accounts Receivable.   Appendix C Case Illustration.

12

THE USE OF VARIABLES SAMPLING IN AUDITING *402*

Comparison with Attributes Sampling.   Population Distributions.
Sampling Distributions.   Statistical Inference.   Statistical Methods.
Confidence Intervals versus Hypothesis Tests.   Beta and Alpha Risks.
Difference Estimation.

13

THE IMPACT OF EDP SYSTEMS ON AUDITING *439*

Impact of EDP on Auditing.   Types of Systems.   Areas of Engagement Concern.
Internal Controls in an EDP System.   Evaluating Internal Control in an EDP System.
Auditing around the Computer.   Auditing with the Use of the Computer.
Generalized Audit Program.   Audit of Computer Service Centers.

14

AUDIT OF THE PAYROLL AND PERSONNEL CYCLE *471*

Nature of the Payroll and Personnel Cycle.   Analytical Review Procedures.
Tests of Transactions.   Direct Tests of Financial Balances.

15

16

17

18

19

AUDIT OF CASH BALANCES   *632*

20

COMPLETING THE AUDIT   *665*

21

SHORT-FORM AUDITOR'S REPORTS   *701*

22

UNAUDITED AND OTHER REPORTS   *737*

PREFACE

OBJECTIVES

The second edition of *Auditing: An Integrated Approach* contains significant changes and revisions, but the objectives and emphasis remain essentially the same.

The book is an introduction to auditing for students who have not had significant experience in auditing. It is intended for either a one quarter or one semester course at the undergraduate or graduate level. The book is also appropriate for introductory professional development courses for CPA firms, internal auditors, and governmental auditors.

The primary emphasis in this text is on the auditor's decision-making process. We believe the most fundamental concepts in auditing relate to determining the nature and amount of evidence the auditor should accumulate after considering the unique circumstances of each engagement. If a student of auditing understands the objectives to be accomplished in a given audit area, the circumstances of the engagement, and the decisions to be made, he or she should be able to determine the appropriate evidence to gather and how to evaluate the evidence obtained.

Thus, as the title of the book reflects, our purpose is to integrate the most important concepts of auditing as well as certain practical aspects in a logical manner to assist students in understanding audit decision-making and evidence accumulation. For example, internal control is integrated into each of the chapters dealing with a particular functional area and is related to tests of transactions; tests of transactions are in turn related to the direct tests of financial statement balances of the accounts for the area; and statistical sampling is applied to the accumulation of audit evidence rather than treated as a separate topic.

MAJOR CHANGES IN THE CURRENT EDITION

The changes incorporated reflect input from four major sources: changes in the profession since the first edition, the authors' classroom experience, comments received over the past several years from textbook adopters, and detailed reviews by a dozen respected auditing educators. The last two sources have been especially influential. The following represent the most important changes:

- Expansion of professional ethics to a full chapter. Special emphasis is placed on independence and the changes in the rules of conduct.
- Expansion of legal liability to a full chapter. The chapter includes a summary of leading cases influencing the profession's development.
- Addition of another chapter on audit reporting. The new material emphasizes special reports and compilation and review.
- Increased emphasis on objectives in determining audit evidence. The internal control, tests of transactions, and direct tests of balances objectives have been modified to make it easier to show their interrelationships.
- Incorporation of the changes in Statements on Auditing Standards throughout the book.
- Introduction to the major influences on the profession in recent years and the resultant changes in the profession. Examples of influence include the Commission on Auditors' Responsibility, Securities and Exchange committees, and the Moss and Metcalf committees.
- Reorganization of certain material. For example, auditing standards and an introduction to audit reports were moved to Chapter 1. Changes of this nature came about because of the authors' teaching experience and comments from reviewers.

ORGANIZATION

It is convenient to think of the book as consisting of eight parts.

Part One includes Chapters 1 through 3. These chapters provide background information and deal with the environment in which auditors function. Chapter 1 defines and describes auditing and different types of audits and auditors. It also introduces the role of the American Institute of CPAs, auditing standards and audit reports, and some of the major challenges facing the profession. Chapter 2 deals with professional ethics of certified public accountants. The chapter emphasizes the importance of auditors' independence and the rules of conduct and their interpretation of the Code of Professional Ethics. Chapter 3 deals with the legal liability of auditors. The emphasis is on the sources and nature of auditors' liability, leading cases affecting auditors, and ways individual auditors and the profession can better protect themselves legally.

Part Two is made up of Chapters 4 and 5. These chapters concern general concepts, audit evidence accumulation, and the documentation of results. Chapter 4 includes a review of the audit process and describes the most important types of evidence and proper documentation of audit tests. Chapter 5 deals with auditors' responsibilities for finding errors and irregularities and the decision-making process that auditors go through in deciding how much evidence to accumulate.

Part Three consists of Chapters 6 through 8. Chapter 6 considers the importance of obtaining an understanding of the client and its business and discusses the means of doing this, including: discussions with client personnel, reference to industry data, examining legal records, calculating ratios, comparing financial information with previous years, and investigating the likelihood of material management fraud. The need to understand the client's business and the environment in which the audit is being conducted is emphasized throughout the book. The study and evaluation of internal control is discussed in Chapter 7 and emphasizes the most important elements in any system, a proper methodology for studying and evaluating the system, and the implications of the results of the study. A unique aspect of Chapter 7 is a set of internal control objectives that relates internal control evaluation to tests of the system. Chapter 8 summarizes Chapters 4 through 7 and integrates them with the remainder of the text. The chapter examines the interrelationship of different types of tests and establishes a general framework for studying tests of transactions and direct tests of balances. It focuses on the importance of the interaction of all tests and the need for specific audit objectives.

Part Four, which includes Chapters 9 through 12, applies the concepts from the first three parts of the book to the audit of sales, cash receipts, and the related income statement and balance sheet accounts. In Chapter 9, the appropriate audit procedures for sales and cash receipts are related to the system of internal control and a set of audit objectives common to all tests of transactions. Determination of an appropriate sample size and deciding which sample items should be tested are considered in Chapter 10, primarily through the use of attributes statistical sampling. Chapter 11 is the study of accounts receivable and the allowance for uncollectible accounts, with emphasis on the relationship of those accounts to the evaluation of internal control and tests of sales and cash receipts transactions. The audit procedures for accounts receivable and all other balance sheet accounts included in the remainder of the text are studied using the audit framework developed in Chapter 8. Chapter 12 discusses the concepts of variables sampling and illustrates their application to accounts receivable.

Part Five includes only Chapter 13, which covers the evaluation of internal control for EDP systems, the audit of systems that include significant

EDP processing, and auditing with and without the use of the computer. The emphasis in this chapter is on the impact of EDP on the way an audit is conducted.

Part Six includes Chapters 14 through 19. Each of these chapters deals with a specific transaction cycle or part of a transaction cycle, in much the same manner as Chapters 9 through 12 deal with the sales and collection cycle. The cycles in Part Five are as follows:

- Payroll and personnel—Chapter 14
- Acquisitions and disbursements—Chapters 15 and 16
- Inventory and warehousing—Chapter 17
- Capital acquisitions and repayments—Chapter 18
- Cash in the bank—Chapter 19 (This chapter indicates the interaction of all of the preceding transaction cycles as they affect cash.)

Each chapter in Part Six is meant to clearly demonstrate the relationship of internal control evaluation and tests of transactions for each broad category of transactions (e.g., general cash disbursements) to the related balance sheet and income statement accounts (e.g., accounts payable and insurance expense). Cash in the bank is studied late in the text to demonstrate how the audit of cash balances is related to most other audit areas.

Part Seven (Chapter 20) is concerned with summarizing all of the audit tests, reviewing working papers, and other aspects of completing the audit.

Part Eight (Chapters 21 and 22) covers the various types of reports issued by auditors. The emphasis in Chapter 21 is on the conditions affecting the type of report the auditor must issue and the type of audit report applicable to each condition under varying levels of materiality. Chapter 22 deals with unaudited and other reports. Compilation and review is examined in detail.

ASSIGNMENT OF CHAPTERS

The book has been designed to provide maximum flexibility in assigning chapters. Certain chapters can be omitted completely without significantly lessening effectiveness. The omitted chapters will reduce the applications of the concepts by studying fewer individual audit areas, but the most important concepts themselves will not be bypassed if the first eleven and last two chapters are studied.

The following are suggestions for assigning chapters:

Chapters 1–11. These chapters include the fundamental concepts in auditing, and, except as modified below, should be studied sequentially. Some instructors may want to delete working papers (last part of Chapter 4), but the other chapters include important fundamental concepts that are interrelated with the remaining chapters of the book. Professional ethics

(Chapter 2) and/or legal liability (Chapter 3) can be studied in sequence or moved to a later part of the course. Some teachers prefer to study these chapters last.

Chapter 12. The study of variables sampling can be conveniently deleted by instructors who are not committed to a heavy emphasis on the use of statistical sampling in auditing. Attributes sampling (Chapter 10) is used more extensively in auditing practice than variables sampling and is such an integral part of the book that it should not be bypassed in ordinary circumstances.

Chapter 13. The study of EDP can be undertaken conveniently after Chapter 7 (internal control) or any time after Chapter 12. It can also be deleted entirely or supplemented with other materials.

Chapters 14–19. One or more of these chapters can be eliminated if the instructor believes that it is unnecessary to study every major audit area in a typical audit. Chapter 14 (payroll) and Chapter 18 (issue and repayment of capital) are likely candidates for omission, but alternative or additional chapters might be deleted. Chapter 16 (accounts payable) should not be studied unless Chapter 15 (acquisitions and disbursements) is assigned first, but it is practical to study Chapter 15 without 16. Certain audit areas in Chapter 16 can also be easily deleted. Chapter 17 (inventory and warehousing) is a useful chapter to demonstrate the interrelationships between different parts of the audit, but it should not be assigned unless Chapter 15, or Chapters 15 and 16, have been studied.

Chapter 20. Completing the audit is an essential part of the book and should be assigned late in the course.

Chapter 21. Short form audit reports can be assigned at any point in the course. Those instructors who believe audit reports should be studied early can assign it as a part of Chapter 1. It would also be acceptable to study the material after Chapters 11, 13, 19, or 20.

Chapter 22. Unaudited and other reports can be assigned at any point in the course as long as they are studied after Chapter 21. The chapter can also be deleted.

ACKNOWLEDGMENTS

We acknowledge the American Institute of Certified Public Accountants for permission to quote extensively from Statements on Auditing Standards, the Code of Professional Ethics, Accounting Principles Board Opinions, Uniform CPA Examinations, and other publications. The willingness of this major accounting organization to permit the use of their materials is a significant contribution to the book.

We also gratefully acknowledge the contributions of the following reviewers for their suggestions: Darwin J. Casler, University of Texas at Arlington; Richard E. Czarnecki, University of Michigan—Dearborn; William L. Felix, Jr., University of Washington; Larry Godwin, Oregon State University; Robert E. Hamilton, University of Minnesota; Robert B. Ilderton, Defense Contract Audit Agency; Henry R. Jaenicke, Franklin and Marshall College; Charles Lawrence, Purdue University; George Mead, Michigan State University; John H. Myers, Indiana University; Don Nichols, University of Kansas; Ernest L. Hicks, Ohio State University, William Timothy O'Keefe, University of Georgia; Larry E. Rittenberg, University of Wisconsin—Madison; Jay M. Smith, Brigham Young University; D. Dewey Ward, Michigan State University; Harold O. Wilson, Middle Tennessee State University; and Alan J. Winters, Louisiana State University.

A special note of thanks is appropriate to Richard L. Hartwick, a Ph.D. student at Michigan State who worked closely with us on all aspects of the book, and to A. Clayton Ostland and Jon Kantrowitz of Touche Ross & Co., who made significant contributions to the professional ethics and legal liability chapters.

The typing and editorial efforts of Ellen Foxman and Marilyn Wenner are also gratefully acknowledged.

Finally, the encouragement and support of our families are acknowledged.

AUDITING

AN OVERVIEW
OF AUDITING

This chapter is intended to present background information about the nature of auditing and the major influences affecting auditing activities.

The first part of the chapter is primarily definitional in nature. It is meant to describe why auditing is needed, what it is, and various types of audits and auditors. Later, the influence of the American Institute of Certified Public Accountants and the nature of generally accepted auditing standards are introduced. A discussion in some detail of the auditor's report is presented, as this is the major tangible result of the audit process. The chapter ends by considering the role of the Securities and Exchange Commission and some of the criticisms currently being leveled against the profession and the profession's response to the criticisms.

NEED FOR RELIABLE INFORMATION

Economic decisions in every society must be based upon the information available at the time the decision is made. For example, the decision of a bank to make a loan to a business is based upon previous financial relationships with that business, the financial condition of the company as reflected by its financial statements, and other factors.

If decisions are to be consistent with the intentions of the decision makers, the information used in the decision process must be *reliable*. Unreliable information can cause inefficient use of resources to the detriment of society and to the decision makers themselves. In the lending decision example, assume that the bank makes the loan on the basis of misleading financial statements and the borrower company is ultimately unable to repay. As a result, the bank has lost both the principal and the interest. In addition, another company that could have used the funds effectively was deprived of the money.

As society becomes more complex, there is an increased likelihood that unreliable information will be provided to decision makers. There are several reasons: remoteness of information, voluminous data, and the existence of complex exchange transactions.

Remoteness of Information

In the modern world it is virtually impossible for a decision maker to have much firsthand knowledge about the organization with which he does business. Information provided by others must be relied on. Whenever information is obtained from others, the likelihood of it being intentionally or unintentionally wrong is increased.

Bias and Motives of Provider

Whenever information is provided by someone whose goals are inconsistent with those of the decision maker, the information will at times be *biased* in favor of the provider of the information. The reason could be an honest optimism about future events or an intentional emphasis designed to influence users in a certain manner. In either case, the result is a misstatement of information. For example, in a lending decision where the borrower provides financial statements to the lender, there is considerable likelihood that the statements will be biased in favor of the borrower to enhance the chance of obtaining a loan. The misstatement could be in the form of outright incorrect dollar amounts being included in the statements or inadequate or incomplete disclosures of information.

Voluminous Data

As organizations become larger, the volume of their exchange transactions increases. This increases the likelihood that improperly recorded information will be included in the records—perhaps buried in a large amount of other information. For example, if a check by a large governmental agency in payment of a vendor's invoice is overstated by $200, there is a fairly good chance it will not be uncovered unless the agency has instituted reasonably complex procedures to check for this type of error. If a large number of minor errors remain undiscovered, the combined total could be significant.

Complex Exchange Transactions

In the past few decades, exchange transactions between organizations have become increasingly complex and hence more difficult to record properly. For example, the correct accounting treatment of the trade-in of manufacturing equipment or the replacement of the roof of a building poses relatively difficult and important problems. Even more difficult is the proper combining and disclosing of the results of operations of subsidiaries in different industries, or the calculation of lease liabilities under Financial Accounting Standards Board Opinion No. 13 (FASB 13) when there are complicated leases and related tax implications.

Need for Independent Verification

As a means of overcoming the problem of unreliable information, the decision maker must develop a method of assuring himself that the information is sufficiently reliable for his decisions. In doing this, he must weigh the cost of obtaining more reliable information against the expected benefits.

A common way to obtain such reliable information is to have some type of verification (*audit*) performed by independent persons. The audited information is then used in the decision-making process on the assumption that it is reasonably complete, accurate, and unbiased. When more than one decision maker uses a particular type of information, it is usually less expensive to have someone perform the audit for all the users than to have each user verify the information individually. Even if only one user relies on the information, it is desirable to have someone with special skills perform the audit function.

NATURE OF AUDITING

Auditing Defined

Auditing is the process of accumulating and evaluating evidence by a competent independent person about quantifiable information of a specific economic entity for the purpose of determining and reporting upon the degree of correspondence between the quantifiable information and established criteria.

This definition includes several key words and phrases that are worth examining briefly at this time. Each of these terms is analyzed more extensively in later chapters. For ease of understanding, the terms are discussed in a different order than they occur in the definition.

Determining the Degree of Correspondence
between Quantifiable Information
and Established Criteria

To do an audit, the information must be in a *verifiable form* and there must be some standards *(criteria)* by which the auditor can determine whether the information is proper.

The quantifiable information can and does take many different forms. It is possible to audit such things as canceled checks and vendors' invoices, the amount of time it takes for an employee to complete an assigned task, the total cost of a government construction contract, and an individual's tax return.

The criteria to evaluate quantitative information can also vary considerably. For example, in auditing a vendor's invoice for the acquisition of raw materials, it is possible to determine whether materials of the quantity and stated description were actually received, whether the proper raw material was acquired considering the production needs of the company, or whether the price charged for the goods was reasonable. The criteria used depend upon the objectives of the audit.

A Specific Economic Entity

Whenever an audit is conducted, boundaries are needed to clarify the scope of the auditor's responsibility. The primary method involves defining the *economic entity* and the *time period*. In most instances the economic entity is also a legal entity, such as a corporation, unit of government, partnership, or proprietorship. In some cases, however, the entity is defined as a division, a department, or even an individual. The time period for conducting an audit is typically one year, but there are also audits for a month, a quarter, several years, and in some cases the lifetime of an entity.

It is not possible to evaluate whether quantifiable information corresponds to established criteria until the economic entity is defined, since one of the primary criteria for evaluating information is whether it is proper for the entity being audited. A simple example is the sole proprietorship, in which the entity under audit is the owner's business. A proper business expense in this situation would be repairs to equipment or the acquisition of raw materials. On the other hand, if the proprietor used funds from the business to buy food for his family or took them on a vacation to the Bahamas, the expenditures would not likely be a proper business expense.

Accumulating and Evaluating Evidence

Evidence is defined as any information used by the auditor to determine whether the quantifiable information being audited is stated in accordance with the established criteria. Evidence takes many different forms, including

4

oral testimony of the auditee (client), written communication with outsiders, and observations by the auditor. It is important to obtain a sufficient quality and volume of evidence in an audit to satisfy the audit objectives. The process of determining the amount of evidence necessary and evaluating whether the quantifiable information corresponds to the established criteria is a critical part of every audit. It is the primary subject of this book.

Competent Independent Person

The auditor must be *qualified* to understand the criteria in use, and he must be *competent* to know the types and amount of evidence to accumulate to reach the proper conclusion after the evidence has been examined. The auditor also must have an *independent mental attitude*. It does little good to have a competent person who is biased performing the evidence accumulation when unbiased information is needed for decision making. Independence is not an absolute concept by any means; there are different degrees of independence. For example, even though an auditor is paid a fee by the company he audits, he may still be sufficiently independent to conduct audits that can be relied upon by users if he is not also an employee of the company.

Reporting

The final stage in the audit process is the *audit report*—the communication of the findings of the audit to users. Reports differ in nature, but in all cases they must inform readers of the degree of correspondence between quantifiable information and established criteria. Reports also differ in form and can vary from a highly technical one of the type usually associated with financial statements to a simple oral report in situations where an audit is conducted for a particular individual. The form and content of any particular report will depend upon the nature of the audit, its purpose, its findings, and the needs of the decision makers who receive it.

TYPES OF AUDITS

The three types of audits discussed in this section are the audit of financial statements, the compliance audit, and the operational audit.

Audit of Financial Statements

An *audit of financial statements* is conducted to determine whether the *overall* financial statements—which are the quantifiable information being verified—are stated in accordance with specified criteria. Normally, the criteria are generally accepted accounting principles, although it is also common to conduct audits of financial statements prepared using the cash basis or some other basis of accounting appropriate for the organization. The financial statements most commonly included are the statement of financial position, the income statement, and the statement of changes of financial position, including accompanying footnotes.

The underlying assumption in auditing financial statements is that they will be used by different groups for different purposes. Therefore, it is more efficient to have one audit firm perform an audit and draw conclusions that can be relied upon by all users than to have each user perform his own audit. If any individual user feels that the general audit does not provide sufficient information for his purposes, he has the option of obtaining more data. For example, a general audit of a business may provide sufficient accounting information for a banker who is considering making a loan to the company, but a corporation considering a merger with that business may also wish to know the replacement cost of fixed assets and other information relevant to the decision. The corporation may use its own auditors to get the information.

Compliance Audit

The purpose of a *compliance audit* is to determine whether the auditee is following specific procedures or rules set down by some higher authority. A compliance audit for a private business could include determining whether accounting personnel are following the procedures prescribed by the company controller, reviewing wage rates for compliance with minimum wage laws, or examining contractual agreements with bankers and other lenders to be sure the company is complying with legal requirements. In the audit of governmental units such as school districts, there is increased compliance auditing due to extensive regulation by higher government authorities. In virtually every private and not-for-profit organization, there are prescribed policies, contractual agreements, and legal requirements that may call for compliance auditing.

Results of compliance audits are generally reported to someone within the organizational unit being audited rather than to a broad spectrum of users. Management, as opposed to outside users, is the primary group concerned with the extent of compliance with certain prescribed procedures and regulations. Hence, a significant portion of all work of this type is done by auditors employed by the organizational units themselves. There are exceptions to this. Whenever an organization wants to determine whether individuals or organizations who are obligated to follow its requirements are actually complying, the auditor is employed by the organization issuing the requirements. An example is the auditing of taxpayers for compliance with the federal tax laws—the auditor is hired by the government to audit the taxpayers' records.

Operational Audit

An *operational audit* is a review of any part of an organization's operating procedures and methods for the purpose of evaluating *efficiency and effectiveness*. At the completion of an operational audit, recommendations to management for improving operations are normally expected.

The conduct of an operational audit and the reported results are normally less well defined than for either compliance or financial statement audits. Efficiency and effectiveness of operations are far more difficult to evaluate objectively than compliance or the presentation of financial statements in accordance with generally accepted accounting principles.

Because of the many different areas in which operational effectiveness can be evaluated, it is impossible to characterize the conduct of a typical operational audit. In one organization the auditor might evaluate the relevancy and sufficiency of the information used by management in making decisions to acquire new fixed assets, while in a different organization he might evaluate the efficiency of the paper flow in processing sales. In operational auditing, the reviews are not limited to accounting. They can include the evaluation of organizational structure, computer operations, production methods, marketing, and any other area where the auditor is qualified.

Establishing criteria for evaluating the quantifiable information in an operational audit is an extremely *subjective* matter. In practice, operational auditors are usually more concerned with making recommendations for improving performance than with reporting on the effectiveness of existing performance. In this sense, operational auditing is more similar to management consulting than to what is generally regarded as auditing.

TYPES OF AUDITORS

In this section the four most widely known types of auditors are discussed briefly. They are: certified public accountants, general accounting office auditors, internal revenue agents, and internal auditors.

Certified Public Accountants

Certified public accountants (CPAs) have as their primary responsibility the performance of the audit function on published financial statements of all publicly traded companies and most other reasonably large companies. Because of the important role of published financial statements in the U.S. economy, as well as businessmen's and statement users' familiarity with these statements, it is common to use the terms *auditor* and *CPA* synonymously even though there are many different types of auditors. Another term frequently used to describe CPAs is *independent auditors*.

The use of the title "certified public accountant" is regulated by state law through the licensing departments of each state. The requirements for becoming a CPA vary among states. All states require that an individual pass a national standardized examination to qualify as a CPA. In addition to the CPA examination, many states require qualifying experience of two or three years in the profession before an individual becomes a CPA. The purpose of these requirements is to protect financial statement users from auditors who do not have minimum qualifications.

A distinction should be made between certified public accountants and public accountants. Some states license public accountants; in other states, individuals refer to themselves as public accountants even though they are not formally designated as such. In most states only individuals designated as certified public accountants are permitted to do audits. Public accountants ordinarily perform bookkeeping services and related tax and consulting services. It is uncommon for CPAs to refer to themselves as public accountants, but the use of a phrase such as "involved in public accounting" is commonly associated with CPAs.

General Accounting Office Auditors

The United States General Accounting Office (GAO) is a nonpartisan agency in the legislative branch of the federal government. The GAO, which is headed by the Controller General, reports to and is responsible solely to Congress. The primary responsibility of the audit staff is to conduct the audit function for Congress.

Many of the GAO's audit responsibilities are basically the same as the CPA's. Much of the financial information prepared by various government agencies is audited by the GAO before it is submitted to Congress. Since the authority for expenditures and receipts of governmental agencies is defined by law, there is considerable emphasis on compliance in these audits.

An increasing portion of the GAO's audit efforts has been devoted to evaluating the *operational efficiency and effectiveness* of various federal programs. A typical example is the evaluation of the computer operations of a particular governmental unit. The auditor can review and evaluate any aspect of the computer system, but he is likely to emphasize the adequacy of the equipment, the efficiency of the operations, the adequacy and usefulness of the output, and similar matters, with the objective of identifying means of providing the same services for less cost.

Because of the immense size of many federal agencies and the similarity of their operations, the GAO has made significant advances in developing better methods of auditing. For example, the use of statistical sampling and computer auditing techniques has been widespread and highly sophisticated for several years.

In many states experience as a GAO auditor qualifies as experience required to become a CPA. In those states, if an individual passes the CPA examination and fulfills the experience stipulations for becoming a GAO auditor, he may then obtain a CPA certificate.

As a result of their great responsibility for auditing the expenditures of the federal government, their use of advanced auditing concepts, their eligibility to be CPAs, and their opportunities for performing operational audits, GAO auditors are highly regarded in the auditing profession.

Internal Revenue Agents

The Internal Revenue Service (IRS), under the direction of the Commissioner of Internal Revenue, has as its responsibility the enforcement of the *federal tax laws* as they have been defined by Congress and interpreted by the courts. A major responsibility of the IRS is to audit the returns of taxpayers to determine whether they have complied with the tax laws. The auditors who perform these examinations are referred to as internal revenue agents. These audits can be regarded as solely compliance audits.

It might seem that the audit of returns for compliance with the federal tax laws would be a simple and straightforward problem, but nothing could be further from the truth. The tax laws are highly complicated, and there are hundreds of volumes of interpretations. The tax returns being audited vary from the simple returns of individuals who work for only one employer and take the standard tax deduction to the highly complex returns of multinational corporations. There are taxation problems involving individual taxpayers, gift taxes, estate taxes, corporate taxes, trusts, and so forth. An auditor involved in any of these areas must have considerable knowledge to conduct an audit.

Internal Auditors

Internal auditors are employed by individual companies to audit for management much as the GAO does for Congress. The internal audit group in some large firms includes over a hundred persons and typically reports directly to the president or another high executive officer.

Internal auditors' responsibilities vary considerably, depending upon the employer. Some internal audit staffs consist of only one or two employees who may spend most of their time doing routine compliance auditing. Other internal audit staffs consist of numerous employees who have diverse responsibilities, including many outside the accounting area. In recent years many internal auditors have become involved in operational auditing or have developed expertise in evaluating computer systems.

A major difference between CPAs and internal auditors is the lack of independence of internal auditors with respect to outside users. To operate effectively, an internal auditor must be independent of the line functions in an organization, but he cannot be independent of the entity as long as an employer-employee relationship exists. Internal auditors provide management with valuable information for making decisions concerning effective operation of its business. Users from outside the entity are unlikely to want to rely on information audited by internal auditors because of their lack of independence.

The major emphasis in this book is the audit of financial statements by CPAs. There are three reasons for this emphasis: a larger percent of students who become auditors initially work for a CPA firm than for any other type of audit organization; CPAs have more clearly defined audit responsibilities than have the other major types; and there are more professional and auditing requirements for CPAs than for the other types because of the reliance of external users on financial statements.

ACTIVITIES AND ORGANIZATIONAL STRUCTURE OF CPA FIRMS

There are currently more than 20,000 CPA firms in the United States. The size of CPA firms ranges from one person in many firms to several thousand staff and partners for the largest firms. There are four size catagories typically used for describing CPA firms.

Big Eight. The eight largest CPA firms in the United States often are referred to as the "Big Eight." Each firm has offices in every major U.S. city and in many cities throughout the world. Each firm has gross revenues in the United States in excess of $200 million and significantly more internationally. The staff size in New York City for one of these firms is more than 1,000 professionals. Some smaller offices have fewer than 20 people. These eight firms audit nearly all of the largest companies in the United States and many smaller companies as well.

Other National Firms. In addition to the Big Eight, several other firms in the United States are referred to as national firms because they have offices in most major cities. These firms perform the same services as the Big Eight and compete directly with them for clients.

Large Local and Regional Firms. There are only a few hundred CPA firms with professional staffs of more than 50 people. Some of these firms have only one office and serve clients primarily within commuting distance of the office. Others have several offices in a state or region and service a larger radius of clients. These firms compete with other CPA firms, including the Big Eight, for clients.

Small Local Firms. More than 95 percent of all CPA firms have fewer than 25 professionals in their single office firm. They perform audits and related services primarily for smaller businesses and not-for-profit entities.

Activities

CPAs perform five major functions:

Audits. The primary reason CPA firms exist is to perform audits that are relied on by external users. CPA firms in their present forms would not exist without the audit function.

Tax Services. CPA firms prepare corporate and individual tax returns for both audit and nonaudit clients. In addition, estate tax, gift tax, tax planning, and other aspects of tax services are provided by most CPA firms. Tax services are now a part of almost every CPA firm, and for many small firms such services are far more important to their practice than auditing.

Management Advisory Services. Most CPA firms provide certain services that enable their clients to operate their businesses more effectively. These services range from simple suggestions for improving the client's accounting system to aids in marketing strategies, computer installations, and actuarial benefit consulting. Many large firms now have departments involved exclusively in management advisory services with little interaction with the audit or tax staff.

Accounting Services. Many small clients who may have a limited accounting staff rely upon CPA firms to prepare their financial statements. Generally, in this type of engagement a large number of adjustments are made by the CPA to properly reflect transactions throughout the period and to adjust for valuation changes or allocations at the end of the period. In many instances the CPA prepares these adjustments as part of an audit. In other instances only accounting services are performed.

Bookkeeping. Some small clients lack the personnel or expertise to prepare even their own journals and ledgers. Many small CPA firms spend much of their time performing this type of work, termed "write-up" work. In recent years some firms have utilized electronic data-processing systems to provide bookkeeping services to clients. In some instances the CPA firm also conducts an audit after the bookkeeping services have been provided, while in other instances financial statements are prepared without an audit.

Organizational Structure

Because of their responsibility for the audit of financial statements, it is essential that CPAs have a high level of *independence* and *competence*. Independence is important to encourage auditors to remain unbiased in drawing conclusions about the financial statements. Both independence and competence in conducting an audit are necessary to enable users to rely upon the statements. The large number of CPAs in the United States makes it impossible for users to evaluate the independence and competence of individual CPAs. Consequently, an organizational structure for CPAs has emerged that encourages, but certainly does not guarantee, both independence and competence.

The organizational form used by CPA firms is that of a *partnership or a professional corporation*. In a typical firm organized as a partnership, several CPAs join together to practice as partners, offering auditing and other services to interested parties. The partners normally hire professional staff persons to assist them in their work. These assistants are, or aspire to become, CPAs.

The existence of a separate entity to perform audits encourages independence by avoiding an employee-employer relationship between the CPAs and their clients. A separate entity also enables CPA firms to become sufficiently large to prevent any one client from representing a significant portion of a partner's total income and thereby endangering the firm's independence. Competence is encouraged by having a large number of professionals with related interests associated in one firm, which facilitates a professional attitude and makes continuing professional education more meaningful.

Thus, the organizational hierarchy in a typical CPA firm includes partners, managers, supervisors, seniors or in-charge auditors, and assistants, with a new employee usually starting as an assistant and spending two or three years in each classification before achieving partner status. The titles of the positions vary from firm to firm, but the structure is basically the same in all firms. When we refer in this text to the *auditor*, we mean the particular person performing some aspect of an audit. It is common to have one or more auditors from each level on larger engagements.

The CPA Examination

It is not necessary to be a CPA to work for a CPA firm, but that designation is required to be a partner. Most firms encourage staff to become certified (designated as a CPA) as quickly as possible.

A common examination is offered twice annually in May and November. The two-and-one-half-day written examination is prepared and graded by the American Institute of Certified Public Accountants (AICPA), the national professional organization. The examination covers four broad fields: auditing, accounting practice, accounting theory, and business law. Subjects such as professional ethics, legal liability of auditors, federal income taxes, and quantitative methods applied to accounting are tested as a part of the four fields. Only approximately 10 percent of those taking the examination pass all parts the first time.

The qualifications needed to take the examination are set by each state and vary from state to state. Typically, an undergraduate college degree but no experience is required before the exam can be attempted. Many states also require a specified minimum number of credits in accounting.

The AICPA obtains background information from individuals taking the CPA exam to aid in determining the major factors affecting success in passing the exam. Individuals wanting more information about the CPA examination will find the booklet, *Information for CPA Candidates*, useful. Past CPA examinations and unofficial solutions are also available. Both can be obtained from the AICPA, 1211 Avenue of the Americas, New York, N.Y. 10036.

Some of the questions and problems at the end of the chapters have been taken from past CPA examinations. They are designated "AICPA" or "AICPA adapted."

AICPA

The CPAs' most important influence has been through their national professional organization, the American Institute of Certified Public Accountants. The AICPA sets professional requirements for CPAs, conducts research, and publishes materials on many different subjects related to accounting, auditing, management advisory services, and taxes.

The membership of the AICPA is restricted to CPAs and currently exceeds 120,000, but not all members are practicing as independent auditors. Many formerly worked for a CPA firm but are currently in government, industry, and education. AICPA membership is not required of CPAs.

The AICPA has three major functions: establishment of standards and rules, research and publication, and continuing education.

Establishing Standards and Rules. The AICPA is empowered to set standards (guidelines) and rules which all members and other practicing CPAs must follow. The requirements are set forth by committees made up of AICPA members. There are three major areas where the AICPA has primary standard and rule-making authority:

- *Auditing Standards.* The Auditing Standards Board (ASB) is responsible for issuing pronouncements in auditing matters. They are referred to as Statements on Auditing Standards (SASs). ASB and its predecessor organizations have been responsible for a considerable portion of the existing auditing literature. The standards are examined in the next section and discussed throughout the text.
- *Compilation and Review Standards.* The Compilation and Review Standards committee is responsible for issuing pronouncements of the CPA's responsibilities when he is associated with financial statements that are not audited. They are referred to as Statements on Standards for Accounting and Review Services (SSARS). SSARS 1, issued in December 1978, supersedes preceding statements of auditing standards in unaudited financial statements. It covers two specific types of services: first, situations where the accountant assists his client in preparing financial statements without giving any assurance about them (i.e., compilation services); second, situations where the accountant performs inquiry and analytical procedures that provide a reasonable basis for expressing limited assurances that there are no material modifications that should be made to the statements (i.e., review services).
- *Code of Professional Ethics.* The Committee on Professional Ethics sets *rules of conduct* that CPAs are required to meet. These rules and their relationships to ethical conduct are the subject of Chapter 2.

Research and Publications. The AICPA supports research through its own research staff and through grants to others. Some of the major periodicals and other publications in accounting and auditing issued by the AICPA are the following:

PERIODIC JOURNALS

- The Journal of Accountancy (monthly)
- Management Adviser (bimonthly)
- The Tax Adviser (monthly)

ACCOUNTING RELATED

- Accounting Research Studies (1 through 15)
- Opinions of the Accounting Principles Board (1 through 31)
- Accounting Trends and Techniques (annual)
- Statements of Position of the Accounting Standards Executive Committee

AUDITING RELATED

- Statement on Auditing Standards No. 1 and beyond
- An Auditor's Approach to Statistical Sampling (vols. 1–6)
- Auditing and EDP
- Internal Control
- Case Studies in Internal Control
- Industry Audit Guides (several volumes in different fields)
- Audit Research Monographs
- Statements on Standards for Accounting and Review Services

GENERAL

- Code of Professional Ethics
- Semiannual CPA examination questions and unofficial answers

Continuing Education. The extensive and ever-changing body of knowledge in accounting, auditing, management services, and taxes is such that continuous study is required for CPAs to stay current. The AICPA provides a considerable number of seminars and education aids to its members in a wide variety of subject matters. An example is a two-day seminar entitled "Professional and Legal Liability of the CPA."

GENERALLY ACCEPTED AUDITING STANDARDS

Auditing Standard is a general guidelines to aid auditors in fulfilling their professional responsibilities. They include consideration of professional qualities such as competence and independence, reporting requirements, and evidence.

The broadest guidelines available are the ten *Generally Accepted Auditing Standards*, which were developed by the AICPA in 1947 and have, with minimum changes, remained the same. These standards are not sufficiently specific to provide any meaningful guidance to practitioners, but they do represent a framework upon which the AICPA can provide interpretations. These ten standards are as follows:

GENERAL STANDARDS

1. The examination is to be performed by a person or persons having adequate technical training and proficiency as an auditor.
2. In all matters relating to the assignment, an independence in mental attitude is to be maintained by the auditor or auditors.
3. Due professional care is to be exercised in the performance of the examination and the preparation of the report.

STANDARDS OF FIELD WORK

1. The work is to be adequately planned and assistants, if any, are to be properly supervised.
2. There is to be a proper study and evaluation of the existing internal control as a basis for reliance thereon and for the determination of the resultant extent of the tests to which auditing procedures are to be restricted.
3. Sufficient competent evidential matter is to be obtained through inspection, observation, inquiries, and confirmations to afford a reasonable basis for an opinion regarding the financial statements under examination.

STANDARDS OF REPORTING

1. The report shall state whether the financial statements are presented in accordance with generally accepted accounting principles.
2. The report shall state whether such principles have been consistently observed in the current period in relation to the preceding period.
3. Informative disclosures in the financial statements are to be regarded as reasonably adequate unless otherwise stated in the report.
4. The report shall either contain an expression of opinion regarding the financial statements, taken as a whole, or an assertion to the effect that an opinion cannot be expressed. When an overall opinion cannot be expressed, the reasons therefore should be stated. In all cases where an auditor's name is associated with financial statements, the report should contain a clear-cut indication of the character of the auditor's examination, if any, and the degree of responsibility he is taking.

Statements on Auditing Standards

The 1973 Statement on Auditing Standards No. 1 (SAS 1) and all subsequent statements on auditing standards are the most *authoritative references* available for auditors. These statements are issued by the AICPA and are interpretations of generally accepted auditing standards. Frequently, these interpretations are referred to as auditing standards or simply as standards, but they should not be called generally accepted auditing standards. Only the ten Generally Accepted Auditing Standards bear that designation.

Statements on Auditing Standards are successors to the Statements on

Auditing Procedure of the AICPA. SAS 1 is a codification of fifty-four previous statements on auditing procedure dating from 1939 to 1972, while subsequent SASs are new pronouncements. New statements are issued whenever an auditing problem arises of sufficient importance to warrant an official interpretation by the AICPA. As of the writing of this book, SAS 26 was the last one issued and incorporated into the text materials. Readers should be alert to subsequent standards that influence auditing requirements.

Periodically, the SASs are codified to integrate the standards. These are called a *Codification of Statements on Auditing Standards*. Generally Accepted Auditing Standards and Statements on Auditing Standards are regarded as authoritative literature because *every member of the profession is required to follow their recommendations*. They obtain their status of authoritative literature through the Code of Professional Ethics, Rule of Conduct 202, which is discussed in Chapter 2.

Even though the Generally Accepted Auditing Standards and the Statements on Auditing Standards are the authoritative auditing guidelines for members of the profession, they provide less direction to auditors than might be suspected. There are almost no specific audit procedures required by the standards; and there are no specific requirements for determining sample size, selecting sample items from the population for testing, or evaluating results. Many practitioners believe the standards should provide more clearly defined guidelines for determining the extent of evidence to be accumulated. Such specificity would eliminate some of the difficult audit decisions and provide a line of defense if a CPA were charged with conducting an inadequate audit. On the other hand, highly specific requirements could turn auditing into mechanistic evidence gathering, void of professional judgment. From the point of view of both the profession and the users of auditing services, there is probably a greater harm in defining authoritative guidelines too specifically than too broadly.

Before the individual standards are discussed, certain overriding points about the general and field work auditing standards must be made. First, these AICPA pronouncements should be looked upon by practitioners as *minimum standards* of performance rather than as maximum standards or ideals. Any professional auditor who is constantly seeking means of reducing the scope of the audit by relying only on the standards, rather than evaluating the substance of the situation, fails to satisfy the spirit of the standards. Second, the existence of auditing standards does not mean the auditor must always follow them blindly. If the auditor sincerely believes the requirement of a standard is impractical or impossible to perform, he is justified in following an alternative course of action. Similarly, if the issue in question is immaterial in amount, it is also unnecessary to follow the standard. It is important to note, however, that the burden of justifying departures from the standards falls upon the practitioner.

When auditors desire more specific guidelines, they must turn to less authoritative sources. These include textbooks, journals, and technical publications. The materials published by the AICPA, mentioned earlier in the chapter, such as the *Journal of Accountancy* and Industry Audit Guides, are particularly useful in furnishing assistance on specific questions.

In the remainder of this section the 10 generally accepted auditing standards and their interpretations are discussed briefly. There is further study of the standards and frequent reference to the SASs throughout the text.

Adequate Technical Training and Proficiency. The general standards stress the important personal qualities the auditor should possess. The first standard is normally interpreted as requiring the auditor to have formal education in auditing and accounting, adequate practical experience for the work being performed, and continuing professional education. Recent court cases clearly demonstrate that the auditor must be technically qualified and experienced in those industries in which his audit clients are engaged.

In any case where the CPA or his assistants are not qualified to perform the work, a professional obligation exists to acquire the requisite knowledge and skills, suggest someone else who is qualified to perform the work, or decline the engagement.

Independence in Mental Attitude. The importance of independence was stressed earlier in the definition of auditing. The *code of professional ethics* and the quality control standards in the Statements on Auditing Standards both stress the need for independence.

Due Professional Care. The third general standard involves *due care* in the performance of all aspects of auditing. Simply stated, this means that the auditor is a professional who is responsible for fulfilling his duties diligently and carefully. As an illustration, "due care" includes consideration of the completeness of the working papers, the sufficiency of the audit evidence, and the adequacy of the audit report. As a professional, the auditor must avoid negligence and bad faith, but he is not expected to make perfect judgments in every instance.

Adequate Planning and Supervision. The field standards concern evidence accumulation and other activities during the actual conduct of the audit in the field. The first field work standard deals with ascertaining that the engagement is sufficiently well planned to ensure an adequate audit and proper supervision of assistants. Supervision is essential in auditing because a considerable portion of the field work is done by inexperienced staff members.

Proper Study and Evaluation of Internal Control. One of the most widely accepted concepts in the theory and practice of auditing is the importance of the client's accounting system (system of internal control) in generating reliable financial information. If the auditor is convinced the client has an excellent system, which includes controls for providing reliable data and for safeguarding assets and records, the amount of audit evidence to be accumulated can be significantly less than if the system is not adequate. On the other hand, in some instances the controls may be so inadequate as to preclude conducting an effective audit.

Sufficient Competent Evidence. The decision as to how much evidence to accumulate for a given set of circumstances is one requiring professional judgment. A major portion of this book is concerned with the study of evidence accumulation and the circumstances affecting the amount needed.

Four Reporting Standards. The four reporting standards require the auditor to prepare a report on the financial statements taken as a whole, including informative disclosures. The report must specifically refer to whether the statements are in accordance with generally accepted accounting principles and have been consistently applied. The reporting requirements for audits are more clearly spelled out in the SASs than for any other aspect of auditing. These requirements are studied in the next section.

AUDIT REPORTS

Audit reporting is studied in some detail at this point to aid in the understanding of the entire audit process. A more detailed study, including specialized reports, is included in Chapter 21.

The profession has defined and enumerated the types of audit reports that should be included with financial statements; the profession recognized the need for uniformity in reporting as a means of avoiding confusion. Users would have considerable difficulty interpreting the meaning of an auditor's report if each report were an original creation. As a result, the wording of audit reports is quite uniform, but there are different audit reports for different circumstances.

Standard Short-Form Report

The most common type of audit report is the *standard short-form report*, used when the following conditions have been met:

- Sufficient evidence has been accumulated by the CPA to enable him to evaluate whether the financial statements are fairly stated.
- The financial statements are presented in accordance with generally accepted accounting principles applied on a basis consistent with that of the preceding period.
- Adequate disclosures have been included in the footnotes and other parts of the financial statements.

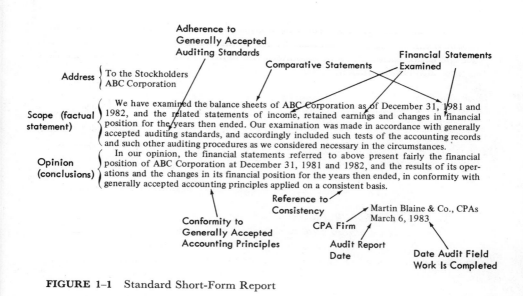

FIGURE 1-1   Standard Short-Form Report

- There are no unusual uncertainties concerning future developments which cannot be reasonably estimated or satisfactorily resolved.

When these conditions are met, the standard short-form audit report on comparative financial statements as shown in Figure 1-1 is issued.

Parts of Short-Form Report

Each standard short-form report includes five distinct parts:

1. *The Audit Report Address.* The report is usually addressed to the company, its stockholders, or the board of directors. In recent years, it has become customary to address the report to the *stockholders*, to indicate that the auditors are independent of the company and the board of directors.

2. *The Scope of the Audit.* In the first paragraph of the audit report, which is referred to as the *scope paragraph*, the auditor lists the financial statements he has examined and informs readers in very general terms about what was done on the audit. The scope paragraph intentionally states the work performed in general terms, rather than enumerating the details, because no reader is in a position to evaluate the adequacy of the evidence unless he has professional experience and knows all the facts about the audit.

3. *The Opinion of the Auditor.* The second paragraph in the short-form report, which is directly related to the four generally accepted auditing standards of reporting, is called the *opinion paragraph*. This part of the report is so important that frequently the entire audit report is referred to simply as the *auditor's opinion*. Here the auditor states his conclusions about the financial statements based upon the results of the audit evidence.

4. *The Date of the Audit Report.* The appropriate date for the report is the one on which the auditor has completed the most important auditing procedures in the field. This date is important to users because it indicates the last day of the auditor's responsibility for the review of significant events that occurred after the date of the financial statements. For example, if the balance sheet is dated December 31, 1981, and the audit report is dated March 6, 1982, this indicates that the auditor has searched for material unrecorded transactions and events that occurred up to March 6, 1978.

5. *The Signature of the Auditor.* This signature identifies the CPA or CPA firm that has performed the audit. Typically, the signature will be that of the CPA firm, since it has the responsibility for making sure the quality of the audit meets its standards.

Conditions Requiring a Departure
from an Unqualified Opinion

There are six conditions that require a departure from an unqualified opinion:

1. *The scope of the auditor's examination has been significantly restricted by the client.* If the client will not permit the auditor to confirm material receivables, physically observe inventories, or perform some other important procedure, it is unlikely that the auditor will be able to determine whether the statements are fairly presented.

2. *The auditor has been unable to perform significant audit procedures or obtain essential information because of conditions beyond either the client's or the auditor's control.* For example, when the engagement is not agreed upon until after the client's year-end, it may not be possible to physically observe inventories, confirm receivables, or perform other important procedures.

3. *The financial statements have not been prepared in accordance with generally accepted accounting principles.* For example, if the client insists upon using replacement costs for permanent assets or values inventory at selling price rather than historical cost, a modification of the unqualified opinion is required. When generally accepted accounting principles are referred to in this context, consideration of the adequacy of all informative disclosures, including footnotes, is important.

4. *The accounting principles used in the financial statements have not been consistently applied.* Even if the auditor recommends the change from one acceptable accounting principle, such as FIFO inventory valuation, to another one, such as LIFO, the audit report must make a specific reference to the change.

5. *There are unusual uncertainties affecting the financial statements which cannot be reasonably estimated at the date of the auditor's report.* There may be such things as significant unresolved lawsuits against the firm in excess of the insurance coverage or questions about the likelihood of the firm's being able to sell its products because of impending changes in state or federal laws.

6. *The auditor is not independent.* Independence ordinarily is determined by Rule 101 of the rules of conduct of the Code of Professional Ethics.

The scope paragraph of the report is important as a means of revealing when the auditor has not followed generally accepted auditing standards or has failed to accumulate the evidence he believes was appropriate for the audit. Whenever this occurs, the auditor must specifically state the shortcoming in the scope paragraph and the effect that it has on his opinion.

The opinion paragraph also becomes particularly pertinent when the auditor lacks sufficient information to form an overall opinion or believes, on the basis of the evidence, that the financial statements are not fairly presented. Under these conditions it is necessary for the auditor to express an opinion as to the overall fairness of the statements or state that it is not possible to give an opinion. It is also necessary to indicate any reservations the auditor has about the statements.

Whenever sufficient evidence has not been accumulated or the results of the tests lead the auditor to believe the statements are not fairly presented, it is necessary to issue some type of report other than an unqualified report. Three primary types of audit reports are issued under these conditions: a *qualified report,* an *adverse opinion,* and a *disclaimer of opinion.*

In addition, *reports on unaudited financial statements* are frequently issued, which, as the name implies, are actually not audit reports. Several types of *special audit reports* are also issued by CPAs for situations such as statements prepared on a cash basis, audits of specific aspects of a company's business other than financial statements, and reviews of internal control. Special unaudited reports are considered in Chapter 21.

Adverse Opinion. This type of report is used only when the auditor believes the overall financial statements are so *materially misstated or misleading* that they do not present fairly the financial position or results of operations in accordance with generally accepted accounting principles (condition 3). The adverse report can arise only when the auditor has knowledge, after an adequate investigation, that the financial statements are not fairly stated. This is not a common occurrence and, thus, the adverse opinion is rarely employed.

Disclaimer of Opinion. A disclaimer is issued whenever the auditor has been *unable to satisfy himself* that the overall financial statements are fairly presented. The necessity for disclaiming an opinion may arise because of (a) a *severe limitation on the scope* of the audit examination (condition 1 or 2), (b) the *existence of unusual uncertainties* concerning the amount of an item or the outcome of a matter materially affecting the financial position (condition 5), or (c) a *nonindependent relationship* under the Code of Professional Ethics between the auditor and the client (condition 6). Any one of these situations prevents the auditor from forming an opinion on the financial statements as a whole.

The disclaimer is distinguished from an adverse opinion in that it can arise only from a *lack* of knowledge by the auditor, whereas to express an adverse opinion the auditor must have knowledge that the financial statements are not fairly stated (condition 1 or 2).

Qualified Opinion. The qualified report can result from a *limitation on the scope* of the audit (condition 1 or 2), failure to follow generally accepted accounting principles (condition 3), the use of different accounting principles during one of the years included in the statements (condition 4), or the *existence of unusual circumstances* that prevented the auditor from knowing whether certain information in the statement was fairly presented (condition 5).

A qualified report *can be used only when the auditor believes that the overall financial statements are fairly presented.* A disclaimer or an adverse report must be used if the auditor believes the exceptions being reported are extremely material. For this reason the qualified report is considered the least severe type of report for disclosing exceptions.

A qualified report can take the form of a *qualification of both the scope and the opinion* or an *opinion qualification only.* The only time a scope and opinion qualification can be issued is when the auditor has not been able to accumulate all the evidence required by generally accepted auditing standards. Therefore the scope and opinion qualification is used only when the auditor's scope has been restricted by the client or when conditions exist that prevent the auditor from conducting a complete audit (conditions 1 and 2). The use of a qualification of the opinion only is restricted to those situations where conditions 3 through 5 exist.

Whenever an auditor uses a qualified opinion, he must use either the term "except for" or the term "subject to" in the opinion paragraph. The implication is that the auditor is satisfied with the overall financial statements "except for" or "subject to" a particular part of the financial statements. The only time a "subject to" qualification is used is when there are unusual uncertainties (condition 5). In all other cases, the opinion in a qualified report must include the expression "except for" (conditions 1 through 4). Examples of both of these qualifications are given in Chapter 2. It is unacceptable to use these two phrases with any type of audit opinion other than a qualified.

The appropriate use of a qualified report is summarized in Figure 1-2.

Materiality. Materiality is an essential consideration in the determination of the appropriate type of report for a given set of circumstances. If an exception is immaterial relative to the financial statement of the entity for the current period and is not expected to have a material effect in future periods, it is appropriate to issue an unqualified report. A common instance is the immediate expensing of office supplies rather than carrying the unused portion in inventory because the amount is insignificant.

At the other extreme are situations in which the amounts are of such great significance that the overall financial statements are materially affected.

FIGURE 1–2

The Auditor Is Satisfied That the Overall Financial Statements Are
Fairly Stated, but There Is a Material Exception

Conditions Requiring a *Departure from an Unqualified Report*	*Nature of the Qualification*
Condition 1—Scope restricted by client.	Scope and opinion—*except for*
Condition 2—Scope restricted by conditions.	Scope and opinion—*except for*
Condition 3—Statements are not in accordance with GAAP.	Opinion only—*except for*
Condition 4—Inconsistent application of GAAP.	Opinion only—*except for*
Condition 5—Unusual uncertainties exist.	Opinion only—*subject to*

In these circumstances it is necessary to issue a *disclaimer of opinion* or an *adverse opinion*, depending on the nature of the exception

Between these two extremes are situations in which the overall financial statements are fairly stated, but there is an exception material enough to require disclosure. A qualified opinion is appropriate in such a situation.

The auditor must make the decision, based upon his professional judgment, as to what constitutes immaterial, reasonably material, or pervasively material circumstances. Unfortunately, at the present time auditors do not have guidelines adequate enough so that reasonably uniform judgments can be assumed among different auditors.

Summary

The requirements for the appropriate auditor's opinion for the six conditions requiring a deviation from the short-form report are summarized in Figure 1-3. Observe that more than one type of audit report is applicable for each condition requiring a deviation, except when the auditor is not independent. The deciding factor in determining the proper type of audit report for any given condition other than independence is the materiality of the amount in question. The determination of materiality is a judgment question requiring a high degree of professional competence.

SECURITIES AND EXCHANGE COMMISSION

The overall purpose of the Securities and Exchange Commission (SEC), an agency of the federal government, is to assist in providing investors with reliable information upon which to make investment decisions. The Securities Act of 1933 contributes to fulfilling this purpose by requiring most companies planning to issue *new securities* to the public to submit a registration statement to the SEC for approval. The Securities Act of 1934 provides additional protection by requiring the same companies and others to file

FIGURE 1-3

Summary of the Proper Audit Report for Each Condition Requiring a Deviation from an Unqualified Report at Different Levels of Materiality

Conditions Requiring a Deviation from an Unqualified Report	The Amounts Are Immaterial	The Amounts Are Material, but They Do Not Overshadow the Overall Statement		The Amounts Are So Material That the Overall Fairness of the Statements Is in Question		No Significant Evidence Was Accumulated
	Unqualified	Qualified Scope and Opinion	Qualified Opinion Only	Adverse	Disclaimer	Unaudited
Auditing related The scope of the examination has been restricted by the client.	✓	✓			✓	✓
The scope of the examination has been restricted by conditions.	✓	✓			✓	✓
Accounting related The financial statements have not been prepared in accordance with generally accepted accounting principles.	✓		✓	✓		
The accounting principles have not been consistently applied.	✓		✓			
Uncertainties Unusual uncertainties affect the financial statements.	✓		✓		✓	
Auditor related The auditor is not independent. (Disclaimer regardless of the materiality.)					✓	

detailed annual reports with the commission. The commission examines these statements for completeness and adequacy before permitting the company to sell its securities through the securities exchanges.

Although the SEC requires considerable information that is not of direct interest to CPAs, the Securities Acts of 1933 and 1934 require financial statements, accompanied by the opinion of an independent certified public accountant, as part of a registration statement and subsequent reports.

Of special interest to auditors are several specific reports that are subject to the reporting provisions of the Securities Acts. The most important of these are as follows:

- *Forms S–1 to S–16.* These forms must be completed and registered with the SEC whenever a company plans to issue new securities to the public. The S–1 form is the general form when there is no specifically prescribed form. The others are specialized forms. For example, S–10 is for restrictions of landholders' royalty interests in gas and oil. All S forms apply to the Securities Act to 1933.
- *Form 8–K.* This report is filed at the end of any month in which significant events have occurred which are of interest to public investors. Such events include the acquisition or sale of a subsidiary, a change in officers or directors, an addition of a new product line, or a change in auditors.
- *Form 10–K.* This report must be filed annually within ninety days after the close of each fiscal year. Extensive detailed financial information is included in this report, including audited financial statements.
- *Form 10–Q.* This report must be filed quarterly for all publicly held companies. It contains certain financial information and requires audit involvement.

Since large CPA firms usually have clients that must file one or more of these reports each year, and the rules and regulations affecting filings with the SEC are extremely complex, most CPA firms have specialists who spend a large portion of their time making sure their clients satisfy all the SEC requirements.

The SEC has considerable influence in setting generally accepted accounting principles and disclosure requirements for financial statements as a result of its authority for specifying reporting requirements considered necessary for fair disclosure to investors. The Accounting Principles Board followed the practice of working closely with the SEC, and the Financial Accounting Standards Board (FASB) has continued this tradition. In addition, the SEC has power to establish rules for any CPA associated with audited financial statements submitted to the commission. Even though the commission has taken the position that accounting principles and auditing standards should be set by the profession, the SEC's attitude is generally considered in any major change proposed by the FASB.

The most important SEC requirements of interest to CPAs are set forth in the commission's *Regulation S-X* and *Accounting Series Releases*. These two publications constitute important basic regulations, as well as decisions and opinions on accounting and auditing issues affecting any CPA dealing with publicly held companies. Some of the major influences the SEC has had on auditors in the past few decades, are discussed in the text under the topics of independence, legal liability, and audit reporting.

CRITICISMS OF THE PROFESSION

One of the changes that is likely to result as a profession matures and increases in importance is an increase of external criticism. Certainly, law and medicine receive considerable criticism from many fronts. In recent years CPAs have also come under growing criticism. In the remainder of the chapter, some of the criticisms of the profession and the profession's responses are discussed.

Metcalf Recommendations

In the late 1970s a U.S. Senate subcommittee chaired by Senator Lee J. Metcalf (now deceased) issued a voluminous report on its investigation of the U.S. accounting profession. The following is a brief summary of some of the major recommendations in the report.

- Congress should exercise stronger oversight of accounting practices promulgated and more leadership in establishing proper goals and policies. The federal government should directly establish financial accounting standards for publicly owned corporations and establish auditing standards used by independent auditors to certify the accuracy of corporate financial statements.
- Congress should establish comprehensive accounting objectives for the federal government to guide agencies and departments in performing their responsiblities.
- The federal government should require the nation's 15 largest accounting firms to report basic operational and financial data annually and act to relieve excessive concentration in the supply of auditing and accounting services to major publicly owned corporations.
- The federal government should define the responsibilities of independent auditors clearly to meet the expectations of Congress, the public, and courts of law.
- The federal government should itself periodically inspect the work of independent auditors for publicly owned corporations. Public confidence in the actual independence of auditors who certify the accuracy of corporate financial statements under the federal securities laws should be restored by promulgating and enforcing strict standards of conduct for such auditors.
- Congress should amend the federal securities laws to restore the right of damaged individuals to sue independent auditors for negligence under the fraud provisions of the securities laws.

Most of these recommendations are unlikely to be passed by Congress in the foreseeable future. They are relevant in that they represent an extreme level of potential involvement in auditing matters by the U.S. government.

Moss Recommendations

Former U.S. Congressman from California John E. Moss, Chairman of the House Subcommittee on Oversight and Investigations, has been an outspoken critic of the CPA profession. He has spoken widely of his opinion that the profession has been unable to properly regulate itself. He has been equally critical of the SEC for their failure to impose harsher requirements on CPAs.

Moss has introduced legislation that, if passed, would have far-reaching implications for the profession. The bill includes a recommendation for establishing a National Association of SEC Accounting which would function much like the one currently existing for the National Association of Security Dealers. CPA firms practicing before the SEC would be required to register. They would be periodically required to have quality reviews for compliance with auditing standards and accounting principles. The bill would also put the responsibility for developing and issuing auditing standards and accounting principle in the hands of the SEC if the AICPA and FASB do not fulfill their responsibilities to the SEC's satisfaction. The legal responsibilities of CPAs would be broadened under the bill and there would be a more extensive ongoing oversight over CPAs involved with publically held companies than currently exists.

Eagleton Recommendations

Senator Thomas Eagleton has replaced Senator Metcalf in the Senate's investigation of the accounting profession. He has prepared a list of existing "Public Policy Goals to Be Achieved by the Accounting Profession and Securities and Exchange Commission." These are still at the discussion stage and do not currently represent a serious problem for the profession.

SEC Annual Report on the Accounting Profession

As a direct result of the congressional activities discussed above, the SEC has committed itself to perform a more active review of the progress of the accounting profession in meeting its responsibilities. Specifically, the commission will prepare a report to Congress as of June 30 of each year relating its oversight activities, the self-regulatory actions of the accounting profession, and the commission's judgments about the appropriateness of these actions and the progress being made.

Implications. What are the implications of harsh criticisms of CPAs by elected officials? The answers are not yet known. There has been no federal legislation passed to this point that changes the role of the federal government in auditing and accounting matters. The future involvement of government will likely depend heavily on the response of the profession, especially through the AICPA, to these criticisms. To this point most critics and members of the profession believe the AICPA has responded positively.

Commission on Auditors' Responsibilities

In 1974, the AICPA appointed a committee of seven members of the AICPA to study the auditing profession. The AICPA gave the charge to

> develop conclusions and recommendations regarding the appropriate responsibilities of independent auditors. It should consider whether a gap may exist between what the public expects or needs and what auditors can and should reasonably expect to accomplish. If such a gap does exist, it needs to be explored to determine how the disparity can be resolved.

The Commission completed its research and issued a 195-page report on its findings in 1978. It was entitled, "The Commission on Auditors' Responsibilities: Report, Conclusions, and Recommendations."

Significant recommendations were made to improve the accounting profession, but the general conclusion was the belief that the accounting profession is likely to do a better job of self-regulation than would result if it were done by government.

Several of the recommendations are included to give the reader an understanding of the nature of the conclusions reached by the Commission:

- Corporate management should present a report that acknowledges its responsibility for the representations in financial statements and that the information is presented in conformity with generally accepted accounting principles.
- The audit function should include greater involvement in a company's financial reporting process on a more current and continuing basis. The audit should be considered a function to be performed during a period of time rather than an audit of a particular set of financial statements.
- The auditor should expand his study and evaluation of the controls over the accounting system, making suggestions to management for the correction of weakness, and reporting on material uncorrected weaknesses not disclosed by management.
- The auditor should be responsible for searching for material fraud, and a concept of "due professional care" should be used as a guide for judging audit performance. The auditor cannot, however, reasonably be expected to detect all frauds. The auditor should seach for illegal or questionable acts and should be expected to detect those acts that his professional skill and care would normally uncover, but management should bear the primary responsibility for meeting the demands of society for corporate accountability.
- Management of public accounting firms should take steps to reduce pressures on independence arising from too-stringent time budgets and too-restrictive cost factors, including resistance against arbitrary deadlines imposed by clients. Principal responsibility for the selection and appointment of auditors and the setting of fees should be that of the client's board of directors or its audit committee.

- The present structure of a private profession regulated by a combination of private and governmental efforts is adequate and capable and should be maintained, but self-regulatory efforts should be improved. The present Auditing Standards Executive Committee should be replaced by an Auditing Standards Board within the AICPA, composed of five to nine full-time members.

A comparison of the Commission on Auditor's Responsibilities to those of Metcalf and Moss makes it clear that the Commissions's recommendations are far less extreme.

PROFESSION'S RESPONSE TO CRITICISMS

It is always difficult and a matter of judgment to assess whether a profession has properly responded to criticism. There is a belief among many segments of the profession that the AICPA and the profession in general has responded positively and quickly. A few of the specific changes that the profession has made are summarized.

Auditing Standards Board

The Auditing Standards Board replaced the predecessor committee, the Auditing Standards Executive Committee, as recommended by the Committee on Auditors' Responsibilities. The objective was to make the committee smaller, better able to quickly respond to needed changes in auditing, and more responsive to the needs of smaller practitioners. It was not made a full-time committee as recommended by the Commission.

The ASB and the predecessor committee have passed far more SASs in the past decade than any other equal time period in the history of the profession. A number of the SASs have been far-reaching and have dramatically changed auditing practice.

Division of CPA Firms

The AICPA has established a division for CPA firms and created two sections, the SEC Practice Section and the Private Companies Practice Section. The intent was to improve the quality of practice by CPA firms. It represents an attempt at self-regulation and is intended to be responsive to the SEC and other critics of the profession. Each practice section has membership requirements and the authority to impose sanctions for noncompliance by members. A firm can choose to belong to one section, both sections, or neither. The SEC Section has the most stringent membership requirements.

The two sections have caused considerable controversy in the profession. Some members feel the change is needed to improve self-regulation.

Others feel it establishes two classes of CPAs and implies a lower performance quality for firms that are not a member of the SEC Practice Section.

The following are the major requirements of belonging to the SEC Practice Section:

- *Reporting on Disagreements.* An auditor is required to report to the audit committee or board of directors of each SEC audit client on the nature of major disagreements with management about accounting, disclosure, or auditing matters.
- *Reporting on Management Advisory Services.* A member firm is required to report annually to the audit committee or board of directors of each SEC audit client on the total fees received from the client for management services during the year under audit and a description of the types of such services rendered.
- *Executive Recruiting Services.* Limits are set on the extent to which members may provide executive recruiting services to SEC audit clients. A CPA firm is, for example, prohibited from searching prospective candidates for managerial, executive, or director positions, acting as negotiator in setting compensation and other conditions of employment, or recommending a specific candidate for a position.
- *Partner Rotation.* The assignment of a new audit partner to be in charge of each SEC engagement is required if another audit partner has been in charge of the engagement for a period of five consecutive years. The incumbent partner is prohibited from returning to in-charge status on the engagement for a minimum of two years.
- *Mandatory Peer Review.* Each firm must have a periodic review of the quality controls and auditing and accounting practices by another qualified CPA firm. A report is to be issued stating the conclusions and recommendations of the reviewer. The standards for the peer review are to be established by the AICPA. A firm not satisfactorily passing a peer review cannot be a member of the SEC Practice Section.

Public Oversight Board

The AICPA has established a special committee to establish policies and solutions for the regulation of the SEC Practice Section. The members of the committee are highly respected individuals from business and the professions, entirely from outside the accounting profession. This Board has the potential for significantly influencing the practice of public accounting.

Peer Review

The review of the practices of a CPA firm by another firm and the reporting of the findings is potentially one of the most significant changes in the profession in recent years. Under peer review, a CPA firm opens itself to significant criticism if the standards of the profession are not properly met.

REVIEW QUESTIONS

1–1. Discuss the major factors in today's society that have made the need for independent audits much greater than it was 50 years ago.

1–2. In the conduct of audits of financial statements it would be a serious breach of responsibility if the auditor did not thoroughly understand accounting. On the other hand, many competent accountants do not have an understanding of the auditing process. What causes this difference?

1–3. Distinguish between generally accepted auditing standards and generally accepted accounting principles, and give two examples of each.

1–4. The first standard of field work requires the performance of the examination by a person or persons having adequate technical training and proficiency as an auditor. What are the various ways auditors can fulfill the requirement of the standard?

1–5. Generally accepted auditing standards have been criticized from different sources for failing to provide useful guidelines for conducting an audit. The critics believe the standards should be more specific to enable practitioners to improve the quality of their performance. As the standards are now stated, they provide little more than an excuse to conduct inadequate audits. Evaluate this criticism of the ten Generally Accepted Auditing Standards.

1–6. What are the differences and similarities in audits of financial statements, compliance audits, and operational audits?

1–7. List five examples of specific operational audits that could be conducted by an internal auditor in an manufacturing company.

1–8. What are the major differences in the scope of the audit responsibilities for CPAs, GAO auditors, IRS agents, and internal auditors?

1–9. State the five major functions CPAs perform, and explain each.

1–10. What major characteristics of the organization and conduct of CPA firms permit them to fulfill their social function competently and independently?

1–11. What role is played by the American Institute of Certified Public Accountants for its members?

1–12. Describe the role of the Securities and Exchange Commission in society and discuss its relationship with and influence on the practice of auditing.

1–13. The conduct of all audits of publicly held companies by auditors reporting to an independent branch of government such as the Securities and Exchange Commission rather than by CPAs would have certain advantages and disadvantages. List the advantages or disadvantages to society as a whole.

1–14. Explain how the Metcalf and Moss Committee reports differ from the report by the Commission on Auditors' Responsibilities.

1–15. What are two sections of practice to which CPA firms may belong? State the arguments for and against these sections.

1–16. State what is meant by the term "mandatory peer review." What are the implications for the profession?

1-17. List the five parts of the standard short-form report and state the purpose of each part.

1-18. Distinguish between an unqualified opinion, a disclaimer of opinion, an adverse opinion, and a qualified opinion. Describe a situation that is appropriate for each type of opinion.

1-19. Distinguish between an "except for" and a "subject to" opinion. Give an example of when each would be used.

1-20. On February 17, 19X7, a CPA completed the field work on the financial statements for the Buckheizer Corporation for the year ended December 31, 19X6. The audit is satisfactory in all respects except for the existence of a change in accounting principles from FIFO to LIFO inventory valuation, which results in a qualified audit opinion as to consistency. On February 26 the auditor completed the tax return and the pencil draft of the financial statement. The final audit report was completed, attached to the financial statements, and delivered to the client on March 7. What is the appropriate date on the auditor's report?

DISCUSSION QUESTIONS AND PROBLEMS

1-21. Feiler, the sole owner of a small hardware business, has been told that the business should have financial statements reported on by an independent CPA. Feiler, having some bookkeeping experience, has personally prepared the company's financial statements and does not understand why such statements should be examined by a CPA. Feiler discussed the matter with Farber, a CPA, and asked Farber to explain why an audit is considered important.

Required:

a. Describe the objectives of an independent audit.

b. Identify 10 ways in which an independent audit may be beneficial to Feiler. (AICPA)

1-22. Four college seniors with majors in accounting are discussing alternative career plans. The first senior plans to become an internal revenue agent because his primary interest is income taxes. He believes the background in tax auditing will provide him with a better exposure to income taxes than will any other available career choice. The second senior has decided to go to work for a CPA firm for at least five years, possibly as a permanent career. She feels the wide variety of experience in auditing and related fields offers a better alternative than any other available choice. The third senior has decided upon a career in internal auditing with a large industrial company because of the many different aspects of the organization with which internal auditors become involved. A fourth senior plans to pursue some aspect of auditing as a career but has not decided upon the particular type of organization to enter. He is especially interested in an opportunity to continue to grow professionally, but meaningful and interesting employment is also an important consideration.

Required:

a. What are the major advantages and disadvantages of each of the three types of auditing careers?

b. What other types of auditing careers are available to those who are qualified?

1–23. In the normal course of performing their responsibilities, auditors frequently conduct examinations or reviews of the following:

a. Federal income-tax returns of an officer of the corporation to determine whether he has included all taxable income in his return.

b. Disbursements of a branch of the federal government for a special research project to determine whether it would have been feasible to accomplish the same research results at a lower cost to the taxpayers.

c. Computer operations of a corporation to evaluate whether the computer center is being operated as efficiently as possible.

d. Annual statements for the use of management.

e. Operations of the Internal Revenue Service to determine whether the internal revenue agents are using their time efficiently in conducting audits.

f. Statements for bankers and other creditors when the client is too small to have an audit staff.

g. Financial statements of a branch of the federal government to make sure the statements present fairly the actual disbursements made during a period of time.

h. Federal income-tax returns of a corporation to determine whether the tax laws have been followed.

i. Financial statements for the use by stockholders when there is an internal audit staff.

j. A bond indenture agreement to make sure a company is following all requirements of the contract.

k. The computer operations of a large corporation to evaluate whether the internal controls are likely to prevent errors in accounting and operating data.

l. Disbursements of a branch of the federal government for a special research project to determine whether the expenditures were consistent with the legislative bill that authorized the project.

Required:

For each of the examples above, state the most likely type of auditor (CPA, GAO, IRS, or internal) and type of audit (audit of financial statements, compliance audit, or operational audit).

1–24. A large conglomerate is considering the possibility of acquiring a medium-sized manufacturing company in a closely related industry. A major consideration by the management of the conglomerate in deciding whether to pursue the merger is the operational efficiency of the company. Management has decided to obtain a detailed report, based on an intensive investigation, of the operational efficiency of the sales department, production department, and research and development department.

Required:

a. Whom should the conglomerate engage to conduct the operational audit?
b. What major problems are the auditors likely to encounter in conducting the investigation and writing the report?

1–25. Consumers Union is a nonprofit organization that provides information and counsel on consumer goods and services. A major part of its function is the testing of different brands of consumer products that are bought on the open market and the reporting on the results of the tests in *Consumer Reports,* a monthly publication. Examples of the types of products it tests are middle-sized automobiles, residential dehumidifiers, canned tuna, and boys' jeans.

Required:

a. Compare the need for the information provided by Consumers Union with the need for audited financial statements by investors and other statement users.
b. In what ways is the service provided by Consumers Union similar to audit services, and in what ways does it differ?

1–26. Ray, the owner of a small company, asked Holmes, CPA, to conduct an audit of the company's records. Ray told Holmes that an audit is to be completed in time to submit audited financial statements to a bank as part of a loan application. Holmes immediately accepted the engagement and agreed to provide an auditor's report within three weeks. Ray agreed to pay Holmes a fixed fee plus a bonus if the loan was granted.

Holmes hired two accounting students to conduct the audit and spent several hours telling them exactly what to do. Holmes told the students not to spend time reviewing the controls but instead to concentrate on proving the mathematical accuracy of the ledger accounts, and summarizing the data in the accounting records that support Ray's financial statements. The students followed Holmes' instructions and after two weeks gave Holmes the financial statements which did not include footnotes. Holmes reviewed the statements and prepared an unqualified auditor's report. The report, did not refer to generally accepted accounting principles nor to the year-to-year application of such principles.

Required:

Briefly describe each of the generally accepted auditing standards and indicate how the action(s) of Holmes resulted in a failure to comply with each standard.

Organize your answer as follows:

Brief Description of Generally Accepted Auditing Standards	*Holmes' Actions Resulting in Failure to Comply with Generally Accepted Auditing Standards*

(AICPA)

1–27. The following two statements are representative of attitudes and opinions sometimes encountered by CPAs in their professional practice:
  a. Today's audit consists of test checking. This is a dangerous practice because test checking depends upon the auditor's judgment, which may be defective. An audit can be relied upon only if every transaction is verified.
  b. An audit by a CPA is essentially negative and contributes to neither the gross national product nor the general well-being of society. The auditor does not create; he merely checks what someone else has done.

Required:

Evaluate each of the above statements and indicate
a. areas of agreement with the statement, if any.
b. areas of misconception, incompleteness, or fallacious reasoning included in the statement, if any. (AICPA adapted)

1–28. The Mobile Home Manufacturing Company is audited by Rossi and Montgomery, CPAs. Mobile Home has decided to issue stock to the public and wants Rossi and Montgomery to perform all the audit work necessary to satisfy the requirements of filing with the SEC. The CPA firm has never had a client go public before.

Required:

a. What are the ethical implications of Rossi and Montgomery's accepting the engagement?
b. List the additional problems confronting the auditors when they file with the SEC as compared with dealing with a regular audit client.

1–29. A CPA's report on financial statements includes his opinion as to whether the statements are presented in accordance with generally accepted accounting principles. In evaluating the general acceptability of an accounting principle, the CPA must determine whether the principle has substantial authoritative support.

Required:

a. Describe the procedure that a CPA should follow in forming an opinion as to whether he should accept an accounting principle proposed by a client for use in preparing the current year's financial statements. Assume that the principle has been consistently applied.
b. Cite primary sources and authorities that a CPA might consult in determining whether an accounting principle has substantial authoritative support. (A source is primary if it is sufficient evidence by itself to constitute substantial authoritative support.)
c. Cite secondary sources and authorities that the CPA might consult in determining whether an accounting principle has substantial authoritative support. (A source is secondary if it must be combined with one or more other secondary sources to constitute substantial authoritative support.)

(AICPA adapted)

1–30. Upon completion of the examination of his client's financial statements, the CPA, in his report, must either express an opinion or disclaim an opinion on the statements taken as a whole. His opinion may be unqualified, qualified, or adverse.

Required:

a. Under what general conditions may a CPA express an unqualified opinion on his client's financial statements?

b. Define and distinguish among (1) a qualified opinion, (2) an adverse opinion, and (3) a disclaimer of opinion on the statements taken as a whole.

(AICPA adapted)

1-31. A careful reading of the short-form unqualified report indicates several important phrases. Explain why each of the following phrases or clauses is used rather than the alternative provided:

a. "In our opinion, the financial statements present fairly" rather than "The financial statements present fairly."

b. "Our examination was made in accordance with generally accepted auditing standards" rather than "Our audit was performed to detect material errors in the financial statements."

c. "The financial statements mentioned above present fairly the financial position" rather than "The financial statements mentioned above are correctly stated."

d. "In conformity with generally accepted accounting principles applied on a basis consistent with that of the preceding year" rather than "are properly stated to represent the true economic conditions on a basis consistent with that of the preceding year."

e. "Brown & Phillips, CPAs (firm name)" rather than "James E. Brown, CPA (individual partner's name)."

1-32. During the year ended December 31, 19X6, Yolly Corporation had its fixed assets appraised and found that they had substantially appreciated in value since the date of their purchase. The appraised values have been reported in the balance sheet as of December 31, 19X6; the total appraisal increment has been included as an extraordinary item in the income statement for the year then ended; and the appraisal adjustment has been fully disclosed in the footnotes. If a CPA believes that the values reported in the financial statements are reasonable, what type of opinion should he issue? Why?

(AICPA adapted)

1-33. Roscoe, CPA, has completed the examination of the financial statements of Excelsior Corporation as of and for the year ended December 31, 1975. Roscoe also examined and reported on the Excelsior financial statements for the prior year. Roscoe drafted the following report for 1975.

March 15, 1976

We have examined the balance sheet and statements of income and retained earnings of Excelsior Corporation as of December 31, 1975. Our examination was made in accordance with generally accepted accounting standards and accordingly included such tests of the accounting records as we considered necessary in the circumstances.

In our opinion, the above mentioned financial statements are accurately prepared and fairly presented in accordance with generally accepted accounting principles in effect at December 31, 1975.

Roscoe, CPA
(Signed)

OTHER INFORMATION:

- Excelsior is presenting comparative financial statements.
- Excelsior does not wish to present a statement of changes in financial position for either year.
- During 1975 Excelsior changed its method of accounting for long-term construction contracts and properly reflected the effect of the change in the current year's financial statements and restated the prior year's statements. Roscoe is satisfied with Excelsior's justification for making the change. The change is discussed in footnote 12.
- Roscoe was unable to perform normal accounts receivable confirmation procedures but alternate procedures were used to satisfy Roscoe as to the validity of the receivables.
- Excelsior Corporation is the defendant in a litigation, the outcome of which is highly uncertain. If the case is settled in favor of the plaintiff, Excelsior will be required to pay a substantial amount of cash which might require the sale of certain fixed assets. The litigation and the possible effects have been properly disclosed in footnote 11.
- Excelsior issued debentures on January 31, 1974, in the amount of $10,000,000. The funds obtained from the issuance were used to finance the expansion of plant facilities. The debenture agreement restricts the payment of future cash dividends to earnings after December 31, 1980. Excelsior declined to disclose this essential data in the footnotes to the financial statements.

Required:

a. Identify and explain any items included in *"Other Information"* that need not be part of the auditor's report.

b. Explain the deficiencies in Roscoe's report as drafted.   (AICPA adapted)

1–34. Various types of "accounting changes" can affect the second reporting standard of the generally accepted auditing standards. This standard reads. "The report shall state whether such principles have been consistently observed in the current period in relation to the preceding period."

Assume that the following list describes changes which have a material effect on a client's financial statements for the current year.

a. A change from the completed-contract method to the percentage-of-completion method of accounting for long-term construction-type contracts.

b. A change in the estimated useful life of previously recorded fixed assets based on newly acquired information.

c. Correction of a mathematical error in inventory pricing made in a prior period.

d. A change from prime costing to full absorption costing for inventory valuation.

e. A change from presentation of statements of individual companies to presentation of consolidated statements.

f. A change from deferring and amortizing preproduction costs to recording such costs as an expense when incurred because future benefits of the costs have become doubtful. The new accounting method was adopted in recognition of the change in estimated future benefits.

g. A change to including the employer share of FICA taxes as "Retirement benefits" on the income statement from including it with "Other taxes."

h. A change from the FIFO method of inventory pricing to the LIFO method of inventory pricing.

Required:

Identify the type of change which is described in each item above, and state whether any modification is required in the auditor's report **as it relates to the second standard of reporting**. Organize your answer sheet as shown below.

For example, a change from the LIFO method of inventory pricing to the FIFO method of inventory pricing would appear as shown.

Assume that each item is material.

Item No.	*Type of Change*	*Should Auditor's Report Be Modified?*
Example	An accounting change from one generally accepted accounting principle to another generally accepted accounting principle.	Yes

(AICPA adapted)

2

PROFESSIONAL ETHICS

The AICPA Code of Professional Ethics and SEC independence requirements have a significant effect on what auditors do. In this chapter the need for rules of ethical conduct is explained along with the current requirements for CPAs. The chapter ends with a discussion of the changes in ethical requirements in the last few years.

NEED FOR ETHICS

The underlying philosophy for a code of ethics for any profession is the need for *public confidence* in the quality of the service, regardless of the individual providing it. For the CPA, it is essential that the client and external financial statement users have confidence in the quality of audits and other services. If users of services do not have confidence in physicians, judges, or CPAs, the ability of the professionals to effectively serve clients and the public is diminished.

It is not practical for users to evaluate the performance of professions because of the *complexity* of what they do. A patient cannot be expected to evaluate whether an operation was properly performed. A user cannot be expected to evaluate the audit performance on an engagement. Most users have neither the competence nor the time to evaluate audit performance. Public confidence in quality performance is enhanced when the profession encourages high standards of performance and conduct on the part of all practitioners. The AICPA Code of Professional Ethics is meant to assist practitioners in achieving a reasonable level of conduct.

A Code of Ethics can be *general statements* of ideal conduct or *specific rules* that define unacceptable behavior. The advantage of the general statements is the emphasis on positive activities that encourage practitioners to strive for a high level of performance. The disadvantage is the difficulty of enforcing general ideals, because there are no minimum standards of behavior. The advantage of specific rules requirements when they are carefully defined is the enforceability of minimum behavior and performance standards. The disadvantage is the tendency of some practitioners to define the rules as maximum behavior and performance standards rather than minimums.

PARTS OF THE CODE

The AICPA Code of Professional Ethics has attempted to accomplish the objectives of both general statements of ideal conduct and of specific rules. The general statements of ideal conduct are included in the concepts of professional ethics and the rules and their interpretations are included in the other three parts. There are four distinct parts of the AICPA Code of Professional Ethics.

Concepts of Professional Ethics

The concepts section of the Code contains a general discussion of the importance of certain characteristics required of a CPA. Independence receives the most attention, but competence, responsibility to clients and colleagues, and other matters are also discussed. In addition to stating the importance of different parts of the Code, the reasons for including each major requirement are brought out.

Ethical Principles. One part of the concepts consists of the five ethical principles that should be followed by all practitioners. The concepts are an elaboration and discussion of these principles.

(*1*) *Independence, integrity, and objectivity.* A certified public accountant should maintain his integrity and objectivity and, when engaged in the practice of public accounting, be independent of those he serves.

(*2*) *Competence and technical standards.* A certified public accountant should observe the profession's technical standards and strive continually to improve his competence and the quality of his services.

(*3*) *Responsibilities to clients.* A certified public accountant should be fair and candid with his clients and serve them to the best of his ability, with professional concern for their best interests, consistent with his responsibilities to the public.

(4) Responsibilities to colleagues. A certified public accountant should conduct himself in a manner which will promote cooperation and good relations among members of the profession.

(5) Other responsibilities and practices. A certified public accountant should conduct himself in a manner which will enhance the stature of the profession and its ability to serve the public.

Rules of Conduct

This part of the Code includes the explicit rules that must be followed by every CPA in the practice of public accounting. (Those individuals holding the CPA certificate, but not actually practicing public accounting, must only follow certain requirements.) Because the Rules of Conduct section is the *only* enforceable part of the Code, it is stated in more precise language than the section on concepts. Because of the enforceability of the Rules of Conduct, many practitioners refer to the Rules as the Code of Ethics.

The Rules of Conduct vary from highly specific to somewhat broad restrictions. Below is an example of a highly specific rule (Rule 503) followed by a broad restriction (Rule 501). Imagine the difficulty of enforcing Rule 501 with any degree of consistency.

Rule 503—Commissions. A member shall not pay a commission to obtain a client, nor shall he accept a commission for a referral to a client of products or services of others. This rule shall not prohibit payments for the purchase of an accounting practice or retirement payments to individuals formerly engaged in the practice of public accounting or payments to their heirs or estates.

Rule 501—Acts Discreditable. A member shall not commit an act discreditable to the profession.

The Rules of Conduct apply to AICPA members as follows:

- The Rules apply to all services in the practice of public accounting, including taxes and management services, except:

    1. When the code specifies otherwise. An example is Rule 102: In tax matters a CPA may resolve doubt in favor of a client if there is reasonable support for his position.
    2. When a CPA is practicing outside the United States, he must follow the rules of the organized accounting profession in the country he is practicing. He must comply with Rule 202 (Auditing Standards) and Rule 203 (Accounting Principles) if a statement user would conclude that U.S. practices were followed.

- A member is responsible for compliance with the Rules of persons under his supervision, partners, and fellow shareholders.

- Others cannot be permitted to do things in behalf of a member that would have been a violation if the member had done it.
- All rules apply to those in the practice of public accounting. Rule 102 (integrity and objectivity) and Rule 501 (acts discreditable) apply to members, such as a controller who is a CPA, who does not practice as a public accountant.

All the Rules of Conduct are included in this chapter. They are tinted and set between horizontal rules.

Interpretation of Rules of Conduct

The need for published interpretations of the Rules of Conduct arises when there are frequent questions from practitioners about a particular rule. The Division of Professional Ethics of the AICPA prepares each Interpretation based upon a consensus of a committee made up principally of public accounting practitioners. Before Interpretations are finalized, they are sent to a large number of key people in the profession for comment. The Interpretations are not enforceable, but it would be difficult for a practitioner to justify a departure from the Interpretations in a disciplinary hearing.

Most of the Interpretations of the Rules are included in this chapter. A portion of several of the Interpretations is omitted because of their length; these omissions are indicated in the text. Interpretations are also tinted.

Ethical Rulings

The Rulings are explanations by the Executive Committee of the Professional Ethics Division of the *specific factual circumstances*. There are a large number of Ethical Rulings which are published in the expanded version of the Code of Professional Ethics.

DEFINITIONS

The Rules of Conduct and Interpretations use well-defined terminology that must be understood before reading the code. Following are the definitions:

Client. The person(s) or entity which retains a member or his firm, engaged in the practice of public accounting, for the performance of professional services.

Council. The Council of the American Institute of Certified Public Accountants.

Enterprise. Any person(s) or entity, whether organized for profit or not, for which a CPA provides services.

Firm. A proprietorship, partnership or professional corporation or association engaged in the practice of public accounting, including individual partners or shareholders thereof.

Financial Statements. Statements and footnotes related thereto that purport to show financial position which relates to a point in time or changes in financial position which relate to a period of time, and statements which use a cash or other incomplete basis of accounting. Balance sheets, statements of income, statements of retained earnings, statements of changes in financial position and statements of changes in owners' equity are financial statements.

Incidental financial data included in management advisory services reports to support recommendations to a client, and tax returns and supporting schedules do not, for this purpose, constitute financial statements; and the statement, affidavit or signature of preparers required on tax returns neither constitutes an opinion on financial statements nor requires a disclaimer of such opinion.

Institute. The American Institute of Certified Public Accountants.

Interpretations of Rules of Conduct. Pronouncements issued by the Division of Professional Ethics to provide guidelines as to the scope and application of the Rules of Conduct.

Member. A member, associate member or international associate of the American Institute of Certified Public Accountants.

Practice of Public Accounting. Holding out to be a CPA or public accountant and at the same time performing for a client one or more types of services rendered by public accountants. The term shall not be limited by a more restrictive definition which might be found in the accountancy law under which a member practices.

Professional Services. One or more types of services performed in the practice of public accounting.

Organization of Sections

The next five sections of the chapter are organized into the five ethical principles previously discussed. For a given ethical principle the first Rule applying to the principle is included (set between rules and tinted). All Interpretations of a given Rule follow immediately if there are any (tinted). The next rule for a principle follows. After all Rules and Interpretations for a given principle have been stated, a discussion follows.

Rule 101—Independence. A member or a firm of which he is a partner or shareholder shall not express an opinion on financial statements of an enterprise unless he and his firm are independent with respect to such enterprise. Independence will be considered to be impaired if, for example: *MUST BE INDEPENDENT IN FACT AS WELL AS APPEARANCE.*

A. During the period of his professional engagement, or at the time of expressing his opinion, he or his firm

   1. Had or was committed to acquire any direct or material indirect financial interest in the enterprise; or

   2. Had any joint closely held business investment with the enterprise or any officer, director or principal stockholder thereof which was material in relation to his or his firm's net worth; or

   3. Had any loan to or from the enterprise or any officer, director or principal stockholder thereof. This latter proscription does not apply to the following loans from a financial institution when made under normal lending procedures, terms and requirements:

     (a) Loans obtained by a member or his firm which are not material in relation to the net worth of such borrower.

     (b) Home mortgages.

     (c) Other secured loans, except loans guaranteed by a member's firm which are otherwise unsecured.

B. During the period covered by the financial statements, during the period of the professional engagement or at the time of expressing an opinion, he or his firm

   1. Was connected with the enterprise as a promoter, underwriter or voting trustee, a director or officer or in any capacity equivalent to that of a member of management or of an employee; or

   2. Was a trustee of any trust or executor or administrator of any estate if such trust or estate had a direct or material indirect financial interest in the enterprise; or was a trustee for any pension or profit-sharing trust of the enterprise.

The examples above are not intended to be all-inclusive.

Interpretations under Rule 101—Independence

101-1—Directorships. Members are often asked to lend the prestige of their name as a director of a charitable, religious, civic or other similar type of nonprofit organization whose board is large and representative of the community's leadership. An auditor who permits his name to be used in this manner would not be considered lacking in independence under Rule 101 so long as he does not perform or give advice on management functions, and the board itself is sufficiently large that a third party would conclude that his membership was honorary.

101-2—*Retired Partners and Firm Independence.* A retired partner having a relationship of a type specified in Rule 101 with a client of his former firm would not be considered as impairing the firm's independence with respect to the client provided that he is no longer active in the firm, that the fees received from such client do not have a material effect on his retirement benefits and that he is not held out as being associated with his former partnership.

101-3—*Accounting Services.* Members in public practice are sometimes asked to provide manual or automated bookkeeping or data processing services to clients who are of insufficient size to employ an adequate internal accounting staff. Computer systems design and programming assistance are also rendered by members either in conjunction with data processing services or as a separate engagement. Members who perform such services and who are engaged in the practice of public accounting are subject to the by-laws and Rules of Conduct.

On occasion members also rent "block time" on their computers to their clients but are not involved in the processing of transactions or maintaining the client's accounting records. In such cases the sale of block time constitutes a business rather than a professional relationship and must be considered together with all other relationships between the member and his client to determine if their aggregate impact is such as to impair the member's independence.

When a member performs manual or automated bookkeeping services, concern may arise whether the performance of such services would impair his audit independence—that the performance of such basic accounting services would cause his audit to be lacking in a review of mechanical accuracy or that the accounting judgments made by him in recording transactions may somehow be less reliable than if made by him in connection with the subsequent audit.

Members are skilled in, and well accustomed to, applying techniques to control mechanical accuracy, and the performance of the record-keeping function should have no effect on application of such techniques. With regard to accounting judgments, if third parties have confidence in a member's judgment in performing an audit, it is difficult to contend that they would have less confidence where the same judgment is applied in the process of preparing the underlying accounting records.

Nevertheless, a member performing accounting services for an audit client must meet the following requirements to retain the appearance that he is not virtually an employee and therefore lacking in independence in the eyes of a reasonable observer.

1. The CPA must not have any relationship or combination of relationships with the client or any conflict of interest which would impair his integrity and objectivity.
2. The client must accept the responsibility for the financial statements as his own. A small client may not have anyone in his employ to maintain accounting records and may rely on the CPA for this purpose. Nevertheless, the client must be sufficiently knowledgeable of the enterprise's activities and financial condition and the applicable accounting principles so that he can reasonably accept such responsibility, including, specifically, fairness of valuation and presentation and adequacy of disclosure. When necessary, the CPA must discuss accounting matters with the client to be sure that the client has the required degree of understanding.
3. The CPA must not assume the role of employee or of management conducting the operations of an enterprise. For example, the CPA shall not consummate transactions, have custody of assets or exercise authority on behalf of the client. The client must prepare the source documents on all transactions in sufficient detail to identify clearly the nature and amount of such transactions and maintain an accounting control over data processed by the CPA, such as control totals and document counts. The CPA should not make changes in such basic data without the concurrence of the client.
4. The CPA, in making an examination of financial statements prepared from books and records which he has maintained completely or in part, must conform to generally accepted auditing standards. The fact that he has processed or maintained certain records does not eliminate the need to make sufficient audit tests.

When a client's securities become subject to regulation by the Securities and Exchange Commission or other federal or state regulatory body, responsibility for maintenance of the accounting records, including accounting classification decisions, must be assumed by accounting personnel employed by the client. The assumption of this responsibility must commence with the first fiscal year after which the client's securities qualify for such regulation.

101-4—Effect of Family Relationships on Independence. (Partially omitted) Relationships which arise through family bloodlines and marriage give rise to circumstances that may impair a member's independence.

1. *Financial and business relationships ascribed to the member.* Independence of a member may be impaired by the financial interests and business relationships of the member's spouse, dependent children, or any relative living in a common household with or supported by the member. The financial interests or business relationships of such family, dependents or relatives in a member's client are ascribed to the member.

2. *Financial and business relationships that may be ascribed to the member.*

Close Kin

Family relationships may also involve other circumstances in which the appearance of independence is lacking. However, it is not reasonable to assume that all kinships, per se, will impair the appearance of independence since some kinships are too remote. The following guidelines to the effect of kinship on the appearance of independence have evolved over the years:

A presumption that the appearance of independence is impaired arises from a significant financial interest, investment, or business relationship by the following close kin in a member's client: non-dependent children, brothers and sisters, grandparents, parents, parent-in-law, and the respective spouses of any of the foregoing.

If the close kin's financial interest in a member's client is material in relationship to the kin's net worth, a third party could conclude that the member's objectivity is impaired with respect to the client since the kinship is so close. In addition, financial interests held by close kin may result in an indirect financial interest being ascribed to the member.

The presumption that the appearance of independence is impaired would also prevail where a close kin has an important role or responsible executive position (e.g., director, chief executive or financial officer) with a client.

Geographical separation from the close kin and infrequent contact may mitigate such impairment.

3. *Financial and business relationships that are not normally ascribed to the member.*

Remote Kin

A presumption that the appearance of independence is impaired would not normally arise from the financial interests and business relationships of remote kin: uncles, aunts, cousins, nephews, nieces, other in-laws, and other kin who are not close.

The financial interests and business relationships of these remote kin are not considered either direct or indirect interests ascribed to the member. However, the presumption of no impairment with remote kin would be negated if other factors indicating a closeness exist, such as living in the same household with the member, having financial ties, or jointly participating in other business enterprises.

101-5—Meaning of the Term "Normal Lending Procedures, Terms and Requirements." (Partially omitted) Rule 101 (A) (3) prohibits loans to a member from his client except for certain specified kinds of loans from a client financial institution when made under "normal lending procedures, terms and requirements." The member would meet the criteria prescribed by this rule if the procedures, terms and requirements relating to his loan are reasonably comparable to those relating to other loans of a similar character committed to other borrowers during the period in which the loan to the member is committed.

101-6—The Effect of Actual or Threatened Litigation on Independence. (Partially omitted) Rule of Conduct 101 prohibits the expression of an opinion on financial statements of an enterprise unless a member and his firm are independent with respect to the enterprise. In some circumstances, independence may be considered to be impaired as a result of litigation or the expressed intention to commence litigation.

Litigation between Client and Auditor

When the present management of a client company commences, or expresses an intention to commence, legal action against the auditor, the auditor and the client management may be placed in adversary positions in which the management's willingness to make complete disclosures and the auditor's objectivity may be affected by self-interest.

. . . Independence may be impaired whenever the auditor and his client company or its management are in threatened or actual positions of material adverse interests by reason of actual or intended litigation. Because of the complexity and diversity of the situations of adverse interests which may arise, however, it is difficult to prescribe precise points at which independence may be impaired. The following criteria are offered as guidelines:

1. The commencement of litigation by the present management alleging deficiencies in audit work for the client would be considered to impair independence.

2. The commencement of litigation by the auditor against the present management alleging management fraud or deceit would be considered to impair independence.

3. An expressed intention by the present management to commence litigation against the auditor alleging deficiencies in audit work for the client is considered to impair independence if the auditor concludes that there is a strong possibility that such a claim will be filed.

4. Litigation not related to audit work for the client (whether threatened or actual) for an amount not material to the member's firm or to the financial statements of the client company would not usually be considered to affect the relationship in such a way as to impair independence.

Litigation by security holders

The auditor may also become involved in litigation ("primary litigation") in which he and the client company or its management are defendants. Such litigation may arise, for example, when one or more stockholders bring a stockholders' derivative action or a so-called "class action" against the client company or its management, its officers, directors, underwriters and auditors under the securities laws. Such primary litigation in itself would not alter fundamental relationships between the client company or its management and auditor and therefore should not be deemed to have an adverse impact on the auditor's independence. These situations should be examined carefully, however, since the potential for adverse interests may exist if cross-claims are filed against the auditor alleging that he is responsible for any deficiencies or if the auditor alleges fraud or deceit by the present management as a defense.

101-7—Application of 101 Rule to Professional Personnel.
The term "he and his firm" as used in the first sentence of Rule 101 means (1) all partners or shareholders in the firm and (2) all full and part-time professional employees participating in the engagement or located in an office participating in a significant portion of the engagement.

Effects of Impairment of Independence

If the auditor believes that the circumstances would lead a reasonable person having knowledge of the facts to conclude that the actual or intended litigation poses an unacceptable threat to the auditor's independence he should either (a) disengage himself to avoid the appearance that his self-interest would affect his objectivity, or (b) disclaim an opinion because of lack of independence as prescribed by Section 517 of *Statement on Auditing Standards No. 1.*

Rule 102—Integrity and Objectivity.
A member shall not knowingly misrepresent facts, and when engaged in the practice of public accounting, including the rendering of tax and management advisory services, shall not subordinate his judgment to others. In tax practice, a member may resolve doubt in favor of his client as long as there is reasonable support for his position.

INDEPENDENCE, INTEGRITY, AND OBJECTIVITY—DISCUSSION

The Rules of Conduct and related Interpretations are dominated by independence. This is as it should be. Independence is no more essential than are integrity and objectivity, but it is more difficult to understand. The discussion in this section is limited to independence.

Independence in auditing means taking an *unbiased viewpoint* in the performance of audit tests, the evaluation of the results, and the issuance of the audit report. If the auditor is an advocate for the client, a particular banker, or anyone else, he cannot be considered independent. Independence must certainly be regarded as one of the auditor's most critical characteristics. The reason that many diverse users are willing to rely upon the CPA's reports as to the fairness of financial statements is their expectation of an unbiased viewpoint.

Not only is it essential that CPAs maintain an independent attitude in fulfilling their responsibility, but it is also important that the users of financial statements have confidence in that independence. These two objectives are frequently identified as *independence in fact* and *independence in appearance*. Independence in fact exists when the auditor is actually able to maintain an unbiased attitude throughout the audit, whereas independence in appearance is dependent on others' interpretations of this independence. If auditors are independent in fact, but users believe them to be advocates for the client, most of the value of the audit function will be lost.

Although it is possible to take the extreme position that anything affecting either independence in fact or in appearance must be eliminated to ensure a high level of respect in the community, it is doubtful whether this would solve as many problems as it would create. The difficulty with this position is that it is likely to significantly restrict the services offered to clients, the freedom of CPAs to practice in the traditional manner, and the ability of CPA firms to hire competent staff. At this point it will be helpful to examine some of the conflicts of independence that have arisen, evaluate the significance of the conflicts, and determine how the profession has resolved them.

Ownership of Stock by a CPA

Although it was once acceptable for CPAs to own a limited amount of stock in a client, it is now regarded as potentially damaging to actual audit independence, and it certainly is likely to affect the users' perceptions of the auditor's independence. Stock ownership and similar investments are specifically prohibited in some circumstances in Rule 101 of the Rules of Conduct. The ownership of stock rule is more complex than it appears at first glance. A more detailed examination of that requirement is included to aid in understanding and to show the complexity of one of the Rules. Three distinctions are important in the Rules as they relate to independence and stock ownership.

Partner or Shareholders versus Nonpartners or Nonstockholders. Rule 101 applies to partners and shareholders for *all clients of a CPA firm*. The rule applies to nonpartners or nonshareholders *only when they are involved in the engagement* or when the engagement is performd by staff in the same office (see Interpretation 101-7). For example, a staff member in a national CPA firm could own stock in a client corporation and not violate Rule 101 if he was never involved in the engagement, but as soon as he became partner he would have to dispose of the stock or the CPA firm must stop doing the audit.

Some CPA firms do not permit any ownership by staff of client's stock regardless of which office serves the client. These firms have decided to have higher requirements than the minimums set by the Rules of Conduct.

Direct versus Indirect Financial Interest. Direct ownership refers to the ownership of a stock or other equity shares by a member or his immediate family. For example, if a partner's wife had a partnership interest in a company, the CPA firm would be prohibitied by Rule 101 from expressing an opinion on the financial statements.

Indirect ownership refers to the nature of the ownership or relationship. Ownership is indirect when there is a close ownership relationship between the auditor and the client, but not a direct relationship. A common example of indirect ownership occurs when a CPA firm audits a mutual fund which owns stock that an audit partner also has in his personal portfolio. Another example of indirect ownership would be the ownership of a stock by a member's grandfather.

Material or Immaterial. Materiality only affects whether an ownership is a violation of Rule 101 for *indirect ownership*. Materiality must be considered in relation to the member person's wealth and income. For example, if a mutual fund client had a large portion of its ownership in the XY Company and a firm partner had a significant amount of his personal wealth invested in XY Company, a violation of the Code exists.

Directorship or Officer of a Company

If a CPA is a member of the board of directors or an officer of a client company, his ability to make independent evaluations of the fair presentation of financial statements could easily be affected. Even if holding one of these positions did not actually affect the auditor's independence, the frequent involvement with management and the decisions it makes is likely to affect how statement users would perceive the CPA's independence. To eliminate this possibility, Rule 101 prohibits being a director or officer of a client company.

Performance of Management Advisory Services and Audits for the Same Client

What is the effect on actual independence and the appearance of independence when an auditor recommends a computer installation or some other improvement in the client's system and at a later date audits the output of the computer installation? If the recommended system turns out to be ineffective, will the auditor evaluate the system as harshly as he would have if someone else had made the recommendation?

The investigation of the accounting profession by both Senator Metcalf and Congressman Moss concluded that management services were a detriment to the independent performance of audits. They recommended restrictions be put on auditors in performing these services. The Commission on Auditors' Responsibilities also concluded that certain types of management services could affect the auditor's independence. The Commission was especially critical of a CPA firm performing executive search services for existing clients.

The SEC has set forth certain disclosure requirements that relate directly to management services and independence. The proxy statement for all SEC clients must include the following:

- A list of all services provided by the principal independent auditors and the fee relationship involved. Specifically, disclosure is required of the percentage relationship the aggregate fees for all nonaudit services bear to the audit fees and the relationship each nonaudit service (amounting to 3 percent or more of the audit fees) bears to the audit fees.
- Whether prior approval for services rendered by independent auditors was granted by the audit committee or board of directors.
- Whether consideration was given by the board of directors to the possible effect of each service rendered, audit and nonaudit, on auditor independence.

AICPA Rules.   There are currently no restrictions in the Rules of Conduct on the management services that can be performed. The apparent determining factor in the AICPA decision to permit the performance of management services on audit clients is the impact on independence compared with the negative effect on CPAs and clients of prohibiting services needed by clients. Some CPA firms have all management advisory services performed by staff members other than the auditors as a means of reducing the problem of independence.

Performance of Bookkeeping Services and Audits for the Same Client

If a CPA records transactions in the journals for the client, posts monthly totals to the general ledger, makes adjusting entries, and subsequently does an audit, there is some question as to whether he can be independent in his audit role. *The AICPA permits a CPA firm to do both bookkeeping and auditing for the same client.* The AICPA's conclusion is presumably based upon a comparison of the effect on independence if both bookkeeping and auditing services are performed by the same CPA firm, to the additional cost of having a different CPA firm do the audit. *The SEC prohibits performing bookkeeping services and auditing for SEC clients* by the same CPA firm.

Dependence upon a Client for a Large Percentage of Audit Fees

Nothing in the Code specifically requires a diversification of clients, but there is pressure from the SEC to discourage the audit of listed companies by a

CPA firm that depends heavily upon a particular client. It is doubtful whether there can be independence in both fact and appearance if the fees from one client make up a significant part of the total income of the firm.

Engagement of the CPA and Payment of Audit Fees by Management

Can an auditor be truly independent in fact and appearance if the payment of fees is dependent upon the management of the audited entity? There is probably no satisfactory answer to this question, but it does demonstrate the difficulty of obtaining an atmosphere of complete independence of auditors. The alternative to engagement of the CPA and payment of audit fees by management would probably be either the use of governmental or quasi-governmental auditors. All things considered, it is questionable whether the audit function would be performed better or cheaper by the public sector. One way to improve independence in fact and appearance in relations between CPAs and management is the use of an audit committee.

Audit Committee. An audit committee is a selected number of members of a company's Board of Directors who have responsibilities for certain relationships with the auditors. The purpose of the committee is to help keep auditors independent of management. Most audit committees are made up of three to five or sometimes as many as seven directors who are not a part of company management.

A typical audit committee is responsible for deciding such things as which CPA firm to retain, the scope of services the CPA firm is to perform, meetings with the CPA firm to discuss audit progress and findings, and helping resolve conflicts between the CPA firm and management. Audit committees are looked upon with favor for larger companies by most auditors, users, and management. The requirement of an audit committee would be costly for smaller companies.

An audit committee is required for all companies listed on the New York Stock Exchange. The AICPA Rules of Conduct and SEC do not require audit committees.

Conclusion. Regardless of the rules set forth by the Code of Professional Ethics, it is essential that the CPA maintain an unbiased relationship with management and all other parties affected by the performance of the CPA's responsibilities. In every engagement, including those involving management advisory and tax services, the CPA must refuse to subordinate his professional judgment to that of others. Even though pressures on the CPA's objectivity and integrity are frequent, the long-run standing of the profession in the financial community demands resisting these pressures. If the conflicts are sufficiently great to compromise the CPA's objectivity, it may be necessary for the CPA firm to resign from the engagement.

COMPETENCE AND TECHNICAL STANDARDS—RULES AND INTERPRETATION

Rule 201—General Standards. A member shall comply with the following general standards as interpreted by bodies designated by Council and must justify any departures therefrom.

A. *Professional Competence.* A member shall undertake only those engagements which he or his firm can reasonably expect to complete with professional competence.

B. *Due Professional Care.* A member shall exercise due professional care in the performance of an engagement.

C. *Planning and Supervision.* A member shall adequately plan and supervise an engagement.

D. *Sufficient Relevant Data.* A member shall obtain sufficient relevant data to afford a reasonable basis for conclusions or recommendations in relation to an engagement.

E. *Forecasts.* A member shall not permit his name to be used in conjunction with any forecast of future transactions in a manner which may lead to the belief that the member vouches for the achievability of the forecast.

Interpretation under Rule 201—General Standards

201-1—Competence. A member who accepts a professional engagement implies that he has necessary competence to complete the engagement according to professional standards, applying his knowledge and skill with reasonable care and diligence, but he does not assume a responsibility for infallibility of knowledge or judgment.

Competence in the practice of public accounting involves both the technical qualifications of the member and his staff and his ability to supervise and evaluate the quality of the work performed. Competence relates both to knowledge of the profession's standards, techniques and the technical subject matter involved, and to the capability to exercise sound judgment in applying such knowledge to each engagement.

The member may have the knowledge required to complete an engagement professionally before undertaking it. In many cases, however, additional research or consultation with others may be necessary during the course of the engagement. This does not ordinarily represent a lack of competence, but rather is a normal part of the professional conduct of an engagement.

However, if a CPA is unable to gain sufficient competence through these means, he should suggest, in fairness to his client and the public, the engagement of someone competent to perform the needed service, either independently or as an associate.

201-2—Forecasts. Rule 201-E does not prohibit a member from preparing, or assisting a client in the preparation of, forecasts of the results of future transactions. When a member's name is associated with such forecasts, there shall be the presumption that such data may be used by parties other than the client. Therefore, full disclosure must be made of the sources of the information used and the major assumptions made in the preparation of the statements and analyses, the character of the work performed by the member, and the degree of the responsibility he is taking.

Rule 202—Auditing Standards. A member shall not permit his name to be associated with financial statements in such a manner as to imply that he is acting as an independent public accountant unless he has complied with the applicable generally accepted auditing standards promulgated by the Institute. Statements on Auditing Procedure issued by the Institute's Committee on Auditing Procedure are, for purposes of this rule, considered to be interpretations of the generally accepted auditing standards, and departures from such statements must be justified by those who do not follow them.

Interpretation under Rule 202—Auditing Standards

202-1—Unaudited Financial Statements. Rule 202 does not preclude a member from associating himself with the unaudited financial statements of his clients. The Rule states in part that "A member shall not permit his name to be associated with financial statements in such a manner as to imply that he is acting as an independent public accountant unless he has complied with the applicable generally accepted auditing standards promulgated by the Institute."

In applying this provision to situations in which a member's name is associated with unaudited financial statements, it is necessary to recognize that the standards were specifically written to apply to audited financial statements. The fourth reporting standard, however, was made sufficiently broad to be applicable to unaudited financial statements as well.

The fourth reporting standard states in part:

". . . In *all* cases where an auditor's name is associated with financial statements, the report should contain a clear-cut indication of the character of the auditor's examination, *if any*, and the degree of responsibility he is taking.''

Rule 203—Accounting Principles. A member shall not express an opinion that financial statements are presented in conformity with generally accepted accounting principles if such statements contain any departure from an accounting principle promulgated by the body designated by Council to establish such principles which has a material effect on the statements taken as a whole, unless the member can demonstrate that due to unusual circumstances the financial statements would otherwise have been misleading. In such cases his report must describe the departure, the approximate effects thereof, if practicable, and the reasons why compliance with the principle would result in a misleading statement.

Interpretations under Rule 203—Accounting Principles

203-1—Departures from Established Accounting Principles. Rule 203 was adopted to require compliance with accounting principles promulgated by the body designated by Council to establish such principles. There is a strong presumption that adherence to officially established accounting principles would in nearly all instances result in financial statements that are not misleading.

However, in the establishment of accounting principles it is difficult to anticipate all of the circumstances to which such principles might be applied. The rule therefore recognizes that upon occasion there may be unusual circumstances where the literal application of pronouncements on accounting principles would have the effect of rendering financial statements misleading. In such cases, the proper accounting treatment is that which will render the financial statements not misleading.

The question of what constitutes unusual circumstances as referred to in Rule 203 is a matter of professional judgment involving the ability to support the position that adherence to a promulgated principle would be regarded generally by reasonable men as producing a misleading result.

Examples of events which may justify departures from a principle are new legislation or the evolution of a new form of business transaction. An unusual degree of materiality or the existence of conflicting industry practices are examples of circumstances which would not ordinarily be regarded as unusual in the context of Rule 203.

203-2—Status of FASB Interpretations. Council is authorized under Rule 203 to designate a body to establish accounting principles and has designated the Financial Accounting Standards Board as such body. Council also has resolved that FASB Statements of Financial Accounting Standards, together with those Accounting Research Bulletins and APB Opinions which are not superseded by action of the FASB, constitute accounting principles as contemplated in Rule 203.

In determining the existence of a departure from an accounting principle established by a Statement of Financial Accounting Standards, Accounting Research Bulletin or APB Opinion encompassed by Rule 203, the division of professional ethics will construe such Statement, Bulletin or Opinion in the light of any interpretations thereof issued by the FASB.

Rule 204—Other Technical Standards. A member shall comply with other technical standards promulgated by bodies designated by Council to establish such standards, and departures therefrom must be justified by those who do not follow them.

COMPETENCE AND TECHNICAL STANDARDS—DISCUSSION

The primary purpose of the requirements for Rules 201 to 203 is to provide support for the ASB and FASB. For example, notice that requirements A to D of Rule 201 are substantially duplications of generally accepted auditing standards. When a practitioner violates an auditing standard, the Rules of Conduct are also automatically violated.

Interpretation 203–1 informs members that it is not acceptable to blindly permit clients to follow generally accepted accounting principles. When an accounting principle would result in misleading financial statements in a certain situation, other accounting principles would be required. Examples of such a situation are rare.

The restriction on forecasts (Rule 201-E) prevents CPAs from providing a service that many members of the profession believe is needed and wanted by statement users. Certainly, forecasts of information are relevant for users' decision-making purposes, and audited forecasts would presumably be more reliable than those submitted by management without verification.

The prime concern over the involvement of CPAs with forecasts is the protection of their credibility in attesting to historical statements. Even if an auditor were to attest to only the reasonableness of the underlying assumptions and to the mechanical accuracy of the forecasts (and thus be in compliance with Rule 201-E), there might be a deterioration of the respect for CPAs whenever a forecast failed. Since forecasts, by their very nature, are often likely to be wrong, the well-established reputation of CPAs for accuracy

57

and reliability in historical financial statements could be adversely affected. There is no simple way to measure the pros and cons of attesting to forecasts, and it is a matter of continuing discussion within the profession.

RESPONSIBILITIES TO CLIENTS—RULES AND INTERPRETATIONS

Rule 301—Confidential Client Information. A member shall not disclose any confidential information obtained in the course of a professional engagement except with the consent of the client.

This rule shall not be construed (a) to relieve a member of his obligation under Rules 202 and 203, (b) to affect in any way his compliance with validly issued subpoena or summons enforceable by order of a court, (c) to prohibit review of a member's professional practices as a part of voluntary quality review under Institute authorization or (d) to preclude a member from responding to any inquiry made by the ethics division or Trial Board of the Institute, by a duly constituted investigative or disciplinary body of a state CPA society, or under state statutes.

Members of the ethics division and Trial Board of the Institute and professional practice reviewers under Institute authorization shall not disclose any confidential client information which comes to their attention from members in disciplinary proceedings or otherwise in carrying out their official responsibilities. However, this prohibition shall not restrict the exchange of information with an aforementioned duly constituted investigative or disciplinary body.

Interpretation under Rule 301—Responsibilities to Clients

301-1—Confidential Information and Technical Standards. The prohibition against disclosure of confidential information obtained in the course of a professional engagement does not apply to disclosure of such information when required to properly discharge the member's responsibility according to the profession's standards. The prohibition would not apply, for example, to disclosure, as required by Statement on Auditing Procedure No. 41 (now section 561 of Statement of Auditing Standards No. 1), of subsequent discovery of facts existing at the date of the auditor's report which would have affected the auditor's report had he been aware of such facts.

> ***Rule 302—Contingent Fees.*** Professional services shall not be offered or rendered under an arrangement whereby no fee will be charged contingent upon the findings or results of such services. However, a member's fees may vary depending, for example, on the complexity of the service rendered.
>
> Fees are not regarded as being contingent if fixed by courts or other public authorities or, in tax matters, if determined based on the results of judicial proceedings or the findings of governmental agencies.

RESPONSIBILITIES TO CLIENTS—DISCUSSION

Confidentiality

During the course of the examination, auditors obtain a considerable amount of information of a confidential nature, including officer salaries, product pricing and advertising plans and product cost data. If auditors divulged this information to outsiders or to client employees who have been denied access to the information, their relationship with management would be seriously strained. Furthermore, having access to the working papers would give employees an opportunity to alter information on the papers. For these reasons, care must be taken to protect the working papers at all times.

Ordinarily, the anditor's working papers can be provided to someone else only with the express permission of the client. This is the case even if a CPA sells his practice to another CPA firm or is willing to permit a successor auditor to examine the working papers prepared for a former client. Permission is not required from the client, however, if the working papers are subpoenaed by a court or are used as part of a voluntary quality review program with other CPA firms. If the working papers are subpoenaed, the client should be informed immediately. The client and its legal council may wish to challenge the subpoena.

Contingent Fees

The charging of fees contingent on the outcome of an audit, such as the granting of a loan by a bank, could easily impair the independence and objectivity of the auditor. Contingent fees are therefore prohibited.

RESPONSIBILITIES TO COLLEAGUES—DISCUSSION

The AICPA recognizes the importance of good relationships between competing members of the profession. The way professionals treat each other affects society's attitude about the profession. The <u>support should include</u> <u>providing highly specialized assistance in technical matters to fellow practi-</u> <u>tioners and reasonable restraint in displacing existing CPA firms from their</u> <u>present clients</u>.

There are now no Rules of Conduct concerning responsibilities to colleagues. They have all been eliminated as a result of pressure from the federal courts and the Justice Department.

Legal counsel for the AICPA advised the AICPA that three formerly existing rules concerning responsibilities to colleagues would be unlikely to hold up in a court of law. The membership of the AICPA voted to eliminate all three rules. They were concerned with competitive bidding, offers of employment, and encroachment.

1. *Competitive Bidding*. The former rule prohibiting competitive bidding was based on the belief by the profession that <u>bidding could result in *excessive competition*</u> and the simultaneous reduction in the quality of audits. The AICPA Rule forbidding a rule against *competitive bidding* was declared void by a U.S. District Court in an antitrust suit in 1972. Bidding is now common practice by CPAs, especially in audits of governmental agencies requiring competitive bids. Nevertheless, bidding is still prohibited in some states.

2. *Offers of Employment.* Until 1978 it was a violation of the Rules of Conduct to make a job offer to an employee of another CPA firm without first contacting the firm. The rule was meant to keep relations friendly between competing firms. The rule was considered a potential violation of employees rights and therefore was eliminated.

3. *Encroachment.* A major issue faced the profession in 1979 when the members were asked to vote on eliminating the former rule on encroachment.

A member shall not endeavor to provide a person or entity with a professional service which is currently provided by another public accountant.

The Professional Ethics Executive Committee recommended eliminating the rule after an inquiry by the U.S. Department of Justice and a recommendation by the Justice Department's staff that the Department initiate a complaint seeking to have the prohibitions against encroachment declared illegal. Legal council for the AICPA concluded that it was unlikely that the profession could defeat the Department of Justice in such an antitrust attack. As a result of this conclusion, members were asked to vote on the rule change. The membership voted in favor of eliminating the encroachment rule in an extremely close vote. Apparently, most CPAs were unwilling to risk action against the profession by the Justice Department

What will be the effect of the changes in these three rules on the practice of public accounting? It is too early to perceive any final conclusions at this early date. The likelihood is high that there will be increased competition between CPA firms, and some firms are likely to be less profitable. Some companies are likely to change CPA firms more frequently to reduce audit costs. There are advantages to newcomers entering the profession as they set up new practices, at least for the first few years. More mature firms may have less of a competitive advantage. Will the quality of audits be endangered?

The existing legal exposure of CPAs, peer review requirement, and the potential for interference by the SEC and government units are likely to keep auditing quality high. In the opinion of the authors, the changes in the rules will cause greater competition in the profession, but not so much competition that high-quality, efficiently run CPA firms will be significantly harmed.

OTHER RESPONSIBILITIES AND PRACTICES—RULES AND INTERPRETATIONS

Rule 501—Acts Discreditable. A member shall not commit an act discreditable to the profession.

Interpretations under Rule 501
Other Responsibilities and Practices

501-1—Client's Records and Accountant's Workpapers. Retention of client records after a demand is made for them is an act discreditable to the profession in violation of Rule 501. The fact that the statutes of the state in which a member practices may specifically grant him a lien on all client records in his possession does not change the ethical standard that it would be a violation of the Code to retain the records to enforce payment.

A member's working papers are his property and need not be surrendered to the client. However, in some instances a member's working papers will contain data which should properly be reflected in the client's books and records but which for convenience have not been duplicated therein, with the result that the client's records are incomplete. In such instances, the portion of the working papers containing such data constitutes part of the client's records, and copies should be made available to the client upon request.

501-2—Discrimination in Employment Practices. Discrimination based on race, color, religion, sex, age or national origin in hiring, promotion or salary practices is presumed to constitute an act discreditable to the profession in violation of Rule 501.

*Rule 502—*A member shall not seek to obtain clients by advertising or other forms of solicitation in a manner that is false, misleading, or deceptive.

Interpretation 502-1—Informational Advertising

Advertising that is informative and objective is permitted. Such advertising should be in good taste and be professionally dignified. There are no other restrictions, such as on the type of advertising media, frequency of placement, size, art work, or type style. Some examples of informative and objective content are—

1. Information about the member and the member's firm, such as—
   a. Names, addresses, telephone numbers, number of partners, shareholders or employees, office hours, foreign language competence, and date the firm was established.
   b. Services offered and fees for such services, including hourly rates and fixed fees.
   c. Educational and professional attainments, including date and place of certifications, schools attended, dates of graduation, degrees received, and memberships in professional associations.
2. Statements of policy or position made by a member or a member's firm related to the practice of public accounting or addressed to a subject of public interest.

Interpretation 502-2—False, Misleading, or Deceptive Acts

Advertising or other forms of solicitation that are false, misleading, or deceptive are not in the public interest and are prohibited. Such activities include those that—

1. Create false or unjustified expectations of favorable results.
2. Imply the ability to influence any court, tribunal, regulatory agency, or similar body official.
3. Consist of self-laudatory statements that are not based on verifiable facts.
4. Make comparisons with other CPAs.
5. Contain testimonials or endorsements.
6. Contain any other representations that would be likely to cause a reasonable person to misunderstand or be deceived.

Interpretation 502-4—Self-Designation as Expert or Specialist

Claiming to be an expert or specialist is prohibited because an AICPA program with methods for recognizing competence in specialized fields has not been developed and self-designations would be likely to cause misunderstanding or deception.

Rule 503—Commissions. A member shall not pay a commission to obtain a client, nor shall he accept a commission for a referral to a client of products or services of others. This rule shall not prohibit payments for the purchase of an accounting practice or retirement payments to individuals formerly engaged in the practice of public accounting or payments to their heirs or estates.

Interpretation under Rule 503—Commissions

503-1—Fees in Payment for Services. Rule 503, which prohibits payment of a commission to obtain a client, was adopted to avoid a client's having to pay fees for which he did not receive commensurate services. However, payment of fees to a referring public accountant for professional services to the successor firm or to the client in connection with the engagement is not prohibited.

Rule 504—Incompatible Occupations. A member who is engaged in the practice of public accounting shall not concurrently engage in any business or occupation which would create a conflict of interest in rendering professional services.

Rule 505—Form of Practice and Name. A member may practice public accounting, whether as an owner or employee, only in the form of a proprietorship, a partnership or a professional corporation whose characteristics conform to resolutions of Council.

A member shall not practice under a firm name which includes any fictitious name, indicates specialization or is misleading as to the type of organization (proprietorship, partnership or corporation). However, names of one or more past partners or shareholders may be included in the firm name of a successor partnership or corporation. Also, a partner surviving the death or withdrawal of all other partners may continue to practice under the partnership name for up to two years after becoming a sole practitioner.

A firm may not designate itself as "Members of the American Institute of Certified Public Accountants" unless all of its partners or shareholders are members of the Institute.

*Interpretation under Rule 505—Form
of Practice and Name*

505-1—Investment in Commercial Accounting Corporation.
A member in the practice of public accounting may have a financial interest
in a commercial corporation which performs for the public services of a
type performed by public accountants and whose characteristics do not
conform to resolutions of Council, provided such interest is no material
to the corporation's net worth, and the member's interest in and relation to
the corporation is solely that of an investor.

OTHER RESPONSIBILITIES
AND PRACTICES—DISCUSSION

All five rules included in the other responsibilities are discussed briefly.

Discreditable Acts

In interpreting Rule 501, do traffic tickets, excessive drinking, and rowdiness
qualify as discreditable acts? Although the rule is not specific, a "discreditable act" has been generally interpreted as covering only a convicted criminal offense. Occasionally, a practitioner is determined to have bribed an
Internal Revenue Agent or willfully failed to file his own tax return. These
are examples of discreditable acts. Notice also that failure to return a client's
records (Interpretation 501–1) and employment discrimination (Interpretation 501–2) are specifically prohibited under Rule 501.

Advertising

Until 1978 advertising in any form was prohibited. Now any advertising that
is not *false, misleading,* or *deceptive* is acceptable. It is not acceptable for a
member CPA firm to state that it is a specialist or limits itself to one or more
types of services. The AICPA feels that the profession has not adequately
defined specialist areas.

This change in the Rules of Conduct is similar to that for other professions. Advertising is now legally acceptable for most professions.

Will significant advertising be used by CPAs? Only time will tell for
certain. Already some *institutional-type advertising* has been done by some of the
larger firms. This type of advertising informs the readers and listeners of some
aspect of the profession such as independence, continuing education, and
qualifications of members.

It is questionable whether most CPAs will benefit much from advertising. Most larger companies are too sophisticated to be affected much by the information that can be communicated by advertising. Many large companies have been asking for detailed proposals from CPA firms several years.

The most likely beneficiaries of advertising are smaller CPA firms currently competing with non-CPAs for preparation of individual tax returns and bookkeeping services. The non-CPAs have been advertising heavily for many years. It is easy to imagine effective advertisement aimed at convincing professionals and small businesses of the advantage of having a CPA doing their accounting and related tax services.

Commissions

The reason for not allowing the payment of commissions to obtain clients (Rule 503) is to prevent overly aggressive obtaining of clients by offering a "finder's fee" to staff, banks, and others in a position to help a firm expand its business.

The reason for prohibiting a CPA from obtaining a referral commission is to prevent a CPA from obtaining clients and subcontracting the services without providing proper supervision. A fee, commission, or profit share cannot be charged to another firm for providing the services unless the first firm actually performed some of the services.

Incompatible Occupations

Until 1975, this rule prohibited concurrent engagement in a business or occupation which impaired the CPA's objectivity or served as a "feeder" to his practice. Now it only prevents occupations that would result in a conflict of interest. Examples of conflicts of interest would be concurrently acting as an attorney and auditor or providing management services and selling a certain brand of EDP equipment. In the first case, the CPA would be protecting the client interests as an attorney and independently evaluating the financial statement as an auditor. In the second the auditor would find it difficult to recommend a competitive EDP equipment even if it suited the client's needs better. Both would be considered a violation of Rule 504.

Form of Practice and Name

The profession has concluded that there are significant advantages for some firms to operate as a corporation rather than a partnership. These include primarily the tax benefits of pension, profit-sharing, and medical-reimbursement plans.

Before corporations were permitted there was a concern among the leadership of the AICPA that the traditional characteristics of a partnership be retained by CPA firms. Under the Rules Conduct, the only allowable form of corporation for CPAs is a professional corporation. The requirements for the name of a professional corporation, its purpose, ownership, and conduct correspond almost identically to that of a partnership. The most important requirement is the unlimited liability of the owners of the stock. Figure 2-1 states the requirements for a professional corporation of CPAs.

ENFORCEMENT

Failure to follow the Rules of Conduct can result in *expulsion* from the AICPA. This by itself would not prevent a CPA from practicing public accounting, but it would certainly be a weighty social sanction. All expulsions from the AICPA for a violation of the Rules are published in the CPA newsletter, a publication that is sent to all AICPA members.

More important than expulsion from the AICPA is the existence of Rules of Conduct, similar to the AICPA's, that have been enacted by the State Board of Accounting of each of the individual states. Since each state grants the individual practitioner a license to practice as a CPA, a significant breach of a State Board's code of ethics can result in the *loss of the CPA certificate and the license to practice*. Although it happens infrequently, this loss removes the practitioner from public accounting.

REVIEW QUESTIONS

2–1. Explain the need for a code of professional ethics for CPAs. In which ways should the CPA's code of ethics be similar to and different from that of other professional groups, such as attorneys or dentists?

2–2. List the four parts of the Code of Professional Ethics, and state the purpose of each part.

2–3. Distinguish between independence in fact and independence in appearance. State three activities that may not affect independence in fact but are likely to affect independence in appearance.

2–4. Why is an auditor's independence so essential?

2–5. Explain how the rules concerning stock ownership apply to partners and non-partners. Give an example of when stock ownership would be prohibited for each.

2–6. What is the profession's position regarding providing management advisory services for an audit client? Compare this position to that presented in the Metcalf and Moss reports.

2–7. Many people believe that a CPA cannot be truly independent when payment of fees is dependent upon the management of the client. Explain two approaches that could reduce this appearance of lack of independence.

2–8. After accepting an engagement a CPA discovers that the client's industry is more technical than he realized and that he is not competent is certain areas of the operation. What are the CPA's options?

RESOLUTION OF COUNCIL APPROVED AT THE SPRING MEETING OF COUNCIL ON MAY 6, 1969 AND AMENDED ON OCTOBER 2, 1974

RESOLVED, that members may be officers, directors, stockholders, representatives or agents of a corporation offering services of a type performed by public accountants only when the professional corporation or association has the following characteristics:

1. *Name.* The name under which the professional corporation or association renders professional services shall contain only the names of one or more of the present or former shareholders or of partners who were associated with a predecessor accounting firm. Impersonal or fictitious names, as well as names which indicate a speciality, are prohibited.

2. *Purpose.* The professional corporation or association shall not provide services that are incompatible with the practice of public accounting.

3. *Ownership.* All shareholders of the corporation or association shall be persons engaged in the practice of public accountancy as defined by the Code of Prefessional Ethics. Shareholders shall at all times own their shares in their own right, and shall be the beneficial owners of the equity capital ascribed to them.

4. *Transfer of Shares.* Provision shall be made requiring any shareholder who ceases to be eligible to be a shareholder to dispose of all of his shares within a reasonable period to a person qualified to be a shareholder or to the corporation or association.

5. *Directors and Officers.* The principal executive officer shall be a shareholder and a director, and to the extent possible, all other directors and officers shall be certified public accountants. Lay directors and officers shall not exercise any authority whatsoever over professional matters.

6. *Conduct.* The right to practice as a corporation or association shall not change the obligation of its shareholders, directors, officers and other employees to comply with the standards of professional conduct established by the American Institute of Certified Public Accountants.

7. *Liability.* The stockholders of professional corporations or associations shall be jointly and severally liable for the acts of a corporation or association, or its employees—except where professional liability insurance is carried, or capitalization is maintained, in amounts deemed sufficient to offer adequate protection to the public. Liability shall not be limited by the formation of subsidiary or affiliated corporations or associations each with its own limited and unrelated liability.

In a report approved by Council at the fall 1969 meeting, the Board of Directors recommended that professional liability insurance or capitalization in the amount of $50,000 per shareholder/officer and professional employee to a maximum of $2,000,000 would offer adequate protection to the public. Members contemplating the formation of a corporation under this rule should ascertain that no further modifications in the characteristics have been made.

FIGURE 2–1 Requirements of a Professional Corporation of CPAs

2–9. What is the purpose of the AICPA's Code of Professional Ethics restriction on the association of the CPA's name with forecasts?

2–10. If an auditor makes an agreement with one of his clients that the amount of his audit fee will be contingent upon the number of days required to complete the engagement, is it a violation of the Code of Professional Ethics? What is the essence of the rule of professional ethics dealing with contingent fees, and what are the reasons for the rule?   (AICPA adapted)

2–11. The auditor's working papers usually can be provided to someone else only with the permission of the client. Give two exceptions to this general rule.

2–12. What is the purpose of the encroachment rule?

2–13. Identify and explain the factors that should keep the quality of audits high even though competitive bidding is allowed.

2–14. Although informational advertising is permitted, a CPA is prohibited from advertising that he is an expert or specialist. Explain.

2–15. What is the purpose of the AICPA's Code of Professional Ethics restriction on commissions as stated in Rule 503?

2–16. What is meant by "incompatible occupations" as used in the Code of Professional Ethics? How would the absence of Rule 504 affect the CPA in conducting an audit?

2–17. State the allowable forms of practice a CPA firm may assume.

DISCUSSION QUESTIONS AND PROBLEMS

2–18. For each of the following questions concerning generally accepted auditing standards, select the best answer.

    a. Triolo, CPA, has a small public accounting practice. One of Triolo's clients desires services that Triolo cannot adequately provide. Triolo has recommended a larger CPA firm, Pinto and Company, to his client, and in return, Pinto has agreed to pay Triolo 10 percent of the fee for services rendered by Pinto for Triolo's client. Who, if anyone, is in violation of the AICPA's Code of Professional Ethics?

    (1) both Triolo and Pinto

    (2) neither Triolo nor Pinto

    (3) only Triolo

    (4) only Pinto

    b. The CPA who regularly examines Viola Corporation's financial statements has been asked to prepare forecasted income statements for the next five years. If the statements are to be based upon the corporation's operating assumptions and are for internal use only, the CPA should

    (1) reject the engagement because the statements are to be based upon assumptions.

    (2) reject the engagement because the statements are for internal use.

    (3) accept the engagement provided full disclosure is made of the assumptions used and the extent of the CPA's responsibility.

(4) accept the engagement provided Viola certifies in writing that the statements are for internal use only.

c. The Code of Professional Ethics considers Statements on Auditing Standards (formerly Statements on Auditing Procedure) issued by the institute's Auditing Standards Board (formerly the Committee on Auditing Procedures) to

(1) supersede generally accepted auditing standards.

(2) be separate and independent of generally accepted auditing standards.

(3) not be part of the Code, since specific rules pertaining to technical standards are established by the Code itself.

(4) be interpretations of generally accepted auditing standards.

(AICPA adapted)

2–19. The following questions concern independence and the Code of Professional Ethics. Choose the best response.

a. What is the meaning of the generally accepted auditing standard which requires that the auditor be independent?

(1) The auditor must be without bias with respect to the client under audit.

(2) The auditor must adopt a critical attitude during the audit.

(3) The auditor's sole obligation is to third parties.

(4) The auditor may have a direct ownership interest in his client's business if it is not material.

b. The independent audit is important to readers of financial statements because it

(1) determines the future stewardship of the management of the company whose financial statements are audited.

(2) measures and communicates financial and business data included in financial statements.

(3) involves the objective examination of and reporting on management-prepared statements.

(4) reports on the accuracy of all information in the financial statements.

c. The appearance of independence of a CPA, or that CPA's firm, could be impaired if the CPA

(1) owns a unit in a cooperative apartment house, where each unit has a vote in the cooperative, and the CPA, who does not participate in the management, has been retained as the auditor for the cooperative.

(2) joins a trade association, which is a client, and serves in a nonmanagement capacity.

(3) accepts a gift from a client.

(4) serves as an executor and trustee of the estate of an individual who owned the majority of the stock of a closely held client corporation.

d. The AICPA Code of Professional Ethics states, in part, that a CPA should maintain integrity and objectivity. Objectivity in the code refers to a CPA's ability

(1) to maintain an impartial attitude on all matters which come under the CPA's review.

(2) to independently distinguish between accounting practices that are acceptable and those that are not.

(3) to be unyielding in all matters dealing with auditing procedures.

(4) to independently choose between alternate accounting principles and auditing standards.

e. Reed, a partner in a local CPA firm, performs free accounting services for a private club of which Reed is treasurer. Which of the following would be the most preferable manner for Reed to issue the financial statements of the club?

(1) On the firm's letterhead with a disclaimer for lack of independence.

(2) On the firm's letterhead with a disclaimer for unaudited financial statements.

(3) On plain paper with no reference to Reed so that Reed will not be associated with the statements.

(4) On the club's letterhead with Reed signing as treasurer.

(AICPA adapted)

2–20. The following questions concern possible violations of the AICPA Code of Professional Ethics. Choose the best response.

a. In which one of the following situations would a CPA be in violation of the AICPA Code of Professional Ethics in determining his fee?

(1) A fee based on whether the CPA's report on the client's financial statements results in the approval of a bank loan.

(2) A fee based on the outcome of a bankruptcy proceeding.

(3) A fee based on the nature of the service rendered and the CPA's particular expertise instead of the actual time spent on the engagement.

(4) A fee based on the fee charged by the prior auditor.

b. The AICPA Code of Professional Ethics states that a CPA shall not disclose any confidential information obtained in the course of a professional engagement except with the consent of his client. In which one of the situations given below would disclosure by a CPA be in violation of the Code?

(1) Disclosing confidential information in order to properly discharge the CPA's responsibilities in accordance with his profession's standards.

(2) Disclosing confidential information in compliance with a subpoena issued by a court.

(3) Disclosing confidential information to another accountant interested in purchasing the CPA's practice.

(4) Disclosing confidential information in a review of the CPA's professional practice by the AICPA Quality Review Committee.

c. A CPA, who is a member of the American Institute of Certified Public Accountants, wrote an article for publication in a professional journal. The AICPA Code of Professional Ethics would be violated if the CPA allowed the article to state that the CPA was

(1) a member of the American Institute of Certified Public Accountants.

(2) a professor at a school of professional accountancy.

(3) a partner in a national CPA firm.

(4) a practitioner specialized in providing tax services.

d. Below are the names of four CPA firms and pertinent facts relating thereto. Unless otherwise indicated, the individuals named are CPAs and partners, and there are no other partners. Which firm name and related facts indicate a violation of the AICPA Code of Professional Ethics?

(1) Green, Lawrence, and Craig, CPAs. (Craig died about five years ago; Green and Lawrence are continuing the firm.)

(2) Clay and Sharp, CPAs. (The name of Andy Randolph, CPA, a third active partner, is omitted from the firm name.)

(3) Fulton and Jackson, CPAs. (Jackson died about three years ago; Fulton is continuing the firm as a sole proprietorship.)

(4) Schneider & Co., CPAs, Inc. (The firm has 10 other stockholders who are all CPAs.)

e. Which of the following is prohibited by the AICPA Code of Professional Ethics?

(1) Use of a firm name which indicates specialization.

(2) Practice of public accounting in the form of a professional corporation.

(3) Use of the partnership name for a limited period by one of the partners in a public accounting firm after the death or withdrawal of all other partners.

(4) Holding as an investment ten of 1,000 outstanding shares in a commercial corporation which performs bookkeeping services.

(AICPA adapted)

2–21. Fred Browning, CPA, has examined the financial statements of Grimm Company for several years. Grimm's president has now asked Browning to install an inventory system for the company.

Required:

Discuss the factors that Browning should consider in determining whether to accept the engagement. (AICPA adapted)

2–22. Your client, Nuesel Corporation, requested that you conduct a feasibility study to advise management of the best way the corporation can utilize electronic data-processing equipment and which computer, if any, best meets the corporation's requirements. You are technically competent in this area and accept the engagement. Upon completion of your study, the corporation accepts your suggestions and installs the computer and related equipment that you recommended.

Required:

a. Discuss the effect the acceptance of this management services engagement would have upon your independence in expressing an opinion on the financial statements of the Nuesel Corporation.

b. Instead of accepting the engagement, assume that you recommended Ike Mackey, of the CPA firm of Brown and Mackey, who is qualified in specialized services. Upon completion of the engagement, your client requests that Mackey's partner, John Brown, perform services in other areas. Should Brown accept the engagement? Discuss.

c. A local printer of data-processing forms customarily offers a commission for recommending him as a supplier. The client is aware of the commission offer and suggests that Mackey accept it. Would it be proper for Mackey to accept the commission with the client's approval? Discuss.

(AICPA adapted)

2-23. The members of the AICPA have recently voted to eliminate Rule 401 on encroachment. Rationalize this position along with other recent changes which permit advertising, competitive bidding, and offers of employment to employees of another firm, all changes that will increase competition.

2-24. For many years the financial and accounting community has recognized the importance of the use of audit committees and has endorsed their formation. At this time the use of audit committees has become widespread. Independent auditors have become increasingly involved with audit committees and consequently have become familiar with their nature and function.

Required:

a. Describe what an audit committee is.
b. Identify the reasons why audit committees have been formed and are currently in operation.
c. What are the functions of an audit committee?   (AICPA adapted)

2-25. Gilbert and Bradley formed a corporation called Financial Services, Inc., each man taking 50 percent of the authorized common stock. Gilbert is a CPA and a member of the American Institute of CPAs. Bradley is a CPCU (Chartered Property Casualty Underwriter). The Corporation performs auditing and tax services under Gilbert's direction and insurance services under Bradley's supervision. The opening of the corporation's office was announced by a three-inch, two-column "card" in the local newspaper.

One of the corporation's first audit clients was the Grandtime Company. Grandtime had total assets of $600,000 and total liabilities of $270,000. In the course of his examination, Gilbert found that Grandtime's building with a book value of $240,000 was pledged as security for a 10-year-term note in the amount of $200,000. The client's statements did not mention that the building was pledged as security for the 10-year-term note. However, as the failure to disclose the lien did not affect either the value of the assets or the amount of the liabilities and his examination was satisfactory in all other respects, Gilbert rendered an unqualified opinion on Grandtime's financial statements. About two months after the date of his opinion, Gilbert learned that an insurance company was planning to loan Grandtime $150,000 in the form of a first-mortgage note on the building. Realizing that the insurance company was unaware of the existing lien on the building, Gilbert had Bradley notify the insurance company of the fact that Grandtime's building was pledged as security for the term note.

Shortly after the events described above, Gilbert was charged with a violation of professional ethics.

Required:

Identify and discuss the ethical implications of those acts by Gilbert that were in violation of the AICPA Code of Professional Ethics.

(AICPA adapted)

2–25. The Lakeland Milk Products Company is a medium-sized company engaged in purchasing unpasteurized milk and processing it into different dairy products. For the past six years Lakeland has had services performed by a CPA firm, which includes an audit, tax services, and management consulting services. Since Lakeland lacks a competent controller, a major part of the fee has consisted of correcting the accounting records, making adjusting entries, and preparing the annual financial statements. The president of Lakeland has approached the CPA in charge of the Lakeland audit for the past three years about the possibility of becoming the full-time combination controller and internal auditor for the company.

Required:

a. Which services currently being provided by the CPA firm could be done by the CPA acting in his new capacity, assuming he is qualified to perform them?

b. Which services must the CPA firm continue to perform, even if the new controller is qualified? Why must they be done by the CPA firm?

c. Explain specific ways the controller can help reduce the CPA's audit fee if he is knowledgeable about the way the audit is conducted.

2–27. The following questions relate to auditors' independence:

a. Why is independence so essential for auditors?

b. Compare the importance of independence of CPAs with that of other professionals, such as attorneys.

c. Explain how an auditor can be independent in fact but not in appearance.

d. Discuss how each of the following could affect independence in fact and independence in appearance, and evaluate the social consequence of prohibiting auditors from doing each one.

(1) Ownership of stock in a client company.

(2) Having bookkeeping services for an audit client performed by the same person who does the audit.

(3) Recommending adjusting entries to the client's financial statements and preparing financial statements, including footnotes, for the client.

(4) Having management services for an audit client performed by individuals in a department that is separate from the audit department.

(5) Having the annual audit performed by the same audit team except for assistants for five years in a row.

(6) Having the annual audit performed by the same CPA firm for 10 years in a row.

(7) Having management select the CPA firm.

e. Which of (1) through (7) of part d are prohibited by the AICPA Code of Professional Ethics? Which are prohibited by the SEC?

2–28. The following situations each involve a possible violation of Rule 502, solicitation and advertising, of the Code of Professional Ethics:

a. Johnson, CPA, has been invited to participate in the tax seminar for industry by the National Association of Accountants. During the seminar, he hands out materials published by his firm, which are relevant to the subject matter under discussion, and includes his business card.

b. Marvin Collins, CPA, sends all existing clients monthly newsletters concerning new developments in taxes and management services. Annually, Collins sends each client brochures describing the nature of the firm's tax and management services capabilities. Included in the list of clients are several who engage other CPA firms for part of their tax or management services.

c. Runckle, CPA, has an office on the first floor of a downtown building. The following is printed on the window of his office in small letters: "R. J. Runckle, CPA, Income Tax Returns Prepared."

d. Every year Oris, CPA, does the audit of a church he does not attend. On the month in which the financial statements are issued, the weekly church bulletin acknowledges the CPA firm and thanks it for its outstanding contribution.

e. The East City State Bank has made arrangements for Patricia Clyde, CPA, to be available in the bank lobby to prepare tax returns for its customers on a fee basis. The bank mails a notice of the service and the hours Mrs. Clyde is available with each customer's monthly bank statement.

f. George and Gordon, CPAs, have recently become partners in the practice of public accounting. They ran an advertisement in the city newspaper under the announcement section stating that they had joined together to practice public accounting at 71262 Norell Street. The ad was in fine print, and the only other information included was their phone number.

g. Frederick, CPA, includes his name in the yellow pages in fine print with his firm name and the statement that he limits his practice to taxes and bookkeeping services for physicians and dentists.

h. In a help-wanted ad for new employees, Grant, CPA, included the required qualifications of prospective employees, starting salary, travel requirements, and the name, address, and telephone number of his CPA firm in the city newspaper. No information was included in bold print.

i. Alexander, CPA, buys several hundred copies of an abbreviated income-tax guide from a publishing company specializing in tax-related materials. The name of the CPA firm and its address are imprinted on the cover of the tax guide and mailed to all existing tax clients.

Required:

a. Indicate for each of these situations whether it is a violation of Rule 502.

b. Discuss the desirable and undesirable aspects of Rule 502 on society, the auditing profession as a whole, existing practitioners who have well-established practices, and newly emerging practitioners who do not have well-established practices.

2-29. The following each involve a possible violation of the AICPA's Code of Professional Ethics. For each situation, state the applicable section of the Rules of Conduct and whether it is a violation.

a. John Brown is a CPA, but not a partner, with three years of professional experience with Lyle and Lyle, CPAs. He owns twenty-five shares of stock in an audit client of the firm, but he does not take part in the audit of the client and the amount of stock is not material in relation to his total wealth.

b. In preparing the personal tax returns for a client, Phyllis Allen, CPA, observed that the deductions for contributions and interest were unusually large. When she asked the client for backup information to support the deductions, she was told, "Ask me no questions, and I will tell you no lies." Allen completed the return on the basis of the information acquired from the client.

c. A client requests assistance of J. Bacon, CPA, in the installation of a computer system for maintaining production records. Bacon had no experience in this type of work, so he obtained assistance from a computer consultant. The consultant is not in the practice of public accounting, but Bacon is confident of his professional skills.

d. Five small Chicago CPA firms have become involved in an information project by taking part in an intrafirm working paper review program. Under the program, each firm designates two partners to review the working papers, including the tax returns and the financial statements of another CPA firm taking part in the program. At the end of each review, the auditors who prepared the working papers and the reviewers have a conference to discuss the strengths and weaknesses of the audit. They do not obtain the authorization from the audit client before the review takes place.

e. Shirley Morris, CPA, applies to Apple and George, CPAs, for a permanent job as a senior auditor. Ms. Morris informs Apple and George that she works for another CPA firm in the same city but will not permit them to contact her present employer. Apple and George hire Ms. Morris without contacting the other CPA firm.

f. James Thurgood, CPA, stayed longer than he should have at the annual Christmas party of Thurgood and Thurgood, CPAs. On his way home he drove through a red light and was stopped by a policeman, who observed that he was intoxicated. In a jury trial, Thurgood was found guilty of driving under the influence of alcohol. Since this was not his first offense, he was sentenced to thirty days in jail and his driver's license was revoked for one year.

g. Bill Wendal, CPA, set up a casualty and fire insurance agency to complement his auditing and tax services. He does not use his own name on anything pertaining to the insurance agency and has a highly competent manager, Frank Jones, who runs it. Wendal frequently requests Jones to review the adequacy of a client's insurance with management if it seems underinsured. He feels that he provides a valuable service to clients by informing them when they are underinsured.

h. Rankin, CPA, provides tax services, management advisory services, and bookkeeping services and conducts audits for the same client. Since the firm is small, the same person frequently provides all of the services.

2–30. The following each involve possible violations of the AICPA's Code of Professional Ethics. For each situation, state whether it is a violation of the code. In those cases where it is a violation, explain the nature of the violation and the rationale for the existing rule.

a. Ralph Williams is the partner on the audit of a nonprofit charitable organization. He is also a member of the board of directors, but this position is honorary and does not involve performing a management function.

b. Pickens and Perkins, CPAs, are incorporated to practice public accounting. The only shareholders in the corporation are existing employees of the organization including partners, staff members who are CPAs, staff members who are not CPAs, and office personnel.

c. Fenn and Company, CPAs, has time available on a computer which it uses primarily for its own record keeping. Aware that the computer facilities of Delta Equipment Company, one of Fenn's audit clients, are inadequate for company needs, Fenn maintains on its computer certain routine accounting records for Delta.

d. Godette, CPA, has a law practice. Godette has recommended one of his clients to Doyle, CPA. Doyle has agreed to pay Godette 10 percent of the fee for services rendered by Doyle to Godette's client.

e. Theresa Barnes, CPA, has an audit client, Smith Inc., which uses another CPA for management services work. Miss Barnes sends her firm's literature covering its mangement services capabilities to Smith on a monthly unsolicited basis.

f. A bank issued a notice to its depositors that it was being audited and requested them to comply with the CPA's effort to obtain a confirmation on the deposit balances. The bank printed the name and address of the CPA in the notice. The CPA had knowledge of the notice.

g. Myron Jones, CPA, is a member of a national CPA firm. His business card includes his name, the firm's name, address, and telephone number, and the word *consultant*.

h. Gutowski, a practicing CPA, has written a tax article which is being published in a professional publication. The publication wishes to inform its readers about Gutowski's background. The information, which Gutowski has approved, includes his academic degrees, other articles he has had published in professional journals, and a statement that he is a tax expert.

i. Poust, CPA, has sold his public accounting practice, which includes bookkeeping, tax services, and auditing, to Lyons, CPA. Poust obtained permission from all audit clients for audit-related working papers before making them available to Lyons.

j. Murphy and Company, CPAs, is the principal auditor of the consolidated financial statements of Lowe, Inc., and subsidiaries. Lowe accounts for approximately 98 percent of consolidated assets and consolidated net income. The two subsidiaries are audited by Trotman and Company, CPAs, a firm with an excellent professional reputation. Murphy insists on auditing the two subsidiaries because he deems this necessary to warrant the expression of an opinion.   (AICPA adapted)

3

LEGAL LIABILITY

This chapter discusses the nature and potential sources of legal liability to CPAs. It starts by discussing the reasons for increasing litigation against CPAs. The nature of the lawsuits and the sources of potential liability are then examined in detail. A summary of significant lawsuits involving CPAs is included. These cases are tinted. The chapter ends with a discussion of the courses of action available to the profession and individual practitioners to minimize liability while meeting society's needs.

CHANGED LEGAL ENVIRONMENT

Professionals have always had a duty of reasonable care while performing work for their clients or patients. This responsibility is an implied part of the contract entered into between any professional and his client.

Under common law the duty of due care is owed to *third-party nonclients* only in limited circumstances, where the third party was a known and intended beneficiary of the professional work. An example is the beneficiary of a will.

In recent years, the courts have frequently interpreted the common law to broaden the availability of legal remedies beyond clients and the narrow, "known beneficiary" group. In addition, the courts have interpreted the federal securities laws broadly to create additional liabilities for CPAs. There are no simple reasons for this trend, but the following are major factors:

Growing Complexity

- The greater complexity of auditing and accounting due to such factors as the increasing size of business, the existence of the computer, and the intricacies of business operations.
- The growing awareness of the responsibilities of public accountants on the part of users of financial statements.
- An increased consciousness on the part of the SEC regarding its responsibility for protecting investors' interests.
- Society's increasing acceptance of lawsuits by injured parties against anyone who might be able to provide compensation, regardless of who was at fault. This is frequently called the "deep-pocket" concept of liability.
- Large civil court judgments against CPA firms in a few cases, which have encouraged attorneys to provide legal services on a contingent-fee basis. This arrangement offers the injured party a potential gain when the suit is successful, but minimal loss when it is unsuccessful.
- The willingness of many CPA firms to settle their legal problems out of court in an attempt to avoid legal fees and adverse publicity rather than resolving them through the judicial process.
- The many alternative accounting principles from which clients can elect to present their financial statements, and the lack of clear-cut criteria for the auditor to evaluate whether the proper alternative was selected.

LEGAL CONCEPTS AFFECTING ALL TYPES OF LIABILITY

The CPA can have liability for every aspect of his public-accounting work, including auditing, taxes, management advisory services, and bookkeeping. For example, if a CPA negligently failed to properly prepare and file a client's tax return, he can be held liable for any penalties and interest the client was required to pay plus the tax preparation fee charged. The court can also assess punitive damages.

Most of the major lawsuits have dealt with auditing and unaudited financial statements. The discussion in this chapter is restricted primarily to those two aspects of public accounting. The areas of liability in auditing can be classified as (1) liability to clients, (2) civil liabilities to third parties under common and statutory law, and (3) criminal liability. Several legal concepts apply to all these types of lawsuits against CPAs. These are the prudent man concept, liability for the acts of others, and the lack of privileged communication.

Prudent Man Concept

There is agreement within the profession and courts that the auditor is not a guarantor or insurer of financial statements. The auditor is only expected to conduct the audit with due care. Even then, the auditor cannot be expected to be perfect.

REASONABLE CARE & diligence (handwritten annotation)

The standard of due care to which the auditor is expected to be held is *NOTE* (handwritten annotation) often referred to as the *prudent man concept*. It is expressed in *Cooley on Torts* as follows:

> Every man who offers his service to another and is employed assumes the duty to exercise in the employment such skill as he possesses with reasonable care and diligence. In all these employments where peculiar skill is prerequisite, if one offers his service, he is understood as holding himself out to the public as possessing the degree of skill commonly possessed by others in the same employment, and, if his pretentions are unfounded, he commits a species of fraud upon every man who employs him in reliance on his public profession. But no man, whether skilled or unskilled, undertakes that the task he assumes shall be performed successfully, and without fault or error. *He undertakes for good faith and integrity, but not for infallibility*, and he is liable to his employer for negligence, bad faith, or dishonesty, but not for losses consequent upon pure errors of judgment [italics added].

Liability for Acts of Others

The partners, or shareholders in the case of a professional corporation, are jointly liable for civil actions against a partner. As stated in Chapter 2, a professional corporation does not have limited liability.

The partners may also be liable for the work of others on whom they rely under the laws of agency. The three most likely groups an auditor is likely to rely on are *employees, other CPA firms* engaged to do part of the work, and *specialists* called upon to provide technical information. For example, if an employee performs improperly in doing an audit, the partners can be held liable for the employee's performance.

Lack of Privileged Communication

CPAs do not have the right under common law to withhold information from the courts on the grounds that the information is privileged. As stated in Chapter 2, information in auditors' working papers can be subpoenaed by a court. Confidential discussions between the client and auditor cannot be withheld from the courts.

Several states have statutes that permit privileged communication between the client and auditor. Even then, the intent at the time of the communication must have been for the communication to remain confidential. A CPA can refuse to testify in a state with privileged communication statutes. The privilege does not extend to federal courts.

DEFINITIONS

The material in the rest of the chapter can be covered more effectively if the most common legal terms affecting CPAs' liability are understood.

Breach of Contract. Failure of one or both parties to a contract to fulfill the requirements of the contract. An example is the failure of a CPA firm to deliver a tax return on the agreed-upon date.

Tort Action for Negligence. Failure of a party to meet its social or professional obligations, contractual or otherwise.

Negligence. Absence of reasonable care that can be expected of a person in a set of circumstances. When negligence of an auditor is being evaluated, it is in terms of what other competent auditors would have done in the same situation.

Contributory Negligence. Absence of reasonable care by the party damaged by another party's negligence. A common example is the failure to give the CPA information that he requested during the preparation of a tax return. The client later sues the CPA for improper preparation of the tax return. The court may hold there was contributory negligence by the client.

Fraud. An intentional wrongful act with the purpose of deceiving or causing harm to another party. An important characteristic of fraud is the intent of the wrongdoer. An example in auditing is for the auditor to give a standard audit opinion (unqualified) on financial statements that will be used to obtain a loan when he knows they are materially misstated.

Constructive Fraud. Existence of extreme or unusual negligence even though there was no intent to deceive or do harm. For example, if a CPA failed to follow most of the generally accepted auditing standards, he may be charged with constructive fraud even though he had no intention of deceiving statement users.

Privity of Contract. A direct relationship between two or more parties to a contract. For an audit, the client and any third party that is named in the audit contract (engagement letter) have privity of contract.

Third-Party Beneficiary. A third party who does not have privity of contract, but is known to the contracting parties and is intended to have certain rights and benefits under the contract. A common example is a bank that has a large loan outstanding at the balance sheet date and requires an audit as a part of its loan agreement.

Common Law. Laws that have been developed through court decisions rather than through government statutes. An example is a claim by a bank related to an auditor's failure to discover material misstatements in financial statements that were relied on to issue a loan.

Statutory Law. Laws that have been passed by the U.S. Congress and other governmental units. The SEC Acts of 1933 and 1934 are important statutory laws affecting auditors.

Liability to Clients

The most traditional source of liability for CPAs has been directly to clients for failure to perform their auditing functions with due care. These lawsuits often involve defalcations which the auditor has failed to uncover. The client claims that the CPA would have uncovered these if he had not been negligent. The lawsuit can be for *breach of contract,* or it can be a *tort action for negligence.* Most lawsuits involving clients are tort rather than breach of contract actions because the amount recoverable under tort is normally larger.

The principal issue in these cases normally concerns the level of care required to perform nonnegligently. Although it is generally agreed that nobody is perfect, not even a professional, in most instances any significant error or mistake of judgment will create at least a presumption of negligence which the professional will have to rebut. In the auditing environment, the failure to meet generally accepted auditing standards is often conclusive evidence of negligence. The reader should recognize from the study of generally accepted auditing standards in Chapter 1 that determining whether there is a violation is highly subjective.

The question of level of care becomes more difficult in the environment of an unaudited review of financial statements, where there are few accepted standards to evaluate performance. In the absence of well-defined standards, the courts are likely to impose standards which are close to those used in audits. A widely known example of a lawsuit for the failure to uncover fraud is the *1136 Tenants* case. It is included as one of the illustrative cases.

Auditor's Defenses

The auditor's defense to claims of negligence for the failure to discover defalcation is normally a lack of responsibility for such discovery or contributory negligence by the clients. The support for the position that the auditor lacked responsibility for discovering the defalcation comes from Section 327 of Statement on Auditing Standards:

> An examination made in accordance with generally accepted auditing standards *is subject to the inherent limitations of the auditing process*. As with certain business controls, the costs of audits should bear a reasonable relationship to the benefits expected to be derived. As a result, the concept of selective testing of the data being examined, which involves judgment both as to the number of transactions to be examined and as to the areas to be tested, has been generally accepted as a valid and sufficient basis for an auditor to express an opinion on financial statements. Thus, the auditor's examination, based on the concept of selective testing of the data being examined, *is subject to the inherent risk that material errors or irregularities, if they exist, will not be detected.* [italics added].

The defense of contributory negligence of the client, in cases of employee fraud, arises when the auditor claims the client knew of the potential for fraud but refused to correct the conditions which permitted the fraud.

This happens frequently when the auditor informs the client of a material weakness in internal control that enhances the likelihood of fraud. Management often does not correct the problem because of cost considerations,

1136 Tenants v. Max Rothenberg and Company (1967)—liability to clients *FAILURE TO PROVIDE AN ENGAGEMENT LETTER FOR UNAUDITED STATEMENTS,*

The 1136 Tenants case was a civil case concerning a CPA's failure to uncover fraud as a part of unaudited financial statements. The tenants recovered approximately $235,000.

A CPA firm was engaged by a real estate managing agent for $600 per year to prepare financial statements, a tax return, and a schedule showing the apportionment of real estate taxes for the 1136 Tenants Corporation, a cooperative apartment house. The statements were sent periodically to the tenants. The statements included the words "unaudited" and there was a cover letter stating that "The statement was prepared from the books and records of the corporation and no independent verifications were taken thereon."

During the period of the engagement, from 1963 to 1965, the manager of the management firm embezzled significant funds from the 1136 tenants. The tenants of the cooperative sued the auditors for negligence and breach of contract for failure to find the fraud.

There were two central issues in the case. Was the CPA firm engaged to do an audit instead of only write-up work, and was there negligence on the part of the CPA firm? The court answered yes on both counts. The reasoning for the court concluding that an audit had taken place was the performance of "some audit procedures" by the CPA firm, including the preparation of a worksheet entitled "missing invoices." Had the CPA followed up on these, the fraud would likely have been uncovered. Most important, the court concluded that even if the engagement had not been considered an audit, the CPA had a duty of follow-up on any potentially significant exceptions uncovered during an engagement.

Two developments resulted from the 1136 Tenants case and similar lawsuits concerning unaudited financial statements:

- Engagement letters between the client and CPA firm have been strongly recommended by the AICPA for all engagements, but particularly unaudited engagements. The letter should clearly define the intent of the engagement, the CPA's responsibilities, and any restrictions imposed on the CPA.
- The Compilation and Review Services Committee was formed as a major committee of the AICPA to set forth guidelines for unaudited financial statements. They issued their first pronouncement in 1979. The Auditing Standards Board has eliminated all references to unaudited statements for non-publicly held Companies in SASs, to avoid confusion between audited and unaudited engagements.

attitudes about employee honesty, or procrastination. In the event of a lawsuit, the auditor is unlikely to lose with the contributory negligence defense, if the client had been informed in writing of the internal control weakness.

Liability to Third Parties under Common Law

Until recently, common law has not recognized any liability of professionals to third parties for negligence. The leading auditing case in the area is *Ultramares* v. *Touche*, and the traditional common-law approach is now known as the *Ultramares doctrine*. The case is included as an illustrative case.

In recent years, some courts have interpreted *Ultramares* more broadly, to allow recovery by third parties *if those third parties were known and recognized to be relying upon the work of the professional* at the time the professional performed his services. *Rusch Factors Case (1968)*

Other jurisdictions and the Restatement of Torts, an authoritative compendium of legal principles, have broadened the CPA's liability for negligence even further to allow recovery by any *reasonably limited and identifiable group that would have relied on the CPA's work, such as creditors, even though these creditors were not specifically known* at the time the CPA performed his or her

Ultramares Corporation v. Touche (1931)—liability to third parties

The creditors of an insolvent corporation relied on the certified financials of Ultramares and subsequently sued the accountants, alleging that they were guilty of negligence and fraudulent misrepresentation. The accounts receivable had been falsified by adding to approximately $650,000 in accounts receivable another item of over $700,000. The creditors alleged that careful investigation would have shown the $700,000 to be fraudulent. The accounts payable contained similar discrepancies.

The court held that the accountants had been negligent but ruled that accountants would not be liable to third parties for honest blunders beyond the bounds of the original contract. The court held that only one who enters into a contract with an accountant for services can sue if those services are rendered negligently.

The court went on, however, to order a new trial on the issue of fraudulent misstatement. The form of certificate then used said, "We further certify that subject to provisions for Federal taxes on income the said statement in our opinion presents a true and correct view of the financial condition." The court pointed out that to make such a representation if one did not have an honest belief in its truth would be *fraudulent misrepresentation*.

work. A leading case relying on the Ultramares doctrine but also referring to the Restatement of Torts is *Stephens Industries* v. *Haskins and Sells*. It is included as an illustrative case.

Still others have rejected the *Ultramares* doctrine entirely and have held that the CPA is *liable to anyone who relies on the CPA's work, if that work is performed negligently.*

In most states, a professional would be liable just as any other person would be for *actually defrauding a third party.* Some courts have stretched the concept of fraud beyond its original bounds to include any known misrepresentation on a financial statement, even if there was no direct intent to defraud. In some cases, fraud can include misrepresentations which were the results of poor judgment. As a further extension of the fraud concept, some courts have held that negligence which is so extreme as to be gross negligence or recklessness will be considered to be constructive fraud, the legal equivalent of fraud.

The liability to third parties under common law continues to be in a state of uncertainty. Some legal jurisdictions still recognize the early precedence of *Ultramares*. At the other extreme, the liability to third parties for negligence is essentially the same as for that to clients. Even the definition of fraudulent behavior is changing.

Stephens Industries v. *Haskins & Sells* (1971)—liability to third parties

The plaintiff, purchaser of two-thirds of the stock of a car rental company, sued Haskins & Sells for negligence in auditing the accounts receivable. The contract provided that the accounts receivable figure on the corporate books should remain "without adjustment to reflect the fact that the auditors may feel certain accounts are or may be uncollectible in whole or in part." The auditor's opinion specifically stated an exception "that in accordance with your instructions we did not request any of the customers to confirm their balances nor did we review the collectability of any trade accounts receivable." The lack of adjustment to reflect uncollectible amounts was also disclosed in the "Notes to the Balance Sheet."

The lower court held that in the absence of privity between the plaintiff and auditor, no liability for negligence existed, citing *Ultramares*. The higher court affirmed, but went on to say that even if the Restatement standard of liability to the third parties known to be relying on the audit applied, there would be no liability here. Haskins & Sells, by reason of the financial statement notes and exception in the audit report, and by not making judgments on others without adequate information, had not been negligent at all, particularly in light of the contract, but had exercised care and competence.

CIVIL LIABILITY UNDER THE FEDERAL SECURITIES LAWS

Although there has been some growth in actions brought against accountants by their clients or third parties under common law, the greatest growth in CPA liability litigation has been in the federal securities law field.

The emphasis on federal remedies has resulted primarily from the recently expanded availability of class-action litigation and the relative ease of obtaining massive recovery from defendants. In addition, several sections of the securities laws impose rather strict liability standards on CPAs. Federal courts are often likely to favor plaintiffs in lawsuits where there are strict standards.

Securities Act of 1933

The Securities Act of 1933 deals with the information in registration statements and prospectuses. It concerns only the reporting requirements for companies issuing new securities.

The Securities Act of 1933 imposes an unusual burden on the auditor. Section 11 of the 1933 Act defines the rights of third parties and auditors. These are summarized as follows:

- Any third party who purchased securities described in the registration statement may sue the auditor. Privity of contract is not applicable under the 1933 Act.
- The third party user does not have the burden of proof that he relied on the financial statements or that the auditor was negligent or fraudulent in doing the audit. He must only prove that the financial statements were misleading or not fairly stated.
- The auditor has the burden of demonstrating as a defense that: (1) the statements were not materially misstated, (2) an adequate audit was conducted in the circumstances, or (3) the user did not incur the loss because of the misleading financial statement.
- The auditor has responsibility for making sure the financial statements were fairly stated beyond the date of the issuance of the statements. He has responsibility up to the date the registration statement became effective, which could be several months later.

Although the burden may appear harsh to auditors, there have been few cases tried under the 1933 Act. The most significant one is *Escott* v. *Bar Chris Construction Corp.* (1968). Because of its effect on audit standards and the auditing profession, a summary of this case is included.

Securities Act of 1934

The liability of auditors under the 1934 Act centers about the audited financial statements submitted to the SEC as a part of annual 10-K reports.

Escott et al. v. *Bar Chris Construction Corporation* (1968)—Securities
Act of 1933   *INADEQUATE*
            S-1 REVIEW

Bar Chris constructed bowling alleys and in most cases sold them to operators on an installment-note basis. The notes were then discounted with a factor. Some of the bowling alleys were also leased by a wholly owned subsidiary of Bar Chris. The construction operations were accounted for on a percentage-of-completion basis.

Bar Chris filed a registration statement in 1961 for the issuance of convertible subordinated debentures. They were thereby subject to the Securities Act of 1933. Approximately 17 months later Bar Chris filed for bankruptcy. The purchasers of the debentures filed suit against the CPA firm under the 1933 Act.

There were several issues involved in the case, including the appropriateness of the percentage-of-completion method of accounting and other related accounting issues, the materiality of the misstatements, and the adequacy of the audit work performed.

The court ruled that the percentage-of-completion method of accounting was appropriate in the circumstances. It concluded that other accounting methods, such as the handling of a sale and subsequent leaseback of a bowling alley and the classification of a cash advance for a subsidiary, were improperly handled.

Materiality was also a significant issue in the case. Bar Chris is one of the few cases in the history of the profession that directly addressed the question of materiality. Earnings per share was misstated by about 15 percent, but the court surprisingly held that the amount was immaterial. There was a significant increase in earnings in the current year of over 25 percent that may have accounted for the court's conclusion. At the same time, the court concluded that the balance sheet was materially misstated when the current ratio was stated at 1.9 to 1 rather than 1.6 to 1.

The most significant issue of the case, especially to audit staff personnel, was the matter of the review for events subsequent to the balance sheet, called an S-1 review for registration statements. The courts concluded that the CPA firm's written audit program was in conformity with generally accepted auditing standards in existence at that time. However, they were highly critical of the reviewer, who was inexperienced in audits of construction companies, for the failure to appropriately follow up on answers by management. The following is an important part of the court's opinion in the case:

> Accountants should not be held to a higher standard than that recognized in their profession. I do not do so here. Richard's review did not come up to that written standard. He did not take the steps which the CPA firm's written program

prescribed. He did not spend an adequate amount of time on a task of this magnitude. *Most important of all, he was too easily satisfied with glib answers to his inquiries.* This is not to say that he should have made a complete audit. But there were enough danger signals in the materials which he did examine to require some further investigation on his part. . . . . It is not always sufficient merely to ask questions [italics added and the name used in the case was changed].

The CPA firm was found liable in the case on the grounds that they had not established due diligence required under the 1933 Securities Act. Two significant results occurred directly from this case:

- Statements on Auditing Standards were changed to require greater emphasis on procedures the auditor must perform on audits regarding subsequent events (Section 560). This change is a good example of the impact that the SEC has on the audits of all companies.
- A greater emphasis began to be placed on the importance of the audit staff understanding the client's business and industry.

Every traded security in national and over-the-counter markets is required to submit audit statements annually. There are obviously a much larger number of statements falling under the 1934 Act than under the 1933 Act.

In addition to annual audited financial statements, there is potential legal exposure to auditors for quarterly (10-Q), monthly (8-K), or other reporting information. The auditor is usually involved in reviewing the information in these other reports; therefore, there is legal responsibility. However, few cases have involved auditors for reports other than the 10-K.

Rule 10b-5 of the 1934 Act   FRAUD

The principal focus on CPA liability litigation under the 1934 act has been Rule 10b-5, a section of the federal Securities Act of 1934 which appears only in the rules and regulations of the Securities and Exchange Commission. Rule 10b-5 states:

> It shall be unlawful for any person directly or indirectly, by the use of any means or instrumentality of interstate commerce, or of the mails or of any facility of any national securities exchange, (a) To employ any device, scheme, or artifice to defraud, (b) To make any untrue statement of a material fact or omit to state a material fact necesary in order to make the statements made, in the light of the circumstances under which they were made, not misleading, or (c) To engage in any act, practice, or course of business which operates or would operate as a fraud or deceit upon any person in connection with the purchase or sale of any security.

The Federal Circuit Courts throughout the country often disagree upon what standard of performance to enforce against a CPA in holding an auditor liable under Rule 10b-5. Some courts have held that negligence alone constituted a fraud on investors. Other courts have held that something more than negligence was required. Still others have said that *actual intent to commit a fraud was required* under the rule.

In 1976, the Supreme Court, in *Hochfelder* v. *Ernst & Ernst*, a leading securities law case as well as CPA liabilities case, ruled that some knowledge and intent to deceive are required before CPAs could be liable for violation of Rule 10b-5. However, the court left open the question of whether or not recklessness would constitute constructive fraud and would also qualify for recovery under Rule 10b-5. *Hochfelder* is included as an illustrative case.

Many auditors believed the Hochfelder case would significantly reduce auditors' exposure to liability. However, subsequently suits have been brought under Rule 10b-5. The knowledge and deceit standard is more easily met by plaintiffs where the auditor knew all the relevant facts but made poor judgments. In such a situation, the courts emphasize that the CPAs had requisite knowledge. The *Herzfeld* case, described below, is an example of that reasoning. Another line of reasoning which has received some judicial support has been to adopt the Supreme Court's requirements of fraud and hold that recklessness or gross negligence constitutes a constructive fraud and is therefore actionable under Rule 10b-5. The *McLean* v. *Alexander* case is a leading case involving allegations of gross negligence and recklessness. It is included as an illustrative case. Even if no intentional misrepresentation or recklessness were evident in the financial statements, lawyers have argued that if the CPA knew that the audit was less than full compliance with all the requirements of the generally accepted auditing standards, the audit opinion stating that generally accepted auditing standards were complied with is in itself fraudulent and therefore actionable.

Hochfelder v. *Ernst & Ernst* (1976)—Securities Act of 1934

This case involved the auditor's responsibility for detecting fraud perpetrated by the president of the firm. Leston Nay, the president of First Securities Co. of Chicago, fraudulently convinced certain customers to invest funds in escrow accounts that he represented would yield a high rate of return. There were no escrow accounts. Nay converted the customers' funds to his own use.

The transactions were not in the usual form of dealings between First Securities and its customers. First, all correspondence with customers was made solely with Nay. Second, checks of the customers were drawn payable to Nay and because of a "mail rule" which Nay imposed, such mail was opened only by him. Third, the escrow accounts were not reflected on the books of First Securities, nor in filings with the SEC, nor in connection with customers' other investment accounts. The fraud was uncovered at the time of Nay's suicide.

Respondent customers originally sued in District Court for damages against Ernst & Ernst as aiders and abetters under Section 10b-5. They alleged that Ernst & Ernst failed to conduct a proper audit which should have led them to discover the "mail rule" and the fraud. No allegations were made as to Ernst & Ernst's fraudulent and intentional conduct. The action was based solely on a claim that Ernst & Ernst failed to conduct a proper audit which should have led them to discover the "mail rule" and the fraud. The District Court dismissed the action, but did not resolve the issue of whether or not a cause of action could be based merely on allegations of negligence.

The Court of Appeals reversed the District Court. The Appeals Court held that one who breaches a duty of inquiry and disclosure owed another is liable in damages for aiding and abetting a third party's violation of Rule 10b-5 if the fraud would have been discovered or prevented had the breach not occurred. The court reasoned that Ernst & Ernst had a common law and statutory duty of inquiry into the adequacy of First Securities' internal control system because it had contracted to audit First Securities and to prepare for filing with the Commission the annual report of its financial condition.

The U.S. Supreme Court reversed the Court of Appeals, concluding that the interpretation of Rule 10b-5 required the "intent to deceive, manipulate or defraud." Justice Powell wrote in the Court's opinion that

> When a statute speaks so specifically in terms of manipulation and deception, and of implementing devices and contrivances—the commonly understood terminology of intentional wrongdoing—and when its history reflects no more expansive intent, we are quite unwilling to extend the scope of the statute to negligent conduct.

The court pointed out that in certain areas of the law, recklessness is considered to be a form of intentional conduct for purposes of imposing liability. This leaves open the possibility that in some circumstances reckless behavior may be sufficient for liability under Rule 10b-5.

Herzfeld v. Laventhol, Krekstein, Horwath & Horwath (1976)—Securities Act of 1934

This case involved a lawsuit by an investor who relied on the audited financial statements of a real estate company in deciding to invest in that real estate company. The lawsuit was brought under Rule 10b-5 of the Securities Exchange Act of 1934.

The real estate company had entered into a contract to purchase some nursing homes for approximately $13 million and sell them for approximately $15 million. Without the nursing homes contracts, the real estate company had a loss of some $169,000. With the profit recognized on the sale of the nursing homes, the real estate company had an additional $2 million of net income. The auditing firm reviewed the contracts. One of the partners, an attorney with one year of practice experience, concluded that the contracts were legally enforceable. He also consulted an attorney over the telephone who, sight unseen, also stated that the contracts were valid and enforceable. The auditors also inquired about the purchaser of the nursing home and found that he had a net worth of $100,000 and a practice of selling contracts before closing. The accounting firm decided that $235,000 of the $2 million profit would be recognized currently. The accounting firm decided that the rest of the $2 million profit would be recognized as "deferred gross profit." In addition, the accounting firm took an exception in its opinion subject to the collectibility of the balance receivable on the contract of sale.

In fact, neither of the transactions was consumated. The real estate company later filed a petition under Chapter XI of the Bankruptcy Act. The lower court found that the financial statements and Laventhol's opinion were materially misleading for failure to disclose the terms of the agreement, the fact that the agreement may have only been an option, the absence of any record on the real estate company's books of the transaction, and the conditions of the contract, which had not yet been met. The court also held that Laventhol had knowledge of the fact that the figures created a false picture, and had actual knowledge of the omitted facts which rendered its report misleading. The court therefore concluded that Laventhol had the necessary knowledge and intent to deceive to be liable under Rule 10b-5. The plaintiff obtained judgment in favor of Herzfeld against Laventhol in the amount of $153,000 plus costs and interest.

McLean v. *Alexander* (1979)—Securities Act of 1934

This is a case in which CPA defendants were found liable by a lower court under Rule 10b-5 and were also found liable for common-law fraud, even though there was no evidence that the accountant knew the financial statements to be incorrect or intended to mislead anyone. The lower court was, however, overruled by a higher court.

The case was brought by a businessman and investor who had purchased all the stock of a speculative company, relying on glowing reports of sales. The financial statement indicated accounts receivable which apparently were based on sales of 16 laser devices which the company manufactured. In fact, all 16 sales were guaranteed sales or consignment sales rather than true sales. Although the 16 sales in the aggregate did not have a material impact on the financial statements in terms of pure numbers, the plaintiff allegedly relied on these accounts receivable as an indication of the business ability of the company.

The auditors did not receive confirmations that they had mailed on these accounts. When pressed by the client to complete the audit, the auditors brought up this problem. The auditors subsequently received two telegram confirmations of purchase orders rather than of accounts receivable. The auditors made no attempt to investigate further and did not find out that, in fact, one of the telegrams was fraudulent.

There were other indications of discrepancies in these accounts which the auditors did not follow up. The lower court held that the information that the auditors obtained during the course of the audit, but did not follow up on, was the kind of information that should have been disclosed. The lower court held that failure to disclose that information constituted reckless disregard for the truth.

The appellate court ruled that the auditors were at most guilty of negligence, but not of bad-faith recklessness. They held the CPAs not liable under Rule 10b-5 and Delaware common-law fraud.

It is clear from the previous discussion that Rule 10b-5 continues to be a basis for lawsuits against auditors, even though *Hochfelder* has limited the liability somewhat.

SEC Sanctions

Closely related to auditors' liability is the SEC's authority to sanction. The SEC has the power in certain circumstances to suspend or sanction practitioners from doing audits for SEC companies. Rule 2(e) of the SEC's Rules of Practice says:

> The Commission may deny, temporarily or permanently, the privilege of appearing or practicing before it in any way to any person who is found by the Commission . . . (1) not to possess the requisite qualifications to represent others, or (2) to be lacking in character or integrity or to have engaged in unethical or improper professional conduct.

The SEC has rarely even temporarily suspended anyone from doing any audits of SEC clients. A more common approach is to prohibit a CPA firm from accepting any new SEC clients for a period, such as 6 months. Recently, the SEC has required an extensive review of a major CPA firm's practices by another CPA firm. In some cases, firms have been required to participate in continuing-education programs and to make changes in their practice. Sanctions such as these are published by the SEC and frequently reported in the business press. These reported sanctions are a significant embarrassment to the CPA firm.

Foreign Corrupt Practices Act of 1977

A significant congressional action affecting both CPA firms and their clients was the passage of the Foreign Corrupt Practices Act of 1977. The Act makes it illegal to offer a bribe to an official of a foreign political party for the purpose of exerting influence and obtaining or retaining business. The prohibition against payments to foreign officials is applicable to all U.S. domestic firms, regardless of whether they are publicly or privately held, and to foreign companies filing with the SEC.

Apart from the bribery provisions that affect publicly held companies, the new law requires SEC registrants under the Securities Act of 1934 to meet additional requirements. These include the maintenance of reasonably complete and accurate records and an adequate system of internal control to prevent bribery. The law significantly affects all SEC companies, but the unanswered question to the profession at this time is how it affects auditors.

The act may affect auditors in that one of their responsibilities is to review and evaluate systems of internal control as a part of doing the audit. Most auditors believe that they are not currently required to do a sufficient review of internal control needed to meet the requirements of the Foreign Corrupt Practices Act.

To date, there have been no legal cases affecting auditors' legal responsibilities under the Foreign Corrupt Practices Act. But there is considerable disagreement about auditors' responsibilities under the law. There is likely to be ongoing discussion and probable legal cases to resolve the issue.

CRIMINAL LIABILITY

It is possible for CPAs to be found guilty for criminal action under both federal and state laws. The most likely statutes to be used under state law are the Uniform Securities Acts, which are similar to parts of the SEC rules. The 1933 and 1934 Securities Acts, as well as the Federal Mail Fraud Statute and the Federal False Statements Statute, are the most relevant federal laws affecting auditors. All of these make it a criminal offense to defraud another person through *knowingly being involved* with false financial statements.

Fortunately for the profession, there have been few criminal actions involving CPAs. The public's reaction to extensive criminal action would be highly damaging to the integrity of the profession. The potential for criminal charges may also have a negative effect on the profession's ability to attract and retain outstanding people. On the positive side, criminal actions may encourage practitioners to use extreme care to act in good faith in all their activities.

The leading case of criminal action against CPAs is *United States* v. *Simon*. It is included as an illustrative case.

United States v. Simon (1969)—criminal liability

The case was a criminal one concerning three auditors prosecuted for filing false statements with a government agency and violation of the 1934 Securities Act. The CPA firm had already settled out of court for civil liability issues for over $2 million after Continental filed for bankruptcy.

The main issue of the trial was the reporting of transactions between Continental Vending Machine Corp. and its affiliate, Valley Commercial Corporation. The dominant figure in both was Harold Roth, who was president of Continental, supervised the day-to-day operations of Valley, and owned about 25 percent of the stock in each company. It is important to the case that Roth had served a jail sentence and was not highly respected in the business community. Valley, which was run by Roth out of a single office on Continental's premises, was engaged in lending money at interest to Continental and others in the vending machine business. Continental would issue negotiable notes to Valley, which would endorse these in blank and use them as collateral for drawing on two lines of credit, of $1 million each. The discounted amount of the notes would then be transferred to Continental. These transactions gave rise to what is called "the Valley payable." In addition to the Valley payable, there was what was known as the "Valley receivable," which resulted from Continental's loans to Valley. Most of these stemmed from Roth's custom of using Continental and Valley as sources of cash to finance his transactions in the stock market. At the end of fiscal 1962, the amount of the Valley receivable was $3.5 million, and by February 15, 1963, the date of certification, it had risen to $3.9 million. By existing accounting rules the Valley payable could not be offset, or "netted," against the Valley receivable.

Before the audit was complete, the auditors had learned that Valley was not in a position to repay its debt, and it was accordingly arranged that collateral would be posted. Roth and members of his family transferred their equity in certain securities to Arthur Field, Continental's counsel, as trustee to secure Roth's debt to Valley and Valley's debt to Continental. Note 2 included with the financial statements read as follows:

> The amount receivable from Valley Commercial Corp. (an affiliated company of which Mr. Harold Roth is an officer, director, and stockholder) bears interest at 12 percent a year. Such amount, less the balance of the notes payable to that company, is secured by the assignment to the Company of Valley's equity in certain marketable securities. As of February 15, 1963, the amount of such equity at current market quotations exceeded the net amount receivable.

The government contended that this note was inadequate and should have disclosed that the amount receivable from Valley was uncollectable at September 30, 1962, since Valley had loaned approximately the same amount to Roth, who was unable to pay. The note should also have stated that approximately 80 percent of the securities Roth had pledged were stock and convertible debentures of Continental Vending. The defendents called eight expert independent accountants as witnesses. They testified generally that, except for the error with respect to netting, the treatment of the Valley receivable in note 2 was in no way inconsistent with generally accepted accounting principles or generally accepted auditing standards. Specifically, they testified that neither generally accepted accounting principles nor generally accepted auditing standards required disclosure of the makeup of the collateral or of the increase in the receivables after the closing date of the balance sheet, although three of the eight stated that in light of hindsight they would have preferred that the makeup of the collateral be disclosed. The witnesses also testified that the disclosure of the Roth borrowings from Valley was not required, and seven of the eight were of the opinion that such disclosure would be inappropriate.

The defendents asked for two instructions which, in substance, would have told the jury that a defendent could be found guilty only if according to generally accepted accounting principles, the statements as a whole did not fairly present the financial condition of Continental at September 30, 1962, and then only if his departure from accepted standards was due to willful disregard of those standards with knowledge of the falsity of the statements and an intent to deceive.

The judge declined to give these instructions and instead said that the critical test was whether the *statements were fairly presented and, if not, whether the defendents had acted in good faith*. Proof of compliance with generally accepted standards was "evidence which may be very persuasive but not necessarily conclusive that he acted in good faith, and that the facts as certified were not materially false or misleading."

The appeals court upheld the earlier conviction of the three auditors with the comment that even without satisfactory showing of motive, "the government produced sufficient evidence of criminal intent. Its burden was not to show that the defendents were wicked men . . . but rather that they had certified a statement knowing it to be false."

The impact on the three men was significant. The total fine was $17,000, but far more important they lost their CPA certificates under Rule 501 of the Code of Ethics (acts discreditable) and were forced to leave the profession. They were ultimately pardoned by President Nixon.

There are several critical lessons in the case:

- An investigation of the integrity of management is an important part of deciding on the acceptability of clients and the extent of work to perform. (Section 315 of the SASs now gives guidance to auditors in investigating new clients.)
- The auditor can be found criminally guilty in the conduct of an audit even if the person's background indicates integrity in his personal and professional life. The criminal liability can extend to partners and staff.

- Independence in appearance and fact by all individuals on the engagement is essential, especially in a defense involving criminal actions. (Section 160 of the SASs requires a firm to implement policies to help assure independence, in fact and in appearance.)
- Transactions with related parties require special scrutiny because of the potential for misstatement. (Section 335 of the SASs now gives guidance in auditing related party transactions.)
- The audit of all major subsidiaries by the same auditor doing the audit of the parent company may be needed to do an adequate audit.
- Generally accepted accounting principles cannot be relied upon exclusively in deciding whether financial statements are fairly presented. The substance of the statements, considering all facts, is required. (The SEC preferability requirement now provides guidelines in selecting accounting principles.)

PROFESSION'S RESPONSE TO LEGAL LIABILITY

There are a number of things the AICPA and the profession as a whole can do to reduce the practioner's exposure to lawsuits. The AICPA's new division for firms into SEC practice and private practice is one positive step in recognizing additional responsibility that the public demands of professionals. Some of the others are discussed briefly.

Research in Auditing. Continued research is important to find better ways to do such things as uncover unintentional material misstatements or management and employee fraud, communicate audit results to statement users, and make sure that auditors are independent. Significant research already takes place through the AICPA, CPA firms, and universities. For example, one CPA firm now has a $1 million research fund available to professors and others that is restricted to research in auditing.

Standards and Rule Setting. The AICPA must constantly set standards and revise them to meet the changing needs of auditing. New Statements on Auditing Standards, revisions of the Code of Ethics, and other pronouncements must be issued as society's needs change and as new technology arises from experience and research.

Set Requirements to Protect Auditors. The AICPA can help protect its members by setting certain requirements that better practitioners already follow. Naturally, these requirements should not be in conflict with meeting users' needs. An example where the auditor has set such standards is the requirement of a written letter of representation from management in all audits (Section 323).

Establish Peer Review Requirements. The periodic examination of a firm's practices and procedures is a way to educate practitioners and identify firms not meeting the standards of the profession.

Opposing Lawsuits. It is important that CPA firms continue to oppose unwarranted lawsuits even if, in the short run, the costs of successfully winning a lawsuit are greater than the costs of settling. The AICPA has aided practioners in fighting an unwarranted expansion of legal liability for accountants by filing briefs as "a friend of the court" known as *amicus curiae* briefs.

Education of Users. It is important to educate investors and others who read financial statements as to the meaning of the auditors' opinion and the extent and nature of the auditors' work. Users must be educated to understand that auditors do not do 100 percent testing of all records and do not guarantee the accuracy of the financial records or the future prosperity of the company. It is also important to educate users to understand that accounting and auditing are arts, not sciences, and that perfection and precision are unachievable.

Sanction Members for Improper Conduct and Performance. One characteristic of a profession is its responsibility for policing its own membership. The AICPA has made progress toward dealing with the problems of inadequate CPA performance, but more rigorous review of alleged failures is still needed.

INDIVIDUAL CPA'S RESPONSE
TO LEGAL LIABILITY

There are also specific actions a practicing auditor can do to minimize his liability. Most of this book deals with that subject. Several of these practices are summarized briefly at this point.

Deal Only with Clients Possessing Integrity. There is an increased likelihood of having legal problems when a client lacks integrity in dealing with customers, employees, government, and others. A CPA firm needs procedures to evaluate the integrity of clients. It should disassociate from clients lacking integrity.

Hire Qualified Personnel and Train and Supervise Them Properly. A considerable portion of most audits is done by young professionals with relatively little experience. Given the high degree of risk CPA firms have in doing audits, it is important that these young professionals be qualified and well trained. Supervision of their work by experienced and qualified professionals is also essential.

Follow the Standards of the Profession. A firm must implement procedures to make sure that all firm members understand and follow the SASs, FASB opinions, Rules of Conduct, and other professional guidelines.

Maintain Independence. Independence is more than merely financial. Independence, in fact, requires an attitude of responsibility separate from the client's interest. Much litigation has arisen from a too-willing acceptance by an auditor of client's representations or of client's pressures.

Understand the Client's Business. The lack of knowledge of industry practices and client operations has been a major factor in auditors failing to uncover errors in several cases. It is important that the audit team be educated in the client's business and industry practices.

Perform Quality Audits. Quality audits require that appropriate evidence be obtained and appropriate judgments be made about the evidence. It is essential, for example, that proper internal control evaluation be made and the evidence be properly modified to reflect the findings. Improved auditing reduces the likelihood of misstatements and the likelihood of lawsuits.

Document the Work Properly. The preparation of good working papers helps in organizing and performing quality audits. Quality working papers are essential if an auditor has to defend an audit in court.

Obtain an Engagement Letter and a Letter of Representation. These two letters are essential in defining the respective obligation of client and auditor. They are helpful especially in lawsuits between the client and auditor, but also in third-party lawsuits.

Maintain Confidential Relations. Auditors are under an ethical and sometimes legal obligation not to disclose client matters to outsiders.

Carry Adequate Insurance. It is essential for a CPA firm to have adequate legal protection in the event of a lawsuit. Although insurance rates have risen considerably in the past few years as a result of increasing litigation, professional liability insurance is still available for all CPAs.

Seek Legal Counsel. Whenever serious problems occur during an audit, a CPA would be wise to consult experienced counsel. In the event of a potential or actual lawsuit, the auditor should seek immediately an experienced attorney.

CONCLUSION

The auditing profession has been under a great deal of attack in recent years, not only in court, but also at the Securities and Exchange Commission (SEC) and in congressional committee proceedings and reports. Demands for increased regulation and increased legal liability are heard frequently. The profession is struggling to respond constructively to these pressures.

The determination of the extent to which auditors should be legally responsible for the reliability of financial statements is relevant to both the professional and to society. Clearly, the existence of legal responsibility is an important deterrent to the inadequate and even dishonest activities of some auditors.

No reasonable CPA would want the profession's legal responsibility for fraudulent or incompetent performance eliminated. The maintenance of public trust in the competent performance of the auditing function is essential to the profession's self-interest.

At the other extreme, it is unreasonable for auditors to be held legally responsible for every misstatement in financial statements. The auditor cannot serve as the insurer or guarantor of financial statement accuracy or business health. The audit costs to society that would be required to achieve such high levels of assurance would exceed the benefits. Moreover, even with increased audit costs, well-planned frauds would not necessarily be discovered, nor errors of judgment eliminated.

In between these two extremes, it is necessary for the profession and society to determine a reasonable trade-off between the degree of responsibility the auditor should take for fair presentation and the audit cost to society. CPAs, Congress, the SEC, and the courts will all have a major influence in shaping the final solution.

REVIEW QUESTIONS

3–1. State seven factors that have affected the increased number of lawsuits against CPAs.

3–2. Lawsuits against CPA firms have increased dramatically in the past decade. State your opinion of the positive and negative effects of the increased litigation on CPAs and society as a whole.

3–3. How does the "Prudent Man Concept" affect the liability of the auditor?

3–4. Name three groups whose work a partner may be held liable for.

3–5. Distinguish between "fraud" and "constructive fraud."

3–6. Discuss why many CPA firms have willingly settled lawsuits out of court. What are the implications to the profession?

3–7. A common type of lawsuit against CPAs is for the failure to detect defalcation. State the auditor's responsibility for such discovery. Give authoritative support for your answer.

3–8. What is meant by "contributory negligence?" Under what conditions will this likely be a successful defense?

3–9. What are the purposes of a letter of representation and an engagement letter?

3–10. What three conditions must exist for an auditor to be liable to third parties under common law?

3–11. Is the auditor's liability affected if the third party was "unknown" rather than "known"? Explain.

3–12. Contrast the auditor's liability under the Security Act of 1933 with that under the Security Act of 1934.

3–13. Distinguish between the auditor's potential legal liability to the client, liability to third parties under common law, civil liability under the securities laws, and criminal liability. Describe one situation for each type of liability where the auditor could be held legally responsible.

3–14. What santions does the SEC have against a CPA firm?

3–15. Discuss the profession's response to the Foreign Corrupt Practices Act of 1977. What are the potential implications of this statute to the profession?

3–16. In what ways can the profession positively respond and reduce liability in auditing?

DISCUSSION QUESTIONS AND PROBLEMS

3–17. The following questions concern accountants' liability. Choose the most appropriate answer.

a. Martinson is a duly licensed CPA. One of his clients is suing him for negligence alleging that he failed to meet generally accepted auditing standards in the current year's audit, thereby failing to discover large thefts of inventory. Under the circumstances:

(1) Martinson is not bound by generally accepted auditing standards unless he is a member of the AICPA.

(2) Martinson's failure to meet generally accepted auditing standards would result in liability.

(3) Generally accepted auditing standards do not currently cover the procedures that must be used in verifying inventory for balance sheet purposes.

(4) If Martinson failed to meet generally accepted auditing standards, he would undoubtedly be found to have committed the tort of fraud.

b. Walters & Whitlow, CPAs, failed to discover a fraudulent scheme used by Davis Corporation's head cashier to embezzle corporate funds during the past five years. Walters & Whitlow would have discovered the embezzlements promptly if they had not been negligent in their annual audits. Under the circumstances, Walters & Whitlow will normally not be liable for

(1) punitive damages.

(2) the fees charged for the years in question.

(3) losses occurring after the time the fraudulent scheme should have been detected.

(4) losses occurring prior to the time the fraudulent scheme should have been detected and which could have been recovered had it been so detected.

c. Martin Corporation orally engaged Humm & Dawson to audit its year-end financial statements. The engagement was to be completed within two months after the close of Martin's fiscal year for a fixed fee of $2,500. Under these circumstances what obligation is assumed by Humm & Dawson?

(1) None, because the contract is unenforceable since it is not in writing.

(2) An implied promise to exercise reasonable standards of competence and care.

(3) An implied obligation to take extraordinary steps to discover all defalcations.

(4) The obligation of an insurer of its work, which is liable without fault.

d. Winslow Manufacturing, Inc., sought a $200,000 loan from National Lending Corporation. National Lending insisted that audited financial statements be submitted before it would extend credit. Winslow agreed to this and also agreed to pay the audit fee. An audit was performed by an independent CPA, who submitted his report to Winslow to be used solely for the purpose of negotiating a loan from National. National, upon reviewing the audited financial statements, decided in good faith not to extend the credit desired. Certain ratios, which as a matter of policy were used by National in reaching its decision, were deemed too low. Winslow used copies of the audited financial statements to obtain credit elsewhere. It was subsequently learned that the CPA, despite the exercise of reasonable care, had failed to discover a sophisticated embezzlement scheme by Winslow's chief accountant. Under these circumstances, what liability does the CPA have?

(1) The CPA is liable to third parties who extended credit to Winslow based upon the audited financial statements.

(2) The CPA is liable to Winslow to repay the audit fee because credit was not extended by National.

(3) The CPA is liable to Winslow for any losses Winslow suffered as a result of failure to discover the embezzlement.

(4) The CPA is not liable to any of the parties.

(AICPA adapted)

3–18. The following questions deal with important cases in accountants' liability. Choose the best response.

a. The most significant aspect of the Continental Vending case was that it

(1) created a more general awareness of the auditor's exposure to criminal prosecution.

(2) extended the auditor's responsibility for financial statements of subsidiaries.

(3) extended the auditor's responsibility for events after the end of the audit period.

(4) defined the auditor's common-law responsibilities to third parties.

b. The 1136 Tenants case was chiefly important because of its emphasis upon the legal liability of the CPA when associated with

(1) a review of interim statements.

(2) unaudited financial statements.

(3) an audit resulting in a disclaimer of opinion.

(4) letters for underwriters.

(AICPA adapted)

3–19. The following questions pertain to liability to third parties. Choose the best response.

a. The traditional common-law rules regarding accountants' liability to third parties for negligence

(1) remain substantially unchanged since their inception.

(2) were more stringent than the rules currently applicable.

(3) are of relatively minor importance to the accountant.

(4) have been substantially changed at both the federal and state levels.

b. A third-party purchaser of securities has brought suit based upon the Securities Act of 1933 against a CPA firm. The CPA firm will prevail in the suit brought by the third party even though the CPA firm issued an unqualified opinion on materially incorrect financial statements if

(1) the CPA firm was unaware of the defects.

(2) the third-party plaintiff had no direct dealings with the CPA firm.

(3) the CPA firm can show that the third-party plaintiff did not rely upon the audited financial statements.

(4) the CPA firm can establish that it was not guilty of actual fraud.

c. An investor seeking to recover stock market losses from a CPA firm, based upon an unqualified opinion on financial statements which accompanied a registration statement, must establish that

(1) there was a false statement or omission of material fact contained in the audited financial statements.

(2) he relied upon the financial statements.

(3) the CPA firm did not act in good faith.

(4) the CPA firm would have discovered the false statement or omission if it had exercised due care in its examination.

d. Which of the following best describes a trend in litigations involving CPAs?

(1) A CPA cannot render an opinion on a company unless the CPA has audited all affiliates of that company.

(2) A CPA may not successfully assert as a defense that the CPA had no motive to be part of a fraud.

(3) A CPA may be exposed to criminal as well as civil liability.

(4) A CPA is primarily responsible for a client's footnotes in an annual report filed with the SEC.   (AICPA adapted)

3–20. The Dandy Container Corporation engaged the accounting firm of Adams and Adams to examine financial statements to be used in connection with a public offering of securities. The audit was completed, and an unqualified opinion was expressed on the financial statements which were submitted to the Securities and Exchange Commission along with the registration statement. Two hundred thousand shares of Dandy Container common stock were offered to the public at $11 a share. Eight months later the stock fell to $2 a share when it was disclosed that several large loans to two "paper" corporations owned by one of the directors were worthless. The loans were secured by the stock of the borrowing corporation which was owned by the director. These facts were not disclosed in the financial report. The director involved and the two corporations are insolvent.

a. The Securities Act of 1933 applies to the above-described public offering of securities in interstate commerce.

b. The accounting firm has potential liability to any person who acquired the stock in reliance upon the registration statement.

c. An investor who bought shares in Dandy Container would make a prima facie case if he alleges that the failure to explain the nature of the loans in question constituted a false statement or misleading omission in the financial statements.

d. The accountants could avoid liability if they could show they were neither negligent nor fraudulent.

e. Accountants' responsibility as to the fairness of the financial statements is determined as of the date of the financial statements and not beyond.

f. The accountants could avoid or reduce the damages asserted against them if they could establish that the drop in price was due in whole or in part to other causes.

g. The Dandy investors would have to institute suit within one year after discovery of the alleged untrue statements or omissions.

h. It would appear that the accountants were negligent in respect to the handling of the secured loans in question—if they discovered the facts regarding the loans to the "paper" corporations and failed to disclose them in their financial statements.

i. The Securities and Exchange Commission would defend any action brought against the accountants in that the SEC examined and approved the registration statement.

Required:

State whether each of items a through i is true or false. For each false item, rephrase the sentence to make it correct.   (AICPA adapted)

3–21. The CPA firm of Bigelow, Barton, and Brown was expanding very rapidly. Consequently, it hired several junior accountants, including a man named Small. The partners of the firm eventually became dissatisfied with Small's production and warned him that they would be forced to discharge him unless his output increased significantly.

   At that time Small was engaged in audits of several clients. He decided that to avoid being fired, he would reduce or omit entirely some of the standard auditing procedures listed in audit programs prepared by the partners. One of the CPA firm's clients, Newell Corporation, was in serious financial difficulty and had adjusted several of the accounts being examined by Small to appear financially sound. Small prepared fictitious working papers in his home at night to support purported completion of auditing procedures assigned to him, although he in fact did not examine the adjusting entries. The CPA firm rendered an unqualified opinion on Newell's financial statements, which were grossly misstated. Several creditors, relying upon the audited financial statements, subsequently extended large sums of money to Newell Corporation.

Required:

Would the CPA firm be liable to the creditors who extended the money because of their reliance upon the erroneous financial statements if Newell Corporation should fail to pay them? Explain.   (AICPA adapted)

3–22. Watts and Williams, a firm of certified public accountants, audited the accounts of Sampson Skins, Inc., a corporation that imports and deals in fine furs. Upon completion of the examination, the auditors supplied Sampson

Skins with twenty copies of the certified balance sheet. The firm knew in a general way that Sampson Skins wanted that number of copies of the auditor's report to furnish to banks and other potential lenders.

The balance sheet in question was in error by approximately $800,000. Instead of having a $600,000 net worth, the corporation was insolvent. The management of Sampson Skins had doctored the books to avoid bankruptcy. The assets had been overstated by $500,000 of fictitious and nonexisting accounts receivable and $300,000 of nonexisting skins listed as inventory when in fact Sampson Skins had only empty boxes. The audit failed to detect these fraudulent entries. Martinson, relying on the certified balance sheet, loaned Sampson Skins $200,000. He seeks to recover his loss from Watts and Williams.

Required:

State whether each of the following is true or false and give your reasons:
a. If Martinson alleges and proves negligence on the part of Watts and Williams, he will be able to recover his loss.
b. If Martinson alleges and proves constructive fraud (i.e., gross negligence on the part of Watts and William) he will be able to recover his loss.
c. Martinson does not have a contract with Watts and Williams.
d. Unless actual fraud on the part of Watts and Williams could be shown, Martinson could not recover.
e. Martinson is a third-party beneficiary of the contract Watts and Williams made with Sampson Skins.   (AICPA adapted)

3–23. Rod Williams, a CPA, was engaged by Jackson Financial Development Company to audit the financial statements of Apex Construction Company, a small closely held corporation. Rod was told when he was engaged that Jackson Financial needed reliable financial statements that would be used to determine whether or not to purchase a substantial amount of Apex Construction's convertible debentures at the price asked by the estate of one of Apex's former directors.

Rod performed his examination in a negligent manner. As a result, he failed to discover substantial defalcations by Brown, the Apex controller. Jackson Financial purchased the debentures but would not have if the defalcations had been discovered. After discovery of the fraud, Jackson Financial promptly sold the debentures for the highest price offered in the market—at a $70,000 loss.

Required:

a. What liability does Rod Williams have to Jackson Financial? Explain.
b. If Apex Construction also sues Rod for negligence, what legal defenses would his attorney probably raise? Explain.
c. Will the negligence of a CPA as described above prevent him from recovering on a liability insurance policy covering the practice of his profession? Explain.   (AICPA adapted)

3–24. Jackson was a junior staff member of an accounting firm. He began the audit of the Bosco Corporation, which manufactured and sold expensive watches.

In the middle of the audit, he quit. The accounting firm hired another person to continue the audit of Bosco. Because of the changeover and the time pressure to finish the audit, the firm violated certain generally accepted auditing standards when they did not follow adequate procedures with respect to the physical inventory. Had the proper procedures been used during the examination, they would have discovered that watches worth more than $20,000 were missing. The employee who was stealing the watches was able to steal an additional $30,000 worth before the thefts were discovered six months after the completion of the audit.

Required:

Discuss the legal problems of the accounting firm as a result of the facts described above.   (AICPA adapted)

3–25. Donald Sharpe recently joined the CPA firm of Spark, Watts, and Wilcox. He quickly established a reputation for thoroughness and a steadfast dedication to following prescribed auditing procedures to the letter. On his third audit for the firm, Sharpe examined the underlying documentation of 200 disbursements as a test of purchasing, receiving, vouchers payable, and cash disbursement procedures. In the process he found twelve disbursements for the purchase of materials with no receiving reports in the documentation. He noted the exceptions in his working papers and called them to the attention of the in-charge accountant. Relying on prior experience with the client, the in-charge accountant disregarded Sharpe's comments, and nothing further was done about the exceptions.

Subsequently, it was learned that one of the client's purchasing agents and a member of its accounting department were engaged in a fraudulent scheme whereby they diverted the receipt of materials to a public warehouse while sending the invoices to the client. When the client discovered the fraud, the conspirators had obtained approximately $70,000, $50,000 of which was after the completion of the audit.

Required:

Discuss the legal implications and liabilities to Spark, Watts, and Wilcox as a result of the facts described above.   (AICPA adapted)

3–26. In confirming accounts receivable on 12-31-X7, the auditor found 15 discrepancies between the customer's records and the recorded amounts in the subsidiary ledger. A copy of all confirmations that had exceptions was turned over to the company controller to investigate the reason for the difference. He, in turn, had the bookkeeper perform the analysis. The bookkeeper analyzed each exception, determined its cause and prepared an elaborate working paper explaining each difference. Most of the differences in the bookkeeper's report indicated that the errors were caused by timing differences in the client's and customer's records. The auditor reviewed the working paper and concluded that there were no material exceptions in accounts receivable.

Two years subsequent to the audit it was determined that the bookkeeper had stolen thousands of dollars in the past three years by taking cash and overstating accounts receivable. In a lawsuit by the client against the

CPA, an examination of the auditor's 12-31-X7 accounts receivable working papers, which were subpoenaed by the court, indicated that one of the explanations in the bookkeeper's analysis of the exceptions was fictitious. The analysis stated the error was caused by a sales allowance granted to the customer for defective merchandise the day before the end of the year. The difference was actually caused by the bookkeeper's theft.

Required:

a. What are the legal issues involved in this situation? What should the auditor use as a defense in the event that he is sued?

b. What was the CPA's deficiency in conducting the audit of accounts receivable?

3–27. Smith, CPA, is the auditor for Juniper Manufacturing Corporation, a privately owned company which has a June 30 fiscal year. Juniper arranged for a substantial bank loan which was dependent upon the bank receiving, by September 30, audited financial statements which showed a current ratio of at least 2 to 1. On September 25, just before the audit report was to be issued, Smith received an anonymous letter on Juniper's stationery indicating that a five-year lease by Juniper, as lessee, of a factory building which was accounted for in the financial statements as an operating lease was, in fact, a capital lease. The letter stated that there was a secret written agreement with the lessor modifying the lease and creating a capital lease.

Smith confronted the president of Juniper, who admitted that a secret agreement existed but said it was necessary to treat the lease as an operating lease to meet the current ratio requirement of the pending loan and that nobody would ever discover the secret agreement with the lessor. The president said that if Smith did not issue his report by September 30, Juniper would sue Smith for substantial damages which would result from not getting the loan. Under this pressure and because the working papers contained a copy of the five-year lease agreement which supported the operating lease treatment, Smith issued his report with an unqualified opinion on September 29.

In spite of the fact that the loan was received, Juniper went bankrupt within two years. The bank is suing Smith to recover its losses on the loan and the lessor is suing Smith to recover uncollected rents.

Required:

Answer the following questions, setting forth reasons for any conclusions stated.

a. Is Smith liable to the bank?

b. Is Smith liable to the lessor?

(AICPA adapted)

3–28. A CPA firm was engaged to examine the financial statements of Martin Manufacturing Corporation for the year ending December 31, 1977. The facts revealed that Martin was in need of cash to continue its operations and agreed to sell its common stock investment in a subsidiary through a private placement. The buyers insisted that the proceeds be placed in escrow because of the possibility of a major contingent tax liability that might result from a pending government claim. The payment in escrow was completed in late November 1977. The president of Martin told the audit partner that the proceeds from the sale of the subsidiary's common stock, held in escrow, should be shown on the balance sheet as an unrestricted current account receivable. The president was of the opinion that the government's claim was groundless and that Martin needed an "uncluttered" balance sheet and a "clean" auditor's opinion to obtain additional working capital from lenders. The audit partner agreed with the president and issued an unqualified opinion on the Martin financial statements which did not refer to the contingent liability and did not properly describe the escrow arrangement.

The government's claim proved to be valid, and pursuant to the agreement with the buyers, the purchase price of the subsidiary was reduced by $450,000. This adverse development forced Martin into bankruptcy. The CPA firm is being sued for deceit (fraud) by several of Martin's unpaid creditors who extended credit in reliance upon the CPA firm's unqualified opinion on Martin's financial statements.

Required:

Based on these facts, can Martin's unpaid creditors recover from the CPA firm? State the reasons for your conclusion.   (AICPA adapted)

3–29. Factory Discount Prices, Inc., is a chain store discount outlet which sells women's clothes. It has an excessively large inventory on hand and is in urgent need of additional cash. It is bordering on bankruptcy, especially if the inventory has to be liquidated by sale to other stores instead of the public. Furthermore, about 15 percent of the inventory is not resalable except at a drastic discount below cost. Faced with this financial crisis, Factory approached several of the manufacturers from whom it purchases. Dexter Apparel, Inc., one of the parties approached, indicated a willingness to loan Factory $300,000 under certain conditions. First, Factory was to submit audited financial statements for the express purpose of providing the correct financial condition of the company. The loan was to be predicated upon these financial statements and Factory's engagement letter with Dunn & Clark, its CPAs, expressly indicated this.

The second condition insisted upon by Dexter was that it obtain a secured position in all unsecured inventory, accounts, and other related personal property. In due course a security agreement was executed and a financing statement properly filed and recorded.

In preparing the financial statements, Factory valued the inventory at cost, which was approximately $100,000 over the current fair market value. Also, Factory failed to disclose two secured creditors to whom substantial amounts are owed and who take priority over Dexter's security interests.

Dunn & Clark issued an unqualified opinion on the financial statements of Factory which they believed were fairly presented.

Six months later Factory filed a voluntary bankruptcy petition. Dexter received $125,000 as its share of the bankrupt's estate. It is suing Dunn & Clark for the loss of $175,000. Dunn & Clark deny liability based upon lack of privity and lack of negligence.

Required:

Is Dexter entitled to recover its loss from Dunn & Clark? State the reasons for your conclusion. (AICPA adapted)

3–30. Gordon & Groton, CPAs, were the auditors of Bank & Company, a brokerage firm and member of a national stock exchange. Gordon & Groton examined and reported on the financial statements of Bank, which were filed with the Securities and Exchange Commission.

Several of Bank's customers were swindled by a fraudulent scheme perpetrated by Bank's president, who owned 90 percent of the voting stock of the company. The facts establish that Gordon & Groton were negligent but not reckless or grossly negligent in the conduct of the audit, and neither participated in the fraudulent scheme nor knew of its existence.

The customers are suing Gordon & Groton under the antifraud provisions of Section 10(b) and Rule 10b-5 of the Securities Exchange Act of 1934 for aiding and abetting the fraudulent scheme of the president. The customer's suit for fraud is predicated exclusively on the nonfeasance of the auditors in failing to conduct a proper audit, thereby failing to discover the fraudulent scheme.

Required:

Answer the following questions, setting forth reasons for any conclusions stated.
a. What is the probable outcome of the lawsuit?
b. What other theory of liability might the customers have asserted?

(AICPA adapted)

3–31. The partnership of Smith, Frank, & Clark, a CPA firm, has been the auditor of Greenleaf, Inc., for many years. During the annual examination of the financial statements for the year ended December 31,19X2, a dispute developed over whether certain disclosures should be made in the financial statements. The dispute resulted in Smith, Frank, & Clark being dismissed and Greenleaf engaging another firm. Greenleaf demanded that Smith, Frank, & Clark turn over all working papers applicable to the Greenleaf audits to it or face a lawsuit. Smith, Frank, & Clark refused. Greenleaf has instituted a suit against Smith, Frank, & Clark to obtain the working papers.

Required:

Answer the following questions, setting forth reasons for any conclusions stated.
a. Will Greenleaf succeed in its suit? Explain.
b. Discuss the rationale underlying the rule of law applicable to the ownership of working papers. (AICPA adapted)

3–32. A CPA firm has been named as a defendant in a class action by purchasers of the shares of stock of the Newly Corporation. The offering was a public offering of securities within the meaning of the Securities Act of 1933. The plaintiffs alleged that the firm was either negligent or fraudulent in connection with the preparation of the audited financial statements which accompanied the registration statement filed with the SEC. Specifically, they allege that the CPA firm either intentionally disregarded, or failed to exercise reasonable care to discover, material facts that occurred subsequent to January 31, 1978, the date of the auditor's report. The securities were sold to the public on March 16, 1978. The plaintiffs have subpoenaed copies of the CPA firm's working papers. The CPA firm is considering refusing to relinquish the papers, asserting that they contain privileged communication between the CPA firm and its client. The CPA firm will, of course, defend on the merits irrespective of the questions regarding the working papers.

Required:

Answer the following questions, setting forth reasons for any conclusions stated.

a. Can the CPA firm rightfully refuse to surrender its working papers?
b. What is the liability of the CPA firm in respect to events that occur in the period between the date of the auditor's report and the effective date of the public offering of the securities?   (AICPA adapted)

4

AUDIT EVIDENCE
AND DOCUMENTATION

Accumulating evidence to evaluate whether financial statements are fairly stated and preparing adequate documentation of the findings are two primary activities of auditors of financial statements. This chapter introduces the subject of audit evidence and documentation.

OVERVIEW OF THE AUDIT PROCESS

A first step in the study of evidence is an understanding of the overall audit process. An overview of the audit of financial statements provides a frame of reference for understanding how each part of the audit relates to the overall objective.

Overall Objective

The overall objective of the ordinary audit of financial statements by CPAs is to determine whether the statements are presented in accordance with generally accepted accounting principles applied on a basis consistent with that of the preceding year. The auditor evaluates whether the financial statements are fairly presented by accumulating audit evidence in a thorough and conscientious manner. When, on the basis of adequate evidence, he reaches the conclusion that the financial statements are unlikely to mislead a prudent user, he gives an audit opinion on their fair presentation and associates his opinion with the statements. If facts subsequent to the issuance of the statements indicate that they were actually not fairly presented, the auditor is likely to have to demonstrate to the courts or regulatory agents that he conducted the audit in a proper manner and drew reasonable conclusions. Although the auditor is not an insurer or a guarantor of the fairness of the presentations in the statements, he has considerable responsibility for notifying users as to whether or not the statements are properly stated. If he believes the statements are not fairly presented or if he is unable to reach a conclusion because of insufficient evidence or prevailing conditions, he has the responsibility for notifying the users of the statements through an auditor's report.

Audit conclusions about whether financial statements are fairly presented are not reached in a precisely defined manner. Instead, evidence is obtained and conclusions are reached by bits and pieces. The auditor starts with relatively little information about whether the client's statements are fairly presented. He has the results of previous audits on a repeat engagement and impressions about integrity and competency, but little else. As the audit proceeds, each additional piece of evidence either confirms or contradicts his initial impression. At the completion of the audit, the auditor should have strong beliefs about the fairness of the presentation, which will lead to his opinion.

Obtain a General Understanding of the Client and Its Circumstances

Each audit is in one sense a replication of all other audits and in another sense a unique experience. Every audit is the same in the sense that a minimum amount of evidence must be obtained and evaluated and certain audit procedures are carried out on practically every audit engagement. On the other hand, some audit procedures—the sample size, the particular items in the population to select for testing, and the timing of the tests—depend upon the unique characteristics of the client. To identify the unique characteristics that affect the accumulation of evidence, the auditor must understand the client and its circumstances.

The general understanding of the client includes four general categories of information:

1. Background Information for the Audit. Background information enables the auditor to better understand the client's industry and the peculiarities of the business.

2. Analytical Tests. Analytical tests include the calculations and comparisons by the auditor of ratios and trends in the client's records as a test of reasonableness of the account balances.

3. Information Concerning the Client's Legal Obligations. The legal commitments of the client, including such items as government regulations, the corporate charter and bylaws, corporate minutes, and contracts of all types, must be understood before it is possible to evaluate whether the financial statements are fairly stated.

4. Information for Evaluation of the Possibility of Management Involvement in Fraud. In recent years there has been an increasing incidence of involvement by management in fraudulent activities. These include the massive theft of company assets and the issuance of intentionally misleading financial statements. A well-known example is the Equity Funding fraud. An evaluation of the environmental factors affecting the predictability of these frauds is useful in helping the auditor decide upon the proper evidence to accumulate. The information described above must be gathered as early in the audit as possible to enable the auditor to decide on the evidence to accumulate. As the audit progresses, a clearer understanding of the client will gradually emerge.

Study and Evaluate the System of Internal Control

One of the most widely accepted concepts in the theory and practice of auditing is the importance of the client's accounting system (system of internal control) in generating reliable financial information. If the auditor is convinced the client has an excellent system, which includes controls for providing reliable data and for safeguarding assets and records, the amount of audit evidence to be accumulated can be significantly less than if the system is not adequate. On the other hand, in some instances the controls may be so inadequate as to preclude conducting an effective audit.

The first step in the study and evaluation of the client's system of internal control is to *determine how it operates.* This is done by means of the auditor's review of organizational charts and procedural manuals, by discussions with client personnel, and by completing internal control questionnaires and flowcharts.

The second step is to make a *preliminary evaluation* of whether the system has been designed to effectively accomplish the objectives of good control, including the prevention of errors. This evaluation involves identifying specific controls that provide substance to the system which the auditor may be willing to rely upon to reduce certain audit tests, and identifying areas of the system where errors are more likely to occur due to the absence of controls. This process is referred to by auditors as *identifying the strengths and weaknesses of the system.*

Test the Effectiveness of the System

Where the auditor has identified an effective control, or strength, in the system, he is entitled to rely on this control to enhance the reliability of financial information. Hence, he can reduce the extent to which the accuracy of that information must be validated through the accumulation of evidence related directly to it. To justify this reliance, however, the auditor must test the effectiveness of the controls. The procedures involved in this type of testing are commonly referred to as *tests of compliance* or *tests of transactions.*

Directly Test the Financial Statement Accounts

The ending balances in the balance sheet and income statement accounts are verified by obtaining various types of evidence. Examples include direct communication in writing with customers for accounts receivable, observation of actual inventory, and examination of vendor's statements for accounts payable. These tests of ending balances are essential to the conduct of the audit because for the most part the evidence is obtained from a source independent of the client, and thus is considered to be of high quality.

There is a close relationship between the general review of the client's circumstances, the results of the evaluation and tests of the system of internal control, and the direct tests of the financial statement accounts. If the auditor has obtained a reasonable level of confidence about the fair presentation of the financial statements through the general review of internal control and tests of its effectiveness, the direct tests can be significantly decreased. In all instances, however, some tests of the financial statement accounts are necessary.

Complete the Audit, Combine the Results of All the Tests, and Draw Conclusions

In addition to direct tests of the financial statement accounts, the auditor must carry out such procedures as testing for material subsequent events and reviewing the working papers.

After the auditor has completed all the procedures, it is necessary to combine the information obtained in some manner to reach an *overall conclusion* as to whether the financial statements are fairly presented. This is a highly subjective process which relies heavily upon the auditor's professional judgment. In practice the auditor continuously combines the information obtained as he proceeds through the audit. The final combination is only a summation at the completion of the engagement.

Issue an Audit Report

At the completion of the audit, the CPA must issue an audit report which accompanies the client's published financial statements. The report must meet the well-defined technical requirements that are affected by the scope of the audit and the nature of the findings.

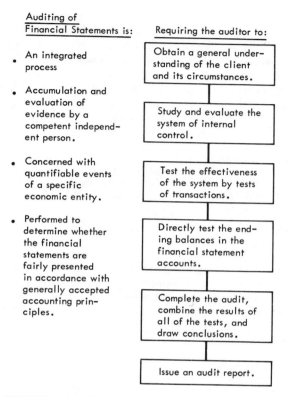

Auditing of Financial Statements is:	Requiring the auditor to:
• An integrated process	Obtain a general understanding of the client and its circumstances.
• Accumulation and evaluation of evidence by a competent independent person.	Study and evaluate the system of internal control.
• Concerned with quantifiable events of a specific economic entity.	Test the effectiveness of the system by tests of transactions.
• Performed to determine whether the financial statements are fairly presented in accordance with generally accepted accounting principles.	Directly test the ending balances in the financial statement accounts.
	Complete the audit, combine the results of all of the tests, and draw conclusions.
	Issue an audit report.

FIGURE 4-1   Overview of the Audit Process

Summary

The overview of the audit process and the most important concepts discussed up to this point are presented schematically in Figure 4-1.

As part of conducting an audit, *working papers* are prepared to provide a frame of reference for planning the audit and to demonstrate that an adequate audit was completed. The working papers include a permanent file, which contains information and records of continuing importance on repeat engagements, and current working papers pertaining to the current year's audit.

AUDIT EVIDENCE DECISIONS

A major judgment problem facing every auditor is determining the appropriate *amount of evidence* to accumulate before the auditor is satisfied that the client's statements are fairly stated. The decision is important because of the prohibitive cost of examining and evaluating all available evidence. For example, in an audit of financial statements of most organizations it is impossible for the CPA to examine all canceled checks, vendors' invoices, documents evidencing the receipt of goods, sales invoices, shipping documents, customer orders, payroll time cards, and the many other types of documents and records.

The auditor's evidence accumulation process can be broken into four interrelated *decisions*:

- The audit procedures to use.
- The sample size to select for a given procedure.
- The particular items to select from the population.
- The appropriate time to perform the procedures.

Audit Procedures

Audit procedures are the detailed instructions for the collections of a particular type of audit evidence that is to be obtained at some time during the audit. For example, such evidence as counting the physical inventory, comparing the canceled checks with the cash disbursements journal for proper payee and amount, and examining a shipping document for proper approval are all collected using audit procedures.

In designing audit procedures, it is common to spell them out in sufficiently specific terms to permit their use as instructions during the audit. For example, the following is an audit procedure for the verification of cash receipts:

> Obtain a listing of daily incoming cash receipts and compare the amount with the postings in the cash receipts journal.

The list of audit procedures for an entire audit is called the *audit program*. Generally, the program also states the sample size and timing of the procedures.

Sample Size

Once an audit procedure is selected, it is possible to vary the sample size from one to all the items in the population being tested. The decision of how many items to test must be made by the auditor for each audit procedure. The sample size for any given procedure is likely to vary from audit to audit and procedure to procedure.

The Particular Items to Select

After the sample size has been determined for a particular audit procedure, it is still necessary to decide upon the particular items to examine. If the auditor decides, for example, to select 200 canceled checks from a population of 10,000 for comparison with the cash disbursements journal, he can use several different methods to select the specific checks to be examined. Three possible methods are: select a week and examine the first 200 checks, select the 200 checks with the largest amounts, or select the checks randomly.

Timing

Since an audit of financial statements normally covers a period of time such as a year, the auditor could start to accumulate evidence soon after the beginning of the accounting period. Because an audit is usually not completed until several weeks or months after the end of the period, the timing of audit procedures can vary from early in the accounting period to long after it has ended. In the audit of financial statements, the client normally desires that the audit be completed from one to three months after year-end.

TYPES OF AUDIT EVIDENCE

There are seven types of evidence used in conducting audits. These are listed below and defined and discussed in this section:

- Physical examination.
- Confirmation.
- Documentation.
- Observation.
- Inquiries of the client.
- Mechanical accuracy.
- Analytical tests.

Factors Affecting Type of Evidence to Use

The appropriate type of evidence to select for a given situation depends on four primary considerations:

Applicability of Evidence to Information Being Verified. The auditor must use care to make sure that the evidence relates to audit areas and objectives under consideration. For example, physical examination of marketable securities is useful evidence to determine the existence of the securities, but not to determine their valuation.

Availability of Evidence. It is rare when only one type of evidence is available for verifying information. All alternative types of evidence should be considered before selecting the best type or types.

Reliability of the Evidence.   Reliability refers to the degree that evidence can be considered believable or worthy of trust. Three factors determine the reliability of evidence.

- *Independence of the provider of the evidence.* Evidence obtained from a source outside of the entity is more reliable than that obtained from within the entity. For example, external evidence such as that received by communications from banks, attorneys, or customers is generally regarded as more reliable than answers obtained from inquiries of the client and from documents that do not leave the client's organization.
- *Qualifications of the individuals providing the information.* Although the source of information is independent, the evidence will not be reliable unless the individual providing it is qualified to provide it. For this reason, confirmations from attorneys and banks are typically more highly regarded than accounts receivable confirmations from persons who are not familiar with the business world. Even evidence obtained directly by the auditor may not be reliable if the auditor lacks the qualifications to obtain the evidence. For example, the physical observation of an inventory of diamonds by an auditor untrained in distinguishing between diamonds and glass would not provide reliable evidence of the existence of diamonds.
- *Degree of objectivity of the evidence.* Evidence that is objective in nature, compared with evidence that requires considerable judgment to determine whether it is correct, is more believable and therefore more reliable. Examples of objective types of evidence include confirmation of accounts receivable and bank balances, the physical count of securities and cash, and adding (footing) a list of accounts payable to determine if it adds to the balance on the general ledger. Examples of subjective evidence include confirmation by a client's attorney of the likely significance of outstanding lawsuits against the client, observation of obsolescence of inventory during physical examination, and inquiring of the credit manager about the collectibility of noncurrent accounts receivable. In evaluating the reliability of subjective evidence, the qualifications of the person providing the evidence is important.

Cost.   The cost of alternative types of evidence must be compared to the other three considerations before the appropriate mix of evidence is decided on. The auditor wants to obtain a sufficient amount of reliable evidence that is applicable to the information being verified at the lowest possible total cost.

Physical Examination

Physical examination is the inspection or count by the auditor of a *tangible asset*. This type of evidence is most often associated with inventory and cash, but it is also applicable to the verification of securities, notes receivable, and tangible fixed assets. The distinction between the physical examination of assets, such as marketable securities and cash, and the examination of documents, such as canceled checks and sales documents, is important for auditing purposes. If the object being examined, such as a sales invoice, has no inherent value, the evidence is called *documentation*. For example, before a check is signed, it is a document; after it is signed, it becomes an asset; and when it is canceled, it becomes a document again. Technically, physical examination of the check can only occur while the check is an asset.

Physical examination, which is a direct means of verifying that an asset actually exists, is regarded as one of the most reliable and useful types of audit evidence. Generally, physical examination is an objective means of ascertaining both the quantity and the description of the asset. In some cases it is also a useful method for evaluating an asset's condition or quality. On the other hand, physical examination is not sufficient evidence to verify that existing assets are owned by the client. Also in many cases the auditor is not qualified to judge such qualitative factors as obsolescence or authenticity. The proper valuation for financial statement purposes can also not usually be determined by physical examination.

Confirmation

Confirmation describes the *receipt* of a *written response* from an *independent third party* verifying the accuracy of information that was *requested by the auditor*. Since confirmations come from sources independent of the client, they are a highly regarded and often used type of evidence. However, confirmations are relatively costly to obtain and may cause some inconvenience to those asked to supply them. Therefore, they are not used in every instance in which they are applicable.

Whether or not confirmations should be used depends on the reliability needs of the situation as well as the alternative evidence available. Traditionally, confirmations are not used to verify individual transactions between organizations, such as sales transactions, because the auditor can use documents to determine the adequacy of the client's system of recording information. Similarly, confirmations are seldom used in the audit of fixed-asset additions because these can be adequately verified by documentation and physical examination.

Whenever practical and reasonable, the confirmation of a sample of accounts receivable is *required* of CPAs. This requirement, which is imposed by the AICPA, exists because accounts receivable usually represent a significant balance on the financial statements, and confirmations are a highly reliable means of verifying the fairness of the balance.

Although confirmation is not required for any account other than accounts receivable, this type of evidence is useful in verifying many types of information. The major types of information that are frequently confirmed, along with the source of the confirmation, are indicated in Figure 4-2.

To be considered as reliable evidence, confirmations must be controlled by the auditor from the time their preparation is completed until they are returned. If the client controls the preparation of the confirmation, performs the mailing, or receives the responses, the auditor has lost control; hence independence is lost, and the reliability of the evidence is reduced.

FIGURE 4–2

Information Frequently Confirmed

Information Confirmed	Confirmation Obtained from
Assets	
Cash in bank	Bank
Accounts receivable	Debtor
Notes receivable	Maker
Owned inventory out on consignment	Consignee
Inventory held in public warehouses	Public warehouse
Cash surrender value of life insurance	Insurance company
Liabilities	
Accounts payable	Creditor
Notes payable	Lender
Advances from customers	Customer
Mortgages payable	Mortgagor
Bonds payable	Bondholder
Owner's Equity	
Shares outstanding	Registrar and transfer agent
Other Information	
Insurance coverage	Insurance company
Contingent liabilities	Company attorneys, bank, etc.
Bond indenture agreements	Bondholder
Collateral held by creditors	Creditor

Documentation

Documentation, which is commonly referred to as *vouching*, is the auditor's examination of the *client's documents and records* to substantiate the information that is or should be included in the financial statements. The documents examined by the auditor are the records used by the client to provide information for conducting its business in an organized manner. Since each transaction in the client's organization is normally supported by at least one document, there is a large volume of this type of evidence available for the auditor's use. For example, the client normally retains a customer order, a shipping document, and a duplicate sales invoice for each sales transaction. These same documents are useful evidence for verification by the auditor of the accuracy of the client's records for sales transactions. Documentation is a widely used form of evidence in every audit because it is usually readily available to the auditor at a relatively low cost. Sometimes it is the only reasonable type of evidence available.

Documents can be conveniently classified as internal and external. An *internal document* is one that has been prepared and used within the client's organization and is retained without its ever going to an outside party such as a customer or a vendor. Examples of internal documents include duplicate sales invoices, employees' time reports, and inventory receiving reports. An *external document* is one that has been in the hands of someone outside the client's organization who is a party to the transaction being documented, but which is either currently in the hands of the client or readily accessible. In some cases, external documents originate outside the client's organization and end up in the hands of the client. Examples of this type of external document are vendor's invoices, canceled notes payable, and insurance policies. In other cases, such as canceled checks, the documents originate with the client, go to an outsider, and are finally returned to the client.

The primary determinant of the auditor's willingness to accept a document as reliable evidence is whether it is an internal or an external document. Since external documents have been in the hands of both the client and another party to the transaction, there is some indication that both members are in agreement about the information and the conditions stated on the document. External documents are therefore regarded as more reliable evidence than internal ones.

Observation

Observation is the use of the senses to assess certain activities. Throughout the audit there are many opportunities to exercise the sensory mechanisms of sight, hearing, touch, and smell to evaluate a wide range of things. For example, the auditor may tour the plant to obtain a general impression of the client's facilities; he may observe whether inventory has rust to evaluate whether it is likely to be obsolete; and he may watch individuals perform accounting tasks to determine whether the person assigned a responsibility is actually doing it. Observation is rarely sufficient by itself. It is necessary to follow up initial impressions with other kinds of corroborative evidence. Nevertheless, observation is useful in most parts of the audit.

Inquiries of the Client

Inquiry is the obtaining of *written* or *oral* information from the client in response to questions from the auditor. Although considerable evidence is obtained from the client through inquiry, it cannot usually be regarded as conclusive because it is not from an independent source and may be biased in the client's favor. Therefore, when the auditor obtains evidence through inquiry, it is normally necessary to obtain further corroborating evidence by other procedures. As an illustration, when the auditor wants to obtain information about the client's method of recording and controlling of accounting transactions, he usually begins by asking the client how the accounting system operates. Later, he performs tests of the system to determine if the transactions are recorded and authorized in the manner stated.

Mechanical Accuracy

Testing of *mechanical accuracy* involves rechecking a sample of the computations and transfers of information made by the client during the period under audit. The rechecking of computations consists of testing the client's arithmetical accuracy. It includes such procedures as extending sales invoices and inventory, adding journals and subsidiary ledgers, and checking the calculation of depreciation expense and prepaid expenses. The rechecking of transfers of information consists of tracing amounts to be confident that when the same information is included in more than one place, it is recorded at the same amount each time. For example, the auditor normally makes limited tests to ascertain that the information in the sales journal has been included for the proper customer and at the correct amount in the subsidiary accounts receivable ledger and accurately summarized in the general ledger.

Analytical Tests

Analytical tests are the use of *comparisons* and *relationships* as a means of isolating accounts or transactions that should be intensively investigated or to help in deciding that additional verification is not needed. An example of this type of evidence is to compare the current period's total repair expense with previous years and to investigate the difference, if it is significant, to determine the cause of the increase or decrease. The auditor's own calculations generally comprise the information used for analytical tests. The tests should be performed early in the audit to aid in determining which audit areas should be more thoroughly investigated, and reviewed again at the end of the audit to corroborate the tentative conclusions reached on the basis of the other evidence.

Summary

It is important to understand the relationship among auditing standards, which were studied in Chapter 1, types of evidence, and audit procedures. Their relationship is shown in Figure 4-3.

WORKING PAPERS

Working papers are the *written records kept by the auditor* of the evidence accumulated during the course of the audit, the methods and procedures followed, and the conclusions reached. They should include all the information the auditor considers necessary to adequately conduct his examination and provide support for his audit report.

Purposes of Working Papers

The overall objective of working papers is to aid the auditor in providing reasonable assurance that an adequate audit was conducted in accordance with generally accepted auditing standards. In more specific terms, the pur-

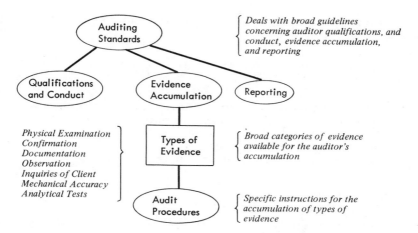

FIGURE 4-3 Relationship among Auditing Standards, Audit Evidence, and Audit Procedures

poses of the working papers as they pertain to the current year's audit include the following:

Basis for Planning the Audit. If the auditor is to adequately plan the current year's audit, the necessary reference information must be available in the working papers to aid him in his decision making. The papers include such diverse planning information as the evaluation of internal control, a time budget for individual audit areas, the audit program, and the results of the preceding year's audit.

Record of the Evidence Accumulated and the Results of the Tests. The working papers are the primary means of documenting that an adequate audit was conducted. If the need arises, the auditor must be able to demonstrate to commissions and courts that the audit was well planned and adequately supervised, the evidence accumulated was both competent and sufficient, and the audit report was proper considering the results of the examination.

Data for Determining the Proper Type of Audit Report. The working papers provide an important source of information to assist the auditor in deciding upon the appropriate audit report to issue in a given set of circumstances. The data in the papers are useful for evaluating the adequacy of audit scope and the fairness of the financial statements. In addition, the working papers contain information needed for the preparation of the financial statements.

Basis for Review by Supervisors and Partners. The working papers are the primary frame of reference used by supervisory personnel to evaluate whether sufficient competent evidence was accumulated to justify the audit report.

In addition to the purposes directly related to the current year's audit, the working papers can also serve as

- The basis for preparing tax returns, filings with the SEC, and other reports.
- A source of information for issuing a management letter to the client for improving operations.
- A frame of reference for training personnel.
- An aid in planning and coordinating subsequent audits.

Contents and Organization

Each CPA firm establishes its own approach to preparing and organizing working papers, and the beginning auditor must adopt his firm's approach. The emphasis in the study of contents and organization in this text is on the general concepts common to all working papers.

Figure 4-4 illustrates the contents and organization of a typical complete set of papers. A look at the contents indicates that they contain virtually

FIGURE 4–4 Working Paper Contents and Organization

everything involved in the examination. There is a definite logic to the type of working papers prepared for an audit and the way they are arranged in the files, even though different firms may follow somewhat different approaches. In Figure 4-4 the working papers start with the more general information such as corporate data in the permanent files and end with the financial statements and audit report. In between are the working papers supporting the auditor's tests.

Permanent Files

Permanent files are intended to contain data of a *historical or continuing nature*, pertinent to the current examination. These files provide a convenient source of information about the audit that is of continuing interest from year to year. The permanent file typically includes the following:

- *Extracts or copies of such company documents of continuing importance as the articles of incorporation, bylaws, bond indentures, and contracts.* The contracts are pension plans, leases, stock options, and so on. Each of these documents is of significance to the auditor for as many years as it is in effect.
- *Analyses from previous years of accounts that have continuing importance to the auditor.* These include accounts such as long-term debt, stockholders' equity accounts, goodwill, and fixed assets. Having this information in the permanent file enables the auditor to concentrate on analyzing only the changes in the current year's balance while retaining the results of previous years' audits in a form accessible for review.
- *Information related to the evaluation of internal control.* This includes organization charts, flowcharts, questionnaires, and other internal control information, including enumeration of strengths and weaknesses in the system.
- *The results of analytical testing from previous years' auditing.* Among these data are ratios and percentages computed by the auditor, and the total balance or the balance by month for selected accounts. This information is useful in helping the auditor decide whether there are unusual changes in the current year's account balance that should be investigated more extensively.

    Analytical tests and internal control review are included in the current period working papers rather than in the permanent file by many CPA firms.

Current Files

The current files include all working papers applicable to the year under audit on a continuing engagement. There is one set of permanent files and a set of current files for each year's audit.

The types of information included in the current file are briefly discussed next.

Audit Program. The *audit program* is ordinarily maintained in a separate file to improve the coordination and integration of all parts of the audit. As the audit progresses, each auditor initials the program for the audit procedures performed and indicates the date of completion. The inclusion in the working papers of a well-designed audit program completed in a conscientious manner is evidence of a high-quality audit.

General Information. Some working papers include current period information that is of a general nature rather than being designed to support specific financial statement amounts. This includes such items as audit planning memos, abstracts or copies of minutes of the board of directors, abstracts of contracts or agreements not included in the permanent file, notes on discussions with the client, working paper review comments, and general conclusions. Documentation of internal control evaluation may also be included.

Working Trial Balance. Since the basis for preparing the financial statements is the general ledger, the amounts included on that record are the focal point of the examination. As early as possible after the balance sheet date, the auditor obtains or prepares a listing of the general ledger accounts and their year-end balances. This schedule is the working trial balance.

The technique used by many firms is to have the auditor's working trial balance in the same format as the financial statements. Each line item on the trial balance is supported by a *lead schedule*, containing the detailed accounts from the general ledger making up the line item total. Each detailed account on the lead schedule is, in turn, supported by appropriate supporting schedules evidencing the audit work performed and the conclusions reached. As an example, the relationship between cash as it is stated on the financial statements, the working trial balance, the lead schedule for cash, and the supporting working papers is presented in Figure 4-5. As the figure indicates, cash on the financial statements is the same as on the working trial balance and the total of the detail on the cash lead schedule. Initially, figures for the lead schedule were taken from the general ledger. The audit work performed resulted in an adjustment to cash which would be evidenced in the detail schedules and reflected in the lead schedule, the working trial balance, and the financial statements.

Adjusting and Reclassification Entries. When the auditor discovers material errors in the accounting records, the financial statements must be corrected. For example, if the client failed to properly reduce inventory for obsolete raw materials, an adjusting entry can be made by the auditor to reflect the realizable value of the inventory. Even though adjusting entries discovered in the audit are typically prepared by the auditor, they must be approved by the client because management is primarily responsible for the fair presentation of the statements. Figure 4-5 illustrates the adjustment of the general cash account for $90.

Reclassification entries are frequently made in the statements to properly present accounting information, even when the general ledger balances are correct. A common example is the reclassification for financial statement

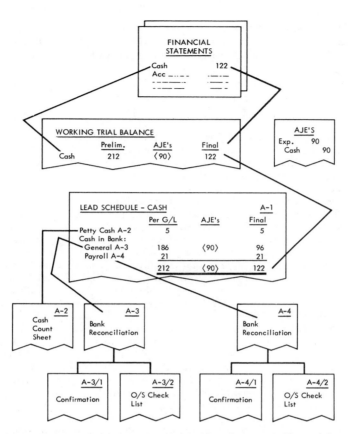

FIGURE 4-5 Relationship of Working Papers to Financial Statements

purposes of material credit balances in accounts receivable to accounts payable. Since the balance in accounts receivable on the general ledger reflects the accounts receivable properly from the point of view of operating the company on a day-to-day basis, the reclassification entry is not included in the client's general ledger.

Only those adjusting and reclassification entries that significantly affect the fair presentation of financial statements must be made. The determination of when an error should be adjusted is based upon *materiality*. The auditor should keep in mind that several immaterial errors that are not adjusted could result in a material overall misstatement when the errors are combined. It is common for auditors to summarize on a separate working paper all entries that have not been recorded as a means of determining their cumulative effect.

Supporting Schedules. The largest portion of working papers includes the detailed schedules prepared by auditors in support of specific financial amounts in the statements. Many different types of schedules are used. Use of the appropriate type of schedule for a given aspect of the audit is necessary to document the adequacy of the audit and to fulfill the other objectives of working papers. Following are the major types of supporting schedules:

- *Analysis.* An analysis is designed to show the *activity in a balance sheet account* during the entire period under examination, tying together the beginning and ending balances. This type of schedule is normally used for accounts such as marketable securities, notes receivable, allowance for doubtful accounts, property, plant, and equipment, long-term debt, and for all equity accounts. The common characteristic of these accounts is the significance of the activity in the account during the year. In most cases the working papers for analyses have cross-references to other working papers.
- *Trial Balance or List.* This type of schedule consists of the *detail making up a year-end balance* of either a balance sheet or an income statement account. It differs from an analysis in that it includes only those items constituting the end-of-the-period balance. Common examples include trial balances or lists in support of trade accounts receivable, trade accounts payable, repair and maintenance expense, legal expense, and miscellaneous income. An example is included in Figure 4–6, page 128.
- *Reconciliation of Amounts.* A reconciliation *supports a specific amount* and is normally expected to tie the amount recorded in the client's records to another source of information. Examples include the reconciliation of bank balances with bank statements, the reconciliation of subsidiary accounts receivable balances with confirmations from customers, and the reconciliation of accounts payable balances with vendor's statements. An example is included in Figure 19–2, page 640.
- *Tests of Reasonableness.* A test of reasonableness schedule, as the name implies, contains information that enables the auditor to evaluate whether the client's balance appears to include an error considering the circumstances in the engagement. Frequently, auditors test depreciation expense, the provision for federal income taxes, and the allowance for doubtful accounts by tests of reasonableness. An example is included in Figure 6–5, page 194.
- *Summary of Procedures.* Another type of schedule *summarizes the results* of a specific audit procedure performed. Examples are the summary of the results of accounts receivable confirmation and the summary of inventory observations.
- *Examination of Supporting Documents.* A number of special-purpose schedules are designed to *show detailed tests performed*, such as examination of documents during tests of transactions or cutoffs. These schedules show no totals, and do not tie into the general ledger because they document only the tests performed and the results found. The schedules must, however, state a definite positive or negative conclusion about the objective of the test. An example is included in Figure 10–10, page 356.
- *Informational.* This type of schedule contains information as opposed to audit evidence. These schedules include information for tax returns and SEC Form 10-K data, and data such as time budgets and the client's working hours, which are helpful in administration of the engagement.

- *Outside Documentation.* Much of the content of the working papers consists of the outside documentation gathered by auditors, such as confirmation replies and copies of client agreements. Although not "schedules" in the real sense, these are indexed and interfiled and procedures are indicated on them in the same manner as the other schedules.

Preparation of Working Papers

The proper preparation of schedules to document the audit evidence accumulated, the results found, and the conclusions reached is an important part of the audit. The auditor must recognize the circumstances requiring the need for a schedule and the appropriate design of schedules to be included in the files. Although the design depends on the objectives involved, working papers should possess certain characteristics:

- Each working paper should be properly identified with such information as the client's name, the period covered, a description of the contents, the initials of the preparer, and the date of preparation, and it should be properly indexed and cross-referenced.
- Working papers should be indexed and cross-referenced to aid in organizing and filing working papers. One type of indexing is illustrated in Figure 4–5. The lead schedule for cash has been indexed as A-1, and the individual general ledger accounts making up the total cash on the financial statements are indexed as A-2 through A-4. The final indexing is for the schedules supporting A-3 and A-4.
- Completed working papers must clearly indicate the audit work performed. This is accomplished in three ways: by a written statement in the form of a memorandum, by initialing the audit procedures in the audit program, and by notations directly on the working paper schedules. Notations on working papers are accomplished by the use of *tick marks*, which are *symbols* written adjacent to the detail on the body of the schedule. These notations must be clearly explained at the bottom of the working paper.
- Each working paper should include sufficient information to fulfill the objectives for which it was designed. If the auditor is to properly prepare working papers, he must be clearly aware of his goals. For example, if a working paper is designed to list the detail and show the verification of support of a balance sheet account, such as prepaid insurance, it is essential that the detail on the working paper reconcile with the trial balance.
- The conclusions that were reached about the segment of the audit under consideration should be plainly stated.
    The common characteristics of proper working paper preparation are indicated in Figure 4–6.

Ownership of Working Papers

The working papers prepared during the engagement, including those prepared by the client for the auditor, are the *property of the auditor*. The only time anyone else, including the client, has a legal right to examine the papers

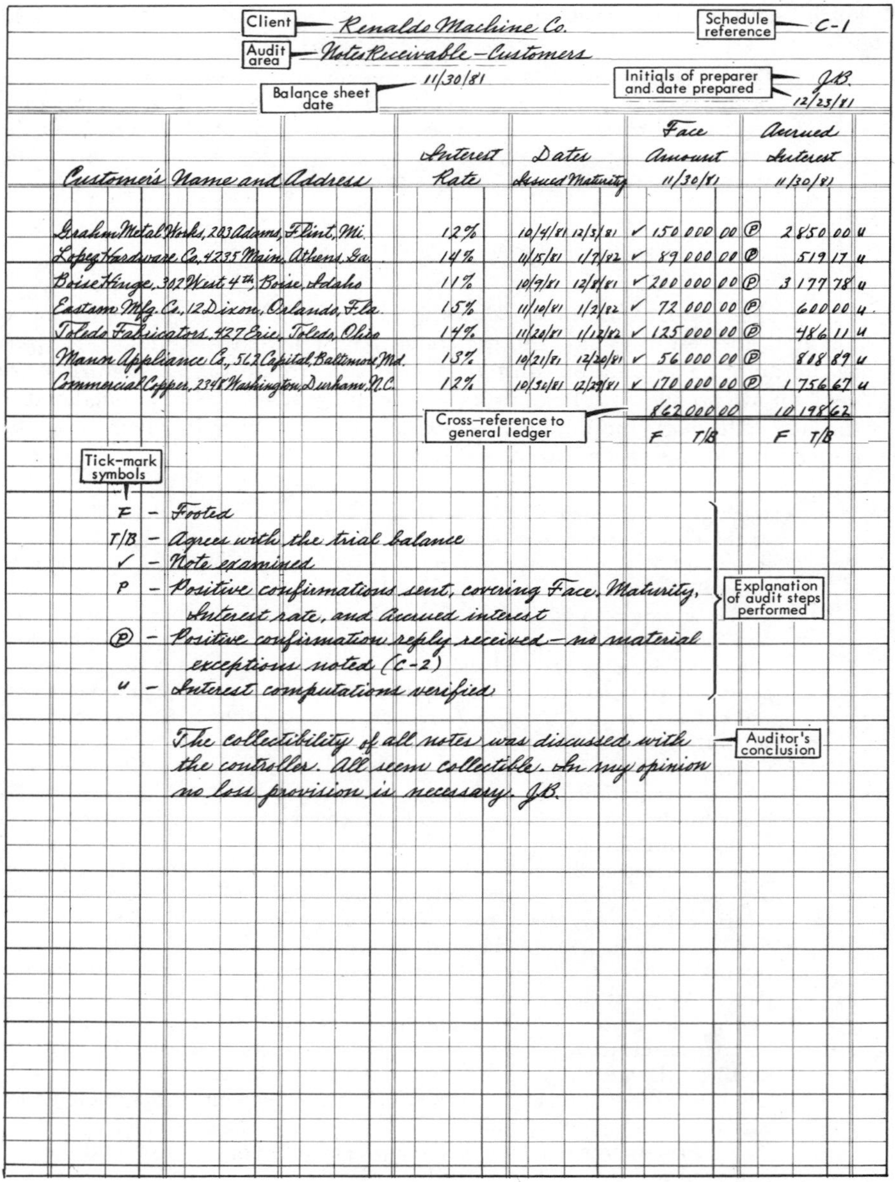

Client — Renaldo Machine Co.
Schedule reference — C-1
Audit area — Notes Receivable—Customers
Balance sheet date — 11/30/81
Initials of preparer and date prepared — J.B. 12/23/81

Customer's Name and Address	Interest Rate	Dates Issued	Dates Maturity		Face Amount 11/30/81		Accrued Interest 11/30/81	
Graham Metal Works, 203 Adams, Flint, Mi.	12%	10/4/81	12/3/81	✓	150 000 00	Ⓟ	2 850 00	u
Lopez Hardware Co. 4235 Main, Athens, Ga.	14%	11/15/81	1/7/82	✓	89 000 00	Ⓟ	519 17	u
Boise Hinge, 302 West 4th, Boise, Idaho	11%	10/9/81	12/8/81	✓	200 000 00	Ⓟ	3 177 78	u
Eastam Mfg. Co., 12 Dixon, Orlando, Fla.	15%	11/10/81	1/2/82	✓	72 000 00	Ⓟ	600 00	u
Toledo Fabricators, 427 Erie, Toledo, Ohio	14%	11/20/81	1/12/82	✓	125 000 00	Ⓟ	486 11	u
Manor Appliance Co., 562 Capital, Baltimore, Md.	13%	10/21/81	12/20/81	✓	56 000 00	Ⓟ	808 89	u
Commercial Copper, 2348 Washington, Durham, N.C.	12%	10/30/81	12/29/81	✓	170 000 00	Ⓟ	1 756 67	u
					862 000 00		10 198 62	
					F T/B		F T/B	

Cross-reference to general ledger

Tick-mark symbols

F – Footed
T/B – Agrees with the trial balance
✓ – Note examined
P – Positive confirmations sent, covering Face, Maturity, Interest rate, and Accrued interest
Ⓟ – Positive confirmation reply received—no material exceptions noted (C-2)
u – Interest computations verified

Explanation of audit steps performed

The collectibility of all notes was discussed with the controller. All seem collectible. In my opinion no loss provision is necessary. J.B.

Auditor's conclusion

FIGURE 4–6 Common Characteristics of Proper Working Papers

is when they are subpoenaed by a court as legal evidence. At the completion of the engagement, working papers are retained on the CPA's premises for future reference. Many firms follow the practice of microfilming the working papers after several years to reduce storage costs.

Confidentiality of Working Papers

The need to maintain a confidential relationship with the client is expressed in Rule 301 of the Code of Professional Ethics, which states:

> A member shall not disclose any confidential information obtained in the course of a professional engagement except with the consent of the client.

During the course of the examination, auditors obtain a considerable amount of information of a confidential nature, including officer salaries, product pricing and advertising plans, and product cost data. If auditors divulged this information to outsiders or to client employees who have been denied access to the information, their relationship with management would be seriously strained. Furthermore, having access to the working papers would give employees an opportunity to alter information on the papers. For these reasons, care must be taken to protect the working papers at all times.

Ordinarily, the working papers can be provided to someone else only with the express permission of the client. This is the case even if a CPA sells his practice to another CPA firm. Permission is not required from the client, however, if the working papers are subpoenaed by a court or are used as part of a voluntary quality review program with other CPA firms.

REVIEW QUESTIONS

4–1. What methods do auditors use to obtain a better understanding of the unique characteristics of the client?

4–2. Explain why the auditor must study and evaluate the system of internal control and test the effectiveness of the system as a part of the ordinary audit.

4–3. Distinguish between tests of the effectiveness of the system of internal control and direct tests of the ending balances in the financial statements.

4–4. How would the conduct of an audit of a medium-sized company be affected by the company's being a small part of a large conglomerate as compared with its being a separate entity?

4–5. List the four major audit evidence decisions that must be made on every audit.

4–6. List the seven types of audit evidence included in this chapter and give two examples of each type.

4–7. List five specific quantifiable events that an auditor can verify, and state specific criteria for evaluating the events.

4–8. Distinguish between internal documentation and external documentation as audit evidence and give three examples of each.

4–9. Explain the importance of analytical tests as evidence in determining the fair presentation of the financial statements.

4–10. Define what is meant by reliability of audit evidence and list the characteristics of evidence that affect its reliability.

4–11. List the purposes of working papers and explain why each purpose is important.

4–12. Explain why it is important for working papers to include each of the following: identification with the name of the client, description of the contents, period covered, initials of the preparer, date of the preparation, indexing, and cross-referencing.

4–13. Define what is meant by a permanent file of working papers, and list several types of information typically included. Why doesn't the auditor include the contents of the permanent file with the current year's working papers?

4–14. Distinguish between the following types of current-period supporting schedules and state the purpose of each: analysis, trial balance, and comparison.

4–15. Why is it essential that the auditor not leave questions or exceptions in the working papers without an adequate explanation?

4–16. What type of working papers can be prepared by the client and used by the auditor as a part of the working paper file? When client assistance is obtained in preparing working papers, describe the proper precautions the auditor should take.

4–17. Define what is meant by a tick mark. What is the purpose of tick marks? What is a standard tick mark?

4–18. Who owns the working papers? Under what circumstances can they be used by other people?

4–19. A CPA sells his auditing practice to another CPA firm and includes all working papers as a part of the purchase price. Under what circumstances is this a violation of the Code of Professional Ethics?

DISCUSSION QUESTIONS AND PROBLEMS

4–20. The following questions concern audit evidence. Choose the best answer.
  a. The following statements were made in a discussion of audit evidence between two CPAs. Which statement is not valid concerning evidential matter?
  (1) "I am seldom convinced beyond all doubt with respect to all aspects of the statements being examined."
  (2) "I would not undertake that procedure because at best the results would only be persuasive and I'm looking for convincing evidence."
  (3) "I evaluate the degree of risk involved in deciding the kind of evidence I will gather."
  (4) "I evaluate the usefulness of the evidence I can obtain against the cost to obtain it."
  b. Which of the following types of documentary evidence should the auditor consider to be the most reliable?
  (1) A sales invoice issued by the client and supported by a delivery receipt from an outside trucker.
  (2) Confirmation of an account payable balance mailed by and returned directly to the auditor.

    (3) A check issued by the company and bearing the payee's indorsement which is included with the bank statements mailed directly to the auditor.

    (4) A working paper prepared by the client's controller and reviewed by the client's treasurer.

  c. The most reliable type of documentary audit evidence that an auditor can obtain is

    (1) physical examination by the auditor.

    (2) documentary evidence calculated by the auditor from company records.

    (3) confirmations received directly from third parties.

    (4) internal documents. (AICPA adapted)

4–21. The following questions concern working papers. Choose the best response.

  a. The third general auditing standard requires that due professional care be exercised in the performance of the examination and the preparation of the report. The matter of due professional care deals with what is done by the independent auditor and how well it is done. For example, due care in the matter of working papers requires that working paper

    (1) format be neat and orderly and include both a permanent file and a general file.

    (2) content be sufficient to provide support for the auditor's report, including the auditor's representation as to compliance with auditing standards.

    (3) ownership be determined by the legal statutes of the state in which the auditor practices.

    (4) preparation be the responsibility of assistant accountants whose work is reviewed by senior accountants, managers, and partners.

  b. Which of the following is not a factor that affects the independent auditor's judgment as to the quantity, type, and content of working papers?

    (1) The timing and the number of personnel to be assigned to the engagement.

    (2) The nature of the financial statements, schedules, or other information upon which the auditor is reporting.

    (3) The need for supervision of the engagement.

    (4) The nature of the auditor's report.

  c. During an audit engagement pertinent data are compiled and included in the audit working papers. The working papers primarily are considered to be

    (1) a client-owned record of conclusions reached by the auditors who performed the engagement.

    (2) evidence supporting financial statements.

    (3) support for the auditor's representations as to compliance with generally accepted auditing standards.

    (4) a record to be used as a basis for the following year's engagement.

  d. Audit working papers are used to record the results of the auditor's evidence-gathering procedures. When preparing working papers the auditor should remember that

    (1) working papers should be kept on the client's premises so that the client can have access to them for reference purposes.

(2) working papers should be the primary support for the financial statements being examined.

(3) working papers should be considered as a substitute for the client's accounting records.

(4) working papers should be designed to meet the circumstances and the auditor's needs on each engagement.

e. Although the quantity, type, and content of working papers will vary with the circumstances, the working papers generally would include the

(1) copies of those client records examined by the auditor during the course of the engagement.

(2) evaluation of the efficiency and competence of the audit staff assistants by the partner responsible for the audit.

(3) auditor's comments concerning the efficiency and competence of client management personnel.

(4) auditing procedures followed, and the testing performed in obtaining evidential matter. (AICPA adapted)

4–22. The following are examples of documentation typically obtained by auditors:
   a. Vendors' invoices
   b. General ledgers
   c. Bank statements
   d. Canceled payroll checks
   e. Payroll time cards
   f. Purchase requisitions
   g. Receiving reports (document prepared when merchandise is received)
   h. Minutes of the board of directors
   i. Remittance advices
   j. Signed W-4s (Employees' Withholding Exemption Certificate)
   k. Signed lease agreements
   l. Duplicate copies of bills of lading
   m. Subsidiary accounts receivable records
   n. Canceled notes payable
   o. Duplicate sales invoices
   p. Articles of incorporation
   q. Title insurance policies for real estate
   r. Notes receivable

Required:

a. Classify each of the preceding items according to types of documentation: (1) internal or (2) external.

b. Explain why external evidence is more reliable than internal evidence.

4–23. The following are examples of audit procedures:
   a. Reviewing the accounts receivable with the credit manager to evaluate their collectibility.
   b. Standing by the payroll time clock to determine whether any employee "punches in" more than one time.

c. Counting inventory items and recording the amount in the audit working papers.

d. Obtaining a letter from the client's attorney addressed to the CPA firm stating the attorney is not aware of any existing lawsuits.

e. Extending the cost of inventory times the quantity on an inventory listing to test whether it is accurate.

f. Obtaining a letter from an insurance company to the CPA firm stating the amount of the fire insurance coverage on building and equipment.

g. Examining an insurance policy stating the amount of the fire insurance coverage on buildings and equipment.

h. Calculating the ratio of cost of goods sold to sales as a test of overall reasonableness of gross margin relative to the preceding year.

i. Obtaining information about the system of internal control by requesting the client to fill out a questionnaire.

j. Tracing the total on the cash disbursements journal to the general ledger.

k. Watching employees count inventory to determine whether company procedures are being followed.

l. Examining a piece of equipment to make sure a major acquisition was actually received and is in operation.

m. Calculating the ratio of sales commissions expense to sales as a test of sales commissions.

n. Examining corporate minutes to determine the authorization of the issue of bonds.

o. Obtaining a letter from management stating there are no unrecorded liabilities.

p. Reviewing the total of repairs and maintenance for each month to determine whether any month's total was unusually large.

q. Comparing a duplicate sales invoice with the sales journal for customer name and amount.

r. Adding the sales journal entries to determine whether they were correctly totaled.

s. Making a petty cash count to make sure the amount of the petty cash fund is intact.

t. Obtaining a written statement from a bank stating the client has $2,671 on deposit and liabilities of $10,000 on a demand note.

Required:

Classify each of the preceding items according to the seven types of audit evidence: (1) physical examination, (2) confirmation, (3) documentation, (4) observation, (5) inquiries of the client, (6) mechanical accuracy, and (7) analytical tests.

4–24. List two examples of audit evidence the auditor can use in support of each of the following:

a. Recorded value of entries in the purchase journal

b. Physical existence of inventory

c. Valuation of accounts receivable

    d. Ownership of permanent assets
    e. Liability for accounts payable
    f. Obsolescence of inventory
    g. Existence of petty cash

4–25. Seven different types of evidence were discussed. The following questions concern the reliability of that evidence:

    a. Explain why confirmations are normally more reliable evidence than inquiry from the client.

    b. Describe a situation where confirmation would be considered highly reliable and another where it would not be reliable.

    c. Under what circumstances is the physical observation of inventory considered relatively unreliable evidence?

    d. Explain why mechanical accuracy tests are highly reliable, but of relatively limited usefulness.

    e. Give three examples of relatively reliable documentation and three examples of less reliable documentation. What characteristics distinguish the two?

    f. Give several examples where the qualifications of the respondent or the qualifications of the auditor affect the reliability of the evidence.

    g. Explain why comparisons and relationships are important evidence even though they are relatively unreliable by themselves.

4–26. The third generally accepted auditing standard of field work requires that the auditor obtain sufficient competent evidential matter to afford a reasonable basis for an opinion regarding the financial statements under examination. In considering what constitutes sufficient competent evidential matter, a distinction should be made between underlying accounting data and all corroborating information available to the auditor.

Required:

    Discuss the nature of evidential matter to be considered by the auditor in terms of the underlying accounting data, all corroborating information available to the auditor, and the methods by which the auditor tests or gathers competent evidential matter.   (AICPA adapted)

4–27. In his examination of financial statements, an auditor must judge the validity of the audit evidence he obtains.

Required:

Assume that you have evaluated internal control and found it satisfactory.

    a. In the course of his examination, the auditor asks many questions of client officers and employees.

       (1) Describe the factors the auditor should consider in evaluating oral evidence provided by client officers and employees.

       (2) Discuss the validity and limitations of oral evidence.

    b. An auditor's examination may include computation of various balance sheet and operating ratios for comparison with previous years and industry averages. Discuss the validity and limitations of ratio analysis.

    c. In connection with his examination of the financial statements of a manufacturing company, an auditor is observing the physical inventory of finished goods, which consists of expensive, highly complex electronic equipment. Discuss the validity and limitations of the audit evidence provided by this procedure. (AICPA adapted)

4–28. A CPA accumulates various kinds of evidence upon which he will base his auditor's opinion as to the fairness of financial statements he examines. Among this evidence are confirmations from third parties.

Required:

a. What is an audit confirmation?

b. What characteristics should an audit confirmation possess if a CPA is to consider it as valid evidence? (AICPA adapted)

4–29. As auditor of the Star Manufacturing Company, you have obtained
a. a trial balance taken from the books of Star one month prior to year-end:

	Dr. (Cr.)
Cash in bank	$ 87,000
Trade accounts receivable	345,000
Notes receivable	125,000
Inventories	317,000
Land	66,000
Buildings, net	350,000
Furniture, fixtures, and equipment, net	325,000
Trade accounts payable	(235,000)
Mortgages payable	(400,000)
Capital stock	(300,000)
Retained earnings	(510,000)
Sales	(3,130,000)
Cost of sales	2,300,000
General and administrative exprenses	622,000
Legal and professional fees	3,000
Interest expense	35,000

b. There are no inventories consigned either in or out.

c. All notes receivable are due from outsiders and held by Star.

Required:

Which accounts should be confirmed with outside sources? Briefly describe from whom they should be confirmed and the information that should be confirmed. Organize your answer in the following format:

Account Name	*From Whom Confirmed*	*Information to Be Confirmed*

(AICPA adapted)

4–30. The preparation of working papers is an integral part of a CPA's examination of financial statements. On a recurring engagement a CPA reviews his audit programs and working papers from his prior examination while planning his current examination to determine their usefulness for the current engagement.

Required:

a. What are the purposes or functions of audit working papers?
b. What records may be included in audit working papers?
c. What factors affect the CPA's judgment of the type and content of the working papers for a particular engagement?   (AICPA adapted)

4–31. An important part of every examination of financial statements is the preparation of audit working papers.

Required:

a. Discuss the relationship of audit working papers to each of the standards of field work.
b. You are instructing an inexperienced staff member on his first auditing assignment. He is to examine an account. An analysis of the account has been prepared by the client for inclusion in the audit working papers. Prepare a list of the comments, commentaries, and notations that the staff member should make or have made on the account analysis to provide an adequate working paper as evidence of his examination. (Do not include a description of auditing procedures applicable to the account.)

(AICPA adapted)

4–32. The first generally accepted auditing standard of field work requires, in part that "the work is to be adequately planned." An effective tool that aids the auditor in adequately planning the work is an audit program.

Required:

What is an audit program, and what purposes does it serve?

(AICPA adapted)

4–33. Auditors frequently refer to the terms "Standards" and "Procedures." Standards deal with measures of the quality of the auditor's performance. Standards specifically refer to the ten generally accepted auditing standards. Procedures relate to those acts that are performed by the auditor while trying to gather evidence. Procedures specifically refer to the methods or techniques used by the auditor in the conduct of the examination.

Required:

List at least eight different types of procedures that an auditor would use during an examination of financial statements. For example, a type of procedure that an auditor would frequently use is the observation of activities and conditions. **Do not discuss specific accounts.**   (AICPA adapted)

4–34. List the deficiencies in the working paper for the ABC Company shown here. For each deficiency, state how the working paper could be improved.

ABC Company, Inc.
Notes Receivable
12/31/81

Acct. 110

	Maker					
	Apex Co.	Ajax, Inc.	J.J. Co.	P. Smith	Martin-Peterson	Tent Co.
Date:						
Made	6/15/80	11/21/80	11/1/80	7/26/81	5/12/80	9/3/81
Due	6/15/82	Demand	$200/mo.	$1000/mo.	Demand	$400/mo.
Face amount	5000<	3591<	13,180<	25,000<	2100<	12,000<
Value of Security	none②	none	24,000©	50,000①	none	10,000②
Notes:						
Beg. bal.	4000^PWP	3591^PWP	12,780^PWP	—	2100^PWP	—
Additions				25,000		12,000
Payments	<1000>	<3,591>	<2400>	<5000>	<2100>	<1600>
End bal.						
① Current	3000✓	—	2400✓	12,000	—	4800
② Long-term	—	—	7980	8000	—	5600
③ Total	3000©	–0–	10,380©	20,000©	–0–	10,400©
	~	~	~	~	~	~
Interest:						
Rate	5%	5%	5%	5%	5%	6%
Pd. to date	none	paid	12/31/81	9/30/81	paid	11/30/81
Beg. bal.	104^PWP	–0–^PWP	24^PWP	–0–	–0–^PWP	–0–
④ Earned	175✓	102✓	577✓	468✓	105✓	162✓
Received	–0–	<102>	<601>	<200>	<105>	<108>
⑤ Accrued at 12/31/81	279	–0–	–0–	268	–0–	54
	~	~	~	~	~	~

< ✓ – Tested
PWP – Agrees with prior year's working papers.
① Total of $22,200 agrees with working trial balance.
② Total of 21,580 agrees with working trial balance.
③ Total of $43,780 agrees with working trial balance.
④ Total of $1,589 agrees with miscellaneous income analysis in operations W/P.
⑤ Total of $601 agrees with A/R lead schedule.
(Over for remainder of legend.)

4–35. James Garold, CPA, was engaged for several years by the Bond Corporation to make annual audits. As a result of a change in control, the corporation discontinued the engagement of Garold and retained another firm of accountants. The Bond Corporation thereupon demanded of Garold surrender of all working papers prepared by the accounting firm in making audits for the corporation. Garold refused on the ground that the working papers were their property. The corporation brought legal action to recover the working papers. State briefly what the law is, in general, as to ownership of accountants' working papers.   (AICPA adapted)

4–36. A major disagreement among CPA firms is whether it is legally advisable to keep review notes by supervisors as an integral part of the working papers.

Required:

a. What are the arguments in favor of maintaining the review notes in the working paper file?

b. What are the arguments in favor of destroying them?

5

AUDITOR'S
RESPONSIBILITIES
AND DECISION PROCESS

The amount of evidence to accumulate in a given audit is among the most important audit decisions. Obtaining too little evidence enhances the likelihood of failing to uncover material errors. Obtaining more evidence than is necessary for the circumstances is costly.

In general terms, it is possible to determine the proper evidence by referring to the third standard of field work, which states:

> *Sufficient competent evidential* matter is to be obtained through inspection, observation, inquiries, and confirmations to afford a *reasonable basis for an opinion* regarding the financial statements under examination [italics added].

The relevance of this standard is certainly difficult to dispute, but like most of the standards it provides little in the way of practical guidelines. What is meant by *sufficient competent evidential matter?* What is a *reasonable basis for an opinion?* These must be understood before the auditor can begin to conduct an audit.

This book taken as a whole is primarily the study of the appropriate amount of evidence for the specific segments of an audit. This chapter addresses general concepts that apply to all segments. The following are the topics included:

- Degree of responsibility.
- Desired levels of assurance.
- The evidence needed to achieve a desired level of assurance.
- The four audit decisions.

DEGREE OF RESPONSIBILITY

As a first step in establishing the amount of evidence to accumulate, it is important to understand the auditor's responsibility for the fairness of the representations made in the financial statements. The professional literature makes it clear that the responsibility for adopting sound accounting policies, maintaining an adequate system of internal control and making fair representations in the financial statements *rests with management* rather than with the auditor.

If the auditor were responsible for making certain that all the representations in the statements were correct, it would make him a guarantor or insurer of the reliability of the financial statements. If auditors had that responsibility, evidence requirements and the resulting cost of the audit function would thereby be increased to such an extent that audits would not be economically feasible.

Management's responsibility for the fairness of the representations in the financial statements carries with it the privilege of determining which disclosures it considers necessary. Although management has the responsibility for the preparation of the financial statements and the accompanying footnotes, it is acceptable for an auditor to prepare a draft for the client or to offer suggestions for clarification. In the event that management insists on financial statement disclosure that the auditor finds unacceptable, the auditor can either issue an adverse or qualified opinion or withdraw from the engagement.

The auditor's responsibility is limited to performing the audit investigation and reporting the results in accordance with *generally accepted auditing standards*. In most cases, any material errors and omissions will be discovered if the audit has been so performed. Yet the possibility always exists that the auditor's selected sample will fail to uncover a material error. In this event, the auditor's best defense is that the audit was performed and the report prepared with due care in accordance with generally accepted auditing standards.

It is usually more difficult for auditors to uncover irregularities (intentional misstatement of financial statements or misappropriation of assets) than errors (unintentional mistakes). The reason is because of the intended deception associated with irregularities. Auditors' responsibility for uncovering irregularities deserves special mention.

Employee Fraud

The profession has been especially emphatic that the auditor is not responsible for the discovery of employee fraud if the examination has been performed in accordance with generally accepted auditing standards. If auditors were responsible for the discovery of all material fraud, auditing tests would have to be greatly expanded, for many types of fraud are extremely difficult if not impossible to detect. The extension of the procedures that would be necessary to uncover all cases of fraud would probably be more expensive than the benefits would justify.

However, the auditor must consider the possibility of intentional errors as a part of internal control evaluation. The audit procedures should be expanded when the auditor finds an absence of adequate controls or the failure to follow prescribed procedures if he believes material errors could result.

Management Fraud

Management fraud is inherently difficult to uncover because it is possible for one or more members of management to override internal controls. The errors may include omissions of transactions, fraudulent amounts, or misstatements of recorded amounts. Audits cannot provide absolute assurance of the detection of material fraud, but the auditor should be especially aware of management fraud under certain circumstances. These include (1) a large number of financial failures in the client's industry, (2) client's lack of working capital, (3) lack of internal auditors by a large client, and (4) previous evidence of dishonest acts by management. The auditor should expand his examination if he is suspicious of fraud. It may be necessary under some circumstances to qualify his opinion or withdraw from the engagement.

Illegal Acts by Clients

The auditor cannot ordinarily be expected to uncover illegal acts, inasmuch as an audit concerns financial, not legal, matters. Nevertheless, the review of internal control, management inquiries, and correspondence with attorneys and other audit procedures may uncover a material illegal act. Upon discovery of illegal acts the auditor should first inform the appropriate client personnel of the illegal act. The auditor must also evaluate the possibility of lack of compliance with generally accepted accounting principles or the existence of a material uncertainty. It may be necessary to withdraw from the engagement if the client will not take corrective action with respect to a known illegal act.

The previous discussion may leave the impression that auditors have little responsibility for making sure that financial statements are fairly stated. That is not the case at all. As a practical matter, if significant errors or omissions exist in the financial statements, the likelihood of the auditor having to defend the adequacy of his performance in the audit is reasonably high. The auditor is likely to have to defend the audit regardless of whether the errors are due to misrepresentation by management, employee fraud, or unintentional omissions. Therefore, the standard of evidence accumulation used by most competent auditors is to proceed until the likelihood of material errors existing in the financial statements is fairly low.

Attention will now be turned to an examination of the auditor's decision process in how low the likelihood of material errors or irregularities needs to be in a given situation.

DESIRED LEVELS OF ASSURANCE

The decision about how much evidence to accumulate comprises two basic steps:

- Set the desired level of assurance the auditor feels he needs in the existing circumstances.
- Accumulate the evidence necessary to achieve the desired level of assurance, considering the existing circumstances.

First the problem of setting a desired level of overall assurance is discussed. In the last part of the chapter the decision process used to determine how much evidence is needed to satisfy the desired level of assurance is examined.

The *desired level of assurance* is the subjectively determined level of confidence that the auditor wants to have about the fair presentation of the financial statements after the audit is completed. The higher the level of assurance attained, the more confident the auditor is that the financial statements contain no material misstatements or omissions. One hundred percent assurance would be certainty, and zero assurance would be complete uncertainty. Complete assurance of the accuracy of the financial statement is not possible. It has already been established that the auditor cannot guarantee the complete absence of material errors and irregularities.

The concept of desired level of assurance can be more easily visualized by thinking in terms of a large number of audits, say 10,000. What portion of these audits could include material errors without having an adverse effect on society? Certainly, the percentage would be below 10 percent. It is probably much closer to 1 percent or one-half of 1 percent or perhaps even one-tenth of 1 percent. If the percent an auditor feels is appropriate is 1 percent, the desired level of assurance is 99 percent.

The auditor achieves assurance through accumulating evidence. The *achieved level of assurance* is that level of confidence the auditor actually has that the statements are not intentionally misstated after the audit is completed. The achieved level of assurance must be greater than the desired level or the auditor should not issue an unqualified opinion.

The higher the desired level of assurance, the more evidence the auditor must obtain. This is true because assurance is achieved by gathering evidence. Since the greater the amount of evidence, the greater the cost, the basic audit decision of the proper level of assurance boils down to a cost-benefit equation. The important question is: At what point does the additional cost of acquiring more evidence exceed the benefit obtained from the additional information? When that level of assurance is reached, the auditor should stop accumulating evidence. If the auditor believes the additional cost of the evidence exceeds the additional benefit from continuing to accumulate, but the level of assurance is still not satisfactory, he has several options. He can negotiate for a higher audit fee; he can issue a disclaimer of opinion; he can bear the additional costs himself; or he can withdraw from the engagement.

It is *not possible to quantify* the overall level of assurance achieved in an audit. It is practical to obtain a measure of the desired and achieved level of assurance for some individual audit procedures by using statistical sampling techniques through the use of the confidence level. But there is no objective measurement method for most audit tests. Furthermore, auditors presently have no means of objectively combining levels of assurance obtained from individual procedures into an overall level of assurance. There are too many different audit procedures and considerations in the audit to make this possible. The idea of a reasonable level of assurance is highly subjective and is determined by the auditor's professional judgment. It is possible to think in terms of high levels of assurance in some circumstances or reasonable levels of assurance and even low levels, but a precise measure is not realistic.

Changing Desired Levels of Assurance
for Different Circumstances

Should the auditor strive for a higher level of assurance in certain situations? The authors believe a reasonably high level of assurance is always desirable. But in some circumstances an even higher level of assurance is needed to protect users. These circumstances fall into two categories.

The Degree to Which External Users Rely upon the Statements. When external users place heavy reliance upon the financial statements, it is appropriate that the auditor's overall level of assurance be increased. When the statements are extensively relied upon, a great social harm could result if a significant error were to remain undetected in the financial statements. The cost of additional evidence can be more easily justified when the loss to users from material errors is substantial. Several factors are good indicators of the degree to which statements are relied upon by external users:

- *Client's Size.* Generally speaking, the larger a client's operations, the more widely used the statements will be. The client's size, measured by total assets or total revenues, will have an effect on the overall level of assurance desired.
- *Distribution of the Client's Ownership.* The statements of publicly held corporations are normally relied upon by many more users than those of closely held corporations. For these companies, the interested parties include the SEC, financial analysts, and the general public.
- *Nature and Amount of the Client's Liabilities.* When statements include a large amount of liabilities, the statements are more likely to be used extensively by actual and potential creditors than when there are few liabilities.

The Likelihood of the Client's Filing Bankruptcy Subsequent to the Audit. If a client is forced to file bankruptcy or even just suffers a significant loss subsequent to the completion of the audit, there is a much greater chance of the auditor being required to defend the quality of the audit than if the client were under no financial strain. There is a natural tendency for those who lose money in a bankruptcy or because of a stock price reversal to file suit against the auditor. This can result from the honest belief that the auditor failed to conduct an adequate audit or from the users' desire to recover part of their loss regardless of the adequacy of the audit work.

In those situations where the auditor believes the chance of bankruptcy or loss is high, the overall level of assurance should be increased. If a subsequent challenge does occur, the auditor will then be in a much better position to successfully defend the audit results. The total audit evidence and the audit costs will increase in this circumstance, but this is justifiable because of the additional risk of lawsuits that the auditor faces.

It is difficult for an auditor to predict a bankruptcy before it occurs, but certain factors are good indicators of an increased probability of bankruptcy:

- *Liquidity Position.* If a client is constantly short of cash and working capital, this is one indication of a future problem in paying bills. The auditor must assess the likelihood and significance of a weak liquidity position getting worse.
- *Profits (losses) in Previous Years.* When a company has rapidly declining profits or increasing losses for several years, the auditor should recognize the future solvency problems the client is likely to encounter. It is also important to consider the changing profits relative to the balance remaining in retained earnings.
- *Method of Financing Growth.* The more a client relies on debt as a means of financing, the greater the risk of financial difficulty if the client's operations become less successful. It is also important to evaluate whether permanent assets are being financed with short-term or long-term loans. Large amounts of required cash outflows during a short period of time can force a company into bankruptcy.
- *Nature of the Client's Operations.* Certain types of businesses are inherently riskier than others. For example, other things being equal, there is a much greater likelihood of bankruptcy of a stockbroker than of a utility.
- *Competence of Management.* Competent management is constantly alert for potential financial difficulties and modifies its operating methods to minimize the effects of short-run problems. The ability of management must be assessed as a part of the evaluation of the likelihood of bankruptcy.

The auditor must investigate his client and assess the importance of each of the factors affecting the degree to which external users rely upon the statements, and the likelihood of the client's filing bankruptcy subsequent to the audit. Based upon this investigation and assessment, the auditor should be able to set a tentative and highly subjective level of the risk that he is willing to take that the financial statements will include a material error after the audit is completed. As the audit progresses, additional information about the client is obtained and the desired level of assurance may be modified.

Similar Assurance Levels for Different Auditors

In an ideal world, different auditors would set the same level of assurance for any one particular audit, and the differing levels of assurance would reflect only differing circumstances.

There have been few studies within the profession to determine whether different auditors strive for approximately the same level of assurance for similar audit clients, but there are several considerations that encourage reasonably uniform standards of assurance:

- *Lawsuits and Other Sanctions.* If auditors in a CPA firm fail to achieve adequate levels of assurance, they may be financially successful in the short run, but they are also likely to fail to discover material errors in the financial statements. When material errors are not detected, lawsuits by users who have been harmed, sanctions by the SEC, and even censure for substandard practice by state societies of CPAs will negatively affect the firm financially and will discredit the firm's professional reputation. Fear of these sanctions has the effect of encouraging CPAs to attain reasonable levels of assurance for all audits.
- *Competition among CPA Firms.* If a firm choose extraordinarily high levels of assurance relative to other CPA firms, the billing submitted to the client will have to reflect the additional time needed to complete the audit. If the total bill is significantly higher than what another CPA firm would charge, the client may change to a less expensive auditor. Competitive forces, then, help to prevent auditing beyond reasonable levels of assurance.
- *Professionalism.* Even without the lawsuits and other sanctions, most auditors want to do high-quality audits, even at some personal financial sacrifice. Most professionals take pride in their work and the quality of the services performed by their firm. Generally, the practitioners who maintain a high degree of professionalism also develop a reputation in their community that pays off in terms of both professional pride and excellent financial rewards.

Different Assurance Levels

There are also several conditions that cause different auditors to end up with different levels of assurance in similar audit situations. The most important of these are as follows:

- *The Difficulty of Measuring Levels of Assurance.* As long as it is difficult to measure levels of assurance, it is unreasonable to expect that all auditors will end up with the same level of evidence under similar circumstances. Such differences might be partially avoided if the profession were to set precise requirements for evidence accumulation, but the result would probably be inflexibility and the failure of auditors to adequately modify evidence under different circumstances.
- *Different Levels of Risk Avoidance.* The level of assurance an auditor selects must take into account the trade-off between the cost of evidence and the risk the auditor is willing to take that material errors exist in the statements. Naturally, auditors differ as to the risks they are willing to accept. Some

are highly conservative and constantly fear a lawsuit or loss of professional reputation. Others are more interested in a high level of income and less concerned with sanctions. The former type of auditor could be expected to seek higher levels of assurance than the latter.
- *Different Levels of Competence.* Unfortunately, in every profession some practitioners do not properly perform their responsibilities. Even requiring a CPA certificate and continuing education cannot eliminate incompetent practitioners. Incompetent practitioners are likely to arrive at lower levels of assurance than competent ones.

It is hoped that competition, legal liability, other sanctions, and professionalism will tend to minimize the differences in levels of assurance in similar circumstances. Nevertheless, it must be recognized that the level of assurance sought by different auditors in similar circumstances is unlikely to be exactly the same.

Segmenting the Audit

Audits are performed by dividing the overall audit into smaller segments. The division is done to make the audit more manageable and to aid in assigning tasks to different audit staffs. The two broadest segments of tests are *tests of transactions* and *direct tests of financial statement balances,* but each of these is also subdivided. The tests of transactions are divided into tests of the various subparts of the client's accounting system, such as the sales and cash receipts area, payroll, and cash disbursements. Similarly, the tests of financial statement balances accounts are typically subdivided into types of accounts such as cash, accounts receivable, inventories, prepaid expenses, fixed assets, and accounts payable. The number of subdivisions depends primarily on the nature of the client's system and the account classifications used in the chart of accounts.

A common way to divide an audit is to keep closely related types of transactions and account balances in the same segment. This is called the *cycle approach.* For example, sales, sales returns, and cash receipts transactions and the accounts receivable balance are all a part of the sales and collection cycle. Similarly, payroll transactions and accrued payroll are a part of the payroll and personnel cycle.

Once the segments (audit areas) have been selected, the auditor must make the four evidence accumulation decisions for each segment (audit procedures, sample size, particular items to select, and timing). For example, in the tests of sales transactions for a given client, the auditor must decide which procedures are appropriate and when they should be performed. For each audit procedure selected, the number of sample items to test must be decided upon. Next, the particular items for testing from the population must be selected. This same decision process must be repeated for cash receipts, accounts receivable, notes payable, and every other audit area being tested.

In assessing whether the desired level of overall assurance for the financial statements taken as a whole has been achieved, it is necessary for the auditor to subjectively combine the level of assurance achieved for each of the individual parts of the audit. It is impossible to achieve a high level of overall assurance if the auditor is uncertain about any one material part of the statements, such as inventory or the adequacy of the disclosure of a significant lawsuit against the client.

A higher overall level of assurance is achieved by obtaining an increased level of assurance in one or more of the components of the financial statements. This increased level of assurance in the individual components is in turn accomplished by accumulating more evidence in certain audit areas. As an illustration, if a partner on an audit feels there is a reasonably high chance of the bankruptcy of a client listed on the New York Stock Exchange, he is likely to test inventory, accounts receivable, accounts payable, and other significant audit areas more carefully than usual.

There may be cases where the auditor wants a higher desired level of assurance for some segments of the engagement than others. For example, if the auditor knows the client always uses inventory as security for short-term loans shortly after the balance sheet date, a higher level of assurance may be appropriate for inventory than other account balances.

EVIDENCE NEEDED TO ACHIEVE
A DESIRED LEVEL OF ASSURANCE

The amount of evidence needed to achieve a given desired level of assurance is considered next. In analyzing this decision, the assumption is made that the auditor has already decided upon the proper desired level of assurance. If the desired level of assurance changes, this means that the evidence needed must also be modified.

It is more convenient at times to refer to assurance in terms of *risks*. This is not a change in concept because the overall level of risk is simply 100 percent minus the overall level of assurance. The auditor's evaluation of when the acceptable desired level of risk has been reached is accomplished by assessing two closely related considerations: the risk that the client makes errors and the risk that the audit tests fail to uncover the material errors.

Risk That the Client Makes Errors

There is always some risk that the client has made errors that are individually or collectively material enough to make the financial statements misleading. The errors can be intentional or unintentional, and they can be errors affecting the dollar balance in accounts or disclosure errors. The risk of the client's making these errors can be low in some instances and extremely high in others.

At the time the audit starts, there is not much that can be done about changing this risk. Instead, the auditor must *assess the factors* making up the risk and *modify his audit evidence* to take them into consideration. If the auditor believes the risk of error is high, the amount of evidence collected must be increased to accomplish the desired overall risk. When this risk is low, the amount of evidence to be collected can be greatly reduced to arrive at the same overall risk.

The auditor should consider several major factors, which will be studied in more detail shortly, when assessing the risk of the financial statements including errors:

- System of internal control
- Materiality
- Population size
- Makeup of the population
- Initial versus repeat engagement
- Results of the current and previous audits
- Integrity of management
- Others

Risk That the Audit Tests Fail to Uncover the Material Errors

Assuming that the audit tests are made with due care, the more evidence the auditor accumulates, the less risk there is of failing to uncover material errors. Even when audit tests are done with due care, there is a risk that a material error will not be uncovered. That risk is inherent in the sampling process.

There are several considerations other than the amount of evidence affecting the likelihood of failing to uncover material existing errors in the financial statements. These are identified at this point and discussed further later in this section:

- Scope of the engagement
- Nature of errors and degree of error concealment
- Reliability of available evidence
- Nature of the client's industry

Auditors do not now and probably never will quantify these two risk factors and combine them into an overall audit risk. There are too many complex factors affecting each risk factor to reduce it to a single quantification. Nevertheless, the decision process that auditors follow is of the nature described, except that it is subjective rather than objective and is frequently carried out informally.

To illustrate the concept, assume that the auditor has a desired level of assurance in the audit of accounts receivable of 98 percent (desired risk is 2 percent). Also assume that the risk of the account being materially misstated is 25 percent. If the auditor believes there is only a 5 percent risk of failing to uncover a material error, if one exists, the overall achieved risk is only 1.25 percent ($.25 \times .05$). Given the foregoing assumptions, the auditor can have an 8 percent risk of failing to uncover a material error if one exists and still meet the overall desired level of assurance requirement (.08 = .02 ÷ .25). The reader is again reminded that it is impractical in practice to assign specific probabilities to overall risk, risk of material errors existing in the statement, or risk that the auditor will fail to uncover them. But the use of high risk and low risk for all three of these risks is frequently used in practice.

The factors discussed in this section are similar to those previously considered as factors affecting the desired level of assurance in that both groups affect the *amount* of evidence that should be accumulated. Both sets of factors are of the utmost importance in the process of professional judgment. Without considering them, the evidence would be the same for each audit.

The major difference between the factors affecting the desired level of assurance and those affecting the auditor's expectation of errors and likelihood of detecting them is the more *specific nature* of the latter factors. Evaluating the factors affecting the proper level of assurance has the effect of requiring higher or lower desired levels of overall assurance; by implication, additional or less evidence is needed in *all* audit areas. For example, the widespread distribution of client ownership implies the need for increased evidence in most facets of the audit because a higher level of overall assurance is desired. The factors affecting the expectation of errors, on the other hand, guide the auditor toward emphasizing particular parts of the audit. For example, if there were numerous errors in the confirmation of accounts receivable in the preceding year's audit, accounts receivable should ordinarily be heavily emphasized in the current year. The relationship between desired and achieved levels of assurance and the factors affecting the desired level of assurance and the factors affecting the amount of evidence needed to achieve a given level of assurance is shown in Figure 5-1.

The remainder of this section deals with the factors affecting the risk of errors existing in the client's statement and those affecting the failure to uncover existing errors.

In dealing with the individual factors affecting the expectation of errors, it is the auditor's responsibility to *identify* the factors in a given audit, *evaluate* the significance of each, and *modify* the evidence to take each significant factor into account. Because of the lack of a precise measurement system, the impact of each factor is evaluated subjectively.

System of Internal Control

The system of internal control is one of the most important determinants of the audit procedures to be performed, the sample size for each procedure and the timing of the procedures. A thorough evaluation of the system must be completed before the audit can be regarded as adequate, and the results of this evaluation will aid the auditor in determining what evidence is to be accumulated throughout the audit. Internal control is such an important factor in evidence accumulation that it is discussed separately in Chapter 8, as well as being integrated into most subsequent chapters.

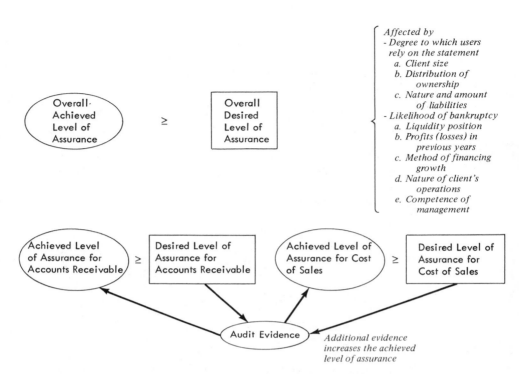

Factors that affect the amount of evidence needed to achieve a given desired level of assurance.

Likelihood of errors:
- System of internal control
- Materiality
- Population size
- Make up of the population
- Initial versus repeat engagement
- Results of the current and previous audits
- Integrity of management
- Others

Likelihood that the evidence will uncover the errors:
- Scope of the engagement
- Reliability of available evidence
- Nature of errors and degree of error concealment
- Nature of the client's industry

FIGURE 5–1 Desired and Achieved Levels of Assurance

Materiality of Account Balances

The concept of materiality as it relates to auditing is simply that the auditor should concentrate on the financial statement information that is important and put less emphasis on the less significant accounts and transactions on the grounds that important information is more likely to be significantly misstated. For example, in most cases the auditor will have a higher level of achieved overall assurance if the verification of a small supplies account is limited to a brief review, and the primary audit emphasis is placed on verifying accounts receivable and inventory, than would occur if an equal amount of time were devoted to each of these accounts.

In deciding on materiality in a given situation, the auditor must establish whether the account or transaction under consideration contains errors or omissions that, when combined with other possible errors in the statements, will make the overall financial statements misleading. Several important facets of materiality make it difficult for the auditor to decide whether any particular item is material:

- *Materiality Is a Relative Concept Rather Than an Absolute One.* An error of a given magnitude might be material for a small company, whereas the same dollar error could be immaterial for a large one. For example, a total error of $100,000 would be extremely material for a company with $200,000 total assets, but it would be immaterial for a company such as General Motors. Hence, it is not possible to establish any dollar-value guidelines applicable to all audit clients.

- *A Basis Is Needed for Evaluating Materiality.* Since materiality is relative, it is necessary to have a basis for establishing whether an error is material. *Net income* is normally the most important basis for deciding what is material, because it is regarded as a critical item of information for users; but it also is important to learn whether the item in question could materially affect the reasonableness of such subtotals as current assets, total assets, current liabilities, and owner's equity, and how it affects longer-run trends. It is the responsibility of the individual auditor to decide whether the item in question contains errors that would be material when compared with any one of these bases.

- *The Combined Errors Are More Important Than Errors in Individual Accounts.* It is not sufficient for the auditor to consider the materiality of the errors in just a particular account. The auditor must ultimately decide whether *all the errors combined* are sufficient to make the overall financial statements misleading. It is possible for individual errors to be immaterial when they are considered separately and for the overall financial statements to be misleading because of their combined effect. Evaluation of the reliability of the overall financial statements becomes especially difficult because the auditor, having only sampled the population, does not know the exact extent of all errors.

- *Accounts with Small Recorded Balances Can Contain Material Errors.* In judging whether an account is material enough to justify extensively verifying the balance, it is not sufficient to make the decision on the basis of the recorded account balance. It is possible for an account with a small balance, or even a zero balance, to contain significant errors.

Certain factors influence the auditor's decision about whether an account with a small recorded balance potentially contains material errors. First, he should consider the materiality of the transactions that affected the balance in the current period. For example, the balance in the cash account may be small, but there usually are material cash receipt and cash disbursement transactions during the year. Second, he should consider the maximum potential size of the account. As an illustration, if the income-tax liability from previous years is recorded at zero, it is still necessary to examine the internal revenue agent's reports for those years, since the unrecorded liability could be material. On the other hand, it is unlikely in most situations that the correct balance of certain accounts (e.g., prepaid insurance) would be material even if the errors relative to the account balances were reasonably large. Finally, the auditor should consider such other factors as the system of internal control and the results of previous audits in deciding whether an account with a small balance is likely to contain a material error.

Materiality is also a consideration in performing tests of transactions. In most cases, tests of transactions areas such as cash receipts, sales, purchases, payroll, and cash disbursements are highly material and require significant audit attention. Certain transactions areas such as sales returns and allowances are frequently immaterial and can be deemphasized. Also, in multifirm or multibranch operations, the segments with the most significant operations should usually receive the greatest audit attention.

Population Size

Population size is closely related to materiality, but it is of sufficient importance to be considered as a separate factor. In general it is reasonable to expect more errors to exist in a large population than in a small one unless there are compensating factors. Therefore, the population size has traditionally been an important determinant of the auditor's sample size. For example, it was traditionally common to audit transactions for a certain period of time such as a month for tests of cash disbursements, or to confirm a certain percentage of the accounts receivable outstanding. In these cases the sample size would be in direct proportion to the population size. The advent of statistical sampling in auditing has dramatically changed this approach. In using statistical sampling, the population size still affects the sample size, but only to a certain point; a doubling of the population, for example, might have little effect on the number of items in the sample where statistical sampling is used.

Makeup of the Population

The individual items making up the total of a population also frequently affect the auditor's expectation of a material errors being included. For example, most auditors would be more concerned about the possibility of a material misstatement in a population of accounts receivable containing a small number of large customer balances than if there were a large number of small accounts. To compensate for the greater possibility of a significant error, a larger percentage of the accounts with bigger customer balances would normally be confirmed and a different type of confirmation would be used. The nature and the source of individual transactions within a total balance also affect the audit tests. Transactions with affiliated companies, amounts due from officers, cash disbursements made payable to cash, and accounts receivable outstanding for several months are examples of situations requiring greater investigation because there is usually a higher likelihood of errors than in more typical transactions.

Initial versus Repeat Engagement

Evidence accumulation is different when the audit is being performed for a new client rather than for one that has been an audit client in previous years. There are three primary reasons for this:

It Is Necessary to Verify the Details Making Up Those Balance Sheet Accounts That Are of a Permanent Nature, Such as Fixed Assets, Patents, and Retained Earnings. On an initial audit it may be necessary to verify transactions that occurred several years earlier in order to establish that the current balance in the account is reasonable, whereas on repeat engagements it is necessary only to audit the transactions that took place in the current period.

It Is Necessary to Verify the Beginning Balances in the Balance Sheet Accounts on an Initial Engagement. This step is essential even if comparative financial statements are not issued because the accuracy of the current year's income statement is dependent on the accuracy of the beginning balances in the balance sheet accounts. In a repeat engagement this step is unnecessary because the prior year-end balances, which were verified in the audit of the preceding year, are the current year's beginning balances.

The Auditor Is Less Familiar with the Client's Operations in an Initial Audit. The lack of knowledge about a client's operations includes such considerations as unfamiliarity with the system of internal control, absence of reliable historical ratios and balances with which to compare the current year's results, and nonexistence of previous years' audit evidence and conclusions as a basis for developing a current year's audit program. As a consequence of the lack of knowledge, it is often necessary to perform more audit procedures for an initial engagement than for a repeat audit. Similarly, larger sample sizes are usually appropriate in new audits.

If a new client has had audits performed in previous years by a reputable CPA firm in which the current auditor has a high degree of confidence, it is acceptable to place some reliance on the previous auditor's results. The extent to which the current auditor should rely on a previous audit depends on his knowledge of the previous auditor, but it is always necessary to at least review the previous auditor's working papers and to perform sufficient procedures on beginning balances to establish that the current-period transactions are recorded on a basis consistent with that of the preceding year. SAS 7 (Section 315) provides guidelines to the successor auditor in communicating with the predecessor auditor about previous years' audit results.

Results of the Current and Previous Audits

An auditor would be considered negligent if the results of the preceding year's examination were ignored during the development of the current year's audit program. If the auditor found a significant number of errors in the preceding year in an audit area such as inventory pricing, extensive testing would have to be done in the current audit as a means of determining whether the deficiency in the client's system had been corrected. On the other hand, if the auditor has found no errors for the past several years in his tests of an audit area, he is justified in reducing the audit tests provided that the internal control review indicates that the system has not deteriorated.

If, during the current-year audit, the auditor finds errors that lead him to believe the total population being tested may be improperly stated, he must ultimately establish whether the population contains material errors. Before the auditor completes his tests, he must either (1) satisfy himself by additional testing that the original sample was not representative of an essentially satisfactory population or (2) take corrective action regarding the population.

Integrity of Management

When management is dominated by a few individuals who lack the integrity to obey the law, the likelihood of significantly misrepresented financial statements is greatly increased. An auditor takes significant legal and professional risks when he does audits for clients lacking in integrity. It is common practice for CPA firms to inquire of sources independent of the client about management integrity, especially for first-year audits. This subject is discussed in greater detail in Chapter 6. Many CPA firms will not do audits for companies where management lacks basic integrity.

Frequently, management has a reasonable level of integrity but cannot be regarded as completely honest in all dealings. For example, management may deduct repairs and maintenance expense on the tax returns that are capital items or a decision might be made not to inform a customer of a duplicate payment received. The CPA firm should first evaluate whether it wants to do an audit for such a client. If the decision is made to do so, extra care should be taken in all areas of the engagement to test for the possibility of intentional misstatements.

Other Factors

Several other factors also affect the expectation of errors. Following are some of the important situations in which the auditor can expect a high probability of errors:

The Transaction Is an Unusual One for the Client. Unusual transactions are more likely to be incorrectly recorded by the client than routine transactions because the client lacks experience in recording them. Therefore, transactions that occur with relative infrequency for a particular client should be carefully scrutinized by the auditor. Examples include fire losses, major property acquisitions, disposals of assets, and lease agreements.

The Account Being Verified Contains Transactions or Information That Requires Considerable Accounting Judgment to Record Properly. Transactions for major repairs or partial replacement of assets are examples of this type of situation. It is common for inexperienced accountants to record these transactions as repairs when in many cases company policy dictates that they should be recorded as assets, or vice versa. When fixed assets are replaced by similar assets, it also requires an adequate knowledge of accounting theory to record the new asset at the correct amount. Another example is the expensing of legal fees which should actually be classified as a patent cost, a part of a property acquisition cost, or a comparable asset.

The Asset Being Verified Is Highly Susceptible to Defalcation. The auditor should be concerned about the risk of possible defalcation in situations where it is relatively easy to convert company assets to personal use. Such is the case when currency or highly marketable inventory is not closely controlled.

There Is Some Motivation for the Client to Misstate the Financial Statements. In many situations, managements may believe that it would be advantageous to misstate the financial statements. For example, if management receives a percentage of total profits as a bonus, there may be a tendency to overstate net income. Similarly, if a bond indenture requirement includes a specification that the current ratio must remain above a certain level, the client may be tempted to overstate current assets or to understate current liabilities by an amount sufficient to meet the requirement. Also, there may be considerable motivation for intentional understatement of income when management wants the company to pay less income taxes. The auditor should constantly be alert to all of these possibilities and adjust his evidence accumulation accordingly.

Scope of the Engagement

The scope of the engagement, along with the next two factors, affects the likelihood of uncovering existing errors rather than affecting the likelihood of errors existing in the statements.

The auditor must have complete freedom in selecting the procedures he believes necessary and the sample size he considers appropriate; otherwise there would be little sense in having an independent person perform the audit function. Nevertheless, occasionally some clients request that the auditor omit certain procedures or not test specific accounts. When the client does impose restrictions on the procedures that can be performed or the extent of the application of the procedures, the auditor must either find *satisfactory alternative means* of verifying the account in question or *qualify his audit report.*

Any restrictions imposed by the client or additions to the responsibilities agreed to by the auditor should be clearly understood by both the auditor and the client before the audit actually begins. This understanding will aid the auditor in modifying the audit procedures and sample size whenever it is possible. In the case where a client has imposed restrictions, this under-standing will facilitate the acceptance of a modified report if the auditor cannot satisfy himself about the fairness of the financial statements by other audit evidence. Any modifications of the normal audit contract should be included as part of the formal *letter of engagement* between the client and the auditor. The letter could become important evidence in a later dispute over the auditor's responsibilities.

Reliability of the Available Evidence

Not all the evidence accumulated by the auditor is equally reliable. Its reliability can vary from nearly useless in the case of a rumor to near certainty in some kinds of physical examination. The three most important deter-minants of the reliability of audit evidence were discussed in Chapter 4.

Nature of Errors and Degree of Error Concealment

All errors are not equally easy for the auditor to uncover. For example, it would be unusual for an auditor to fail to uncover a large number of uninten-tional errors of pricing inventory at replacement cost rather than FIFO. At the other extreme, it is extremely difficult for an auditor to uncover a care-fully concealed illegal act by management such as the bribery of foreign officials by first paying commissions to foreign sales personnel, who in turn remit the payments to the officials.

To illustrate how the nature of errors affects the likelihood of uncover-ing them, four comparisons are made between different types of errors. In each of the four comparisons, the most difficult of the errors to uncover is listed first and both types of errors are assumed equally material.

Intentional versus Unintentional. Regardless of whether an intentional error is a defalcation, a misstatement of assets or liabilities to improve reported earnings, or an omitted footnote, it is usually more difficult to uncover them than to uncover mistakes or wrong judgment. This is because a person commiting an intentional error attempts to conceal the error.

A Large Number of Small Errors versus a Small Number of Large Errors. When several population errors are included in the auditor's sam-ple, it is relatively easy to evaluate whether the total population error is material. Careful use of statistical sampling methods minimizes the likelihood of overlooking a material error in this situation. When there are a small number of large errors in a population, there is a risk of not including any population items containing errors in the sample. It is easy to conclude that the population is fairly stated when it is actually materially misstated in such a situation.

Omitted Disclosures and Amounts versus Incorrectly Recorded Amounts.
The client's failure to record transactions or footnotes and other disclosures is difficult to uncover because the auditor must first find related information to aid in uncovering the omission. For example, if a company has failed to disclose a contingent liability resulting from a lawsuit, the auditor may fail to uncover the lawsuit, especially if the client attempts to conceal the facts. For example, the client may deal with an attorney it has never used before, and no mention of the lawsuit may exist in any documentation.

When information is recorded, but has been recorded incorrectly, it is often easy to find and evaluate the errors. The auditor can start with recorded information and examine supporting documentation and other evidence to determine whether the material is correctly recorded.

Judgment Errors versus Mechanical Errors. Audit problems occur frequently when the client makes errors where significant judgment is required, such as frequently happens in charging off obsolete inventory or estimating waranty liabilities. These types of problem areas are often difficult to find. Even when they are found, it may be difficult to obtain evidence to determine that the statements are not fairly stated. For example, it is easy for an auditor to overlook obsolete inventory entirely unless he has extensive knowledge of the client's business. Even if the auditor knows that there is an obsolescence problem, it is difficult to determine the appropriate obsolescence charge-off.

The nature of expected errors and likely degree of error concealment affect the auditor's evidence accumulation in three ways. First, the auditor must be alert to the different types of errors that can occur and assess their likelihood of occurrence. Second, he must recognize that some types are more difficult to uncover, if they exist, than others. Third, he must use special precautions and perhaps significantly expand the evidence when there is a high risk of the existence of material hard-to-find errors.

Reliability of the Available Evidence

The reliability of the evidence affects the audit procedures performed and, in some cases, the sample size. Less reliable evidence must be combined with other information to provide a level of competent evidence sufficient to satisfy the auditor. If the type of evidence being collected is highly reliable, the overall level of assurance can usually be increased by testing additional sample items. On the other hand, it does no good to increase sample size if the evidence is extremely low in reliability in the first place.

A major consideration affecting the audit procedures used by auditors is the industry in which the client is engaged. In most cases it is undesirable for the auditor to use the same audit procedures for widely differing industries. For example, many of the audit procedures for testing revenue for a life insurance company will be significantly different from those for an automobile manufacturer. Similarly, many of the procedures for the valuation of inventory for a building contractor will be different from those for a department store using the retail method. However, it is important to keep in mind that even for different industries a considerable portion of the audit is similar in nature. For example, the audit of cash in the bank is likely to be almost identical for most clients, regardless of the type of industry.

The AICPA has recognized the differences in auditing in various industries by publishing specific audit guides for somewhat unusual types of audits. The categories covered by these audit guides include the following:

- Banks
- Brokers and dealers in securities
- Colleges and universities
- Construction contractors
- State and local governmental units
- Voluntary health and welfare organizations

THE FOUR AUDIT DECISIONS

Now that the factors that determine the amount of evidence for the auditor to accumulate have been discussed, it is appropriate to turn directly to the four decisions the auditor must make and discuss each of them briefly.

Appropriate Audit Procedures

There are some procedures for each audit area that will almost always be used. These are the *minimum audit procedures*. If many actual audit programs of highly regarded CPA firms for many different clients in a given situation were examined, those audit procedures common to all of them would be the minimum audit program. Neither the AICPA nor any other group serving more than one firm has ever specified a set of minimum audit procedures for each audit area. It is the responsibility of every firm to decide for itself its minimum standard of performance. Fortunately, the communication system between CPA firms is sufficient to provide some agreement as to what these minimum procedures should be.

The minimum audit program is insufficient for most audits. The auditor must perform other audit procedures beyond these to take into account unusual situations in the engagement. Professional judgment comes into play in recognizing such situations and modifying the procedures accordingly. In making this judgment, the factors of interest to the auditor include all those previously discussed in this chapter.

A Proper Sample Size

Sample size should vary depending upon the same circumstances in the audit that affect the adequacy and selection of audit procedures. In most cases the same factors that determine whether additional audit procedures should be used will have a major influence on the actual sample size. For example, an inadequacy in the system of internal control requires an increase in the number of audit procedures; it is also likely to cause a need for an increased sample size for some tests.

For most audits, determining the proper sample size is a more difficult decision than selecting the proper audit procedures because most of the procedures are likely to be a part of the minimum audit program. In such situations it is only necessary to decide whether to add one or two more procedures. It would be rare, even in those audit areas where the minimum audit program is not extensive, to add more than four or five. On the other hand, in selecting the proper sample size, the variation can be anywhere from a small number to all the items in the population. Since population sizes for different clients can vary in certain audit areas, such as cash disbursements and inventory, from a few dozen to hundreds of thousands, the sample size decision is indeed difficult. The problem is further complicated by the fact that a minimum sample size has not been well defined by either the organized profession or individual practitioners.

Wherever it is applicable, the use of statistical sampling is desirable in helping the auditor select the appropriate sample size. Statistical sampling techniques do not change the basic sample size decision, but they do help the auditor formalize his judgment. This will become apparent in Chapters 11 and 13, where the use of statistical sampling is discussed in detail.

The Timing of the Procedures

The decision as to when to perform audit procedures is less difficult and less important than the decisions about proper audit procedures and sample size. Nevertheless, timing cannot be ignored. As a means of better understanding the audit-timing decision, it is necessary to be familiar with the time framework in which the auditor operates.

Figure 5-2 shows points of time and time periods of special significance in the audit. The time period from 1-1-80 to 12-31-80 is the reporting period of the income statement and statement of changes of financial position and is therefore the most important period shown. The most important single date

```
                                              Last Day    Date the Audit
                                                 of        Report and Com-
                                              Fieldwork    pleted State-
                                                           ments Are De-
                                                           livered to Client

1-1-80                              12-31-80           2-27-81    3-8-81
|----------------------------------------|---------------|---------------|
             Financial Statement              Subsequent
                  Period                        Events
```

FIGURE 5-2 Significant Points of Time and Time Periods

is 12-31-80, since the statement of financial position is at that point of time. For continuing audits, the 1-1-80 date has already been verified in the previous year. The last day of field work is important because it signifies that the auditor has reviewed for important subsequent events from 12-31-80 to 2-27-81. The date the audit report is sent to the client is important only for the relationship between the client and the auditor. In normal circumstances, the report will be delivered on or before a date specified in a preliminary discussion between a representative of management and the partner responsible for the audit.

Certain audit procedures should normally be *done as close to the balance sheet date as possible.* These are primarily tests of the most important current assets, such as the physical count of cash, securities, and inventory, and the confirmation of accounts receivable. The reason for testing these types of assets near year-end is their relatively fast turnover. If the assets are not tested at that time, it is often difficult to verify them at a later date. When the client's system of internal control is considered highly reliable, it is possible to perform the tests somewhat earlier or later than the balance sheet date.

The tests of transactions of the client's system of internal control should be done *for the entire period under audit,* and they should be done before the direct tests of balances. This is because the results of the tests of transactions are a major determinant of the remaining audit evidence needed to reach a conclusion about the fair presentation of the financial statements.

The timing of audit tests other than tests of transactions and certain direct tests of current assets depends upon when the client has the records and documents prepared. After the end of the client's fiscal year, such *accounting tasks* as the pricing of inventory, computation of depreciation, and adjustment of prepaid expenses must be completed before the financial statements are ready for audit. It typically takes several weeks before the client's financial records are sufficiently complete to perform many of the necessary audit tests.

A major consideration affecting the timing of audit tests is the CPA firm's difficulty of *scheduling personnel.* Scheduling would not be a significant problem if the year-end dates of a firm's clients were evenly distributed throughout the year. Since this is not the case for most CPA firms, there is a shortage of personnel during certain periods of the year and an excess at other times. To overcome this problem, CPA firms schedule audit tests earlier than the end of the year to the extent that it is practical. It is usually possible to update the permanent asset records maintained in the auditor's working papers, examine new loan agreements and other legal records, analyze changes in the client's system, and perform other similar procedures throughout the accounting period. These tests have to be finalized after the end of the year, but some early testing will aid in spreading the audit work throughout the year. As already mentioned, it may also be possible to perform some direct tests of balances earlier than the end of the year if the client has an adequate system of internal control.

The timing of the audit tests for a typical audit is shown in Figure 5-3. Each of these parts of the audit will be studied in greater depth as we proceed through the text.

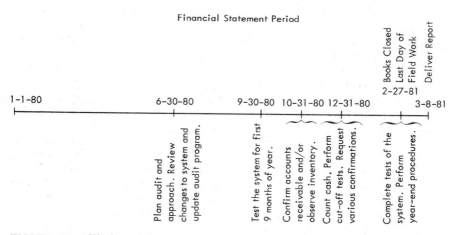

FIGURE 5-3 Timing of the Audit Tests

The Particular Items Selected for Testing

The most important considerations in selecting the sample items from a population are (1) obtaining a representative sample of the entire population and (2) emphasizing those items most likely to be in error. These can both be accomplished by taking a larger portion of certain types of items, and at the same time making sure that some of each type of item is included. For example, in confirming accounts receivable, the auditor is likely to want to test the large balances and the balances that have been outstanding for a long period of time more extensively than the small and current balances. If the combined total of all the small balances is material, a representative sample of these accounts should also be selected. More will be said about this decision in Chapter 12.

SUMMARY

This chapter examines the process the auditor goes through in deciding upon the appropriate evidence to accumulate. The emphasis is on the nature of these decisions in every audit and the most important factors the auditor considers in determining the proper level of evidence.

The underlying concept throughout the chapter is the auditor's need to consider the risk of failing to discover material errors if they exist in the financial statements. Even though the auditor is not a guarantor of the financial statements, the risk must be kept to a reasonable level if the profession is to retain credibility in the financial community.

The proper level of assurance or overall level of risk for which the auditor should strive in a given audit is dependent upon two major considerations: the degree to which users rely upon the statements and the likelihood of the client's filing bankruptcy subsequent to the audit. In determining the permissible overall level of risk, the factors affecting these two considerations should be carefully assessed before a decision is made. The desired overall level of risk has a direct effect on accumulation of sufficient competent evidence.

In conducting the audit, it is necessary to evaluate several factors that enable the auditor to perceive the overall risk of the financial statements' including a material error. These factors include the system of internal control, materiality, the results of previous audits, and so forth. The auditor must modify his evidence to take such factors into consideration because the greater the risk of error in the statements, the greater the need for more extensive evidence. These factors must be evaluated early in the audit if the evidence is to be effectively modified. As the auditor obtains the additional information from the audit, he may change his assessment of the factors.

Figure 5-4 summarizes and integrates the most important concepts presented in Chapters 1, 4 and 5. A careful review of the figure at this point will clarify the interrelationship of the concepts.

REVIEW QUESTIONS

5-1. Distinguish between the auditor's responsibility for fraud and his responsibility for unintentional errors.

5-2. Describe what is meant by an overall level of assurance. Explain why each of the following statements is true:
   a. A CPA firm should attempt to achieve the same overall level of assurance for all audit clients with approximately the same circumstances.
   b. A CPA firm should increase the overall level of assurance for audit clients where external users rely heavily upon the statements.
   c. A CPA firm should increase the overall level of assurance for audit clients where there is a reasonably high likelihood of a client's filing bankruptcy.
   d. Different CPA firms should attempt to achieve reasonably uniform overall levels of assurance for clients with similar circumstances.

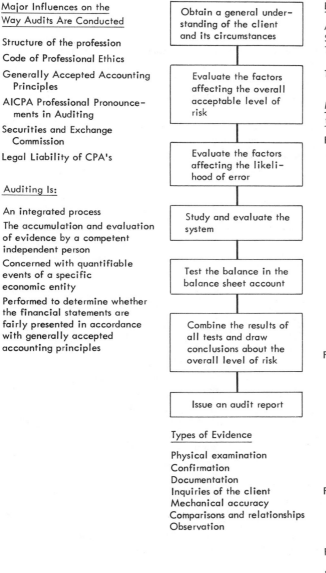

Major Influences on the Way Audits Are Conducted

Structure of the profession

Code of Professional Ethics

Generally Accepted Accounting Principles

AICPA Professional Pronouncements in Auditing

Securities and Exchange Commission

Legal Liability of CPA's

Auditing Is:

An integrated process

The accumulation and evaluation of evidence by a competent independent person

Concerned with quantifiable events of a specific economic entity

Performed to determine whether the financial statements are fairly presented in accordance with generally accepted accounting principles

---

Obtain a general understanding of the client and its circumstances

Evaluate the factors affecting the overall acceptable level of risk

Evaluate the factors affecting the likelihood of error

Study and evaluate the system

Test the balance in the balance sheet account

Combine the results of all tests and draw conclusions about the overall level of risk

Issue an audit report

Types of Evidence

Physical examination
Confirmation
Documentation
Inquiries of the client
Mechanical accuracy
Comparisons and relationships
Observation

Evidence Decisions

Audit procedures
Sample size
The particular items to select
Timing

Major Determinants of the Evidence Decision

Factors affecting the proper level of assurance:

The degree to which users rely on the statements:

Client size
Distribution of ownership
Nature and amount of liabilities

The likelihood of bankruptcy:

Liquidity position
Profits (losses) in previous years
Method of financing growth
Nature of the client's operation
Competence of management

Factors affecting the auditor's expectation of error:

System of internal control
Materiality
Population size
Makeup of the population
Initial versus repeat engagement
Results of the current and previous audits
Integrity of management
Others

Factors affecting the risk of failing to discover existing material errors:

Scope of the engagement
Nature of errors
Reliability of the available evidence
Degree of error concealment
Nature of the client's industry

FIGURE 5–4 Expanded Overview of the Audit Process

5–3. When an auditor issues an unqualified opinion, it is the same for a publicly held company and a small closely held firm. What justification is there for providing lower levels of assurance for closely held companies than for listed companies if the audit report is the same? Justify it from the point of view of auditors and users of financial statements.

163

5–4. Explain the relationship between the desired level of assurance and the legal liability of auditors.

5–5. State the two categories of circumstances that determine the overall level of assurance and list the factors that the auditor can use to indicate the degree to which each category exists.

5–6. Auditors have not been successful in measuring the levels of assurance achieved in different audits. How is it possible to think in terms of obtaining increased or decreased levels of assurance without a precise means of measuring the level achieved?

5–7. Explain the relationship between the factors affecting the expectation of error, the desired overall level of assurance, and the accumulation of audit evidence.

5–8. List the factors affecting the auditor's expectation of error and explain why each factor should affect the evidence needed to achieve a given level of assurance.

5–9. Assume that the client's internal controls over the recording and classifying of permanent assets additions are considered weak because the individual responsible for recording new acquisitions has inadequate technical training and limited experience in accounting. How would this situation affect the evidence you should accumulate in auditing permanent assets as compared with another audit where the controls are excellent? Be as specific as possible.

5–10. Each of the following questions concerns the concept of materiality in auditing:
   a. What criteria should the auditor use in deciding whether an estimated error in inventory, based on a sample, is sufficiently material to require an adjustment to the financial statements?
   b. What criteria should the auditor use in deciding whether an account balance is sufficiently immaterial to justify performing minimal tests rather than extensive procedures? Using your criteria, state the conditions when extensive audit procedures are required for cash in the bank, federal income taxes payable, petty cash, and unexpired insurance.
   c. Assume the auditor has decided to perform no detailed tests of factory supplies on hand in the audit of a manufacturing company. List the overall reasonableness tests the auditor should use.

5–11. Brad Jackson was assigned to the audit of a client that had not been audited by any CPA firm in the preceding year. In conducting the audit, he did no testing of the beginning balance of accounts receivable, inventory, or accounts payable on the grounds that the audit report is being limited to the ending balance sheet, the income statement, and the statement of changes in financial position. No comparative financial statements are to be issued.
   a. Explain the error in Jackson's reasoning.
   b. Suggest an approach Jackson can follow in verifying the beginning balance in accounts receivable.
   c. Why doesn't the same problem exist in the verification of beginning balances on continuing audit engagements?

5–12. Why do auditors frequently consider it desirable to perform audit tests throughout the year rather than wait until year-end? List several examples of evidence that can be accumulated prior to the end of the year.

5–13. Distinguish between a minimum audit program and the minimum evidence for a particular engagement that must meet the requirements of the third generally accepted auditing standard of field work. Under what circumstances could these two be the same?

5–14. Once the auditor has determined the amount of evidence to accumulate, what decisions must be made?

5–15. Why do auditors frequently perform tests prior to the client's year-end? Give three example of such tests and circumstances that would be necessary for these tests to be performed at this time.

5–16. State whether each of the following statements is true or false, and give your reason:

a. The audit evidence accumulated for every client should be approximately the same, regardless of the circumstances.

b. If the audit evidence accumulated for two different clients is approximately the same, the overall level of assurance achieved is approximately the same.

c. If the desired level of assurance is the same for two different clients, the audit evidence for the two clients should be approximately the same.

d. If the desired level of assurance, the factors affecting the expectation of error, and the factors affecting the auditor's likelihood of failing to discover existing errors are approximately the same for two different clients, the audit evidence for the two clients should be approximately the same.

DISCUSSION QUESTIONS AND PROBLEMS

5–17. Select the best response for each of the following questions.

a. The primary responsibility for the adequacy of disclosure in the financial statements and footnotes rests with the
   (1) partner assigned to the engagement.
   (2) auditor in charge of field work.
   (3) staff member who drafts the statements and footnotes.
   (4) client.

b. When a CPA expresses an opinion on financial statements, his responsibilities extend to
   (1) the underlying wisdom of the client's management decisions.
   (2) whether the results of the client's operating decisions are fairly presented in the financial statements.
   (3) active participation in the implementation of the advice given to the client.
   (4) an ongoing responsibility for the client's solvency.

c. The concept of materiality will be least important to the CPA in determining the
   (1) scope of his audit of specific accounts.
   (2) specific transactions that should be reviewed.
   (3) effects of audit exceptions upon his opinion.
   (4) effects of his direct financial interest in a client upon his independence.

(AICPA adapted)

5–18. Select the best response for each of the following questions.

a. Although the discovery of fraud is not the objective of the CPA's ordinary audit engagement, the CPA would be responsible for the detection of fraud if he failed to detect the fraud because
  (1) of management's failure to disclose an unrecorded transaction. The documents pertaining to the transaction are kept in a confidential file.
  (2) of management's description of the system of internal control.
  (3) of management's misstatement of the value of an inventory of precious gems.
  (4) the amount of fidelity bond coverage for certain employees is not compatible with the amount of potential defalcation that might be committed.

b. What is the independent auditor's responsibility prior to completion of field work when he believes that a material fraud may have occurred?
  (1) Notify the appropriate law enforcement authority.
  (2) Investigate the persons involved, the nature of the fraud, and the amounts involved.
  (3) Reach an understanding with the appropriate client representatives as to the desired nature and extent of subsequent audit work.
  (4) Continue to perform normal audit procedures and write the audit report in such a way as to disclose adequately the suspicions of material fraud.   (AICPA adapted)

5–19. Select the best response for each of the following questions.

a. The ultimate risk against which the auditor requires reasonable protection is a combination of two separate risks. The first of these is that material errors will occur in the accounting process by which the financial statements are developed, and the second is that
  (1) a company's system of internal control is not adequate to detect errors and irregularities.
  (2) those errors that occur will not be detected in the auditor's examination.
  (3) management may possess an attitude that lacks integrity.
  (4) evidential matter is not competent enough for the auditor to form an opinion based on reasonable assurance.

b. In determining validity of accounts receivable, which of the following would the auditor consider most reliable?
  (1) Documentary evidence that supports the accounts receivable balance.
  (2) Credits to accounts receivable from the cash receipts book after the close of business at year end.
  (3) Direct telephone communication between auditor and debtor.
  (4) Confirmation replies received directly from customers.
                                                                    (AICPA adapted)

5–20. The following questions deal with errors and fraud. Choose the best response.

a. When the auditor's regular examination leading to an opinion on financial statements discloses specific circumstances that make him suspect that fraud may exist and he concludes that the results of such fraud, if any, could not be so material as to affect his opinion, he should

      (1) make a note in his working papers of the possibility of a fraud of immaterial amount so as to pursue the matter next year.

      (2) reach an understanding with the client as to whether the auditor or the client, subject to the auditor's review, is to make the investigation necessary to determine whether fraud has occurred and, if so, the amount thereof.

      (3) refer the matter to the appropriate representatives of the client with the recommendation that it be pursued to a conclusion.

      (4) immediately extend his audit procedures to determine if fraud has occurred and, if so, the amount thereof.

b. When is the auditor responsible for detecting fraud?

      (1) When the fraud did not result from collusion.

      (2) When third parties are likely to rely on the client's financial statements.

      (3) When the client's system of internal control is judged by the auditor to be inadequate.

      (4) When the application of generally accepted auditing standards would have uncovered the fraud.

c. The ordinary examination of financial statements is not primarily designed to disclose defalcations and other irregularities although their discovery may result. Normal audit procedures are more likely to detect a fraud arising from

      (1) collusion on the part of several employees.

      (2) failure to record cash receipts for services rendered.

      (3) forgeries on company checks.

      (4) theft of inventories.

d. If an independent auditor's examination leading to an opinion on financial statements causes the auditor to believe that material errors or irregularities exist the auditor should

      (1) consider the implications and discuss the matter with appropriate levels of management.

      (2) make the investigation necessary to determine whether the errors or irregularities have in fact occurred.

      (3) request that the management investigate to determine whether the errors or irregularities have in fact occurred.

      (4) consider whether the errors or irregularities were the result of a failure by employees to comply with existing internal control procedures.

e. An auditor should recognize that the application of auditing procedures may produce evidential matter indicating the possibility of errors or irregularities and therefore should

      (1) design audit tests to detect unrecorded transactions.

      (2) extend the work to audit most recorded transactions and records of an entity.

      (3) plan and perform the engagement with an attitude of professional skepticism.

      (4) not depend on internal accounting control features that are designed to prevent or detect errors or irregularities.   (AICPA adapted)

5–21. Jordan Finance Company opened four personal loan offices in neighboring cities on January 2, 19X6. Small cash loans are made to borrowers who repay the principal with interest in monthly installments, over a period not exceeding two years. Ralph Jordan, president of the company, uses one of the offices as his headquarters and visits the other offices periodically for supervision and internal auditing purposes.

Mr. Jordan is concerned about the honesty of his employees. He came to your office in December 19X6. "I want to engage you to install a system to prohibit employees from embezzling cash," he stated. "Until I went into business for myself I worked for a nationwide loan company with five hundred offices, and I am familiar with that company's system of accounting and internal control. I want to describe that system so you can install it for me because it will absolutely prevent fraud."

Required:

a. How would you advise Mr. Jordan on his request that you install the large company's system of accounting and internal control for his firm? Discuss.

b. How would you respond to the suggestion that the new system would prevent embezzlement? Discuss.

c. Assume that in addition to undertaking the system's engagement in 19X7, you agreed to examine Jordan Finance Company's financial statements for the year ended December 31, 19X6. No scope limitations were imposed.

   (1) How would you determine the scope necessary to satisfactorily complete your examination? Discuss.

   (2) Would you be responsible for the discovery of fraud in this examination? Discuss.   (AICPA adapted)

5–22. You have examined Hagren Appliance Corporation's financial statements for several years and have always rendered an unqualified opinion. To reduce its current auditing cost, Hagren limited the scope of your examination of its financial statements for the year just ended to exclude accounts receivable and commissions payable. Hagren's officers stated that the type of auditor's opinion you would render was not important because your report would be used for internal management purposes only and would not be distributed externally. The materiality of the accounts not examined required you to disclaim an opinion on the fairness of the financial statements as a whole.

Required:

a. Why does a CPA prefer that the scope of his auditing engagement not be limited? Discuss.

b. How would a client's assurance to a CPA that his auditor's report will be used only for internal purposes affect the scope of the CPA's examination and the kind of opinion rendered? Discuss.   (AICPA adapted)

5–23. Frequently, questions have been raised ". . . regarding the responsibility of the independent auditor for the discovery of fraud (including defalcations and other similar irregularities), and concerning the proper course of conduct of the independent auditor when his examination discloses specific circumstances which arouse his suspicion as to the existence of fraud."

Required:

a. What are (1) the function and (2) the responsibilities of the independent auditor in the examination of financial statements? Discuss fully, but in this part do not include fraud in the discussion.
b. What are the responsibilities of the independent auditor for the detection of fraud? Discuss fully.
c. What is the independent auditor's proper course of conduct when his examination discloses specific circumstances that arouse his suspicion as to the existence of fraud? (AICPA adapted)

5–24. Kim Bryan is confused by the inconsistency of the three audit partners she has been assigned to on her initial three audit engagements. On the first engagement she spent a considerable amount of time in the audit of cash disbursements by examining canceled checks and supporting documentation, but almost no testing was done in the verification of permanent assets. On the second engagement a different partner had her do less intensive tests in the cash disbursements area and take smaller sample sizes than in the first audit even though the company was much larger. On her most recent engagement under a third audit partner, there was a thorough test of cash disbursement transactions, far beyond that of the other two audits, and an extensive verification of permanent assets. In fact, this partner insisted on a complete physical examination of all permanent assets recorded on the books. The total audit time on the most recent audit was longer than that of either of the first two audits in spite of the smaller size of the company. Bryan's conclusion is that the amount of evidence to accumulate depends on the audit partner in charge of the engagement.

Required:

a. State several factors that could explain the difference in the amount of evidence accumulated in each of the three audit engagements as well as the total time spent.
b. What could the audit partners have done to help Bryan understand the difference in the audit emphasis on the three audits?
c. Explain how these three audits are useful in developing Bryan's professional judgment. How could the quality of her judgment have been improved on the audits?

5–25. The following are different types of errors that can be encountered on an audit:
a. The use of a method of valuing inventory that is not in accordance with generally accepted accounting principles.
b. Failure to disclose a lawsuit for patent infringement where the amount of the liability is unknown.
c. The recording of expenditures as permanent assets which should have been recorded as repairs and maintenance.

d. The inclusion of invalid amounts in accounts receivable by preparing fictitious sales invoices to nonexisting customers.

Required:

a. Assuming the amounts are equally material, rank the types of errors listed above in terms of the difficulty of uncovering the error. (*Most difficult* is first.) Give reasons to support your answers.
b. Discuss whether auditors should have the same responsibility for uncovering the most difficult error as for discovering the least difficult one. Consider this from the point of view of the auditors and the users of financial statements.

5-26. A competent auditor has done a conscientious job of conducting an audit, but because of a clever fraud by management, a material fraud is included in the financial statements. The fraud, which is an overstatement of inventory, took place over several years, and it covered up the fact that the company's financial position was rapidly declining. The fraud was accidentally discovered in the latest audit by an unusually capable audit senior, and the SEC was immediately informed. Subsequent investigation indicated the company was actually near bankruptcy, and the value of the the stock dropped from $26 per share to $1 in less than one month. Among the losing stockholders were pension funds, university endowment funds, retired couples, and widows. The individuals responsible for perpetrating the fraud were also bankrupt.

After making an extensive investigation of the audit performance in previous years, the SEC was satisfied that the auditor had done a high-quality audit and had followed generally accepted auditing standards in every respect. The commission concluded that it would be unreasonable to expect auditors to uncover this type of fraud.

Required:

State your opinion as to who should bear the loss of the management fraud. Include in your discussion a list of potential bearers of the loss, and state why you believe they should or should not bear the loss.

5-27. In a preliminary discussion before beginning your audit of the Mark Company, the president states that he would like to ascertain whether any key employees have interests that conflict with their duties at the company. He asks that, during your regular audit, you be watchful for signs of these conditions and report them to him.

Required:

Briefly discuss your professional position in this matter. Include the following aspects in your discussion:

a. The responsibility of the CPA for the discovery of conflicts of interest. Give reasons for your position.
b. At the same time that you are conducting the audit of Mark Company you are also conducting the audit of Timzin Company, a supplier of Mark Company. During your audit of Timzin Company you determine that an employee of Mark Company is receiving kickbacks.

(1) Discuss your responsibility, if any, to reveal this practice to the president of Mark Company.

(2) Discuss your professional relationship with Timzin Company after discovering the kickbacks.　　　　　　　　　　(AICPA adapted)

5–28. Gale Brewer, CPA, has been the partner in charge of the Merkle Manufacturing Company, a client listed on the Midwest Stock Exchange for thirteen years. Merkle has had excellent growth and profits in the past decade, primarily as a result of the excellent leadership provided by Bill Merkle and other competent executives. Brewer has always enjoyed a close relationship with the company and prides himself on having made several constructive comments over the years which have aided in the success of the firm. Several times in the past few years Brewer's CPA firm has considered rotating a different audit team on the engagement, but this has been strongly resisted by both Brewer and Merkle.

For the first few years of the audit, the system of internal control was inadequate and the accounting personnel had inadequate qualifications for their responsibilities. Extensive audit evidence was required during the audit, and numerous adjusting entries were necessary. However, because of Brewer's constant prodding, the system of internal control improved gradually and competent personnel were hired. In recent years there were normally no audit adjustments required, and the extent of the evidence accumulation was gradually reduced. During the past three years Brewer was able to devote less time to the audit because of the relative ease of conducting the audit and the cooperation obtained throughout the engagement.

In the current year's audit, Brewer decided the total time budget for the engagement should be kept approximately the same as in recent years. The senior in charge of the audit, Phil Warren, was new on the job and highly competent, and he had the reputation of being able to cut time off of the budget. The fact that Merkle had recently acquired a new division through merger would probably add somewhat to the time, but Warren's efficiency would probably compensate for it.

The interim tests of the system of internal control took somewhat longer than expected because of the use of several new assistants, a change in the accounting system to computerize the inventory and several other aspects of the accounting records, a change in accounting personnel, and the existence of a few more errors in the tests of the system. Neither Brewer nor Warren was concerned about the budget deficit, however, because they could easily make up the difference at year-end.

At year-end Warren assigned the responsibility for inventory to an assistant who had also not been on the audit before but was competent and extremely fast at his work. Even though the total value of inventory increased, he reduced the size of the sample from that of other years because there had been few errors the preceding year. He found several items in the sample that were overstated due to errors in pricing and obsolescence, but the combination of all of the errors in the sample was immaterial. He completed the tests in 25 percent less time than the preceding year. The entire audit was completed on schedule and in slightly less time than the preceding year. There were only a few adjusting entries for the year, and only two of them were material. Brewer was extremely pleased with the results and wrote a special letter to Warren and the inventory assistant complimenting them on the audit.

Six months later Brewer received a telephone call from Merkle and was informed that the company was in serious financial trouble. Subsequent investigation revealed that the inventory had been significantly overstated in the preceding audit. The major cause of the misstatement was the inclusion of obsolete items in inventory (especially in the new division), errors in pricing due to the new computer system, and the inclusion of nonexistent inventory in the final inventory listing. The new controller had intentionally overstated the inventory to compensate for the reduction in sales volume from the preceding year.

Required:

a. List the major deficiencies in the audit and state why they took place.
b. What things should have been apparent to Brewer in the conduct of the audit?
c. If Brewer's firm is sued by stockholders or creditors, what is the likely outcome of the suit?

5-29. During the course of an audit engagement an independent auditor gives serious consideration to the concept of *materiality*. This concept of materiality is inherent in the work of the independent auditor and is important for planning, preparing, and modifying audit programs. The concept of materiality underlies the application of all the generally accepted auditing standards, particularly the standards of field work and reporting.

Required:

a. Briefly describe what is meant by the independent auditor's concept of materiality.
b. What are some common relationships and *other considerations* used by the auditor in judging materiality?
c. Identify how the planning and execution of an audit program might be affected by the independent auditor's concept of materiality.   (AICPA)

6

UNDERSTANDING
THE CLIENT'S BUSINESS
AND PLANNING
THE ENGAGEMENT

Before an audit begins, the CPA firm must decide whether it is willing to do the audit—whether to accept the client. After the audit begins, it is necessary to obtain *general information* about the organization, as well as to perform detailed tests of individual audit areas. The detailed tests receive the greatest emphasis in the auditing literature, but the more general information is equally important in the audit. This chapter concerns that general information. The following main topics are covered.

- Background information for the audit and planning
- Information about the client's legal obligations
- Analytical review procedures

CLIENT ACCEPTANCE

Even though obtaining and retaining clients is not easy in a competitive profession such as public accounting, a CPA firm must use care in deciding which clients are acceptable. The firm's legal and professional responsibilities are such that clients lacking in integrity or constantly arguing about the proper conduct of the audit and fees can cause more problems than they are worth.

Communications between
Predecessor and Successor Auditors

On prospective new clients which have been previously audited by another CPA firm, the new auditor (successor) in *required* by SAS 7 (Section 3.15) to communicate with the predecessor auditor. The purpose of the requirement is to help the successor auditor evaluate whether to accept the engagement. The communication may, for example, inform the successor auditor that the client lacks integrity or that there have been disputes over accounting principles, audit procedures, or fees.

The burden of initiating the communication rests with the successor auditor. *Permission must be obtained* from the client before the communication can be made because of the confidentiality requirement in the Code of Ethics. The predecessor auditor is required to respond to the request for information. In the event there are legal problems or disputes between the client and the predecessor, the predecessor's response can be limited to stating that no information will be provided. The successor should seriously consider the desirability of accepting a prospective engagement, without considerable other investigation, if a client will not permit the communication.

When a prospective client has not been audited by another CPA firm, other investigations are needed. Ways to get the information include contacting local attorneys, other CPAs, banks, and other businesses. In some cases the auditor may hire a professional investigator to obtain information about the reputation and background of the key members of management. The same approach can be followed when a predecessor auditor will not provide the desired information or if any indications of problems arise from the communication.

Evaluate the Possibility of Management Fraud

In recent years there have been several known instances of *deliberate management action to materially misrepresent financial statement information* for the personal benefit of various members of management. In some cases the motive was to cover up a massive fraud; in other cases management attempted to portray significantly more favorable financial statements than actually existed in order to prevent undesirable effects such as bankruptcy, a significant decline in value of securities, or the termination of employment. Three cases involving management fraud are briefly summarized to illustrate the nature of the fraudulent activity.

U.S. Financial, Inc. The chief executive officer of the company did not disclose his personal guarantees of down-payment funds used by purportedly independent parties to purchase real property from the company. The SEC's suit against this officer and the company also alleged the "manufacturing" of transactions in an endeavor to stimulate or maintain the price of the company's stock on which his personal fortune may have been dependent.

National Student Marketing. Among the many issues in this complex case, at least two fall into the management involvement area. First, revenues were prematurely recorded and subsequently proved not to have been realized. The reporting of favorable results at the earliest possible time ostensibly stimulated the market valuation of the company's stock, making it attractive for acquisition purposes. Second, the chairman of National Student Marketing also used his own stock in the company as an inducement for employment or as additional compensation, without disclosing such activities.

Equity Funding. The activities in this case were of three types: creation and inflation of assets, failure to record liabilities for borrowed cash, and creation of bogus insurance which was coinsured with other insurance companies. The effect of these practices was to inflate earnings and assets and to create the appearance of sustained growth at a substantial but measured rate. The insurance fraud also provided funds for critical cash needs. Equity Funding has incorrectly been referred to as the "great computer fraud," and although electronic data processing was substantial, a rational analysis leads to the conclusion that persons, not computers, perpetrate fraud.

Auditor's Responsibility. What is the auditor's responsibility for the discovery of material fraud perpetrated by management? The AICPA's position is that the auditor has responsibility for the failure to detect fraud only when the failure results from the inadequate performance of auditing procedures. In recent years, however, the courts, the SEC, and even some CPA firms are beginning to recognize the need for auditors to make *reasonable efforts* to discover management fraud. The cost to society for the losses caused by management frauds and the effect on the CPA's image in the financial community when the auditor fails to discover the fraud are too significant to ignore. How far the responsibility should extend has not yet been established, and none of these groups are willing to go so far as to make auditors responsible for the discovery of all material management frauds.

Evaluation of Environmental Considerations. Before the auditor begins an investigation of the possibility of management fraud, there are four environmental considerations he should evaluate:

- *Motivation of Management.* Management is unlikely to become involved in fraudulent transactions without a strong reason. It is difficult to assess the likelihood that personal reasons, such as heavy gambling or alcoholism, will cause one or two individuals in management to commit fraud. Certain *economic factors*, however, may motivate management to intentionally misrepresent the statements. These factors are basically similar to the factors affecting the likelihood of filing bankruptcy—the lack of sufficient capital to continue business, the urgent desire for a continued favorable earnings record in the hope of supporting the price of the stock, numerous unsuccessful business acquisitions and significant obsolescence dangers because the company is in a high-technology industry.

- *Business Structure.* Experience has shown that the structure and style of operating a business may be *deliberately designed* by management to facilitate management fraud. Of course, in the vast majority of cases, the business structure and style adopted are meant to be responsive to the abilities of management as well as business geography and product diversification, but an evaluation should be made of the effect of the business structure on the likelihood of management fraud. For example, when management is dominated by one or two individuals or when the accounting and financial functions are always significantly understaffed, the potential for management fraud is enhanced.
- *Integrity of Management.* An analysis of recent court cases involving management fraud shows that in most instances the individuals responsible for the fraud had also been previously involved in illegal or unethical business practices. The decision in the previous section on client investigation is pertinent to getting information about that integrity.
- *Reliance on Computers.* While the basic objectives of accounting control do not actually change with the method of data processing used, organization and control procedures utilized in EDP applications may differ significantly from those utilized in manual or mechanical applications. There are risks inherent in business activities involving massive volumes of individual transactions when total reliance is placed on computer operations.

Impact on Audit.   After the auditor evaluates the potential for management fraud, the firm decision should be whether to do the audit or withdraw. If the auditor decides to do the audit even though there is some potential, the entire staff should be made aware of the potential. They should also be advised to be constantly alert to any indications that fraud may exist.

BACKGROUND INFORMATION
FOR THE AUDIT AND PLANNING

Background information should help the auditor to thoroughly understand the client's industry, the nature of the client's business, and past relationships and existing agreements between the auditor and the client. Some of the information is useful in deciding upon the appropriate evidence to accumulate, whereas other information is useful in interpreting the evidence, planning the audit, and making constructive comments to the client. Planning is needed to enable the effective and efficient completion of the engagement on a timely basis. Both understanding the client's business and proper planning are required by SAS 22 (Section 311).

Obtain an Engagement Letter

The first step in the engagement is to make sure there is a clear understanding between the client and auditor as to the terms of the engagement. The understanding should be specified in the engagement letter.

The *engagement letter* is the agreement between the CPA firm and the auditor for the conduct of the audit and related services (see Figure 6-1). It should specify whether the auditor will prepare the client's tax returns and also a letter recommending improvements in the client's system based upon observations made during the audit (*management letter*). It should also state whether any restrictions will be imposed on the auditor's work, deadlines for completing the audit, assistance to be provided by the client's personnel for obtaining records and documents and schedules to be prepared for the auditor. The engagement letter is also a means of informing the client that the auditor is not responsible for the discovery of fraud. The engagement letter does not affect the auditor's responsibilities to external users of audited financial statements, but the responsibility to the client can be modified by the agreement.

Engagement letter information is important in planning the audit principally because it affects the timing of the tests and the total amount of time the audit and other services will take. If the deadline for submitting the audit report is soon after the balance sheet date, a significant portion of the audit must be done before the end of the year. When the auditor is preparing tax returns and a management letter, or if client assistance is not available, arrangements must be made to extend the amount of time on the engagement. Restrictions on the audit imposed by the client could affect the audit procedures performed and possibly even the type of audit opinion issued.

Obtain Knowledge of the Client's Industry

To adequately interpret the meaning of information obtained throughout the audit, an understanding of the *client's industry* is essential. Certain unique aspects of different industries must be reflected in the financial statements. An audit for a life insurance company could not be performed with due care without an understanding of the unique characteristics of the life insurance business. Imagine attempting to audit a client in the bridge construction industry without understanding the construction business and the percentage-of-completion method of accounting. A reasonable understanding of the client's industry is required by SAS 22 (Section 311).

Knowledge of the client's industry can be obtained in different ways. These include discussions with the auditor who was responsible for the engagement in previous years and auditors currently on similar engagements, as well as conferences with the client's personnel. There are AICPA industry audit guides, text books and technical magazines available for the auditor to

```
                                    Berger and Wild, CPAs
                                    Gary, Indiana 46405

        6-11-81
        Merchant's Steel
        2146 Willow St.
        Gary, Indiana 46405

        Dear Mr. Hocking:

                This letter confirms our arrangements for
        the audit of Merchant's Steel for the year ended
        12-31-81.

                The purpose of our engagement is to
        examine the Company's financial statements for the
        year ended 12-31-81 and evaluate the fairness of
        presentation of the statements in conformity with
        generally accepted accounting principles applied
        on a basis consistent with that of the preceding
        period.

                Our examination will be conducted in
        accordance with generally accepted auditing
        standards which will include a review of the
        system of internal control and tests of trans-
        actions to the extent we believe necessary.
        Accordingly, it will not include a detailed audit
        of transactions to the extent which would be re-
        quired if intended to disclose defalcations or
        other irregularities, although their discovery may
        result.

                We direct your attention to the fact that
        management has the responsibility for the proper
        recording of transactions in the books of account,
        for the safeguarding of assets, and for the sub-
        stantial accuracy of the financial statements.
        Such statements are the representations of manage-
        ment.
```

FIGURE 6–1 Engagement Letter

The timing of our examination will be scheduled for performance and completion as follows:

	Begin	Complete
Preliminary tests	9-11-81	9-24-81
Internal control letter		10-3-81
Year-end closing	2-3-82	2-18-82
Delivery of report and tax return		3-10-82

Assistance to be supplied by your personnel, including the preparation of schedules and analyses of accounts, is described on a separate attachment. Timely completion of this work will facilitate the conclusion of our examination.

Our fees are based on the amount of time required at various levels of responsibility, plus actual out-of-pocket expenses (travel, typing, telephone, etc.), payable upon presentation of our invoices. We will notify you immediately of any circumstances we encounter that could significantly affect our initial estimate of total fees of $23,000.

If the foregoing is in accordance with your understanding, please sign and return to us the duplicate copy of this letter.

Yours very truly,

John Wild

Accepted:

By: *Virgil Hocking*
Date: *6-21-81*

FIGURE 6-1 (cont.)

study in most major industries. Some auditors follow the practice of subscribing to specialized industry journals for those industries in which they spend a large amount of time. Considerable knowledge can also be obtained by participating actively in industry associations and training programs.

Obtain General Information about the Client's Business

A knowledge of the important aspects of the business that differentiate it from other firms in its industry is needed by the auditor in making industry comparisons. Similarly, information such as organizational structure, marketing and distribution practices, method of inventory valuation, and other unique characteristics of the client's business should be understood before the audit is started because such facts are continuously used in interpreting auditing information as it is obtained.

Companies filing with the SEC are required under FASB 14 to disclose segment information for different lines of business in the financial statements. SAS 21 provides audit guidelines for auditing the segment information. The auditor must have sufficient knowledge of a company's business to enable him to evaluate whether there are segments requiring separate disclosure. Since SAS 21 requires audit testing of the segment information, it is important for the auditor to identify the segments early.

The auditor's *permanent file* frequently includes the history of the company, a listing of the major lines of business, and a record of the most important accounting policies in previous years. The study of this information and discussions with the client's personnel aid in understanding the business.

Tour the Plant and Offices

A *tour of the facilities* is helpful in obtaining a better understanding of the client's business and operations because it provides an opportunity to meet key personnel. Discussions with nonaccounting employees during the tour and throughout the audit are useful in maintaining a broad perspective. The actual viewing of the physical facilities aids in understanding physical safeguards over assets and in interpreting accounting data by providing a frame of reference in which to visualize such assets as inventory in process and factory equipment. A knowledge of the physical layout also facilitates getting answers to questions later in the audit.

Review the Permanent File for Company Policies

Regardless of the quality of the system of internal control, many company policies and authorizations reflected in the financial statements are outside the scope of the accounting system. These include such things as authorization for disposal of a portion of the business, credit policies, loans to affiliates, and accounting policies for recording assets and recognizing revenue. Basic policy decisions must always be carefully evaluated as part of the audit to determine whether management has authorization from the board of directors to make certain decisions, and to be sure the decisions of management are properly reflected in the statements.

A useful approach followed by many CPA firms is to include a record in the *permanent file* of the most important policies followed by the client and the name of the person or group authorized to change the policy. The inclusion in the permanent file of the primary generally accepted accounting principles, such as the costs to be included in inventory valuation, is especially useful in helping the auditor determine whether the client has changed accounting principles. A periodic review of the information is important.

Investigate the Results of the Previous Audits

An important source of information in determining the parts of the current audit that are likely to cause the auditor difficulty is the results of previous years. Two major indicators of problem areas from previous years are the *amount of time* that was spent on each audit area and the *errors discovered* during the audit. If a particular audit area received unusual attention, the reasons for the emphasis should be obtained. If the conditions have not changed, increased attention may also be warranted in the current audit. Similarly, consideration should be given to heavy emphasis in the current year on those parts of the audit where significant errors were discovered in the past. The best source of information for reviewing the results of a previous audit is that year's *working papers*.

Evaluate Existence of Related Parties Transactions

Transactions with related parties are important to auditing because they will be *disclosed in the financial statements* if they are material. Generally accepted accounting principles require disclosure of the nature of the related party relationship, a description of transactions including dollar amounts, and amounts due from and to related parties.

A related party is defined in SAS (Section 335) as affiliated companies, principal owners of the client company, or any other party with which the client deals where one of the parties can influence the management or operating policies of the other. A related party transaction is any transaction between related parties. Common examples include sales or purchase transactions between a parent and its subsidiary, exchanges of equipment between two companies owned by the same person, and loans to officers. A less common example is the exercise of significant management influence on an audit client by its most significant customer.

Because related party transactions must be disclosed, it is important that all related parties be *identified and included in the permanent file* early in the engagement. Finding undisclosed related party transactions is thereby enhanced. Common ways of identifying related parties include inquiry of management, reviewing SEC filings, and examining stockholders' listings to identify principal stockholders.

Evaluate the Need for Outside Specialists

When the auditor encounters situations requiring specialized knowledge, it may be necessary to consult a specialist. SAS 11 (Section 336) establishes the requirements for selecting a specialist and reviewing the specialist's work. Examples include using a diamond expert in evaluating the replacement cost of diamonds and an actuary for determining the appropriateness of the recorded value of insurance loss reserves. Another common use of a specialist is consulting with attorneys on the legal interpretation of contracts and titles.

The auditor needs a sufficient understanding of the client's business to recognize the need for a specialist. Proper planning is needed to make sure that a specialist is available when he is needed. He should be both competent and, if possible, independent of the client.

Develop an Audit Strategy

Once the auditor understands the client's business, it is possible to begin thinking of the most efficient and effective way to complete the audit. Several of the decisions that are a part of a strategy are identified to illustrate audit strategies. Proper planning is needed for each strategy.

- Should there be heavy reliance on the system of internal control?
- Should tests of the system be performed at an interim date?
- Will EDP audit techniques be used?
- Should statistical sampling methods be followed?
- Is it more desirable to use a large audit team for a short period of time or a smaller team for a longer period?

Write an Audit Program

An essential part of planning is the development of an audit program. The program should be tailored to meet the audit strategy and circumstances of the engagement. For example, if there are significant weaknesses in the system of internal control, the audit program should be modified accordingly. The program should therefore be developed only after the auditor understands the client's business and has evaluated internal control.

An audit program should be as specific as possible. An example of a partial audit program is included in Figure 6-2. Written audit programs are required by SAS 22 (Section 311), but their form or the amount of detail to be included is not specified.

FIGURE 6–2

Partial Audit Program—Accounts Payable
June 30, 1982

Time (minutes)			Date and Initials	Working Paper Reference
Budget	Actual			
		1. Obtain a trial balance of accounts payable.	ᎫᏒ 7–21	L–1
15	20	2. Foot the balance and reconcile with general ledger.	ᎫᏒ 7–21	L–1
30	25	3. Compare the balance in the trial balance to the related subsidiary ledger for 25 vendors.	ᎫᏒ 7–21	L–1
120	130	4. Send a request for vendors' statements to 45 vendors. Emphasize larger balances, and those with significant activity but also include 5 with zero balances.	ᎫᏒ 7–22	L–2

INFORMATION ABOUT THE CLIENT'S LEGAL OBLIGATIONS

The fair presentation of financial statements in accordance with generally accepted accounting principles requires compliance with governmental regulations and other legal commitments in which the organization has become involved. Information about the client's legal obligations, if material, must be disclosed in the financial statements.

It is important to understand the most important legal requirements and agreements affecting the client *before* the audit begins. This will enable the auditor to properly interpret evidence obtained throughout the audit. If knowledge of a legal requirement is not obtained until the end of the engagement, it will be difficult to recall transactions or events encountered early in the audit that might have been affected by the requirement.

A distinction should be made between providing *legal advice* or interpreting legal documents and obtaining a reasonable understanding of the meaning of legal requirements from an audit point of view. The Code of Professional Ethics *prohibits CPAs from providing legal advice and making legal interpretations* if they are also acting as the independent auditor. On the other hand, it is essential that auditors be familiar with the client's legal requirements to the extent that they directly or indirectly affect the financial statements. If any difficulties arise in interpreting legal documents, either the client's legal counsel or the auditor's own attorney should be consulted.

Four general types of legal documents are discussed in this section:

- Governmental regulations affecting the client
- Corporate charter and bylaws

- Minutes of directors' and stockholders' meetings
- Contracts

Governmental Regulations Affecting the Client

Every organization's operations are affected in some way by local, state, or federal laws. These laws are frequently complex, and in some instances it may be impractical for CPAs to evaluate them. As an illustration, the determination of whether a company is living within the legal requirement of local zoning laws is outside of the CPA's scope of responsibility. On the other hand, many regulations directly affect the financial statements and are within the CPA's domain. In addition, SAS 17 (Section 328) requires the auditor to be aware of the possibility of illegal acts. When the auditor knows that an illegal act has taken place, the CPA's legal counsel should be contacted. The auditor should be familiar with the following:

Federal and State Securities Acts. The SEC Acts of 1933 and 1934 have special significance to both the client and the auditor. For an auditor involved with publicly held companies, a thorough understanding of these requirements is essential. Most clients rely heavily upon their auditor in complying with SEC regulations. State laws regulating publicly held companies are normally less difficult to comply with than the federal laws, but nevertheless must be understood.

Regulations Relating to Labor. Numerous regulations affect matters relating to employees. Of special significance are the laws relating to payroll taxes. These include requirements for withholding federal, state, and local income taxes and FICA taxes, as well as the client's tax requirements for federal and state unemployment taxes and the employer's share of FICA taxes. Minimum wage laws, regulations for payment of overtime rates, and nondiscrimination laws should also be understood. The requirements of the 1974 pension reform act are important for the fair presentation of financial statements.

Antitrust Laws. Price discrimination in interstate commerce is prohibited by the Robinson-Patman Act. Although it is difficult to determine when a violation of this federal law has taken place, the auditor should at least be familiar with the regulations.

Wage and Price Controls. At various times the federal government institutes controls on such things as prices, wages, interest, and dividends. A violation of these regulations during the time they are in effect can result in significant fines, including the possibility of a payment to individuals or businesses harmed by the violation of the law. Excess profits taxes are another example of this type of government regulation. The auditor must understand the nature of these regulations and know the periods to which the regulations apply.

Income Tax Laws. It is essential that auditors involved with businesses for profit understand the state and federal tax laws affecting the business. Even though the study of taxes can be a separate career in itself, auditors must know the tax implications of various accounting transactions and business decisions. Most CPA firms expect their auditors to understand the tax regulations well enough to recognize the possibility of a tax problem. Otherwise it would be difficult to determine whether federal income tax expense and the related liability account are fairly stated. Once a tax problem is recognized, the CPA firm's tax department is typically responsible for resolving the issues and advising the auditor of the proper solution. Many clients also rely on the CPA firm to provide tax advice.

Industry Regulations. Many clients in specialized industries are regulated by state and federal regulatory commissions. Examples include banks, railroads, insurance companies, brokers, and dealers in securities. The audits of municipal governments and state and federal governmental agencies also require an understanding of specialized regulations.

Corporate Charter and Bylaws

The *corporate charter* is granted by the state in which the company is incorporated and is the legal document necessary for recognizing a corporation as a separate entity. It includes the exact name of the corporation, the date of incorporation, the kinds and amounts of capital stock the corporation is authorized to issue, and the types of business activities the corporation is authorized to conduct. In specifying the kinds of capital stock, there is also included such information as the voting rights of each class of stock, par or stated value of the stock, preferences and conditions necessary for dividends, and prior rights in liquidation.

The *bylaws* include the rules and procedures adopted by the stockholders of the corporation. They specify such things as the fiscal year of the corporation, the frequency of stockholder meetings, the method of voting for directors, and the duties and powers of the corporate officers.

The auditor must understand the requirements of the corporate charter and the bylaws in order to determine whether the financial statements are properly presented. The correct disclosure of the stockholders' equity, including the proper payment of dividends, depends heavily upon these requirements.

Minutes of Directors' and Stockholders' Meetings

The *corporate minutes* are the official record of the meetings of the board of directors and stockholders. They include summaries of the most important topics discussed at these meetings and the decisions made by the directors and stockholders. A considerable portion of the information in the minutes has no direct relationship to the fair presentation of the financial statements and is useful to the auditor only as a means of obtaining a better understanding of the client's business. On the other hand, there is some essential information the auditor could easily overlook if he failed to examine the minutes. Information such as the following is usually included in the minutes:

- Declaration of dividends
- Authorized compensation of officers
- Acceptance of contracts and agreements
- Authorization for the acquisition of property
- Approval of mergers
- Authorization of long-term loans
- Approval to pledge securities
- Authorization of individuals to sign checks
- Reports on the progress of operations

While examining the corporate minutes, the auditor normally obtains information about those portions having significance to the fair presentation of the financial statements for inclusion in the working papers. This can be done by making an *abstract* of the minutes or obtaining a *copy* and underlining significant portions. At some time before the audit is completed, there must be a follow-up of this information to be sure management has complied with actions taken by the stockholders and the board of directors. As an illustration, the authorized compensation of officers should be traced to each individual officer's payroll record as a test of whether the correct total compensation was paid. Similarly, the auditor should compare the authorizations for the acquisition of equipment in the minutes with the equipment records if the board of directors must approve all new acquisitions of equipment over a specified amount, such as $100,000.

Contracts

Clients become involved in many different types of contracts that are of interest to the auditor. These contracts can include such diverse items as long-term notes and bonds payable, stock options, pension plans, contracts with vendors for future delivery of supplies, government contracts for completion and delivery of manufactured products, royalty agreements, union contracts, and leases.

Most of these contracts are of primary interest in individual parts of the audit and, in practice, receive special attention during the different phases of the detailed tests. As an example, the provisions of a pension plan would receive substantial emphasis as a part of the audit of the unfunded liability for pensions. The auditor should review and abstract the documents early in the engagement to gain a better perspective of the organization and to familiarize himself with potential problem areas. Later these documents can be examined more carefully as a part of the tests of individual audit areas.

In examining contracts, primary attention should focus on any aspect of the legal agreement affecting financial disclosure. Contracts can have an important effect on the statements when the subject of the contract must be directly included at a specific dollar value on the statements, as in the case of a mortgage or bond liability. The potential effect of a contract on the statements will naturally depend upon the nature of the contract. A long-term note has a completely different kind of disclosure requirement than a government contract for the delivery of finished goods.

ANALYTICAL REVIEW PROCEDURES

Analytical review procedures are defined by SAS 23 (Section 318) as *substantive tests of financial information* made by a study of *comparisons and relationships among data*. For example, comparison of the current year's gross margin percent to the previous year's to determine whether the percentage is approximately the same is an analytical review procedure.

Purposes

The most important reasons for analytical tests are as follows:

A Better Understanding of the Client and Its Industry. A better understanding of the client's industry can be accomplished by comparing current period ratios and other analytical information with the same industry for prior years and determining the reasons for any changes in the industry. Another useful approach is to compare the current-period industry average with other industries as a means of better understanding the unique financial characteristics of the client's line of business.

Indication of Financial Difficulty. If the analytical tests for the client are unfavorable relative to the average firm of its size in the same industry, this may indicate the inability to adequately fund current operations, difficulty in repaying debt, and possible financial failure. For example, if a higher than normal ratio of long-term debt to net worth is coupled with a lower-than-average ratio of profits to total assets, a relatively high risk of financial failure is indicated.

Reduction of Other Audit Tests. When analytical tests are performed and the comparisons indicate that the financial statements are likely to be fairly stated, it is possible to perform fewer other substantive tests. For example, if analytical test results of a small account balance such as unexpired insurance are favorable, no other substantive tests may be necessary. In other cases, sample sizes or certain audit procedures can be reduced.

Indication of Errors in the Financial Statements. When there are significant differences indicated by comparisons and relationships, the likelihood of a material error existing in the statements is increased. If a difference is large, the auditor should determine the reason and investigate the possibility that one or more of the client's account balances is materially wrong.

Recommendations to the Client. When the auditor discovers areas where the client's analytical test results are significantly different from those of other firms in its industry or have changed relative to previous years, these areas can be discussed with the client. In some instances the client may be unaware of the changes in its operations or of the differences between its practices and those of the other firms in the same industry. For example, if the ratio of sales to accounts receivable is higher than that of the average firms in the industry, it could indicate that the client is losing sales because of an overly restrictive credit policy.

Industry versus Internal Comparisons

Industry Ratios and Percentages. Dun and Bradstreet, Robert Morris Associates, and other publishers accumulate financial information for thousands of companies and compile the data for different lines of business. Many CPA firms purchase these publications for use as a basis for industry comparisons in their audits.

Robert Morris Associates, for example, publishes *ratios* and *percentages* for manufacturing, wholesaling, retailing, contractors, finance, and miscellaneous industries. Within the manufacturing category alone there are approximately 110 different lines of business included in such diverse areas as men's work clothing, poultry-dressing plants, and iron and steel forgings. For each industry area, the publication includes several different calculations for different sizes of businesses. Figure 6-3 contains the data shown for one business line in the retail section of the Robert Morris Annual Statement Studies.

The most important benefits of industry comparisons are as an indication of financial failure and to aid in understanding the client's business. The ratios in Robert Morris Associates, for example, are primarily of a type that bankers and other credit executives use in evaluating whether a company will be able to repay a loan. That same information is useful to auditors in assessing the likelihood of financial failure.

A major weakness of using industry ratios for auditing is the difference between the nature of the client's financial information and that of the firms making up the industry totals. Since no two companies are the same, the comparisons may not be meaningful in some cases. Many times the client's line of business is not the same as the industry standards. In addition, different companies follow different accounting methods, and this affects the comparability of data. If most companies in the industry use FIFO inventory valuation and straight-line depreciation, while the audit client uses LIFO and double-declining-balance depreciation, the results are not too significant. This does not mean that industry comparisons should not be made. Rather, it is an indication of the need for care in interpreting the results.

Internal Ratios, Percentages, and Other Comparisons. A second approach to analytical testing is to calculate important relationships from the client's accounting records and compare the results with previous years, standards, or other available information. There are several advantages in emphasizing this approach:

- There are no restrictions on the number and type of calculations to make. For most comparisons to industry sources there are a limited number of ratios published.
- The ratios can be much more specific and directly related to the auditor's areas of interest. For example, when the auditor wants to calculate sales returns and allowances on a monthly basis, it is possible to do so if the data are available in the records.
- The comparisons are made only within the firm; therefore, there is no problem of determining the client's industry.
- There is little difficulty encountered in comparing data based upon different methods of accounting. In fact, one of the uses of analytical testing is discovering instances where the client has changed accounting methods without disclosing this fact in the financial statements.

There are many different *types of internal analytical tests* available for auditors to compute. The appropriate ones to use depend upon the auditor's information needs and his personal preferences. Following are six categories of internal analytical tests which are potentially useful in different situations:

Comparison of Budgets with Actual Operating Results. Since budgets represent the client's expectations for the period, an investigation of the most significant areas where differences exist between budget and actual results may disclose errors in the financial statements. The starting point for the investigation should be a discussion with management as to why the differences exist. In many instances, additional evidence is also necessary to satisfy the auditor that the explanations provided by management are a reasonable interpretation rather than a rationalization of the differences.

Comparison of the Current-Year Absolute Total Balance with the Balance of the Preceding Year. One of the easiest ways to make this test is to include the preceding year's adjusted trial balance results in a special column of the current year's trial balance worksheet. This gives the auditor an opportunity to find out early in the audit whether a particular account should receive more than the normal amount of attention because of a significant change in the balance. For example, if the auditor observes a substantial increase in supplies expense, this would indicate the need to determine whether the cause of the increase was the increased use of supplies, a mis-

FIGURE 6–3

Retailers of Family Clothing

Asset Size Number of Statements	61(6/30-9/30/77) 0–250M 40	250M– 1MM 76	98(10/1/77–3/31/78) 1–10MM 43	All 159
ASSETS	%	%	%	%
Cash & Equivalents	9.4	8.6	6.7	8.5
Accts. & Notes Rec.-Trade (net)	10.4	15.3	18.2	15.2
Inventory	59.1	53.7	44.7	52.1
All Other Current	.3	2.4	2.1	1.7
Total Current	79.2	79.9	71.7	77.5
Fixed Assets (net)	17.1	15.3	21.0	17.3
Intangibles (net)	.8	.3	.5	.4
All Other Non-Current	2.9	4.6	6.8	4.8
Total	100.0	100.0	100.0	100.0
LIABILITIES				
Notes Payable-Short Term	10.3	11.0	8.1	9.9
Cur. Mat.-L/T/D	4.6	1.5	3.8	2.8
Accts. & Notes Payable-Trade	15.2	16.9	15.8	16.1
Accrued Expenses	3.2	5.3	5.2	4.9
All Other Current	1.5	3.5	3.5	3.0
Total Current	34.8	38.2	36.4	36.8
Long Term Debt	21.7	13.8	16.6	16.4
All Other Non-Current	.1	.6	1.5	.8
Net Worth	43.4	47.4	45.5	46.1
Total Liabilities & Net Worth	100.0	100.0	100.0	100.0
INCOME DATA				
Net Sales	100.0	100.0	100.0	100.0
Cost Of Sales	60.2	62.5	60.5	61.3
Gross Profit	39.8	37.5	39.5	38.7
Operating Expenses	32.4	34.4	37.6	34.7
Operating Profit	7.3	3.1	1.9	4.0
All Other Expenses (net)	1.7	.5	−.5	.5
Profit Before Taxes	5.7	2.6	2.4	3.4
RATIOS				
	3.6	3.3	2.7	3.3
Current	2.4	2.2	1.9	2.2
	1.6	1.5	1.5	1.6
	.9	1.2	1.3	1.2
Quick	.6	.5	.6	.6
	.2	.3	.3	.2
	0 426.3	1 355.5	2 185.2	1 390.7
Sales/Receivables	5 81.0	17 22.0	25 14.7	13 27.5
	22 16.5	44 8.3	62 5.9	48 7.6
	111 3.3	99 3.7	101 3.6	101 3.6
Cost of Sales/Inventory	174 2.1	140 2.6	126 2.9	140 2.6
	281 1.3	192 1.9	166 2.2	192 1.9

FIGURE 6–3 (cont.)

Asset Size Number of Statements	61(6/30–9/30/77)	250M– 1MM	98(10/1/77–3/31/78) 1–10MM	All
	0–250M 40	76	43	159
Sales/Working Capital	2.9 4.8 7.0	3.7 4.8 11.1	4.4 5.7 9.2	3.7 4.9 9.4
EBIT/Interest	10.2 4.0 1.8	7.4 3.5 1.7	6.4 3.2 1.7	8.3 3.5 1.7
Cash Flow/Cur. Mat. L/T/D		6.6 2.9 1.2	2.7 1.4 .8	5.8 2.2 .9
Fixed/Worth	.1 .3 .6	.1 .3 .5	.2 .4 .8	.2 .3 .6
Debt/Worth	.5 1.2 2.8	.6 1.1 2.4	.6 1.4 2.2	.6 1.1 2.4
% Profit Before Taxes/Tangible Net Worth	47.9 29.1 6.9	27.5 15.4 5.1	23.1 9.7 3.9	30.4 14.2 5.6
% Profit Before Taxes/Total Assets	20.0 8.6 2.5	12.6 6.4 1.7	11.1 4.0 2.0	13.8 6.2 1.9
Sales/Net Fixed Assets	59.2 14.8 7.2	37.5 20.9 10.8	24.1 10.7 6.6	33.7 16.6 8.7
Sales/Total Assets	2.4 2.1 1.4	2.7 2.3 1.8	2.6 2.0 1.6	2.6 2.1 1.7
% Depr., Dep., Amort./Sales	.5 1.2 2.1	.7 .9 1.6	.9 1.2 1.8	.7 1.1 1.8
% Lease & Rental Exp./Sales	2.2 3.4 5.1	2.3 4.1 5.2	2.4 3.6 5.6	2.4 3.8 5.2
% Officers' Comp./Sales	4.4 6.5 9.2	2.9 4.9 7.3	1.5 1.9 4.0	2.8 4.6 7.5
Net Sales ($)	**12049M**	**96087M**	**251382M**	**533356M**
Total Assets ($)	**5701M**	**40671M**	**116899M**	**252776M**

M = $ thousand   **MM** = $ million

statement in the account due to a misclassification, or an error in the supplies inventory.

Comparison of the Detail of a Total Balance with Similar Detail for the Preceding Year. If there have been no significant changes in the client's operations in the current year, much of the detail making up the totals in the financial statements should also remain relatively unchanged. By briefly comparing the detail of the current period with similar detail of the preceding period, it is often possible to isolate information that needs further examination. A common example is comparing the monthly totals for the current and preceding year for sales, repairs, and other accounts. The auditor should perform a more detailed analysis and investigation of any month that shows a significantly different total.

Scanning Details for Unusual Items. When the auditor properly understands the client's business, the examination of the detail making up journals, ledgers, and lists often uncovers amounts that are improperly recorded. For example, the accounts receivable general ledger account may include large credits other than those arising from the cash journal, or the name of an affiliated company may be included in the list of accounts receivable. These unusual items should be followed up to evaluate the possibility of an error.

Calculation of the Approximate Balance in an Expense or Revenue Account Using Relationships to Other Accounts. In this type of calculation the auditor makes an estimate of what an account balance should be by relating it to some other balance sheet or income statement balance. If the auditor's estimate of the balance is materially different from the actual balance, detailed investigation of the reason for the difference is necessary. An example of this is the independent calculation of interest expense on long-term notes payable by multiplying the ending monthly balance in notes payable by the average monthly interest rate. This total should approximate the total balance of interest expense (see Figure 6-4). In some instances it is also possible to estimate commission expense in the same manner, but if commission rates vary substantially on different types of sales, this would not be feasible. Similarly, it may be possible by overall calculations to make a useful estimate of total sales, depreciation expense, interest income, and similar account balances.

Computation of Ratios and Percentage Relationships for Comparison with Previous Years. The computation of ratios and percentage relationships for comparison with previous years is another way to obtain an indication of whether an account is materially misstated. For example, one of the most important percentage relationships is the gross margin percentage. A significant change in this amount could be due to an error either in sales or in cost of goods sold. An error in the cost of goods sold could be caused by

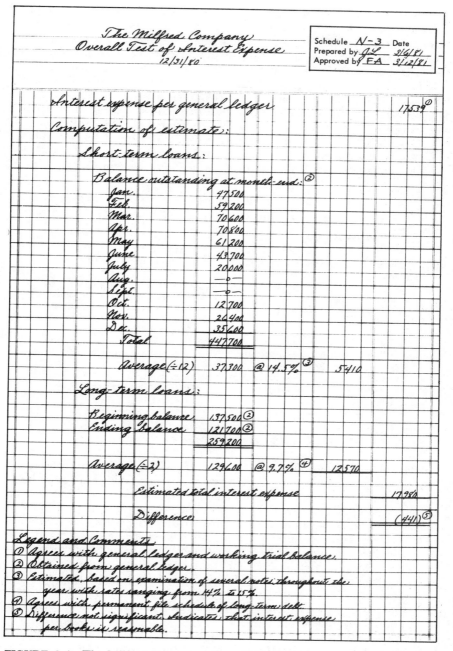

The Milfred Company
Overall Test of Interest Expense
12/31/80

Schedule __N-3__ Date
Prepared by _GL_ 3/6/81
Approved by _FA_ 3/12/81

Interest expense per general ledger   17,539 ①

Computation of estimate:

Short-term loans:

Balance outstanding at month-end: ②
        Jan.   47,500
        Feb.   59,200
        Mar.   70,600
        Apr.   70,800
        May   61,200
        June   43,700
        July   20,000
        Aug.   —0—
        Sept.   —0—
        Oct.   12,700
        Nov.   26,400
        Dec.   35,600
        Total   447,700

        Average (÷12)   37,300 @ 14.5% ③   5,410

Long-term loans:

        Beginning balance 137,500 ②
        Ending balance   121,700 ②
                           259,200

        Average (÷2)   129,600 @ 9.7% ④   12,570

                    Estimated total interest expense   17,980

                    Difference   (441) ⑤

Legend and Comments:
① Agrees with general ledger and working trial balance.
② Obtained from general ledger.
③ Estimated, based on examination of several notes throughout the
     year with rates ranging from 14% to 15%.
④ Agrees with permanent file schedule of long-term debt.
⑤ Difference not significant. Indicates that interest expense
     per books is reasonable.

FIGURE 6-4 The Milford Company—Overall Tests of Interest Expense, 12-31-80

errors in the quantities or pricing of physical inventory, inadequate cutoff of accounts payable, or other factors. Sales could be misstated due to improper cutoff, the failure to bill, and other reasons. A large change in the gross margin percentage would indicate to the auditor the need for a detailed investigation to determine the cause of the difference. Of course, a major change in gross margin percentage might not be the result of an error; a change in product mix or selling price could also be responsible for the change. It is the auditor's responsibility to determine the cause of the change so he can be sure it did not result from misstated financial statements.

A few of the *types of ratios and internal comparisons* are included in Figure 6-5 to show the usefulness of ratio analysis. In all cases the comparisons should be made with calculations made in previous years for the same client.

FIGURE 6–5

Examples of Internal Comparisons and Relationships

Ratio or Comparison	*Possible Errors in Statement*
Raw material turnover for a manufacturing company	Misstatement of inventory or cost of goods sold or obsolescence of raw material inventory
Sales commissions ÷ net sales	Misstatement of sales commissions
Sales returns and allowances ÷ gross sales	Misclassified sales returns and allowances or unrecorded returns or allowances subsequent to year-end
Cash surrender value of life insurance (current year) ÷ cash surrender value of life insurance (preceding year)	Failure to record the change in cash surrender value or an error in recording the change
Each of the individual manufacturing expenses as a percentage of total manufacturing expense	Significant misstatement of individual expenses within the total

Timing of Analytical Review Procedures

Analytical review procedures may be performed at any time during an engagement, depending on the circumstances. Some analytical procedures, ideally, are performed in the planning stages of the year-end work to assist in determining the nature, extent, and timing of work to be performed. Performance of analytical review procedures at this time helps identify significant matters requiring special consideration later in the engagement. For example, the calculation of inventory turnover before inventory price tests are done may indicate the need for special care during price tests. Many times, the analytical tests are done during the audit in conjunction with other procedures; for example, the prepaid portion of each insurance policy might be compared to the same policy for the previous year as a part of doing tests of unexpired insurance.

Most analytical review procedures, however, are done after the balance sheet date. The reason is that since the procedures are substantive tests, the primary concern is the balances and disclosures in the statements.

Obtaining Meaningful Results

In making calculations using analytical techniques, certain procedures are helpful in obtaining more meaningful results:

- Various methods may be used to make the comparisons. They may be made using dollars, physical quantities, ratios, or percentages. Mathematical techniques such as trend analysis, graphs and charts, and financial models may be used. The methods selected are a matter of professional judgment.
- To determine trends that enable meaningful analysis, it is normally desirable to compare ratios, percentages, and absolute amounts with more periods than just the preceding one. Ideally, at least *four periods* should be included for each ratio and percentage used. To facilitate this, carry forward schedules of ratio and trend calculations should be included in the permanent file.
- It is desirable to compute *separate ratios* for different divisions, products, or types of expenses. Aggregation of data seldom enhances the meaningfulness of ratio and trend analysis.
- Ratio and trend analysis should be concerned only with significant differences. This tool is meant to isolate significant differences relative to previous periods or other totals. In most uses, analytical techniques are not able to distinguish small differences.
- It is important that the auditor know when the current period's calculations *should be different* from those of previous periods *because of changed conditions.* If conditions within the organization change, such as a major decrease in the selling price of its products or the obsolescence of inventory due to a change in technology, affected ratios and comparisons should also change. The auditor is unlikely to recognize situations where ratios should change unless he has a good knowledge of the client's business and industry.
- Ratio and trend analysis requires considerable *professional judgment* both in deciding upon the appropriate ratios to use and in interpreting their results. It is essential that an experienced professional be responsible for determining the appropriate ratios to compute. As much care should be taken in selecting ratios and comparisons for a given client as in the case of any other audit procedure.

Follow-Up of Differences

It is imperative that there be *follow-up* on all material differences discovered through analytical techniques. It would be regarded as a failure to fulfill the requirement of due care if a comparison indicated the possibility of a material error and the auditor failed to investigate the cause of the difference. The following factors affect the investigation:

Materiality of the Amount. If the *potential* error indicated by the analytical test is large enough to materially affect net income, more extensive follow-up is needed than when the potential error is small. In many cases no follow-up is needed because of immateriality.

Auditor's Knowledge of the Entity's Business. For example, the auditor may know that there was a strike during the year. He may conclude that this is a satisfactory explanation for a decline in sales volume.

Results of Other Auditing Procedures. For example, in performing his auditing procedures with respect to property accounts, the auditor would become aware of major additions and retirements. He may use this information in deciding what other procedures to apply to explain an unusual fluctuation in depreciation expense.

Purpose of the Analytical Review. If the objective is to assist the auditor in planning his examination by identifying areas that may need special consideration, the audit program should be modified to reflect the results of the analytical review. For example, identifying any significant increases in inventories by inventory locations could affect whether to send someone to physically observe inventory. Other objectives should have a different impact.

REVIEW QUESTIONS

6–1. What are the responsibilities of the successor and predecessor auditors when a company is changing auditors?

6–2. Distinguish between management fraud and employee fraud. Discuss the likely difference between these two types of fraud on the fair presentation of financial statements.

6–3. "It is well accepted in auditing that throughout the conduct of the ordinary examination, it is essential to obtain large amounts of information from management and to rely heavily on management's judgments. After all, the financial statements are management's representations, and the primary responsibility for their fair presentation rests with management, not the auditor. For example, it is extremely difficult, if not impossible, for the auditor to evaluate the obsolescence of inventory as well as management can in a highly complex business. Similarly, the collectibility of accounts receivable and the continued usefulness of machinery and equipment is heavily dependent on management's willingness to provide truthful responses to questions." Reconcile the auditor's responsibility for discovering material misrepresentations by management with the above comments.

6–4. List three major considerations that are useful in predicting the likelihood of management fraud in an audit. For each of the considerations, state two things the auditor can do to evaluate its significance in the engagement.

6–5. What are the factors that an auditor should consider prior to accepting an engagement? Explain.

6–6. What is the purpose of an engagement letter? What subjects should be covered in such a letter?

6–7. List the five types of information the auditor should obtain or review as a part of gaining background information for the audit, and provide one specific example of how the information will be useful in conducting the audit.

6–8. When a CPA has accepted an engagement from a new client who is a manufacturer, it is customary for the CPA to tour the client's plant facilities. Discuss the ways in which the CPA's observations made during the course of the plant tour will be of help to him as he plans and conducts his audit.

(AICPA adapted)

6–9. An auditor often tries to acquire background knowledge of his client's industry as an aid to him in his audit work. How does the acquisition of this knowledge aid the auditor in distinguishing between obsolete and current inventory?

(AICPA adapted)

6–10. Jennifer Bailey is an experienced senior who is in charge of several important audits for a medium-sized firm. Her philosophy of conducting audits is to ignore all previous years and permanent working papers until near the end of the audit as a means of keeping from prejudicing herself. She believes this enables her to perform the audit in a more independent manner because it eliminates the tendency of simply doing the same things in the current audit that were done on previous audits. Near the end of the audit Bailey reviews the working papers from the preceding year, evaluates the significance of any items she has overlooked, and modifies her evidence if she considers it necessary. Evaluate Bailey's approach to conducting an audit.

6–11. List five federal or state regulations the auditor should be familiar with, and state how they would affect the fair presentation of the financial statements.

6–12. Your firm has performed the audit of the Rogers Company for several years and you have been assigned the audit responsibility for the current audit. How would your review of the corporate charter and bylaws for this audit differ from that of the audit of a client that was audited by a different CPA firm in the preceding year?

6–13. For the audit of Radline Manufacturing Company, the audit partner asks you to carefully read the new mortgage contract with the First National Bank and abstract all pertinent information. List the information that is likely to be relevant to the auditor in a mortgage.

6–14. Your client, Harper Company, has a contractual commitment as a part of a bond indenture to maintain a current ratio of 2.0. If the ratio falls below that level on the balance sheet date, the entire bond becomes payable immediately. In the current year the client's financial statements show that the ratio has dropped from 2.6 to 2.05 over the past year. How should this situation affect your audit plan?

6–15. When should analytical tests be performed? Why?

6–16. The following questions refer to the use of industry ratios, internal ratios, percentages, and other comparisons:
   a. List five industry ratios the auditor can compute, explain how to calculate each one, and state the most important information provided by each ratio.
   b. List five types of internal comparisons the auditor can make, state the purpose of each one, and provide two examples for each comparison.

    c. What are the primary advantages of internal comparison over industry ratios?

    d. What are the primary advantages of industry ratios over internal comparison?

6–17. Explain why the statement "Analytical tests are essential in every part of an audit, but these tests are rarely sufficient by themselves for any audit area" is correct or incorrect.

6–18. Gale Gordon, CPA, has found ratio and trend analysis relatively useless as a tool in conducting audits. For several engagements he computed the industry ratios included in publications by Robert Morris Associates and compared them with industry standards. For most engagements the client's business was significantly different from the industry data in the publication and the client would automatically explain away any discrepancies by attributing them to the unique nature of its operations. In cases where the client had more than one branch in different industries, Gordon found the ratio analysis no help at all. How could Gordon improve the quality of his analytical tests?

6–19. At the completion of every audit, Roger Morris, CPA, calculates a large number of ratios and trends for comparison with industry averages and prior year calculations. He believes the calculations are worth the relatively small cost of doing them because they provide him with an excellent overview of the client's operations. If the ratios are out of line, Morris discusses the reasons with the client and frequently makes suggestions on how to bring the ratio back in line in the future. In some cases these discussions with management have been the basis for management services engagements. Discuss the major strengths and shortcomings in Morris's use of ratio and trend analysis.

6–20. It is imperative that the auditor follow up on all material differences discovered through analytical techniques. What factors will affect such investigations?

DISCUSSION QUESTIONS AND PROBLEMS

6–21. The following questions pertain to the predecessor/successor auditor relationship. Choose the best response.

    a. A CPA is conducting the first examination of a nonpublic company's financial statements. The CPA hopes to reduce the audit work by consulting with the predecessor auditor and reviewing the predecessor's working papers. This procedure is

        (1) acceptable if the client and the predecessor auditor agree to it.

        (2) acceptable if the CPA refers in the audit report to reliance upon the predecessor auditor's work.

        (3) required if the CPA is to render an unqualified opinion.

        (4) unacceptable because the CPA should bring an independent viewpoint to a new engagement.

    b. Rusk, CPA, succeeded Boone, CPA, as auditor of Moonlight Corporation. Boone had issued an unqualified report for the calendar year 1975. What can Rusk do to establish the basis for expressing an opinion on the 1976 financial statements with regard to opening balances?

(1) Rusk may review Boone's working papers and thereby reduce the scope of audit tests Rusk would otherwise have to do with respect to opening balances.

(2) Rusk must apply appropriate auditing procedures to account balances at the beginning of the period so as to be satisfied that they are properly stated and may not rely on the work done by Boone.

(3) Rusk may rely on the prior year's financial statements since an unqualified opinion was issued and must make reference in the auditor's report to Boone's report.

(4) Rusk may rely on the prior year's financial statements since an unqualified opinion was issued and must refer in a middle paragraph of the auditor's report to Boone's report of the prior year.

c. If, during an audit examination, the successor auditor becomes aware of information that may indicate that financial statements reported on by the predecessor auditor may require revision, the successor auditor should

(1) ask the client to arrange a meeting among the three parties to discuss the information and attempt to resolve the matter.

(2) notify the client and the predecessor auditor of the matter and ask them to attempt to resolve it.

(3) notify the predecessor auditor who may be required to revise the previously issued financial statements and auditor's report.

(4) ask the predecessor auditor to arrange a meeting with the client to discuss and resolve the matter.

d. A CPA may reduce the audit work on a first-time audit by reviewing the working papers of the predecessor auditor. The predecessor should permit the successor to review working papers relating to matters of continuing accounting significance such as those that relate to

(1) extent of reliance on the work of specialists.

(2) fee arrangements and summaries of payments.

(3) analysis of contingencies.

(4) staff hours required to complete the engagement. (AICPA adapted)

6–22. The following questions concern the planning of the engagement. Select the best response.

a. Which of the following is an effective audit planning and control procedure that helps prevent misunderstandings and inefficient use of audit personnel?

(1) Arrange to make copies, for inclusion in the working papers, of those client supporting documents examined by the auditor.

(2) Arrange to provide the client with copies of the audit programs to be used during the audit.

(3) Arrange a preliminary conference with the client to discuss audit objectives, fees, timing, and other information.

(4) Arrange to have the auditor prepare and post any necessary adjusting or reclassification entries prior to final closing.

b. An auditor is planning an audit engagement for a new client in a business that is unfamiliar to the auditor. Which of the following would be the most useful source of information for the auditor during the preliminary planning stage, when the auditor is trying to obtain a general understanding of audit problems that might be encountered?

(1) Client manuals of accounts and charts of accounts.
(2) AICPA Industry Audit Guides.
(3) Prior-year working papers of the predecessor auditor.
(4) Latest annual and interim financial statements issued by the client.

c. The independent auditor should acquire an understanding of a client's internal audit function to determine whether the work of internal auditors will be a factor in determining the nature, timing, and extent of the independent auditor's procedures. The work performed by internal auditors might be such a factor when the internal auditor's work includes

(1) verification of the mathematical accuracy of invoices.
(2) review of administrative practices to improve efficiency and achieve management objectives.
(3) study and evaluation of internal accounting control.
(4) preparation of internal financial reports for management purposes.

d. Which of the following is the most likely first step an auditor would perform at the beginning of an initial audit engagement?

(1) Prepare a rough draft of the financial statements and of the auditor's report.
(2) Study and evaluate the system of internal administrative control.
(3) Tour the client's facilities and review the general records.
(4) Consult with and review the work of the predecessor auditor prior to discussing the engagement with the client management.

(AICPA adapted)

6–23. For each of the following questions, state the one best response:

a. With respect to proceedings of the meetings of the board of directors of a client corporation, the normal auditing procedure is to

(1) obtain from the company secretary a minutes representation letter that summarizes actions pertinent to the financial statements.
(2) discuss proceedings of the board with its chairman or his designated representative.
(3) review the minutes of all meetings.
(4) obtain tapes or written transcripts of all meetings or attend all meetings.

b. An auditor should examine minutes of board of directors' meetings

(1) through the date of his report.
(2) through the date of the financial statements.
(3) on a test basis.
(4) only at the beginning of the audit.

c. Your independent examination of the Dey Company reveals that the firm's poor financial condition makes it unlikely that it will survive as a going concern. Assuming that the financial statements have otherwise been prepared in accordance with generally accepted accounting principles, what disclosure should you make of the company's precarious financial position?

(1) You should issue an unqualified opinion, but in a paragraph between the scope and opinion paragraphs of your report, direct the reader's attention to the poor financial condition of the company.

(2) You should insist that a note to the financial statements clearly indicate that the company appears to be on the verge of bankruptcy.

(3) You need not insist on any particular disclosure, since the company's poor financial condition is clearly indicated by the financial statements themselves.

(4) You should provide adequate disclosure and appropriately modify your opinion because the company does not appear to be a going concern.

d. Which potential error or questionable practice will most likely be discovered by a tour of the plant when the auditor is accompanied by the production manager?

(1) Depreciation expense was recognized in the current year for a machine that is fully depreciated.

(2) Overhead has been underapplied

(3) Necessary plant maintenance was not performed during the year.

(4) Insurance coverage on the plant has been allowed to lapse.

(AICPA adapted)

6–24. Brown, CPA, received a telephone call from Calhoun, the sole owner and manager of a small corporation. Calhoun asked Brown to prepare the financial statements for the corporation and told Brown that the statements were needed in two weeks for external financing purposes. Calhoun was vague when Brown inquired about the intended use of the statements. Brown was convinced that Calhoun thought Brown's work would constitute an audit. To avoid confusion Brown decided not to explain to Calhoun that the engagement would only be to prepare the financial statements. Brown, with the understanding that a substantial fee would be paid if the work were completed in two weeks, accepted the engagement and started the work at once.

During the course of the work, Brown discovered an accrued expense account labeled "professional fees" and learned that the balance in the account represented an accrual for the cost of Brown's services. Brown suggested to Calhoun's bookkeeper that the account name be changed to "fees for limited audit engagement." Brown also reviewed several invoices to determine whether accounts were being properly classified. Some of the invoices were missing. Brown listed the missing invoice numbers in the working papers with a note indicating that there should be a follow-up on the next engagement. Brown also discovered that the available records included the fixed asset values at estimated current replacement costs. Based on the records available, Brown prepared a balance sheet, income statement and statement of stockholder's equity. In addition, Brown drafted the footnotes but decided that any mention of the replacement costs would only mislead the readers. Brown suggested to

Calhoun that readers of the financial statements would be better informed if they received a separate letter from Calhoun explaining the meaning and effect of the estimated replacement costs of the fixed assets. Brown mailed the financial statements and footnotes to Calhoun with the following note included on each page:

> "The accompanying financial statements are submitted to you without complete audit verification."

Required:

Identify the inappropriate actions of Brown and indicate what Brown should have done to avoid each inappropriate action.

Organize your answer sheet as follows:

Inappropriate Action	What Brown Should Have Done to Avoid Inappropriate Action

(AICPA)

6–25. In late spring you are advised of a new assignment as in-charge accountant of your CPA firm's recurring annual audit of a major client, the Lancer Company. You are given the engagement letter for the audit covering the current calendar year, and a list of personnel assigned to this engagement. It is your responsibility to plan and supervise the field work for the engagement.

Required:

Discuss the necessary preparation and planning for the Lancer Company annual audit *prior to* beginning field work at the client's office. In your discussion include the sources you should consult, the type of information you should seek, the preliminary plans and preparation you should make for the field work, and any actions you should take relative to the staff assigned to the engagement.   (AICPA adapted)

6–26. One of the major means of perpetrating management fraud is for a company to become involved in non-arm's-length transactions for the personal benefit of management. When an auditor is attempting to evaluate whether management has been involved in fraudulent transactions, it is possible to think of the problem at two levels: determining whether there have been any significant transactions with related parties, and evaluating whether any of the transactions resulted in a personal benefit to any individual in management to the detriment of the entity being audited.

Required:

a. Distinguish between a valid and proper non-arm's-length transaction and a fraudulent transaction.

b. List several different types of legal or illegal non-arm's-length transactions that could take place in a company.

c. List the most important related parties who are likely to be involved in non-arm's-length transations involving management.

d. Discuss different ways the auditor can determine the existence of legal or illegal material transactions with related parties.

e. For each type of non-arm's-length transaction in part b, discuss different ways the auditor can evaluate whether any are fraudulent, assuming that he knows the transactions exist.

6–27. In the audit of Whirland Chemical Company, a large publicly traded company, you have been assigned the responsibility for obtaining background information for the audit. Your firm is auditing the client for the first time in the current year as a result of a dispute between Whirland and the previous auditor over the proper valuation of work-in-process inventory and the inclusion of sales of inventory that has not been delivered but has for practical purposes been completed and sold.

Whirland Chemical has been highly successful in its field in the past two decades, primarily because of many successful mergers negotiated by Bert Randolph, the president and chairman of the board. Even though the industry as a whole has suffered dramatic setbacks in recent years, Whirland continues to prosper, as evidenced by its constantly increasing earnings and growth. Only in the last two years have the company's profits turned downward. Randolph has a reputation for having been able to hire an aggressive group of young executives by the use of relatively low salaries combined with an unusually generous profit-sharing plan.

A major difficulty you face in the new audit is the lack of highly sophisticated accounting records for a company the size of Whirland. Randolph believes that profits come primarily from intelligent and aggressive action based on forecasts, not by relying on historical data that come after the fact. Most of the forecast data are generated by the sales and production department rather than by the accounting department. The personnel in the accounting department do seem competent, but somewhat overworked and underpaid relative to other employees. One of the recent changes that will potentially improve the record keeping is the installation of sophisticated computer techniques. All the accounting records are not computerized yet, but such major areas as inventory and sales are included in the new system. Most of the computer time is being reserved for production and marketing on the grounds that these areas are more essential to operations than the record-keeping function.

The first six months' financial statements for the current year include a profit of approximately only 10 percent less than the first six months of the preceding year, which is somewhat surprising considering the reduced volume and the disposal of a segment of the business, Mercury Supply Co. The disposal of this segment was considered necessary because it had become increasingly unprofitable over the past four years. At the time of its acquisition from Roger Randolph, who is a brother of Bert Randolph, the company was highly profitable and it was considered a highly desirable purchase. The major customer of Mercury Supply Co. was the Mercury Corporation, which is owned by Roger Randolph. Gradually the market for its products declined as the Mercury Corporation began diversifying and phasing out its primary products in favor of more profitable business. Even though Mercury Corporation is no longer buying from Mercury Supply Company, it compensates for it by buying a large volume of other products from Whirland Chemical.

The only major difficulty Whirland faces right now, according to financial analysts, is a fairly severe underfinancing. There is an excessive amount of current debt and long-term debt because of the depressed capital markets. Management is reluctant to obtain equity capital at this point because the increased number of shares would decrease the earnings per share even more than 10 percent. At the present time Randolph is negotiating with several cash-rich companies in the hope of being able to merge with them as a means of overcoming the capital problems.

Required:

a. List the major concerns you should have in the audit of Whirland Company and explain why they are potential problems.
b. State the appropriate approach to investigating the significance of each item you listed in part a.

6–28. The inspection of the minutes of meetings is an integral part of a CPA's examination of a corporation's financial statements.

Required:

a. A CPA should determine if there is any disagreement between transactions recorded in the corporate records and actions approved by the corporation's board of directors. Why is this so and how is it accomplished?
b. Discuss the effect each of the following situations would have on specific audit steps in a CPA's examination and on his audit opinion:
   (1) The minute book does not show approval for the sale of an important manufacturing division which was consummated during the year.
   (2) Some details of a contract negotiated during the year with the labor union are different from the outline of the contract included in the minutes of the board of directors.
   (3) The minutes of a meeting of directors held after the balance sheet date have not yet been written, but the corporation's secretary shows the CPA notes from which the minutes are to be prepared when the secretary has time.
c. What corporate actions should be approved by stockholders and recorded in the minutes of the stockholders' meetings?   (AICPA adapted)

6–29. You are engaged in the annual audit of the financial statements of Maulack Company, a medium-sized wholesale company that manufactures light fixtures. The company has 25 stockholders. During your review of the minutes you observe that the president's salary has been increased substantially over the preceding year by action of the board of directors. His present salary is much greater than salaries paid to presidents of companies of comparable size and is clearly excessive. You determine that the method of computing the president's salary was changed for the year under audit. In previous years, the president's salary was consistently based on sales. In the latest year, however, his salary was based on net income before income taxes. The Maulack Company is in a cyclical industry and would have had an extremely profitable year except that the increase in the president's salary siphoned off much of the income that would have accrued to the stockholders. The president is a substantial stockholder.

Required:

a. What is the implication of this condition on the fair presentation of the financial statements?
b. Discuss your responsibility for disclosing this situation.
c. Discuss the effect, if any, that the situation has upon your auditor's opinion as to
   (1) The fairness of the presentation of the financial statements
   (2) The consistency of the application of accounting principles
   (AICPA adapted)

6–30. A CPA has been asked to audit the financial statements of a publicly held company for the first time. All preliminary verbal discussions and inquiries have been completed between the CPA, the company, the predecessor auditor, and all other necessary parties. The CPA is now preparing an engagement letter.

Required:

List the items that should be included in the typical engagement letter in these circumstances and describe the benefits derived from preparing an engagement letter. (AICPA adapted)

6–31. The CPA firm of Whipple and White is defending its audit of the Merkle Construction Company, a builder of apartments, in a legal liability case. The firm had audited the client for several years and had observed a gradual deterioration of the client's financial position, but it was surprised when the client filed for bankruptcy three months after the completion of the audit.

Several major issues are involved in the lawsuit, including the following:
a. The construction in process on the balance sheet included an overhead rate based upon all construction overhead and 40 percent of all administrative costs. Management contended that this is normal practice for the industry. There are more buildings in progress in the current year than in any previous year. The same practice was followed in previous years.
b. Two weeks after the balance sheet date, Merkle repurchased an apartment building from a customer for the same amount as the original sale price, which was $10,500,000. One month later the apartment building was resold to a syndicate for $8,200,000 cash. The original sale was included in the audited financial statements at $10,500,000. The audit report was dated 87 days after the balance sheet date.

    c. One of the apartment buildings has been included as a completed building available for rent at year-end. This same building was also included as a contract receivable and a sale. Thirty apartments were completed during the year, but only one was recorded more than once.

    d. A major mortgage on one of the apartments for the amount of $2,400,000 was not included as a liability. The auditor had confirmed all mortgages, but the unrecorded mortgage was owed to a bank the client had not done business with before. All 26 apartments owned and operated by the company were mortgaged, and all but the unrecorded one were properly valued.

Required:

    a. How could each of the errors described above have been discovered in the audit?

    b. What appears to be the primary weakness in the auditor's approach to the audit?

6–32. In auditing the financial statements of a manufacturing company that were prepared by electronic data-processing equipment, the CPA has found that his traditional "audit trail" has been obscured. As a result, the CPA may place increased emphasis upon overall checks of the data under audit. These overall checks, which are also applied in auditing visibly posted accounting records, include the computation of ratios, which are compared with prior year ratios or with industry-wide norms. Examples of such overall checks or ratios are the computation of the rate of inventory turnover and the computation of the number of days in receivables.

Required:

    a. Discuss the advantages to the CPA of the use of ratios as overall checks in an audit.

    b. In addition to the computations given above, list the ratios that a CPA may compute during an audit as overall checks on balance sheet accounts and related nominal accounts. For each ratio listed, name the two (or more) accounts used in its computation.

    c. When a CPA discovers that there has been a significant change in a ratio when compared with the preceding year's ratio, he considers the possible reasons for the change. Give the possible reasons for the following significant changes in ratios:

        (1) The rate of inventory turnover (ratio of costs of sales and average inventory) has decreased from the preceding year's rate.

        (2) The number of days sales in receivables (ratio of average daily accounts receivable and sales) has increased over the prior year.

(AICPA adapted)

6–33. Your comparison of the gross margin percentage for Jones Drugs for the years 19X3 through 19X6 indicates a significant decline. This is shown by the following information:

	19X6	19X5	19X4	19X3
Sales (thousands)	$14,211	$12,916	$11,462	$10,351
CGS (thousands)	9,223	8,266	7,313	6,573
Gross margin	$ 4,988	$ 4,650	$ 4,149	$ 3,778
Percent	35.1	36.0	36.2	36.5

A discussion with Marilyn Adams, the controller, brings to light two possible explanations. She informs you that the industry gross profit percentage in the retail drug industry declined fairly steadily for three years, which accounts for part of the decline. A second factor was the declining percentage of the total volume resulting from the pharmacy part of the business. The pharmacy sales represent the most profitable portion of the business, yet the competition from discount drugstores prevents it from expanding as fast as the nondrug items such as magazines, candy, and the many other items sold. Adams feels strongly that these two factors are the cause of the decline.

The following additional information is obtained from independent sources and the client's records as a means of investigating the controller's explanations:

	Drug Sales	Non-drug Sales	Drug Cost of Goods Sold	Nondrug Cost of Goods Sold	Industry Gross Profit Percent for Retailers of Drugs and Related Products
19X6	$5,126	$9,085	$3,045	$6,178	32.7
19X5	$5,051	$7,865	$2,919	$5,347	32.9
19X4	$4,821	$6,641	$2,791	$4,522	33.0
19X3	$4,619	$5,732	$2,665	$3,908	33.2

Required:

a. Evaluate the explanation provided by Adams. Show calculations to support your conclusions.
b. Which specific aspects of the client's financial statements require intensive investigation in this audit?

6–34. In the audit of the Worldwide Wholesale Company, you performed extensive ratio and trend analysis. No material exceptions were discovered except for the following:

a. Commission expense as a percentage of sales has stayed constant for several years but has increased significantly in the current year. Commission rates have not changed.
b. The rate of inventory turnover has steadily decreased for four years.

c. Inventory as a percentage of current assets has steadily increased for four years.

d. The number of days sales in accounts receivable has steadily increased for three years.

e. Allowance for uncollectible accounts as a percentage of accounts receivable has steadily decreased for three years.

f. The absolute amount of depreciation expense and depreciation expense as a percentage of gross fixed assets are significantly smaller than in the preceding year.

Required:

a. Evaluate the potential significance of each of the exceptions above for the fair presentation of financial statements.

b. State the follow-up procedures you would use to determine the possibility of material errors.

6–35. Wholesale Gourmet, Inc., is a highly successful wholesaler in the gourmet food supply industry. The company sells all types of bottled and canned gourmet foods to small, medium-sized, and large grocery stores and other retailers throughout the Midwest. At this point the client has twenty-six different wholesale grocery subsidiaries operating out of various midwestern regions under different names. In some cases the subsidiaries compete against each other, but for the most part they operate in different sales territories.

The success of the firm is primarily due to the majority owner of the business, Cecil VanDowen. He permits each subsidiary to operate somewhat independently under a manager. The manager is permitted to buy his own products from any source, set sales policies, and hire and discharge employees. At the same time, VanDowen frequently advises the managers and is able to get them to follow similar policies because of his excellent management skills. Sales policies, inventory policies, accounts receivable policies, and most other business practices are amazingly similar between the subsidiaries. Each subsidiary is treated somewhat as a franchise by the main store inasmuch as accounting policies, physical facilities, and records of all kinds are identical. This enables VanDowen to keep better control over the operations.

No store is completely dominant in the operation, but four stores do make up about 40 percent of the total inventory and 45 percent of the sales. Fourteen stores, including the four biggest, account for about 75 percent of the sales and inventory.

The audit is conducted out of Chicago by a single-office, medium-sized CPA firm. A major problem it faces is deciding how many of those subsidiaries must be visited annually. The subsidiaries are spread out widely and most of the records are kept in the subsidiary offices, but monthly statements are sent to the home office in Chicago and retained.

This is the fourth year of the audit of the client. Previous audits have indicated outstanding results. There is rarely an adjusting entry of any kind, and the client is cooperative. The client is not publicly listed, has few loans outstanding, and is highly profitable. In the past every subsidiary has been audited as if it were a separate company, but the client is now putting some pressure on the CPA firm to reduce audit fees. The client feels strongly that previous results warrant a significant reduction in testing, since only a consolidated opinion is issued. The CPA firm discussed the possibility of reducing the audit tests with two larger firms in the Chicago area, and they agree the situation merits a reduction in the number of subsidiaries audited if conditions within the client's organization remain stable.

The most significant assets by far are accounts receivable and inventory. Accounts receivable are collected quickly, but because of the nature of the product, inventory turnover is low. The most significant expense is cost of goods sold. Expenses are well controlled by managers, with strong pressures from VanDowen. Internal control is considered excellent.

Required:

a. Must the CPA firm visit each subsidiary annually? What conditions exist that reduce the need for a test of every subsidiary?
b. Discuss how ratio analysis could be used effectively in this situation.
c. Assume the decision is made to visit twelve subsidiaries. How could ratio analysis help the auditor in this situation to decide which subsidiaries to visit?
d. State several ratios the auditor should calculate for all twenty-six subsidiaries.

6-36. As part of the analytical review of Mahogany Products, Inc., you perform calculations of the following ratios:

Ratio	Industry 19X6	Averages 19X5	Mahogany 19X6	Products 19X5
1. Current ratio	3.3	3.8	2.2	2.6
2. Days to collect receivables	87	93	67	60
3. Days to sell inventory	126	121	93	89
4. Purchases ÷ accounts payable	11.7	11.6	8.5	8.6
5. Inventory ÷ current assets	.56	.51	.49	.48
6. Operating earnings ÷ tangible assets	.08	.06	.14	.12
7. Operating earnings ÷ net sales	.06	.06	.04	.04
8. Gross margin percent	.21	.27	.21	.19
9. Earnings per share	$14.27	$13.91	$2.09	$1.93

For each of the ratios above:

a. State whether there is a need to investigate the results further and, if so, the reason for further investigation.
b. State the approach you would use in the investigation.
c. Explain how the operations of Mahogany Products appear to differ from those of the industry.

6-37. Following are the auditor's calculations of several key ratios for Cragston Star Products. The primary purpose of this information is to assess the risk of financial failure, but any other relevant conclusions are also desirable.

Ratio	19X6	19X5	19X4	19X3	19X2
Current ratio	2.08	2.26	2.51	2.43	2.50
Quick ratio	.97	1.34	1.82	1.76	1.64
Earnings before taxes ÷ interest expense	3.5	3.2	4.1	5.3	7.1
Accounts receivable turnover	4.2	5.5	4.1	5.4	5.6
Days to collect receivables	108.2	83.1	105.2	80.6	71.6
Inventory turnover	2.03	1.84	2.68	3.34	3.36
Days to sell inventory	172.6	195.1	133.9	107.8	108.3
Net sales ÷ tangible assets	.68	.64	.73	.69	.67
Operating earnings ÷ net sales	.13	.14	.16	.15	.14
Operating earnings ÷ tangible assets	.09	.09	.12	.10	.09
Net earnings ÷ common equity	.05	.06	.10	.10	.11
Earnings per share	$4.30	$4.26	$4.49	$4.26	$4.14

a. What major conclusions can be drawn from this information for the company's future?

b. What additional information would be helpful in your assessment of this company's financial condition?

c. Based on the ratios above, which particular aspects of the company do you believe should receive special emphasis in the audit?

6–38. During the audit of the Railine Manufacturing Company, you observe that the net sales and manufacturing operations have increased tremendously relative to the preceding year. Despite this apparently healthy expansion, the client's net income decreased significantly. In the course of the engagement, the auditor did not find any explanation for the decrease in net income. During the ensuing discussion, one of the staff members on the engagement suggested the need to perform additional tests to explain the decline in profits. Another staff member disagreed with this point of view. He felt that additional testing to discover the cause of the decline was beyond the audit responsibilities required by generally accepted auditing standards. "Our audit fees do not include troubleshooting a client's operating efficiency problems," he remarked. "I will not agree to an extension of auditing procedures if I am satisfied a client's financial statements are presented fairly."

Required:

a. State five possible causes of the decline in profits when volume has expanded.

b. Discuss the auditor's responsbility for determining the cause of the decline in profits when the detailed tests of the records do not indicate the existence of material errors.

c. Ordinarily, when should the auditor determine the cause of a decline in profits? Why?

7

THE STUDY
AND EVALUATION
OF INTERNAL CONTROL

SAS 1 (Section 320) defines internal control as follows:

> Internal control comprises the plan of organization and all of the coordinate methods and measures adopted within a business to safeguard its assets, check the accuracy and reliability of its accounting data, promote operational efficiency, and encourage adherence to prescribed managerial policies.

This chapter focuses on the meaning and objectives of internal control from both the client's and the auditor's point of view. The elements of internal control are examined, along with the auditor's methodology for fulfilling the requirement of the second standard of field work.

OBJECTIVES

Client's Concerns about Internal Control

The reason companies establish a system of internal control is to aid the organization in more effectively meeting its own goals. The types of controls adopted are selected by comparing the cost to the organization relative to the benefit expected. One of the benefits to management, but certainly not the most important one, is the reduced cost of an audit when the auditor evaluates the controls as good or excellent.

Management typically has the following four concerns in setting up a good system of internal control:

To Provide Reliable Data. Management must have accurate information for carrying out its operations. A wide variety of information is used for making critical business decisions. For example, the price to charge for products is based in part on information about the cost of the products.

To Safeguard Assets and Records. The physical assets of a company can be stolen, misused, or accidentally destroyed unless they are protected by adequate controls. The same is true of nonphysical assets such as accounts receivable, important documents (e.g., confidential government contracts), and records (e.g., the general ledger and journals). The safeguarding of certain assets and records has become increasingly important since the advent of computer systems. Large amounts of information stored on computer media such as magnetic tape can be destroyed permanently if care is not taken to protect them.

To Promote Operational Efficiency. The controls within an organization are meant to prevent unnecessary duplication of effort, protect against waste in all aspects of the business, and discourage other types of inefficient use of resources.

To Encourage Adherence to Prescribed Policies. Management institutes procedures and rules to provide a means of meeting the goals of the company. The system of internal control is meant to provide reasonable assurance that these are followed by company personnel.

There may at times be a conflict between operational efficiency and the safeguarding of assets and records or the providing for reliable information. There is a cost of fulfilling the first two objectives, and to the extent the cost exceeds the benefits, the results may be operationally inefficient.

Foreign Corrupt Practices Act of 1977. A concern of all companies subject to the Securities Exchange Act of 1934 is the requirement that the company maintain "proper record keeping systems." These have not yet been defined by the 1977 law, but they include a sufficient system to:

- Enable the preparation of reliable external financial statements
- Prevent off-the-books slush funds and payments of bribes

The penalties for violation of the act are severe. They include both fines and imprisonment for company officials. The SEC has already brought its first court action under the law. The act makes maintaining proper internal control systems a high-priority item for publicly held companies.

Auditor's Concerns about Internal Control

Standard of Field Work. The study and evaluation of the client's system of internal control are important to auditors and are specifically included as a generally accepted auditing standard. The second standard of field work is:

> There is to be a *proper study and evaluation of the existing internal control* as a basis for reliance thereon and for the *determination of the resultant extent of the tests* to which auditing procedures are to be restricted [italics added].

Reliable Data and Safeguarding Assets and Records. In complying with this standard, the auditor is interested primarily in the first two of management's internal control concerns: the reliability of data and the safeguarding of assets and records. This emphasis stems from the auditor's need to determine whether the financial statements are fairly presented in accordance with generally accepted accounting principles. The financial statements are unlikely to be correct if the controls affecting the reliability of financial data and the safeguarding of assets and records are inadequate, but the statements can still be properly stated even if the company's controls do not promote efficiency in its operations and the employees fail to follow prescribed policies.

The auditor should emphasize controls concerned with the reliability of data for *external reporting purposes*, but controls affecting internal management information, such as statistical analyses, budgets, and internal performance reports, should not be completely ignored. These are important in helping the auditor decide whether the financial statements are fairly presented. If the controls over these internal reports are considered inadequate, the value of the reports as evidence is diminished.

The auditor's interest in the client's controls also should not be limited to those directly affecting the reliability of financial data and the safeguarding of assets. It is inappropriate to disregard controls concerned with operational efficiency and adherence to prescribed policies. If a company fails to follow the rules and procedures set forth by management or is highly inefficient, it is less likely to have accurate financial records. Even though the auditor should be alert for operational efficiency and adherence to prescribed policy controls, the remainder of this chapter is devoted primarily to controls directly related to the reliability of financial data and the physical safeguard of assets and records.

Ways the Study and Evaluation Are Used. The study and evaluation of the client's system of internal control are used by the auditor to perform the following three functions:

- *Determine Whether An Audit Is Possible.* The adequacy of the system of internal control is crucial to the client's accumulation of accounting data for preparation of the financial statements. If the system is inadequate or non-existent, it is virtually impossible for the auditor to evaluate whether the financial statements are fairly presented. The major problem arising from inadequate internal control is the possibility of material unrecorded amounts, such as sales made by the company but not recorded, loans made in the company name but not included in the records, and permanent assets used in the business without their being included as assets.

A second problem is the impracticality of assessing the proper valuation of some assets without relying on the client's internal control. An extreme example is construction in process for a bridge builder using the percentage-of-completion method of accounting. An adequate cost accumulation system must exist for the auditor to reach conclusions about the valuation of this asset.

If the internal control is so inadequate as to prohibit basic reliance, the auditor must either *refuse to conduct an audit* or *disclaim an opinion* on the financial statements.

- *Determine the Audit Evidence to Accumulate.* The client's system of internal control is an essential consideration affecting audit procedures, sample size, timing of the tests, and particular items to select. This aspect of internal control is the primary subject of this chapter and several subsequent chapters.

- *Inform Senior Management and the Board of Directors.* When the auditor identifies significant weaknesses in the system affecting the control over assets or any other aspect of internal control, including instances of inefficiency in production and clerical operations, there is a professional responsibility to inform the client of the findings. The client is informed by a letter, which is referred to as a *required communication of material weaknesses of internal control.* The letter is required by SAS 20 (Section 323). It must be sent to senior management and the board of directors or the audit committee. The letter is discussed further at the end of the chapter.

DIVIDE THE SYSTEM INTO TRANSACTION CYCLES

As a means of making a meaningful study and evaluation of internal control, it is necessary for the auditor to divide the overall system into a number of major segments called *transaction cycles.* This concept was introduced in Chapter 5. The use of cycles enables the auditor to manage the engagement without separating parts of the system that are closely intertwined. Every industry has its own set of major transaction cycles consistent with the nature of the economic events that affect it. In this text we consider the following five major cycles that are common to most commercial and manufacturing enterprises, although those of a bank or an insurance company could just as well be used:

- Sales and collection cycle
- Payroll and personnel cycle
- Acquisition of goods and services and payment cycle
- Inventory and warehousing cycle
- Capital acquisition and repayment cycle

Figure 7-1 illustrates the relationship of the cycles to each other. In addition to the five cycles, general cash is also shown. Each of these cycles is studied in subsequent chapters.

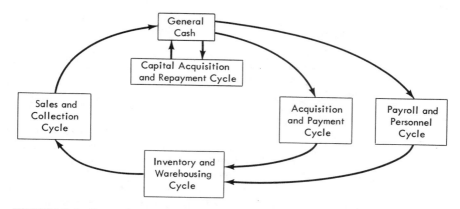

FIGURE 7-1 Interrelationship between Transaction Cycles

There is no start and end to the cycles except at the origin of a company. A company starts by obtaining capital, usually in the form of cash. The cash is used in a manufacturing company to acquire raw materials, permanent assets, and related goods and services to produce inventory (acquisition and payment cycle). The cash is also used to acquire labor for the same reason (payroll and personnel cycle). Acquisitions and payments and payroll and personnel are similar in nature, but the functions are sufficiently different to justify separate cycles. The combination of the effort of these two cycles results in inventory (inventory and warehousing cycle). At a subsequent point, the inventory is sold and collections result (sales and collection cycle). The cash is used to pay dividends and interest and to start the cycles again. The cycles interrelate much the same for a service company, but of course there is no inventory.

Transaction cycles are of major importance in the conduct of the audit. For the most part, auditors treat each transaction cycle separately as the audit is being performed. Internal control questionnaires and flowcharts, used in gaining a preliminary understanding of the system, are normally prepared independently for each transaction cycle. Similarly, a preliminary evaluation of the controls and the tests of the controls and account balances in one cycle can be made with relatively little regard for the other cycles. Although care should be taken to interrelate different cycles at different times, the auditor must treat the cycles somewhat independently in order to effectively manage complex audits.

DEFINE DETAILED INTERNAL CONTROL OBJECTIVES

There are eight detailed internal control objectives which embrace the primary concerns the auditor has for the prevention of errors in the recording of transactions in the journals and records. The client's system of internal control in every transaction cycle must be sufficient to provide reasonable assurance that

1. *Transactions as recorded are reasonable.* This objective encompasses all of the other seven. It is important that the transaction appears reasonable to management in all regards.

2. *Recorded transactions are valid.* The system cannot permit the inclusion of fictitious or nonexistent transactions in the system.

3. *Transactions are properly authorized.* If a transaction that is not authorized takes place, it could result in a fraudulent transaction, and it could also have the effect of wasting or destroying company assets.

4. *Existing transactions are recorded.* The procedures must provide controls to prevent the omission of actual transactions from the records.

5. *Transactions are properly valued.* An adequate system includes procedures to avoid errors in calculating, recording, and summarizing transactions at various stages in the recording process.

6. *Transactions are properly classified.* The proper account classification must be made in the journals if the financial statements are to be properly stated. Classification also includes such categories as division and product.

7. *Transactions are recorded at the proper time.* The recording of transactions either before or after the point of time they actually took place increases the likelihood of failing to record transactions, or recording them at the improper amount. If late recording occurs at year-end, the financial statements can be misstated.

8. *Transactions are properly included in subsidiary records and correctly summarized.* In many instances individual transactions are summarized and totaled before they are recorded in the journals. The journals are then posted to the general ledger, and the general ledger is summarized and used to prepare the financial statement. Regardless of the method used to enter transactions in the subsidiary's records and to summarize transactions, the procedures must provide for adequate controls to make sure that this is properly handled.

These eight internal control objectives can be related to any of the five transaction cycles identified in the previous section as a part of internal control evaluation. For example, if the internal controls over sales transactions are adequate to provide reasonable assurance of fulfilling each of the eight objectives, the likelihood of errors in that system is small.

ELEMENTS OF INTERNAL CONTROL

It is necessary that a system have certain elements or characteristics to increase the likelihood of reliable accounting data and safeguarding of assets and records. These elements are directly related to the internal control objectives. The elements are the way a company satisfies the objectives.

The following six elements are discussed in this section:

- Competent, trustworthy personnel with clear lines of authority and responsibility
- Adequate segregation of duties
- Proper procedures for authorization
- Adequate documents and records
- Physical control over assets and records
- Independent checks on performance

The relationship between elements and internal control objectives is shown in Figure 7-2. The figure shows that some elements are more important to a given objective than others. The relationship will become more clear in the following discussion.

Competent, Trustworthy Personnel with Clear Lines of Authority and Responsibility

The most important element of any system of internal control is personnel. If employees are competent and trustworthy, some of the other elements can be absent and reliable financial statements can still result. Honest, efficient people are able to perform at a high level even when there are few other controls to support them. On the other hand, even if the other five elements of control are strong, incompetent or dishonest people can reduce the system to a shambles. The importance of competent trustworthy personnel is shown in Figure 7-2. Every internal control objective is significantly affected by this element.

Still, the employment of competent and trustworthy personnel is not by itself sufficient to make a system completely adequate. People have a number of innate shortcomings due to their highly complex nature. They can, for example, become bored or dissatisfied, personal problems can disrupt their performance, or their goals may change. From an audit standpoint, it is important to make a judgment of the competence and integrity of employees, even though it is difficult to do, and to use this as a part of the total evaluation of the system.

Specific responsibility for the performance of duties must be assigned to specific individuals if the system is to operate effectively and work is to be properly performed. If a duty is not adequately performed, it is then possible to place responsibility with the person who did the work. The one assigned is thus motivated to work carefully, and corrective action by management is made possible.

Adequate Segregation of Duties

There are four general types of segregation of duties for the prevention of both intentional and unintentional errors that are of special significance to auditors. These are as follows:

Internal Control Objectives	Elements of Internal Control	Competent trustworthy personnel	Adequate segregation of duties	Proper procedures for authorization	Adequate documents and records	Physical control over assets and records	Independent checks on performance
Transactions as recorded are reasonable		M	S	S	S	S	M
Recorded transactions are valid		M	M	M	S	M	M
Transactions are properly authorized		M	S	M	S	L	M
Existing transactions are recorded		M	M	L	M	M	M
Transactions are properly valued		M	S	M	S	L	M
Transactions are properly classified		M	S	S	M	L	M
Transactions are recorded at the proper time		M	S	L	M	L	M
Transactions are properly included in subsidiary records and correctly summarized		M	S	L	S	L	M

M - The element has <u>a major effect</u> on the related internal control objective

S - The element has <u>some effect</u> on the related internal control objective

L - The element has <u>little or no effect</u> on the related internal control objective

FIGURE 7–2 Matrix Relating Internal Control Objectives to Elements of Internal Control

Separation of the Custody of Assets from Accounting. This type of segregation is the most important in a company. The reason for not permitting the person who has temporary or permanent custody of an asset to account for that asset is to protect the firm against fraud. When one person performs both functions, there is an excessive risk of his disposing of the asset for personal gain and adjusting the records to relieve himself of responsibility for the asset. If the cashier, for example, receives cash and maintains both the cash and accounts receivable records, it is possible for him to take the cash received from a customer and adjust the customer's account by failing to record a sale or by recording a fictitious credit to the account. Other examples of inadequate segregation of the custodial function include the distribution of payroll checks by the payroll clerk and the maintenance of inventory records by storeroom personnel.

In an EDP system, any person with custody of assets should be prevented from performing the programming function, and be denied access to punched cards or other input records. As a general rule it is desirable that any person performing an accounting function, whether it be in an EDP or in a manual system, be denied access to assets that can be converted to personal gain.

Figure 7-1 indicates the importance of segregation of asset custody from accounting by including a major effort for both the validity and recording of existing transactions objectives. Validity refers to recording fictitious entries to cover up a fraud. Recording of existing transactions refers to failing to record a transaction and taking the related asset. The other three types of segregations affect the objective, but to a lesser degree of importance.

Separation of the Authorization of Transactions from the Custody of Related Assets. It is desirable, to the extent that it is possible, to prevent persons who authorize transactions from having control over the related asset. For example, the same person should not authorize the payment of a vendor's invoice and also sign the check in payment of the bill. Similarly, the authority for adding newly hired employees to the payroll or eliminating those who have terminated employment should be performed by someone other than the person responsible for distributing checks to the employees. As illustrated, the authorization of a transaction and the handling of the related asset by the same person increases the possibility of fraud within the organization.

Separation of Duties within the Accounting Function. The least desirable accounting system is one in which one employee is responsible for recording a transaction from its origin to its ultimate posting in the general ledger. This enhances the likelihood that unintentional errors will remain undetected, and it encourages sloppy performance of duties.

There are many opportunities for automatic cross-checking of different employees' work in a manual system by simply segregating the recording in journals from the recording in related subsidiary ledgers. It is also possible to segregate the responsibility for recording in related journals, such as the sales and cash receipts journals.

Separation of Operational Responsibility from Record Keeping Responsibility. If each department or division in an organization was responsible for preparing its own records and reports, there would be a tendency to bias the results to improve its reported performance. In order to ensure unbiased information, record keeping is typically included in a separate department under the controllership function.

The overall organization structure of a business must provide proper segregation of duties, yet still promote operational efficiency and effective

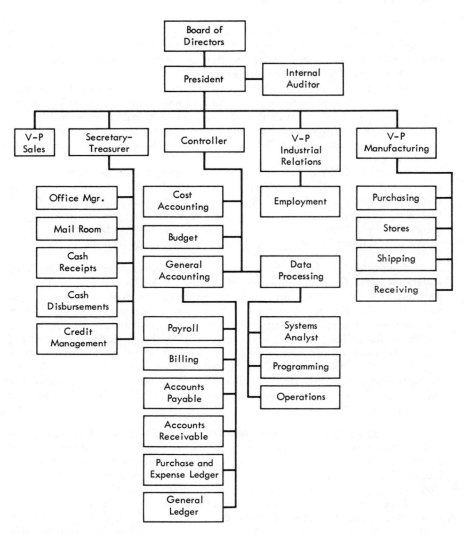

FIGURE 7–3 Organization Chart

communication. Figure 7-3 shows one typical *organization chart* where these objectives could be achieved. This is not a complete organization chart, but it does indicate the broad segregation of duties. Three of the most important segregations should be apparent:

- Accounting is completely isolated under the controller, who has no custodial or operating responsibility.
- The custodianship of cash, including receipts and disbursements, is the responsibility of the secretary-treasurer.
- The internal auditor reports directly to the president.

Proper authorization significantly affects the authorization objective, of course, but authorization is important to prevent invalid transactions. Since authorization often concerns unit or total price and the quality of goods and services acquired or sold, there is also an important effect on valuation.

Proper Procedures for Authorization

Every transaction must be properly authorized if control is to be satisfactory. If any person in an organization could acquire or expend assets at will, complete chaos would result.

Authorization can be either *general* or *specific*. In performing its function of general authorization, management establishes policies for the organization to follow. Subordinates are instructed to implement these general authorizations by approving all transactions within the limits set by the policy. Examples of general authority are the issuance of fixed price lists for the sale of products, credit limits for customers, and fixed automatic reorder points for making purchases.

Specific authority has to do with individual transactions. For some transactions, management is unwilling to establish a general policy of authorization. Instead, it prefers to make authorizations on a case-by-case basis. An example is the authorization of a sales transaction by the sales manager for a used-car company.

The individual or group who can grant either specific or general authority for transactions should hold a position commensurate with the nature and significance of the transactions, and the policy for such authority should be established by top management. For example, a common policy is to have all acquisitions of capital assets over a set amount authorized by the board of directors.

Adequate Documents and Records

Documents and records are the physical objects upon which transactions are entered and summarized. They include such diverse items as sales invoices, purchase orders, subsidiary ledgers, sales journals, time cards, and bank reconciliations. Both documents of original entry and records upon which transactions are entered are important elements of a system, but the inadequacy of documents normally causes greater control problems.

Documents perform the function of transmitting information throughout the client's organization and between different organizations. The documents must be adequate to provide reasonable assurance that all assets are properly controlled and all transactions correctly recorded. For example, if the receiving department fills out a receiving report when material is obtained, the accounts payable department can verify the quantity and description on the vendor's invoice by comparing it with the information on the receiving report.

Certain relevant principles dictate the proper design and use of documents and records. Documents and records should be

- Prenumbered consecutively to facilitate control over missing documents, and as an aid in locating documents when they are needed at a later date. (Significantly affects recording-of-existing-transactions objective.)
- Prepared at the time a transaction takes place, or as soon thereafter as possible. When there is a longer time interval, records are less credible and the chance for error is increased. (Affects recording-at-the-proper-time objective.)
- Sufficiently simple to make sure that they are clearly understood.
- Designed for multiple uses whenever possible, to minimize the number of different forms. For example, a properly designed and used sales invoice can be the basis for recording sales in the journals, the authority for shipment, the basis for developing sales statistics, and the support for salesmen's commissions.
- Constructed in a manner that encourages correct preparation. This can be done by providing a degree of internal check within the form or record. For example, a document might include instructions for proper routing, blank spaces for authorizations and approvals, and designated column spaces for numerical data.

Chart of Accounts. A control closely related to documents and records is the *chart of accounts*, which classifies transactions into individual balance sheet and income statement accounts. The chart of accounts is an important control because it provides the framework for determining the information presented to management and other financial statement users. It must contain sufficient information to permit the presentation of financial statements in accordance with generally accepted accounting principles, but in addition the classification of the information should help management make decisions. Information by divisions, product lines, responsibility centers, and similar breakdowns should be provided for. The chart of accounts is helpful in preventing misclassification errors if it accurately and precisely describes which type of transactions should be in each account. It is especially important that the descriptions clearly distinguish between capital assets, inventories, and expense items, since these are the major categories of concern to external users of the financial statements. (Significantly affects the proper-classification-of-transactions objective.)

Procedures Manual. The procedures for proper record keeping should be spelled out in *procedures manuals* to enourage consistent application. The manuals should define the flow of documents throughout the organization and should provide for sufficient information to facilitate adequate record keeping and the maintenance of proper control over assets. For example, to ensure the proper recording of the purchase of raw materials, a copy of the purchase order for acquiring the merchandise and a copy of the receiving report when the raw materials are received should be sent to accounts payable. This procedure aids in properly recording purchases in the accounts payable journal, and it facilitates the determination of whether the vendor's invoice from the supplier should be paid.

Physical Control over Assets and Records

The most important type of protective measure for safeguarding assets and records is the use of physical precautions. An example is the use of storerooms for inventory to guard against pilferage. When the storeroom is under the control of a competent employee, there is also further assurance that obsolescence is minimized. Fireproof safes and safety deposit vaults for the protection of assets such as currency and securities are other important physical safeguards.

Physical safeguards are also necessary for records and documents. The redevelopment of lost or destroyed records is costly and time consuming. Imagine what would happen if an accounts receivable master file were destroyed. The considerable cost of backup records and other controls can be justified to prevent this loss. Similarly, such documents as insurance policies and notes receivable should be physically protected.

Mechanical protective devices can also be used to obtain additional assurance that accounting information is currently and accurately recorded. Cash registers and certain types of automatic data-processing equipment are all potentially useful additions to the system of internal control for this purpose.

Independent Checks on Performance

The last specific element of control is the careful and continuous review of the other five elements in the system. The need for a system of *internal checks* arises because a system tends to change over time unless there is a mechanism for frequent review. Personnel are likely to forget procedures, become careless, or intentionally fail to follow them unless someone is there to observe and evaluate their performance. In addition, both fraudulent and unintentional errors are always possible, regardless of the quality of the controls.

An essential characteristic of the persons performing internal verification procedures is *independence* from the individuals originally responsible for preparing the data. A considerable portion of the value of checks on performance is lost when the individual doing the verification is a subordinate of the person originally responsible for preparing the data, or lacks independence in some other way. The importance of this element is indicated in Figure 7-2. Every internal control objective is significantly affected by internal verification.

The least expensive means of internal verification is the separation of duties in the manner previously discussed. For example, when the bank reconciliation is performed by a person independent of the accounting records and handling of cash, there is an opportunity for verification without incurring significant additional costs. Some important types of verification can only be accomplished by a duplication of effort. For example, the counting of inventory by two different teams to make certain that the count is correct is costly, but frequently necessary.

Internal Audit Staff. The existence of an *internal audit staff* is usually a highly effective method of verifying the proper recording of financial information. If the internal audit staff is independent of both the operating and the accounting departments, and if it reports directly to top management, there is an excellent opportunity for extensive verification within the client's organization.

Although the independent outside auditor is not permitted to rely entirely on evidence obtained by the internal audit staff, the existence of an adequate internal audit staff can greatly reduce the evidence he must gather during the external audit. SAS 9 (Section 322) defines the way internal auditors affect the independent auditor's evidence accumulation. For example, it is inappropriate for the CPA to completely forgo the confirmation of accounts receivable even if it has already been done by internal auditors. However, it is proper for him to review and evaluate the internal auditors' confirmation procedures and working papers, and significantly reduce the sample size for the audit confirmations if the internal audit results are satisfactory. The reliance on internal auditors as an internal control depends heavily on their competence, integrity, and independence from operating departments.

Overall Control Considerations

In addition to the controls that apply to each audit area, several overall controls within the system should be evaluated. These include the following:

- Adequate budgets and other reports prepared with sufficient frequency to meet management's needs.
- Bonding of employees in a position of trust as a deterrent to fraud and a means of recovering the loss if one should occur.
- A mandatory vacation policy. If every employee is required to take a vacation, and have his normal duties performed by someone else, the likelihood of a defalcation is reduced.
- A well defined conflict-of-interest policy strictly adhered to as a means of reducing temptation to employees in their relationship with the organization. Personnel in a position of trust who are related, employees having personal business dealings with the client's major customers or suppliers, and transactions between the company and officers, directors, or major stockholders are common examples where conflicts of interest can occur.
- Reasonable record retention policies in accordance with state and federal laws.

Relationship between Size of Business and Controls

An adequate system of internal control is important for small companies as well as for large ones. If there are inadequate controls, the likelihood of errors in the records is enhanced. This can be highly damaging to the effective operation of the company inasmuch as unreliable information frequently leads to poor decisions. Similarly, the safeguarding of assets and operational efficiency is as important for small companies as for large ones.

The size of a company does have a significant effect on the nature of the controls likely to exist. Obviously it is more difficult to establish adequate separation of duties in a small company. It would also be unreasonable to expect a small firm to have internal auditors. On the other hand, if the seven elements of internal control are examined, it becomes apparent that most of the controls are applicable to both large and small companies. Even though it may not be common to formalize policies in manuals, it is certainly possible for a small company to have competent, trustworthy personnel with clear lines of authority; proper procedures for authorization, execution, and recording of transactions; adequate documents, records, and reports; physical controls over assets and records; and, to a limited degree, checks on performance.

A major control available in a small company is the knowledge and concern of the top operating person, who is frequently an *owner-manager*. His interest in the organization and close relationship with the personnel enable him to evaluate the competence of the employees and the effectiveness of the overall system. For example, the system can be significantly strengthened if the owner conscientiously performs such duties as signing all checks after carefully reviewing supporting documents, reviewing bank reconciliations, examining accounts receivable statements sent to customers, approving credit, examining all correspondence from customers and vendors, and approving bad debts.

OVERVIEW OF AUDIT PROCESS

There are eight phases in doing an audit. Each phase is related to the review and evaluation of internal control. The purpose of this overview is to show briefly how the review and evaluation affects the entire audit process. Each phase is studied in greater detail in this and the next chapter. The phases are summarized in Figure 7-4.

Obtain a General Understanding of the Client's Business. This phase was studied in Chapter 6. It relates to internal control in that it provides background information about the client's business. The nature of the business affects the controls a company must have to safeguard assets and provide reliable data.

Review of the Existing System of Internal Control. The purpose of the review is to find out how the client believes the internal controls operate. The review is done by interviewing client personnel, examining procedures manuals, describing the flow of documents and records by the use of flowcharts and narrative descriptions, and using an internal control questionnaire. No testing of the system has occurred at this point.

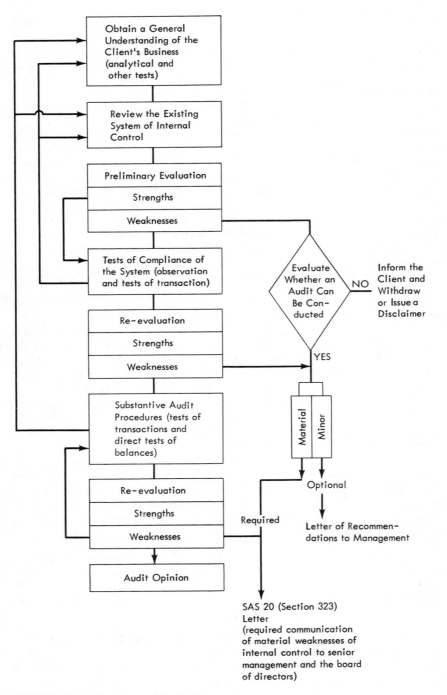

FIGURE 7–4 Overview of Audit Process

Preliminary Evaluation. Each audit area must be evaluated for strengths and weaknesses.

Strengths are the existence of adequate controls in a system that are intended to reduce the likelihood of errors. If the auditor identifies strengths (controls) that can be considered effective and if they are properly tested, the auditor can reduce certain audit tests.

Weaknesses are the lack of adequate controls. When there are significant weaknesses, the likelihood of material error is enhanced. The auditor must first identify material weaknesses in this phase of internal control evaluation. Audit evidence is then modified during the audit because of the increased likelihood of errors. The auditor also informs the client of all material weaknesses by letter during or at the end of the engagement.

Tests of Compliance of the System. Each control that is to be relied upon to reduce direct tests of balances must be tested to determine if the control is actually effective. These are referred to as tests of compliance.

Reevaluation. When the tests of the various controls have been completed, the results must be carefully analyzed to determine whether the system is operating as effectively as the auditor originally believed. Those controls that are operating satisfactorily can be relied upon, and as a result, other audit tests can be reduced. For those controls where the system is not operating effectively, the auditor cannot rely upon the system. In those circumstances, he must act as if the control did not exist and increase other tests accordingly.

Substantive Tests of Financial Balances. Substantive audit tests are tests for monetary errors in transactions and balances. They are based in part upon the auditor's evaluation of the strengths and weaknesses of the client's system after it has been tested for compliance. But other variables also affect the nature of the tests. Considerations such as the overall level of assurance desired, the materiality of the balance in question, the first-year versus a subsequent-year audit, the results of previous audits, and other factors discussed in Chapter 5 must be taken into account.

Reevaluation. After all substantive tests are completed, the auditor summarizes the information to determine if sufficient evidence has been accumulated to issue an opinion.

Audit Opinion. The type of audit opinion given depends on the evidence accumulated and the results found in the audit tests. The results of the substantive tests also provide additional information about the system. If significant errors are found, it may be necessary to rechallenge the quality of internal controls and to perform additional tests to determine whether the financial statements are fairly presented.

REVIEW OF THE SYSTEM

With the previous background, it is appropriate to examine the first phase, review of the system, in greater detail.

Obtain Information from the Organization

A thorough review of the client's system enables the auditor to identify existing controls, which is an essential part of internal control evaluation. If the auditor understands the way documents and records flow through a transaction cycle, he can identify the procedures employed for processing and recording each transaction. If he knows which person performs each procedure, the existing controls can be easily identified.

Interviews and Manuals. The starting point for developing an understanding of the client's system is to interview the chief accounting officer and other key personnel and to review the formal procedures the organization has established. A detailed *organization chart* and the *procedures manuals* are key information for understanding the system. As a part of reviewing these documents, it is desirable to obtain a job description for the most important individuals involved in any aspect of record keeping and the custody of assets. The procedures manuals should be studied and discussed with company personnel to ensure an understanding of the prescribed procedures. If the company is small and has no organization chart or procedures manuals, a description of the system should be obtained through discussion with management.

Flowcharts and Internal Control Questionnaire. After obtaining an overview of the system, it is necessary to obtain more specific information about the flow of documents and records and the nature of specific controls. *Flowcharts* and *internal control questionnaires* are useful for this purpose. These two topics and their relationship to the audit as a whole are discussed in the following sections. It is desirable to use the client's flowcharts and have the client fill out the internal control questionnaire, but this often has the disadvantage of depriving the auditor of the opportunity to interview client personnel and observe procedures. When understandable and reliable flowcharts and questionnaires are not available, which is frequently the case, the auditor must prepare his own.

Flowcharting

A *flowchart* of internal control is a symbolic, diagrammatic representation of the client's documents and their sequential flow in the organization. An adequate flowchart shows the origin of each document and record in the system, the subsequent processing, and the final disposition of any document or record included in the chart. In addition, it is possible for the flowchart to show the separation of duties, authorizations, approvals, and internal verifications that take place within the system.

Flowcharting is advantageous primarily because it can provide a concise overview of the client's system, which is useful to the auditor as an analytical tool in his evaluation. A well-prepared flowchart aids in identifying inadequacies by facilitating a clear understanding of how the system operates. For most uses, it is superior to written descriptions as a method of communicating the characteristics of a system. It is simply easier to follow a diagram than to read a description. It is also usually easier to update a flowchart than a narrative description.

Elements of Flowcharting. The three basic elements of a flowchart are symbols, flow lines, and areas of responsibility. Each of these three elements is examined briefly.

Symbols are used to show predefined items, steps, and actions. No matter what symbols are used, the concept of flowcharting remains unchanged, but naturally the symbols must be defined. Different audit firms use different symbols, but most of them have been derived from the United States of America Standards Institute symbols and are similar in form. Figure 7-5 shows the basic symbols that have been adopted for this textbook and gives an example of each symbol.

Flow lines are used to show how documents and records are related. Arrowheads are used to indicate the direction of the flow. The flowcharting convention for arrowheads is that they should be used for all directions of flow except down and to the right. We recommend the use of arrowheads whenever it adds clarification.

Areas of responsibility are established on flowcharts as vertical columns or sections through which the flow of documents takes place horizontally (from left to right). This technique enables the reader to clearly identify changes in responsibility as the documents flow through the system. An example of separation by areas of responsibility is given in Figure 7-6.

Guidelines for Preparation. The overall objectives of a flowchart are to help the preparer understand the system, to communicate a description of a system to all subsequent readers, and to aid in evaluating internal control. Following are a few general guidelines to help accomplish these objectives:

- Use notations in addition to symbols to make the flowchart more understandable.
- Where the information on the flowchart is not completely self-explanatory, use supplementary information and refer specifically to its source.
- Show the source and disposition of every document included in the flowchart.

Illustration. A brief flowcharting illustration is useful at this point. Figure 7-6 furnishes a flowchart for the following narrative description of the sales, billing, and shipping departments of a small wholesale company. A more extensive illustration is given in Figure 9-6.

Document – paper documents and
reports of all types
Example: a sales invoice

Process Symbol – any processing function;
 defined operation causing a change in
 value, form, or location of information
Example: a billing clerk prepares a sales invoice

Off–line Storage – off–line storage of
 documents, records, and EDP files
Example: a duplicate sales invoice is filed
  in numerical order

Transmittal Tape – a proof or adding machine
 tape used for control purposes
Example: an adding machine tape of sales invoices

Input/Output Symbol – used to indicate
 information entering or leaving system
Example: a receipt of order from customer

Decision – used to indicate a decision is made
requiring different action for a yes or no answer
(this symbol is rarely used)
Example: is customer credit satisfactory

No

Yes

Annotation – the addition of descriptive
 comments or explanatory notes as clarification
Example: a billing clerk checks credit before
  preparing an invoice

Directional Flow–Lines – the direction of
 processing or data flow

Connector – exit to, or entry from, another part
 of chart; keyed in by using numbers
Example: a document transfer from one department
  into another department

Symbols Unique to EDP Systems

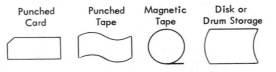

| Punched Card | Punched Tape | Magnetic Tape | Disk or Drum Storage |

FIGURE 7–5 Basic Flowcharting Symbols

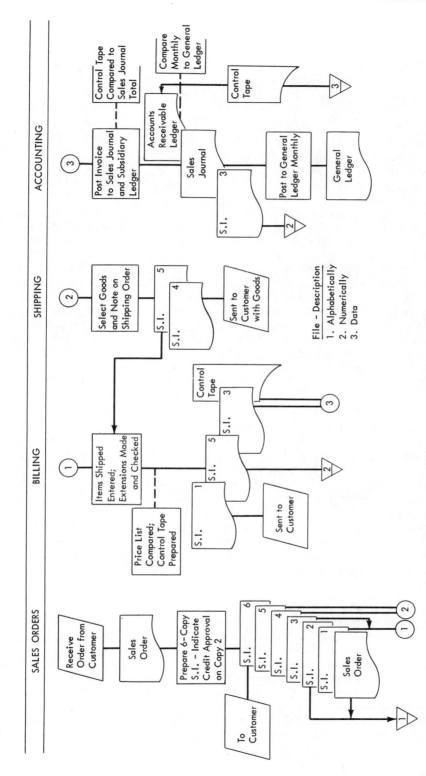

FIGURE 7-6 Flowchart

231

The sales department prepares a six-part sales invoice form from the customer's sales order. The sales order is filed alphabetically by customer after the sales invoice is prepared. Credit approval is indicated on copy 2, which is then filed with the customer's order. Parts 1 (sales invoice) and 3 (ledger) are sent to billing; part 4 (packing slip) and part 5 (shipping order) are sent to shipping; and part 6 is sent to the customer as acknowledgment of the order.

Shipping physically collects the items for shipment and notes that the goods were shipped on the shipping order. The packing slip is sent to the customer with the goods, and the shipping order is sent to billing.

Billing enters the shipped items marked on the shipping order on the sales invoice and ledger copy, makes extensions and checks them, compares the prices with the price list, and runs a tape of the amounts on the ledger copy. The shipping order is then filed numerically. The sales invoice is sent to the customer, and the ledger copy and the tape are sent to accounting.

In accounting, invoices are posted to the sales journal and subsidiary ledger. The journal is totaled daily and compared to the tape received from billing. The control tape and sales invoices (copy 3) are filed daily. Monthly the journal is added and posted to the general ledger. The balances in accounts receivable subsidiary ledgers are also totaled monthly and compared to the general ledger control account.

Obtaining Information. Frequently, flowcharts are initially prepared in rough form only because as the review progresses the auditor is likely to need to redraw and refine them. It may be convenient to base the rough charts on the client's manuals and information already included in the current or previous audit working papers. Ultimately, the flowcharts must describe the system and procedures *actually in force:* these may differ materially from those management believes to be in effect. The information for the final flowchart can come either from the personnel responsible for performing the work or from the observations of the auditor. A combination of these two can be accomplished by asking the responsible individuals questions and requesting to actually see the documents and records.

Walk-Through Test. After the flowcharting is completed, it is desirable to follow an example of every document described in the chart from its origin to its final disposition. Common terminology to describe this procedure is a *walk-through test*, a *cradle-to-grave test*, or a *sample of one*. This not only provides a better understanding of the system but also helps to disclose errors or incomplete parts of the flowchart. The tracing of one or two transactions through the system should not be confused with testing the system. To meet the standards of the profession, a test of the system requires a larger sample size than one or two transactions.

Internal Control Questionnaires

An *internal control questionnaire* is designed to ask a series of questions about the controls in each audit area as a means of indicating to the auditor aspects of the system that may be inadequate. In most instances it is designed to require a yes or a no response, with "no" responses indicating potential internal control deficiencies. Figure 7-7 illustrates a part of an internal control questionnaire for sales.

Cash Receipts and Accounts Receivable

The partial questionnaire in Figure 7-7 combines sales, cash receipts, and accounts receivable. All of these accounts are a part of the sales and collection cycle discussed previously. The questionnaire is also designed for use with the eight internal control objectives. Notice that for sales the letters refer to the detailed objectives applied to sales transactions. The same is true for all other audit areas.

The primary advantage of the questionnaire approach is the relative completeness of coverage of each audit area that a good instrument affords. Furthermore, a questionnaire can usually be prepared reasonably quickly at the beginning of the audit engagement. The primary disadvantage is that individual parts of the client's system are examined without providing an overall view of the entire cycle. In addition, a standard questionnaire is often inapplicable to some audit clients, especially the smaller ones.

In using questionnaires, it is important to determine whether the controls believed by management to exist are actually being followed. Questioning the personnel actually performing each procedure, observation, and verification by examining documents and records are convenient methods of obtaining information for completing the questionnaire.

We believe the use of both questionnaires and flowcharts is highly desirable for understanding the client's system. The flowcharts provide an overview of the entire system, and the questionnaire is a useful checklist to remind the auditor of many different types of controls that should exist. A combination of these two approaches when properly used should provide the auditor with an excellent description of the system.

PRELIMINARY EVALUATION

Once the auditor understands how management and other personnel believe the system operates, he is in a position to make a preliminary evaluation of the controls in the system and those aspects of the system that are likely to permit errors due to the absence of adequate controls. The evaluation is only preliminary because a final evaluation cannot take place until the actual operation of the system is tested for congruence with the apparent system. The evaluation must concern both strengths and weaknesses. The evaluation is done separately for each transaction cycle.

SALES, CASH RECEIPTS, AND ACCOUNTS RECEIVABLE

Sales and Sales Returns and Allowances	Yes	No	Verified by	Date
A. Sales and sales returns and allowances are reasonable as recorded.				
1. Are sales transactions periodically reviewed by a responsible member of management for reasonableness?	—	—	——	—
B. Recorded sales are for shipments actually made to nonfictitious customers.				
1. Is the recording of sales supported by authorized shipping documents and approved customer orders?	—	—	——	—
C. Sales transactions are properly authorized.				
1. Is customers' credit approved by a responsible official?	—	—	——	—
2. Is a prenumbered written shipping order required for any merchandise to leave the premises?	—	—	——	—
3. Is an authorized price list used?	—	—	——	—
4. Are sales returns and allowances and discounts approved by a responsible official?	—	—	——	—
5. Are charged-off bad debts approved by a responsible official?	—	—	——	—

FIGURE 7–7 Partial Internal Control Questionnaire

234

SALES, CASH RECEIPTS, AND ACCOUNTS RECEIVABLE

Sales and Sales Returns and Allowances	Yes	No	Verified by	Date
D. Existing sales transactions are recorded.				
1. Is a record of shipments maintained?	___	___	___	___
2. Is the shipping document controlled from the office in a manner which helps ensure that all shipments are billed?	___	___	___	___
3. Are shipping documents prenumbered and accounted for?	___	___	___	___
4. Are sales invoices prenumbered and accounted for?	___	___	___	___
5. Are credit memos prenumbered and accounted for?	___	___	___	___
6. Are prenumbered sales invoices prepared on all sales (cash, charge, property and equipment, miscellaneous, scrap sales, etc.)?	___	___	___	___
Cash Receipts				
A. Recorded cash receipts are for funds actually received.				
1. Are authenticated duplicate deposit tickets received by the bank reconciler or by a person who does not handle or record cash?	___	___	___	___
2. Are authenticated duplicate deposit tickets compared to the cash receipts journal?	___	___	___	___
B. Cash discounts are authorized.				
1. Are cash discounts periodically reviewed by an independent person?	___	___	___	___
C. All cash received is recorded in the cash receipts journal and receipts deposited in the amount received.	___	___	___	___

FIGURE 7–7 (cont.)

Identify and Evaluate Existing Controls

For each of the detailed internal control objectives, the auditor must identify the existing controls to prevent errors. Where such controls exist, they are referred to as the *strengths in the system*. Most of these controls should have been identified as a part of understanding the system. The identification of strengths is the association of these controls with each detailed objective. If a control providing strength exists and is functioning properly, the auditor's expectation of certain types of errors is reduced, which means he can reduce the extent of tests for the substance of the error. For example, in the audit of purchase journal transactions there are several controls a client can use to fulfill the "recorded transactions are valid" objective. These include the following:

- Approval of all purchase requisitions and purchase orders by an authorized person.
- Issuance of a receiving report at the time goods are received.
- Matching and comparing of vendor's invoices, receiving reports, and purchase orders before entries are made in the purchases journal.
- Internal verification by the internal audit staff to determine whether the three above controls are being properly followed.

Compliance Tests

If the auditor plans to rely upon the strengths, the pertinent controls must be tested through *tests of compliance*. These tests are intended to provide assurance that the controls believed to exist do exist and are functioning properly. An example of a strength which might be relied upon is a clerk examining and initialing all vendor's invoices and other supporting documents after they have been paid. If the clerk is properly performing his duties, the likelihood of errors in recording purchases is significantly reduced. As a compliance test of whether the clerk is performing his duties, a sample of documents can be examined for the clerk's initials. If, as a result of this and other tests, the independent auditor concludes that the clerk is competent and conscientious, the extent of the verification of the propriety and proper classification of recorded purchase transactions could be reduced (but not eliminated). An example of a compliance test for the first control in the previous section is to examine a sample of purchase requisitions and purchase orders to determine if each one has been approved by an authorized person. Examples of compliance tests for controls concerning each of the eight detailed objectives are included in Figure 9-3.

Identify and Evaluate Weaknesses

Weaknesses are defined as the *absence of controls*. If there are inadequate controls to prevent a specific type of error, the auditor's expectation of such an error increases. Therefore, the audit evidence must be modified to make sure the potential error is not material. For example, if no internal verification of the recording of purchase transactions is taking place, the auditor must test recorded transactions more extensively than he would if adequate internal verification did exist.

A six-step methodology is appropriate in determining weaknesses and their effect on the audit.

Identify the Weaknesses. Internal control questionnaires and flow-charts are useful to identify areas where controls are lacking.

Consider the Possibility of Compensating Controls. A compensation control is a different control that offsets a weakness in the system. A common example in a smaller company is active involvement of the owner of the company. When a compensatory control exists, the weakness is no longer a concern.

Determine the Potential Errors That Could Result. This step is intended to identify the potential impact of the weakness on the financial statements.

Evaluate the Materiality of the Potential Errors. The auditor is only concerned about weaknesses that are likely to result in material errors or irregularities.

Modify the Audit Evidence. The audit evidence should be increased to compensate for the increased likelihood of material errors.

Inform the Client. SAS 20 (Section 323) requires the communication of material weaknesses of internal control to the client.

A working paper showing the methodology and how it can be documented is included in Figure 7-8.

Required Communication of Material Weaknesses of Internal Control

The purpose of the requirement that all material weaknesses of internal control be communicated to the client is twofold. First, it is fulfilling a social responsibility to management to give it the benefit of the auditor's knowledge acquired during the audit. Most CPA firms would do this as a part of good business practice even if it were not required. Second, it protects the audit from potential lawsuits from the client. If a proper communication has taken place, management would likely be unsuccessful in a suit in which it claimed the auditor failed to inform management of a significant weakness.

Although SAS 20 (Section 323) does not require that the communication be in writing, most firms use the standard format suggested by the AICPA. An example of a required communication letter is included in Figure 7-9. The subject matter was taken from the information in Figure 7-8.

SUMMARY

Figure 7-10 summarizes the major internal control concepts and applications introduced in this chapter. They will be referred to throughout the remainder of the book.

AIRTIGHT MACHINE CO.

Weakness in Internal Control – Sales and Collections
12/31/80

Schedule __P-3__
Prepared by __JR__

Weakness	Compensating Control	Potential Error	Materiality	Effect on Audit Evidence
1. The accounts receivable clerk approves credit memos and has access to cash.	The owner reviews all credit memos after they are recorded. He knows all customers.	N/A	N/A	N/A
2. There is no internal verification of unit prices, extensions, footing or postings of sales invoices and credit memos.[1]	None	Clerical errors in billings to customers and posting to subsidiary ledger.	Potentially material	Increase the audit tests of sales transactions to 125 transactions and confirm 75 accounts receivable at the balance sheet date.

[1]Included in the required communication of material weakness of internal control letter.

FIGURE 7-8 Weaknesses in Internal Control and the Effect on the Audit Process

JOHNSON and SEYGROVES
Certified Public Accountants
2016 Village Boulevard
Troy, Michigan 48801

February 12, 1981

Board of Directors
Airtight Machine Company
1729 Athens Street
Troy, Michigan 48801

Gentlemen:

We have examined the financial statements of Airtight
Machine Company for the year ended December 31, 1980, and have issued
our report thereon dated February 12, 1981. As part of our examination, we made a study and evaluation of the Company's system of
internal accounting control to the extent we considered necessary to
evaluate the system as required by generally accepted auditing
standards. Under these standards, the purposes of such evaluation
are to establish a basis for reliance on the system of internal
accounting control in determining the nature, timing, and extent of
other auditing procedures that are necessary for expressing an opinion
on the financial statements and to assist the auditor in planning and
performing his examination of the financial statements. Our examination of the financial statements made in accordance with generally
accepted auditing standards, including the study and evaluation of
the Company's system of internal accounting control for the year
ended December 31, 1980, that was made for the purposes set forth in
the first paragraph of this report, would not necessarily disclose
all weaknesses in the system because it was based on selective tests
of accounting records and related data. However, such study and
evaluation disclosed the following condition that we believe to be
a material weakness:

There is a lack of independent verification of unit prices,
extensions, footings or postings of sales invoices and credit memos.
This internal control weakness is especially important because of
the large size of the average sale of Airtight Machine Company.

The foregoing condition was considered in determining the
nature, timing, and extent of audit tests to be applied in our examination of the financial statements, and this report of such conditions
does not modify our report dated December 31, 1980, on such financial
statements.

Very truly yours,

Johnson + Seygroves

JOHNSON and SEYGROVES, CPAs

FIGURE 7-9 Required Communication of Material Weaknesses of Internal Control

FIGURE 7–10

Summary of Major Internal Control Concepts and Applications

Concerns about Internal Control

Client's concerns

$\left\{\begin{array}{l}\text{• Provide reliable data} \\ \text{• Safeguard assets and records}\end{array}\right\}$ Auditor's primary concerns

$\left\{\begin{array}{l}\text{• Promote operational efficiency} \\ \text{• Encourage adherence to prescribed} \\ \text{~~policies}\end{array}\right\}$ Auditor's secondary concerns

*Ways the Study and
Evaluation Are Used by Auditor*

- Determine whether an audit is possible
- Determine the audit evidence to accumulate
- Inform senior management and the board of directors

Detailed Internal Control Objectives

- Transactions as recorded are reasonable
- Recorded transactions are valid
- Transactions are properly authorized
- Existing transactions are recorded
- Transactions are properly valued
- Transactions are properly classified
- Transactions are recorded at the proper time
- Transactions are properly included in subsidiary records and correctly summarized

Elements of Internal Control

- Competent, trustworthy personnel with clear lines of authority and responsibility
- Adequate segregation of duties
- Proper procedures for authorization
- Adequate documents and records
- Physical control over assets and records
- Independent checks on performance

Overview of Audit Process

- Obtain a general understanding of the client
- Review of the existing system of internal control
- Preliminary evaluation
- Tests of compliance
- Reevaluation
- Substantive tests of financial balances
- Reevaluation
- Audit opinion

*Methodology for Determining
Weaknesses and Their Effect on the Audit*

- Identify the weaknesses
- Consider the possibility of compensating controls
- Determine the potential errors that could result
- Evaluate the materiality of the potential errors
- Modify the audit evidence
- Inform the client

REVIEW QUESTIONS

7-1. Compare management's concerns about internal control with the auditor's concerns about internal control.

7-2. In what ways does the auditor use the study and evaluation of internal control?

7-3. Frequently, management is more concerned about internal controls that promote operational efficiency than about obtaining reliable financial data. How can the independent auditor persuade management to devote more attention to controls affecting the reliability of accounting information when management has this attitude?

7-4. Give an illustration of a situation where the controls are so inadequate as to preclude the possibility of conducting an adequate audit. What are the auditor's options under these circumstances?

7-5. List the six elements of internal control and provide one specific illustration of a control in the payroll area for each element.

7-6. The separation of duties within the accounting department is meant to prevent different types of errors than the separation of the custody of assets from accounting. Explain the difference in the purposes of these two types of segregation of duties.

7-7. In recent years there has been an increased tendency of the internal audit staff to report directly to the president rather than to the controller. What is the major shortcoming of having the internal auditor report to the controller?

7-8. Distinguish between general and specific authorization of transactions and give one example of each type.

7-9. Define what is meant by a chart of accounts and explain how it relates to an adequate system of internal control.

7-10. For each of the following, give an example of a physical control the client can use to protect the asset or record:
   a. Petty cash
   b. Cash received by retail clerks
   c. Accounts receivable records
   d. Raw material inventory
   e. Perishable tools
   f. Manufacturing equipment
   g. Marketable securities

7-11. Explain what is meant by internal checks on performance and give five specific examples of internal checks.

7-12. Distinguish between the auditor gaining an understanding of the system of internal control and the auditor's preliminary evaluation of the system. Also explain the methodology the auditor uses for each of them.

7-13. Define what is meant by a strength and a weakness in a system of internal control. Give three examples of each in the sales and collection cycle.

7–14. Frank James was a highly competent employee of Brinkwater Sales Corporation who had been responsible for accounting-related matters for two decades. His devotion to the firm and his duties had always been exceptional, and over the years he had been given increased responsibility. Both the president of Brinkwater and the partner of the independent CPA firm in charge of the audit were shocked and dismayed to discover that James had embezzled more than $500,000 over a 10-year period by not recording billings in the sales journal and subsequently diverting the cash receipts. What major factors permitted the defalcation to take place?

7–15. Jeanne Maier, CPA, believes it is appropriate to review the system of internal control about halfway through the audit, after she is familiar with the client's operations and the way the system actually works. She has found through experience that filling out internal control questionnaires and flowcharts early in the engagement is not beneficial because the system rarely functions the way it is supposed to. Later in the engagement, it is feasible to prepare flowcharts and questionnaires with relative ease because of the knowledge already obtained on the audit. Evaluate her approach to internal control review.

7–16. Explain why the system of internal control is reevaluated after both compliance and substantive tests.

7–17. Explain what is meant by a transaction cycle and discuss the need to separate different cycles as a part of the study and evaluation of internal control.

7–18. Distinguish between the objectives of an internal control questionnaire and the objectives of a flowchart for obtaining information about a client's system. State the advantages and disadvantages of each of these two methods.

7–19. What does the terminology "walk-through test" mean when used in connection with flowcharting? Why is this procedure used?

7–20. State the eight detailed internal control objectives.

DISCUSSION QUESTIONS AND PROBLEMS

7–21. Select the best response for each of the following questions.
 a. What is the independent auditor's principal purpose for conducting a study and evaluation of the existing system of internal control?
  (1) To comply with generally accepted accounting principles.
  (2) To obtain a measure of assurance of management's efficiency.
  (3) To maintain a state of independence in mental attitude in all matters relating to the audit.
  (4) To determine the nature, timing, and extent of subsequent audit work.
 b. When evaluating internal control, the auditor's primary concern is to determine
  (1) the possibility of fraud occurring.
  (2) compliance with policies, plans, and procedures.
  (3) the reliability of the accounting information system.
  (4) the type of an opinion he will issue.

   c. In evaluating internal control, the first step is to prepare an internal control questionnaire or a flowchart of the system. The second step should be to

     (1) determine the extent of audit work necessary to form an opinion.

     (2) gather enough evidence to determine if the internal control system is functioning as described.

     (3) write a letter to management describing the weaknesses in the internal control system.

     (4) form a final judgment on the effectiveness of the internal control system. (AICPA adapted)

7–22. The following questions deal with flowcharts. Choose the best response.

   a. One reason why an auditor uses a flowchart is to aid in the

     (1) evaluation of a series of sequential processes.

     (2) study of the system of responsibility accounting.

     (3) performance of important, required, dual-purpose tests.

     (4) understanding of a client's organizational structure.

   b. During which phase of an audit examination is the preparation of flowcharts most appropriate?

     (1) Review of the system of internal accounting control.

     (2) Tests of compliance with internal accounting control procedures.

     (3) Evaluation of the system of internal administrative control.

     (4) Analytic review of operations.

   c. When preparing a record of a client's system of internal accounting control, the independent auditor sometimes uses a systems flowchart, which can best be described as a

     (1) pictorial presentation of the flow of instructions in a client's internal computer system.

     (2) diagram which clearly indicates an organization's internal reporting structure.

     (3) graphic illustration of the flow of operations which is used to replace the auditor's internal control questionnaire.

     (4) symbolic representation of a system or series of sequential processes.

(AICPA adapted)

7–23. The following questions concern internal accounting control. Choose the best response.

   a. Which of the following is an effective internal accounting control used to prove that production department employees are properly validating payroll timecards at a time-recording station?

     (1) Time cards should be carefully inspected by those persons who distribute pay envelopes to the employees.

     (2) One person should be responsible for maintaining records of employee time for which salary payment is not to be made.

     (3) Daily reports showing time charged to jobs should be approved by the foreman and compared to the total hours worked on the employee time cards.

     (4) Internal auditors should make observations of distribution of paychecks on a surprise basis.

b. Which of the following policies is an internal accounting control weakness related to the acquisition of factory equipment?

(1) Acquisitions are to be made through and approved by the department in need of the equipment.

(2) Advance executive approvals are required for equipment acquisitions.

(3) Variances between authorized equipment expenditures and actual costs are to be immediately reported to management.

(4) Depreciation policies are reviewed only once a year.

c. Which of the following best describes how an auditor, when evaluating internal accounting control, considers the types of errors and irregularities that could occur and determines those control procedures that should prevent or detect such errors or irregularities?

(1) Discussions with management with respect to the system of internal accounting control and how management determines that the system is functioning properly.

(2) Review of questionnaires, flowcharts, checklists, instructions or similar generalized materials used by the auditor.

(3) Exercise of professional judgment in evaluating the reliability of supporting documentation.

(4) Use of attribute sampling techniques to gather information for tests of compliance.

d. To avoid potential errors and irregularities a well-designed system of internal accounting control in the accounts payable area should include a separation of which of the following functions?

(1) Cash disbursements and invoice verification.

(2) Invoice verification and merchandise ordering.

(3) Physical handling of merchandise received and preparation of receiving reports.

(4) Check signing and cancellation of payment documentation.

e. Which of the following is a standard internal accounting control for cash disbursements?

(1) Checks should be signed by the controller and at least one other employee of the company.

(2) Checks should be sequentially numbered and the numerical sequence should be accounted for by the person preparing bank reconciliations.

(3) Checks and supporting documents should be marked "Paid" immediately after the check is returned with the bank statement.

(4) Checks should be sent directly to the payee by the employee who prepares documents that authorize check preparation.

(AICPA adapted)

7–24. Select the best response for each of the following questions and explain the reason for your choice.

a. Which of the following is a responsibility that should *not* be assigned to only one employee?

(1) Access to securities in the company's safe deposit box.

(2) Custodianship of the cash working fund.

(3) Reconciliation of bank statements.

(4) Custodianship of tools and small equipment.

b. A company holds bearer bonds as a short-term investment. Custody of these bonds and submission of coupons for interest payments is normally the responsibility of the

  (1) treasury function.

  (2) legal counsel.

  (3) general accounting function.

  (4) internal audit function.

c. Operating control of the check-signing machine normally should be the responsibility of the

  (1) general accounting function.

  (2) treasury function.

  (3) legal counsel.

  (4) internal audit function.

d. Matching the supplier's invoice, the purchase order, and the receiving report should normally be the responsibility of the

  (1) warehouse-receiving function.

  (2) purchasing function.

  (3) general accounting function.

  (4) treasury function.   (AICPA adapted)

7–25. Adherence to generally accepted auditing standards requires, among other things, a proper study and evaluation of the existing internal control. The most common approaches to reviewing the system of internal control include the use of a questionnaire, preparation of a memorandum, preparation of a flowchart, and combinations of these methods.

Required:

a. What is a CPA's objective in reviewing internal control for an opinion audit?

b. Discuss the advantages to a CPA of reviewing internal control by using

  (1) an internal control questionnaire.

  (2) a flowchart.

c. If the CPA, after completing his evaluation of internal control for an opinion audit is satisfied that no material weaknesses in the client's internal control system exist, is it necessary for him to test transactions? Explain.

        (AICPA adapted)

7–26. For each of the following errors or inefficiencies, provide a control procedure the client could institute to reduce its likelihood of occurrence.

a. The incorrect price is used on sales invoices for billing shipments to customers.

b. A vendor's invoice is paid twice for the same shipment. The second payment arose because the vendor sent a duplicate copy of the original two weeks after the payment was due.

c. Employees in the receiving department for a retail meat market take sides of beef for their personal use. When a shipment of meat is received, the receiving department fills out a receiving report and forwards it to the accounting department for the amount of goods actually received. At that time, one or two sides of beef are put in an employee's pickup truck rather than in the storage freezer.

d. Assembly workers in a furniture shop go to the raw materials wood bin whenever a piece of wood they are using to make furniture doesn't fit properly. Even though company policy requires the employee to correct the deficiency in the original piece by planing it, he usually throws it away and gets a new piece.

e. The factory foreman of a medium-sized manufacturing company is responsible for delivering weekly paychecks to the employees under his supervision. Last September when his brother-in-law quit working without informing anyone, the factory foreman continued to punch his daily time card. The foreman approves the time card and submits it to the payroll department. On the weekend the foreman delivers the check to his brother-in-law's house and they split the money.

7-27. The division of the following duties is meant to provide the best possible controls for the Meridian Paint Company, a small wholesale store.

 *a. Assemble supporting documents for disbursements and prepare checks for signature.
 *b. Sign general disbursement checks.
 *c. Record checks written in the cash disbursements and payroll journal.
 d. Mail disbursement checks to suppliers.
 e. Cancel supporting documents to prevent their reuse.
 *f. Approve credit for customers.
 *g. Bill customers and record the invoices in the sales journal and subsidiary ledger.
 *h. Open the mail and prepare a prelisting of cash receipts.
 *i. Record cash receipts in the cash journal and subsidiary ledger.
 *j. Prepare daily cash deposits.
 *k. Deliver daily cash deposits to the bank.
 *l. Assemble the payroll time cards and prepare the payroll checks.
 *m. Sign payroll checks.
 n. Post the journals to the general ledger.
 o. Reconcile the accounts receivable subsidiary account with the control account.
 p. Prepare monthly statements for customers by copying the subsidiary ledger account.
 q. Reconcile the monthly statements from vendors with the subsidiary accounts payable account.
 r. Reconcile the bank account.

Required:

You are to divide the accounting-related duties a through r among Robert Smith, James Cooper, and Bill Miller. All of the responsibilities marked with an asterisk are assumed to take about the same amount of time and must be divided equally between the two employees, Smith and Cooper. Both employees are equally competent. Miller, who is president of the company, is not willing to perform any functions designated by an asterisk and a maximum of two of the other functions. (AICPA adapted)

7–28. The Y Company, a client of your firm, has come to you with a problem it would like you to solve. It has three clerical employees who must perform the following functions:

a. Maintain general ledger.
b. Maintain accounts payable ledger.
c. Maintain accounts receivable ledger.
d. Prepare checks for signature.
e. Maintain disbursements journal.
f. Issue credits on returns and allowances.
g. Reconcile the bank account.
h. Handle and deposit cash receipts.

Assuming that there is no problem as to the ability of any of the employees, the company requests that you assign the functions to the three employees in such a manner as to achieve the highest degree of internal control. It may be assumed that these employees will perform no other accounting functions than the ones listed and that any accounting functions not listed will be performed by persons other than these three employees.

Required:

a. State how you would distribute the functions among the three employees. Assume that, with the exception of the nominal jobs of the bank reconciliation and the issuance of credits on returns and allowances, all functions require an equal amount of time.
b. List four possible unsatisfactory combinations of the functions.

(AICPA adapted)

7–29. Recently, while eating lunch with your family at a local cafeteria, you observe a practice that is somewhat unusual. As you reach the end of the cafeteria line, an adding machine operator asks how many persons are in your party. He then totals the food purchases on the trays for all of your family and writes the number of persons included in the group on the adding machine tape. He hands you the tape and asks you to pay when you finish eating. Near the end of the meal, you decide you want a piece of pie and coffee so you return to the line, select your food, and again go through the line. The adding machine operator again goes through the same procedures, but this time he staples the second tape to the original and returns it to you.

When you leave the cafeteria, you hand the stapled adding machine tapes to the cash register operator, who totals the two tapes, takes your money, and puts the tapes on a spindle.

Required:

a. What internal controls has the cafeteria instituted for its operations?
b. How can the manager of the cafeteria evaluate the effectiveness of the control procedures?

c. How do these controls differ from those used by most cafeterias?

d. What are the costs and benefits of the cafeteria's system?

7–30. Lew Pherson and Vern Collier are friends who are employed by different CPA firms. One day during lunch they are discussing the importance of internal control in determining the amount of audit evidence required for an engagement. Pherson expresses the view that internal control must be carefully evaluated in all companies, regardless of their size, in basically the same manner. His CPA firm requires a standard internal control questionnaire on every audit as well as a flowchart of every transaction area. In addition, he says the firm requires a careful evaluation of the system and a modification in the evidence accumulated based on the strengths and weaknesses in the syatem.

Collier responds by saying he believes internal control cannot be adequate in many of the small companies he audits, therefore he simply ignores the evaluation of internal control and acts under the assumption of inadequate controls. He goes on to say, "Why should I spend a lot of time evaluating a system of internal control when I know it has all kinds of weaknesses before I start? I would rather spend the time it takes to fill out all those forms in testing whether the statements are correct."

Required:

a. Express in general terms the most important difference between the nature of the potential controls available for large and small companies.

b. Criticize the positions taken by Pherson and Collier, and express your own opinion about the similarities and differences that should exist in evaluating internal control for different-sized companies.

7–31. Internal auditing is a staff function found in virtually every large corporation. The internal audit function is also performed in many small companies as a part-time activity of individuals who may or may not be called internal auditors. The differences between the audits by independent public accountants and the work of internal auditors are more basic than is generally recognized.

Required:

a. Briefly discuss the auditing work performed by the independent public accountant and the internal auditor with regard to
   (1) auditing objectives.
   (2) general nature of auditing work.

b. In conducting his audit, the independent public accountant must evaluate the work of the internal auditor. Discuss briefly the reason for this evaluation.

c. List the auditing procedures used by an independent public accountant in evaluating the work of the internal auditor.   (AICPA adapted)

7–32. Each of the following internal control procedures has been taken from a standard internal control questionnaire used by a CPA firm for evaluating controls in the payroll and personnel cycle.

Required:

a. For each internal control procedure, identify the element(s) of internal control to which it applies (e.g., adequate documents and records or physical control over assets and records).

b. For each procedure, identify one audit test the auditor could use to evaluate whether an existing control is effective.

	Procedure Employed by Client		
Internal Control Procedure	*N/A*	*Yes*	*No*
1. Approval of department head or foreman on time cards is required prior to preparing payroll.			
2. All prenumbered time cards are accounted for before the preparation of checks begins.			
3. Persons preparing the payroll do not perform other payroll duties (e.g., timekeeping, distribution of checks) or have access to other payroll data or cash.			
4. All clerical operations in payroll are double-checked before payment is made.			
5. All voided and spoiled payroll checks are properly mutilated and retained.			
6. Personnel requires an investigation of an employment application from new employees. Investigation includes checking employee's background, former employers, and references.			
7. Written termination notices are required, must properly document reasons for termination, and require approval of an appropriate official.			

c. For each procedure, list a specific error that could result from the absence of the control.

d. For each procedure, identify one audit test the auditor could use to uncover errors resulting from the absence of the control if the errors exist.

7–33. Western Meat Processing Company buys and processes livestock for sale to supermarkets. In connection with your examination of the company's financial statements, you have prepared the following notes based on your review of procedures:

a. Each livestock buyer submits a daily report of his purchases to the plant superintendent. This report shows the dates of purchase and expected delivery, the vendor, and the number, weights, and type of livestock purchased. As shipments are received, any available plant employee counts the number of each type received and places a check mark beside the quantity on the buyer's report. When all shipments listed on the report have been received, the report is returned to the buyer.

b. Vendor's invoices, after a clerical check, are sent to the buyer for approval and returned to the accounting department. A disbursement voucher and a check for the approved amount are prepared in the accounting department. Checks are forwarded to the treasurer for his signature. The treasurer's office sends signed checks directly to the buyer for delivery to the vendor.

c. Livestock carcasses are processed by lots. Each lot is assigned a number. At the end of each day a tally sheet reporting the lots processed, the number and type of animals in each lot, and the carcass weight is sent to the accounting department where a perpetual inventory record of processed carcasses and their weights is maintained.

d. Processed carcasses are stored in a refrigerated cooler located in a small building adjacent to the employee parking lot. The cooler is locked when the plant is not open, and a company guard is on duty when the employees report for work and leave at the end of their shifts. Supermarket truck drivers wishing to pick up their orders have been instructed to contact someone in the plant if no one is in the cooler.

e. Substantial quantities of by-products are produced and stored, either in the cooler or elsewhere in the plant. By-products are initially accounted for as they are sold. At this time, the sales manager prepares a two-part form—one copy serves as authorization to transfer the goods to the customer and the other becomes the basis for billing the customer.

Required:

For each of parts a through e, state

a. what the specific internal control objective(s) should be at the stage of the operating cycle described.

b. the control weaknesses in the present procedures, if any; and suggestions for improvements, if any. (AICPA adapted)

7–34. The following are descriptions of systems of internal control for companies engaged in the manufacturing business:

a. When Mr. Clark orders materials for his machine-rebuilding plant, he sends a duplicate purchase order to the receiving department. During a delivery of materials, Mr. Smith, the receiving clerk, records the receipt of shipment on this purchase order. After recording, Mr. Smith sends the purchase order to the accounting department, where it is used to record materials purchased and accounts payable. The materials are transported to the storage area by forklifts. The additional purchased quantities are recorded on storage records.

b. Every day hundreds of employees clock in using time cards at Generous Motors Corporation. The timekeepers collect these cards once a week and deliver them to the tabulating machine department. There the data on these time cards are transferred to punch cards. The punched cards are used in the preparation of the labor cost distribution records, the payroll journal, and the payroll checks. The treasurer, Mrs. Webber, compares the payroll journal with the payroll checks, signs the checks, and returns the payroll checks to Mr. Strode, the supervisor of the tabulating department. The payroll checks are distributed to the employees by Mr. Strode.

c. The smallest branch of Connor Cosmetics in South Bend employs Mary Cooper, the branch manager, and her sales assistant, Janet Hendrix. The branch uses a bank account in South Bend to pay expenses. The account is kept in the name of "Connor Cosmetics—Special Account." To pay expenses, checks must be signed by Mary Cooper or by the treasurer of Connor Cosmetics, John Winters. Ms. Cooper receives the canceled checks and bank statements. She reconciles the branch account herself and files canceled checks and bank statements in her records. She also periodically prepares reports of disbursements and sends them to the home office.

Required:

a. List the weaknesses in internal control for each of the above.
b. For each weakness, state the type of error(s) that is (are) likely to result. Be as specific as possible.
c. How would you improve each of the three systems?   (AICPA adapted)

7–35. Charting, Inc., a new audit client of yours, processes its sales and cash receipts documents in the following manner:

a. *Cash receipts.* The mail is opened each morning by a mail clerk in the sales department. The mail clerk prepares a remittance advice (showing customer and amount paid) if one is not received. The checks and remittance advices are then forwarded to the sales department supervisor, who reviews each check and forwards the checks and remittance advices to the accounting department supervisor. The accounting department supervisor, who also functions as the credit manager, reviews all checks for payments of past due accounts and then forwards the checks and remittance advices to the accounts receivable clerk, who arranges the advices in alphabetical order. The remittance advices are posted directly to the accounts receivable ledger cards. The checks are endorsed by stamp and totaled. The total is posted to the cash receipts journal. The remittance advices are filed chronologically.

   After receiving the cash from the preceding day's cash sales, the accounts receivable clerk prepares the daily deposit slip in triplicate. The third copy of the deposit slip is filed by date, and the second copy and the original accompany the bank deposit.

b. *Sales.* Salesclerks prepare the sales invoices in triplicate. The original and the second copy are presented to the cashier. The third copy is retained by the salesclerk in the sales book. When the sale is for cash, the customer pays the salesclerk, who presents the money to the cashier with the invoice copies.

   A credit sale is approved by the cashier from an approved credit list after the salesclerk prepares the three-part invoice. After receiving the cash or approved invoice, the cashier validates the original copy of the sales invoice and gives it to the customer. At the end of each day the cashier recaps the sales and cash received and forwards the cash and the second copy of all sales invoices to the accounts receivable clerk. The accounts receivable clerk balances the cash received with cash sales invoices and prepares a daily sales summary. The credit sales invoices are posted to the accounts receivable ledger, and then all invoices are sent to the inventory control clerk in the sales department for posting to the inventory control catalog. After posting, the inventory control clerk files all invoices numerically. The accounts receivable clerk posts the daily sales summary to the cash receipts journal and sales journal and files the sales summaries by date.

The cash from cash sales is combined with the cash received on account, and this constitutes the daily bank deposit.

c. *Bank deposits.* The bank validates the deposit slip and returns the second copy to the accounting department where it is filed by date by the accounts receivable clerk.

Monthly bank statements are reconciled promptly by the accounting department supervisor and filed by date.

Required:

a. Flowchart the sales and cash receipts functions for Charting, Inc., using good form. Include the segregation of duties.
b. List the most important weaknesses in the system.
c. For each weakness, identify the type of error that is likely to occur.

(AICPA adapted)

7–36. The town of Commuter Park operates a private parking lot near the railroad station for the benefit of town residents. The guard on duty issues annual prenumbered parking stickers to residents, who submit an application form and show evidence of residency. The sticker is affixed to the auto and allows the resident to park anywhere in the lot for 12 hours if four quarters are placed in the parking meter. Applications are maintained in the guard office at the lot. The guard checks to see that only residents are using the lot and that no resident has parked without paying the required meter fee.

Once a week the guard on duty, who has a master key for all meters, takes the coins from the meters and places them in a locked steel box. The guard delivers the box to the town storage building, where it is opened, and the coins are manually counted by a storage department clerk, who records the total cash counted on a "Weekly Cash Report." This report is sent to the town accounting department. The storage department clerk puts the cash in a safe and on the following day the cash is picked up by the town's treasurer, who manually recounts the cash, prepares the bank deposit slip, and delivers the deposit to the bank. The deposit slip, authenticated by the bank teller, is sent to the accounting department, where it is filed with the "Weekly Cash Report."

Required:

Describe weaknesses in the existing system and recommend one or more improvements for each of the weaknesses to strengthen the internal control over the parking lot cash receipts.

Organize your answer sheet as follows:

Weakness	*Recommended Improvement(s)*

(AICPA)

7–37. Anthony, CPA, prepared the accompanying flowchart (page 254), which portrays the raw materials purchasing function of one of Anthony's clients, a medium-sized manufacturing company, from the preparation of initial documents through the vouching of invoices for payment in accounts payable. The flowchart was a portion of the work performed on the audit engagement to evaluate internal control.

Required:

Identify and explain the systems and control weaknesses evident from the flowchart. Include the internal control weaknesses resulting from activities performed or not performed. All documents are prenumbered.

(AICPA adapted)

7–38. The partially completed charge sales systems flowchart (page 255) shown depicts the charge sales activities of the Bottom Manufacturing Corporation. A customer's purchase order is received and a six-part sales order is prepared therefrom. The six copies are initially distributed as follows:

- Copy 1—Billing copy—to billing department.
- Copy 2—Shipping copy—to shipping department.
- Copy 3—Credit copy—to credit department.
- Copy 4—Stock request copy—to credit department.
- Copy 5—Customer copy—to customer.
- Copy 6—Sales order copy—file in sales order department.

When each copy of the sales order reaches the applicable department or destination, it calls for specific internal control procedures and related documents. Some of the procedures and related documents are indicated on the flowchart. Other procedures and documents are labeled letters a to r.

Required:

List the procedures or the internal documents that are labeled letters c to r in the flowchart of Bottom Manufacturing Corporation's charge sales system. Organize your answer as follows (note that an explanation of the letters a and b which appear in the flowchart are entered as examples):

Flowchart Symbol Letter	Procedures or Internal Document
a.	Prepare six-part sales order.
b.	File by order number.

(AICPA)

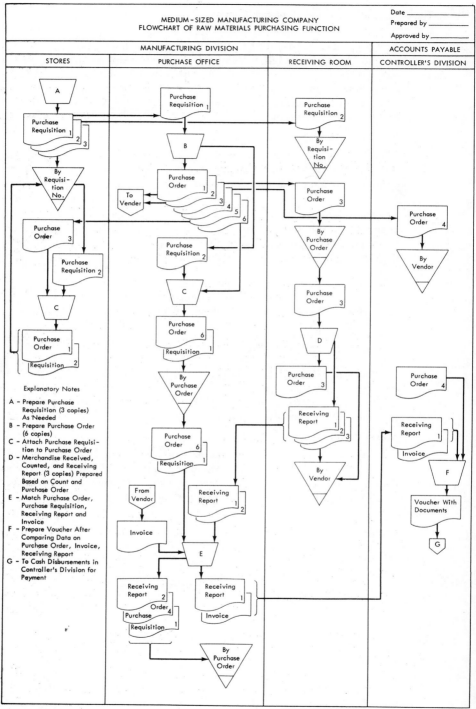

MEDIUM – SIZED MANUFACTURING COMPANY
FLOWCHART OF RAW MATERIALS PURCHASING FUNCTION

Date _____
Prepared by _____
Approved by _____

MANUFACTURING DIVISION			ACCOUNTS PAYABLE
STORES	PURCHASE OFFICE	RECEIVING ROOM	CONTROLLER'S DIVISION

Explanatory Notes

A – Prepare Purchase Requisition (3 copies) As Needed
B – Prepare Purchase Order (6 copies)
C – Attach Purchase Requisition to Purchase Order
D – Merchandise Received, Counted, and Receiving Report (3 copies) Prepared Based on Count and Purchase Order
E – Match Purchase Order, Purchase Requisition, Receiving Report and Invoice
F – Prepare Voucher After Comparing Data on Purchase Order, Invoice, Receiving Report
G – To Cash Disbursements in Controller's Division for Payment

QUESTION 7–37

254

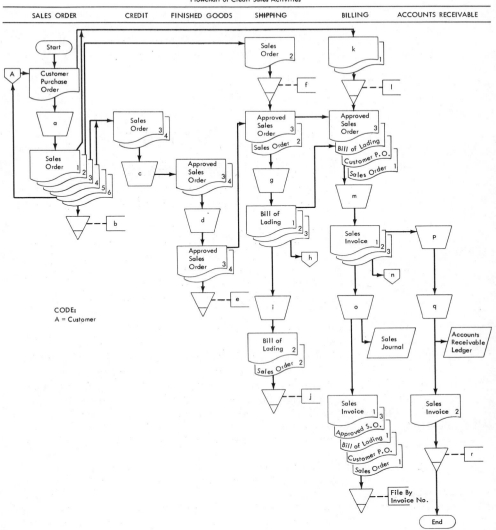

BOTTOM MANUFACTURING CORPORATION
Flowchart of Credit Sales Activities

SALES ORDER   CREDIT   FINISHED GOODS   SHIPPING   BILLING   ACCOUNTS RECEIVABLE

CODE:
A = Customer

QUESTION 7-38

8

NATURE
OF AUDIT TESTS

In this chapter there is a transition from the general concepts that apply to all aspects of the audit to the accumulation of evidence for specific transaction cycles. In making this transition, it is essential to understand certain terms and to have a thorough knowledge of basic evidence accumulation concepts. The following main topics are included in this chapter as a means of accomplishing the transition:

- Types of audit tests.
- A framework for determining audit procedures for tests of transactions.
- A framework for determining audit procedures for direct tests of financial balances.
- An integration of the different parts of the audit.

TYPES OF AUDIT TESTS

Auditing students often misunderstand the distinction between the terminology used in the professional literature for the purpose of discussing the important concepts of evidence accumulation and the terminology used by auditors in actually conducting audit tests. It is important to be able to distinguish between the two sets of terminology, and it is also necessary to understand the purpose of each type of test and the interrelationships of the different types of tests. Three types of audit tests are commonly discussed in the professional literature:

- Analytical review procedures.
- Tests of compliance with the system of internal control.
- Tests for substantive verification of financial statement balances.

Four types of audit tests are commonly referred to in the actual conduct of audits:

- Analytical tests
- Observations
- Tests of transactions
- Direct tests of balances

Types of Tests—Professional Literature

Analytical Review Procedures. These are the general tests discussed in Chapter 6, which include *ratios and trend analysis* for comparison with previous years and with industry standards. These tests are meant to aid the auditor in understanding the client's business better and in identifying areas where more intensive investigation may be needed. When the analytical review procedures show a significant deviation from the auditor's expectations, follow-up with one of the other types of tests is necessary. SAS 23 defines analytical review procedures as substantive tests.

Compliance Tests. These tests are audit procedures designed to verify whether the client's controls are being applied in the manner described in the flowchart and internal questionnaire. If, after the tests, the auditor believes the client's controls are operating effectively, he is justified in placing reliance upon the system and thereby reducing the substantive tests. Compliance tests are concerned primarily with three aspects of the client's controls:

- *The Frequency with Which the Necessary Control Procedures Are Performed.* Before controls can be relied upon to reduce substantive testing, the prescribed procedures in the system must be consistently complied with. An example of a compliance test is the examination of a sample of duplicate sales invoices to determine whether each one has been initialed for the approval of credit.
- *The Quality of the Performance of the Control Procedure.* Even if a control procedure has been performed, it may not necessarily have been done properly. Quality of performance of a procedure can be tested, for example, by discussing with the credit manager the criteria used in deciding when credit sales should be approved and examining the details of approval documents for exceptions.
- *The Person Performing the Procedures.* The individual responsible for a control procedure must be independent of incompatible functions if the control is to be effective. This is accomplished by segregation of duties. An example is the segregation of duties between the handling of cash receipts and the recording of the transactions in the cash receipts journal and subsidiary accounts receivable ledger. Initials on documents can be inspected to determine who performed such procedures.

The client's control procedures can be conveniently divided into two types: those that leave a visual indication of having been performed (*an audit trail*) and those that do not. Examples of the former are the initials of an employee verifying the price and extensions on sales invoices, an internal auditor's initial indicating he has reviewed a bank reconciliation, and the signature of an authorized employee approving credit. The most likely control where no audit trail is available is the segregation of duties. An example is the opening of mail and the prelisting of cash receipts by an employee who does not prepare the cash receipts records.

When the auditor plans to rely upon a control that leaves an audit trail, it is usually tested for compliance by examining underlying documentation. For example, if the assistant credit manager approves sales returns and allowances, the auditor should discuss with him the criteria he uses to grant credit memos to determine if they are consistent with company policy and then test a sample of returns and allowances for missing approvals.

In testing compliance for the segregation of duties, documents and records are usually not available for the auditor's examination. In those instances it is necessary to make inquiries of personnel and observe the procedures as they are being performed to evaluate compliance. For example, a compliance test of the segregation of duties between the custody of cash and the recording of cash receipts can be accomplished by asking each person to describe his duties. During the audit the auditor should also observe who receives and deposits cash and who prepares cash receipts journal records.

Substantive Tests. A substantive test is a procedure designed to *test for dollar errors* directly affecting the fair presentation of financial statement balances. Such errors (often termed *monetary errors*) are a clear indication of the misstatement of the accounts. The only question the auditor must resolve is whether the errors are sufficiently material to require adjustment or disclosure. Examples of substantive tests are the comparison of a duplicate sales invoice with a shipping document to determine whether the quantity shipped equals the quantity billed, the footing of a duplicate sales invoice for accuracy, and the confirmation of customers' accounts receivable.

Relationship between Compliance and Substantive Tests. To better understand the nature of compliance and substantive tests, an examination of their differences is useful. Compliance tests differ from substantive tests in that an error in a compliance test is only an indication of the *likelihood* of errors affecting the dollar value of the financial statements. Compliance errors are material only if they occur with sufficient frequency to cause the auditor to believe there may be material dollar errors in the statements. Substantive tests should then be performed to determine whether *dollar errors have actually occurred*. As an illustration, assume the client's system requires an independent clerk to verify the quantity, price, and extension of each sales invoice, after which he must initial the duplicate invoice to indicate performance. A compliance audit procedure would be to examine a sample of duplicate sales invoices for the initials of the person who verified the quantitative data. If there are a significant number of documents without a signature, the auditor should follow this up with substantive tests. This can be done by extending the test of the duplicate sales invoices to include verifying prices, extensions, and footings or by increasing the sample size for the confirmation of accounts receivable. Of course, even though the compliance procedure is not operating effectively, the actual invoices may be correct. This will be the result if the person originally preparing the sales invoices did a conscientious and competent job.

There are two circumstances in which the auditor may decide not to perform compliance tests on a particular control in the system:

- *He concludes that the control procedure is not effective.* For example, if a person performing internal verification is incompetent or not independent, the control procedure would not be tested. The justification for not testing is that there is no reason to test a control the auditor considers too ineffective to rely upon.
- *When the audit cost required to test for compliance is greater than the cost savings from reduced substantive tests that would result from relying upon the client's controls.* An example is in the tests of sales invoices discussed in the preceding paragraph. The auditor could simply ignore the initials of the individual who had verified the calculations and act as if no internal verification had taken place. Naturally, substantive tests would have to be increased accordingly.

Even if the auditor's compliance tests yield good results, some substantive tests are necessary. It would be inappropriate, for example, to limit the testing of duplicate sales invoices to examining the initials of a person who has performed internal verification. The presence of the initials is some evidence of clerical accuracy, but additional assurance is needed. Even if a control procedure exists, errors are still possible if the procedure is performed improperly. The audit procedures, sample size, selection of the items for testing, and timing of substantive tests can be modified and reduced by compliance tests, but they cannot be eliminated.

Types of Tests—Conduct of the Audit

The preceding discussion of the three methods of verifying financial statement information is useful as a means of understanding the relationship between the review and evaluation of internal control and the rest of the audit, but it is an inadequate description of the way audits are actually conducted. There are specific audit procedures that are easily identified as tests of overall reasonableness, but there are few if any tests that are used solely for compliance or substantive testing. Instead, most other procedures accomplish both objectives simultaneously (commonly referred to as *dual-purpose tests*). The four types of tests actually used in conducting audits will now be examined.

Analytical Tests. These are the same as analytical review procedures previously discussed in this and other chapters.

Observations.   These are the observations of activities in the client's organization to test compliance with the client's system of internal control. Such an observation could be a tour of the data-processing facility for the purpose of determining whether tapes and disks are properly safeguarded and programmers prohibited from operating the computer. Similarly, watching an individual do a bank reconciliation to determine who is doing it and when it is being performed is a test of the client's control procedures. Observations are compliance tests to determine the effectiveness of the client's system.

Tests of Transactions.   The purpose of tests of transactions is to determine whether individual transactions are *correctly recorded and summarized* in the journals, subsidiary records, and general ledger. Being correctly recorded and summarized refers to meeting the eight detailed internal control objectives identified in Chapter 7. For example, in tests of sales transactions, the auditor is concerned that recorded sales transactions were *reasonable, valid, authorized, properly valued, correctly classified, recorded on a timely basis,* and *correctly summarized and posted* to the accounts receivable subsidiary ledger and general ledger. The auditor is also concerned that actual sales transactions were recorded.

The primary purpose of tests of transactions is to verify the effectiveness of the client's system of internal control. This is compliance testing. When the auditor determines that the system is effective, it is then possible to reduce substantive tests.

Tests of transactions are also used for substantive testing. For example, assume an accounting clerk stamps a vendor's invoice after he has tested the document for clerical accuracy, proper classification in the purchases journal, and consistency with supporting documentation. A compliance test is performed by examining the invoice for the initials of the accounting clerk, and a substantive test is accomplished by actually performing the same procedures that were done by the clerk to determine if monetary errors exist. If the clerk's initials are on all the invoices, and the auditor believes the clerk is independent and competent, the substantive tests can be greatly reduced but they cannot be eliminated. In virtually all tests of transactions, some substantive testing is performed simultaneously with compliance testing (*dual-purpose tests*).

A problem the auditor faces with dual-purpose tests is the impact of compliance tests of transactions on substantive tests of transactions. If the compliance test indicates that the control is effective, it is possible to reduce the substantive tests. But since both types of tests are normally performed simultaneously (dual-purpose tests), how can compliance tests influence substantive tests? The auditor solves the problem by designing the substantive tests under the assumption that the compliance tests will indicate that the controls are effective. If the compliance tests show that the controls are actually ineffective, additional substantive tests of transactions or other substantive tests will need to be performed.

Direct Tests of Balances. The auditor does direct tests of balances by obtaining and verifying the details of ending balances in specific accounts in the general ledger.

For example, accounts receivable is made up of the subsidiary account balances of individual customers. The usual approach is to obtain a list of customers with the balance due from each customer at a point in time (*"a trial balance of accounts receivable"*), reconcile the total with the general ledger, and directly confirm the balances with customers. The same basic approach is used for accounts such as notes receivable and accounts payable.

Direct tests of balances are primarily concerned with monetary errors in accounts. They therefore can be considered primarily substantive tests. Yet, whenever an error is discovered in a test, the auditor investigates the cause of the error with special emphasis on the control breakdown that permitted the error. Thus, these audit procedures also have a compliance aspect.

Since direct tests of balances are directly concerned with the balances on the financial statements, they are essential to the audit and are used extensively in all engagements.

It is important to distinguish between tests of transactions and direct tests of balances. The important distinction is that tests of transactions concern *classes of transactions* such as cash receipts, payroll, and acquisitions, whereas direct tests of balances concern individual accounts such as accounts receivable, inventory, notes payable, and depreciation expense. An example follows to clarify that distinction.

The example is taken from Figure 9-6 on page 303 which includes sales and accounts receivable from the sales and collection cycle.

> The tests of transactions are done to test the effectiveness of the system of recording sales transactions. Following are seven tests of transactions audit procedures the auditor might perform to test the effectiveness of the system.
>
> - Examine customer order for an indication of credit approval (compliance).
> - Compare sales invoice copy 4 to the sales order as to product description and quantity (substantive) and attachment of order to invoice (compliance).
> - Compare unit selling price on sales invoice copy 3 to an approved price list (substantive).
> - Compare sales invoice copy 3 to bill of lading copy 3 for name, quantity, and date (substantive).
> - Account for a sequence of sales invoice copy 3 (compliance).
> - Compare name, amount, and date on sales invoice copy 3 to the sales journal and subsidiary ledger (substantive).
> - Foot the sales journal and trace the balance to the general ledger (substantive).
>
> Assuming that the system is considered effective after the tests of transactions, the auditor should have achieved a certain level of assurance through the tests of transactions. Following are some of the typical direct tests of balances that concern the ending balance in accounts receivable.

- Obtain a trial balance of accounts receivable from the client, foot the list, and trace the balance to the general ledger (substantive).
- Compare individual amounts on the trial balance to the related subsidiary ledger for customer name and balance (substantive).
- Select a sample of accounts from the trial balance and send confirmations directly to customers (substantive).
- Examine the credit file for a sample of receivables to see whether one exists, as a basis for evaluating the collectibility of accounts receivable (compliance).

In addition, the auditor is likely to do analytical tests of both sales and collections. An example is to review the sales journal and accounts receivable subsidiary ledger for unusual amounts.

The matrix in Figure 8-1 summarizes the discussion of the types of audit tests.

Types of Tests — Conduct of the Audit	Types of Tests — Professional Literature		
	Analytical review procedures	Compliance with the system of internal control	Substantive verification of financial statement balances
Analytical tests	P		
Observations		P	
Tests of transactions		P	S
Direct tests of balances		S	P

P - Primary purpose of the test
S - Secondary purpose of the test

FIGURE 8–1   Matrix of Types of Audit Tests—Professional Literature and Conduct of the Audit

A FRAMEWORK—TESTS OF TRANSACTIONS

A major decision the auditor must make in every audit is the appropriate audit procedures, sample size, items to be included in the sample for testing, and timing of the tests. One of the most important conclusions that has been reached in previous chapters is the need to adapt the audit program to the unique circumstances of a particular client. For this reason, we do not believe there is such a thing as a single audit program. In this section we are concerned with establishing a framework to aid in developing a tailor-made audit program for performing tests of transactions that will permit the auditor to consider the unique circumstances of the engagement.

The approach used in this text is to establish *detailed audit objectives* that are common to every transaction cycle and use these objectives as a point of departure for deciding on the audit tests in a particular engagement. The objectives used are identical to the eight internal control objectives discussed in Chapter 7. The same objectives are used because the purpose of performing tests of transactions is to determine whether the internal controls are effective. Thus they are relevant in determining the proper evidence to accumulate to evaluate the reliability of existing controls. These eight objectives for any given audit area are listed below, together with examples of the types of errors for which the auditor is searching in each objective. The type of error that results when the objective is not satisfied is included in parentheses.

Transactions as Recorded in the Journal Are Reasonable (Any of the Other Seven Types of Errors). This objective concerns the possibility of any type of large or unusual error. There may be large sales transactions that require special scrutiny or related party transactions that must be described in the footnotes.

Recorded Transactions Are Valid (Invalid, Illegal, or Duplicate Transactions). This objective deals with the possibility of invalid transactions being included in the records. Instances include the recording of a sale when no shipment took place, or a charge-off of an uncollectible account that has actually been paid.

Transactions Are Properly Authorized (Unauthorized Transactions). If a transaction takes place without proper authorization at the key points, an improper transaction may have occurred. Examples of transactions without proper authorization include the failure to authorize shipments and the acceptance of unauthorized sales returns and allowances.

Existing Transactions Are Recorded (Omitted Transactions). An error under this objective occurs whenever the client fails to record a transaction. An example is the shipment of goods without billing or inclusion in the accounting records. This objective is the opposite of the validity of the recorded transactions objective inasmuch as it deals with existing transactions not being recorded rather than recorded transactions not being valid.

Transactions Are Properly Valued (Valuation Errors). Even though all transactions included in the records are authorized and valid, they may be stated at an incorrect amount. For the financial statements to be fairly stated, the individual transactions must be recorded at the correct amount.

As an illustration, the quantities, prices, extensions, and footings on sales invoices must be correctly stated to meet this objective, and the amount of the sale must be correctly included in the sales journal and subsidiary ledgers.

Transactions Are Properly Classified (Classification Errors). This objective deals with the possibility of a transaction in the cycle being classified improperly. Examples of misclassifications include the recording of the disposal of a permanent asset as a sale, the recording of the receipt of loan proceeds as a collection of an outstanding account receivable, the recording of a collection of an account receivable as a cash sale, and the recording of a sale to a residential customer as a commercial sale.

Transactions Are Recorded at the Proper Time (Recorded in Wrong Period). In addition to being correctly recorded, transactions must be recorded on a timely basis. The failure to record a transaction reasonably soon after its occurrence may result in including the amount in the wrong time period, especially if the transaction took place near the end of the accounting period. This is referred to as a *cutoff error*. The failure to record transactions on a timely basis can also result in the complete omission of the recording due to the loss or mishandling of the records.

Transactions Are Properly Included in the Subsidiary Records and Correctly Summarized (Footing and Posting Errors). Since the individual transactions are the source of the balances in the financial statements, they must be correctly summarized and posted to subsidiary records, the general ledger, and other reports. Although it is not difficult to perform tests to fulfill this objective, an audit is inadequate if it has not been done. A fraud error can be covered up in sales by underfooting the sales journal or posting the amounts in the journal to the general ledger incorrectly. Examples of unintentional errors are debiting a wrong general ledger account when the journals are posted or crediting a sales return to the wrong customer in the subsidiary ledger.

A FRAMEWORK—DIRECT TESTS OF FINANCIAL BALANCES

Once the tests of the system have been completed for a transaction cycle and their results evaluated, tests of the related financial statement balances are performed. These tests concentrate on the verification of the balance sheet accounts in the cycle, but income and expense accounts are also included. Tests of many balance sheet accounts relate to specific income statement accounts as well. For example, in testing accounts receivable, the auditor is also verifying sales and sales returns and allowances. However, it is also necessary to verify some of the income statement accounts directly.

When the auditor does direct tests of balances, the starting point for doing the tests is typically a list obtained from the client that ties out to the general ledger. An example is a trial balance of accounts receivable that agrees in total with the accounts receivable control account.

In completing the tests of account balances, it is desirable to set up a framework similar to the one used for tests of transactions. This procedure facilitates approaching the audit of the account balance in a logical manner without specifying a required set of inflexible audit procedures for each account balance.

The framework used to test account balances is the use of *detailed objectives for direct tests of financial balances* in the same manner as was done for tests of transactions. The detailed objectives serve both as a guide to understanding what the auditor is trying to accomplish and as an aid in developing audit programs. The nine detailed objectives for the direct tests of financial balances are examined briefly at this point. The type of error for each objective is included in parentheses.

The list referred to is the one that ties to the general ledger. To illustrate, the use of the objectives of the audit of accounts receivables is used as a frame of reference.

Amounts as Listed Are Reasonable (Any of the Other Types of Errors). Tests for overall reasonableness are intended to aid the auditor in evaluating whether the balances in the asset and related revenue accounts appear to include material errors. For accounts receivable, the auditor should compare the individual total balances of the current year with those of previous years and compute selected ratios.

Amounts as Listed Are Valid (Invalid Amounts). This objective concerns whether the amounts included are valid. The possibility of invalid accounts receivable could be verified by confirmation of accounts included in the trial balance.

Assets as Listed Are Owned (Non-Owned Items Included as Assets). In addition to existing, most assets must be owned before it is acceptable to include them in the financial statements. Naturally, this objective does not apply to the verification of liability and owner's equity accounts. Determining ownership of accounts receivable is usually not much of a problem. Examination of the minutes and confirmation is usually sufficient to inform the auditor of pledged or factored accounts receivable.

Existing Amounts Are Included on the List (Omitted Amounts). This objective concerns the possibility that all amounts that should be included have actually been included. For accounts receivable, the likelihood of an omitted receivable is small because the listing will be compared to the control account. The objective is far more important for accounts payable or inventory.

Amounts as Listed Are Properly Valued (Valuation Errors). The correct valuation of the individual balances making up the total account balance, including the arithmetic accuracy of ali calculations, is one of the concerns in this objective. Accounts receivable confirmation is the most common audit test for valuation. A second aspect of valuation as it relates to many asset balances is determining whether the overall balance is stated at its realizable value. For example, in accounts receivable, this requires the auditor to satisfy himself that the allowance for uncollectible accounts is reasonably stated, since it is a valuation account relating to accounts receivable.

Amounts in the Trial Balance Are Properly Classified (Classification Errors). Classification in balance sheet accounts involves determining whether amounts are separated as to short-term and long-term assets and amounts due from affiliates, officers, and directors are separated from amounts due from customers. In accounts receivable, the auditor would require the receivables listing for such things as related party, interest-bearing, and noncurrent receivables.

Transactions Near the Balance Sheet Date Are Recorded in the Proper Period (Cutoff Errors). In testing for cutoff, the objective is to determine whether transactions are recorded in the proper period. The transactions that are most likely to be misstated are those recorded near the end of the accounting period. It is proper to think of cutoff tests as a part of verifying either the balance sheet accounts or the selected revenue and expense accounts, but for convenience auditors usually perform them as a part of auditing balance sheet accounts. In account receivables, auditors could test the cutoff for sales, cash receipts, and sales returns and allowances.

Details in the List Agree with Related Subsidiary Ledger Amounts, Foot to the Total in the List and Agree to the Total in the General Ledger (Footing or Reconciliation Errors). The auditor is verifying that the detail from which the list supposedly comes actually corresponds to the list. For accounts receivable, the auditor would compare individual amounts on the list to the subsidiary ledger, foot the list, and trace the total to the general ledger.

Account Balance and Related Disclosure Requirements Are Properly Disclosed on the Financial Statements (Disclosure Errors). In fulfilling the disclosure objective, the auditor tests to make certain that all balance sheet and income statement accounts are correctly set forth in the financial statements and properly described in the body and footnotes of the statements. In accounts receivable, the receivables balance, allowance, and any liens on receivables must be disclosed.

Audit Procedures for Each Objective

A thorough understanding of the detailed audit objectives for internal control, tests of transactions, and direct tests of financial balances is essential to the development of adequate audit programs. If an auditor clearly understands the audit objectives, it is relatively easy to develop a tailor-made audit program that takes into account the available evidence, the strengths and weaknesses in the internal control system, and the special circumstances in the audit.

In designing audit procedures to satisfy the audit objectives for any given account, several key points should be kept in mind:

- A given audit procedure is likely to fulfill more than one objective. The objectives are kept separate at this point to provide a better understanding of the purpose of the procedures. This text often refers to the same audit procedure several times. This repetition does not mean the auditor will perform the procedure more than once, but rather that multiple objectives are met.
- More than one procedure is frequently necessary to satisfactorily verify any given objective. The procedures tend to complement each other, but in some instances they may be substitutes.
- The appropriate procedures for the audit of any audit area depend upon all of the circumstances of the audit discussed in previous chapters, but special emphasis is put on internal control.
- It is relatively easy to combine the objectives and procedures into an audit program after the auditor has decided on the proper tests in a given audit area.

To summarize the audit objectives, Figure 8-2 shows the detailed audit objectives for a typical audit of acquisitions of inventory (tests of transactions) and the related tests of the inventory balance (direct tests of financial balances). In the example it is assumed that acquisitions of inventory are recorded in the acquisitions or purchases journal. The ending balance of inventory is determined by a physical count, after which the inventory is costed, extended, and totaled. The general ledger is adjusted to reflect the inventory total.

It is important to note two things:

- The objectives for internal control and tests of transactions are identical.
- The objectives for tests of transactions and direct tests of balances are nearly the same. The major differences are that the tests of transactions objectives refer to transactions and the direct tests refer to the actual inventory on hand and the list of inventory that reflects the actual inventory.

INTEGRATION OF THE DIFFERENT PARTS OF THE AUDIT

At this point it is appropriate to summarize the concepts discussed in previous chapters to facilitate an understanding of how the entire audit ties together in an integrated process. Figure 8-3 presents a summary of the overview of the audit process.

There are four phases to the process:

FIGURE 8–2

Internal Control, Tests of Transactions, and Direct Tests of Financial
Balances Objectives Illustrated for Acquisitions of Inventory

Internal Control Objectives	Tests of Transactions Objectives	Direct Tests of Financial Balances Objectives
• Acquisition transactions as recorded in the journal are reasonable.	• Acquisition transactions as recorded in the journal are reasonable.	• Inventory as listed in the inventory listing is reasonable.
• Recorded acquisitions are for goods and services received, in the best interests of the client.	• Recorded acquisitions are for goods and services received, in the best interests of the client.	• The inventory on the listing actually exists.
• Acquisition transactions are authorized.	• Acquisition transactions are authorized.	• The inventory on the listing is owned.
• Existing acquisition transactions are recorded.	• Existing acquisition transactions are recorded.	• Existing inventory is included in the inventory list.
• Recorded acquisition transactions are correctly valued.	• Recorded acquisition transactions are correctly valued.	• The inventory on the listing is correctly valued as to quantity, unit price, extensions, and realizable value.
• Acquisition transactions are properly classified.	• Acquisition transactions are properly classified.	• The inventory on the listing is properly classified as to raw material, work in process, and finished goods.
• Acquisitions are recorded on a timely basis.	• Acquisitions are recorded on a timely basis.	• The inventory cutoff is correct.
• Acquisition transactions are properly included in the accounts payable subsidiaries; they are correctly summarized.	• Acquisition transactions are properly included in the accounts payable subsidiaries; they are correctly summarized.	• The inventory on the listing is correctly totaled and agrees with the general ledger.
		• Inventory and related liabilities are properly disclosed on the financial statements.

Phase I: Planning and Designing an Audit Approach

In this phase the auditor is obtaining information and deciding on the most efficient way to complete the engagement within the time deadline. There are five parts to this phase.

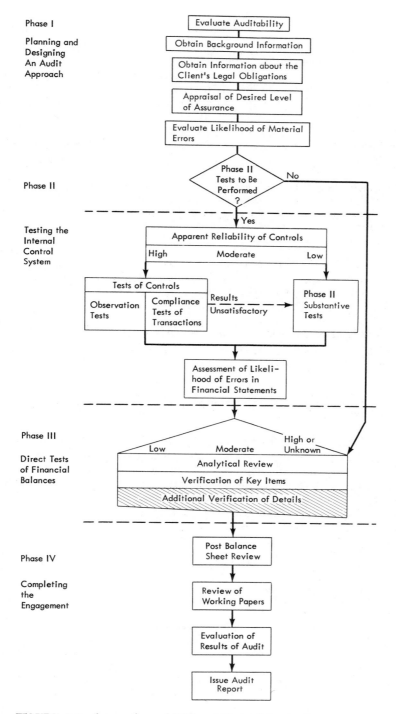

Phase I

Planning and Designing An Audit Approach

Evaluate Auditability

Obtain Background Information

Obtain Information about the Client's Legal Obligations

Appraisal of Desired Level of Assurance

Evaluate Likelihood of Material Errors

Phase II

Phase II Tests to Be Performed ? — No

Yes

Testing the Internal Control System

Apparent Reliability of Controls

High · Moderate · Low

Tests of Controls

Observation Tests · Compliance Tests of Transactions

Results Unsatisfactory

Phase II Substantive Tests

Assessment of Likelihood of Errors in Financial Statements

Phase III

Direct Tests of Financial Balances

Low · Moderate · High or Unknown

Analytical Review

Verification of Key Items

Additional Verification of Details

Phase IV

Completing the Engagement

Post Balance Sheet Review

Review of Working Papers

Evaluation of Results of Audit

Issue Audit Report

FIGURE 8–3 Interactions of Different Parts of the Audit

Evaluate Auditability. The auditor may decide not to do the audit because of the potential for management fraud, the likelihood of bankruptcy, or an inadequate system of internal control. Although this is the first step, the decision not to do the audit can take place later when more information is obtained.

Obtain Background Information. Several aspects of obtaining knowledge about the engagement were discussed in Chapter 6, including:

- Obtain an engagement letter.
- Obtain knowledge of the client's industry and business.
- Tour the plant and offices.
- Review permanent and current working paper files.
- Identify related parties.

Obtain Information about the Client's Legal Obligations. Chapter 6 also discussed obtaining information about government requirements pertaining to the client, the corporate charter and bylaws, minutes of directors, and contracts.

Appraisal of Desired Level of Assurance. Chapter 5 included a discussion of how sure the auditor needs to be, after the audit was finished, that there were no material errors in the statements. Two factors affect that decision:

- The degree to which external users rely upon the statements.
- The likelihood of the client's filing bankruptcy subsequent to the audit.

Evaluate Likelihood of Material Errors. Chapter 5 also included a discussion of the importance of evaluating where material errors were most likely to exist for a given client. This part of the phase includes the evaluation of internal control as discussed in Chapter 6. The following are the most important factors affecting the auditor's expectation of errors:

- System of internal control
- Materiality
- Population size
- Makeup of the population
- Initial versus repeat engagement
- Results of the current and previous audits
- Integrity of management

At the completion of phase I, several major decisions should have been made. They are subject to revision as the engagement progresses.

- The planned degree of reliance on internal controls.
- The planned extent of substantive tests in phases II and III.
- The timing of all audit procedures and intended completion date of the engagement.

- The size of the audit team needed and the allocation of the work among the team.
- The extent to which firm specialists such as computer audit or industry specialists are needed (either from within the firm or external).
- The degree to which related services such as management services and taxes are to be provided.

Phase II: Testing the Internal Control System

The objective of phase II is to evaluate the effectiveness of the internal controls the auditor plans to rely on. The controls are tested by observation and compliance tests of transactions. At the same time the compliance tests of transactions are being done, some substantive tests (tests of transactions) are also performed. They are done at this point to maximize audit efficiency. When the controls are not considered effective, substantive tests of transactions can be expanded in this phase or in phase III.

At the completion of phase II, the auditor will have more information about the expectation of errors. If the controls are considered effective, direct tests of balances can be reduced.

Phase III: Direct Tests of Financial Balances

The objective of phase III is to obtain sufficient additional evidence to determine whether the ending balances and footnotes in financial statements are fairly stated. The nature and extent of the work will depend heavily on the findings of the two previous phases.

There are two general categories of phase III procedures—analytical and detailed. Analytical procedures are those which assess the overall reasonableness of transactions and balances. Detailed procedures are intended to test primarily for monetary errors in the balances in the financial statements. Certain key transactions and amounts are so important that each one must be audited. Other items can be sampled.

Phase IV: Completing the Engagement

After the first three phases are completed, it is necessary to summarize the results and issue the audit report. There are four main parts to this phase:

Post-Balance-Sheet Review. Occasionally, events occurring subsequent to the balance sheet date but before the issuance of the financial statements and auditor's report will have an effect on the information presented in the financial statements. Specific review procedures are designed to bring to the auditor's attention any subsequent events that may require recognition in the financial statements. Post-balance-sheet review is studied in Chapter 20.

Review of Working Papers. The review of working papers by persons more experienced than the original preparer is important to uncover mistakes and evaluate the judgments and conclusions of the preparer. Adequate working paper review is an essential way to assure quality performance and independent judgments by the entire audit team.

Evaluation of Results of Audit. At this point the engagement partner evaluates the results of the audit and decides whether sufficient evidence has been accumulated.

Issue Audit Report. The final step in Phase IV is to issue the appropriate audit report, given the evidence accumulated and the audit findings.

REVIEW QUESTIONS

8-1. State and explain the three aspects of the client's controls that compliance tests are designed to evaluate.

8-2. Distinguish between a compliance test and a substantive test of transactions. Give two examples of each.

8-3. Distinguish between a compliance test and a substantive test of account balances. Give two examples of each.

8-4. Distinguish between tests of transactions and direct tests of balances.

8-5. A considerable portion of the compliance and substantive tests of transactions are performed simultaneously as a matter of audit convenience. But the substantive tests of transaction procedures and sample size are in part dependent upon the results of the compliance tests. How can the auditor resolve this apparent inconsistency?

8-6. Evaluate the following statement: "Observations of people by an auditor are a waste of time. It is unreasonable to expect anyone to behave in a normal manner when they know the auditor is watching what they do. People will perform properly when the auditor is around and the auditor will make incorrect inferences about their normal behavior."

8-7. Explain what is meant by a dual-purpose test. Give an example of one.

8-8. Explain the difference between a control procedure that leaves an audit trail and one that does not. Give one example of each. For each example, state a compliance procedure to test the effectiveness of the control.

8-9. Evaluate the following statement: "Tests of sales and collection transactions are such an essential part of every audit that I like to perform them as near the end of the audit as possible. By that time I have a fairly good understanding of the client's business and internal controls because confirmations, cutoff tests, and other procedures have already been completed."

8-10. State the relationship between the preliminary evaluation of an internal control system and tests of compliance.

8-11. In testing sales transactions using the framework developed in this chapter, explain the difference between these two objectives: "recorded transactions are valid" and "existing transactions are recorded." State one audit procedure that could be used to test each of these objectives.

8–12. An auditor is testing the purchases of raw material transactions by examining vendors' invoices, purchase orders, and receiving reports. Which of the documents would be the most important as a test of whether the recorded transaction is properly authorized? Which would be most important to test for the valuation objective? Which would be most important to test for the proper timing objective?

8–13. Explain how the calculation and comparison to previous years of the gross margin percent and the ratio of accounts receivable to sales is related to the confirmation of accounts receivable and other tests of the accuracy of accounts receivable.

8–14. List the circumstances under which it is acceptable to limit the tests of transactions to an interim date.

8–15. "Most of my clients have only two or three people in the entire office staff, including bookkeepers and secretaries; therefore, internal control is virtually nonexistent. My approach to auditing is not to rely on the system of internal control. I don't perform tests of transactions, but I compensate for it by extensively testing the ending balances in all balance sheet accounts." Evaluate these comments.

8–16. List the nine valuation objectives in the verification of the ending balance in inventory, and provide one useful audit procedure for each of the objectives.

8–17. Compare and contrast internal control objectives, tests of transaction objectives and direct tests of financial balances objectives.

8–18. Explain what is meant by a complementary and a substitutability relationship among analytical tests, compliance tests, and substantive tests.

8–19. Identify the four phases to an audit. What are the most important components of each phase?

DISCUSSION QUESTIONS AND PROBLEMS

8–20. The following questions deal with audit tests. Choose the best response.
　a. Which of the following statements relating to compliance tests is most accurate?
　　(1) Auditing procedures cannot concurrently provide both evidence of compliance with accounting control procedures and evidence required for substantive tests.
　　(2) Compliance tests include physical observations of the proper segregation of duties which ordinarily may be limited to the normal audit period.
　　(3) Compliance tests should be based upon proper application of an appropriate statistical sampling plan.
　　(4) Compliance tests ordinarily should be performed as of the balance sheet date or during the period subsequent to that date.
　b. The primary purpose of tests of compliance is to provide reasonable assurance that

(1) the accounting and administrative control procedures are adequately designed to assure employee compliance therewith.

(2) the accounting and administrative control procedures are being applied as prescribed.

(3) the administrative control procedures are being applied as prescribed.

(4) the accounting control procedures are being applied as prescribed.

c. The auditor looks for an indication on punched cards to see if the cards have been verified. This is an example of a

    (1) substantive test.

    (2) compliance test.

    (3) transactions test.

    (4) dual-purpose test.

d. The two phases of the auditor's study of internal accounting control are referred to as "review of the system" and "tests of compliance." In the tests of compliance phase, the auditor attempts to

(1) obtain a reasonable degree of assurance that the client's system of controls is in use and is operating as planned.

(2) obtain sufficient, competent evidential matter to afford a reasonable basis for the auditor's opinion.

(3) obtain assurances that informative disclosures in the financial statements are reasonably adequate.

(4) obtain knowledge and understanding of the client's prescribed procedures and methods.

e. Before relying on the system of internal control, the auditor obtains a reasonable degree of assurance that the internal control procedures are in use and operating as planned. The auditor obtains this assurance by performing

    (1) substantive tests.

    (2) transaction tests.

    (3) compliance tests.

    (4) tests of trends and ratios.   (AICPA adapted)

8–21. The following questions concern analytical tests. Choose the best response.

a. One reason why the independent auditor makes an analytic review of the client's operations is to identify

(1) weaknesses of a material nature in the system of internal control.

(2) noncompliance with prescribed control procedures.

(3) improper separation of accounting and other financial duties.

(4) unusual transactions.

b. Which of the following situations has the best chance of being detected when a CPA compares 1976 revenues and expenses with the prior year and investigates all changes exceeding a fixed percentage?

(1) An increase in property tax rates has not been recognized in the company's 1976 accrual.

(2) The cashier began lapping accounts receivable in 1976.

(3) Because of worsening economic conditions, the 1976 provision for uncollectible accounts was inadequate.

(4) The company changed its capitalization policy for small tools in 1976.

    c. An auditor uses analytical review during the course of an audit. The most important phase of this review is the
       (1) computation of key ratios such as inventory turnover and gross profit percentages.
       (2) investigation of significant variations and unusual relationships.
       (3) comparison of client-computed statistics with industry data on a quarterly and full-year basis.
       (4) examination of the client data that generated the statistics that are analyzed. (AICPA adapted)

8–22. Indicate whether each of the eleven audit procedures listed below is (1) an analytical test, (2) a compliance test, or (3) a substantive test. Also indicate whether it is (4) an observation, (5) a test of transactions, or (6) a direct test of account balances.
    a. Foot the trial balance of accounts payable and compare the total with the general ledger.
    b. Examine vendors' invoices to verify the ending balance in accounts payable.
    c. Compare the balance in payroll tax expense with previous years. The comparison takes the increase in payroll tax rates into account.
    d. Discuss the duties of the cash disbursements bookkeeper with him and observe whether he has responsibility for handling cash or preparing the bank reconciliation.
    e. Confirm accounts payable balances directly with vendors.
    f. Account for a sequence of checks in the cash disbursements journal to determine whether any have been omitted.
    g. Examine the internal auditor's initials on monthly bank reconciliations as an indication of whether they have been reviewed.
    h. Examine vendors' invoices and other documentation in support of recorded transactions in the purchases journal.
    i. Multiply the commission rate by total sales and compare the result with commission expense.
    j. Examine vendors' invoices and other supporting documents to determine whether large amounts in the repair and maintenance account should be capitalized.
    k. Examine the initials on vendors' invoices that indicate internal verification of pricing, extending, and footing by a clerk.

8–23. The following are independent internal control procedures commonly found in the purchases and cash disbursements cycle. Each control is to be considered independently.
    a. At the end of each month an accounting clerk accounts for all pre-numbered receiving reports (documents evidencing the receipt of goods) issued during the month, and he traces each one to the related vendor's invoice and purchase journal entry. The clerk's tests do not include testing quantity or description of the merchandise received.
    b. The cash disbursements bookkeeper is prohibited from handling cash. The bank account is reconciled by another person even though the bookkeeper has sufficient expertise and time to do it.

c. Before a check is prepared to pay for purchases by the accounts payable department, the related purchase order and receiving report are attached to the vendor's invoice being paid. A clerk compares the quantity on the invoice with the receiving report and purchase order, compares the price with the purchase order, recomputes the extensions, reads the total, and examines the account number indicated on the invoice to determine whether it is properly classified. He indicates his performance of these procedures by initialing the invoice.

d. Before a check is signed by the controller, he examines the supporting documentation accompanying the check. At that time he initials each vendor's invoice to indicate his approval.

e. After the controller signs the checks, his secretary writes the check number and the date the check was issued on each of the supporting documents to prevent their reuse.

Required:

a. For each of the internal control procedures, state the internal control objective(s) the control is meant to fulfill.

b. List one compliance procedure for each control procedure the auditor could perform to test the effectiveness of the control.

c. List one substantive test for each control the auditor could perform to determine whether financial errors are actually taking place.

8–24. For each of the following controls, identify whether the control leaves an audit trial, and list a compliance procedure the auditor can use to test the effectiveness of the control.

a. An accounting clerk accounts for all shipping documents on a monthly basis.

b. The bank reconciliation is prepared by the controller, who does not have access to cash receipts.

c. As employees check in daily by using time clocks, a supervisor observes to make certain no individual "punches in" more than one time card.

d. Vendor's invoices are approved by the controller after he examines the purchase order and receiving report attached to each invoice.

e. The cashier, who has no access to accounting records, prepares the deposit slip and delivers the deposit directly to the bank on a daily basis.

f. An accounting clerk verifies the prices, extensions, and footings of all sales invoices in excess of $300 and initials the duplicate sales invoice when he has completed the procedure.

g. All mail is opened and cash is prelisted daily by the president's secretary, who has no other responsibility for handling assets or recording accounting data.

8–25. Ron Blanch, CPA, spends considerable time evaluating internal control and performing compliance tests of the system. When he identifies controls in the system that can be relied upon to reduce the likelihood of errors, he tests the controls until he is confident no significant errors are possible. At that point he performs no additional tests of any kind, since he feels he has achieved an adequate level of assurance. In several audits he has performed no substantive tests of any kind in certain areas such as accounts payable and property, plant, and equipment because of extraordinary controls in the system. Blanch feels that this approach saves time on audits with good internal control, and it enables him to concentrate on helping the client improve the effectiveness of the system.

Required:

Evaluate Blanch's approach to conducting audits. Include a discussion of both the strengths and the weaknesses in his approach.

8–26. Jennifer Schaefer, CPA, follows the philosophy of performing interim tests of transactions on every December 31 audit as a means of keeping overtime to a minimum. Typically, the interim tests are performed some time between August and November.

Required:

a. Evaluate her decision to perform interim tests of transactions.
b. Under what circumstances is it acceptable for her to perform no additional tests of transactions work as a part of the year-end audit tests?
c. If she decides to perform no additional testing, what is the effect on other tests she performs during the remainder of the engagement?

8–27. You are the in-charge accountant examining the financial statements of the Gutzler Company for the year ended December 31, 19X7. During late October 19X7, you, with the help of Gutzler's controller, completed an internal control questionnaire and prepared the appropriate memoranda describing Gutzler's accounting procedures. Your comments relative to cash receipts are as follows.

All cash receipts are sent directly to the accounts receivable clerk with no processing by the mail department. The accounts receivable clerk keeps the cash receipts journal, prepares the bank deposit slip in duplicate, posts from the deposit slip to the subsidiary accounts receivable ledger, and mails the deposit to the bank.

The controller receives the validated deposit slips directly (unopened) from the bank. He also receives the monthly bank statement directly (unopened) from the bank and promptly reconciles it.

At the end of each month, the accounts receivable clerk notifies the general ledger clerk by journal voucher of the monthly totals of the cash receipts journal for posting to the general ledger.

Each month, with regard to the general ledger cash account, the general ledger clerk makes an entry to record the total debits to cash from the cash receipts journal. In addition, the general ledger clerk on occasion makes debit entries in the general ledger cash account from sources other than the cash receipts journal (e.g., funds borrowed from the bank).

Required:

a. List the controls in the system for handling and recording cash.
b. List the weaknesses in the system.
c. For each control, list a compliance test that can be used to test the effectiveness of the system.

d. Considering Gutzler's internal control over cash receipts, list all other auditing procedures and reasons therefor which should be performed to obtain sufficient audit evidence regarding cash receipts. Do not discuss the procedures for cash disbursements and cash balances. Also do not discuss the extent to which any of the procedures are to be performed. Assume adequate controls exist to assure that all sales transactions are recorded.   (AICPA adapted)

8–28. A large portion of the audit clients of Miller and Jordan, CPAs, have a December 31 year-end. The partners would like to do more interim testing on these engagements but most of the clients are small and have relatively weak systems of internal control. The clients have been asked to consider changing to a fiscal year-end, but with minor exceptions they have resisted the change. The effect on Miller and Jordan's professional practice is heavy peak loads during the period from January 1 to April 1 and significant idle time the rest of the year. How can the CPA firm reduce this problem and still meet the standards of the profession?

9

AUDIT OF THE SALES
AND COLLECTION CYCLE

OVERVIEW

This chapter presents information on the nature of the sales and collection cycle, primary internal control considerations for the cycle, and tests of transactions procedures used for verifying sales, cash receipts, sales returns and allowances, and the charge-off of uncollectible accounts. The intent in this chapter is to emphasize the methodology for deciding on the appropriate evidence to accumulate for testing transactions in the sales and collection cycle. An illustration of an audit program for sales and cash receipts and how it was developed is included in Appendix A at the end of the chapter. Audit procedures relating to the direct tests of accounts receivable, allowance for uncollectible accounts, and bad debts expense are the subject of Chapter 11.

The overall objective in the audit of the sales and collection cycle is to evaluate whether the account balances affected by the cycle are fairly presented in accordance with generally accepted accounting principles. More specifically, the auditor determines whether the account balances are consistent with the detailed objectives identified on pages 263 and 266 for tests of transactions and direct tests of balances. The following are typical accounts included in the sales and collection cycle:

- Sales
- Sales Returns and Allowances
- Bad Debts Expense
- Trade Discounts Taken

- Trade Accounts and Notes Receivable
- Allowance for Uncollectible Accounts
- Cash in the Bank (debits for cash receipts)

The names and the nature of the accounts may of course vary depending upon the industry and client involved. There are differences in account titles for a service industry, such as medical clinics, a retail company, and an insurance company, but regardless of the industry or account titles the basic concepts are the same. To provide a frame of reference for understanding the material, a wholesale merchandising company is assumed for this chapter.

A brief summary of the way accounting information flows through the various accounts in the sales and collection cycle is illustrated by the use of T-accounts in Figure 9-1. This figure shows that with the exception of cash sales, every transaction and amount ultimately is included in the accounts receivable or allowance for doubtful accounts balances. For the purpose of simplicity the assumption is made that the same control procedures are used for both cash and credit sales.

For the most part, the audit of the sales and collection cycle can be performed independently of the audit of other cycles and subjectively combined with the other parts of the audit as the evidence accumulation process proceeds. The auditor must keep in mind that the concept of materiality requires him to consider the combination of errors in all parts of the audit before making a final judgment on the fair presentation in the financial statements. This is done by stopping at various times throughout the engagement and integrating the parts of the audit.

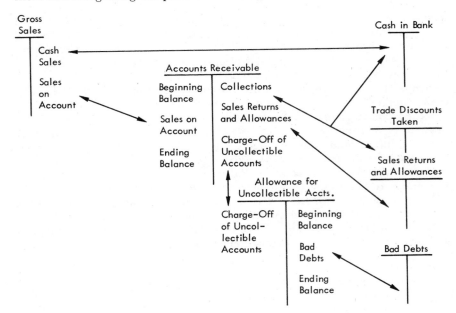

FIGURE 9-1 Accounts in the Sales and Collection Transaction Cycle

NATURE OF THE SALES AND COLLECTION CYCLE

Flow of Transactions

The sales and collection cycle involves the decisions and processes necessary for the transfer of the ownership of goods to customers after goods are made available for sale. It begins with a request for goods by a customer and ends with the conversion of material or service into an account receivable, and ultimately into cash.

The sales transaction cycle for a typical wholesale company is illustrated in Figure 9-2 with an *overview flowchart*. This type of flowchart is meant to aid readers in understanding the sales and collection function rather than to serve as a means of evaluating internal control. Therefore, it does not include all documents in the system nor all internal controls. A detailed flowchart for evaluating internal control is illustrated in Figure 9-6 on page 303.

Documents and Records

Several important documents and records are typically used in the sales and collection cycle:

Customer Order. A request for merchandise by a customer. It may be received by telephone, letter, a printed form that has been sent to prospective and existing customers, salesmen, or in other ways.

Sales Order. A document for recording the description, quantity, and related information for goods ordered by a customer. This is frequently used to show credit approval and authorization for shipment.

Bill of Lading or Other Shipping Document. A document prepared at the time of shipment, indicating the description of the merchandise, the quantity shipped, and other relevant data. Formally, it is a written contract of the receipt and shipment of goods between the seller and the carrier. It is also used as a signal to bill the customer. The original is sent to the customer and one or more copies are retained.

Sales Invoice. A document indicating the description and quantity of goods sold, the price including freight, insurance, terms, and other relevant data. It is the method of indicating to the customer the amount of a sale and due date of a payment. The original is sent to the customer and one or more copies are retained. It is also the basic document for recording sales in the accounting records.

Sales Journal. A journal for recording sales. It usually indicates gross sales for different classifications, such as product lines, the entry to

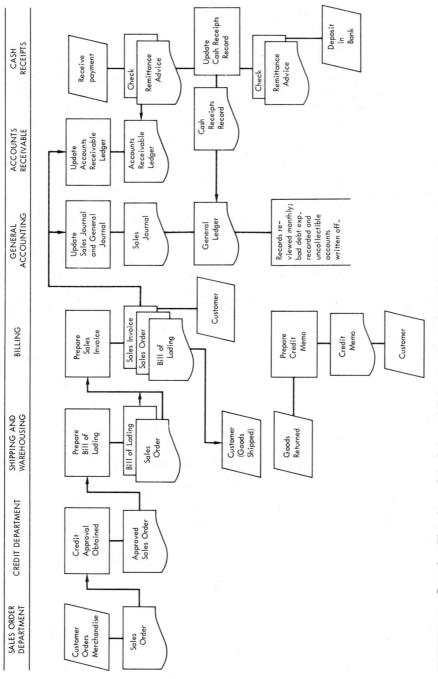

FIGURE 9-2 Overview Flowchart of the Sales and Collection Cycle of a Wholesale Company

accounts receivable, and miscellaneous debits and credits. It is common to include only daily summaries in the journals. Copies of each day's duplicate sales invoices are retained, and these copies are totaled to equal the total sales recorded in the journal. Totals of details in the journal are typically posted to the general ledger monthly.

Credit Memo. A document indicating a reduction in the amount due from a customer because of returned goods or an allowance granted. It often takes the same general form as a sales invoice, but it supports reductions in accounts receivable rather than increases.

Sales Returns and Allowances Journal. A journal that is basically the same as the sales journal for recording sales returns and allowances. Frequently the sales journal is designed to accommodate such transactions.

Remittance Advice. A document that accompanies the sales invoice mailed to the customer and can be returned to the seller with the cash payment. It is used to indicate the customer name, the sales invoice number, and the amount of the invoice when the payment is received. If the customer fails to include the remittance advice with his payment, it is common for the person opening the mail to prepare one at that time. A remittance advice is used to permit the immediate deposit of cash and to improve control over the custody of assets.

Cash Receipts Journal. A journal for recording cash receipts from collections, cash sales, and all other cash receipts. It indicates total cash received, the credit to accounts receivable at the gross amount of the original sale, trade discounts taken, and other debits and credits. The daily entries in the cash receipts journal are supported by remittance advices.

Uncollectible Account Authorization Forms. A document used internally, indicating authority to write an account receivable off as uncollectible.

Accounts Receivable Subsidiary Ledger. A subsidiary ledger for recording individual sales, cash receipts, and sales returns and allowances for each customer. The total of the individual account balances in the subsidiary ledger equals the total balance of accounts receivable in the general ledger.

Monthly Statement. A document sent to each customer indicating the beginning balance of accounts receivable, the amount and date of each sale, cash payments received, credit memos issued, and the ending balance due. It is, in essence, a copy of the customer's portion of the accounts receivable subsidiary ledger.

Functions in the Cycle

An understanding of the functions that take place in a typical client's organization for the sales and collection cycle is useful for understanding how an audit of the cycle is conducted. Students often find it difficult to envision which documents exist in any given audit area and how they flow through the client's organization. It is unlikely for anyone to understand the audit process without an understanding of accounting systems. The following functions for the sales and collection cycle are examined briefly at this point:

- Processing customer orders
- Granting credit
- Shipping goods
- Billing customers and recording sales
- Processing and recording cash receipts
- Processing and recording sales returns and allowances
- Charging off uncollectible accounts receivable
- Providing for bad debts

Processing Customer Orders. The request for goods by a customer is the starting point for the entire cycle. Legally, it is an offer to buy goods under specified terms. The receipt of a customer order results in the fairly immediate creation of a sales order and a sales invoice.

Granting Credit. Before goods are shipped, a properly authorized person must *approve credit* to the customer for sales on account. Weak practices in credit approval frequently result in excessive bad debts and accounts receivable that may be uncollectible. For most firms, an indication of credit approval on the sales order is the approval to ship the goods.

Shipping Goods. This critical function is the first point in the cycle where company assets are given up. Most companies recognize sales when goods are shipped. A shipping document is prepared at the time of shipment. This document, which is frequently a multicopy bill of lading, is essential to the proper billing of shipments to customers. Companies that maintain perpetual inventory records also update them by the use of shipping records.

Billing Customers and Recording Sales. Since the billing of customers is the means by which the customer is informed of the amount due for the goods, it must be done correctly and on a timely basis. The most important aspects of billing are to be sure all shipments made have been billed, no shipment has been billed more than once, and each one is billed for the proper amount. Billing at the proper amount is dependent upon charging the customer for the quantity shipped at the authorized price. The authorized price includes consideration of freight charges, insurance, and terms of payment. The proper recording of sales in the sales journal and the accounts receivable subsidiary ledger is also an important part of billing customers.

Errors in any part of the billing process can result in significant errors in the financial statements.

Processing and Recording Cash Receipts.

Processing and Recording Cash Receipts. The preceding four functions are necessary for getting the goods into the hands of customers, properly billing them, and reflecting the information in the accounting records. The remaining functions involve the collection and recording of cash and the other means of reducing accounts receivable.

In processing and recording cash receipts, the most important concern is the possibility of the theft of cash. Theft can occur before receipts are entered in the records or at a later point in time. The most important consideration in the handling of cash receipts is that all cash must be recorded in the cash receipts journal and subsidiary ledger and deposited in the bank at the proper amount on a timely basis. Remittance advices are important for this purpose.

Processing and Recording Sales Returns and Allowances. When a customer is dissatisfied with the goods, the seller frequently accepts the return of the goods or grants a reduction in the charges. Returns and allowances must be correctly and promptly recorded in the sales returns and allowances journal as well as in the subsidiary record. *Credit memos* are normally issued for returns and allowances to aid in maintaining control and to facilitate record keeping.

Charging Off Uncollectible Accounts Receivable. Regardless of the aggressiveness of credit departments, it is not unusual if some customers do not pay their bills. When the company concludes that an amount is no longer collectible, it must be charged off. Typically, this occurs after a customer files bankruptcy or the account is turned over to a collection agency. Proper accounting requires an adjustment for these uncollectible accounts.

Providing for Bad Debts. The provision for bad debts must be sufficient to allow for the current period sales that the company will be unable to collect in the future. For most companies the provision represents a residual, resulting from management's year-end adjustment of the allowance for uncollectible accounts.

INTERNAL CONTROLS AND AUDIT TESTS FOR SALES

All of the types of tests used in the conduct of the audit are used for the sales and collection cycle, and it is important to keep their interrelationships in mind. First, *analytical tests* are used to consider overall fairness of the balances in the accounts affected by the cycle. Analytical tests should be performed sufficiently early in the audit so that they can be used as an aid in understanding the client and isolating problem areas for further investigation. On the other hand, it is desirable to wait until after the balance sheet date to do these tests so that the full year's financial information will be reflected in the ratios and trends. Since tests of the system are frequently performed on an interim basis, it is common to perform analytical tests after the tests of transactions but before most of the direct tests of financial balances. This practice is reflected in the text by including analytical tests as a part of direct tests of balances rather than as a part of tests of transactions.

Second, significant assurance of the fair presentation of accounts in the cycle is obtained through the *study and evaluation of internal control*, including *tests of transactions*. If the controls are good and compliance tests indicate the procedures are being followed, this is evidence of fair presentation. If substantive tests of transactions disclose no monetary errors, further evidence of fair presentation is obtained.

Finally, assurance is gained through *direct tests of financial balances* by the use of substantive procedures. These procedures are designed primarily to directly test the ending balance sheet accounts, but errors found in the balance sheet accounts will indicate the types of errors taking place in the recording of transactions.

For the two primary areas, sales and cash receipts, the audit procedures are studied in the tests of transactions framework discussed in Chapter 8. This approach is meant to facilitate an understanding of the concepts involved in performing the tests by concentrating on the objectives rather than procedures. The problem of how to determine the proper sample size for tests of the system is studied in Chapter 10, and the direct tests of the financial statement balances for the sales and collection transaction cycle are the subject of Chapter 11.

Summary of Objectives, Controls, and Tests for Sales Transactions

Figure 9-3 is a summary of the application of the concepts discussed in previous chapters to the audit of sales. This summary integrates internal control and audit objectives with key internal controls and tests of transactions. Its most important points are discussed in detail in the following pages.

Internal Control and Audit Objectives.   The objectives are included in the framework developed in Chapter 8. Although certain controls and audit procedures satisfy more than one objective, it is convenient to consider each objective separately to facilitate a better understanding of the entire audit process.

Key Controls.   The internal controls in sales are designed to achieve the eight objectives discussed in Chapter 8. If the controls necessary to satisfy any one of the objectives are inadequate, the likelihood of errors related to that objective is enhanced, regardless of the controls for the other objectives.

Compliance Tests. For each internal control there exists a related compliance test to verify its effectiveness. In most audits it is relatively easy to determine the nature of the compliance tests from the nature of the control. For example, if the internal control is to initial customer orders after they have been approved for credit, the compliance test is to examine the customer order for a proper initial.

In Figure 9-3 observe that the compliance tests relate directly to the controls. For each control there should be at least one compliance test.

Substantive Tests. In deciding on substantive tests of transactions, some procedures are commonly employed on every audit regardless of the circumstances, whereas others are dependent upon the adequacy of the controls and the results of compliance tests. In Figure 9-3, the substantive tests are related to the objectives in the first column. The audit procedures used are affected by the internal controls and compliance tests for that objective. Materiality, results of the prior year, and the other factors discussed in Chapter 5 also affect the procedures used. Some of the audit procedures employed when internal controls are inadequate are discussed in a later section.

Design and Performance Format

The methodology used in Figure 9-3 is intended to help auditors *design audit programs* that satisfy the audit objectives in a given set of circumstances. If the auditor feels that certain objectives are important in a given audit or when the controls are different for one client than for another, the methodology aids in designing an effective and efficient audit program.

After the appropriate audit procedures for a given set of circumstances have been designed, they must be performed. It is likely to be inefficient to actually do the audit procedures in the design format. The procedures are converted from a design to a performance format by combining procedures. This will accomplish several things:

- Eliminate duplicate procedures.
- Make sure that when a given document is examined all procedures to be performed on that document are done at that time.
- Enable the auditor to do the procedures in the most effective order. For example, by footing the journal and reviewing the journal for unusual items first, it helps the auditor keep a better perspective in doing the detailed tests.

The process of converting from a design to a performance format is illustrated in Appendix A. The design format is shown on pages 304–07. The performance format is shown on page 310.

Internal Controls and Compliance Tests

In this section the key internal controls and related tests of compliance included in Figure 9-3 are discussed in greater detail. For convenience they

FIGURE 9-3

Summary of Objectives, Controls, and Tests for Sales Transactions

Internal Control and Audit Objectives	Key Internal Controls	Common Compliance Tests	Common Substantive Tests
Sales transactions as recorded in the sales journal are reasonable.	• Sales transactions are periodically reviewed by an independent person for reasonableness.	• Inquiry of independent person and examination of reports and recommendations prepared by reviewer.	• Review the sales journal, general ledger, and accounts receivable subsidiary ledger for large or unusual items.
Recorded sales are for shipments actually made to nonfictitious customers.	• Recording of sales is supported by authorized shipping documents and approved customer orders. • Sales invoices are prenumbered and properly accounted for. • Monthly statements are sent to customers; complaints receive independent follow-up.	• Examine copies of sales invoices for supporting bills of lading and customers' orders. • Account for integrity of numerical sequences of sales invoices. • Observe whether statements are mailed and examine customer correspondence files.	• Trace sales journal entries to bills of lading. • Trace shipments on bills of lading to entry of shipment in perpetual inventory records. • Trace sales journal entries to sales orders for credit approval and shipping authorization. • Trace credit entries in accounts receivable subsidiary ledger to valid source.
Sales transactions are properly authorized.	• Specific or general authorization must occur, through proper procedures, at three key points: —Granting of credit before shipment takes place —Shipment of goods —Determination of prices and terms, freight, and discounts.	• Examine documents for proper approval at these three points.	• Compare prices on sales invoices with authorized price lists or properly executed contracts.
Existing sales transactions are recorded.	• Shipping documents (e.g., bills of lading) are prenumbered and accounted for. • Sales invoices are prenumbered and accounted for.	• Account for integrity of numerical sequence of shipping documents. • Account for integrity of numerical sequence of sales invoices.	• Trace shipping documents to resultant sales invoice and entry into sales journal and accounts receivable ledger.

FIGURE 9-3 (cont.)

Internal Control and Audit Objectives	Key Internal Controls	Common Compliance Tests	Common Substantive Tests
Recorded sales are for the amount of goods ordered and are correctly billed and recorded.	• Internal verification of invoice preparation and posting by an independent person.	• Examine indication of internal verification on affected documents.	• Recompute information on sales invoices. • Trace entries in sales journal to sales invoices and posting to accounts receivable ledger. • Trace details on sales invoices to shipping records, price lists, and customers' orders.
Sales transactions are properly classified.	• Use of adequate chart of accounts. • Internal review and verification.	• Review chart of accounts for adequacy. • Examine indication of internal verification on affected documents.	• Examine documents supporting sales transactions for proper classification.
Sales are recorded on a timely basis.	• Procedures requiring billing and recording of sales on a daily basis as close to time of occurrence as possible. • Internal verification.	• Examine documents for unbilled shipments and unrecorded sales at any point in time. • Examine indication of internal verification on affected documents.	• Compare dates of recorded sales transactions with dates on shipping records.
Sales transactions are properly included in the subsidiary records and are correctly summarized.	• Segregation of duties for recording of the sales journal and the accounts receivable ledger. • Regular monthly statements to customers. • Internal verification.	• Observe procedures. • Observe whether statements are mailed. • Examine indication of internal verification.	• Tests of clerical accuracy, e.g., footing journals and tracing postings to general ledger and accounts receivable ledger.

are discussed in terms of individual internal controls rather than internal control objectives.

Adequate Documents and Records. Since each company has a somewhat unique system of originating, processing, and recording transactions, it may be difficult to evaluate whether its procedures are designed for maximum control; nevertheless, adequate record-keeping procedures must exist before most of the internal control objectives can be met. Some companies, for example, automatically prepare a multicopy prenumbered sales invoice at the time a customer order is received. Copies of this document are used to approve credit, authorize shipment, record the number of units shipped, and bill customers. Under this system, there is almost no chance of the failure to bill a customer if all invoices are accounted for periodically. Under a different system, where the sales invoice is prepared only after a shipment has been made, the likelihood of the failure to bill a customer is much higher, unless some compensating control exists.

Proper compliance procedures for testing record keeping, including the adequacy of documents and the timeliness of recording, depend on the nature of the control being relied upon. For example, if the client requires that a duplicate sales invoice be attached to every shipping order to prevent failing to bill a customer for shipped goods, a useful compliance test is to account for a sequence of shipping orders and examine each one to make sure a duplicate sales invoice is attached.

Prenumbered Documents. The use of prenumbered documents is meant to prevent both the *failure* to bill or record sales and the occurrence of *duplicate* billings and recordings. Of course, it does not do much good to have prenumbered documents unless they are properly accounted for. An example of the use of this control is where the billing clerk files a copy of all shipping documents in sequential order after each shipment is billed, with someone else periodically accounting for all numbers and investigating the reason for any missing documents.

A common compliance test for this control is to account for a sequence of various types of documents, such as duplicate sales invoices selected from the sales journal, watching for omitted and duplicate numbers, or invoices outside of the normal sequence. This test simultaneously provides evidence of both the "validity" and "failure to record" objectives.

Monthly Statements Are Mailed. The mailing of monthly statements by someone who has no responsibility for handling cash or preparing the sales and accounts receivable records is a useful control because it encourages a response from customers if the balance is improperly stated. For maximum effectiveness, all disagreements about the balance in the account should be directed to a designated official who has no responsibility for handling cash or recording sales or accounts receivable.

The auditor's observations of the mailing of statements by a properly designated person and the examination of customer correspondence files are useful compliance procedures for testing whether monthly statements have been sent to customers.

Proper Authorization. The auditor is concerned about authorization at *three key points*: credit must be properly authorized before a sale takes place; goods should be shipped only after proper authorization; and prices, including base terms, freight, and discounts, must be authorized. The first two of these controls are meant to prevent the loss of company assets by shipping to fictitious customers or those who will fail to pay for the goods. Price authorization is meant to make sure the sale is billed at the price set by company policy.

It is easy to test for compliance with the system for authorization by examining documents for proper approval of each of these three types.

Adequate Segregation of Duties. Proper segregation of duties within accounting is useful to prevent various types of errors, both fraudulent and unintentional. For example, if the sales register is prepared independently of the accounts receivable subsidiary records and the subsidiary record is reconciled with the control account periodically by someone independent of the persons preparing the records, an automatic cross-check exists. For the prevention of fraudulent errors, it is important that anyone responsible for recording the sales journal or subsidiary records be denied access to cash. It is also desirable to separate the credit-granting function from the sales function, since credit checks are intended to offset the natural tendency of sales personnel to optimize volume even at the expense of high bad debt write-offs.

The appropriate compliance tests for segregation of duties are ordinarily restricted to the auditor's observations of activities and discussions with personnel. For example, it is possible to observe whether the billing clerk also prepares the subsidiary ledger or has access to cash by opening incoming mail.

Internal Verification Procedures. The use of internal auditors or other independent persons for checking the processing and recording of sales transactions is essential for fulfilling each of the eight internal control objectives. The following are typical internal verification procedures for each objective.

The examination of internal auditors' reports and initials of independent persons on documents they have tested are examples of compliance procedures the external auditor can use.

Substantive Tests of Sales Transactions

Determining the proper substantive tests of transactions procedures for sales is relatively difficult because they vary considerably depending on the circumstances. In subsequent paragraphs, the procedures frequently *not*

Internal Control Objective	Example of an Internal Verification Procedure
Sales as recorded are reasonable.	Periodic review of recorded sales by an independent person who is knowledgeable about the business.
Recorded sales are valid.	Account for a sequence of sales invoices and examine supporting documentation.
Sales are properly authorized.	Examine Dun and Bradstreet reports for customers to determine if credit was approved in accordance with company policy.
Existing sales transactions are recorded.	Account for a sequence of bills of lading and trace them to the sales journal.
Recorded sales are properly valued.	Compare quantity on sales invoices with shipping document records.
Recorded sales are properly classified.	Compare supporting documents for recorded sales with the chart of accounts.
Sales are recorded on a timely basis.	Examine unbilled shipping documents in the possession of the billing clerk to determine whether shipments that should already have been billed are included.
Sales transactions are properly included in the subsidiary records and correctly summarized.	Trace sales transactions from the sales journal to the subsidiary ledgers.

performed are emphasized, since they are the ones requiring an audit decision. The substantive procedures are discussed in the same order in which they were included in Figure 9-3. It should be noted that some procedures fulfill multiple objectives.

Sales as Recorded Are Reasonable. In addition to detailed tests, analytical review tests must be made to make sure there are no transactions that appear suspicious on the surface. Auditors typically test a small percentage of the population and therefore are unlikely to include unusual transactions in the sample. Analytical review tests help the auditor find these transactions for further investigation. Examples of sales transactions frequently requiring further investigation are unusually large sales, the sale of a building or equipment, or sales to officers, directors, or affiliates. In addition, the auditor should review the general ledger and subsidiary records for unusual debits and credits or extraordinary amounts. Analytical review tests are ordinarily done even when controls are considered good.

Recorded Sales Are Valid. For this objective, the auditor is concerned with the possibility of *two types of errors*: sales being included in the journals for which no shipment was made, and alternatively, shipments being made to fictitious customers and recorded as sales. As might be imagined, the inclusion of invalid sales is rare, but the potential consequences are significant.

The appropriate substantive tests for detecting invalid transactions depend upon where the auditor believes the errors are likely to take place. Normally, the auditor tests for invalid sales only if he believes a control weakness exists; therefore, the nature of the tests depends upon the nature of the weakness. As a test of recorded sales for which there were no actual shipments, the auditor can trace from selected entries in the sales journal to make sure a related copy of the bill of lading and other supporting documents exist. If the auditor is also concerned about the possibility of a fictitious duplicate copy of a bill of lading, it may be necessary to trace the amounts to the perpetual inventory records as a test of whether inventory was reduced. A test of the possibility of a shipment to a fictitious customer is to examine the sales orders corresponding to a sales transaction entry in the sales journal for the existence of credit approval and shipping authorization. Another effective approach to auditing for invalid sales transactions is to trace the *credit* for the accounts receivable in the subsidiary ledger to its source. If the receivable was actually collected in cash or the goods returned, there must have originally been a valid sale. If the credit was for a bad debt charge-off or a credit memo, or if the account was still unpaid at the time of the audit, intensive follow-up by examining shipping and customer order documents is required, since each of these could indicate a fictitious sales transaction.

It should be kept in mind that *the ordinary audit is not primarily intended to detect fraud.* The preceding substantive tests should be necessary only if the auditor is particularly concerned about the occurrence of fraud errors due to inadequate controls.

Sales Are Properly Authorized.

It is normally necessary to test by substantive procedures whether the company's general credit, shipping, and pricing policies are being properly followed in the day-to-day operations. This is especially important with regard to the pricing of sales. Substantive pricing tests are done by comparing the actual price charged for different products, including freight and terms, with the price list authorized by management. If product prices are negotiated on an individual sale basis, the tests usually involve determining that the proper authorization by the sales manager or other appropriate official has occurred. Also, contracts which exist are examined, and in some cases even confirmed directly with the customer. Procedures to test pricing are normally necessary regardless of the quality of the controls, but the sample size can be reduced if the controls are adequate.

Existing Sales Transactions Are Recorded.

In many audits, no substantive transaction tests are made for this objective on the grounds that overstatements of assets are a greater concern in the audit of sales transactions than their understatement. If there are inadequate controls, as is likely in the case where no independent internal tracing from shipping documents to the sales journal takes place, substantive tests are necessary.

An effective procedure to test for unbilled shipments is to trace selected shipping documents from a file in the shipping department to related duplicate sales invoices, the sales journal, and accounts receivable subsidiary ledgers. To conduct a meaningful test using this procedure, the auditor must be confident that all shipping documents are included in the file. This can be done by accounting for a numerical sequence of the documents.

It is important that auditors understand the difference between tracing from source documents to the journals and tracing from the journals back to supporting documents. The former is a test for *omitted transactions*, whereas the latter is a test for *invalid transactions*.

Recorded Sales Are Properly Valued. The correct valuation of sales transactions concerns shipping the amount of goods ordered, correctly billing for the amount of goods shipped, and correctly recording the amount billed in the accounting records. Substantive tests to make sure that each of these aspects of valuation is correct are ordinarily conducted in every audit.

Typical substantive tests include recomputing information in the accounting records to verify whether it is proper. A common approach is to start with entries in the sales journal and compare the total of selected transactions with accounts receivable subsidiary ledgers and duplicate sales invoices. Prices on the duplicate sales invoices are normally compared with an approved price list, extensions and footings are recomputed, and the products listed on the invoices are compared with shipping records for description, quantity, and customer identification. Frequently, customer orders and sales orders are also examined for the same information.

The comparison of compliance and substantive tests for the valuation objective is a good example of the saving in audit time that can result when effective internal controls exist. It is obvious that the compliance test for this objective takes almost no time because it involves examining only an initial or other evidence of internal verification. Since the sample size for substantive tests can be reduced if this control is effective, there can be a significant saving from performing the compliance test due to its lower cost.

Recorded Sales Are Properly Classified. Charging the correct account is less of a problem in sales than in some other transaction cycles, but it is still of some concern. When there are cash and credit sales, it is important not to debit accounts receivable for a cash sale, or credit sales for collection of a receivable. It is also important not to classify sales of operating assets, such as buildings, as sales. For those companies using more than one sales classification, such as companies issuing segmented earnings statements, proper classification is essential.

It is common to test sales for proper classification as part of testing for valuation. The auditor examines supporting documents to determine the proper classification of a given transaction and compares this with the actual account to which it is charged.

Sales Are Recorded on a Timely Basis. It is important that sales be billed and recorded as soon after shipment takes place as possible to prevent the unintentional omission of transactions from the records and to make sure sales are recorded in the proper period. At the same time that substantive valuation procedures are being performed, it is common to compare the date on selected bills of lading or other shipping documents with the date on related duplicate sales invoices, the sales journal, and subsidiary ledgers. Significant differences indicate a potential cutoff problem.

Sales Transactions Are Properly Included in the Subsidiary Records and Correctly Summarized. The proper inclusion of all sales transactions in the accounts receivable subsidiary ledger is essential because the accuracy of these records affects the client's ability to collect outstanding receivables. Similarly, the sales journal must be correctly footed and posted to the general ledger if the financial statements are to be correct. In every audit, it is necessary to perform some clerical accuracy tests by footing the journals and tracing the totals and details to the general ledger and subsidiary records. Only the sample size is affected by the quality of the internal controls. Tracing from the sales journal to subsidiary records is typically done as a part of fulfilling other objectives, but footing the sales journal and tracing the totals to the general ledger is done as a separate procedure.

AUDIT PROCEDURES FOR PROCESSING OF SALES RETURNS AND ALLOWANCES

The audit objectives and the client's methods of controlling errors are essentially the same for processing credit memos as the ones described for sales, with two important differences. The first relates to *materiality.* In many instances sales returns and allowances are so immaterial that they can be ignored in the audit altogether. The second major difference relates to *emphasis on objectives.* For sales returns and allowances, the primary emphasis is normally on testing the validity of recorded transactions as a means of uncovering any diversion of cash from the collection of accounts receivable that has been covered up by a fictitious sales return or allowance.

Naturally, the other objectives should not be ignored. But because the objectives and methodology for auditing sales returns and allowances are essentially the same as for sales, we will not include a detailed study of the area. The reader should be able to go through the same logic process used for sales to arrive at suitable controls, compliance tests to test the controls, and substantive tests to verify the amounts.

INTERNAL CONTROLS AND AUDIT TESTS FOR CASH RECEIPTS

The audit procedures for verifying cash receipts are developed around the same framework used for sales; i.e., considering internal control and audit objectives, key internal controls for each objective, compliance tests for each control, and substantive tests for each objective. As in all other audit areas, the compliance tests depend on the controls the auditor intends to rely upon to reduce substantive tests and the substantive tests depend on the results of the compliance tests and the other considerations in the audit. Thus it is inappropriate to think of a single audit program for cash receipts as being useful for all engagements.

Key internal controls, common compliance tests, and common substantive tests to satisfy each of the internal control and audit objectives for cash receipts are listed in Figure 9-4. Since this summary follows the same format as the previous one for sales, no further explanation of its meaning is necessary.

A detailed discussion of the internal controls, compliance tests, and substantive tests such as the one included for the audit of sales is not included for cash receipts. Instead, the audit procedures that are most likely to be misunderstood by students of auditing are explained in more detail.

An essential part of the auditor's responsibility in auditing cash receipts is the identifying of weaknesses in the system that increase the likelihood of fraud. In expanding on Figure 9-4, the emphasis will be on those audit procedures that are designed primarily for the discovery of fraud. However, the reader should keep in mind throughout this discussion that the nonfraud procedures included in Figure 9-4 are the auditor's primary responsibility. Those procedures that are not discussed in the following paragraphs are omitted only because their purpose and the methodology for applying them should be apparent from their description.

Procedures Designed to Determine Whether All Cash Received Was Recorded

The most difficult type of cash defalcation for the auditor to detect is that which occurs *before the cash is recorded* in the cash receipts journal or other cash listing. For example, if a grocery store clerk takes cash and intentionally fails to register the receipt of cash on the cash register, it is extremely difficult to subsequently discover the theft. To prevent this type of fraud, internal controls such as those included in the third objective in Figure 9-4 are implemented by many companies. The type of control will of course depend on the type of business. For example, the controls for a retail store where the cash is received by the same person who sells the merchandise and rings up the cash receipts should be different from the controls for a company where all receipts are received through the mail several weeks after the sales have taken place.

It is normal practice to trace from *prenumbered remittance advices* or *prelists of cash receipts* to the cash receipts journal and subsidiary accounts receivable records as a *substantive* test of the recording of actual cash received. This test will only be effective if the cash was listed on a cash register tape or some other prelisting at the time it was received.

If the auditor is particularly concerned about weaknesses in the internal control system that could lead to fraudulently omitted cash receipts, there is an effective but time consuming approach that combines a part of the cash receipts tests with the audit of sales transactions. When the auditor traces a sales transaction to the debit in the customer's subsidiary ledger, he can also trace the subsequent *credit* that reduces the account receivable to its source. The credit must arise from cash received, sales returns and allowances, or accounts charged off as uncollectible. In testing the credits to the sales transactions, the auditor traces the cash receipts to the cash receipts journal, the sales returns and allowances to a properly authorized credit memo and the sales returns and allowances journal, and the accounts charged off to proper authorization. Any sales transactions not credited are still a part of accounts receivable and are tested as a part of the confirmation of a sample of the outstanding balances in accounts receivable. In this approach the auditor is looking for sales *without a valid credit* in the accounts receivable subsidiary ledger, which would be an indication of a possible defalcation. Of course, if an employee is able to omit the recording of a sale and subsequently takes the cash receipt from the customer before it is recorded, the procedure described here would be ineffective.

Proof of Cash Receipts

A useful audit procedure to test whether all recorded cash receipts have been deposited in the bank account is a proof of cash receipts. In this test the total cash receipts recorded in the cash receipts journal for a period of time, such as a month, are reconciled with the actual deposits made to the bank during the same time period. There may be a difference in the two due to deposits in transit and other items, but the amounts can be reconciled and compared. The procedure is not useful in discovering cash receipts that have not been recorded in the journals or time lags in making deposits, but it is useful in discovering recorded cash receipts that have not been deposited, unrecorded deposits, unrecorded loans, bank loans deposited directly into the bank account, and similar errors. A proof of cash receipts and cash disbursements is illustrated in Chapter 19 on page 647. This somewhat time-consuming procedure is ordinarily used only when the controls are weak. In rare instances where controls are extremely weak, the period covered by the proof of cash receipts may be the entire year.

Tests to Discover Lapping

Lapping, which is one common type of fraud, is the postponement of entries for the collection of receivables to *conceal an existing cash shortage*. The fraud is perpetrated by a person who records cash in both the cash receipts journal and subsidiary accounts receivable ledger. He defers recording of the cash receipts from one customer and covers the shortages with receipts of another customer. These in turn are covered from the receipts of a third customer a few days later. The employee must continue to cover the shortage through repeated lapping, replace the stolen money, or find another way to conceal the shortage.

FIGURE 9-4

Summary of Objectives, Controls, and Tests for Cash Receipts Transactions

Internal Control and Audit Objectives	Key Internal Controls	Common Compliance Tests	Common Substantive Tests
Cash receipts transactions as recorded in the cash receipts journal are reasonable.	• Cash receipts transactions are periodically reviewed by an independent person for reasonableness.	• Inquiry of independent person and examination of reports and recommendations prepared by reviewer.	• Review the cash receipts journal, general ledger, and accounts receivable subsidiary ledger for large and unusual amounts.
Recorded cash receipts are for funds actually received by the company.	• Separation of duties between handling cash and record keeping. • Independent reconciliation of bank accounts.	• Observation. • Observation.	• Trace from cash receipts journal to bank statements. • Proof of cash receipts.
Cash discounts are authorized.	• A policy on granting cash discounts must exist. • Approval of cash discounts.	• Discussion with management. • Examine remittance advice for proper approval.	• Examine remittance advices and sales invoices to determine whether discounts allowed are consistent with company policy.
Cash received is recorded in the cash receipts journal.	• Separation of duties between handling cash and record keeping. • Use of prenumbered remittance advices or a prelisting of cash. • Immediate endorsement of incoming checks. • Internal verification of the recording of cash receipts. • Regular monthly statements to customers.	• Discussion with personnel and observation. • Account for numerical sequence or examine prelisting. • Observation. • Examine indication of internal verification. • Observation.	• Trace from remittances or prelisting to cash receipts journal.

FIGURE 9-4 (cont.)

Internal Control and Audit Objectives	Key Internal Controls	Common Compliance Tests	Common Substantive Tests
Recorded cash receipts are deposited at the amount received.	• Same as previous objective. • Regular reconciliation of bank accounts.	• Same as previous objective. • Review monthly bank reconciliations.	• Proof of cash receipts.
Cash receipts are properly classified.	• Use of adequate chart of accounts. • Internal review and verification.	• Review chart of accounts. • Examine indication of internal verification.	• Examine documents supporting cash receipts for proper classification.
Cash receipts are recorded on a timely basis.	• Procedure requiring recording of cash receipts on a daily basis. • Internal verification.	• Observe unrecorded cash at any point of time. • Examine indication of internal verification.	• Compare dates of deposits with dates in the cash receipts journal and prelisting of cash receipts.
Cash receipts are properly included in the subsidiary records and are correctly summarized.	• Segregation of duties for recording of the cash receipts journal and accounts receivable ledger. • Regular monthly statements to customers. • Internal verification.	• Observation. • Observation. • Examine indication of internal verification.	• Tests of clerical accuracy, e.g., footing journals and tracing postings to general ledger and accounts receivable ledger.

This fraud can be detected by comparing the name, amount, and dates shown on remittance advices with cash receipts journal entries and related duplicate deposit slips. Since the procedure is relatively time consuming, auditors ordinarily perform the procedure only when there is specific concern with fraud because of a weakness in the system.

AUDIT PROCEDURES FOR CHARGING OFF AND RECORDING UNCOLLECTIBLE ACCOUNTS

Validity and *proper authorization* are the most important considerations the auditor should keep in mind in the verification of the write-off of individual uncollectible accounts. A major concern in testing accounts charged off as uncollectible is the possibility of the client covering up a defalcation by charging off accounts receivable that have already been collected. The major control for preventing this type of error is proper authorization of the write-off of uncollectible accounts by a designated level of management only after the thorough investigation of the reason the customer has not paid.

Normally, the verification of the accounts charged off takes relatively little time. Typical procedures include the examination of approvals by the appropriate persons. For a sample of accounts charged off, it is also usually necessary for the auditor to examine correspondence in the client's files establishing their uncollectibility. In some cases the auditor will also examine Dun and Bradstreet and other credit reports. After the auditor has concluded that the accounts charged off by general journal entries are proper, selected items should be traced to the accounts receivable subsidiary ledger as a test of the records.

EFFECT OF THE RESULTS OF TESTS OF TRANSACTIONS ON THE REMAINDER OF THE AUDIT

The results of the compliance and substantive tests of transactions will have a significant effect on the remainder of the audit, especially on the direct tests of balances. The parts of the audit most affected by the tests of the sales and collection cycle transactions are the balances in *accounts receivable, cash, bad debts expense*, and *allowance for doubtful accounts*. Furthermore, if the results of the tests are unsatisfactory, it is necessary to do additional substantive testing for the propriety of sales, sales returns and allowances, charge-off of uncollectible accounts, and processing of cash receipts.

At the completion of the tests of transactions, it is essential to *analyze each compliance and substantive test exception* to determine its cause and the implication of the exception on the system and the audit of the affected accounts. The methodology and implications of exceptions analysis are explained more fully in Chapter 10.

The most significant effect of the results of the tests of the system in the sales and collection cycle is on the confirmation of accounts receivable. The type of confirmation, the size of the sample, and the timing of the test are all affected by the results of both compliance and substantive tests of transactions. The effect of the tests on accounts receivable, bad debts expense, and allowance for uncollectible accounts is considered in Chapter 11.

appendix a

case illustration

The concepts for testing the sales and collection cycle presented in this chapter are now illustrated by the case of the Hillsburg Hardware Company. A description of the system is followed by a preliminary evaluation of the system and, for each objective, the tests of the system a prudent auditor might consider appropriate for the circumstances.

The Hillsburg Hardware Company is a small wholesale distributor of hardware to independent, high-quality hardware stores in the southeastern part of the United States. This is the fourth year of the audit for this client, and there have never been any significant errors discovered in the tests. During the current year, a major change has occurred. The chief accountant left the firm and has been replaced by Erma Swanson. There has also been some turnover of other accounting personnel.

The overall assessment by management is that the accounting personnel are reasonably competent and highly trustworthy. The president, Rick Chulick, has been the chief operating officer for approximately ten years. He is regarded as a highly competent, honest individual who does a conscientious job. The following information is provided from the auditor's files:

- *The organization chart and a flowchart of the system prepared for the audit.* This information is included in Figures 9–5 and 9–6. Sales returns and allowances for this client are too immaterial to include in the flowchart or to verify in the audit.
- *Evaluation of internal controls and the related tests of transaction procedures for each objective.* An appropriate approach to evaluating a system of internal control and developing tests of transactions is included for sales in Figure 9–7 and cash receipts in Figure 9–8. A study of these two figures indicates the importance of isolating strengths (controls) and weaknesses (absence of controls) in the system. The compliance tests are designed to test the strengths and are shown separately from the substantive tests only to illustrate the differences in their nature.
- *The strengths in the system and their effect.* These represent the controls the auditor is willing to rely upon to reduce substantive tests if the compliance

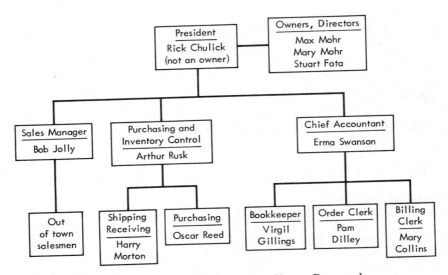

FIGURE 9-5 Hillsburg Hardware Organization Chart—Personnel

tests indicate they are operating effectively. Figure 9–9 presents the strengths along with the effect of the strengths on specific errors, the compliance tests necessary to test the controls, and the effect on substantive tests if the controls are in fact operating effectively. The information for this figure is taken from Figures 9–7 and 9–8 to show the importance of strengths in designing tests of transactions.

- *The weaknesses in the system and their effect.* These represent aspects of the system the auditor believes may result in significant errors because of the lack of adequate controls. The weaknesses are included in Figure 9–10, along with the effect of the weaknesses on specific errors and on audit procedures. The information for this figure is taken from Figures 9–7 and 9–8 to show the importance of weaknesses in designing tests of transactions.
- *The analytical, compliance, and substantive procedures for sales, cash receipts, and charge-off of uncollectible accounts.* These audit procedures were developed after consideration of the strengths and weaknesses of the system and all other relevant factors of the audit. Figure 9–11 lists these procedures in the manner in which they are typically included in audit programs in a performance format. The procedures in Figures 9–7 and 9–8 are keyed to indicate where they appear in the performance format audit program in Figure 9–11. Sample size and the particular items for inclusion in the sample are not included here, but they are considered in an extension of the case in the illustration in Appendix B at the end of Chapter 10.

NOTES TO FIGURE 9–6:

1. All correspondence is sent to the president.

2. All sales order numbers are accounted for weekly by the accountant.

3. All bills of lading numbers are accounted for weekly by the accountant.

4. Sales amount recorded on sales invoice is based on standard price list.

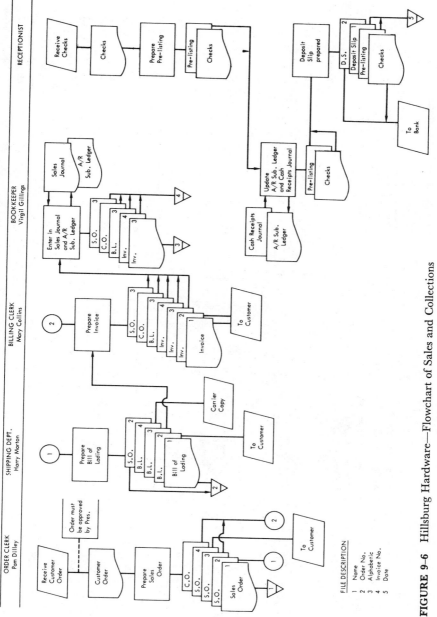

FIGURE 9-6 Hillsburg Hardware—Flowchart of Sales and Collections

303

FIGURE 9–7

Hillsburg Hardware–Evaluation of Internal Controls and Tests of Transactions—Design Format*

Sales

Objective	Existing Controls	Compliance Tests	Weaknesses	Substantive Tests
Sales transactions as recorded are reasonable.	President reviews journals and ledgers monthly.	Discuss with Chulick the extent to which he reviews the journals and the nature of his findings. (1)		Review the sales journal and ledgers for unusual transactions and amounts. (2)
Recorded sales are for shipments actually made to nonfictitious customers	Pam Dilley examines underlying documents after billing.	Account for a sequence of sales invoices in the sales journal. (12) Examine underlying documents for indication of internal verification by Pam Dilley. (13b)	Lack of internal verification for the possibility of sales invoices being recorded more than once.	Trace recorded sales from the sales journal to the file of supporting documents, which includes a duplicate sales invoice, bill of lading, sales order, and customer order. (14)
Sales transactions are properly authorized.	Credit is approved by the president before shipment.	Examine customer order for credit approval by Rick Chulick. (13e)		
Existing sales transactions are recorded.	Bills of lading are accounted for weekly by accountant to make sure they are billed.	Account for a sequence of shipping documents. (10)	Lack of internal verification that sales invoices are included in the sales journal (also see objective 3, weakness for cash receipts).	Trace selected shipping documents to sales journal to be sure they are all included. (11)
Recorded sales are for the amount of goods ordered and are correctly billed and recorded.	Internal verification of pricing, extension, and footings by Dilley.	Examine underlying documents for indication of internal verification by Pam Dilley. (13b)		Trace selected duplicate invoice numbers from the sales journal to a. Duplicate sales invoice, and test for total amount recorded in journal, date, customer name, and classification. Check the pricing, extensions, and footings. (13b)

Transaction-related audit objective	Existing internal control	Deficiency	Test of control	Substantive test of transactions
				b. Bill of lading and test for customer name, product description, quantity, and date. (13c)
				c. Duplicate sales order, and test for customer name, product description, quantity, date, and approval by Pam Dilley. (13d)
				d. Customer order, and test for customer name, product description, quantity, and date. (13e)
Sales transactions are properly classified.	None.	Not a problem, because of lack of cash sales.		Examine duplicate sales invoice for proper account classification. (13b)
Sales are recorded on a timely basis.	None.	Lack of control for test of timely recording.		Compare dates on the bill of lading, duplicate sales invoice, and sales journal. (15)
Sales transactions are properly included in the subsidiary records and are correctly summarized.	Accountant reconciles subsidiary ledger with control account.	No internal verification of footing the journal and posting totals to the general ledger.	Observe whether accountant reconciles subsidiary ledger with control account. (9)	Foot and crossfoot the sales journal, and trace totals to the general ledger. (4)
	Monthly statements are sent to customers.		Observe whether monthly statements are mailed. (7)	Trace selected duplicate invoice numbers from the sales journal to the accounts receivable subsidiary ledger, and test for amount, date, and invoice number. (13a)

*The procedures are summarized into a performance format in Figure 9–11. The number and letter in parentheses after the procedure refers to Figure 9–11.

FIGURE 9-8

Hillsburg Hardware—Evaluation of Internal Controls and Tests of Transactions—Design Format*

Cash Receipts

Objectives	Existing Controls	Compliance Tests	Weaknesses	Substantive Tests
Cash receipts transactions as recorded are reasonable.	President reviews journals and ledgers monthly.	Discuss with Chulick the extent to which he reviews the journals and the nature of his findings. (1)		Review the cash receipts journal and the ledgers for unusual transactions and amounts. (2) Review the subsidiary ledger for miscellaneous credits. (3)
Recorded cash receipts are for funds actually received by the company.	Accountant reconciles bank account.	Observe who performs the bank reconciliation. (5)		Prepare a proof of cash receipts. (18) Trace the total from the cash receipts journal to the bank statement, testing for dates and amounts of deposit. (17)
Cash discounts are authorized.	Not applicable.			
Cash received is recorded in the cash receipts journal.	Checks are stamped with a restrictive endorsement. Statements are sent to customers monthly.	Observe whether a restricted endorsement is used on cash receipts. (6) Observe whether monthly statements are mailed. (7)	Prelisting of cash is not used to verify recorded cash receipts. Receptionist handles cash after it is returned from cash receipts. Bookkeeper has access to cash receipts and maintains accounts receivable records.	Compare prelisting of cash receipts with the duplicate deposit slip, testing for names, amounts, and dates. (17) Obtain the prelisting of cash receipts, and trace amounts to the cash receipts journal, testing for names, amounts, and dates. (17)

FIGURE 9-8 (cont.)

Cash Receipts

Objectives	Existing Controls	Compliance Tests	Weaknesses	Substantive Tests
Recorded cash receipts are deposited at the amount received	Statements are sent to customers monthly. Accountant reconciles bank account.	Observe whether a restricted endorsement is used on cash receipts. (6) Observe whether accountant reconciles bank account. (8)		The procedures for the first two objectives also fulfill this objectives.
Cash receipts are properly classified.	None.		Not a problem, because of lack of cash sales.	Not tested.
Cash receipts are recorded on a timely basis.	None.		Cash receipts are not deposited daily.	Trace the total from the cash receipts journal to the bank statement, testing for a delay in deposit. (17)
Cash receipts are properly included in the subsidiary records and are correctly summarized.	Accountant reconciles subsidiary ledger with control account.	Observe whether accountant reconciles subsidiary ledger with control account. (9)	No internal verification of footing the journal and posting totals to the general ledger.	Foot and crossfoot the cash receipts journal, and trace totals to the general ledger. (4) Trace selected entries from the cash receipts to entries in the subsidiary ledger, and test for date and amount. (19) Trace selected credits from the subsidiary ledger to the cash receipts journal, and test for date and amount. (20)

*The procedures are summarized into a performance format in Figure 9–11. The number in parentheses after the procedure refers to Figure 9–11.

FIGURE 9–9

Hillsburg Hardware—Strengths in the System and Their Effect

Major Strengths	Effect on Likely Errors	Compliance Tests Performed to Verify the Strengths (Effect on the Substantive Tests Is in Parentheses)
The accountant accounts for all bills of lading and traces them to sales invoices.	Reduces the likelihood of failing to bill shipments. An important control due to weakness 1 in Figure 9–10.	Account for a series of bills of lading. (Because of weakness 1, it will be necessary to trace from bills of lading to the duplicate sales invoices.)
Credit is approved by the president.	Reduces the likelihood of failing to follow company policy.	Examine credit approval on customer order. (Do not do any other tests of credit until balance sheets tests are done.)
The bank statement is reconciled by the accountant.	Reduces the likelihood of fraudulent errors.	Observation. (No effect until balance sheet tests are performed.)
The accountant reconciles the balance in the accounts receivable subsidiary ledger with the control accounts.	Reduces the likelihood of undetected errors in the subsidiary ledgers.	Observation and asking questions. (No effect until balance sheet tests are performed.)
The sales invoices are internally verified for pricing, extensions, and footings.	Reduces the likelihood of clerical errors.	Examination of duplicate invoices for initials. (Reduce substantive tests of invoices as well as confirmations.)
Statements are mailed to customers monthly, and all correspondence is sent directly to the president.	Reduces the likelihood of errors remaining undetected.	Observation and questions. (The effect is a reduction in all tests concerned with the overstatement of receivables. This includes pricing, extensions, footings, etc.)
Checks are stamped with a restrictive endorsement.	Reduces the likelihood of fraud.	Observation. (Reduction in tests for fraud.)
Journals and ledgers are reviewed monthly by the president.	Reduces the likelihood of all types of large errors.	Inquiry (small reduction of all other audit tests).

Notes to Figure 9–6 (cont.)

5. Duplicate sales invoice is compared with bill of lading, and prices are checked daily by Pam Dilley and initialed before the original invoice is mailed to the customer.

6. Statements are sent to customers monthly.

7. Accounts receivable subsidiary ledger is reconciled with general ledger by the accountant on a monthly basis.

8. Sales invoices are recorded individually in the journal in the order they are received rather than sequentially.

FIGURE 9–10

Hillsburg Hardware—Weaknesses in the System and Their Effect

Weaknesses	Effect on Likely Errors	Effect on Audit Procedures
The bookkeeper maintains the accounts receivable records and also has access to cash receipts.	Potential for fraud by the bookkeeper. Significantly offset by the lack of currency and restrictive endorsement.	Trace a larger sample than normal from the prelisting of cash receipts to the cash receipts journal. Test a larger sample than normal of the billing of shipments and the recording of invoices (as a test of omitting the invoice and theft of the check). It is not possible to test remittance advices because they are not retained. Instead trace the detail of the prelist of cash receipts to the duplicate deposit slip and the bank statement.
Cash receipts are not deposited daily.	Potential for loss of checks, and it enhances the likelihood of fraud in the preceding entry.	Trace a larger sample than normal from the prelisting of cash receipts to the cash receipts journal, and prepare a proof of cash.
Receptionist handles cash after it is returned from the A/R clerk.	A potential for fraud.	Trace a larger sample than normal from the prelisting of cash receipts to the bank statement.
The prelisting of cash is not used to verify cash receipts.	The failure to use this information enhances the likelihood of fraud in 1 above and unintentional loss of checks or other errors.	Trace a larger sample than normal from the prelisting of cash receipts to the cash receipts journal and bank statement.
There is no internal verification of the inclusion of all sales invoices in the sales journal.	There may be an intentional or an unintentional omission or duplicate recording of sales invoices. This weakness is enhanced by the recording of invoices in a manner other than sequential order. The likelihood of duplicate recording is partially offset by the president's receiving all correspondence from customers.	Account for a large sequence of duplicate sales invoices in the sales journal, watching for omissions and duplications. Because of the way the sales journal is organized, this procedure will have to be done with great care.
Lack of internal verification of footing and posting of journals.	Potential for fraud.	Foot and crossfoot journals, and trace the balances to the general ledger.

```
Audit Procedures for Sales and Cash Receipts
(Sample Size and the Items in the Sample Are Not Included)
```

General
1. Discuss with Chulick the extent to which he reviews the journals and the nature of his findings.
2. Review the journals and the ledgers for unusual transactions and amounts.
3. Review the subsidiary ledger for miscellaneous credits.
4. Foot and crossfoot the journals, and trace the totals to the general ledger.
5. Observe who performs the bank reconciliation.
6. Observe whether a restricted endorsement is used on cash receipts.
7. Observe whether monthly statements are mailed.
8. Observe whether accountant reconciles bank account.
9. Observe whether accountant reconciles subsidiary ledger with control account.

Shipment of Goods
10. Account for a sequence of shipping documents.
11. Trace selected shipping documents to a duplicate sales invoice and the sales journal for assurance that each one has been billed and included in the journal.

Billing of Customers and Recording the Sales in the Records
12. Account for a sequence of sales invoices in the sales journal.
13. Trace selected duplicate invoice numbers from the sales journal to
    a. Accounts receivable subsidiary ledger, and test for amount, date, and invoice number.
    b. Duplicate sales invoice, and test for the total amount recorded in the journal, date, customer name, and account classification. Check the pricing, extensions, and footings. Examine underlying documents for indication of internal verification by Pam Dilley.
    c. Bill of lading, and test for customer name, product description, quantity, and date.
    d. Duplicate sales order, and test for customer name, product description, quantity, date, and approval by Pam Dilley.
    e. Customer order, and test for customer name, product description, quantity, date, and credit approval by Rick Chulick.
14. Trace recorded sales from the sales journal to the file of supporting documents, which includes a duplicate sales invoice, bill of lading, sales order, and customer order.
15. Compare dates on the bill of lading, duplicate sales invoice, and sales journal.

Processing Cash Receipts and Recording the Amounts in the Records
16. Obtain the prelisting of cash receipts, and trace amounts to the cash receipts journal, testing for name, amount, and date.
17. Compare the prelisting of cash receipts with the duplicate deposit slip, testing for names, amounts, and dates. Trace the total from the cash receipts journal to the bank statement, testing for dates, amounts of deposit, and delay in deposit.
18. Prepare a proof of cash receipts.
19. Trace from the cash receipts journal to entries in the subsidiary ledger, and test for date and amount.
20. Trace selected credits from the subsidiary ledger to the cash receipts journal, and test for date and amount.

FIGURE 9–11 Hillsburg Hardware—Audit Program Sales and Cash Receipts—Performance Format

9. Unpaid invoices are filed separately from paid invoices.

10. The sales journal, accounts receivable subsidiary ledger, and cash receipts journal are sent to the accountant on a monthly basis for posting to the general ledger.

11. The receptionist stamps incoming checks with a restrictive endorsement immediately upon receipt.

12. There are no cash sales.

13. Deposits are made at least weekly.

14. The bank account is reconciled by the accountant on a monthly basis.

15. All bad debts expense and charge-off of bad debts are approved by the president after being initiated by the chief accountant.

16. All journals and ledgers are reviewed monthly by the president.

REVIEW QUESTIONS

9–1. Describe the nature of the following documents and records and explain their use in the sales and collection cycle: bill of lading, sales invoice, credit memo, remittance advice, monthly statement to customers.

9–2. Explain the importance of proper credit approval for sales. What effect do adequate controls in the credit function have on the auditor's evidence accumulation?

9–3. Distinguish between bad debts expense and the charge-off of uncollectible accounts. Explain why they are audited in completely different ways.

9–4. List the detailed audit objectives for the verification of sales transactions. For each objective, state one internal control the client can use to reduce the likelihood of errors.

9–5. State one compliance and one substantive test the auditor can use to verify the sales objective, "Recorded sales are stated at the proper amount."

9–6. List the most important duties that should be segregated in the sales and collection cycle. Explain why it is desirable that each of these duties be segregated.

9–7. Explain how prenumbered shipping documents and sales invoices can be useful controls for preventing errors in sales.

9–8. What three types of authorizations are commonly used in an internal control system for sales? For each authorization, state a substantive test the auditor could use to verify whether the control was effective in preventing errors.

9–9. Explain the purpose of footing and crossfooting the sales journal and tracing the totals to the general ledger.

9–10. What is the difference between the auditor's approach in verifying sales returns and allowances compared to sales? Explain the reasons for the difference.

9–11. Explain why auditors usually emphasize the detection of fraud in the audit of cash. Is this consistent or inconsistent with the auditor's responsibility in the audit? Explain.

9–12. List the detailed audit objectives for the verification of cash receipts. For each objective, state one internal control the client can use to reduce the likelihood of errors.

9–13. List several audit procedures the auditor can use to determine whether all cash received was recorded.

9–14. Explain what is meant by *proof of cash receipts*, and state its purpose.

9–15. Explain what is meant by *lapping*, and discuss how the auditor can uncover it. Under what circumstances should the auditor make a special effort to uncover lapping?

9–16. What audit procedures are most likely to be used to verify accounts receivable charged off as uncollectible? State the purpose of each of these procedures.

9–17. State the relationship between the confirmation of accounts receivable and the results of the tests of transactions.

9–18. Under what circumstances is it acceptable to perform tests of transactions for sales and cash receipts at an interim date?

9–19. Diane Smith, CPA, tested sales transactions for the month of March in an audit of the financial statements for the year ended December 31, 19X7. Based on the excellent results of both the compliance and the substantive tests, she decided to significantly reduce her direct tests of the financial balances at year-end. Evaluate this decision.

DISCUSSION QUESTIONS AND PROBLEMS

9–20. For each of the following questions, select the best response:

a. The CPA tests sales transactions. One step is tracing a sample of sales invoices to debits in the accounts receivable subsidiary ledger. Based upon this step, he will form an opinion as to whether
   (1) each sales invoice represents a valid sale.
   (2) all sales have been recorded.
   (3) all debit entries in the accounts receivable subsidiary ledger are properly supported by sales invoices.
   (4) recorded sales invoices have been properly posted to customer accounts.

b. For good internal control, the credit manager should be responsible to the
   (1) sales manager.
   (2) customer-service manager.
   (3) controller.
   (4) treasurer.

c. For good internal control, the billing department should be under the direction of the
   (1) controller.
   (2) credit manager.
   (3) sales manager.
   (4) treasurer.

    d. The authorization for write-off of accounts receivable should be the responsibility of the
      (1) credit manager.
      (2) controller.
      (3) accounts receivable clerk.
      (4) treasurer.

    e. A CPA is examining the financial statements of a small telephone company and wishes to test whether customers are being billed. One procedure that he might use is to
      (1) check a sample of listings in the telephone directory to the billing control.
      (2) trace a sample of postings from the billing control to the subsidiary accounts receivable ledger.
      (3) balance the subsidiary accounts receivable ledger to the general ledger control account.
      (4) confirm a representative number of accounts receivable.

                                    (AICPA adapted)

9–21. For each of the following types of errors (parts a through e), select the control that should have prevented the error.

    a. A manufacturing company received a substantial sales return in the last month of the year, but the credit memorandum for the return was not prepared until after the auditors had completed their field work. The returned merchandise was included in the physical inventory.
      (1) Aging schedules of accounts receivable are prepared periodically.
      (2) Credit memoranda are prenumbered, and all numbers are accounted for.
      (3) A reconciliation of the trial balance of customers' ledgers with the general ledger control is prepared periodically.
      (4) Receiving reports are prepared for all materials received, and such reports are numerically controlled.

    b. The sales manager credited a salesman, Jack Smith, with sales that were actually "house account" sales. Later, Smith divided his excess sales commissions with the sales manager.
      (1) The summary sales entries are checked periodically by persons independent of sales functions.
      (2) Sales orders are reviewed and approved by persons independent of the sales department.
      (3) The internal auditor compares the sales commission statements with the cash disbursements record.
      (4) Sales orders are prenumbered, and all numbers are accounted for.

    c. A sales invoice for $5,200 was computed correctly but, in error, was posted as $2,500 to the sales journal and to the accounts receivable ledger. The customer remitted only $2,500, the amount on his monthly statement.
      (1) Prelistings and predetermined totals are used to control postings.
      (2) Sales invoice serial numbers, prices, discounts, extensions, and footings are independently checked.

(3) The customers' monthly statements are verified and mailed by a responsible person other than the bookkeeper who prepared them.

(4) Unauthorized remittance deductions made by customers or other matters in dispute are investigated promptly by a person independent of the accounts receivable function.

d. Copies of sales invoices show different unit prices for apparently identical items.

(1) All sales invoices are checked as to all details after their preparation.

(2) Differences reported by customers are satisfactorily investigated.

(3) Statistical sales data are compiled and reconciled with recorded sales.

(4) All sales invoices are compared with the customers' purchase orders.

e. The cashier diverted cash received over the counter from a customer to his own use and wrote off the receivable as a bad debt.

(1) Aging schedules of accounts receivable are prepared periodically and reviewed by a responsible official.

(2) Journal entries are approved by a responsible official.

(3) Receipts are given directly to the cashier by the person who opens the mail.

(4) Remittance advices, letters, or envelopes that accompany receipts are separated and given directly to the accounting department.

(AICPA adapted)

9–22. The following sales procedures were encountered during the regular annual audit of Marvel Wholesale Distributing Company.

Customer orders are received by the sales order department. A clerk computes the dollar amount of the order and sends it to the credit department for approval. Credit approval is stamped on the order and returned to the sales order department. An invoice is prepared in two copies and the order is filed in the "customer order" file.

The customer copy of the invoice is sent to the billing department and held in the "pending" file awaiting notification that the order was shipped.

The shipping copy of the invoice is routed through the warehouse and the shipping department as authority for the respective departments to release and ship the merchandise. Shipping department personnel pack the order and prepare a three-copy bill of lading: the original copy is mailed to the customer, the second copy is sent with the shipment, and the other is filed in sequence in the bill of lading file. The invoice shipping copy is sent to the billing department.

The billing clerk matches the received shipping copy with the customer copy from the pending file. Both copies of the invoice are priced, extended, and footed. The customer copy is then mailed directly to the customer, and the shipping copy is sent to the accounts receivable clerk.

The accounts receivable clerk enters the invoice data in a sales accounts receivable journal, posts the customer's account in the subsidiary customers' accounts ledger, and files the shipping copy in the sales invoice file. The invoices are numbered and filed in sequence.

a. In order to gather audit evidence concerning the proper credit approval of sales, the auditor would select a sample of transaction documents from the population represented by the

   (1) customer order file.
   (2) bill of lading file.
   (3) subsidiary customers' accounts ledger.
   (4) sales invoice file.
   b. In order to determine whether the system of internal control operated effectively to minimize errors of failure to post invoices to customers' accounts ledger, the auditor would select a sample of transactions from the population represented by the
   (1) customer order file.
   (2) bill of lading file.
   (3) subsidiary customers' accounts ledger.
   (4) sales invoice file.
   c. In order to determine whether the system of internal control operated effectively to minimize errors of failure to invoice a shipment, the auditor would select a sample of transactions from the population represented by the
   (1) customer order file.
   (2) bill of lading file.
   (3) subsidiary customers' accounts ledger.
   (4) sales invoice file.
   d. In order to gather audit evidence that uncollected items in customers' accounts represented valid trade receivables, the auditor would select a sample of items from the population represented by the
   (1) customer order file.
   (2) bill of lading file.
   (3) subsidiary customers' accounts ledger.
   (4) sales invoice file. (AICPA adapted)

9-23. Items a through h are selected questions of the type generally found in internal control questionnaires used by auditors in evaluating controls in the sales and collection cycle. In using the questionnaire for a particular client, a "yes" response to a question indicates a possible strength in the system, whereas a "no" indicates a potential weakness.
   a. Are sales invoices independently compared to customers' orders for prices, quantities, extensions, and footings?
   b. Are sales orders, invoices, and credit memoranda issued and filed in numerical sequence and are the sequences accounted for periodically?
   c. Are the selling function and sales register preparation independent of the cash receipts, shipping, delivery, and billing functions?
   d. Are all COD, scrap, equipment, and cash sales accounted for in the same manner as charge sales and is the record keeping independent of the collection procedure?
   e. Is the collection function independent of, and does it constitute a check on, the accounts receivable function and accounts receivable bookkeepers?
   f. Are receivable subsidiary ledgers balanced regularly to control accounts by an employee independent of the detail posting functions?
   g. Are cash receipts entered in books of original entry by persons independent of the mail-opening and receipts-listing functions?
   h. Are receipts deposited intact daily on a timely basis?

Required:

a. For each of the questions above, state the internal control objectives being fulfilled if the control is in effect.

b. For each control, list a compliance procedure to test its effectiveness.

c. For each of the questions above, identify the nature of the potential financial errors.

d. For each of the potential errors in part c, list a substantive audit procedure to determine whether a material error exists.

9–24. The following errors or omissions are included in the accounting records of the Joyce Manufacturing Company:

a. A sales invoice was misadded by $1,000.

b. A material sale was unintentionally recorded for the second time on the last day of the year. The sale had originally been recorded two days previously.

c. Cash paid on accounts receivable was stolen by the mail clerk when the mail was opened.

d. Cash paid on accounts receivable that had been prelisted by a secretary was stolen by the bookkeeper who records cash receipts and accounts receivable. He failed to record the transactions.

e. A shipment to a customer was not billed because of the loss of the bill of lading.

f. Merchandise was shipped to a customer, but no bill of lading was prepared. Since billings are prepared from bills of lading, the customer was not billed.

g. A sale to a residential customer was unintentionally classified as a commercial sale.

Required:

a. For each error, state a control that should have prevented the error from occurring on a continuing basis.

b. For each error, state a substantive audit procedure that could uncover the error.

9–25. The following are commonly performed tests of transactions audit procedures in the sales and collection cycle:

a. Examine sales returns for approval by an authorized official.

b. Account for a sequence of shipping documents and examine each one to make sure a duplicate sales invoice is attached.

c. Account for a sequence of sales invoices and examine each one to make sure a duplicate copy of the shipping copy is attached.

d. Compare the quantity and description of items on shipping documents with the related duplicate sales invoices.

e. Trace recorded sales in the sales journal to the related subsidiary ledgers and compare the customer name, date, and amount for each one.

f. Review the prelisting in the cash receipts book to determine whether cash is prelisted on a daily basis.

g. Reconcile the recorded cash receipts on the prelisting of cash receipts with the cash receipts journal and the bank statement for a one-month period.

Required:

a. Identify whether each audit procedure is a compliance or a substantive test.

b. State which of the eight detailed objectives each of the audit procedures fulfills.

9–26. Your client is the Quaker Valley Shopping Center, Inc., a shopping center with thirty store tenants. All leases with the store tenants provide for a fixed rent plus a percentage of sales, net of sales taxes, in excess of a fixed dollar amount computed on an annual basis. Each lease also provides that the landlord may engage a CPA to audit all records of the tenant for assurance that sales are being properly reported to the landlord.

You have been requested by your client to audit the records of the Bali Pearl Restaurant to determine that the sales totaling $390,000 for the year ended December 31, 19X7, have been properly reported to the landlord. The restaurant and the shopping center entered into a five-year lease on January, 19X7. The Bali Pearl Restaurant offers only table service. No liquor is served. During meal times there are four or five waitresses in attendance who prepare handwritten prenumbered restaurant checks for the customers. Payment is made at a cash register, manned by the proprietor, as the customer leaves. All sales are for cash. The proprietor also is the bookkeeper. Complete files are kept of restaurant checks and cash register tapes. A daily sales book and general ledger are also maintained.

Required:

a. For purposes of this audit, which audit objectives are you primarily concerned with?

b. List the auditing procedures that you would employ to verify the total annual sales of the Bali Pearl Restaurant. (Disregard vending machines sales and counter sales of chewing gum, candy, etc.)   (AICPA adapted)

9–27. The following auditing procedures are customarily applied in connection with the verification of cash balances or the testing of cash receipts transactions. Indicate a type of irregularity that could be expected to be disclosed by the application of each procedure and explain how the procedure would disclose the irregularity.

a. Verification of the detail of deposit slips.

b. Comparison of deposits as shown by the bank statement for several days prior to the end of the period under examination with receipts as shown by the cash book.

c. Reconcilement of cash receipts by months as shown by the cash book with deposits as shown by the bank statements.   (AICPA adapted)

9–28. Jerome Paper Company engaged you to review its internal control system. Jerome does not prelist cash receipts before they are recorded and has other weaknesses in processing collections of trade receivables, the company's largest asset. In discussing the matter with the controller, you find he is chiefly interested in economy when he assigns duties to the 15 office personnel. He feels the main considerations are that the work should be done by people who are most familiar with it, capable of doing it, and available when it has to be done.

The controller says he has excellent control over trade receivables because receivables are pledged as security for a continually renewable bank loan and the bank sends out positive confirmation requests occasionally, based on a list of pledged receivables furnished by the company each week.

Required:

a. Explain how prelisting of cash receipts strengthens internal control over cash.
b. Assume that an employee handles cash receipts from trade customers before they are recorded. List the duties which that employee should not do to withhold from him the opportunity to conceal embezzlement of the receipts. (AICPA adapted)

9–29. You have been asked by the board of trustees of a local church to review its accounting procedures. As a part of this review you have prepared the following comments relating to the collections made at weekly services and record keeping for members' pledges and contributions:

• The church's board of trustees has delegated responsibility for financial management and audit of the financial records to the finance committee. This group prepares the annual budget and approves major disbursements but is not involved in collections or record keeping. No audit has been considered necessary in recent years because the same trusted employee has kept church records and served as financial secretary for fifteen years.

• The collection at the weekly service is taken by a team of ushers. The head usher counts the collection in the church office following each service. He then places the collection and a notation of the amount counted in the church safe. Next morning the financial secretary opens the safe and recounts the collection. He withholds about $100 to meet cash expenditures during the coming week and deposits the remainder of the collection intact. In order to facilitate the deposit, members who contribute by check are asked to draw their checks to "cash."

• At their request a few members are furnished prenumbered predated envelopes in which to insert their weekly contributions. The head usher removes the cash from the envelopes to be counted with the loose cash included in the collection and discards the envelopes. No record is maintained of issuance or return of the envelopes, and the envelope system is not encouraged.

• Each member is asked to prepare a contribution pledge card annually. The pledge is regarded as a moral commitment by the member to contribute a stated weekly amount. Based upon the amounts shown on the pledge cards, the financial secretary furnishes a letter to requesting members to support the tax deductibility of their contributions.

Required:

Describe the weaknesses and recommend improvements in procedures for
a. collections made at weekly services.
b. record keeping for members' pledges and contributions.
Organize your answer sheets as follows:

Weakness	Recommended Improvement

(AICPA adapted)

9–30. You are auditing the Alaska Branch of Far Distributing Co. This branch has substantial annual sales which are billed and collected locally. As a part of your audit you find that the procedures for handling cash receipts are as follows:

Cash collections on over-the-counter sales and COD sales are received from the customer or delivery service by the cashier. Upon receipt of cash the cashier stamps the sales ticket "paid" and files a copy for future reference. The only record of COD sales is a copy of the sales ticket which is given to the cashier to hold until the cash is received from the delivery service.

Mail is opened by the secretary to the credit manager, and remittances are given to the credit manager for his review. The credit manager then places the remittances in a tray on the cashier's desk. At the daily deposit cutoff time the cashier delivers the checks and cash on hand to the assistant credit manager who prepares remittance lists and makes up the bank deposit which he also takes to the bank. The assistant credit manager also posts remittances to the accounts receivable ledger cards and verifies the cash discount allowable.

You also ascertain that the credit manager obtains approval from the executive office of Far Distributing Co., located in Chicago, to write off uncollectible accounts, and that he has retained in his custody as of the end of the fiscal year some remittances that were received on various days during the last month.

Required:

a. Describe the irregularities that might occur under the procedures now in effect for handling cash collections and remittances.
b. Give procedures that you would recommend to strengthen internal control over cash collections and remittances. (AICPA adapted)

9–31. The customer billing and collection functions of the Robinson Company, a small paint manufacturer, are attended to by a receptionist, an accounts receivable clerk, and a cashier who also serves as a secretary. The company's paint products are sold to wholesalers and retail stores.

The following describes *all* the procedures performed by the employees of the Robinson Company pertaining to customer billings and collections:

a. The mail is opened by the receptionist, who gives the customers' purchase orders to the accounts receivable clerk. Fifteen to twenty orders are received each day. Under instructions to expedite the shipment of orders, the accounts receivable clerk at once prepares a five-copy sales invoice form which is distributed as follows:

(1) Copy 1 is the customer billing copy and is held by the accounts receivable clerk until notice of shipment is received.
(2) Copy 2 is the accounts receivable department copy and is held for ultimate posting of the accounts receivable records.
(3) Copies 3 and 4 are sent to the shipping department.
(4) Copy 5 is sent to the storeroom as authority for release of the goods to the shipping department.

b. After the paint order has been moved from the storeroom to the shipping department, the shipping department prepares the bills of lading and labels the cartons. Sales invoice copy 4 is inserted in a carton as a packing slip. After the trucker has picked up the shipment, the customer's copy of the bill of lading and copy 3, on which are noted any undershipments, are returned to the accounts receivable clerk. The company does not "back order" in the event of undershipments; customers are expected to reorder the merchandise. The Robinson Company's copy of the bill of lading is filed by the shipping department.

c. When copy 3 and the customer's copy of the bill of lading are received by the accounts receivable clerk, copies 1 and 2 are completed by numbering them and inserting quantities shipped, unit prices, extensions, discounts, and totals. The accounts receivable clerk then mails copy 1 and the copy of the bill of lading to the customer. Copies 2 and 3 are stapled together.

d. The individual accounts receivable ledger cards are posted by the accounts receivable clerk by a bookkeeping machine procedure whereby the sales register is prepared as a carbon copy of the postings. Postings are made from copy 2 which is then filed, along with staple-attached copy 3, in numerical order. Monthly the general ledger clerk summarizes the sales register for posting to the general ledger accounts.

e. Since the Robinson Company is short of cash, the deposit of receipts is also expedited. The receptionist turns over all mail receipts and related correspondence to the accounts receivable clerk who examines the checks and determines that the accompanying vouchers or correspondence contain enough detail to permit posting of the accounts. The accounts receivable clerk then endorses the checks and gives them to the cashier who prepares the daily deposit. No currency is received in the mail, and no paint is sold over the counter at the factory.

f. The accounts receivable clerk uses the vouchers or correspondence that accompanied the checks to post the accounts receivable ledger cards. The bookkeeping machine prepares a cash receipts register as a carbon copy of the postings. Monthly the general ledger clerk summarizes the cash receipts register for posting to the general ledger accounts. The accounts receivable clerk also corresponds with customers about unauthorized deductions for discounts, freight or advertising allowances, returns, etc., and prepares the appropriate credit memos. Disputed items of large amount are turned over to the sales manager for settlement. Each month the accounts receivable clerk prepares a trial balance of the open accounts receivable and compares the resultant total with the general ledger control account for accounts receivable.

Required:

a. Discuss the internal control weaknesses in the Robinson Company's procedures related to customer billings and remittances and the accounting for these transactions. In your discussion, in addition to identifying the weaknesses, explain what could happen as a result of each weakness.

b. For each weakness, list one substantive audit procedure for testing the significance of the potential error. (AICPA adapted)

9–32. The Meyers Pharmaceutical Company, a drug manufacturer, has the following system for billing and recording accounts receivable:

   a. An incoming customer's purchase order is received in the order department by a clerk who prepares a prenumbered company sales order form in which is inserted the pertinent information, such as the customer's name and address, customer's account number, quantity and items ordered. After the sales order form has been prepared, the customer's purchase order is stapled to it.

   b. The sales order form is then passed to the credit department for credit approval. Rough approximations of the billing values of the orders are made in the credit department for those accounts on which credit limitations are imposed. After investigation, approval of credit is noted on the form.

   c. Next the sales order form is passed to the billing department where a clerk types the customer's invoice on a billing machine that crossmultiplies the number of items and the unit price, then adds the automatically extended amounts for the total amount of the invoice. The billing clerk determines the unit prices for the items from a list of billing prices.

      The billing machine has registers that automatically accumulate daily totals of customer account numbers and invoice amounts to provide "hash" totals and control amounts. These totals, which are inserted in a daily record book, serve as predetermined batch totals for verification of computer inputs.

      The billing is done on prenumbered, continuous, carbon-interleaved forms having the following designations:

   (1) "Customer's copy."

   (2) "Sales department copy," for information purposes.

   (3) "File copy."

   (4) "Shipping department copy," which serves as a shipping order. Bills of lading are also prepared as carbon copy by-products of the invoicing procedure.

   d. The shipping department copy of the invoice and the bills of lading are then sent to the shipping department. After the order has been shipped, copies of the bill of lading are returned to the billing department. The shipping department copy of the invoice is filed in the shipping department.

   e. In the billing department one copy of the bill of lading is attached to the customer's copy of the invoice and both are mailed to the customer. The other copy of the bill of lading, together with the sales order form, is then stapled to the invoice file copy and filed in invoice numerical order.

   f. A keypunch machine is connected to the billing machine so that punched cards are created during the preparation of the invoices. The punched cards then become the means by which the sales data are transmitted to a computer for preparation of the sales journal, subsidiary ledger, and perpetual inventory records.

      The punched cards are fed to the computer in batches. One day's accumulation of cards comprises a batch. After the punched cards have been processed by the computer, they are placed in files and held for about two years.

Required:

a. Flowchart the billing system as a means of understanding the system.
b. List the internal controls over sales for each for the eight internal control objectives.
c. For each control, list a useful compliance test to verify the effectiveness of the control.
d. For each audit objective for sales, list appropriate audit procedures, considering the system of internal control.
e. Combine the audit procedures from parts c and d into an efficient audit program for conducting the audit. (The listed procedures should be limited to the verification of the sales data being fed into the computer. Do not carry the procedures beyond the point at which the cards are ready to be fed to the computer.)   (AICPA adapted)

9-33. You are engaged in your first audit of the Licitra Pest Control Company for the year ended December 31, 19X8. The company began doing business in January 19X8 and provides pest control services for industrial enterprises.
Additional information:

a. The office staff consists of a bookkeeper, a typist, and the president, Tony Licitra. In addition, the company employs twenty service personnel on an hourly basis who are assigned to individual territories to make both monthly and emergency visits to customers' premises. The servicemen submit weekly time reports which include the customer's name and the time devoted to each customer. Time charges for emergency visits are shown separately from regular monthly visits on the report.

b. Customers are required to sign annual contracts which are prenumbered and prepared in duplicate. The original is filed in numerical order by contract anniversary date, and the copy is given to the customer. The contract entitles the customer to pest control services once each month. Emergency visits are billed separately.

c. Fees for monthly services are payable in advance—quarterly, semiannually, or annually—and are recorded on the books as "income from services" when the cash is received. All payments are by checks received by mail.

d. Prenumbered invoices for contract renewals are prepared in triplicate from information in the contract file. The original invoice is sent to the customer twenty days prior to the due date of payment, the duplicate copy is filed chronologically by due date, and the triplicate copy is filed alphabetically by customer. If payment is not received by fifteen days after the due date, a cancellation notice is sent to the customer and a copy of the notice is attached to the customer's contract. The bookkeeper notifies the servicemen of all contract cancellations and reinstatements and requires written acknowledgment of receipt of such notices. Mr. Licitra approves all cancellations and reinstatements of contracts.

e. Prenumbered invoices for emergency services are prepared weekly from information shown on servicemen's time reports. The customer is billed at 20 percent of the servicemen's hourly rate. These invoices, prepared in triplicate and distributed as shown above, are recorded on the books as "income from services" at the billing date. Payment is due thirty days after the invoice date.

f. All remittances are received by the typist, who prepares a daily list of collections and stamps a restrictive endorsement on the checks. A copy of the list is forwarded to the bookkeeper, who posts the date and amount received on the copies of the invoice in both the alphabetical and chronological files. After posting, the copy of the invoice is transferred from the chronological file to the daily cash receipts binder, which serves as a subsidiary record for the cash receipts book. The bookkeeper totals the amounts of all remittances received, posts this total to the cash receipts book, and attaches the daily remittance tapes to the paid invoices in the daily cash receipts binder.

g. The typist prepares a daily bank deposit slip and compares the total with the total amount shown on the daily remittance tapes. All remittances are deposited in the bank the day they are received. (Cash receipts from sources other than services need not be considered.)

Required:

List the audit procedures you would employ in the examination of the *income from services* account for 19X8. In developing the procedures, consider the strengths and weaknesses in the system of internal control.

(AICPA adapted)

10

DETERMINING SAMPLE SIZE USING ATTRIBUTES SAMPLING, AND SELECTING THE ITEMS FOR TESTING

Once the auditor has decided which procedures to select and when they should be performed, it is still necessary to determine the proper *number* of items to sample from the population and *which ones* to choose. This chapter examines the process the auditor goes through in making these two decisions for tests of transactions and the methodology followed after the decisions are made. The sales and collection cycle is used as a frame of reference for discussing these concepts. In the early part of the chapter, the selection of items from the population by the use of *judgmental* and *random sampling* is examined. The remainder of the chapter concerns the use of *attributes sampling* as it is applied to tests of transactions. The use of *variables sampling* is studied in Chapter 12.

THE NATURE OF THE PROBLEM

The difficulty facing the auditor in testing most populations is the prohibitive *cost of testing the entire population*. There are a few audit procedures, such as confirming bank balances and analyzing legal expense, where it is typical to sample 100 percent of the population, but these are exceptions. Once the decision has been made to test less than 100 percent of the population, it becomes necessary to decide *how many* and *which specific items* to test.

When a sample is obtained and audit procedures are performed on the sample items, the sample becomes a *representation* of the entire population.

This is true regardless of the method used to select the sample. In using an audited sample to draw conclusions about the population, the auditor must evaluate the sample from four different standpoints:

- A *quantitative* evaluation must be made to estimate the characteristics of interest about the total population. For example, in testing compliance with internal control, an estimate of the error rate of all transactions processed is made on the basis of the sample.
- A *qualitative* evaluation must be made with respect to the system that generated any errors found. Regardless of the approach taken in the audit, the auditor must always determine the cause of the errors he finds and expand his procedures if follow up is necessary.
- An appraisal of the *effectiveness* of the audit procedures employed must be made. If the procedures used are not effective, the sample results will not represent competent evidential matter, no matter how large a sample is taken.
- An appraisal of the *sampling risk* inherent in the sampling process must be made. There is always a risk that the quantitative conclusions about the total population above are wrong, unless 100 percent of the population is examined. Such is the nature of all sampling, whether it be judgmental or statistical.

JUDGMENTAL SAMPLING

A *judgmental sample* is the determination of the sample size and the selection of the individual items in the sample on the basis of sound reasoning by the auditor. It differs from statistical sampling primarily in the lack of objectivity in selecting the sample items and the inability to measure sampling risk.

The use of judgmental sampling is widespread even among those auditors who are strong advocates of statistical methods. There are many parts of every audit where statistical methods are not applicable, and most CPAs have clients where judgmental sampling is preferable because of cost considerations. Therefore, it is important that auditors understand the characteristics of both statistical and judgmental sampling.

Regardless of the method of selecting the sample, the foremost consideration is the *need to make correct generalizations* about the population on the basis of the sample. In selecting a sample, the auditor is primarily concerned with its *representativeness* of the entire population, in terms of the characteristics of audit interest. This does not mean that the sample must be exactly the same as the population, but it should be approximately the same to be representative. For example, if the population contains significant errors, but the sample is almost free of errors, the sample is *nonrepresentative*, and likely to result in an improper audit decision. To improve the likelihood of a judgmental sample being a representative one for tests of transactions, there are several things the auditor should keep in mind:

- In selecting items for examination, *each major type of transaction* in the cycle should be included in the sample. For example, in testing purchases of goods and services, it is inappropriate to test only raw materials purchases if the auditor is also interested in transactions such as advertising, repairs, and donations.
- When different personnel are responsible for processing transactions during the accounting period, some *transactions prepared by each person* should be tested. If there is a change of accounting personnel during the year or if transactions at different locations are handled differently, the likelihood of a nonrepresentative sample is increased when the tests are restricted to the transactions prepared by only one of the employees.
- When the auditor is testing for errors in amounts, *population items with large balances* should be tested more heavily than those with small balances. In compliance testing the auditor is interested in the adequacy of the controls, but for substantive tests the emphasis should be on testing larger dollar balances, since they are normally likely to contain any material errors.
- The size of the sample should be modified to take into account the *circumstances of the audit*. For example, when the population size is large, the auditor's exposure to legal liability is high, and if internal controls are weak, the sample size for substantive tests of transactions should be larger than when these conditions do not prevail.
- Tests of transactions should not be limited to interim testing when the internal controls are inadequate or when certain other conditions affect the auditor's timing of his tests.
- Increasing the sample size cannot compensate for audit procedures that are ineffective. Careful selection of the proper audit procedures is always essential.

Two common approaches to selecting judgmental samples from accounting populations are *block sampling* and *haphazard selection: Random selection* is used for statistically evaluated samples. The first two are discussed briefly below and the third is examined in more detail separately.

Block Sampling

A *block sample* is the selection of several items in sequence. Once the first item in the block is selected, the remainder of the block is chosen automatically. One example of a block sample is the selection of a *sequence* of 100 sales transactions from the sales journal for the third week of March. A total sample of 100 could also be selected by taking five blocks of 20 items each, ten blocks of 10, or fifty blocks of 2.

It is acceptable to use block samples for compliance testing only if a reasonable number of blocks is used. If few blocks are used, the probability of obtaining a nonrepresentative sample is too great, considering the possibility of such things as employee turnover, changes in the accounting system, and the seasonal nature of many businesses. The exact number has not been specified, but a "reasonable number" for most situations is probably at least nine blocks from nine different months.

Haphazard Selection

When the auditor goes through a population and selects items for the sample without regard to their size, source, or other distinguishing characteristics, he is attempting to select without bias. This is called a *haphazard sample.*

The most serious shortcoming of haphazard sampling is the difficulty of really remaining completely unbiased in selecting sample items. Due to the auditor's training and "cultural bias," certain population items are more likely to be included in the sample than others. For some auditors, sales to certain customers and sales journal entries at the top of the page are more likely to be included in a sample than sales to unknown customers and entries in the middle of the page. For other auditors, entries in the middle of the page or large amounts would be more likely to be selected.

Haphazard and block sampling are often useful and should not be automatically discarded as audit tools. In many situations the cost of unbiased or more complex selection methods outweighs the benefits obtained from using them. For example, assume the auditor wants to trace credits from the accounts receivable subsidiary ledger to the cash receipts journal and other authorized sources as a test for the possibility of fictitious credits in the subsidiary records. A haphazard or block approach is simpler and less costly than random selection in this situation and would be employed by most auditors. It is preferable to use random selection methods for selecting samples whenever it is practical, but it is also necessary to consider the relationship between cost and benefit.

It is improper and a serious breach of due care to use *statistical measurement techniques* if the sample is selected by the haphazard, block or any other judgmental approach. Only *random selection* is acceptable when the auditor intends to evaluate a population statistically.

RANDOM SELECTION

Defined

A *random sample* is one in which every possible combination of elements (items) in the population has an equal chance of constituting the sample. The only way the auditor can be confident a random sample has been obtained is by adopting a formal methodology that is designed to accomplish this. Three methods of random selection are discussed in this book: *random number tables, computer terminals,* and *systematic sampling.* Each of these methods is commonly used in practice.

Random Number Tables

A *random number table* is a listing of independent random digits conveniently arranged in tabular form to facilitate the selection of random numbers with multiple digits. An example of such a table, taken from the Interstate Com-

FIGURE 10–1

Random Number Table

Column

Item	(1)	(2)	(3)	(4)	(5)	(6)	(7)	(8)
1000	37039	97547	64673	31546	99314	66854	97855	99965
1001	25145	84834	23009	51584	66754	77785	52357	25532
1002	98433	54725	18864	65866	76918	78825	58210	76835
1003	97965	68548	81545	82933	93545	85959	63282	61454
1004	78049	67830	14624	17563	25697	07734	48243	94318
1005	50203	25658	91478	08509	23308	48130	65047	77873
1006	40059	67825	18934	64998	49807	71126	77818	56893
1007	84350	67241	54031	34535	04093	35062	58163	14205
1008	30954	51637	91500	48722	60988	60029	60873	37423
1009	86723	36464	98305	08009	00666	29255	18514	49158
1010	50188	22554	86160	92250	14021	65859	16237	72296
1011	50014	00463	13906	35936	71761	95755	87002	71667
1012	66023	21428	14742	94874	23308	58533	26507	11208
1013	04458	61862	63119	09541	01715	87901	91260	03079
1014	57510	36314	30452	09712	37714	95482	30507	68475
1015	43373	58939	95848	28288	60341	52174	11879	18115
1016	61500	12763	64433	02268	57905	72347	49498	21871
1017	78938	71312	99705	71546	42274	23915	38405	18779
1018	64257	93218	35793	43671	64055	88729	11168	60260
1019	56864	21554	70445	24841	04779	56774	96129	73594
1020	35314	29631	06937	54545	04470	75463	77112	77126
1021	40704	48823	65963	39359	12717	56201	22811	24863
1022	07318	44623	02843	33299	59872	86774	06926	12672
1023	94550	23299	45557	07923	75126	00808	01312	46689
1024	34348	81191	21027	77087	10909	03676	97723	34469
1025	92277	57115	50789	68111	75305	53289	39751	45760
1026	56093	58302	52236	64756	50273	61566	61962	93280
1027	16623	17849	96701	94971	94758	08845	32260	59823
1028	50848	93982	66451	32143	05441	10399	17775	74169
1029	48006	58200	58367	66577	68583	21108	41361	20732
1030	56640	27890	28825	96509	21363	53657	60119	75385

merce Commission "Table of 105,000 Random Decimal Digits," is included as Figure 10-1. This table has numbered lines and columns, with five digits in each column, as a convenience in reading the tables and documenting the portion of the table used.

The proper use of random number tables is important to ensure the selection of an unbiased sample. Four major steps are involved in the use of the tables:

Establish a Numbering System for the Population. Before a set of random numbers can be selected from the table, each item in the population must be identified with a *unique number*. This is usually not a problem, because many of the populations from which the auditor wants a random sample consist of prenumbered documents. When prenumbered records are not used, some type of numbering system must be developed. In rare instances the entire population may have to be renumbered, but ordinarily a simple approach can be devised to meet the objective. An illustration is the selection of a random sample of accounts receivable for confirmation from a trial balance that contains forty pages with up to ninety lines per page. The sampling unit can be defined as a line on the listing with an outstanding balance. The combination of page numbers and line numbers provides a unique identifying number for every line in the population.

Establish Correspondence between the Random Number Table and the Population.

Once the numbering system has been established for the population, correspondence is established by deciding upon the *number of digits* to use in the random number table and their *association with the population numbering system*. For example, assume the auditor is selecting a sample of one hundred duplicate sales invoices from a file of prenumbered sales invoices beginning with document number 3272 and ending with 8825. Since the invoices contain a four-digit number, it is necessary to use four digits in the random number table. If the first four digits of each five-digit set are used and the starting point in the random number table in Figure 10-1 is item 1000, column 1, the first invoice for inclusion in the sample is 3703. The next three numbers are *outside the range* of the population and are *discarded*. The next sample item is invoice 7804, and so forth.

Establish a Route for Using the Table.

The route defines which digits the auditor uses in a column and the method of reading the table. For a three-digit number, it is, for example, acceptable to use the first three digits, the middle three, or the last three. It is also acceptable to select numbers by reading vertically down columns or horizontally along rows. The route is an *arbitrary decision*, but it needs to be *established in advance* and *followed consistently*.

Select a Starting Point.

Selecting a random starting point in the table is necessary only to eliminate the predictability of the sample. If an employee of the client has a copy of the random number tables used in selecting the random numbers and knows the starting point for their selection, he can determine which items the auditor will be testing. It is acceptable to pick a starting point by simply using a *"blind stab"* into the table with a pencil. The number the pencil falls on is the first item included in the sample and the place from which the established route begins.

Special Considerations

Discards. A difficulty in the use of random number tables occurs when there are a large number of *discards*. Discards increase the time it takes to select the sample and enhance the likelihood of making errors in using the table. Certain shortcuts can be used to reduce the discards, but care must be taken to avoid unequal probability of selection. An example is the selection of a random sample from a population of prenumbered shipping documents numbered from 14067 to 16859. If a five-digit number is used in the tables, only about three numbers out of one hundred are usable (16,859 − 14,067 ÷ 100,000 = .028). The discards can be greatly reduced by ignoring the first digit, which is common to all population items, and using a four-digit number in the table. The discards can be further reduced by carefully redefining the way the first digit in the four-digit random number is used. For example, 1 through 3 could be defined to produce a first digit 4, 4 through 6 a first digit 5, and 7 through 9 a first digit 6. Thus, the random number 7426 from the table would be shipping document number 16426 in the population. This method reduces the discards to only about 10 percent, but it is fairly complicated and difficult to use.

   Documentation.   Regardless of the method used in selecting a random sample, it is necessary to have *proper documentation.* This is beneficial as a means of rechecking and reviewing the selection of the numbers, expanding the sample if additional items are desired, and defending the methodology if the quality of the audit is questioned. *Minimum documentation* would include sufficient information in the working papers to permit the reproduction of the numbers at a later date. This includes the name and page number of the table, the correspondence between the population and the table used, the route, the starting point, and the sample size. Many auditors simply include in the working papers a copy of the table they used, with the random numbers identified. (For an example, see Figure 10-9.)

   Replacement versus Nonreplacement Sampling.   In selecting a random sample, there is a distinction between replacement and nonreplacement sampling. In *replacement sampling,* an element in the population can be included in the sample more than once if the random number corresponding to that element is selected from the table more than once; whereas in *nonreplacement sampling,* an element can be included only once. If the random number corresponding to an element is selected more than once in nonreplacement sampling, it is simply treated as a discard the second time. Although both selection approaches are consistent with sound statistical theory, auditors rarely use replacement sampling.

Computer Terminals

Most CPA firms now rent or have access to computer time-sharing programs which include programs for the selection of random numbers. The advantages of this approach over random number tables are *time saving, reduced likelihood of auditor error* in selecting the numbers, and *automatic documentation.*
   In using computer terminals, it is still necessary for each population

element to have a *unique identification number*, and *correspondence* must be established between the population numbers and the random numbers generated by the computer. There is no need for concern about discards in establishing correspondence because the computer can eliminate most types of discards.

For a typical computer program, it is necessary to input the smallest and largest numbers in the population sequence, the quantity of random numbers desired, and in some cases a random number to start the program. In addition, the auditor usually has the option of getting the list of random numbers in *selection order*, in *ascending numerical sequence*, or both. The input and output from a computer terminal are illustrated in Figure 10-2. In this illustration the auditor is selecting a sample of thirty shipping documents from

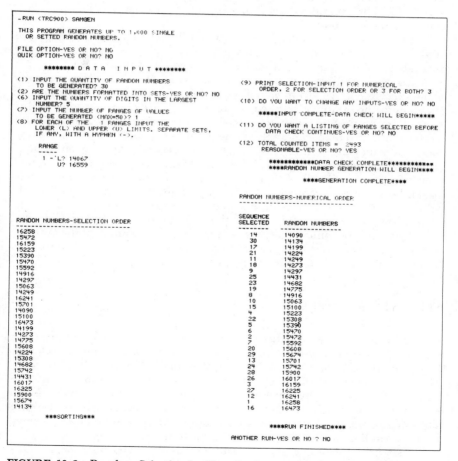

FIGURE 10-2 Random Selection by Use of a Computer Terminal

the same prenumbered population sequence illustrated in the preceding section where the document numbers ranged from 14067 to 16859.

Systematic Selection

In systematic selection, the auditor calculates an *interval* and then methodically selects the items for the sample based on the size of the interval. The interval is determined by dividing the population size by the number of sample items desired. For example, if a population of sales invoices ranges from 652 to 3151 and the desired sample size is 125, the interval is 20 (3,151 — 652 ÷ 125). The auditor must now select a random number between 0 and 19 to determine the starting point for the sample. If the randomly selected number is 9, the first item in the sample is invoice number 661 (652 + 9). The remaining 124 items are 681 (661 + 20), 701 (681 + 20), and so to the last item (3141).

The advantage of systematic sampling is its *ease of use*. In most populations a systematic sample can be drawn quickly, the approach automatically puts the numbers in sequential order, and documentation is easy.

A major problem with the use of systematic sampling is the possibility of *bias*. Because of the way in which systematic samples are selected, once the first item in the sample is selected, all other items are chosen automatically. This causes no problem if the characteristic of interest, such as compliance errors, are distributed randomly throughout the population; however, in many cases they are not. If compliance errors occurred at a certain time of the month or with certain types of documents, a systematic sample would have a higher likelihood of failing to obtain a representative sample than would the two methods previously discussed. This shortcoming is sufficiently serious that some CPA firms do not permit the use of systematic sampling. Other firms require a careful examination of the way the population is listed to evaluate the possibility of a systematic error. In the opinion of the authors, *the use of systematic sampling is not advisable* unless the two other approaches discussed in this section are impractical.

ATTRIBUTES SAMPLING

Attributes sampling is a statistical method used to estimate the *proportion* of items in a population containing a characteristic or attribute of interest. This proportion is called the *occurrence rate* and is the ratio of the items containing the specific attribute to the total number of population items. The occurrence rate is usually expressed as a percent. Auditors are usually interested in the occurrence of errors in populations and refer to the occurrence rate as an error rate. An error may be a compliance deviation or a monetary error, depending on the nature of the audit test.

Assume, for example, that the auditor wants to determine the percentage of duplicate sales invoices which do not have shipping documents attached. There is an actual but unknown percent of unattached shipping documents. The error rate in the sample is used to statistically estimate the population error rate. The estimate is expressed as an *interval estimate* of the population error rate and is a *statement of probability* that the interval does contain the actual population error rate. Furthermore, the interval may be *one-sided* or *two-sided*. A two-sided interval gives upper and lower bounds of probable population error rate, which are referred to as the *computed lower precision limit* (CLPL) and *computed upper precision limit* (CUPL). The auditor might conclude, for example, that the percent of unattached invoices is between 1 percent (computed lower precision limit) and 4 percent (computed upper precision limit) at a 95 percent confidence level.

A one-sided interval specifies a CUPL only and represents the probable "worst likely error rate." This type of attributes estimate is the one most commonly used in tests of transactions.

Purpose of Using Attributes Sampling

Auditors use attributes sampling in order to measure the *sampling risk* inherent in every sampling process. If an auditor selects a sample of 100 items from a population and finds two exceptions without using a statistical method, the auditor can conclude the *sample error rate* is 2 percent. But the auditor is interested in the population error rate, not the sample error rate. The only objective way to obtain a measure of "the worst likely population error rate" (CUPL) at a specified probability (confidence level) is to use statistical methods.

Stated differently, statistical sampling enables auditors to objectively determine the appropriate sample size once an allowable CUPL and confidence level are specified. Determining sample size in this manner aids auditors in achieving greater uniformity for different audits. It may also help auditors defend themselves in the event of a lawsuit.

Attributes sampling measures error rates, whereas *variables* sampling, which is studied in Chapter 12, measures the dollar value of errors. Attributes sampling is typically used for tests of transactions and variables sampling for direct tests of balances. Direct tests of balances deal mostly with monetary errors and therefore are suitable for variables sampling. Since compliance tests of transactions do not directly involve dollar errors, attributes sampling is generally used. Either variables or attributes sampling can be used for substantive tests of transactions; however, most auditors use attributes sampling for substantive tests of transactions for convenience.

Sampling Distribution

The determination of the CUPL at a specified confidence level for a given number of errors in a sample is based upon the use of mathematically determined sampling distributions. Assume that a population of sales invoices exists in which 5 percent of them have no shipping document attached. If the auditor takes a random sample of 50 invoices, how many will have missing shipping documents? The sample could contain no errors or it might contain six or seven. The *probability* of each possible number of errors that would exist in the sample forms the *sampling distribution*. The sampling distribution for the described sample population is shown in Figure 10-3.

FIGURE 10–3

Probability of Each Error Rate for a Sample of 50 Items
from a Population with a Known 5 Percent Error Rate

Number of Errors	Percent of Errors	Probability	Cumulative Probability
0	0	.0769	.0769
1	2	.2025	.2794
2	4	.2611	.5405
3	6	.2199	.7604
4	8	.1360	.8964
5	10	.0656	.9620
6	12	.0260	.9880
7	14	.0120	1.0000

It can be seen in Figure 10-3 that, with a sample of 50 items from a population with a population error rate of 5 percent, the likelihood of obtaining a sample with at least one error is 92.31 percent (1 — .0769).

There is a unique sampling distribution for each population error rate and sample size, which is mathematically determined. The distribution for a sample size of 100 from a population with a 5 percent error rate is different from the previous one, as is the distribution for a sample of 60 from a population with a 3 percent error rate.

In actual audit situations, the auditor does not take repeated samples from known populations. He takes one sample from an unknown population and gets a specific number of errors in that sample. But knowledge about sampling distributions enables the auditor to make statistical statements about the population. For example, if the auditor selected a sample of 50 sales invoices to test for attached shipping documents and found one exception, he could examine the previous probability table and know there is a 20.25 percent probability that the sample came from a population with a 5 percent error rate, and a 79.75 percent (1 — .2025) probability that the sample was taken from a population having some other error rate. Since it is similarly possible to calculate the probability distributions for other population error rates, these can be examined in the aggregate to draw more specific statistical conclusions about the unknown population being sampled. These sampling distributions are the basis for the tables used by auditors for attributes sampling.

NATURE OF ATTRIBUTES ESTIMATES

Assume that an auditor takes a random sample of two hundred sales invoices from a population of 10,000 to determine if their quantities and descriptions on the related shipping documents are the same as on the invoices. The auditor carefully compares the documents and finds eight exceptions in the sample. What is the error rate in the population? Is it 4 percent? The auditor will never know the true population error rate, but he can be fairly certain that it is more or less than exactly 4 percent. Fortunately, the exact percent is not that important. In fact, usually the auditor is primarily concerned about whether the population error rate exceeds a certain upper percent, such as 5 percent. If he believes that the population error rate may be more than the upper percent which is set before the testing is done, some additional audit work is needed; otherwise, no more testing is necessary.

As previously discussed, the statistical upper limit of the population error rate based on the sample results is referred to as the *computed upper precision limit* (CUPL) and is determined using a *one-sided attribute estimate*. The probability that the true population error rate does not exceed the computed upper precision limit is called the *confidence level*, or, alternatively, the *reliability level*. After the audit tests are completed for attributes sampling, the statistical result is stated as a computed upper precision limit and a confidence level.

Use of Tables

Auditors use statistical tables to determine the statistical results of attributes sampling in audit tests as a way of saving time. Tables that are prepared from the sampling distributions previously described are readily available and simple to use. The only difficulty is the occasional lack of availability of the information on the table in exactly the form the auditor wants it. Usually, this problem can be overcome using interpolation.

The computed upper precision limit can be determined using tables with the following steps:

1. Select the attributes table for the desired confidence level.
2. Locate the actual number of sample items in the far left column and read to the right.
3. Locate the actual *sample occurrence rate* in the sample in the "occurrence rate" column and read downward.
4. Locate the intersection of steps 2 and 3. The result is the computed upper precision limit *in percent* at the confidence level stated for the table.

Using Figure 10-4, it can be seen that the computed upper precision limit at a 90 percent confidence level for the previous example is 6.4 percent (eight exceptions from a sample of 200). The result means that the auditor can state with a 90 percent confidence level that the true population error

FIGURE 10–4

One-Sided Upper Precision Limits for Confidence Level of 90.0 Percent

Sample Size												Occurrence Rate									
	0.0	.5	1.0	2.0	3.0	4.0	5.0	6.0	7.0	8.0	9.0	10.0	12.0	14.0	16.0	18.0	20.0	25.0	30.0	40.0	50.0
50	4.5			7.6		10.3		12.9		15.4		17.8	20.1	22.7	24.7	27.2	29.1		39.8	50.0	59.9
100	2.3		3.8	5.2	6.6	7.8	9.1	10.3	11.7	12.7	14.0	15.0	17.3	19.6	21.7	24.0	26.1	31.4	36.6	46.9	56.8
150	1.5			4.4		6.9		9.3		11.6		13.9	16.1	18.4	20.5	22.7	24.8		35.2	45.5	55.4
200	1.1	1.9	2.6	4.0	5.2	6.4	7.6	8.8	10.0	11.0	12.2	13.3	15.5	17.7	19.8	22.0	24.0	29.3	34.5	44.4	54.4
250	.9			3.7		6.1		8.4		10.7		12.9	15.1	17.2	19.3	21.5	23.6		33.7	43.7	53.7
300	.8		2.2	3.5	4.7	5.9	7.0	8.2	9.3	10.4	11.5	12.6	14.7	16.9	19.0	21.1	23.2	28.2	33.2	43.2	53.2
350	.7			3.3		5.7		8.0		10.2		12.3	14.5	16.7	18.8	20.9	22.8		32.8	42.8	52.8
400	.6	1.3	2.0	3.2	4.4	5.6	6.7	7.8	8.9	10.0	11.1	12.2	14.3	16.5	18.5	20.5	22.5	27.5	32.5	42.5	52.5
450	.5			3.1		5.5		7.7		9.9		12.0	14.2	16.3	18.3	20.3	22.3		32.3	42.3	52.2
500	.5		1.8	3.1	4.2	5.4	6.5	7.6	8.7	9.8	10.9	11.9	14.1	16.1	18.1	20.1	22.1	27.1	32.1	42.1	52.0
550	.4			3.0		5.3		7.5		9.7		11.8	13.9	15.9	17.9	19.9	21.9		31.9	41.9	51.9
600	.4	1.1	1.7	2.9	4.1	5.2	6.3	7.4	8.5	9.6	10.7	11.7	13.7	15.7	17.7	19.7	21.7	26.7	31.7	41.7	51.7
650	.4			2.9		5.2		7.4		9.5		11.6	13.6	15.6	17.6	19.6	21.6		31.6	41.6	51.6
700	.3		1.7	2.9	4.0	5.1	6.2	7.3	8.4	9.5	10.5	11.5	13.5	15.5	17.5	19.5	21.5	26.5	31.5	41.5	51.5
750	.3			2.8		5.1		7.3		9.4		11.4	13.4	15.4	17.4	19.4	21.4		31.4	41.4	51.4
800	.3	1.0	1.6	2.8	3.9	5.0	6.1	7.2	8.3	9.3	10.3	11.3	13.3	15.3	17.3	19.3	21.3	26.3	31.3	41.3	51.3
850	.3			2.8		5.0		7.2		9.2		11.2	13.2	15.3	17.3	19.3	21.3		31.3	41.3	51.3
900	.3		1.6	2.7	3.9	5.0	6.0	7.1	8.2	9.2	10.2	11.2	13.2	15.2	17.2	19.2	21.2	26.2	31.2	41.2	51.2
950	.2			2.7		4.9		7.1		9.1		11.1	13.1	15.1	17.1	19.1	21.1		31.1	41.1	51.1
1000	.2	.9	1.5	2.7	3.8	4.9	6.0	7.1	8.1	9.1	10.1	11.1	13.1	15.1	17.1	19.1	21.1	26.1	31.1	41.1	51.1
1500	.2		1.4	2.5	3.6	4.7	5.7	6.7	7.7	8.7	9.7	10.7	12.7	14.7	16.7	18.7	20.7	25.7	30.7	40.7	50.7
2000	.1	.8	1.3	2.5	3.5	4.5	5.5	6.5	7.5	8.5	9.5	10.5	12.5	14.5	16.5	18.5	20.5	25.5	30.5	40.6	50.6
2500	.1		1.3	2.4	3.4	4.4	5.4	6.4	7.4	8.4	9.4	10.4	12.4	14.4	16.4	18.4	20.4	25.4	30.4	40.4	50.4
3000	.1	.7	1.3	2.4	3.4	4.4	5.4	6.4	7.4	8.4	9.4	10.4	12.4	14.4	16.4	18.4	20.4	25.4	30.4	40.4	50.4
4000	.1	.7	1.2	2.3	3.3	4.3	5.3	6.3	7.3	8.3	9.3	10.3	12.3	14.3	16.3	18.3	20.3	25.3	30.3	40.3	50.3
5000	.0	.7	1.2	2.3	3.2	4.2	5.2	6.2	7.2	8.2	9.2	10.2	12.2	14.2	16.2	18.2	20.2	25.2	30.2	40.2	50.2

FIGURE 10-4 (cont.)

One-Sided Upper Precision Limits for Confidence Level of 95.0 Percent

Sample Size	\multicolumn{21}{c}{Occurrence Rate}

Sample Size	0.0	.5	1.0	2.0	3.0	4.0	5.0	6.0	7.0	8.0	9.0	10.0	12.0	14.0	16.0	18.0	20.0	25.0	30.0	40.0	50.0
50	5.8			9.1		12.1		14.8		17.4		19.9	22.3	25.1	27.0	29.6	31.6		42.4	52.6	62.4
100	3.0	4.7		6.2	7.6	8.9	10.2	11.5	13.0	14.0	15.4	16.4	18.7	21.2	23.3	25.6	27.7	33.1	38.4	48.7	56.6
150	2.0			5.1		7.7		10.2		12.6		15.0	17.3	19.6	21.7	24.0	26.1		36.7	47.0	56.8
200	1.5	2.4	3.1	4.5	5.8	7.1	8.3	9.5	10.8	11.9	13.1	14.2	16.4	18.7	20.9	23.1	25.2	30.5	35.7	45.7	55.6
250	1.2			4.2		6.7		9.1		11.4		13.7	15.9	18.1	20.3	22.4	24.6		34.8	44.8	54.7
300	1.0		2.6	3.9	5.2	6.4	7.6	8.8	10.0	11.1	12.2	13.3	15.5	17.7	19.8	22.0	24.1	29.1	34.1	44.1	54.1
350	0.9			3.7		6.2		8.5		10.8		13.0	15.2	17.4	19.5	21.7	23.6		33.6	43.6	53.6
400	0.7	1.6	2.3	3.6	4.8	6.0	7.2	8.3	9.5	10.6	11.7	12.8	15.0	17.2	19.2	21.2	23.2	28.2	33.2	43.2	53.2
450	0.7			3.5		5.9		8.2		10.4		12.6	14.8	16.8	18.9	20.9	22.9		32.9	42.9	52.9
500	0.6		2.1	3.4	4.6	5.8	6.9	8.0	9.2	10.3	11.4	12.5	14.6	16.7	18.6	20.7	22.6	27.6	32.6	42.6	52.6
550	0.5			3.3		5.7		7.9		10.1		12.3	14.4	16.4	18.4	20.4	22.4		32.4	42.4	52.4
600	0.5	1.3	2.0	3.2	4.4	5.6	6.7	7.8	9.0	10.0	11.2	12.2	14.2	16.2	18.2	20.2	22.2	27.2	32.2	42.2	52.2
650	0.5			3.2		5.5		7.7		10.0		12.1	14.1	16.1	18.1	20.1	22.1		32.1	42.1	52.1
700	0.4		1.9	3.1	4.3	5.4	6.6	7.7	8.8	9.9	10.8	11.9	13.9	15.9	17.9	19.9	21.9	26.9	31.9	41.9	51.9
750	0.4			3.1		5.4		7.6		9.8		11.8	13.8	15.8	17.8	19.8	21.8		31.8	41.8	51.8
800	0.4	1.1	1.8	3.0	4.2	5.3	6.4	7.5	8.7	9.7	10.7	11.7	13.7	15.7	17.7	19.7	21.7	26.7	31.7	41.7	51.7
850	0.4			3.0		5.3		7.5		9.6		11.6	13.6	15.6	17.6	19.6	21.6		31.6	41.6	51.6
900	0.3		1.7	3.0	4.1	5.2	6.3	7.5	8.5	9.5	10.5	11.5	13.5	15.5	17.5	19.5	21.5	26.5	31.5	41.5	51.5
950	0.3			2.9		5.2		7.4		9.4		11.4	13.4	15.5	17.4	19.5	21.4		31.4	41.5	51.5
1000	0.3	1.0	1.7	2.9	4.0	5.2	6.3	7.4	8.4	9.4	10.4	11.4	13.4	15.4	17.4	19.4	21.4	26.4	31.4	41.4	51.4
1500	0.2		1.5	2.7	3.8	4.9	5.9	6.9	7.9	8.9	9.9	10.9	12.9	14.9	16.9	18.9	20.9	25.9	30.9	40.9	50.9
2000	0.1	.8	1.4	2.6	3.7	4.7	5.7	6.7	7.7	8.7	9.7	10.7	12.7	14.7	16.7	18.7	20.7	25.7	30.7	40.7	50.7
2500	0.1		1.4	2.6	3.6	4.6	5.6	6.6	7.6	8.6	9.6	10.6	12.6	14.6	16.6	18.6	20.6	25.6	30.6	40.6	50.6
3000	0.1	.8	1.4	2.5	3.5	4.5	5.5	6.5	7.5	8.5	9.5	10.5	12.5	14.5	16.5	18.5	20.5	25.5	30.5	40.5	50.5
4000	0.1	.7	1.3	2.4	3.4	4.4	5.4	6.4	7.4	8.4	9.4	10.4	12.4	14.4	16.4	18.4	20.4	25.4	30.4	40.4	50.4
5000	0.1	.7	1.3	2.3	3.3	4.3	5.3	6.3	7.3	8.3	9.3	10.3	12.3	14.3	16.3	18.3	20.3	25.3	30.3	40.3	50.3

rate does not exceed 6.4 percent. Stated another way, it means there is a 10 percent statistical risk (100 percent — 90 percent) of the true population error rate exceeding 6.4 percent. Does this result indicate that if 100 percent of the population were tested, the true error rate would be 6.4 percent? No, the true error rate is unknown, but there is only a 10 percent chance of the true rate being more than 6.4 percent. There is a 90 percent chance of it being 6.4 percent or less.

Use of Attributes Sampling in Auditing

With this basic background about attributes sampling, it is now possible to examine its use in auditing. The most important part of attributes sampling is the decision process the auditor goes through in determining the sample size and evaluating the results.

In studying attributes sampling for tests of transactions, it is useful to separate the main steps and to study each one separately. The following steps provide an outline of the methodology for using attributes sampling:

- State the objectives of the audit test.
- Define the population.
- Define the sampling unit.
- Define the attributes of interest.
- Specify the desired upper precision limit.
- Specify the desired confidence level.
- Estimate the population error rate.
- Determine the initial sample size.
- Randomly select the sample.
- Perform the audit procedures.
- Generalize from the sample to the population.
- Perform error analysis.
- Decide on the acceptability of the population.

State the Objectives of the Audit Test

The overall objectives of the test must be stated in terms of the particular transactions cycle being tested. Generally, the overall objective of tests of transactions is to test the controls in a particular cycle. In the test of the sales and collection cycle, the overall objective is usually to test the reliability of controls over sales or cash receipts.

Define the Population

The population represents the body of data about which the auditor wishes to generalize. The auditor can define the population to include whatever data he desires but he must *randomly sample from the entire population* as he has defined it and he may *generalize only about that population from which he has sampled*. For example, in performing tests of recorded sales transactions, the auditor generally defines the population as all sales invoices for the year.

If the auditor randomly samples from only one month's transactions, it is invalid to draw statistical conclusions about the invoices for the entire year. It is important that the auditor carefully define the population in advance, consistent with the objectives of the audit tests. Furthermore, in some cases it may be necessary to define more than one population for a given set of audit objectives. For example, if the auditor intends to trace from shipping documents to sales invoices to test for unrecorded sales, and from sales invoices to shipping documents to test validity, there are two populations.

Define the Sampling Unit

The major consideration in defining the sampling unit is to make it consistent with the objectives of the audit tests. Thus, the definition of the population and the planned audit procedures usually dictate the appropriate sampling unit. For example, if the auditor wants to determine how frequently the client fails to fill a customer's order, the sampling unit must be defined as the customer's order. On the other hand, if the objective is to determine whether the proper quantity of the goods described on the customer's order is correctly shipped and billed, it is possible to define the sampling unit as the customer's order, the shipping document, or the duplicate sales invoice.

Define the Attributes of Interest

The auditor must carefully define the *characteristics (attributes)* being tested whenever attributes sampling is used. Unless a precise statement of what constitutes the attribute is made in advance, the staff person who performs the audit procedure will have no guidelines for identifying exceptions. The following is an example of five different attributes being tested as a part of one attributes sampling application. For each attribute, the related internal control objective and whether the audit test is compliance or substantive are also included.

Attribute	Internal Control Objective	Compliance or Substantive
The duplicate sales invoice is approved.	Sales transactions are properly authorized.	Compliance
A copy of the shipping document is attached to the duplicate sales invoice.	Recorded sales are for shipments actually made to nonfictitious customers.	Compliance
The quantity on the sales invoice is the same as on the shipping document.	Recorded sales are properly valued.	Substantive
The account number charged is included on the duplicate sales invoice.	Recorded sales are properly classified.	Compliance
The amount and date on the duplicate sales invoice are the same as on the related subsidiary ledger.	Sales transactions are properly included in the subsidiary records.	Substantive

Each of these five attributes is verified for every item randomly selected for the sample. The absence of the attribute for any sample item is an error for that attribute.

Specify the Desired Upper Precision Limit

Establishing the *desired* upper precision limit (DUPL) requires the auditor to make a *professional judgment*. It represents the error rate the auditor will permit in the population and still be willing to rely upon the controls in the system. The suitable DUPL is a question of *materiality* and is therefore affected by the *definition of the attribute* and the *importance of the attribute*.

The DUPL has a significant effect on the sample size. If it is close to the sample error rate, a larger sample is needed than for a higher DUPL.

Specify the Desired Confidence Level

Whenever a sample is taken, there is always a risk that the quantitative conclusions about the population will be incorrect. This is always true unless 100 percent of the population is tested. As has been stated, this is the nature of both judgmental and statistical sampling.

When the auditor determines the CUPL from a table on the basis of a random sample, there is still a chance that the true population error rate will exceed the computed value if the sample happens to be nonrepresentative. In attributes testing, the confidence level is the statistical means of expressing the probability that the true population error rate does not exceed the stated upper precision limit. The confidence level is traditionally expressed as a percent.

Referring to the foregoing example, assume that the auditor specifies the confidence level at 90 percent when the DUPL is 5 percent. The auditor is saying that he wants to be 90 percent confident that the true population error rate is 5 percent or less. Another way of saying this is that he is willing to take a *statistical risk* of 10 percent (100 percent − 90 percent) that the true population error rate exceeds 5 percent. The auditor must decide for himself if the desired confidence level and DUPL are satisfactory to meet his audit objectives.

Choosing the appropriate confidence level in a particular situation is difficult, and the auditor must make this decision using his best judgment. Since the confidence level is a measure of the level of audit assurance the auditor desires, the important considerations affecting its choice are the *degree to which the auditor wishes to rely upon the system* and the *potential for adverse actions* against the client by the SEC, creditors, or other statement users. If the auditor plans to rely heavily upon the system as a basis for reducing substantive tests, a high level of assurance is desirable. Similarly, if the auditor feels the exposure to legal liability is great, it is desirable to set high confidence levels to minimize the likelihood of the true error rate being greater than the computed results.

The auditor can establish different upper precision limit and confidence level requirements for different attributes of a particular audit test. For example, it is common for auditors to use a higher desired upper precision limit and lower confidence level for tests of credit approval than for tests of the existence of duplicate sales invoices and a bill of lading.

Figures 10-5 and 10-6 are illustrative guidelines for establishing desired upper precision limits and confidence levels for tests or transactions. They should not be interpreted as representing AICPA or anyone else's recommendations. They are illustrative of guidelines a CPA firm could issue to its staff.

Estimate the Population Error Rate

In attributes sampling, an *advance estimate* of the population error rate is necessary to plan the appropriate sample size. If the estimated population error rate is low, a relatively small sample size will satisfy the auditor's desired upper precision limit. It is common to use the *results of the preceding year's audit* as information to help make this estimate; but if last year's results are not available or if they are considered unreliable, the auditor can take a small *preliminary sample* of the current year's population for this purpose. It is not critical that the estimates be absolutely correct because the current year's sample error rate is ultimately used to estimate the population characteristics.

Determine the Initial Sample Size

Four factors determine the initial sample size for attributes sampling: *population size, DUPL, desired confidence level,* and *advance estimate of the population error rate.* The population size is not a major factor in the early part of the following discussion and is examined later. The initial sample size is called an initial one because the errors in the actual sample must be evaluated before it is possible to decide whether the sample is sufficiently large to achieve the audit objectives.

When the three major factors affecting sample size have been determined, it is possible to compute an initial sample by using tables. These tables were developed using the same concepts that were shown in the calculations in Figure 10-3. The same tables (Figure 10-4) are used for determining sample size as for determining the CUPL. It should be kept in mind that these are "one-sided tables," which means that they represent the *upper* precision limit for the given confidence level.

Use of the Tables. In using the tables to compute the initial sample size, three steps are required:

1. Select the table corresponding to the desired confidence level.
2. Locate the expected occurrence rate at the top of the table.

FIGURE 10–5

Guidelines for Statistical Sample Sizes—Compliance Tests of Transactions

Factor	Judgment	Guideline
		Confidence level (1)
Planned degree of reliance on internal controls being tested. Consider:	High reliance	95% reliability
• Nature, extent, and timing of substantive tests: i.e., greater substantive tests, lesser reliance on internal control, and vice versa	Moderate reliance	90% reliability
• Quality of evidence about compliance available: i.e., the lower the quality of evidence, the lesser the reliance on internal control will be	Low reliance	80% reliability
		Upper precision limit
• Significance of the transactions and related account balances the internal controls are intended to affect	Highly significant balances	4%
	Significant balances	5%
	Less significant balances	6%

Notes: (1) Confidence levels are for one-sided estimates.
(2) Certain significant items may be judgmentally selected in addition to the statistical sample.
(3) The guidelines should also recognize that there may be variations in confidence levels based on overall audit assurance considerations. The guildelines above are the most conservative that should be followed.

FIGURE 10–6

Guidelines for Statistical Sample Sizes—Substantive Tests of Transactions

Planned Reduction in Substantive Tests of Details of Balances	Results of Evaluation of Internal Control and Compliance Tests	Confidence Levels for Substantive Tests of Transactions (1)	DUPL for Substantive Tests of Transactions
Large	Excellent (2)	60%	Percent or amount
	Good	80%	based on materiality
	Not good	95%	considerations for
Moderate	Excellent (2)	60%	related accounts
	Good	75%	
	Not good	90%	
Small (3)	Excellent (2)	60%	
	Good	70%	
	Not good	80%	

Notes: (1) Confidence levels are for one-sided estimates.
(2) This situation is where internal control and evidence about it are both good. Substantive tests of transactions are least likely to be performed at all in these cases.
(3) This situation is where little emphasis is being placed on the system at all. Neither compliance nor substantive tests of transactions are likely in this situation.
(4) The guidelines should also recognize that there may be variations in confidence levels based on overall audit assurance considerations. The guidelines above are the most conservative that should be followed.

3. Read down the table in that column to the line that contains the desired upper precision limit. The left-hand column for that line contains the initial sample size to use. Interpolation for values not in the table is valid, but a minimum sample size of 50 items is required.

To illustrate the use of the table, assume an auditor is willing to rely upon the system of credit approval if the rate of missing credit approvals in the population (DUPL) does not exceed 6 percent at a 95 percent confidence level. On the basis of past experience, the sample error rate has been about 4 percent. Using the 95 percent confidence level table in Figure 10-4, the initial sample size is determined to be 400. (Occurrence rate is 4 percent; read down until 6 percent is reached in the table.)

Is this a large enough sample size for this audit? It is not possible to answer that question until after the tests have been performed. If the actual error rate in the sample turns out to be somewhat over 4 percent, but less than 6 percent, the auditor will be unsure of the adequacy of the controls. The will become apparent as we proceed.

Effect of Population Size. In the preceding discussion the size of the population was ignored in determining the initial sample size. It may seem strange to some readers, but statistical theory proves that in most types of populations where attributes sampling applies, the population size is only a *minor* consideration in determining sample size. This is true because representativeness is ensured by the random selection process. Once an adequate sample size is obtained to include a good cross-section of items, additional items are not needed.

The tables used by most auditors, including the tables in this text, are based upon infinite population sizes. It is possible to take the population size into effect in determining the initial sample size by making an adjustment called the *finite correction factor*. The finite correction factor has the effect of significantly reducing the sample size only when more than 10 percent of the population is included in the sample. The calculation is as follows:

$$n = \frac{n'}{1 + n'/N}$$

where n' = sample size before considering the effect of the population size
N = population size
n = revised sample size after considering the effect of the population size

As an example, assume the size of the population of sales orders in the previous problem to be 2,000. The revised sample size is computed as follows:

$$n = \frac{400}{1 + 400/2,000} = 333$$

If the population is 20,000 rather than 2,000, the revised sample size is 392, which is not significantly lower than the 400 shown in the table.

It is never improper to use the finite correction factor. The determining factor in its use is whether the reduction in sample size is worth the additional calculation cost.

Effect of a Change in the Factors. In order to properly understand the concepts underlying statistical sampling in auditing, the reader should understand the effect of individually changing any of the four factors that determine sample size when the other factors remain unchanged. The following table illustrates the effect of increasing each of the four factors. A decrease of any of the factors will have the opposite effect.

Type of Change	*Effect on Preliminary Sample Size*
Increase the desired confidence level.	Increase
Increase the desired upper precision limit.	Decrease
Increase the estimate of the population error rate.	Increase
Increase the population size.	Increase (minor effect)

Randomly Select the Sample

After the auditor has computed the initial sample size for the attributes sampling application, he must choose the particular elements in the population to be included in the sample. It is essential that the selection be random whenever statistical sampling is used. This can be done by the use of random tables, computers, or systematic sampling, as previously discussed.

Perform the Audit Procedures

The audit procedures are performed in the same manner in statistical sampling as in judgmental sampling. The auditor examines each item in the sample to determine whether it is consistent with the definition of the attribute, and he maintains a record of all the errors found.

In performing the audit procedures, it is essential that the auditor avoid *nonsampling errors.* A nonsampling error occurs when the auditor fails to recognize the existence of an actual error in the sample items. This can result from many causes, including the lack of understanding of the objectives of the test, fatigue or boredom, carelessness, and deception on the part of the client by using fictitious documents or records. Nonsampling errors have the effect of understating the population error rate because of the omission of actual errors in the sample. For example, assume that the auditor is comparing the quantity and description of merchandise shipped as they are stated on the shipping document with the corresponding data on the duplicate sales invoice for a sample of three hundred items. If the actual number of exceptions in the sample is nine, but the auditor unintentionally overlooks four of them because his mind wanders, a serious nonsampling error has occurred. Because of the auditor's failure to follow due care, an unacceptable population may be accepted.

A related consideration is the identification of types of *errors not defined as attributes* during planning. These must never be overlooked just because they were not expected. Unexpected errors usually result in the auditor's revising his initial definition of attributes of interest, and may even necessitate a revision of planned sample size.

Generalize from the Sample to the Population (*Determine CUPL*)

After the auditor has completed his tests of the sample, he is in a position to generalize about the population. It would be wrong for him to conclude that the population error rate is exactly the same as the sample error rate; the odds of this being the case are just too low. Instead, he must *compute the upper precision limit* for the population error rate at the *confidence level he desires* based on the *actual sample results*. This is easily accomplished by using the same attributes sampling table that was used for determining the initial sample size previously shown.

If the auditor has tested the random sample of four hundred items from the population of two thousand sales orders from the previous example and has determined that there are twelve missing credit approvals (3 percent), the table in Figure 10-4 indicates a CUPL of 4.8 percent at a 95 percent confidence level (using the 95 percent confidence level table, a sample size of 400 and a 3.0 occurrence rate). This result means the auditor can state with a 95 percent confidence level that the true population error rate does not exceed 4.8 percent. Stated another way, it means there is a 5 percent statistical risk (100 percent − 95 percent) of the true population error rate exceeding 4.8 percent. Does this result indicate that if 100 percent of the population were tested, the true error rate would be 4.8 percent? No, the true error rate is unknown, but there is only a 5 percent chance of the true rate being more than 4.8 percent. There is a 95 percent chance of it being 4.8 percent or less.

A useful way of looking at the statistical results is by a combination of the *point estimate of the error rate* and the *computed precision interval*. The point estimate of the population error rate is the same as the sample error rate; in this case 3 percent. The computed precision interval is 1.8 percent (4.8 percent − 3 percent). It represents a statistical measure of the inability to accurately measure the population error rate due to the restriction of the test to a sample. The combination of the two is the "worst likely error rate," which is called the computed upper precision limit, at the confidence level specified.

The *finite correction factor* can also be used to adjust the computed upper precision limit. This is done by multiplying the *computed precision interval* by $\sqrt{(N - n)/N}$ and adding the result to the sample error rate ($N =$ population size; n = actual sample size). In the previous example the revised precision interval is approximately 1.6 percent (1.8 percent $\times \sqrt{(2{,}000 - 400)/2{,}000}$). This means the revised computed upper precision limit is 4.6 percent (3.0 percent + 1.6 percent). The reduction in the computed upper precision limit is ordinarily not worth the effort to calculate it unless more than 10 percent of the population has been tested.

Perform Error Analysis

In addition to determining the CUPL for each attribute, it is necessary to *analyze the individual errors* to determine the breakdown in the internal control that caused them. The errors could have been caused by carelessness of employees, misunderstood instructions, intentional failure to perform procedures, or many other factors. The nature of an error and its cause have a significant effect on the qualitative evaluation of the system. For example, if all the errors in the tests of internal verification of sales invoices occurred while the person normally responsible for performing the tests was on vacation, this would affect the auditor's evaluation of the system and the subsequent investigation.

Decide on the Acceptability of the Population

It is important to distinguish between the DUPL and *confidence level* that were *chosen* by the auditor before the tests were performed and the CUPL and *confidence level* that *resulted* from the sample. The first set represents the *standards that were deemed necessary* by the auditor, and the second set is the *result that is objectively computed* on the basis of the sample.

Before the population can be considered acceptable, the CUPL determined on the basis of the actual sample results must be *less than or equal to* the desired upper precision limit when both are based upon the desired confidence level. In the example just given where the auditor had prespecified that he would accept a 6 percent population error rate at a 95 percent confidence level and the computed upper precision limit was 4.6 percent, the requirements of the sample have been met. In this case the control being tested can be relied upon to reduce the substantive tests as planned, provided a careful analysis of the cause of errors does not indicate the possibility of a significant problem in a particular aspect of the controls not previously considered.

When the CUPL is greater than DUPL requirements, it is necessary to take specific action. Four courses of action can be followed:

Revise the DUPL or Confidence Level Desired. This alternative should be followed only when the auditor has concluded that the original specifications were too conservative. The relaxing of either the DUPL or the confidence level may be difficult to defend if the auditor is ever subject to review by a court or a commission. If these requirements are changed, it should be on the basis of well thought out reasons.

Expand the Sample Size. An increase in the sample size has the effect of decreasing the CUPL if the actual sample error rate does not increase. This can be demonstrated with the table in Figure 10-4 by keeping the sample error rate constant and observing the decrease in the CUPL for increases in sample size.

The decision of whether to increase the sample size until the computed upper precision limit is less than the DUPL must be made on the basis of the cost versus the benefits. If the sample is not expanded, it is necessary to perform additional substantive tests due to the unacceptability of the controls. The cost of the additional compliance testing must be compared with the additional cost of the substantive tests. Of course there is always a chance that an expanded attributes sample will continue to produce unacceptable results. Therefore, additional substantive tests will still be necessary. Another examination of Figure 10-4 will demonstrate that when the sample error rate is close to the DUPL precision limit, a large sample size is needed to satisfy the statistical requirements.

Alter the Substantive Procedures. Instead of expanding the sample in order to rely upon the controls, it is acceptable instead to perform additional substantive procedures. For example, if the compliance tests of the internal verification procedures for verifying the price, extension, and quantities on sales invoices indicate they are not being properly followed, the auditor may increase the substantive tests of the pricing, extension, and footing. An expansion of the confirmation of accounts receivable may also help to discover whether there are material errors.

Write a Management Letter. This action is desirable, in combination with one of the other three actions, regardless of the nature of the errors. When the auditor determines that the control system is not operating effectively, management should be informed.

In some instances it may be acceptable to limit the action to writing a management letter when the CUPL exceeds the DUPL. This occurs if the auditor has no intention of relying on the control being tested or has already carried out substantive procedures to his own satisfaction as a part of the tests of transactions.

Other Considerations

In the preceding discussions, we bypassed several important considerations involving selecting the proper sample size and drawing conclusions about the results for the sake of better continuity. These topics are discussed at this time.

Distinction between Random Selection and Statistical Measurement.
Auditors often do not understand the distinction between random selection
and statistical measurement. It should now be clear that random selection
is a part of statistical sampling but is not, by itself, statistical measurement.
To have statistical measurement, it is necessary to mathematically generalize
from the sample to the population.

It is acceptable to use random selection procedures without drawing
statistical conclusions, but this practice is questionable if a reasonably large
sample size has been selected. Whenever the auditor takes a random sample,
regardless of his basis for determining the size of the sample, there is a *statistical measurement inherent in the sample*. Since there is little or no cost involved
in computing the upper precision limit, we believe it should be done whenever it is possible. It would of course be inappropriate to draw a statistical
conclusion unless the sample were randomly selected.

Need for Adequate Documentation. It is important that the auditor
retain adequate records of the procedures performed, the methods used to
select the sample and perform the tests, the results found in the tests, and
the conclusions drawn. This is necessary as a means of *evaluating the results*
of all tests when they are combined and as a basis for *defending the audit* if
the need arises. An example of the type of documentation commonly found
in practice is included in the appendix at the end of the chapter.

Need for Professional Judgment. A criticism occasionally levied
against statistical sampling is that it embodies a reduction in the use of
professional judgment. An examination of the thirteen steps given previously
indicates how unwarranted this criticism is. To have a proper application
of attributes sampling, it is necessary to use professional judgment in most of
the steps. For example, the selection of the initial sample size is dependent
primarily upon the desired confidence level, DUPL, and estimated error
rate. The first two of these require the exercise of high-level professional
judgment. The latter requires a careful estimate. Similarly, the final evaluation of the adequacy of the entire application of attributes sampling,
including the adequacy of the sample size, must also be based upon high-level
professional judgment.

Use of Judgmental Sampling. The preceding discussion of attributes
sampling should not be interpreted as a criticism of performing audit tests
without the use of statistical sampling. First of all, many audit tests must
be performed outside of a statistical sampling context. This includes footing
of journals, reviewing records, and having discussions with personnel.
Second, in many instances the cost of performing random selection or testing
a sufficient number of items to warrant a statistical inference exceeds the
benefits of using a statistical approach.

The primary reason for not criticizing judgmental sampling, however,
is the fact that in most instances it *does not differ* substantially from statistical
methods. A careful examination of the steps in applying attributes sampling
indicates that except for the degree of formality required, the methods are

essentially the same for a judgmental or a statistical approach. The most important differences are in specifying the desirable upper precision limit, the confidence level, and the estimated error rate. In addition, there is a difference in the way the auditor generalizes from the sample to the population. Nevertheless, the same decisions that are made when the auditor uses statistical sampling must also be made, on a more intuitive basis, for judgmental sampling.

The most important advantage of attributes sampling for tests of transactions as compared with judgmental sampling is the requirement of *formally* specifying the auditor's judgments. We believe this encourages more careful and precise thinking about the *objectives* of the audit tests. We also believe the ability to determine the *results achieved* in terms of a computed upper precision limit and a confidence level is a significant benefit of attributes sampling.

Discovery Sampling

For some audit procedures the auditor expects to find no exceptions, but if even one exception is found, it is sufficient to require extensive follow-up. Examples might be fraud-oriented procedures or the failure to bill a customer when all shipments are for large dollar amounts. The use of a statistical method called discovery sampling is sometimes used for such "critical errors."

Discovery sampling deals with the probability of discovering *at least one error* in a given sample size if the population error rate is a certain percent. Tables derived from sampling distributions of the type illustrated in Figure 10-3 are used to determine the probabilities. Such a table is included in Figure 10-7. For example, if an auditor selected a random sample of 300 from a population and found no errors in the sample, he could conclude from the table in Figure 10-7 at an 78 percent confidence level that the true population error rate does not exceed .5 percent. He could also conclude at a 45 percent confidence level that the population error rate does not exceed .2 percent and at a 95 percent confidence level that it does not exceed 1 percent.

Notice that by using attributes sampling with a 95 percent confidence level and a zero error rate (Figure 10-4), the same conclusions would have been reached. The reason is that both tables are prepared using the same types of sampling distributions. A 95 percent confidence level table for attributes uses one probability (95 percent), with different sample sizes and different expected error rates. The discovery sampling table uses one expected error rate (zero), with different sample sizes and different probabilities.

The discovery sampling table can also be used to determine the appropriate sample size for critical errors. For example, assume that the auditor is willing to accept a .5 percent population error rate (DUPL) at a confidence level of 90 percent for a certain critical error. (The expected error rate is always zero.) Using the table in Figure 10-7, the sample size required for the test is 460. Except for a minor difference due to a rounding in the table, the same sample size would be required by the table in Figure

FIGURE 10–7

Probability in Percent of Including at Least One Occurrence in a Sample

Rate of Occurrence in the Population (%)

Sample Size	.01	.05	.1	.2	.3	.5	1	2
50		2	5	9	14	22	39	64
60	1	3	6	11	16	26	45	70
70	1	3	7	13	19	30	51	76
80	1	4	8	15	21	33	55	80
90	1	4	9	16	24	36	60	84
100	1	5	10	18	26	39	63	87
120	1	6	11	21	30	45	70	91
140	1	7	13	24	34	50	76	94
160	2	8	15	27	38	55	80	96
200	2	10	18	33	45	63	87	98
240	2	11	21	38	51	70	91	99
300	3	14	26	45	59	78	95	99+
340	3	16	29	49	64	82	97	99+
400	4	18	33	55	70	87	98	99+
460	5	21	37	60	75	90	99	99+
500	5	22	39	63	78	92	99	99+
600	6	26	45	70	84	95	99+	99+
700	7	30	50	75	88	97	99+	99+
800	8	33	55	80	91	98	99+	99+
900	9	36	59	83	93	99	99+	99+
1,000	10	39	63	86	95	99	99+	99+
1,500	14	53	78	95	99	99+	99+	99+
2,000	18	63	86	98	99+	99+	99+	99+
2,500	22	71	92	99	99+	99+	99+	99+
3,000	26	78	95	99+	99+	99+	99+	99+

10-4 when an expected error rate of zero, a DUPL of .5, and a confidence level of 95 percent is used. The only advantage of the discovery table is the availability of a wider confidence level option. If the auditor has attributes tables for all confidence levels he considers necessary, there is no need to use discovery sampling. Discovery sampling cannot be used to evaluate results statistically when one or more errors are found in the sample.

appendix b

case illustration

To illustrate the concepts discussed in this chapter, the Hillsburg Hardware case from Appendix A in Chapter 9 is extended to include the determination of sample size, the selection of items for testing, and the conclusions drawn on the basis of the results of the tests. The only parts of the tests of the sales and collection cycle included here are the tests of credit approval, the shipment of goods, the billing of customers, and recording the amounts in the records. It should be kept in mind that the procedures for Hillsburg Hardware were developed specifically for that client and would probably not be applicable for a different audit. The audit procedures for these tests are repeated at this time, along with comments to indicate the relationship of each procedure to attributes sampling.

In applying attributes sampling to the procedures for Hillsburg Hardware, there are only two functions where statistical sampling is being used: the shipment of goods and the billing of customers. The emphasis is put on the billing of customers in the illustration because the duplicate sales invoice is the sampling unit for most of the audit procedures. In order to concentrate on the attributes sampling applications for the billing function, comments about the shipping function are restricted to the ones shown adjacent to the list of audit procedures. The reader should recognize, however, that the attributes sampling methodology followed for the shipping function would be essentially the same as the methodology illustrated for the billing function in the remainder of the case.

Objectives, Population, and the Sampling Unit

Most auditors use some type of preprinted form to document each attributes sampling application. An example of a commonly used form is given in Figure 10-8. The top part of the form includes a definition of (1) the objective, (2) the population, and (3) the sampling unit.

Define the Attributes of Interest

The attributes used in this application are taken directly from the audit program. The procedures that can be used as attributes for a particular application of attributes sampling depend upon the definition of the sampling unit. In this case all the procedures in the billing function can be included. The nine attributes used for this case are illustrated in Figure 10-8.

The definition of the attribute is a critical part of the use of attributes sampling. The decision as to which attributes to combine and which ones to keep separate is the most important aspect of defining the attributes. If all possible types of attributes, such as customer name, date, price, and quantity, are separated for each procedure, the large number of attributes makes the problem unmanageable. On the other hand, if all the procedures are combined into one or two attributes, greatly dissimilar errors are evaluated together. Somewhere in between, a reasonable compromise is needed.

Establishing the DUPLs and the Desired Confidence Levels, Estimating Expected Error Rates, and Determining the Initial Sample Size

The DUPL for each attribute is decided on the basis of the auditor's judgment of what error rate is material. The failure to record a sales invoice would be highly significant, especially considering this particular system; therefore,

Procedure	*Comments*

General

    Random selection and statistical sampling are not applicable for the 9 general audit procedures in Figure 9–11. Advanced statistical techniques, such as regression analysis, could be applicable for analysis of the results of analytical tests. Random selection could be used for procedure 4.

Shipment of Goods

10. Account for a sequence of shipping documents.	It is possible to do this by selecting a random sample and accounting for all customer orders selected. This requires a separate set of random numbers, since the sampling unit is different than for the other tests.
11. Trace selected shipping documents to a duplicate sales invoice and the sales journal for assurance that each one has been billed and included in the journal.	No errors are expected, and a 2 percent error rate is considered acceptable at a 95 percent confidence level. A sample size of 200 is selected. The shipping documents are traced to the duplicate sales invoices and sales journal. This is done for all 200 items. There are no exceptions for either test. The results are considered acceptable. There is no further information about this portion of the tests in this illustration.

Billing of Customers and Recording the Sales in the Records

12. Account for a sequence of sales invoices in the sales journal.	The audit procedures for billing and recording sales are the primary ones tested using attributes sampling for this case illustration. The attributes sampling data sheet includes each of these procedures as attributes.

13. Trace selected duplicate sales invoice numbers from the sales journal to
    a. Accounts receivable subsidiary ledger, and test for amount, date, and invoice number.
    b. Duplicate sales invoice, and test for the total amount recorded in the journal, date, customer name, and account classification. Check the pricing, extensions, and footings. Examine underlying documents for indication of internal verification by Pam Dilley.
    c. Bill of lading, and test for customer name, product description, quantity, and date.
    d. Duplicate sales order, and test for customer name, product description, quantity, date, and approval by Pam Dilley.

Procedure	*Comments*
e. Customer order, and test for customer name, product description, quantity, date, and credit approval by Rick Chulick.	
14. Trace recorded sales from the sales journal to the file of supporting documents, which includes a duplicates sales invoice, bill of lading, sales order, and customer order.	
15. Compare dates on the bill of lading, duplicate sales invoice, and sales journal.	

as indicated in Figure 10-8, the lowest upper precision limit is chosen for attribute 1. The incorrect billing of the customer represents potentially significant errors, but no error is likely to be for the full amount of the invoice. As a result, a 4 percent desired upper precision limit is chosen for each of the attributes directly related to billing of shipments and recording the amounts in the records. The last four attributes have higher DUPLs since they are of less importance for the audit.

A confidence level of 95 percent is desired for all tests due to the change in personnel in the past year and the potential for relying on internal control if the controls are proven effective.

The expected error rate is based upon previous years' results, modified upward slightly due to the change in personnel. The preliminary sample size for each attribute is determined from Figure 10-4 on the basis of the above considerations. This information is summarized for all attributes in Figure 10-8.

Random Selection

The random selection for the case is straightforward except for the need for a sample of 150 items for attributes 1 through 5 and only 50 items for attributes 6 through 8. This problem can be easily overcome by selecting a random sample of 50 for use on all nine attributes followed by another sample of 100 for the first five attributes. The documentation for the selection of the first fifty numbers is illustrated in Figure 10-9.

Perform the Audit Procedures and Generalize to the Population

The audit procedures that are included in the audit program and summarized in the attributes sampling data sheet must be carefully performed for every element in the sample. As a means of documenting the tests and

Client *Hillsburg Hardware* Year end *12/31/8x*
Audit Area *Compliance Tests – Billing Function* Pop. size *5,764*

Define the objective(s) *Examine duplicate sales invoices and related documents to determine if the system is functioning as intended and as described in the audit program.*

Define the population precisely (including stratification, if any) *Sales invoices for the period 11/1/8x to 12/31/8x. First invoice number = 3689. Last invoice number = 9452.*

Define the sampling unit, organization of population items, and random selection
procedures *Sales invoice number, recorded in the sales journal sequentially; random number table.*

| Description of Attributes | Planned Audit | | | | Actual Results | | | |
	Expect. error rate	Dupl.	Conf. level	Sample size	Sample size	Number of errors	Sample error rate	Cupl.
1. Existence of the sales invoice number in the sales journal.	0	2	95	150				
2. Amount and other data in the subsidiary ledger agree with sales journal entry.	1	4	95	150				
3. Amount and other data in the sales invoice agree with the sales journal entry.	1	4	95	150				
4. Evidence that pricing, extensions, and footings are checked (initials and correct amount).	1	4	95	150				
5. Quantity and other data on the bill of lading agree with the duplicate sales invoice.	1	4	95	150				
6. Quantity and other data on the sales order agree with the duplicate sales invoice.	1	6	95	50				
7. Quantity and other data on the customer order agree with the duplicate sales invoice.	2	8	95	50				
8. Credit is approved by Rick Chulik.	3	8	95	50				
9. The file of supporting documents includes a duplicate sales invoice, bill of lading, sales order, and customer order.	1	6	95	50				

Intended use of sampling results:

1. Effect on Audit Plan:

2. Recommendations to Management:

FIGURE 10–8 Hillsburg Hardware—Statistical Sampling Data Sheet—Attributes

Hillsburg Hardware
Random Sample for Testing Sales

	(1)	(2)	(3)	(4)	(5)	(6)
1036	77339	64605	4 82583	18 85011	00955	50 84348
1087	61714	57933	5 37342	26000	33 93611	93346
1088	15232	48027	15832	19 62924	11509	95853 End
1089	41447	34275	10779	20 83515	34 63899	30932
1090	23244	43524	16382	21 36340	35 73581	76780
1091	53460	83542	25224	22 70378	36 49604	14609
1092	53442	16897	6 61578	05032	37 81825	76822
1093	55543	19096	04130	23104	38 60534	44842
1094	18185	63329	02340	23 63111	39 41768	74409
1095	02372	45690	7 38595	23121	40 73818	74454
1096	51715	35492	8 61371	24 87132	41 81585	55439
1097	24717	16785	9 42786	25 86585	21858	39489
1098	78002	32604	10 87295	26 93702	99438	68184
1099	35995	08275	11 62405	27 43313	03249	74135
1100	29152	86922	31508	28 42703	42 59638	31226
1101	84192 Start	90150	02904	26835	17174	42301
1102	21791	24764	12 53674	30093	43 45134	24073
1103	63501	05040	13 71881	17759	44 91881	69614
1104	07149	1 69285	14 55481	24889	45 67061	06631
1105	59443	98962	15 74778	29 96920	46 65620	36794
1106	39059	2 58021	28485	30 43052	99001	44400
1107	73176	3 58913	22638	31 69769	21102	72292
1108	11851	09065	96033	02752	47 58232	56504
1109	37515	25668	16 55785	32 66463	48 52758	67588
1110	45324	00016	17 46818	04373	49 75360	87519

Population = 3689 to 9453.
Correspondence — First 4 digits in table.
Route — Read down to end of column; start at top of the next column.
Sample size — 50, represented by sequential numbers 1 to 50.

FIGURE 10–9 Hillsburg Hardware—Random Sample for Testing Sales

providing information for review, it is common to include a worksheet of the results. Some auditors prefer to include a worksheet containing a listing of all the elements in the sample, while others prefer to limit the documentation to identifying the errors. This latter approach is followed in the example (Figure 10-10).

At the completion of the testing, the errors are tabulated to determine the number of errors in the sample for each attribute. This enables the auditor to compute the sample error rate and determine the CUPL from the tables. This information is summarized in Figures 10-10 and 10-11.

Error Analysis and Decision on the Acceptability of the Population

The final part of the application consists of analysis of the errors to determine their cause and drawing conclusions about each attribute tested. For every attribute where the CUPL exceeds the DUPL it is essential that some con-

Prepared by MSW
Date 2/3/8y

Hillsburg Hardware Co.

INSPECTION OF SAMPLE ITEMS FOR ATTRIBUTES

12/31/8x

Identity of Item Selected	Attribute Present										
Voucher No.	1	2	3	4	5	6	7	8	9	10	11
3679					X						
3859				X				X			
3990				X							
4071		X		X							
4270								X			
4222					X						
4331								X			
4513				X	X						
4681						X		X			
4859				X							
5367								X			
5578								X			
5802								X			
5823								X			
5963								X			
6157		X		X							
6229				X							
6311								X			
7188					X						
7536				X							
8351								X			
8517				X							
8713								X			
9545				X							
No. Errors	0	2	0	10	4	1	0	12	0		
Sample Size	150	150	150	150	150	50	50	50	50		

FIGURE 10–10 Hillsburg Hardware Co.—Inspection of Sample Items for Attributes

Client *Hillsburg Hardware*
Audit Area *Compliance Tests — Billing Function*

Year end 12/31/8x
Pop. size 5,764

Define the objective(s) *Examine duplicate sales invoices and related documents to determine if the system is functioning as intended and as described in the audit program.*

Define the population precisely (including stratification, if any) *Sales invoices for the period 11/1/8x to 12/31/8x. First invoice number = 3689. Last invoice number = 9452.*

Define the sampling unit, organization of population items, and random selection procedures *Sales invoice number, recorded in the sales journal sequentially; random number table.*

Description of Attributes	Planned Audit					Actual Results		
	Expect. error rate	Dupl.	Conf. level	Sample size	Sample size	Number of errors	Sample error rate	Cupl.
1. Existence of the sales invoice number in the sales journal.	0	2	95	150	150	0	0%	2.0%
2. Amount and other data in the subsidiary ledger agree with sales journal entry.	1	4	95	150	150	2	1⅓	4.0
3. Amount and other data in the sales invoice agree with the sales journal entry.	1	4	95	150	150	0	0	2.0
4. Evidence that pricing, extensions, and footings are checked (initials and correct amount).	1	4	95	150	150	10	6⅔	11
5. Quantity and other data on the bill of lading agree with the duplicate sales invoice.	1	4	95	150	150	4	2⅔	6.0
6. Quantity and other data on the sales order agree with the duplicate sales invoice.	1	6	95	50	50	1	2	9.1
7. Quantity and other data on the customer order agree with the duplicate sales invoice.	2	8	95	50	50	0	0	5.8
8. Credit is approved by Rick Chulik.	3	8	95	50	50	12	24	35.9
9. The file of supporting documents includes a duplicate sales invoice, bill of lading, sales order, and customer order.	1	6	95	50	50	0	0	5.8

Intended use of sampling results:

1. Effect on Audit Plan: *All controls tested can be relied upon as illustrated on working paper 7-6. Additional emphasis is needed in confirmation, allowance for uncollectible accounts, cut-off tests, and price tests.*

2. Recommendations to Management: *Each of the errors should be discussed with management. Specific recommendations are needed to correct the internal verification of sales invoices and to improve the approach to credit approvals.*

FIGURE 10–11 Hillsburg Hardware—Statistical Sampling Data Sheet—Attributes

Hillsburg Hardware
ANALYSIS OF ERRORS
12/31/8x

Prepared by
MSW

Attribute	Number of Exceptions	Nature of Exceptions	Effect on the Audit and Other Comments
1	—0—		
2	2	Both errors were posted to the wrong account and were still outstanding after several months. The amounts were for $125.00 and $393.00.	Even though the upper control limit is equal to the desired limit, additional substantive work is needed, owing to the nature of the errors. Perform expanded confirmation procedures and review older uncollected balances thoroughly.
3	—0—	—	—
4	10	In 6 cases there were no initials for internal verification. In 2 cases the wrong price was used but the errors were under $10 in each case. In 1 case freight was not charged. In 1 case there was an extension error of $1,000. (Three of the last 4 errors had initials for internal verification.)	There is a lack of internal verification, and dollar errors appear to be occurring with excessive frequency. The internal verification cannot be relied upon. As a result test the 50 largest sales transactions for the year for proper price and expand the confirmation of accounts receivable.
5	4	In each case the date on the duplicate sales invoice was several days later than the shipping date.	Do extensive tests of the sales cut-off by comparing recorded sales to the shipping documents.
6	1	Just 106 items were shipped and billed though the sales order was for 112 items. The reason for the difference was an error in the perpetual records. The perpetual indicated that 112 items were on hand, when there were actually 106. The system does not backorder for undershipments smaller than 25%.	No expansion of compliance or substantive tests. The system appears to be working effectively.
7	—0—	—	—
8	12	Credit was not approved. Four of these were for new customers. Discussed with Chulik, who stated his busy schedule did not permit approving all sales.	Expand the year-end procedures extensively in evaluating allowance for uncollectible accounts. This includes scheduling of cash receipts subsequent to year end and for all outstanding accounts receivable.

FIGURE 10–12 Hillsburg Hardware—Analysis of Errors

clusion concerning follow up action be drawn and documented. The error analysis and conclusions reached are illustrated in Figure 10-12 and summarized at the bottom of the data sheet in Figure 10-11.

REVIEW QUESTIONS

10–1. Distinguish between a quantitative and a qualitative evaluation of a population and state the importance of each.

10–2. State what is meant by a representative sample and explain its importance in sampling audit populations.

10–3. In using judgmental sampling, what major considerations should be kept in mind to increase the likelihood of a representative sample?

10–4. Explain what is meant by block sampling and describe how an auditor could obtain five blocks of twenty sales invoices from a sales journal.

10–5. Compared with judgmental selection, what are the major advantages of random selection?

10–6. Why is the pursuit of every item in the sample essential when statistical sampling techniques are used?

10–7. Explain the difference between "sampling with replacement" and "sampling without replacement." Which method do auditors usually follow? Why?

10–8. Explain what is meant by a random number table. Describe how an auditor would select thirty-five random numbers from a population of 1,750 items by using a random number table.

10–9. Describe systematic sampling and explain how an auditor would select thirty-five numbers from a population of 1,750 items using this approach. What are the advantages and disadvantages of systematic sampling?

10–10. Describe what is meant by a sampling unit. Explain why the sampling unit for verifying the validity of recorded sales differs from the sampling unit for testing for the possibility of omitted sales.

10–11. Distinguish between the desired upper precision limit and the computed upper precision limit. How is each of them determined?

10–12. Distinguish between a "sampling error" and a "nonsampling error." How can each of them be reduced?

10–13. State the relationship between the following:
   a. Confidence level and sample size.
   b. Population size and sample size.
   c. Desired upper precision limit and sample size.
   d. Expected error rate and sample size.

10–14. Assume that the auditor has selected 100 sales invoices from a population of 10,000 to test for an indication of internal verification of pricing and extensions. Determine the upper precision limit of the error at a 95 percent confidence level if three exceptions existed in the sample. Explain the meaning of the statistical results in auditing terms.

10–15. Explain what is meant by error analysis and discuss its importance.

10–16. When the computed upper precision limit exceeds the desired upper precision limit, what courses of action are available to the auditor? Under what circumstances should each of these courses of action be followed?

10–17. Distinguish between random selection and statistical measurement. State the circumstances under which one can be used without the other.

10–18. List the decisions the auditor must make in using attributes sampling. State the most important considerations involved in making each decision.

10–19. Define what is meant by discovery sampling. Under what circumstances would an auditor use discovery samples?

DISCUSSION QUESTIONS AND PROBLEMS

10–20. The following items apply to random sampling from large populations for attributes sampling. Select the most appropriate response for each question.

a. A CPA wishes to determine the percentage of items in his client's inventory with annual sales of less than 50 percent of the units on hand at the inventory date. Which of the following exhibits the characteristic the CPA is measuring?

Item	Units in Inventory	Units Sold This Year
1. Firs	251	525
2. Furs	243	124
3. Friezes	198	98
4. Furzes	144	92

b. A CPA specifies that a sample shall have a confidence level of 90 percent. The specified confidence level assures him of
(1) a true estimate of the population characteristic being measured.
(2) an estimate that is at least 90 percent correct.
(3) a measured precision for his estimate.
(4) how likely he can estimate the population characteristic being measured.

c. If all other factors specified in a sampling plan remain constant, changing the specified confidence level from 90 percent to 95 percent would cause the required sample size to
(1) increase.
(2) remain the same.
(3) decrease.
(4) become indeterminate.

d. If all other factors specified in a sampling plan remain constant, changing the desired upper precision limit from 8 percent to 12 percent would cause the required sample size to
(1) increase.
(2) remain the same.

(3) decrease.

(4) become indeterminate.

e. If all other factors specified in a sampling plan remain constant, changing the estimated occurrence rate from 2 percent to 4 percent would cause the required sample size to

(1) increase.

(2) remain the same.

(3) decrease.

(4) become indeterminate.

f. In the evaluation of the results of a sample of a specified confidence level, the fact that the occurrence rate in the sample was 2 percent rather than the estimated occurrence rate of 4 percent would cause the computed upper precision limit to

(1) exceed the desired upper precision limit.

(2) equal the desired upper precision limit.

(3) be less than the desired upper precision limit.

(4) cannot be determined from the information given.

(AICPA adapted)

10–21. The following items apply to random sampling from large populations using attributes sampling. For each question, select the best response.

a. In a random sample of 1,000 records, a CPA determines that the rate of occurrence of errors is 2 percent. He can state that the error rate in the population is

(1) not more than 3 percent.

(2) not less than 2 percent.

(3) probably about 2 percent.

(4) not less than 1 percent.

b. From a random sample of items listed from a client's inventory count, a CPA estimates with 90 percent confidence that the error occurrence rate is between 4 percent and 6 percent. The CPA's major concern is that there is one chance in twenty that the true error rate in the population is

(1) more than 6 percent.

(2) less than 6 percent.

(3) more than 4 percent.

(4) less than 4 percent.

c. If from a particular random sample a CPA can state with 90 percent confidence that the occurrence rate in the population does not exceed 20 percent, he can state that the occurrence rate does not exceed 25 percent with

(1) 95 percent confidence.

(2) greater reliability on his sample.

(3) the same reliability on his sample.

(4) less reliability on his sample.

d. If a CPA wishes to select a random sample that must have a 90 percent confidence level and a desired upper precision limit of 10 percent, the size of the sample he must select will decrease as his estimate of the

(1) occurrence rate increases.

(2) occurrence rate decreases.

(3) population size increases.

(4) reliability of the sample decreases.

e. If a CPA selects a random sample for which he specified a confidence level of 99 percent and an upper precision limit of 5 percent and subsequently changes the confidence level to 90 percent, the sample will produce an estimate that is

(1) more reliable and more precise.

(2) more reliable and less precise.

(3) less reliable and more precise.

(4) less reliable and less precise.

f. If the result obtained from a particular sample will be critical, e.g., the CPA would not be able to render an unqualified opinion (unless every item in the population were examined), which of the following is the most important to the CPA?

(1) Size of the population.

(2) Estimated occurrence rate.

(3) Desired upper precision limit.

(4) Desired confidence level.

g. Which of the following need not be known to evaluate the results of a sample for a particular attribute?

(1) Occurrence rate in the population.

(2) Size of the sample.

(3) Desired confidence level.

(4) Occurrences in the sample.   (AICPA adapted)

10–22. You are now conducting your third annual audit of the financial statements of Elite Corporation for the year ended December 31, 19X7. You decide to employ unrestricted random number statistical sampling techniques in testing the effectiveness of the company's internal control procedures relating to sales invoices, which are all sequentially numbered. In prior years, after selecting one representative two-week period during the year, you tested all invoices issued during that period and resolved all the errors which were found to your satisfaction.

Required:

a. Explain the statistical procedures you would use to determine the size of the sample of sales invoices to be examined.

b. Once the sample size has been determined, how would you select the individual invoices to be included in the sample? Explain.

c. Would the use of statistical sampling procedures improve the examination of sales invoices as compared with the selection procedure used in prior years? Discuss.

d. Assume that the company issued fifty thousand sales invoices during the year and the auditor specified a confidence level of 95 percent with a desired upper precision limit of 4 percent. Does this mean that the auditor would be willing to accept the reliability of the sales invoice data if errors are found on no more than four sales invoices out of every ninety-five invoices examined? Discuss.   (AICPA adapted)

10–23. In each of the following independent problems, design an unbiased random sampling plan using the random number table in Figure 10–1. The plan should include defining the sampling unit, establishing a numbering system for the population, and establishing a correspondence between the random number table and the population. After the plan has been designed, select the first five sample items from the random number table for each problem. Use a starting point of item 1009, column 1, for each problem. Read down the table using the leftmost digits in the column. When you reach the last item in a column, start at the top of the next column.

   a. Prenumbered sales invoices in a sales journal where the lowest invoice number is 1 and the highest is 6211.

   b. Prenumbered bills of lading where the lowest document number is 21926 and the highest is 28511.

   c. Accounts receivable on 10 pages with 60 lines per page. Each line has a customer name and an amount receivable, except the last page, which has only 36 full lines.

   d. Prenumbered invoices in a sales journal where each month starts over with number 1. (Invoices for each month are designated by the month and document number.) There are a maximum of 20 pages per month with a total of 185 pages for the year. All pages have 75 invoices, except for the last page for each month.

10–24. You desire a random sample of 80 sales invoices for the examination of supporting documents. The invoices range from numbers 1 to 9500 for the period January 1 through December 31. There are 128 pages of sales invoices numbered 1 through 128. Each page has 75 lines, but the last page in each month sometimes has a few less.

Required:

   a. Design four different methods of selecting random numbers from the above population using a random number table or systematic sampling.

   b. Which method do you consider the most desirable? Why?

10–25. The use of statistical sampling techniques in an examination of financial statements does not eliminate judgmental decisions.

Required:

   a. Identify and explain four areas where judgment may be exercised by a CPA in planning a statistical sampling test.

   b. Assume that a CPA's sample shows an unacceptable error rate. Describe the various actions that he may take based upon these findings.

   c. A nonstratified sample of 80 accounts payable vouchers is to be selected from a population of 3,200. The vouchers are numbered consecutively from 1 to 3,200 and are listed, 40 to a page, in the voucher register. Describe four different techniques for selecting a random sample of vouchers for review. (AICPA adapted)

10–26. Lenter Supply Company is a medium-sized distributor of wholesale hardware supplies in the central Ohio area. It has been a client of yours for several years and has instituted an excellent system for the control of sales at your recommendation.

In providing control over shipments, the client has prenumbered "warehouse removal slips" that are used for every sale. It is company policy never to remove goods from the warehouse without an authorized warehouse removal slip. After shipment, two copies of the warehouse removal slip are sent to billing for preparation of a sales invoice. One copy is stapled to the duplicate copy of a prenumbered sales invoice, and the other copy is filed numerically. In some cases more than one warehouse removal slip is used for billing one sales invoice. The smallest warehouse removal slip number for the year is 14682 and the largest is 37521. The smallest sales invoice number is 47821 and the largest is 68507.

In the audit of sales, one of the major concerns is the effectiveness of the system in making sure all shipments are billed. The auditor has decided to use attributes sampling in testing the system.

Required:

a. State an effective audit procedure for testing whether shipments have been billed. What is the sampling unit for the audit procedure?
b. Assuming that the auditor expects no error in the sample but is willing to accept a maximum error rate of 3 percent, at a 90 percent confidence level, what is the appropriate sample size for the audit test?
c. Design a random selection plan for selecting the sample from the population using the random number table. Select the first ten sample items from the table in Figure 10–1. Use a starting point of item 1013, column 3.
d. Your supervisor suggests the possibility of performing other sales tests with the same sample as a means of efficiently using your audit time. List two other audit procedures that could conveniently be performed using the same sample and state the purpose of each of the procedures.
e. Is it desirable to test the validity of sales with the random sample you have designed in part c? Why?

10–27. Mavis Stores had two billing clerks during the year. Snow worked three months and White worked nine months. As the auditor for Mavis Stores, Jones, CPA, uses attributes sampling to test clerical accuracy for the entire year, but due to the lack of internal verification, the system depends heavily upon the competence of the billing clerks. The quantity of bills per month is constant.

Required:

a. Jones decided to treat the billing by Snow and White as two separate populations. Discuss the advisability of this approach, considering the circumstances.
b. Jones decided to use the same confidence level, expected error rate, and desired upper precision limit for each population. Assuming that he decided to select a sample of 200 to test Snow's work, approximately how large a sample is necessary to test White's?   (AICPA adapted)

10–28. The following questions concern the determination of the proper sample size in attributes sampling:
a. For each of the columns numbered 1 through 7 determine the initial sam-

ple size needed to satisfy the auditor's requirements from the appropriate table in Figure 10–4. Wherever the sample size is more than 10 percent of the population, adjust it with the finite correction factor.

	1	2	3	4	5	6	7
Confidence level	90%	95%	95%	95%	95%	95%	95%
Desired upper precision limit	6%	6%	4%	6%	8%	6%	5%
Estimated population error rate	3%	3%	3%	3%	3%	3%	0%
Population size	1,000	100,000	6,000	1,000	500	500	1,000,000

b. Using your understanding of the relationship between the foregoing factors and sample size, state the effect on the initial sample size (increase or decrease) of changing each of the following factors while the other three are held constant:
   (1) An increase in confidence level.
   (2) An increase in the desired upper precision limit.
   (3) An increase in the estimated population error rate.
   (4) An increase in the population size.
c. Compare your answers in part b with the results you determined in part a. Which of the four factors appears to have the greatest effect on the initial sample size? Which one appears to have the least effect?
d. Why is the sample size referred to as the initial sample size?

10–29. The following questions relate to determining the computed upper precision limit in attributes sampling:
   a. For each of columns 1 through 8, determine the computed upper precision limit from the appropriate table in Figure 10–4. Wherever the sample size is more than 10 percent of the population, adjust the computed upper precision limit with the finite correction factor.

	1	2	3	4	5	6	7	8
Confidence level	90%	95%	95%	95%	95%	95%	95%	95%
Population size	5,000	5,000	5,000	50,000	500	900	5,000	500
Sample size	200	200	50	200	400	100	100	200
Number of error occurrences	4	4	1	4	8	10	0	4

b. Using your understanding of the relationship between the four factors above and the computed upper precision limit, state the effect on the computed upper precision limit (increase or decrease) of changing each of the following factors while the other three are held constant:
   (1) a decrease in the confidence level
   (2) a decrease in the population size
   (3) a decrease in the sample size
   (4) a decrease in the number of occurrences in the sample

c. Compare your answers in part b with the results you determined in part a. Which of the factors appears to have the greatest effect on the computed upper precision limit? Which one appears to have the least effect?

d. Why is it necessary to compare the computed upper precision limit with the acceptable upper precision limit?

10–30. For the examination of the financial statements of Mercury Fifo Company, Stella Mason, CPA, has decided to apply attributes sampling in the tests of sales transactions. Based upon her knowledge of Mercury's operations in the area of sales, she decides that the expected rate of error occurrence is likely to be 3 percent and that she would like to be 90 percent confident that the true error rate is not greater than 6 percent. Given this information, Mason selects a random sample of 150 sales invoices from the 5,000 written during the year and examines them for errors. She notes the following exceptions in her workpapers. There is no other documentation.

Invoice No.	Comments
5028	Sales invoice was originally footed incorrectly but was corrected by client before the bill was sent out.
6791	Voided sales invoice examined by auditor.
6810	Shipping document for a sale of merchandise could not be located.
7364	Sales invoice for $2,875 has not been collected and is six months past due.
7625	Client unable to locate the duplicate sales invoice.
8431	Check was dated three days later than the date entered in the sales journal.
8528	Customer order is not attached to the duplicate sales invoice.
8566	Billing is for $100 less than it should be due to a pricing error. No indication of internal verification is included on the invoice.
8780	Client unable to locate the duplicate sales invoice.
9169	Credit not authorized, but the sale was for only $7.65.
9974	Lack of indication of internal verification of price extensions and postings of sales invoice.

Required:

a. Which of the exceptions stated above are actually errors?

b. Explain why it is inappropriate to set a single accepted upper precision limit and expected rate of occurrence for the combined errors.

c. For each attribute as tested in the population, determine the computed upper precision limit assuming a 95 percent confidence level for each attribute. (You must decide which attributes should be combined, which should be kept separate, and which exceptions are actually errors, before you can determine the computed upper precision limit.)

d. State the appropriate error analysis for each of the errors in the sample.

10–31. In performing tests of transactions of sales for the Oakland Hardware Company, Ben Frentz, CPA, is concerned with the internal verification of pricing, extensions, and footings of sales invoices and the accuracy of the actual calculations. In testing sales using attributes sampling, a separate attribute is used for the compliance test (the existence of internal verification) and the substantive test (the actual accuracy of the calculation). Since the internal control is considered excellent, Frentz uses a 90 percent confidence level, a zero estimated population error rate, and a 5 percent desired upper precision limit for both attributes; therefore, the initial sample size is 50 items.

In conducting the tests, the auditor finds three sample items where there was no indication of internal verification on the sales invoice, but no sales invoices tested in the sample had a financial error.

Required:

a. Determine the computed upper precision limit for both the attributes, assuming a population of 5,000 sales invoices.

b. Compare the computed upper precision limit with the desired upper precision limit.

c. Discuss the most desirable course of action the auditor should follow in deciding upon the effect of the computed upper precision limit exceeding the desired upper precision limit.

d. Which type of error analysis is appropriate in this case?

10–32. For the audit of Carbald Supply Company, Carole Wever, CPA, is conducting a test of sales for nine months of the year ended 12-31-8X. Included among her audit procedures are the following:

a. Foot and crossfoot the sales journal and trace the balance to the general ledger.

b. Review all sales transactions for reasonableness.

c. Select a sample of recorded sales from the sales journal and trace the customer name and amounts to duplicate sales invoices and the related shipping document.

d. Select a sample of shipping document numbers and perform the following tests:

(1) Trace the shipping document to the related duplicate sales invoice.

(2) Examine the duplicate sales invoice to determine whether a copy of the shipping document, shipping order, and customer order are attached.

(3) Examine the shipping order for an authorized credit approval.

(4) Examine the duplicate sales invoice for an indication of internal verification of quantity, price, extensions, footings, and tracing the balance to the subsidiary ledger.

(5) Compare the price on the duplicate sales invoice with the approved price list and the quantity with the shipping document.

(6) Trace the balance in the duplicate sales invoice to the sales journal and subsidiary ledger for customer name, amount, and date.

Required:

a. For which of these procedures could attributes sampling be conveniently used?

b. Considering the audit procedures Wever has developed, what is the most appropriate sampling unit for conducting most of the attributes-sampling tests?

c. Set up an attributes sampling data sheet. For all compliance tests, assume an acceptable upper precision limit of 3.5 percent and an expected population error rate of 1 percent. For all substantive tests, use 2.5 percent for the upper precision limit and a zero expected population error rate. Use a 90 percent confidence level for all tests.

d. For the audit procedures not included in the attributes sampling test in part c, describe appropriate judgmental sampling procedures to determine the items to include in the sample.

COMPLETING THE TESTS
IN THE SALES
AND COLLECTION CYCLE—
ACCOUNTS RECEIVABLE

Chapter 11 is concerned with the analytical and direct tests of balances for the accounts in the sales and collection cycle and the relationship of these tests to the review and evaluation of internal control and tests of transactions. The detailed objectives for direct tests of financial balances presented in Chapter 8 are the frame of reference used to discuss the audit tests. Confirmation of accounts receivable, which is the most important direct test in the cycle, receives particular emphasis. The relationship between confirmations and tests of transactions and the factors affecting the auditor's confirmation decisions are the most important part of this discussion.

Before examining a methodology for completing the audit of the sales and collection cycle, a brief review of the tests of the cycle that were discussed in previous chapters is appropriate. These tests have a direct effect on the evidence needed to complete the audit of the cycle.

REVIEW OF THE TESTS OF THE SYSTEM

The overall objective in auditing the sales and collection cycle is to evaluate whether sales, sales returns and allowances, bad debts, accounts receivable, allowance for uncollectible accounts, and cash receipts are properly reflected in the financial records in accordance with the detailed tests of transactions and direct tests of balances objectives discussed in Chapter 8.

The emphasis to this point has been on understanding, evaluating, and testing the system of internal control. An understanding of the system comes about through flowcharting the client's sales and collection system, completing an internal control questionnaire, and tracing one or two transactions through the system from the customer's order to the collection of cash. The evaluation of internal control is accomplished by relating the eight objectives of internal control to the flowchart and internal control questionnaire for the purpose of identifying strengths and weaknesses in the system. The tests of transactions for the cycle include compliance tests to enable the the auditor to evaluate the effectiveness of the controls and substantive tests to enable him to evaluate the correctness of the dollar amounts in the records.

In accumulating evidence for the sales and collection cycle, the importance of modifying the evidence for the circumstances of the audit cannot be overemphasized. The determination of the proper audit procedures, sample size, timing of the tests, and particular items to include in the sample can only be made after a careful analysis of the system and the other relevant factors in the engagement. The decision-making involved in this process is one of the most important aspects of the study of auditing.

Audit Procedures. Compliance procedures for testing effectiveness need to be performed for those controls in the system the auditor intends to rely upon to reduce substantive tests. Whether or not to perform compliance tests is a cost-benefit question and should be decided on the basis of the cost to test the controls versus the savings if substantive tests are reduced.

Proper substantive procedures for testing the system depend upon the auditor's evaluation of internal control and the results of the compliance tests. Since some substantive procedures must always be performed to test whether transactions and balances are correctly recorded, it is convenient to carry out compliance and substantive tests of transactions simultaneously. If the compliance procedures indicate that the controls are inadequate, the substantive tests may need to be expanded.

Sample Size. Three major factors affect the number of sample items for tests of transactions: the error rate the auditor is willing to accept in the population, the error rate expected in the sample, and the risk the auditor is willing to take of obtaining a nonrepresentative sample. The first factor is a question of materiality, and the second one is based primarily on experience with the client in previous years. The risk factor is affected by the extent to which the auditor plans to rely on the system to reduce substantive tests and the overall level of assurance the auditor considers necessary. Population size has some effect on sample size, but it is generally not significant in transactions testing.

When the system of internal control is of high quality, the auditor can accept a lower confidence level for substantive tests of the system. In addition, the expected magnitude of errors is smaller when there are good controls. The combination of these two factors normally permits the auditor to reduce considerably the sample size for substantive tests.

Timing. Several factors determine whether the system should be tested at an interim date without a thorough test for the remainder of the year. These factors include the length of the untested time period, the results of the interim tests, discussions with the client about changes in the system, personnel changes, the nature of the transactions for the untested period, and the results of the preliminary substantive tests. Even when conditions are ideal, it is not possible to completely ignore the untested time period.

Items to Select for the Sample. In testing the system, it is essential to obtain a representative sample. Therefore, random selection is generally desirable, and it is a requirement when statistical methods are used. On the other hand, if the auditor observes unusual transactions or amounts, they should be investigated even if they are not included in the random sample. In addition, many auditors feel it is also important to review all large transactions.

DIRECT TESTS OF FINANCIAL BALANCES

After the auditor has completed the internal control evaluation and tests of transactions, it is appropriate to design and perform audit procedures for *analytical* and *direct tests* of the financial balances. Frequently a time lapse of several months occurs before the direct tests are performed when tests of transactions are conducted at an interim date. In many cases confirmation of accounts receivable also takes place before the balance sheet date, but some direct tests are always performed as of the balance sheet date.

Confirmation of accounts receivable is the most important audit procedure for direct tests of the sales and collection cycle. Confirmation is discussed briefly in studying the appropriate tests for each of the nine objectives of direct tests of balances, then in more detail in a separate section.

The direct tests of the cycle emphasize the fair presentation of accounts receivable and allowance for uncollectible accounts. The income statement accounts are not ignored in these tests, but they are verified more as a by-product of the balance sheet tests rather than directly. In analytical tests, income statement and balance sheet accounts are examined concurrently for reasonableness and receive equal attention.

The following discussion is in terms of the nine objectives for direct tests of balances that were introduced in Chapter 8. For convenience, they are discussed in a slightly different order than in Chapter 8.

Account balances and details included in the accounts in the sales and collection cycle are reasonable for accounts receivable.

The individual accounts that typically deserve special attention are large balances, accounts that have been outstanding for a long period of time, and receivables from affiliated companies, officers, directors, and other related parties. The auditor should review the accounts receivable confirmation at the confirmation date and the balance sheet date to determine which accounts should be investigated further.

The following are examples of the major types of ratios and comparisons for the sales and collection cycle:

- Gross margin by product line
- Sales returns and allowances as a percentage of gross sales by product line or segment
- Trade discounts taken as a percentage of net sales
- Bad debts as a percentage of gross sales
- Days sales in receivables outstanding
- Aging categories as a percentage of accounts receivable
- Allowance for uncollectible accounts as a percentage of accounts receivable
- Comparison of individual customers' balances over a stated amount with their balances in the preceding year

Accounts Receivable in the Aged Trial Balance Agree with Related Subsidiary Ledger Amounts, and the Total Is Correctly Added and Agrees with the General Ledger

Most tests of accounts receivable and the allowance for uncollectible accounts are based on the *aged trial balance*. An aged trial balance is a listing of the balances in the subsidiary accounts receivable ledger at the balance sheet date. It includes the individual total balances outstanding and a breakdown of each balance by the length of time passed between the date of sale and the balance sheet date. An illustration of a typical aged trial balance is given in Figure 11-1.

Testing the information on the aged trial balance for mechanical accuracy is a necessary audit procedure. The total column and the columns depicting the aging must be footed, and the total on the trial balance must be reconciled with the general ledger. In addition, a sample of individual balances should be traced to the detailed subsidiary ledger or other supporting data to verify the customer name, balance, and proper aging. The extent of the testing for mechanical accuracy depends on the number of accounts involved and the degree to which the schedule has been verified by an internal auditor or other independent person before it is given to the auditor.

Accounts Receivable in the Aged Trial Balance Are Valid

The most important tests for determining the validity of recorded accounts receivable are the confirmation of customers balances, the examination of supporting documents evidencing the shipment of the goods, and the examination of subsequent cash receipts to determine whether the accounts were collected. Normally, auditors do not examine shipping documents or evidence of subsequent cash receipts for any account in the sample that is

ABC Company, Inc.
Accounts Receivable
Aged Trial Balance
12/31/80

Schedule _____ Date _____
Prepared by *Miess 1/5/81*
Approved by _____

Account Number	Customer	Balance 12/31/80	Aging based on Service Date				
			0–30 days	31–60 days	61–90 days	91–120 days	Over 120
01011	Adams Supply	7,329	4,511	2,818			
01044	Agonault, Inc.	1,542	1,542				
01100	Awater Brothers	10,519	10,519				
01191	Beekman Bearings	4,176	3,676		500		
01270	Brown and Phillips	3,000				3,000	
01301	Christopher Plumbing	789					789
09733	Traveler Equipment	2,976	2,976				
09742	Underwood Paint and Maintenance	8,963	8,763	1,700			
09810	O'Toy Co.	5,111	1,811	1,700	1,600		
09907	Zephyr Plastics	14,800	9,200	5,000			1,100
		229,716	183,773	26,414	11,486	6,891	1,100

FIGURE 11–1 Aged Trial Balance

confirmed, but these documents are used extensively as alternative evidence for nonresponses. The tests of transactions discussed in Chapters 9 and 10 are also useful in testing the validity of recorded transactions.

Existing Accounts Receivable Are Included in the Aged Trial Balance

It is difficult to test for omitted account balances in accounts receivable except by relying upon the self-balancing nature of the subsidiary accounts. For example, if the client decided to exclude an account receivable from the trial balance to deceive the auditor, the only likely way it will be discovered is by footing the accounts receivable trial balance and reconciling the balance with the control account in the general ledger.

If all sales to a customer are omitted from the sales journal, the understatement of accounts receivable is almost impossible to uncover by direct tests of balances. The understatement of sales and accounts receivable may be uncovered by tests of transactions for shipments made but not recorded.

Accounts Receivable in the Trial Balance Are Owned

The ownership of accounts receivable ordinarily causes no audit problems because the receivables usually belong to the client, but in some cases a portion of the receivables may have been factored or sold at a discount. Generally, the client's customers are not aware of the existence of discounting; therefore, the confirmation of receivables will not bring it to light. A review of the minutes, discussions with the client, confirmation with banks, and the examination of correspondence files are usually sufficient to uncover instances where the receivables are not owned.

Accounts Receivable in the Trial Balance Are Properly Valued

Confirmation of the gross value of selected customers' balances is the most common direct test for valuation of accounts receivable. Tests of the debits and credits to particular customers' balances by examining supporting documentation for shipments and collections and tests of transactions of the type discussed in Chapter 10 are also helpful. The interrelationship of these tests is discussed in greater detail later in this chapter.

A second part of the valuation objective for accounts receivable is determining the *realizable value* of the outstanding balances; that is, the amount which will ultimately be collected. The client's estimate of the total amount that is uncollectible is represented by the allowance for uncollectible accounts. Although it is not possible to precisely predict the future, it is necessary for the auditor to evaluate whether the allowance is reasonable considering all of the available facts.

The starting point for the evaluation of the allowance for uncollectible accounts is to review the results of the tests of the system that are concerned with the client's credit policy. If the client's credit policy has remained unchanged and the results of the tests of credit policy and credit approval are consistent with those of the preceding year, the change in the balance in the allowance for uncollectible accounts should reflect only changes in economic conditions and sales volume. On the other hand, if the client's credit policy or the degree of compliance has significantly changed, great care must be taken to consider the effects of these changes as well.

A common way to evaluate the adequacy of the allowance is to examine carefully the noncurrent accounts in the aged trial balance to determine which ones have not been paid subsequent to the balance sheet date. The size and age of unpaid balances can then be compared with similar information from previous years to evaluate whether the amount of noncurrent receivables is increasing or decreasing over time. The examination of Dun and Bradstreet reports, discussions with the credit manager, and review of the client's correspondence file may also provide insights into the collectibility of the accounts. These procedures are especially important if a few large balances are noncurrent and are not being paid on a regular basis.

There are two pitfalls in evaluating the allowance by reviewing individual noncurrent balances in the aged trial balance. First, the current accounts are ignored in establishing the adequacy of the allowance even though some of these amounts will undoubtedly become uncollectible. Second, it is difficult to compare the results of the current year with those of previous years on such an unstructured basis. If the accounts are becoming progressively uncollectible over a period of several years, this fact could be overlooked. A way to avoid these difficulties is to establish the history of bad debt charge-offs over a period of time as a frame of reference for evaluating the current year's allowance. As an example, if historically a certain percentage of the total of each age category becomes uncollectible, it is relatively easy to compute whether the allowance is properly stated. If 2 percent of current accounts, 10 percent of 30- to 90-day accounts, and 35 percent of all balances over 90 days ultimately become uncollectible, these percentages can easily be applied to the current year's aged trial balance totals and the result compared with the balance in the allowance account. Of course, the auditor has to be careful to modify the calculations for changed conditions.

After the auditor is satisfied with the allowance for uncollectible accounts, it is easy to verify bad debts expense. Let it be assumed that (1) the beginning balance was verified as a part of the previous audit, (2) the uncollectible accounts charged off were verified as a part of the tests of transactions, and (3) the ending balance in the allowance account has been verified by various means. Then bad debts expense is simply a residual balance that can be verified by a mechanical test.

Accounts Receivable in the
Aged Trial Balance Are Properly Classified

It is normally relatively easy to evaluate the classification of accounts receivable by reviewing the aged trial balance for material receivables from affiliates, officers, directors, or other related parties. If there are notes receivable included with the regular accounts or accounts that should not be classified as a current asset, these should also be segregated. Finally, if the credit balances in accounts receivable are significant, it is appropriate to reclassify them as accounts payable.

Transactions in the Sales and Collection Cycle Are Recorded in the Proper Period

Cutoff errors can occur for *sales, sales returns and allowances,* and *cash receipts.* They take place when current period transactions are recorded in the subsequent year or subsequent period transactions are recorded in the current year.

The objective of cutoff tests is the same regardless of the type of transaction, but the procedures vary. The objective is simply to verify whether the client has recorded transactions near the end of the year in the proper period. The cutoff objective is one of the most important in the cycle because errors in cutoff can significantly affect current period income. For example, the intentional or unintentional inclusion of several large, subsequent period sales in the current period and the exclusion of several current period sales returns and allowances can materially overstate net earnings. In determining the reasonableness of the cutoff, it is necessary to use a threefold approach: first, decide on the appropriate *criteria for cutoff;* second, evaluate whether the client has established *adequate procedures* to ensure a reasonable cutoff; and third, *test* whether a reasonable cutoff was obtained.

Sales Cutoff. The criterion used by most clients for determining when a sale takes place is the *shipment of goods,* but some companies record invoices at the time title passes. The passage of title can take place before shipment (as in the case of custom-manufactured goods), at the time of shipment, or subsequent to shipment. For the proper measurement of current period income, the method must be in accordance with generally accepted accounting principles, and it must also be consistently applied.

The most important part of evaluating the client's method of obtaining a reliable cutoff is to determine the procedures in use. When a client issues prenumbered shipping documents sequentially, it is usually a simple matter to evaluate and test cutoff. Moreover, the segregation of duties between the shipping and the billing function also enhances the likelihood of recording transactions in the proper period. On the other hand, if shipments are made by company truck, the shipping records are unnumbered, and there is no independence between the shipping and the billing departments, it may be difficult, if not impossible, to be assured of an accurate cutoff.

When the client's records and procedures are adequate, the cutoff can usually be verified by obtaining the shipping document number for the last shipment made at the end of the period and comparing this number with current and subsequent period recorded sales. As an illustration, assume the shipping document number for the last shipment in the current period is 1489. All recorded sales before the end of the period should bear a shipping document number preceding number 1490. There should also be no sales recorded in the subsequent period for a shipment with a bill of lading numbered 1489 or lower. This can be easily tested by comparing recorded sales with the related shipping document for the last few days of the current period and the first few days of the subsequent period.

If the system is unusual or inadequate, it is necessary to carefully study and evaluate it before cutoff tests are determined. In extreme circumstances, physical observation of shipments and control of documents by the auditor during the period around year end may be required.

Sales Returns and Allowances. Generally accepted accounting principles require that sales returns and allowances be *matched with related sales* if the amounts are material. For example, if current period shipments are returned in the subsequent period, the proper treatment of the transaction is the inclusion of the sales return in the current period. (The returned goods would be treated as current period inventory.) For most companies, however, sales returns and allowances are recorded in the *period they occur*, under the assumption of approximately equal, offsetting errors at the beginning and end of the period. This is acceptable as long as the amounts are not significant.

When the auditor is confident that the client records all sales returns and allowances on a timely basis, the cutoff tests are simple and straightforward. The auditor can examine supporting documentation for a sample of sales returns and allowances recorded during several weeks subsequent to the closing date to determine the date of the original sale. If the amounts recorded in the subsequent period are significantly different from unrecorded returns at the beginning of the year, an adjustment must be considered. If the system for recording sales returns and allowances is evaluated as ineffective during the review and tests of the system, a larger sample is needed to verify cutoff.

Cash Receipts. For most audits a proper cash receipts cutoff is *less important* than either the sales or the sales returns and allowances cutoff because the improper cutoff of cash affects only the cash and the accounts receivable balances, and does not affect earnings. Nevertheless, if the misstatement is material, it could affect the fair presentation of these accounts, particularly when cash is a small or negative balance.

It is easy to test for a cash receipts cutoff error, which is frequently referred to as "*holding the cash receipts book open*," by tracing recorded cash receipts to subsequent period bank deposits on the bank statement. If there is a delay of several days, this could indicate a cutoff error.

The confirmation of accounts receivable may also be relied upon to some degree to uncover cutoff errors for sales, sales returns and allowances, and cash receipts, especially when there is a long time span between the date the transaction took place and the recording date. However, when the cutoff error is for only a few days, the delays caused by the time it takes to deliver the mail confuse cutoff errors with normal reconciliation differences. For example, if a customer mails and records a check to a client for payment of an unpaid account on December 30 and the client receives and records the amount on January 2, the records of the two organizations will be different on December 31. This is not a cutoff error, but a *reconcilable difference* due to the delivery time; it will be difficult for the auditor to evaluate whether it is a cutoff error or a normal reconciling item if it is reported on a confirmation reply.

Accounts in the Sales and Collection Cycle Are Properly Disclosed

In addition to testing for the proper statement of the dollar amount in the general ledger, the auditor must also determine that the account balances resulting from the sales and collection cycle are properly disclosed in the financial statements. The disclosure problem is to decide whether the client has properly combined amounts and disclosed related information in the statements. To evaluate the adequacy of the disclosure, the auditor must have a thorough understanding of generally accepted accounting principles and disclosure requirements.

An important part of evaluating proper disclosure involves deciding whether material amounts requiring separate disclosure have actually been separated in the statements. For example, receivables from officers and affiliated companies must be segregated from accounts receivable from customers if the amounts are material. Similarly, under SEC requirements, it is necessary to separately disclose sales for different business segments. The proper aggregation of general ledger balances in the financial statements also requires combining account balances that are not relevant for external users of the statements. If all the accounts included in the general ledger were separately disclosed on the statements, most statement users would be more confused than enlightened.

As a part of proper disclosure, the auditor is also required to evaluate the adequacy of the *footnotes*. One of the major lawsuits in the history of the profession, the *Continental Vending* case, revolved primarily around the adequacy of the footnote disclosure of a major receivable from an affiliated company. The required footnote disclosure includes information about the pledging, discounting, factoring, and assignment of accounts receivable. Of course, in order to evaluate the adequacy of these disclosures, it is first necessary to know of their existence and to have complete information about their nature. This information is generally obtained in other parts of the audit by such procedures as examining the minutes, reviewing contracts and agreements, confirming the bank accounts, and discussing the existence of information requiring disclosure with management.

CONFIRMATION OF ACCOUNTS RECEIVABLE

One of the most important audit procedures used by auditors is the *confirmation of accounts receivable*. The primary purpose of accounts receivable confirmation is to satisfy the *existence*, *valuation*, and *cutoff* objectives.

AICPA Requirements

Only two audit procedures are formally required by the AICPA: the *confirmation of accounts receivable* and the *physical examination of inventory*. These two requirements are a direct result of the 1938 landmark legal case, *McKesson and Robbins*, in which a massive fraud involving fictitious accounts receivable and inventory was not uncovered in the audit. There was ample legal support to demonstrate that the confirmation of receivables and the physical observation of inventory would have brought the fraud to light, but at that time neither of these procedures was normally performed. Because of a strong reaction in the financial community, the membership of the AICPA voted in 1939 to require these two procedures whenever an unqualified report is issued.

In 1970 the requirement for confirmation was modified somewhat to permit an unqualified report even when accounts receivable are not confirmed when two conditions are met: first, the reason for not confirming the accounts must be that it is impractical or impossible to do so; second, the auditor must satisfy himself that accounts receivable is fairly stated by means of other auditing procedures. The modified requirement also specifically states that the auditor who fails to confirm accounts receivable has the burden of justifying the audit report he issues. The practical implication is that accounts receivable must be confirmed when the amount is material, except in unusual circumstances.

Relationship between Confirmation and Tests of Sales Transactions

The value of accounts receivable confirmation as evidence can be visualized more clearly by relating it to the compliance and substantive tests of transactions discussed in Chapters 9 and 10. If the beginning balance in accounts receivable can be assumed to be correct and a careful evaluation of the tests of the controls has been conducted, the auditor should be in an excellent position to evaluate the fairness of the ending balance in accounts receivable. (A review of Figure 9-1 may help refresh your memory regarding this important concept.)

Confirmations are typically more effective than tests of transactions for discovering certain types of errors. These include invalid accounts, disputed amounts, and uncollectible accounts resulting from the inability to locate the customer. Although confirmations cannot ensure the discovery of any of these types of errors, they are more reliable than tests of transactions because confirmations are evidence obtained from an independent source, whereas tests of transactions rely upon internally created documents.

Confirmations are less likely to uncover omitted transactions and amounts than tests of the system for two reasons. First, in order to send a confirmation it is necessary to have a list of accounts receivable from which to select. Naturally, an omitted account will not be included in the population from which the sample is selected. Second, if an account with an omitted transaction is circularized, customers may ignore the confirmation or, alternatively, state that the amount is correct.

Clerical errors in billing customers and recording the amounts in the accounts can be effectively discovered by confirmation and tests of transactions. Confirmations are typically more effective in uncovering overstatements of accounts receivable than understatements, whereas tests of the system are effective for discovering both types.

The important concept in this discussion is the existence of both a *complementary* and a *supplementary* relationship between tests of sales transactions and confirmations. They are complementary in the sense that both types of evidence, when combined, provide a higher level of overall assurance of the fair presentation of sales, sales returns and allowances, and accounts receivable than can result from either type considered separately. The strengths of tests of transactions together with the strengths of confirmation result in a highly useful combination. The two types of evidence are supplementary in the sense that the auditor can obtain a given level of assurance by decreasing the tests of transactions if there is an offsetting increase in the confirmation of accounts receivable. The extent to which the auditor should rely upon the tests of transactions is dependent upon his evaluation of the effectiveness of the system. If he has carefully evaluated the controls, tested them for compliance, and concluded that the system is likely to provide correct results, it is appropriate to reduce the confirmation of accounts receivable. On the other hand, it would be inappropriate to bypass confirmation altogether.

Although the remaining sections in this chapter refer specifically to the confirmation of accounts receivable from customers, the concepts apply equally to other receivables such as notes receivable, amounts due from officers, and employee advances.

Confirmation Decisions

In performing confirmation procedures, the auditor must make four major decisions: the type of confirmation to use, the timing of the procedures, the sample size, and the individual items to select. Each of these is discussed along with the factors affecting the decision.

Type of Confirmation. Two common types of confirmations are used for confirming accounts receivable: *positive* confirmations and *negative* confirmations. A *positive* confirmation is a communication addressed to the debtor requesting him to confirm directly whether the balance as stated on the confirmation request is correct or incorrect. Figure 11-2 illustrates a positive confirmation. A *negative* confirmation is also a communication addressed to the debtor, but it requests a response only when he disagrees with the stated amount. Figure 11-3 illustrates a negative confirmation which has been attached to a customer's monthly statement with a gummed label.

A positive confirmation is *more reliable* evidence because the auditor can perform follow-up procedures if a response is not received from the debtor. With a negative confirmation, failure to reply must be regarded as a correct response even though the debtor may have ignored the confirmation request.

Offsetting the reliability disadvantage, negative confirmations are *less expensive* to send than positive confirmations, and thus more of them can be distributed for the same total cost. The determination of which type of confirmation to use is an auditor's decision, and it should be based on the facts in the audit. Positive confirmation should be used in the following circumstances:

- Where there are a small number of large customers who account for a significant portion of total accounts receivable.
- Where the auditor believes there may be disputed or inaccurate accounts. This would be the case when internal controls are considered inadequate or previous years' results are unsatisfactory.
- Where the rules of certain regulatory agencies require them, such as those governing brokers and dealers in securities.

When the conditions above do not exist, it is acceptable to use negative confirmations, but negatives should not be used if the auditor believes the customer is likely to ignore the confirmation. Typically, when negatives are used, the auditor places great reliance upon the system as evidence of the fairness of accounts receivable. Negatives are often used for audits of hospitals, retail stores, and other industries where the receivables are due from the general public. In these cases far more reliance is placed on the tests of the system of internal control than on confirmations.

It is also common to use a combination of negatives and positives by sending the positives to accounts with large balances and negatives to those with small balances.

Timing. The most reliable evidence from confirmations is obtained when they are sent as close to the balance sheet date as possible, as opposed to confirming the accounts several months before year-end. This permits the auditor to directly test the accounts receivable balance on the financial statements without making any inferences about the transactions taking place between the confirmation date and the balance sheet date. On the other hand, as a means of completing the audit on a timely basis, it is frequently convenient to confirm the accounts at an interim date. This is permissible if the system of internal control is adequate and can provide reasonable

ABC COMPANY, INC.

Middletown

January 5, 198Y

Middletown Supply Co.
19 South Main Street
Middletown

Gentlemen:

In connection with an examination of our financial statements,
please confirm directly to our auditors

SMART & ALLEN
New York, New York

the correctness of the balance of your account with us as of
December 31, 198X, as shown below.

This is not a request for payment; please do not send your remittance to our auditors.

Your prompt attention to this request will be appreciated. An
envelope is enclosed for your reply.

———————————————
Martin Abrams, Controller

No._____

Smart & Allen
New York, New York

The balance receivable from us of $29,700 as of December 31, 198X.
is correct except as noted below:

_____

_____

_____

_____

Date_____   By_____

FIGURE 11–2   Positive Confirmation

FIGURE 11-3 Negative Confirmation

assurance that sales, cash receipts, and other credits are properly recorded between the date of the confirmation and the end of the accounting period. Other factors the auditor is likely to consider in making the decision are the materiality of accounts receivable and the auditor's exposure to lawsuits because of the risk of client bankruptcy and similar risks.

If the decision is made to confirm accounts receivable prior to year-end, it is necessary to test the transactions occurring between the confirmation date and the balance sheet date by examining such internal documents as duplicate sales invoices, shipping documents, and evidence of cash receipts.

Sample Size. The considerations affecting the number of confirmations to send are essentially the same for judgmental as for statistical sampling:

- The materiality of total accounts receivable. If accounts receivable is highly material relative to the other asset balances, a larger sample size is necessary than when it is immaterial.
- The number of accounts receivable.
- The distribution in the size of the accounts. If all the accounts are approximately the same size, fewer need to be confirmed than when their size is distributed over a wide range of values.
- The results of the internal control evaluation and the tests of the system.
- The results of the confirmation tests in previous years.
- The likelihood of client bankruptcy and similar risks.
- The type of confirmation being used. More confirmations are usually required for negative than for positive confirmation.

A discussion of these factors in the context of variables statistical sampling is given in Chapter 11.

Selection of the Items for Testing. Some type of *stratification is desirable* with most confirmations. A typical approach to stratification is to consider both the size of the outstanding balance and the length of time an account has been outstanding as a basis for selecting the balances for confirmation. In most audits the emphasis should be on confirming larger and older balances, since these are the ones that are most likely to include a significant error. But it is also important to sample some items from every material stratum of the population. In many cases the auditor selects all accounts above a certain dollar amount and selects a random sample from the remainder.

In selecting the items for confirmation, it is important that the auditor have complete *independence* in choosing the accounts to be confirmed. If the client dictates which accounts to select or refuses to grant permission to confirm certain accounts, the ability to operate independently is seriously threatened. On the other hand, clients do frequently request that certain accounts not be confirmed. Although this is undesirable and should be resisted, it is acceptable if the amounts are not material, the client's reasons appear valid, and it is possible to verify the balance in the accounts by other means. If the account balances that the client will not grant permission to confirm are material in relation to the financial statements as a whole, the standards of the profession do not permit the issuance of an unqualified opinion.

Maintaining Control

After the items have been selected for confirming, the auditor must maintain control of the confirmations until they are returned from the customer. If the client's assistance is obtained in preparing the confirmations, enclosing them in envelopes, or putting stamps on the envelopes, close supervision by the auditor is required. A return address must be included on all envelopes to make sure that undelivered mail is received by the CPA firm. Similarly, self-addressed return envelopes accompanying the confirmations must be addressed for delivery to the CPA firm's office. It is even important to mail the confirmations in a post-office box outside of the client's office. All of these steps are necessary to ensure an independent communication between the customer and the auditor.

When a confirmation request is returned as undelivered mail by the post office, it is necessary to carefully evaluate the reason why the request was not delivered. In most cases it represents a customer who has moved without paying his bill, but there is always the possibility of its being a fraudulent account. Even if it is a valid receivable, the existence of a large number of these accounts could indicate a serious collectibility problem which must be reflected in the allowance for uncollectible accounts.

Follow-up on Nonresponses

If the amounts are material, it is necessary to perform follow-up procedures for positive confirmations not returned by the customer. It is common to send second requests for confirmations and sometimes even third requests.

Even with these efforts, some customers do not return the confirmation, so it is necessary to follow up with a method referred to as *alternative procedures*. The objective of alternative procedures is to determine by a means other than confirmation whether the nonconfirmed account was valid and properly stated at the confirmation date. For any positive confirmation not returned, the following documentation can be examined to verify the validity and valuation of individual sales transactions making up the ending balance in accounts receivable:

Subsequent Cash Receipts. Evidence of the receipt of cash subsequent to the confirmation date includes examining remittance advices, entries in the cash receipts records, or perhaps even subsequent credits in the accounts receivable subsidiary records. The examination of evidence of subsequent cash receipts is a highly useful alternative procedure because it is reasonable to assume that a customer would not make a payment unless it was a valid receivable. On the other hand, the fact of payment does not establish whether there was an obligation on the date of the confirmation. In addition, care should be taken to specifically match each unpaid sales transaction with evidence of its payment as a test for disputes or disagreements over individual outstanding invoices.

Duplicate Sales Invoices. These are useful in verifying the actual issuance of a sales invoice and the actual date of the billing.

Shipping Documents. These are important in establishing whether the shipment was actually made and as a test of cutoff.

Correspondence with the Client. Usually, the auditor does not need to review correspondence as a part of alternative procedures, but correspondence can be used to disclose disputed and questionable receivables not uncovered by other means.

The extent and nature of the alternative procedures depend primarily upon the materiality of the nonresponses, the types of errors discovered in the confirmed responses, the subsequent cash receipts from the nonresponses, and the auditor's evaluation of the system of internal control. It is normally desirable to account for all unconfirmed balances with alternative procedures even if the amounts are small, as a means of properly generalizing from the sample to the population.

Analysis of Differences

When the confirmation requests are returned by the customer, it is necessary to determine the reason for any reported differences. In many cases they are caused by timing differences between the client's and the customer's records. It is important to distinguish between these and *exceptions*, which represent misstatements of the accounts receivable balance. The most commonly reported types of differences on confirmations are as follows:

Payment Has Already Been Made. These typically arise when the customer has made a payment prior to confirmation date, but the client has not received the payment in time for posting before the confirmation date. Such instances should be carefully investigated to determine the possibility of a cash receipts cutoff error, lapping, or a theft of cash.

Goods Have Not Been Received. These typically result because the client records the sale at the date of shipment and the customer records the purchase when the goods are received. The lapse of time during which the goods are in transit is frequently the cause of differences reported on confirmations. These should be investigated to determine the possibility of the customer not receiving the goods at all or the existence of a cutoff error on the client's records.

The Goods Have Been Returned. The client's failure to record a credit memo could result from timing differences or the improper recording of sales returns and allowances. Like other differences, these must be investigated.

Clerical Errors and Disputed Amounts. The most likely case of the client's records being in error occurs when the customer states that there is an error in the price charged for the goods, the goods are damaged, the proper quantity of goods was not received, and so forth. These differences must be investigated to determine whether the client is in error and what the amount of the error is.

In most instances the auditor will ask the client to reconcile the difference and, if necessary, communicate with the customer to resolve any disagreements. Naturally, the auditor must carefully verify the client's conclusions on each significant difference.

Drawing Conclusions

When all differences have been resolved, including those discovered in performing alternative procedures, it is important to *reevaluate the system* of internal control. Each client error must be analyzed to determine whether it was consistent or inconsistent with the original evaluation of the strengths and weaknesses in the system. If a significant number of errors take place which are inconsistent with the strengths of the system, it indicates that the original evaluation of the system was incorrect. In such a case it is necessary to revise the evaluation and consider the impact of the revision on the audit.

It is also necessary to generalize from the sample to the entire population of accounts receivable. Even though the sum of the errors in the sample may not significantly affect the financial statements, the auditor must consider whether the population is likely to be materially misstated. This conclusion can be arrived at by using statistical sampling techniques or on a purely judgmental basis.

The final decision that must be reached about accounts receivable and sales is whether sufficient evidence has been obtained through analytical tests, tests of the system, cutoff procedures, confirmations, and other substantive tests to justify drawing conclusions about the fairness of the stated balance.

appendix c

case illustration

The Hillsburg Hardware case from Appendixes A and B is extended to include the determination of the direct tests of balances audit procedures in the sales and collection cycle. The following information, needed to design the direct tests of balances audit program, is included in the case:

- Comparative trial balance information for the sales and collection cycle (Figure 11–4).
- A summary of the weaknesses of internal control in sales and collection (Figure 11–5).
- A summary of the existing controls and the results of the audit tests (Figure 11–6).

FIGURE 11–4

Hillsburg Hardware—Comparative Information
for the Sales and Collection Cycle

in Thousands

	12–31–80	*12–31–79*	*12–31–78*
Sales	$7,216	$6,321	$5,937
Sales returns and allowances	62	57	50
Gross margin	1,992	1,738	1,621
Accounts receivable	1,033	898	825
Allowance for uncollectible accounts	86	77	69
Bad debts	166	164	142
Total current assets	2,607	2,239	2,099
Total assets	3,709	3,301	3,057
Net earnings before taxes	506	436	397
Number of accounts receivable	258	221	209
Number of accounts receivable with balances over $5,000	37	32	30

FIGURE 11–5

Hillsburg Hardware—Weaknesses in the System

Weaknesses (*from Figure 9–10*)	Comments
The bookkeeper maintains the accounts receivable records and also has access to cash receipts.	Compensated in part by tests of transactions. Confirmations may also be effective to uncover potential errors.
Cash receipts are not deposited daily.	Compensated by tests of transactions. Confirmations may also be effective to uncover potential errors.
Receptionist handles cash after it is returned from accounts receivable clerk.	Compensated by tests of transactions. Confirmations may also be effective to uncover potential errors.
The prelisting of cash is not used to verify cash receipts.	Compensated by tests of transactions. Confirmations may also be effective to uncover potential errors.
There is no internal verification of the inclusion of all sales invoices in the sales journal.	Compensated by tests of transactions. Accounts receivable confirmation would not likely be effective for uncovering unrecorded sales.
Lack of internal verification of footing and posting of journals.	Compensated by tests of transactions. Direct tests would not uncover this error.

FIGURE 11–6

Hillsburg Hardware—Strengths in the System

Strengths (*from Figure 9–9*)	Comments
The accountant accounts for all bills of lading and traces them to sales invoices.	No effect; tested by tests of transactions to offset a weakness.
Credit is approved by the president.	The control was not found effective in tests of transactions. See Figure 11–7 and the effect as stated in Figure 11–8.
The bank statement is reconciled by the accountant.	Affects the audit of cash in the bank, but not accounts receivable.
The accountant reconciles the balance in the accounts receivable subsidiary ledger with the control accounts.	Reduce footing the accounts receivable subsidiary ledger and tracing customer balances to the subsidiary ledgers.
The sales invoices are internally verified for pricing, extensions, and footings.	The control was not found effective in tests of transactions. See Figure 11–7 and the effect as stated in Figure 11–8.
Statements are mailed to customers monthly, and all correspondence is sent directly to the president.	This control would permit the reduction of confirmations if it were not for the other weaknesses and compliance deviations found in tests of transactions.
Checks are stamped with a restrictive endorsement.	No effect; tested by tests of transactions to offset a weakness.
Journals and ledgers are reviewed monthly by the president.	This reduces tests of transactions somewhat but it has no effect on direct tests of balances.

An audit program in a design format (Figure 11-7) and in a performance format (Figure 11-8) is then presented.

FIGURE 11-7

Hillsburg Hardware—Direct Tests of Balances Objectives and Audit Program—
Sales and Collections Cycle—Design Format*

Objective	*Audit Procedures*
Account balances and details of sales, sales returns and allowances, accounts receivable, bad debts, and the allowance are reasonable.	Review accounts receivable trial balance for large and unusual receivables. (1)
	Calculate ratios indicated in carry-forward working papers (not included) and follow up on any significant changes from prior years. (2)
Accounts receivable in the aged trial balance agree with related subsidiary ledger amounts, and the total is correctly added and agrees with the general ledger.	Trace 20 accounts from the trial balance to the related subsidiary ledger. (5)
	Foot two pages of the trial balance, and total all pages. (6)
	Trace the balance to the general ledger. (7)
The accounts receivable in the aged trial balance are valid.	Confirm accounts receivable using positive confirmations. Confirm all amounts over $5,000 and a judgment sample of the remainder. (9)
	Perform alternative procedures in all confirmations not returned on the first or second request. (10)
Existing accounts receivable are included in the aged trial balance.	Trace 10 accounts from the subsidiary ledger to the aged trial balance. (8)
Accounts receivable in the trial balance are owned.	Confirm accounts receivable using positive confirmations. (9)
	Review the minutes of the board of directors for any indication of pledged or factored accounts receivable. (3)
	Inquire of management whether any receivables are pledged or factored. (4)
Accounts receivable in the trial balance are properly valued.	Confirm accounts receivable using positive confirmations. Confirm all amounts over $5,000 and a judgment sample of the remainder. (9)
	Perform alternative procedures for all confirmations not returned on the first or second request. (10)
	Trace 20 accounts from the aging schedule to the subsidiary ledger to test for the correct aging on the trial balance. (5)
	Foot the aging columns on the trial balance and total the pages. (6)
	Crossfoot the aging columns. (6)
	Discuss with the credit manager the likelihood of collecting older accounts. Examine

---

*The procedures are summarized into a performance format in Figure 11–8. The number in parentheses after the procedure refers to Figure 11–8.

FIGURE 11–7 (cont.)

Objective	*Audit Procedures*
	subsequent cash receipts and the credit file on all accounts over 120 days and evaluate whether the receivables are collectible. (11)
	Evaluate whether the allowance is adequate after performing other audit procedures relating to collectibility of receivables. (12)
Accounts receivable in the aged trial balance are properly classified.	Review the receivables listed on the aged trial balance for notes and related party receivables. (3)
	Inquire of management whether there are any related party notes or long-term receivables included in the trial balances. (4)
Transactions in the sales and collection cycle are recorded in the proper period.	Select the last 10 sales transactions from the current year's sales journal and the first 10 from the subsequent year's and trace each one to the related shipping documents, checking for the date of actual shipment and the correct recording. (13)
	Review large sales returns and allowances after the balance sheet date to determine whether any should be included in the current period. (14)
Accounts in the sales and collection cycle are properly disclosed.	Review the minutes of the board of directors for any indication of pledged or factored accounts receivable. (3)
	Inquire of management whether any receivables are pledged or factored. (4)

FIGURE 11–8

Hillsburg Hardware—Direct Tests of Balances—Audit Program Sales and Collection Cycle—Performance Format

1. Review accounts receivable trial balance for large and unusual receivables.
2. Calculate ratios indicated in carry-forward working papers (not included) and follow-up any significant changes from prior years.
3. Review the receivables listed on the aged trial balance for notes and related party receivables.
4. Inquire of management whether there are any related party, notes, or long-term receivables included in the trial balance. Inquire as to whether any receivables are pledged or factored.
5. Trace 20 accounts from the trial balance to the related subsidiary ledger for aging and the balance.
6. Foot two pages of the trial balance for aging columns and balance and total all pages and crossfoot the aging.
7. Trace the balance to the general ledger.
8. Trace 10 accounts from the subsidiary ledger to the aged trial balance.
9. Confirm accounts receivable using positive confirmations. Confirm all amounts over $5,000 and a judgment sample of the remainder.
10. Perform alternative procedures on all confirmations not returned on the first or second request.

FIGURE 11-8 (cont.)

11. Discuss with the credit manager the likelihood of collecting older accounts. Examine subsequent cash receipts and the credit file on all larger accounts over 120 days and evaluate whether the receivables are collectible.
12. Evaluate whether the allowance is adequate after performing other audit procedures relating to collectibility of receivables.
13. Select the last 10 sales transactions from the current year's sales journal and the first 10 from the subsequent year's and trace each one to the related shipping documents, checking for the date of actual shipment and the correct recording.
14. Review large sales returns and allowances after the balance sheet date to determine whether any should be included in the current period.

REVIEW QUESTIONS

11-1. Distinguish between direct tests of financial balances and tests of transactions for the sales and collection cycle. Explain how the tests of transactions affect the direct tests.

11-2. Cynthia Roberts, CPA, expresses the following viewpoint: "I do not believe in performing tests of transactions for the sales and collection cycle. As an alternative, I send a lot of negative confirmations on every audit at an interim date. If I find a lot of errors I analyze them to determine their cause. If the system is inadequate, I send positives at year-end to evaluate the amount of the errors. If the negatives result in minimal errors, which is often the case, I have found that the system is effective without bothering to perform tests of transactions, and the AICPA's confirmation requirement has been satisfied at the same time. In my opinion the best test of the system is to go directly to third parties." Evaluate her point of view.

11-3. List five analytical tests for the sales and collection cycle. For each test, describe an error that could be identified.

11-4. State the purpose of footing the total column in the client's trial balance, tracing individual customer names and amounts to the subsidiary ledger, and tracing the total to the general ledger. Is it necessary to trace each amount to the subsidiary ledger? Why?

11-5. Distinguish between valuation tests of gross accounts receivable and tests of the realizable value of receivables.

11-6. Explain why you agree or disagree with the following statement: "In most audits it is more important to carefully test the cutoff for sales than for cash receipts." Describe how you perform each type of test, assuming the existence of prenumbered documents.

11-7. Evaluate the following statement: "In many audits where accounts receivable is material, the requirement of confirming customer balances is a waste of time and would not be performed by competent auditors if it was not required by the AICPA. When the system of internal control is excellent and there are a large number of small receivables from customers who do not recognize the function of confirmation, it is a meaningless procedure.

Examples are well-run utilities and department stores. In these situations tests of transactions are far more effective tests than confirmations."

11–8. Distinguish between a positive and a negative confirmation and state the circumstances when each should be used. Why do CPA firms frequently use a combination of positives and negatives on the same audit?

11–9. Under what circumstances is it acceptable to confirm accounts receivable prior to the balance sheet date?

11–10. State the most important factors affecting the sample size in confirmations of accounts receivable.

11–11. In Chapter 10 one of the points brought out was the need to obtain a representative sample of the population. How can this concept be reconciled with the statement in this chapter that the emphasis should be on confirming larger and older balances, since these are the most likely to contain errors?

11–12. Define what is meant by "alternative procedures" and explain their purpose. Which alternative procedures are the most reliable? Why?

11–13. Explain why the analysis of exceptions is important in the confirmation of accounts receivable, even if the errors in the sample are not material.

11–14. State three types of differences observed on the confirmation of accounts receivable that do not constitute errors. For each difference state an audit procedure that would verify the difference.

11–15. With regard to the sales and collection cycle, explain the relationship between flowcharts, preliminary evaluation, tests of compliance, and substantive tests.

DISCUSSION QUESTIONS AND PROBLEMS

11–16. For each of the following questions concerning the account balance in the sales and collection cycle, select the best response.

a. In connection with his examination of the Beke Supply Company for the year ended August 31, 19X1, Derek Lowe, CPA, has mailed accounts receivable confirmations to three groups as follows:

Group Number	Type of Customer	Type of Confirmation
1	Wholesale	Positive
2	Current retail	Negative
3	Past-due retail	Positive

The confirmation responses from each group vary from 10 percent to 90 percent. The most likely response percentages are

(1) Group 1 90%   Group 2 50%   Group 3 10%
(2) Group 1 90%   Group 2 10%   Group 3 50%
(3) Group 1 50%   Group 2 90%   Group 3 10%
(4) Group 1 10%   Group 2 50%   Group 3 90%

   b. Of the following, the most common argument against the use of negative accounts receivable confirmations is that

     (1) the cost-per-response is excessively high.

     (2) statistical sampling techniques cannot be applied to selection of the sample.

     (3) recipients are more likely to feel that the confirmation is a request for payment.

     (4) the implicit assumption that no response indicates agreement with the balance may not be warranted.

   c. In connection with his review of key ratios, the CPA notes that Pyzi had accounts receivable equal to 30 days' sales at December 31, 19X0, and to 45 days' sales at December 31, 19X1. Assuming that there had been no changes in economic conditions, clientele, or sales mix, this change most likely would indicate

     (1) a steady increase in sales in 19X1.

     (2) an easing of credit policies in 19X1.

     (3) a decrease in accounts receivable relative to sales in 19X1.

     (4) a steady decrease in sales in 19X1.

   d. Balmes Company asks its CPA's assistance in estimating the proportion of its active 30-day charge account customers who also have an active installment credit account. The CPA takes an unrestricted random sample of 100 accounts from the 6,000 active 30-day charge accounts. Of the accounts selected, 10 also have active installment credit accounts. If the CPA decides to estimate with 95 percent confidence, the estimate is that

     (1) at most 10 percent of the active 30-day charge account customers also have active installment credit accounts.

     (2) at least 10 percent of the active 30-day charge account customers also have active installment credit accounts.

     (3) between 7 percent and 13 percent of the active 30-day charge account customers also have active installment credit accounts.

     (4) between 4 percent and 16 percent of the active 30-day charge account customers also have active installment credit accounts.

   e. The CPA learns that collections of accounts receivable during the first 10 days of January were entered as debits to cash and credits to accounts receivable as of December 31. The effect generally will be to

     (1) leave both working capital and the current ratio unchanged at December 31.

     (2) overstate both working capital and the current ratio at December 31.

     (3) overstate working capital with no effect on the current ratio at December 31.

     (4) overstate the current ratio with no effect on working capital at December 31.

   f. The return of a positive account receivable confirmation without an exception attests to the

     (1) collectibility of the receivable balance.

     (2) accuracy of the receivable balance.

(3) accuracy of the aging of accounts receivable.

(4) accuracy of the allowance for bad debts.   (AICPA adapted)

11–17. Dodge, CPA, is examining the financial statements of a manufacturing company with a significant amount of trade accounts receivable. Dodge is satisfied that the accounts are properly summarized and classified and that allocations, reclassifications, and valuations are made in accordance with generally accepted accounting principles. Dodge is planning to use accounts receivable confirmation requests to satisfy the third standard of field work as to trade accounts receivable.

Required:

a. Identify and describe the two forms of accounts receivable confirmation requests and indicate what factors Dodge will consider in determining when to use each.

b. Assume that Dodge has received a satisfactory response to the confirmation requests. Describe how Dodge could evaluate collectibility of the trade accounts receivable.   (AICPA)

11–18. a. What are the implications to a CPA if during his examination of accounts receivable some of a client's trade customers do not respond to his request for positive confirmation of their accounts?

b. Should the CPA send second requests? Why?

c. What auditing steps should a CPA perform if there is no response to a second request for a positive confirmation?   (AICPA adapted)

11–19. In a properly planned examination of financial statements, the auditor coordinates his reviews of specific balance sheet and income statement accounts.

Required:

a. Why should the auditor coordinate his examinations of balance sheet accounts and income statement accounts in the sales and collection cycle? Discuss and illustrate by examples.

b. A properly designed audit program enables the auditor to determine conditions or establish relationships in more than one way.

Cite various procedures that the auditor employs that might lead to detection of each of the following two conditions:

(1) Inadequate allowance for doubtful accounts receivable.

(2) Unrecorded sales commissions.   (AICPA adapted)

11–20. During the past few years your audit client, Commercial Dry Wall, has been in somewhat of an income slump, as competition for dry wall and newly developed interior wall materials has been intensive. Losses have occurred because of the need to diversify and expand in different areas. In discussing the current year's audit, Brian Curtis, the controller, expresses dissatisfaction with the approach to auditing your firm and the profession as a whole takes in verifying financial statements. He feels that the entire approach emphasizes only the overstatement of assets and the understatement of liabilities. His criticisms are especially intense in auditing accounts receivable, where the customer is likely to say nothing about understatements and respond to overstatements or even questionable items. He asserts that even the emphasis in the accounts normally selected for testing is on overstatements, since large balances and disputed amounts are frequently confirmed. After ranting on for about fifteen minutes, he talks about switching CPA firms to someone who is more interested in a balanced picture of overstatements and understatements, rather than only overstatements.

You feel an immediate response is necessary in this case, and you decide to restrict yourself to a discussion of accounts receivable. How would you answer him?

11–21. You have been assigned to the confirmation of accounts receivable for the Blank Paper Company audit. You have tested the trial balance and selected the accounts for confirming. Before the confirmation requests are mailed, the controller asks to look at the accounts you intend to confirm to determine whether he will permit you to send them.

He reviews the list and informs you that he does not want you to confirm six of the accounts on your list. Two of them are credit balances, one is a zero balance, two of the other three have a fairly small balance, and one balance is highly material. The reason he gives is that he feels the confirmations will upset these customers, because "they are kind of hard to get along with." He doesn't want the credit balances confirmed because it may encourage the customer to ask for a refund.

In addition, the controller asks you to send an additional twenty confirmations to customers he has listed for you. He does this as a means of credit collection for "those stupid idiots who won't know the difference between a CPA and a credit collection agency."

Required:

a. Is it acceptable for the controller to review the list of accounts you intend to confirm? Discuss.
b. Discuss the appropriateness of sending the twenty additional confirmations to customers.
c. Assuming the auditor complies with all the controller's requests, what is the effect on the auditor's opinion?

11–22. In your examination of the financial statements of the Kay Savings and Loan Association for year ended December 31, 19X5, you find a new account in the general ledger, Home Improvement Loans. You determine that these are unsecured loans not insured by any government agency, made on a discount basis to homeowners who are required to secure life insurance coverage provided by the association under a group life insurance policy for the outstanding amount and duration of the loan. Borrowers are issued coupon books which require monthly installment payments; however, borrowers may prepay the outstanding balance of the loan at any time in accordance with the terms of their loan contract. This account constitutes a material amount of the total assets of the association at December 31, 19X5.

Required:

a. Prepare an audit program for the examination of the new account, Home Improvement Loans.

b. During your examination of the Home Improvement Loans account the vice-president in charge of the loan department hands you a list of 25 accounts with balances from $300 to $8,000 representing approximately 40 percent of the total account balance. He states that confirmation requests are not to be prepared for these 25 accounts under any circumstances because the borrowers have requested "no correspondence."

(1) Would you comply with the vice-president's request? Discuss.

(2) Assuming you complied with the vice-president's request and did not send confirmation requests to the "no correspondence" accounts, what effect, if any, would this compliance have upon your auditor's short form report? (AICPA adapted)

11-23. Maria Nolan, CPA, in examining the financial statements of the Quinn Helicopter Corporation for the year ended September 30, 19X7, found a material amount of receivables from the federal government. The governmental agencies replied neither to the first nor to the second confirmation requests, nor to a third request made by telephone.

Required:

a. How could Nolan satisfy herself as to the fairness of the receivables as of the balance at September 30, 19X7?

b. Assuming she was able to satisfy herself, what is the effect on the auditor's report? (AICPA adapted)

11-24. In connection with his examination of the financial statements of Houston Wholesalers, Inc., for the year ended June 30, 19X7, a CPA performs several cutoff tests.

Required:

a. (1) What is a cutoff test?

(2) Why must cutoff tests be performed for both the beginning and the end of the audit period on initial engagements?

b. The CPA wishes to test Houston's sales cutoff at June 30, 19X7. Describe the steps that he should include in this test.

c. Describe steps the CPA should use to test cash receipts cutoff.

(AICPA adapted)

11-25. You have been assigned to the first examination of the accounts of the Chicago Company for the year ending March 31, 19X8. The accounts receivable were circularized at December 31, 19X7, and at that date the receivables consisted of approximately 200 accounts with balances totaling $956,750. Seventy-five of these accounts with balances totaling $650,725 were selected for circularization. All but 20 of the confirmation requests have been returned; 30 were signed without comments, 14 had minor differences which have been cleared satisfactorily, while 11 confirmations had the following comments:

a. We are sorry but we cannot answer your request for confirmation of our account as the PDQ Company uses an accounts payable voucher system.

b. The balance of $1,050 was paid on December 23, 19X7.

c. The balance of $7,750 was paid on January 5, 19X8.

d. The balance noted above has been paid.

e. We do not owe you anything at December 31, 19X7, as the goods, represented by your invoice dated December 30, 19X7, number 25,050, in the amount of $11,550, were received on January 5, 19X8, on FOB destination terms.

f. An advance payment of $2,500 made by us in November 19X7 should cover the two invoices totaling $1,350 shown on the statement attached.

g. We never received these goods.

h. We are contesting the propriety of this $12,525 charge. We think the charge is excessive.

i. Amount okay. As the goods have been shipped to us on consignment, we will remit payment upon selling the goods.

j. The $10,000, representing a deposit under a lease, will be applied against the rent due to us during 19X9, the last year of the lease.

k. Your credit memo dated December 5, 19X7, in the amount of $440 cancels the balance above.

Required:

What steps would you take to clear satisfactorily each of the above eleven comments?   (AICPA adapted)

11–26. You have examined the financial statements of the Heft Company for several years. The system of internal control for accounts receivable is very satisfactory. The Heft Company is on a calendar year basis. An interim audit, which included confirmation of the accounts receivable, was performed at August 31 and indicated that the accounting for cash, sales, sales returns and allowances, and receivables was very reliable.

The company's sales are principally to manufacturing concerns. There are about 1,500 active trade accounts receivable of which about 35 percent represent 65 percent of the total dollar amount. The accounts receivable are maintained alphabetically in five subledgers which are controlled by one general ledger account.

Sales are machine-posted in the subledgers by an operation that produces simultaneously the customer's ledger card, his monthly statement, and the sales journal. All cash receipts are in the form of customers' checks and are machine-posted simultaneously on the customer's ledger card, his monthly statement, and the cash receipts journal. Information for posting cash receipts is obtained from the remittance advice portions of the customers' checks. The bookkeeping machine operator compares the remittance advices with the list of checks that was prepared by another person when the mail was received.

Summary totals are produced monthly by the bookkeeping machine operations for posting to the appropriate general ledger accounts such as cash, sales, accounts receivable. Aged trial balances by subledgers are prepared monthly.

Required:

Prepare the additional audit procedures necessary for testing the balances in the sales and collection cycle. (Ignore bad debts and allowance for uncollectible accounts.)   (AICPA adapted)

11–27. In the confirmation of accounts receivable for the Reliable Service Company, 85 positive confirmations and no negatives were mailed to customers. This represents 35 percent of the dollar balance of the total accounts receivable. For all nonresponses second requests were sent, but there were still 10 customers who had not responded. The decision was made to perform alternative procedures on the 10 unanswered confirmation requests. An assistant is requested to conduct the alternative procedures and report to the senior auditor after he has completed his tests on two accounts. He prepared the following information for the working papers:

    1. Confirmation request #9
       Customer name—Jolene Milling Co.
       Balance—$3,621 at 12-31-X7
       Subsequent cash receipts per the subsidiary ledger   1-15-X8—$1,837
                                                 1-29-X8—$1,263
                                                 2-6-X8—$1,429

    2. Confirmation request #26
       Customer name—Rosenthal Repair Service
       Balance—$2,500 at 12-31-X7
       Subsequent cash receipts per the subsidiary ledger   2-9-X8—$ 500
       Sales invoices per the subsidiary ledger   9-1-X7—$4,200
       (I examined the duplicate sales invoice)

Required:

   a. If you were called upon to evaluate the adequacy of the sample size, the type of confirmation used, and the percentage of accounts confirmed, what additional information would you need?
   b. Discuss the need to send second requests and perform alternative procedures for nonresponses.
   c. Evaluate the adequacy of the alternative procedures used for verifying the two nonresponses.

11–28. Your client took a complete physical inventory under your observation as of December 15 and adjusted the inventory control account (perpetual inventory method) to agree with the physical inventory. You have decided to accept the balance of the control account as of December 31, after reflecting transactions recorded therein from December 16 to December 31, in connection with your examination of financial statements for the year ended December 31.

     Your examination of the sales cutoff as of December 15 and December 31 disclosed the following items not previously considered. What adjusting journal entries, if any, would you make for each of these items?

		Date		
Cost	Sales Price	Shipped	Billed	Credited to Inventory Control
$2,840	$3,690	12–14	12–16	12–16
3,910	5,020	12–10	12–19	12–10
1,890	2,130	1–2	12–31	12–31

(AICPA adapted)

11–29. You are considering using the services of a reputable outside mailing service for the confirmation of accounts receivable balances. The service would prepare and mail the confirmation requests and remove the returned confirmations from the envelopes and give them directly to you.

Required:

What reliance, if any, could you place upon the services of the outside mailing service? Discuss and state the reasons for your answer.

(AICPA adapted)

11–30. The following errors are commonly found in the sales and collection account balances:

a. Cash received from collections of accounts receivable in the subsequent period are recorded as current period receipts.

b. The allowance for uncollectible accounts is inadequate due to the client's failure to reflect depressed economic conditions in the allowance.

c. Several accounts receivable are in dispute due to claims of defective merchandise.

d. The pledging of accounts receivable to the bank for a loan is not disclosed in the financial statements.

e. Goods shipped and included in current period sales were returned in the subsequent period.

f. Several sales are not recorded due to the loss of shipping documents by the shipping department.

g. Uncollectible accounts are included in current period accounts receivable.

h. An accounts receivable bookkeeper who has access to cash is covering an embezzlement by lapping.

i. Long-term interest-bearing notes receivable from affiliated companies are included in accounts receivable.

j. The trial balance total does not equal the amount in the general ledger.

Required:

a. For each of these errors, list an internal control that should prevent the error.

b. List two audit procedures for each of these errors that the auditor can use to detect its existence.

11–31. You are a senior accountant on the staff of Marin and Matthews, certified
public accountants. You are conducting the annual audit of the Never-Slip
Corporation for the calendar year 19X9.

　　　You are now working on the audit of the accounts receivable and
related allowance for bad debts accounts.

　　　All the data included in the client's general ledger and supporting
schedules are summarized below.

General Ledger

Accounts Receivable

19X9		
Dec. 31	Balance	$184,064.20

Allowance for Uncollectible Accounts

19X9			19X9		
July 31	G.J.	$570.00	Jan. 1	Balance	$2,712.50
Oct. 31	G.J.	954.16	Dec. 31	G.J.	2,698.10

Bad Debts

19X9			19X9		
Dec. 31	G.J.	$2,698.10	Aug. 1	C.R.J.	$85.00

General Journal

July 31

Allowance for uncollectible accounts	$570.00	
Accounts receivable		$570.00
To charge off bad accounts (detail omitted)		

October 31

Allowance for uncollectible accounts	954.16	
Accounts receivable		954.16
Accounts charged off:		
Baker, J. A.	$110.00	
Dehner & Son	9.75	
Meek, Roger	350.00	
Wagner, James	494.41	
	$954.16	

December 31

Bad debts	2,698.10	
Allowance for uncollectible accounts		2,698.10
Annual charge based on $\frac{1}{2}\%$ of net credit sales		

Cash Receipts Journal

　　　On August 1 the $85 account of John Smith, previously charged off as
of July 31, was collected in full. Credit was to bad debts.

Summary of Aging Schedule

The summary of the aged trial balance prepared by the client as of December 31, 19X9, was totaled as follows:

Under one month	$ 92,715.60
One to three months	58,070.15
Three to six months	29,126.89
Over six months	4,624.10
	$184,536.74

Credit balances:

Dabney Cleaners ..	$ 16.54	—O.K.—Additional billing in January 19X0
Britting Cafeteria ..	72.00	—Should have been credited to Britt Motor Co.
Wehby & Son	384.00	—Advance on a sales contract
	$472.54	

Additional Information:

The accounts receivable clerk has access to cash, maintains accounts receivable subsidiary records, and approves the charge-off of uncollectible accounts receivable.

The auditor and the client have agreed on the following allowance for uncollectible account requirements:

It is agreed that $\frac{1}{2}$ percent is adequate for accounts under one month.

Accounts one to three months are expected to require a reserve of 1 percent.

Accounts three to six months are expected to require a reserve of 2 percent.

Accounts over six months are analyzed as follows:

Definitely bad	$ 416.52
Doubtful (estimated 50% collectible)	516.80
Apparently good, but slow (estimated 90% collectible)	3,690.78
	$4,624.10

Required:

a. List the audit procedures you would consider necessary for the verification of bad debts, the charge-off of uncollectible accounts, and allowance for uncollectible accounts, assuming no testing has been done to this point.

b. Assuming you verify and are satisfied with the amounts charged off as uncollectible during the current year, what is the proper ending balance in allowance for uncollectible accounts? (AICPA adapted)

12

THE USE
OF VARIABLES SAMPLING
IN AUDITING

Both attributes sampling and variables sampling are valuable techniques in carrying out audit tests. But there are significant differences in the application of these two methods. The first part of this chapter discusses these differences. The remainder of the chapter concerns the different types of variables sampling methods available to auditors and the concepts and uses of the methods. The chapter ends with the application of one method, difference estimation, to the confirmation of accounts receivable.

COMPARISON WITH ATTRIBUTES SAMPLING

Many of the basic concepts underlying attributes sampling apply to variables sampling as well. The auditor wants to generalize from a sample to the entire population but needs a method that takes into account the imperfection of sampling as opposed to testing the entire population. The two measures of this imperfection are the *precision interval* and the *confidence level*. The calculations for the two methods are different, but the objectives and methodology are similar.

The major difference between the two methods is in the characteristic the auditor wants to measure. In *attributes sampling* the objective is to measure the *frequency of error* in the population. When attributes sampling is used in a compliance test, the statistical result obtained is a *computed upper precision limit at the desired confidence level;* this can also be stated as a "point estimate" plus a precision interval at the desired confidence level. For example, assume the auditor tests the percentage of duplicate sales invoices not supported by shipping documents by examining one hundred sales invoices from a population of ten thousand. If he found three invoices with no shipping documents attached, the point estimate of the error rate would be 3 percent, and the computed upper precision limit determined from the tables in Chapter 10 would be 7.6 percent at a 95 percent confidence level. Another way of stating this result is to say that it is a point estimate of 3 percent plus a precision interval of 4.6 percent at a 95 percent confidence level.

In *variables sampling* as it is used in auditing, the objective is almost always to measure the *true dollar amount* of an account balance or some similar total. The computed result is stated in terms of *the dollar amount of the point estimate plus and minus the dollar amount of the precision interval at the confidence level desired.* It is common to calculate both an upper and a lower limit for variables sampling because an account balance can be understated or overstated. As an example, assume the auditor is confirming accounts receivable and computes the point estimate of the total balance as $1,470,000 with a $200,000 computed precision interval at a confidence level of 95 percent. This means the auditor estimates that, at a 95 percent confidence level, the true value of the accounts receivable is between $1,270,000 and $1,670,000 ($1,470,000 $\pm$ $200,000). At this early stage in the study of variables sampling, it is not possible for the reader to determine how these values are computed, but it is possible to observe that the results are stated in the same basic form as attributes.

Whenever it is practical to use variables sampling for substantive tests, it is a more useful measurement device than attributes sampling because auditors are generally more interested in the monetary amount of errors than in the frequency of errors. As an illustration, assume the auditor could use either attributes or variables sampling in confirming accounts receivable. If attributes sampling is used, the statistical conclusion is stated in terms of the percentage of the accounts receivable that are in error regardless of the amount of the individual errors in the sample. In variables sampling, the auditor is measuring the correct dollar value of the accounts in the sample. Which of these is more useful? Variables sampling, because the correct dollar value of total accounts receivable is of primary interest to the auditor. As a result, attributes sampling is normally applied to tests of transactions and variables sampling is applied to direct tests of balances. The only time attributes sampling is used for direct tests of balances is when the cost of variables sampling is prohibitive or the method does not give useful results.

The major advantage of using variables sampling rather than judgmental sampling for measuring the dollar amount of errors or account balances is the *objectivity* of the results. At the completion of a test using variables sampling, the auditor can use his professional judgment in deciding whether he is satisfied with the potential error in the population considering the measurable statistical risk in the result.

POPULATION DISTRIBUTIONS

Populations that are audited by variables sampling methods are made up of various items, the sum of which equals the population total value. For example, a client may have 15,000 accounts receivable, which have recorded values ranging from $0 to $90, that total $450,000. The dollar values of all the elements of this population can be plotted on a continuous distribution curve such as the one shown in Figure 12-1.

It is apparent from the population distribution shown that some population items have a zero value and none have a value over $90. There are more population items with a value between 0 and $20 than with a value between $50 and $90. The population has a mean of $30 (total value of $450,000 divided by the population size of 15,000) and a mode of approximately $22 (value appearing most frequently, which is the highest point in the distribution).

The population also has a *standard deviation*, which is a measure of the variability of the population. The larger the variability, the larger the standard deviation. Calculation of the standard deviation is shown later in the chapter.

Population distributions can have different shapes, depending upon the makeup of the population. A few are shown in Figure 12-2.

Distributions A, B, and C are symmetrical curves. The mean, median, and mode are the same and the left side of the distribution is equal to the right side. Distributions A and B are a special type of symmetrical distribution called a *normal curve*. The two characteristics of a normal curve for a population are: (1) it must be symmetrical and (2) known proportions of the population are contained within fixed distances from the arithmetic mean. These fixed portions are measured by the standard deviation. For example, approximately 68 percent of the population items of a normal curve must fall within *one* standard deviation on each side of the mean, and about 95 percent within *two* standard deviations of each side of the mean.

There is a difference between distributions A and B in Figure 12-2, even though they are both normal. The values of population items are closer to the mean for A than for B. This means that the population standard deviation is smaller for A.

Distribution C is symmetrical, but not normal. It is apparent by inspection that condition 2 for normality has not been met.

Distributions D and E are referred to as *skewed distributions*. Distribution D has a large number of population items with small values and few items with large values. It is called a "positively skewed" or a "skewed to the right" distribution. A large number of accounting populations are shaped somewhat like D. For example, it is not unusual to have a large number of accounts receivable with small balances and a few with large balances. The conditions for distribution E are the reverse of D. A distribution of this type is negatively skewed or skewed to the left.

Distribution F indicates the existence of an exceptionally large number

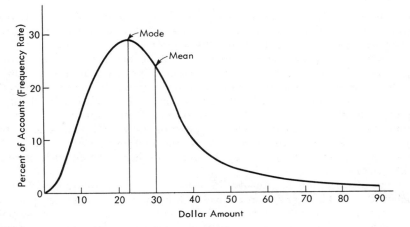

FIGURE 12-1 Continuous Population Distribution Curve

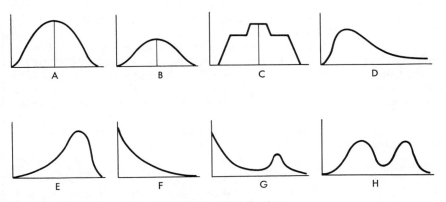

FIGURE 12-2 Examples of Population Distributions

of small items in the population and some larger items. The same conditions exist for distribution G except that there are also a reasonably large number of items with high values.

Distribution H appears to be a combination of two distributions. It is called a *bimodal distribution*.

Importance of Population Distributions to Auditors

Auditors are usually concerned about one or both of two characteristics of accounting populations, the *audited value* and the *errors* in the population. The audited value is the amount that the auditor believes should be recorded for a population. The errors are the difference between the client's recorded value and the audited value. The nature of the distribution of an accounting population determines whether the variables sampling statistical method the auditor uses should emphasize audited values or errors.

There has been almost no research on the exact nature of accounting populations. The reason is that auditors rarely test every item in the population to determine the audited values or the population errors. However, there is reason to believe that the distribution of the *audited value* of many populations is shaped much like distribution D in Figure 12-2. Many accounting populations have a large number of fairly small values and some large values. There are many possible shapes for those skewed to the right distributions. Some are highly skewed, whereas others may be fairly close to symmetrical.

The distribution of the *absolute value of errors* in many populations is believed to be like F and G in Figure 12-2. Frequently, accounting populations have a large number of items without error (i.e., error amount equals zero) or a large number of small errors and a small number of large errors (distribution F). Notice in distribution G that there would be a large number of small errors, but there also would be quite a few large errors. It is possible that the total dollar value of the combined large errors is considerably larger than the total of all small errors.

The shape and standard deviation of the population are essential to auditors. These two considerations determine the appropriate statistical methods to use in a given audit situation and also impact sample size. If an auditor uses an improper statistical method he can easily reach an incorrect audit conclusion or take a larger sample size than would have been necessary with an alternative method.

The problem of selecting an appropriate statistical method is complicated by three considerations:

- *The auditor does not know the exact shape of the distribution either before or after the audit has been completed.* The client's recorded values of individual transactions and balances are normally available, but the auditor is interested in the correct balance for each population element. If there are significant errors in a population, the auditor may erroneously conclude that the client's recorded distribution is the actual distribution. For example, if the auditor of the population shown in distribution G in Figure 12–2 is not aware of the hump in the right side of the distribution, it would be easy to draw wrong conclusions about the population.
- *The auditor estimates the population's standard deviation on the basis of a sample.* If the auditor's estimate of the standard deviation based on a sample is materially different from the actual standard deviation, the statistical estimate will not be a good measure of the actual population value.
- *The auditor must know which statistical method to use in a given set of circumstances.* Certain statistical methods are so likely to result in incorrect audit decisions in certain situations that it is improper to use those methods in those situations at all.

SAMPLING DISTRIBUTIONS

Auditors do not know the mean value or the distribution of the populations they are testing in audit engagements. The population characteristics must be estimated from samples. In this section there is a discussion of sampling distributions, which are essential to drawing conclusions about populations on the basis of samples using variables estimation methods.

Assume that an auditor, as an experiment, took thousands of repeated samples of equal size from a population of accounting data having a mean value of $\bar{X}$. For each sample the auditor calculates the mean value of the items in the sample as follows:

$$\bar{x} = \frac{\sum x_j}{n}$$

where $\bar{x}$ = mean value of the sample items
  x_j = value of each individual sample item
  n = sample size

After the auditor calculates $\bar{x}$ for each sample, he plots them into a *frequency distribution*. The frequency distribution of the sample will likely be as shown in Figure 12-3.

A distribution of the sample means such as this is *always normal*, and has all the characteristics of the normal curve stated earlier: the curve is symmetrical, and the sample means fall within known portions of the sampling distribution around the mean, measured by the distance along the horizontal axis in terms of standard deviations. Further, the mean of the sample means (the midpoint of the sampling distribution) is equal to the population mean and the standard deviation of the sampling distribution is equal to $SD/\sqrt{n}$. SD is the population standard deviation and n is the sample size.

To illustrate, assume a population with a mean of $40 and a standard deviation of $15 ($\bar{X}$ = $40 and SD = $15), from which we elected to take many random samples of 100 items each. The standard deviation of our

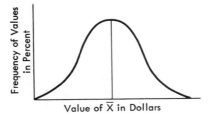

Value of $\overline{X}$ in Dollars

FIGURE 12-3 Frequency Distribution of Sample Means

sampling distribution would be $1.50 (SD$/\sqrt{n} = 15/\sqrt{100} = 1.50$). The reference to "standard deviation" of the population and to "standard deviation" of the sampling distribution often is confusing. To avoid the confusion the standard deviation of the distribution of the sample means is often called the *standard error of the mean* (SE). With this information, the tabulation of the sampling distribution can be made, as shown in Figure 12-4.

FIGURE 12-4

Calculated Sampling Distribution from a Population
with a Known Mean and Standard Deviation

(1) Number of Standard Errors of the Mean (Confidence Coefficient)	*(2)* Value [(1) × $1.50]	*(3)* Range Around $\bar{X}$ [$40 ± (2)]	*(4)* Percent of Sample Means Included in Range
1	$1.50	$38.50–$41.50	68.2
2	$3.00	$37.00–$43.00	95.4
3	$4.50	$35.50–$44.50	99.7 (taken from table for normal curve)

To summarize, three things are important about the results of the experiment of taking a large number of samples from a known population.

- The sample mean value ($\bar{x}$) with the highest frequency of occurrence is equal to the population mean ($\bar{X}$).
- The shape of the frequency distribution is that of a normal curve if the sample is reasonably large, *regardless of the distribution of the population.* A graphic representation of this conclusion is shown in Figure 12–5.
- The percentage of sample means between any two values of the sampling distribution is measurable. The percentage can be calculated by (1) deter-

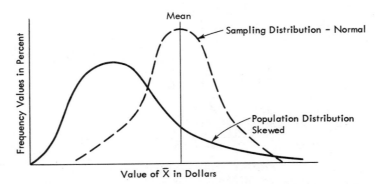

FIGURE 12-5 Sampling Distribution for a Population Distribution

mining the number of standard errors of the mean between any two values and (2) the percentage of sample means represented determined from a table for normal curves.

STATISTICAL INFERENCE

Naturally when the auditor samples from a population in an actual audit situation he does not know the population's characteristics and there is ordinarily only one sample taken from the population. But the *knowledge of sampling distributions* enables auditors to draw statistical conclusions (i.e., make statistical inferences) about the population. For example, assume that the auditor takes a sample from a population and calculates $\bar{x}$ as $46 and SE as $9 (the way to calculate SE will be shown later). We can now calculate a confidence interval of the population mean using the logic gained from the study of sampling distributions. It is

$$CI_{\bar{x}} = \hat{X} \pm Z \cdot SE$$

where $CI_{\bar{x}}$ = confidence interval for the population mean
$\hat{X}$ = point estimate of the population mean
Z = confidence coefficient (1 = 68.2 confidence level
            2 = 95.4 confidence level
            3 = 99.7 confidence level)
   SE = standard error of the mean

For the example:

$CI_{\bar{x}} = \$46 \pm 1(\$9) = \$46 \pm \$9$ at a 68.2% confidence level
$CI_{\bar{x}} = \$46 \pm 2(\$9) = \$46 \pm \$18$ at a 95.4% confidence level
$CI_{\bar{x}} = \$46 \pm 3(\$9) = \$46 \pm \$27$ at a 99.7% confidence level

The results can also be stated in terms of confidence limits (CL $\bar{X}$). The upper confidence limit (UCL $\bar{X}$) is $\hat{X} + Z$ SE ($46 + $18 = $64 at a 95 percent confidence level) and a lower confidence limit (LCL $\bar{X}$) is $\hat{X} - Z$ SE ($46 - $18 = $28 at 95 percent confidence level). Graphically, the results are as follows:

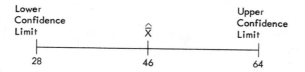

The conclusion about the confidence interval based on a sample from an unknown population can be stated in different ways, but care must be taken to avoid incorrect conclusions. In making statistical inferences the auditor should remember that the true population value is unknown. There is always a possibility that the sample is not representative of the true population value if the sample result is significantly different from the population value. The auditor can say in the previous example that the confidence interval for the true population mean value is $46 $\pm$ $18 at a 95 percent confidence level or that the true population mean value is between $28 and $64 at a 95 percent confidence level.

Efficiency and Reliability

Recent research has indicated that there is no *one* variables statistical sampling method which is adequate for all situations. Different methods suit different audit objectives, perform well or poorly under different population conditions, and are more or less practical in difference circumstances.

There are two important factors affecting the desirability of alternative methods: *efficiency* and *reliability of the estimator*.

Efficiency. The efficiency of an estimation method is a function of the sample size required to satisfy the auditor that no material error exists for a population compared to an alternative variables estimation method. For example, if the sample size needed to satisfy the auditor that inventory is not misstated by more than $50,000 is smaller when a stratified difference estimate is used than for an unstratified mean-per-unit estimate, the difference estimate is more efficient. The most important factor that affects the efficiency of the estimate is the population standard deviation. When the population standard deviation is small, the sample size needed to meet a given materiality requirement is also smaller.

Reliability of the Estimator. The reliability of an estimator is a measure of how likely the computed confidence limits for a population conform to the results that should be expected from a normal distribution. An example should help to understand this idea. Assume that a researcher has a *known population* with a mean of $1,200 and a population standard deviation of $200. The researcher knows that if he takes repeated samples of, say 100 items, approximately 95 percent of the sample means should be between $1,160 and $1,240 [$1,200 $\pm$ 2 $(200/\sqrt{100})$]. Assume that the researcher takes 1,000 such samples and finds that 995 (99.5 percent) fell within the expected limits of $1,160 to $1,240. He would conclude that the statistical method was not a reliable estimator. If the researcher found that 750 (75 percent) of the samples fell within the range, he would also conclude that the estimator was not reliable. The estimator is reliable only if the actual results fall within the confidence limits approximately the same percent of the time as the stated confidence level (in this case 95 percent). Stating this conclusion in terms of a single sample from an unknown population: an estimate of a population using a statistical method is considered reliable when the *actual* probability that the confidence interval obtained contains the true population value is equal to the *nominal* (expected) probability.

It is important for auditors to use reasonably reliable estimators because this is the basis for controlling sampling risk. A judgment error could easily result if the auditor's statistical conclusion is that he has a 95 percent confidence level that a population value is between two values, such as $45,000 and $55,000, when a reliable estimator would have concluded that it is actually between $35,000 and $65,000.

Determining the reliability of an estimator is difficult in practice because the auditor takes only one sample from an unknown population. He may conclude that a population is correctly stated when it actually is not, because of the use of an unreliable estimator. Alternatively, the auditor may select larger sample sizes than are necessary in order to reduce the effects of an unreliable estimator. Naturally, the larger sample is costly.

STATISTICAL METHODS

Several variables methods are applicable to auditing. These include unstratified difference, ratio and mean-per-unit estimation, stratified sampling, and dollar unit sampling.

Difference Estimation

Difference estimation is used to measure the estimated total error amount in a population when there is both a recorded value and an audited value for each item in the sample. An example is to confirm a sample of accounts receivable and determine the difference (error) between the client's recorded amount and the amount the auditor considers correct for each selected account. The auditor makes an estimate of the population error based on the number of errors, average error size, and individual error size in the sample. The result is stated as a point estimate plus or minus a computed precision interval at a stated confidence level. An illustration using difference estimation is shown later.

Difference estimation is frequently more efficient than any other method and it is relatively easy to use. For that reason difference estimation is used extensively by auditors.

The problem with difference estimation is its lack of reliability in certain situations. When the population error rate is small or if most of the errors are in one direction, difference estimation is an unreliable estimator and should not be used. Before using difference estimation it is important to evaluate whether the population error rate is likely to exceed approximately 10 percent with a maximum of 75 percent of the errors in one direction. Unless these two conditions exist, there is a risk of the estimator being unreliable.

Ratio Estimation

Ratio estimation is similar to difference estimation except that the point estimate of the population error is determined by multiplying the portion of sample dollars in error times the total recorded population book value.

The ratio estimate is even more efficient than difference estimation *if the size of the errors in the population is proportionate to the recorded value of the population items.* If the size of the individual errors is independent of the recorded value, the difference estimate is more efficient.

Unfortunately, the same reliability problems for difference estimation also apply to ratio estimation. Therefore, to be useful, ratio estimation should only be applied where the error rate is reasonably high and errors are not predominantly in one direction.

Mean-per-Unit Estimation

In *mean-per-unit estimation*, the auditor is concerned with the *audited value* rather than the error amount of each item in the sample. Except for the definition of what is being measured, the mean-per-unit estimate is calculated in exactly the same manner as the difference estimate. The *point estimate* of the audited value is the average audited value of items in the sample times the population size. The *computed precision interval* is computed on the basis of the audited value of the sample items rather than the errors. When the auditor has computed the upper and lower confidence limits, a decision is made about the acceptability of the population by comparing these amounts with the recorded book value.

There are two advantages to mean-per-unit estimation. First, it can be used when the client has no recorded value for individual population items. Neither difference nor ratio estimation can be used in such a situation because the difference between audited and recorded values is needed. Typically, clients have recorded values for all population items, but occasionally, such as when the client does not want to take a 100 percent inventory count, recorded values do not exist. Second, mean-per-unit is ordinarily highly reliable, unless the population values are extremely skewed.

The disadvantage of mean-per-unit estimation is that it is almost always highly inefficient. This is because of the large standard deviation for the audited values of most accounting populations. Owing to the large sample size requirements, unstratified mean-per-unit is typically used only when no alternative method is suitable.

Stratification

Stratified sampling is a method of sampling in which all the elements in the total population are divided into two or more subpopulations. Each subpopulation is then independently tested and statistically measured in the manner described for variables estimation. After the results of the individual parts have been computed, they are combined into one overall population estimate in terms of a confidence interval. Stratification is applicable to difference, ratio, and mean-per-unit estimation.

Subdividing or stratifying a population is not unique to statistical sampling, of course. Auditors have traditionally emphasized certain types of items when they are testing a population. For example, in confirming accounts receivable, it has been customary to place more emphasis on large accounts than on small ones. The major difference is that in statistical stratified sampling the approach is more objective and better defined than it is under most traditional stratification methods.

The purpose of stratified sampling is to *reduce the effect of skewness* in population distributions on samples, thereby gaining efficiency and reliability. This is done by controlling overall sample mix through sampling selectively from each stratum. It is very important to define the strata so they contain items as homogeneous as possible. For example, with difference estimation, the population should be divided into segments in such a manner as to make sure that errors of a similar size are included in the same strata. For example, a population of accounts receivable could be divided by including the large errors in the population in one stratum, the medium-sized errors in a second stratum, and the small errors (including the items with no errors) in a third stratum.

The difficulty is that the auditor must stratify the population before the sample is selected, and of course he does not know which population items include which size errors. Therefore the stratification must be based upon the auditor's professional judgment of where the different types of errors are likely to exist. For example, in accounts receivable, it may be reasonable to expect the large accounts to contain the large errors and the small ones to contain the small errors, even though this need not necessarily be true.

A further difficulty with stratified sampling is the relatively high cost of stratifying population items, sample selection, and making calculations when the population data is not in a computer-readable form. When the population data are computerized, it is common to use mean-per-unit stratification with as many as 20 strata. Both efficiency and reliability can be achieved in this manner. The use of more than three or four strata is uncommon for populations where the data is not computerized.

Dollar Unit Sampling

In recent years a variables sampling technique has been developed which combines the concepts of attributes and variables estimation. Instead of defining the sampling unit as an individual accounts receivable balance, a sale to a customer, or a similar characteristic, it is defined as an individual dollar in an account balance. This method is referred to as *dollar unit sampling, cumulative monetary sampling,* or *sampling with probability proportional to size.* To illustrate, if there are four thousand accounts receivable with a book value of $1,872,500, the sampling unit is the individual dollar and the population size is 1,872,500. The auditor takes a random sample of the population of 1,872,500 and confirms the individual account balances which include the individual random dollars selected in the sample. The statistical results are calculated in a manner similar to attributes sampling, but the results are stated in terms of an upper confidence limit for dollar overstatement errors.

One significant feature of dollar unit sampling is its *automatic stratification* on the basis of dollar balances. Since the random sample is selected on the basis of individual dollars, an account with a large balance has a greater chance of being included than an account with a small one. In accounts receivable confirmation, an account with a $5,000 balance has a ten times greater probability of being included than one with a $500 balance.

There are also some difficulties in applying dollar unit sampling. In those situations where there are a large number of errors in a population, the sample size required to satisfy most auditors' allowable error standards is much higher than would be required with many other variables sampling techniques. In addition, in many instances the difficulty of obtaining a random sample without the use of a computer makes dollar unit sampling a costly application. Nevertheless, this highly innovative technique has great potential as an audit tool and is likely to be more widely used as it becomes better understood by the profession.

Summary

In evaluating the five variables estimation methods, it becomes apparent that *no single one is clearly superior* in every audit situation. Where there are large numbers of errors of approximately the same size in the population, either difference or ratio estimation is likely to be most suitable. On the other hand, when there are large populations in a computer-readable form with few errors, dollar unit sampling or stratified mean-per-unit estimation is more appropriate. It is necessary to understand which technique should be applied in a given situation if an auditor is to intelligently use statistical sampling as an audit tool.

CONFIDENCE INTERVALS VERSUS HYPOTHESIS TESTING

Whenever variables sampling is used, an auditor can choose between calculating confidence intervals or doing hypothesis testing.

When the auditor calculates confidence intervals, *the objective is to determine the total value of an account balance or other total*. The most likely circumstance where confidence intervals are calculated by auditors is when the client wants the auditor to determine the appropriate amount to record for an account balance. A somewhat common example is for the auditor to help the client determine the book value of inventory by statistical methods rather than the client taking a 100 percent count of the entire inventory.

When the auditor uses hypothesis testing, *the objective is to determine whether the client's recorded balance is correct.* Hypothesis tests are much more commonly used in auditing than is calculation of confidence intervals because the objective in most audits is to evaluate whether an account balance is correctly recorded. Hypothesis tests are emphasized in the rest of the chapter.

In a hypothesis test the auditor is testing the hypothesis that a balance is correct as stated, within an allowable error which is defined in terms of materiality. If the auditor accepts the hypothesis, the population is accepted as fairly stated. If the hypothesis is rejected, some other course of action is required.

Beta and Alpha Risks

There are two risks that auditors must be concerned about when hypothesis tests are used: Beta and Alpha risk.

Beta Risk. After an audit test is performed and statistical results calculated, the auditor must either conclude that the population is not materially misstated or conclude that it is materially misstated. Beta risk is the statistical risk that the auditor has accepted a population that is actually *materially misstated.* Beta risk is a serious concern to auditors because there are potential legal implications in concluding that an account balance is fairly stated when it is in error by a material amount.

An account balance can be either overstated or understated but not both; therefore, Beta risk is a one-tailed statistical test. The confidence coefficients for Beta are therefore different than for the confidence level. (Confidence level = 1–2 Beta; for example, if Beta is 10 percent, the confidence level is 80 percent.) The confidence coefficients for various Betas are shown in Figure 12-6, together with confidence coefficients for the confidence level and Alpha risk.

Alpha Risk. Alpha risk is the statistical risk that the auditor has concluded that a population is materially misstated when actually it is not. The only time Alpha risk affects auditor's actions is when an auditor concludes that a population is not fairly stated. The most likely action when the auditor finds a balance not fairly stated is to increase the sample size. An increased sample size will usually lead the auditor to conclude that the balance was actually fairly stated if the account actually is not materially in error.

Alpha risk is important only when there is a high cost to increase the sample size. Beta risk is always important. Confidence coefficients for Alpha risk are shown in Figure 12-6.

FIGURE 12–6

Confidence Coefficient for Confidence Levels, Beta Risks,
and Alpha Risks

Confidence Level (%)	Beta Risk (%)	Alpha Risk (%)	Confidence Coefficient
99	.5	1	2.58
95	2.5	5	1.96
90	5	10	1.64
80	10	20	1.28
75	12.5	25	1.15
70	15	30	1.04
60	20	40	.84
50	25	50	.67
40	30	60	.52
30	35	70	.39
20	40	80	.25
10	45	90	.13
0	50	100	.0

Alpha and Beta risks are summarized in Figure 12-7. It may seem from Figure 12-7 that the auditor should attempt to minimize Alpha (α) and Beta (β) risk. The way to accomplish that is by increasing the sample size, thus minimizing the risks. Since that is costly, having reasonable Alpha and Beta risks is a more desirable goal.

FIGURE 12–7

Alpha and Beta Risks

	Actual State of the Population		
Actual Audit Decision	Materially Misstated	Not Materially Misstated	
Conclude that the population is materially misstated	Correct conclusion— no risk	Incorrect conclusion— risk is α	100%
Conclude that the population is not materially misstated	Incorrect conclusion risk is β	Correct conclusion no risk	100%

DIFFERENCE ESTIMATION

As previously discussed, there are several different types of variables sampling techniques that may be applicable to auditing in different circumstances. One of these, *difference estimation using hypothesis testing* (without stratification), has been selected as a means of illustrating the concepts and methodology of variables sampling. The reason for using difference estimation is its relative simplicity and extensive use by practitioners. When the method is considered reliable in a given set of circumstances, it is preferred by most auditors.

In explaining the concepts, the steps in determining whether the account balance in the audit of accounts receivable is fairly stated are illustrated. Positive confirmations in the audit of Hart Lumber company are used as a frame of reference to illustrate the use of difference estimation. There are 4,000 accounts receivable listed on the aged trial balance with a recorded value of $600,000. Internal controls are considered somewhat weak and a large number of small errors in recorded amounts are expected in the audit. Total assets are $2,500,000 and net earnings before tax are $400,000. The desired level of assurance is considered reasonably low because of the limited users of the statements and the good financial health of Hart Lumber. Analytical tests results indicated no significant problem.

The assumptions throughout are either that all confirmations were returned or that effective alternative procedures were carried out. Hence, the sample size is the number of positive confirmations mailed.[1]

Audit Decisions Needed to Determine Sample Size

The auditor must make three decisions before the sample size can be determined for a hypothesis test using difference estimation:

The Minimum Dollar Amount of Errors the Auditor Is Willing to Accept in the Population for the Audit Test. The amount of error the auditor is willing to accept is a *materiality* question which must be based upon the factors discussed in Chapter 4. Major considerations affecting the total acceptable error are the amount of reported net earnings, the size of the total account balance being tested, and the expected amount of errors in other account balances in the audit. The auditor decides to accept a minimum error of $21,000 in the audit of Hart Lumber.

Beta Risk. The risk of accepting accounts receivable as correct if it is actually misstated by more than $21,000 is affected by the overall desired level of assurance, the achieved level of assurance obtained through tests of the system and analytical tests, and the relative significance of accounts receivable in the financial statements. In Hart Lumber a Beta risk of 10 percent is used.

---

[1]The use of statistical sampling for the measurement of results obtained by positive confirmation is questioned by some auditors. If errors exist in the balances being confirmed, but the customer signs the confirmation and returns it without noting the exception, the statistical results do not accurately measure the errors in the population. Recent empirical studies indicate that this frequently occurs in accounts receivable confirmation. Virtually all auditors agree that it is not proper to statistically measure the results of negative confirmations because any sample items ignored by customers would automatically be treated as if they were correct.

After the auditor specifies the allowable error and Beta risk, the hypothesis can be stated. The auditor's hypothesis for the audit of accounts receivable for Hart Lumber is: accounts receivable is not misstated by more than $21,000 at a Beta risk of 10 percent.

Alpha Risk. The risk of accepting accounts receivable as correct if it is actually misstated by a material amount is affected by the additional cost of resampling. Since it is fairly costly to confirm receivables a second time, an Alpha risk of 25 percent is used. For audit tests where it is not costly to increase the sample size, a much higher Alpha is common.

Other Information Needed to Determine Sample Size

Three additional pieces of information are needed to determine sample size:

Population Size. The population size is determined by count, the same as for attributes sampling. An accurate count is much more important in variables sampling because sample size and the computed precision limits are directly affected by population size. The population size for Hart Lumber's accounts receivable is 4,000.

Expected Point Estimate. An advanced estimate of the population point estimate is needed for difference estimation, much like the expected error rate is needed for attributes. The advanced estimate is $1,500 (overstatement) for Hart, based on the previous year's audit tests.

Advanced Population Standard Deviation Estimate—Variability of the Population. An advanced estimate of the variation in the errors in the population as measured by the population standard deviation is needed to determine the initial sample size. The calculation of the standard deviation is shown later. It is estimated to be 20, based on the previous year's audit tests.

Calculation of the Initial Sample Size

The initial sample size for Hart Lumber can be now calculated from the formula in Figure 12-8. An examination of the formula indicates the effect on sample size of independently changing each of the factors in the formula. The relationships are as follows:

Type of Change	Effect of Factors on Preliminary Sample Size
Decrease the confidence level	Decrease
Decrease the acceptable precision interval	Increase
Decrease the estimate of the population standard deviation	Decrease
Decrease the population size	Decrease

FIGURE 12–8

Sample Size Determination

$$n = \left[\frac{N(Z_\beta + Z_\alpha)SD^*}{API^*} \right]^2$$

where n = preliminary estimate of the sample size
N = population size
Z_β = confidence coefficient for Beta risk (see Figure 12–7)
Z_α = confidence coefficient for Alpha risk (see Figure 12–7)
SD^* = advanced estimate of the standard deviation
$API^* = AE - E^*$
AE = acceptable error in the population (materiality)
E^* = estimated point estimate of the population error

Applied to Hart Lumber, this equation yields

$$n = \left[\frac{4,000(1.28 + 1.15)20}{21,000 - 1,500} \right]^2 = (9.97)^2 = 100$$

The results are consistent with the conclusions reached in Chapter 10 when the four factors that affect attributes sampling were individually changed.

The sample size may or may not be large enough to meet the auditor's materiality and risk requirements. The auditor must select the sample, determine the error for each sample item, and calculate the confidence limits based on the actual sample results. At that point the auditor will determine whether the hypothesis that accounts receivable is fairly stated is accepted or rejected.

Take a Random Sample

The *sampling unit* is defined as the individual balance on the accounts receivable aged trial balance. The random sample is selected in the same manner as for attributes sampling, probably on the basis of page number and line number. The number of confirmations mailed is the sample size. The number of confirmations that must be sent for Hart Lumber is 100.

Determine the Value of Each Error in the Sample

For confirmations, the error is the *difference* between the confirmation response and the client's balance after the reconciliation of all timing differences and customer errors. For example, if a customer returns a confirmation and states the correct balance is $887.12, and the balance in the client's records is $997.12, the difference of $110 is an overstatement error if the auditor concludes the client's records are incorrect. For *nonresponses*, the errors discovered by alternative procedures are treated identically to those discovered through confirmation. At the end of this step, there is an error value for each item in the sample, many of which are likely to be zero. The errors for Hart Lumber are shown in Figure 12–9, Step 2.

Compute the Point Estimate of the Total Errors

The *point estimate* is a direct extrapolation from the errors in the sample to the errors in the population. The calculation of the point estimate is shown in Figure 12-9, Step 3 for Hart Lumber.

It is unlikely, of course, for the actual, but unknown, error to be *exactly* the same as the point estimate. It is more realistic to estimate the error in terms of a *confidence interval determined by the point estimate plus and minus a computed precision interval*. It should be apparent at this point that the calculation of the confidence interval is an essential part of variables sampling, and that the process used to develop it depends on the obtaining of a *representative sample*.

Compute an Estimate of the Population Standard Deviation

The population *standard deviation* is a statistical measure of the *variability* in the values of the individual items in the population. If there is a large amount of variation in the values of population items, the standard deviation is larger than when the variation is small. For example, in the confirmation of accounts receivable, errors of $4, $14, and $26 have far less variation than the set $2, $275, and $812. Hence the standard deviation is smaller in the first set.

The standard deviation has a significant effect on the computed precision interval. As might be expected, the ability to predict the value of a population is better when there is a small rather than a large amount of variation in the individual values of the population.

A reasonable estimate of the value of the population standard deviation is computed by the auditor using the standard statistical formula shown in Figure 12-9, Step 4. The size of the standard deviation estimate is determined solely by the characteristics of the auditor's sample results and is not affected by his professional judgment.

Compute the Precision Interval

The *precision interval* is calculated by a statistical formula. The results are a dollar measure of the inability to predict the true population error because the test was based on a sample rather than on the entire population. In order for the computed precision interval to have any meaning, it must be associated with a Beta risk.

An examination of the formula indicates that the effect of changing each factor while the other factors remain constant is as follows:

Type of Change	Effect on the Upper Precision Limit
Increase Beta risk	decrease
Increase the point estimate of the errors	increase
Increase the standard deviation	increase
Increase the sample size	decrease

The formula for determining the sample size (Figure 12-8) is derived from the one for calculating the computed precision interval (Figure 12-9, Step 5), but there are important differences:

- The formula for sample size uses allowable precision interval (allowable error minus expected point estimate) instead of computed precision interval. The use of these two terms in the formulas is equivalent to the use of desired upper precision limit and computed upper precision limit for attributes sampling.
- The only confidence coefficient included in calculating CPI is for Beta risk. The reason is that after the audit tests are performed the auditor wants to find out if the population is acceptable. If it is, only Beta risk is relevant because there can be no Alpha risk when the population is accepted.
- The actual standard deviation, based on the sample results, is used for calculating CPI instead of the advanced estimate used for calculating sample size.
- The actual point estimate, based on the sample result, is used for calculating CPI instead of the advanced estimate used for calculating sample size.

Compute the Confidence Limits

The *confidence limits*, which define the confidence interval, are calculated by combining the point estimate of the total errors and the computed precision interval at the desired confidence level (point estimate ± computed precision interval). The formula to calculate the confidence limits is shown in Figure 12-9, Step 6.

The lower and upper confidence limits for Hart Lumber are ($1,760) and $19,840, respectively. There is a 10 percent statistical risk that the population is understated by more than $1,760 and the same risk that it is overstated by $19,840 or more.

Application of the Decision Rule

A *decision rule* in auditing is the prespecifying of a set of conditions that must exist before the hypothesis is accepted. The following decision rule assumes an equal concern for understatements and overstatements and requires the auditor to specify an exact amount that is material. The decision rule is:

FIGURE 12-9

Calculation of Confidence Limits

Steps	Statistical Formulas	Illustration for Hart Lumber
1. Take a random sample of size n	n = sample size	100 accounts receivable are selected randomly from the aged trial balance containing 4,000 accounts.
2. Determine the value of each error in the sample		75 accounts are confirmed by customers, and 25 accounts are verified by alternative procedures. After reconciling timing differences and customer errors, the following twelve items were determined to be client errors (understatements):

1. 12.75	7. (.87)
2. (69.46)	8. 24.32
3. 85.28	9. 36.59
4. 100.00	10. (102.16)
5. (27.30)	11. 54.71
6. 41.06	12. 71.56

$$\text{Sum} = 226.48$$

3. Compute the point estimate of the total errors

$$\bar{e} = \frac{\sum e_j}{n}$$

$$\hat{E} = N\bar{e} \text{ or } N \frac{\sum e_j}{n}$$

where $\bar{e}$ = average error in the sample
$\sum$ = summation
e_j = an individual error in the sample
n = sample size
$\hat{E}$ = point estimate of the total error
N = population size

$$\bar{e} = \frac{226.48}{100} = 2.26$$

$$\hat{E} = 4,000(2.26) = \$9,040$$

or

$$\hat{E} = 4,000 \frac{226.48}{100} = \$9,040$$

4. Compute the population standard deviation of the errors from the sample

$$SD = \sqrt{\frac{\sum (e_j)^2 - n(\bar{e})^2}{n-1}}$$

where SD = standard deviation
e_j = an individual error in the sample

	e_j (rounded to nearest dollar)	$(e_j)^2$
1.	13	169
2.	(69)	4,761
3.	85	7,225

FIGURE 12-9 (cont.)

Steps	Statistical Formulas	Illustration for Hart Lumber

Illustration for Hart Lumber:

4.	100	10,000
5.	(27)	729
6.	41	1,681
7.	(1)	1
8.	24	576
9.	36	1,296
10.	(102)	10,404
11.	55	3,025
12.	72	5,184
	227	45,051

$$SD = \sqrt{\frac{45{,}051 - 100(2.26)^2}{99}}$$

$$SD = 21.2$$

Statistical Formulas:

n = sample size
$\bar{e}$ = average error in sample

5. Compute the precision interval for the estimate of the population of the errors at the desired confidence level

$$CPI = NZ_\beta \frac{SD}{\sqrt{n}} \sqrt{\frac{N-n}{N}}$$

where CPI = computed precision interval
N = population size
Z_β = confidence coefficient for Beta risk (see Figure 12-6)
SD = population standard deviation
n = sample size
$\sqrt{\dfrac{N-n}{N}}$ = finite correction factor

Illustration:

$$CPI \text{ at Beta risk} = 4{,}000 \cdot 1.28 \cdot \frac{21.2}{\sqrt{100}} \sqrt{\frac{4{,}000-100}{4{,}000}}$$
$$= 4{,}000 \cdot 1.28 \cdot \frac{21.2}{10} \cdot .99$$
$$= 4{,}000 \cdot 1.28 \cdot 2.11 = \$10{,}800$$

6. Compute the confidence limits at the CL desired

$$UCL = \hat{E} + CPI$$
$$LCL = \hat{E} - CPI$$

where UCL = computed upper confidence limit
LCL = computed lower confidence limit
$\hat{E}$ = point estimate of the total error
CPI = computed precision interval at desired CL

Illustration:

$$UCL = \$9{,}040 + \$10{,}800 = \$19{,}840$$
$$LCL = \$9{,}040 - \$10{,}800 = \$(1{,}760)$$

If the two-sided confidence interval for the total audit value is completely within the book value plus and minus the amount considered material, accept the hypothesis that the book value is not misstated by a material amount. Otherwise, accept the hypothesis that the book value is misstated by a material amount. This decision rule may be illustrated graphically as follows:

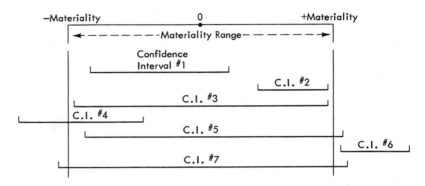

The auditor should conclude:

- Confidence intervals 1, 2, and 3 fall completely within both bounds of the materiality range. Therefore, the hypothesis that the population is not misstated by a material amount is accepted.
- For confidence intervals 4, 5, 6, and 7, the confidence limits do not fall entirely within the materiality range. Therefore, the population book value is rejected.

Application of the decision rule to Hart Lumber leads the auditor to the conclusion that the population should be accepted, since both confidence limits are within the materiality range:

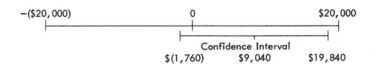

Analysis. Given that the actual standard deviation (21.2) was larger than the advanced estimate (20) and the actual point estimate $9,000 was larger than the advanced estimate ($1,500), it may seem surprising that the population was accepted. The reason is that the use of a reasonably small Alpha risk caused the sample size to be larger than if Alpha risk was 100 percent. If Alpha risk had been 100 percent, which is common when the additional audit cost to increase the sample size is small, the required sample size would have been only 28:

$$\left[\frac{4,000(1.28 + 0)20}{21,000 - 1,500} \right]^2$$

Assuming a sample size of 28 and the same actual point estimate and standard deviation, the upper confidence limit would have been $29,559 and therefore rejected $(9,040 + 4,000(1.28)(21.2)/\sqrt{28})$. The reason that auditors use Alpha risk is to reduce the likelihood of needing to increase the sample size if the standard deviation or point estimate is larger than was expected.

Action When a Hypothesis Is Rejected

When one or both of the confidence limits lie outside the materiality range, the population is not considered acceptable. There are several possible courses of action.

Perform Expanded Audit Tests in Specific Areas. If an analysis of the errors indicates that most of the errors are of a particular type, it may be desirable to restrict the additional audit effort to the problem area. For example, if an analysis of the exceptions in confirmations indicates that most of the errors result from shipping cutoff, an extended search could be made of the year-end sales cutoff to be sure it is proper. However, great care must be taken to evaluate the cause of all errors in the sample before a conclusion is drawn about the proper emphasis in the expanded tests; there may be more than one problem area.

Adjust the Account Balance. When one of the computed confidence limits is larger than the auditor will accept, the client may be willing to adjust the book value. For example, in the Hart Lumber case, if the confidence level had been $9,040 ± $15,800 and the client is willing to reduce the book value by $9,040, the results are now 0 ± $15,800. The new computed lower confidence limit would be an understatement of $15,800, and the upper confidence limit an $15,800 overstatement, which are both acceptable. The minimum adjustment the auditor could make and still have the population acceptable is $3,840 [($9,040 + $15,800) − $21,000].

The client, however, may be unwilling to adjust the balance on the basis of a sample. Furthermore, if the computed precision interval exceeds the allowable error, an adjustment to the books cannot be made that will satisfy the auditor. This would be the case in the above example if the acceptable error were only $15,000.

Increase the Sample Size. When the auditor increases the sample size, the point estimate of the population remains approximately the same and the computed precision interval gets smaller *if* the number of errors and their amount and direction in the expanded sample are similar in nature to those in the original sample. When this occurs, the computed lower confidence limit gets larger and the upper confidence limit gets smaller, which may satisfy the auditor's materiality standards. The additional sample size needed can be determined using the formula in Figure 12-8. The standard deviation and point estimate determined by the actual sample results should now be used to determine the revised sample size.

Increasing the sample enough to satisfy the auditor's materiality standards is often *costly*, especially when the confidence limits are well beyond the auditor's standards of acceptability. And even if the sample size is increased, there is no assurance of a satisfactory result. If the number, amount, and direction of the errors in the extended sample are proportionately greater or more variable than in the original sample, the results are still likely to be unacceptable. For accounts receivable confirmation it is also difficult to increase the sample size because the requests should be sent out near the end of the month being confirmed. By the time the auditor finds out the sample was not large enough, several weeks have usually passed. In spite of all of these difficulties, in many instances the auditor must extend the sample to obtain more information about the population. It is much more common to increase sample size in other audit areas where variables sampling is used than in confirming receivables, but even for confirmations it is occasionally necessary.

Request the Client to Correct the Population.   In some cases the client's records are so inadequate that a correction of the entire population is required before the audit can be completed. For example, in accounts receivable, the client may be asked to prepare the aging schedule again if the auditor concludes that it has significant errors. Whenever the client changes the valuation of some items in the population, it is of course necessary to audit the results again.

Refuse to Give an Unqualified Opinion.   If the auditor believes the recorded amount in accounts receivable, or any other account, is not fairly stated, it is necessary to follow at least one of the above alternatives or *qualify the audit opinion* in an appropriate manner. If the auditor believes there is a reasonable chance that the financial statements are materially misstated, it would be a serious breach of auditing standards to issue an unqualified audit report.

REVIEW QUESTIONS

12–1. Distinguish between attributes sampling and variables sampling. When would each of these be a useful audit tool?

12–2. Explain why variables sampling is considered a more useful audit tool than attributes sampling when it is applicable.

12–3. Distinguish between difference estimation, mean-per-unit estimation, and ratio estimation. Give one example where each could be used.

12–4. Assume an auditor decided to select a random sample of accounts receivable for confirming from a 60-page aged trial balance where each page is numbered. There are no more than 75 customer names per page, but the lines are not prenumbered. Describe how an auditor could obtain a random sample of 100 accounts by using a random number table.

12–5. In using difference estimation, an auditor took a random sample of 100 inventory items from a large population to test for proper pricing. Several of the inventory items were in error, but the combined net amount of the sample error was not material. In addition, a review of the individual errors indicated that no error was by itself material. As a result, the auditor did not investigate the errors or make a statistical evaluation. Explain why this practice is improper.

12–6. Distinguish between the point estimate of the total errors and the true value of the errors in the population. How can each be determined?

12–7. Evaluate the following statement made by an auditor: "On every aspect of the audit where it is possible, I calculate the point estimate of the errors and evaluate whether the amount is material. If it is, I investigate the cause and continue to test the population until I determine whether there is a serious problem. The use of statistical sampling in this manner is a valuable audit tool."

12–8. Distinguish among the following terms: confidence level, confidence limits, confidence interval, and computed precision interval. For the statistical statement "The population value of the errors is $50,000 \pm $16,000 with a reliability of 90 percent," calculate or identify the value for each of the four terms.

12–9. Define what is meant by the population standard deviation and explain its importance in variables sampling. What is the relationship between the population standard deviation and the required sample size?

12–10. Define what is meant by Alpha and Beta risk for hypothesis testing and distinguish between the two risks. Explain the advantages and disadvantages of a small Beta risk. Do the same for Alpha risk.

12–11. State the decision rule using hypothesis testing for difference estimation. Assume a confidence interval at a 95 percent confidence level of $25,000 \pm $15,000 and a materiality limit of $45,000. What is the decision in that circumstance?

12–12. An essential step in difference estimation is the comparison of each computed confidence limit with the acceptable error. Why is this step so important and what should the auditor do if one of the confidence limits is larger than the acceptable error?

12–13. Define what is meant by a normal distribution in difference estimation and explain its importance in making auditing decisions.

12–14. Explain the circumstances under which a preliminary sample in variables sampling may not be large enough for the statistical requirements the auditor specifies.

12–15. Explain the circumstances where unrestricted difference estimation may not be a useful audit tool.

12–16. Define *stratified sampling* and explain its importance in auditing. How could an auditor obtain a stratified sample of thirty items from each of three strata in the confirmation of accounts receivable?

12–17. Explain how the methodology for calculating confidence limits using mean-per-unit estimation is the same as and different from difference estimation.

12–18. Define *dollar unit sampling* and explain its importance in auditing. How does it combine the features of attributes and variables estimation?

12–19. List the decisions the auditor must make in using variables sampling. What considerations influence the auditor in making each decision?

DISCUSSION QUESTIONS AND PROBLEMS

12–20. Each of the following 10 items is concerned with the use of unrestricted random sampling without replacement for variables sampling. State whether each one is true or false.

a. If the auditor wishes to use a table of random digits to select a random sample, he must first find a table conforming to the numbering employed by the items in the population he wishes to sample.

b. If a usable number appears more than once in the table of random digits during the selection of the sample, the item should be included in the sample only once and another number selected from the table.

c. A random sample of at least 30 items would have to be discarded if it produced one item disproportionately large in relation to the other items selected.

d. The effect of the inclusion by chance of a very large or a very small item in a random sample can be lessened by increasing the size of the sample.

e. The reliability specified by the auditor for a sample estimate expresses the degree of confidence that the true value will be within the computed confidence interval.

f. The standard deviation is a measure of variability of items in the population.

g. Variability of items in the population is a factor that usually causes the point estimate of the population, and its true value, to be different.

h. It is necessary to determine the true standard deviation for a population in order to determine the size of the sample to be drawn from that population.

i. The computed precision interval of the mean will always be less than the estimated standard deviation computed on the basis of a sample.

(AICPA adapted)

12–21. The following apply to difference estimation variables sampling. Choose the best response.

a. The auditor's failure to recognize an error in an amount or an error in an internal control data-processing procedure is described as a
   (1) statistical error.
   (2) sampling error.
   (3) standard error of the mean.
   (4) nonsampling error.

b. An auditor makes separate compliance and substantive tests in the accounts payable area which has good internal control. If the auditor uses statistical sampling for both of these tests, the confidence level established for the substantive test is normally
   (1) the same as that for tests of compliance.
   (2) greater than that for tests of compliance.
   (3) less than that for tests of compliance.
   (4) totally independent of that for tests of compliance.

c. How should an auditor determine the precision required in establishing a statistical sampling plan?
   (1) By the materiality of an allowable margin of error the auditor is willing to accept.
   (2) By the amount of reliance the auditor will place on the results of the sample.
   (3) By reliance on a table of random numbers.
   (4) By the amount of risk the auditor is willing to take that material errors will occur in the accounting process.

12–22. The following questions refer to the use of stratified sampling in auditing. For each one, select the best response.

a. Mr. Murray decides to use stratified sampling. The basic reason for using stratified sampling rather than unrestricted random sampling is to
   (1) reduce as much as possible the degree of variability in the overall population.
   (2) give every element in the population an equal chance of being included in the sample.
   (3) allow the person selecting the sample to use his own judgment in deciding which elements should be included in the sample.
   (4) reduce the required sample size from a nonhomogeneous population.

b. In an examination of financial statements, a CPA will generally find stratified sampling techniques to be most applicable to
   (1) recomputing net wage and salary payments to employees.
   (2) tracing hours worked from the payroll summary back to the individual time cards.
   (3) confirming accounts receivable for residential customers at a large electric utility.
   (4) reviewing supporting documentation for additions to plant and equipment.

c. From prior experience, a CPA is aware that cash disbursements contain a few unusually large disbursements. In using statistical sampling, the CPA's best course of action is to

    (1) eliminate any unusually large disbursements that appear in the sample.

    (2) continue to draw new samples until no unusually large disbursements appear in the sample.

    (3) stratify the cash-disbursements population so that the unusually large disbursements are reviewed separately.

    (4) increase the sample size to lessen the effect of the unusually large disbursements.   (AICPA adapted)

12–23. An audit partner is developing an office training program to familiarize his professional staff with statistical decision models applicable to the audit of dollar-value balances. He wishes to demonstrate the relationship of sample sizes to population size and variability and the auditor's specifications as to precision and confidence level. The partner prepared the following table to show comparative population characteristics and audit specifications of two populations.

	Characteristics of Population 1 Relative to Population 2		Audit Specifications as to a Sample from Population 1 Relative to a Sample from Population 2	
	Size	Variability	Acceptable Precision Interval	Specified Confidence Level
Case 1	Equal	Equal	Equal	Higher
Case 2	Equal	Larger	Wider	Equal
Case 3	Larger	Equal	Narrower	Lower
Case 4	Smaller	Smaller	Equal	Lower
Case 5	Larger	Equal	Equal	Higher

In items (1) through (5) below you are to indicate for the specific case from the table above the required sample size to be selected from population 1 relative to the sample from population 2.

Your Answer Choice Should Be Selected from the Following Responses:

a. Larger than the required sample size from population 2.

b. Equal to the required sample size from population 2.

c. Smaller than the required sample size from population 2.

d. Indeterminate relative to the required sample size from population 2.

    (1) In case 1 the required sample size from population 1 is ____

    (2) In case 2 the required sample size from population 1 is ____

    (3) In case 3 the required sample size from population 1 is ____

    (4) In case 4 the required sample size from population 1 is ____

    (5) In case 5 the required sample size from population 1 is ____

                                       (AICPA adapted)

12–24. During a professional development program at a CPA firm, an audit manager was instructing several younger staff members on how to calculate confidence intervals in the accounts receivable area by using difference estimation. As part of the discussion, he explained the importance of the population size in calculating the point estimate of the total error and the precision interval for the population. He ended his talk by informing the group that a 20 percent error in counting the number of accounts in the population would probably result in a misleading statistical calculation.

At that point one of the staff members raised his hand and stated that these conclusions were inconsistent with what he had learned about using attributes sampling. He also described how a statistics professor had explained to him when he was in college that the finite correction factor, which is affected by the population size, could frequently be ignored in variables sampling.

Required:

a. Explain why the population size is far more important for making variables sampling calculations than it is for attributes sampling.
b. Explain how the population size affects the statistical results in variables sampling in more ways than only the finite correction factor.

12–25. In auditing the valuation of inventory, the auditor, Claire Butler, decided to use difference estimation. She decided to select an unrestricted random sample of 80 inventory items from a population of 1,840 that had a book value of $175,820. Butler had decided in advance that she was willing to accept a maximum error in the population of $6,000 at a confidence level of 95 percent. There were eight errors in the sample and they were as follows:

Audit Value	Book Value	Sample Errors
$ 812.50	$ 740.50	$ (72.00)
12.50	78.20	65.70
10.00	51.10	41.10
25.40	61.50	36.10
600.10	651.90	51.80
.12	0	(.12)
51.06	81.06	30.00
83.11	104.22	21.11
Total $1,594.79	$1,768.48	$173.69

Required:

a. Calculate the point estimate, the computed precision interval, the confidence interval, and the confidence limits for the population. Label each calculation.
b. Should Butler accept the book value of the population? Explain.
c. What options are available to her at this point?

12–26. In confirming accounts receivable with a recorded value of $6,250,000 for the Blessman Wholesale Drug Company, Gerald Bloomstad, CPA, has decided that if the total error in the account exceeds $60,000, he will consider the error material. He believes the point estimate of the error will approximate $20,000. He has decided to use unrestricted random sampling for difference estimation, and he believes a 90 percent confidence level is appropriate considering the circumstances of the engagement. Although Bloomstad doesn't know the standard deviation, he decides to estimate it a little bit high to make sure he does not undersample. The standard deviation is estimated at $22. There are 14,300 total accounts receivable in the trial balance.

Required:

a. Calculate the number of accounts receivable Bloomstad should confirm.
b. Assuming only 100 confirmation responses are received in the first and second requests, what should the auditor do at this point?
c. What would the sample size in part a have been if the estimated standard deviation was $32 instead of $22?
d. What would the sample size in part a have been if the allowable error were $80,000 and the expected point estimate were $20,000?
e. What would the sample size in part a have been if the allowable error were $90,000 and the expected point estimate were $50,000? Explain the relationship between your answers in a and e.

12–27. The following are five different sets of sample information from a population of 5,000 accounts receivable with a book value of $4,600,000. (In each situation, the net book value of the items in the sample exceeds the audit value.)

Situation	Sample Size	Total Net Error in the Sample	Population Standard Deviation Estimated from the Sample	Desired Confidence Level
1	100	1,000	25	95%
2	200	2,000	25	95%
3	200	2,000	50	95%
4	200	2,000	25	90%
5	200	1,000	25	95%

Required:

a. Using difference estimation, calculate the point estimate of the errors in the population, the computed precision interval, and the confidence limits for each of the five situations.
b. In general for a given population, state the effect on the computed upper confidence limit for each of the following (increase, decrease, no effect, or cannot determine from the information given):
(1) An increase in the sample size (the average error in the sample,

population standard deviation, and confidence level remain constant).

(2) An increase in the average error in the sample (the sample size, population standard deviation, and confidence level remain constant).

(3) An increase in the population standard deviation (the sample size, average error in the sample, and confidence level remain constant).

(4) An increase in the confidence level (the sample size, average error in the sample, and population standard deviation remain constant).

(5) An increase in the sample size and population standard deviation (the average error in the sample and confidence level remain constant).

(6) An increase in the confidence level and the population standard deviation (the average error in the sample and sample size remain constant).

12–28. a. Calculate confidence limits for a through e using difference estimation from the information provided.

	a	b	c	d	e
Population size	2,000	2,000	5,000	5,000	1,000
Confidence level	90%	80%	80%	80%	99%
Sum of sample errors (net)	320	320	1,750	1,750	250
Standard deviation	17	17	30	40	50
Sample size	100	100	400	400	50
Materiality	13,000	9,000	30,000	35,000	15,000

b. In general, what is the effect on the upper confidence limits (increase, decrease, no affect, or cannot determine without additional information) of each of the following independent changes, assuming that the other components are held constant?

Effect on Upper Confidence Limit

(1) Increase confidence level
(2) Increase sample size
(3) Increase standard deviation
(4) Increase population size
(5) Increase allowable error and decrease the sum of the sample errors
(6) Add two more sample errors: one for $450 and one for ($450)

12–29. In reviewing the results of a difference estimation calculation, an in-charge auditor, Roger Murphy, concluded that the confidence limits were larger than he could accept. In examining the details of the calculation, he determined that the point estimate of the population was nearly zero, but the standard deviation was large. He decided that there must be an error in the calculation, since it was impossible to get a small point estimate and a large standard deviation. His assistant, Lannell Tigg, expressed a different view-point. She stated that the problem was simply the failure to take a sufficiently large sample size. Tigg ended her explanation by informing Murphy that an increase in the sample size would automatically reduce the standard deviation and thereby reduce the confidence limits.

Required:

a. Explain how it is possible to have a small point estimate in the population and a large standard deviation when difference estimation is used.
b. Was Tigg's explanation of the way to reduce the population standard deviation correct? Discuss.

12–30. Items (1) through (5) apply to an examination by Lee Melinda, CPA, of the financial statements of Summit Appliance Repair Company for the year ended June 30, 19X7. Summit has a large fleet of identically stocked repair trucks. It establishes the total quantities of materials and supplies stored on the delivery trucks at year-end by physically inventorying a random sample of trucks.

Melinda is evaluating the statistical validity of Summit's 19X7 sample. He knows that there were seventy-four trucks in the 19X6 required sample. Assumptions about the size, variability, precision interval, and confidence level for the 19X7 sample are given in each of the following five items. You are to indicate in each case the effect upon the size of the 19X7 sample as compared with the 19X6 sample. Each case is independent of the other four and is to be considered separately. *Your answer choice for each of items (1) through (5) should be selected from the following responses:*

a. Larger than the 19X6 sample size.
b. Equal to the 19X6 sample size.
c. Smaller than the 19X6 sample size.
d. Of a size that is indeterminate based upon the assumptions as given

(1) Summit has the same number of trucks in 19X7 but supplies are replenished more often, meaning that there is less variability in the quantity of supplies stored on each truck. The acceptable precision interval and confidence level remain the same.

Under these assumptions, the required sample size for 19X7 should be _____

(2) Summit has the same number of trucks; supplies are replenished less often (greater variability). Summit specifies the same precision interval but decides to change the confidence level from 95 percent to 90 percent.

Under these assumptions, the required sample size for 19X7 should be _____

(3) Summit has more trucks in 19X7. Variability and confidence level remain the same, but with Melinda's concurrence, Summit decides upon a wider acceptable precision interval.

Under these assumptions, the required sample size for 19X7 should be _____

(4) The number of trucks and variability remain the same, but with

Melinda's concurrence, Summit decides upon a wider precision interval and a confidence level of 90 percent rather than 95 percent.

Under these assumptions, the required sample size for 19X7 should be _____

(5) The number of trucks increases, as does the variability of quantities stored on each truck. The confidence level remains the same, but the acceptable precision interval is narrowed.

Under these assumptions, the required sample size for 19X7 should be _____ (AICPA adapted)

12–31. For each of the following populations, the auditor has established an acceptable precision interval as a part of using difference estimation and has calculated actual statistical results after he conducted the audit tests:

Population	The Acceptable Precision Interval (at the Same Confidence Level as the Computed Precision Interval)	Point Estimate of the Population Error. Understated Book Value Is ( )	Computed Precision Interval
1	$25,000	$6,000	$16,000
2	25,000	0	24,000
3	25,000	(14,000)	18,000
4	25,000	21,000	30,000
5	25,000	(12,000)	11,000

Required:

a. Determine which of the calculated results satisfy the acceptable precision interval the auditor set before the sample was selected.

b. For any result in part a that does not satisfy the acceptable precision interval, state the minimum adjustment in the client's book value, if any, that will make the sample result satisfactory.

c. What options does the auditor have for any sample result that does not satisfy the acceptable precision interval established by the auditor?

12–32. An auditor is using difference estimation for the confirmation of accounts receivable in the audit of Lafferty Hardware Supply. A random sample of 100 positive confirmations has been sent to customers. Second requests have been mailed to all no responses. Alternative procedures have been established for all confirmations not received.

After all responses have been received and alternative procedures performed, follow-up procedures are used to determine the value of each error in the sample. Difference estimation is then used to calculate the confidence interval.

Required:

a. Why would difference estimation probably be a better statistical method than attributes in this situation?

    b. Define what is meant by a nonsampling error. Why might nonsampling errors be a serious problem in the circumstances described in the case?

    c. Evaluate the following statement: "The calculation of the confidence interval for hypothesis testing and interval estimation is identical. The difference between the two methods is the use of the results."

    d. Describe how the auditor would use the calculated confidence interval for a hypothesis test.

    e. Explain the circumstances when an adjusting journal entry would be necessary and appropriate when a hypothesis has been used.

    f. Under what circumstances would unstratified difference estimation be an appropriate statistical method for the confirmation of accounts receivable?

12–33. Marjorie Jorgensen, CPA, is verifying the accuracy of outstanding accounts payable for Marygold Hardware, a large single-location retail hardware store. There are 650 vendors listed on the outstanding accounts payable list. She has eliminated 40 vendors which have large ending balances from the population and will audit them separately from the planned test for this problem. (There are now 610 vendors.)

    She plans to do one of three tests for each item in the sample: examine a vendor's statement in the client's hands, obtain a confirmation when no statement is on hand, or extensive search for invoices when neither of the first two are obtained. There are no accounts payable subsidiary records available and a large number of errors is expected. Marjorie has obtained facts or made audit judgments as follows:

Alpha risk	20%	Beta risk	10%
Allowable error	$45,000	Expected error	$20,000
Recorded book value	$600,000	Estimated standard deviation	$280

    a. Under what circumstances is it desirable to use unstratified difference estimation in the situation described? Under what circumstances would it be undesirable?

    b. Calculate the required sample size for the audit tests of accounts payable assuming that Alpha risk is ignored.

    c. Assume that the auditor selects exactly the sample size calculated in part b. The point estimate calculated from the sample results is $21,000 and the estimated population standard deviation is 267. Is the population fairly stated as defined by the decision rule? Explain what causes the result to be acceptable or unacceptable.

    d. Calculate the required sample size for the audit tests of accounts payable assuming that Alpha risk is considered.

    e. Explain the reason for the large increase of the sample size resulting from including Alpha risk in determining sample size.

    f. Fred Lehne calculates the required sample size using the formula without consideration of alpha risk. After the sample size is determined, he increases the sample size by 25 percent. Fred believes that this does the same thing as using Alpha risk without having to bother to make the calculation. Is this approach appropriate? Evaluate the desirability of the approach.

12–34. For a number of years the accounts receivable confirmation process at John's Printing Company has been more time-consuming than is considered desirable. Typically about 20 percent of the 500 active accounts were sent positive confirmations. About 70 percent of these were returned either initially or after a second request, but these represented only about 40 percent of the dollar amount. The problem was that larger customers had as many as 100 invoices listed on their statements and they simply were unwilling to take the time to check the detail. Considerable time had to be spent following up on these items.

In an attempt to combat this problem, you have decided to redefine the population of accounts receivable this year. Specifically, you have defined the population of accounts receivable as the 4,000 individual invoices listed by the open invoice system. The total book value of accounts receivable (open invoices) is $875,350. You feel that an error of $25,000 would be material. The internal control system and prior year results are such that you set Beta risk at 10 percent. The cost of selecting and sending out an additional sample of confirmations would be high, so you want an Alpha risk of only 10 percent.

Based on prior years' work and this year's tests of invoices for other purposes, you estimate the standard deviation of the population of errors at $17. Your advance estimate of the point estimate of the population error is $4,000.

a. What is the sample size necessary to achieve your audit objectives?

b. Ignoring your answer to part a, assume that you select a sample of 80 invoice amounts. Confirmations are mailed and 80 percent are returned either initially or after a second request. Alternative procedures are used to evaluate the remaining invoices in the sample. Based on these confirmation and tests, the following errors are noted:

Item	Difference
1	$ (70)
2	40
3	134
4	12
5	(93)
6	(8)
7	78
8	74
9	(51)
10	40
Total	$156

Calculate the confidence interval at the required confidence level based on the sample results.

c. Graph the materiality requirements and the confidence limits calculated in part b. What is the appropriate audit conclusion about the population?
d. Explain the conclusion in part c, given the actual sample size compared to the planned sample size, the actual standard deviation compared to the expected standard deviation, and the actual point estimate compared to the expected point estimate.

13

THE IMPACT
OF EDP SYSTEMS
ON AUDITING

There is no distinction between the audit concepts applicable to electronic data processing (EDP) and those applicable to manual systems. When computers or other aspects of EDP systems are introduced, generally accepted auditing standards and their interpretations, the Code of Professional Ethics, legal liability, and the basic concepts of evidence accumulation remain the same.

At the same time, the specific methods appropriate for implementing the basic auditing concepts do change with the introduction of EDP systems. An understanding of the impact of EDP on auditing becomes increasingly important as the use of computers by clients increases. In this chapter we study the way the conduct of an audit changes when an EDP system is a part of the client's preparation of financial records.

The first part of the chapter examines the impact of an EDP system on a typical client's organizational structure, its method of processing transactions, and its internal controls. The remainder of the chapter is devoted to a study of evaluating internal controls in an EDP system and auditing with and without the use of the computer.

IMPACT OF EDP ON AUDITING

The most important effect of EDP on auditing results directly from *changes in the client's organization* and the *information available* for auditors to examine. The major changes involved are considered in this section.

Changes in the Organizational Structure

The establishment of an EDP center generally brings the data gathering and accumulation activities of different parts of the organization into one department. This change has the advantage of *centralizing data* and permitting *higher-quality controls* over operations. On the other hand, a frequent disadvantage of this change toward centralization is the *elimination* of the control provided by *division of duties* of independent persons who perform related functions and compare their results. As an illustration, in many manual systems different individuals prepare the sales journal and subsidiary records. The accuracy of their results is tested by comparing the subsidiary ledger with the total balance in the general ledger. Both these records will be prepared simultaneously by the computer with EDP.

The organizational structure also frequently changes by taking the record keeping function out of the hands of those who have custody of assets and putting it into the EDP center. This is a desirable change if it does not merely change the opportunity for defalcation from operating personnel to EDP personnel. The latter are in a position to take company assets for their own use if they also have the opportunity to prepare or process documents that result in the disposal of the assets. For example, if EDP personnel have access to documents authorizing the shipment of goods, in essence they have direct access to inventory.

The combining of functions in an EDP center generally causes more organizational problems than it solves. Auditors must use great care in evaluating inadequate segregation of duties for the possibility of both fraudulent and unintentional errors.

Changes in the Traditional Audit Trail

The *audit trail* is the accumulation of *source documents and records* maintained by the client which are the support for the transactions that occurred during the period. It includes such things as duplicate sales invoices, vendor's invoices, canceled checks, general and subsidiary ledgers, and all types of journals. Since the audit trail is a primary source of evidence used by auditors, it is important that an adequate trail be available for verification needs. Traditionally, every transaction should be supported by one or more visible source documents and a record in a journal and sometimes in a subsidiary ledger.

The effect of the computer on the audit trail depends on the level of sophistication of the system. When the computer is used only as an accurate high-speed calculator, the audit trail may not be affected, especially if management desires to maintain the traditional source documents and records. In highly integrated on-line systems, on the other hand, the traditional audit trail can be nearly eliminated unless specific provision is made for some detailed records. A common change that occurs in the audit trail is the *elimination or reduction of some source documents*, such as payroll time

440

cards and inventory receiving reports. Even if they are not eliminated, they are frequently filed in a manner that makes them difficult to retrieve for audit purposes. A second change in the system is the transfer of data and activities into a *form that is not visually observable* by the auditors. For example, the ledger summaries are included in master files in machine-readable form, the journals and records are not printed out but instead are retained on magnetic tapes or disks, and the methods of processing records are not observable because they are done by the computer.

Changes in the Method of Processing Transactions

The most important effect of the computer on the processing of transactions is that it provides *uniformity*. Once information is put into the system, the auditor can be confident it will be processed consistently with previous or subsequent information unless some aspect of the system itself is changed. This is important from an audit point of view because it means the system will process a particular type of transaction consistently correctly or consistently incorrectly. As a result, the emphasis in auditing EDP systems for processing is likely to be on testing for unusual transactions and on testing for changes in the system over time rather than on testing a large sample of similar transactions.

The use of the computer also facilitates the inclusion of many different types of controls directly in the computer as a means of automatically detecting errors. It is possible to program automatic authorization controls such as credit limits for customers and price lists for products. It is also possible for the computer to review the reasonableness of a transaction within certain limits and the completeness of the information provided for a transaction. These procedures reduce the likelihood of errors.

Changes in the Approach to Auditing

The advent of EDP has challenged auditors to devise new methods for testing complex systems because of the loss of the audit trail. For a short time after audit trails began to disappear, auditors insisted upon extensive special printouts; but the high cost to clients forced auditors to think about alternative approaches.

The most important aspects of EDP that have affected auditing are the review and evaluation of internal control and the use of the computer in the conduct of audits. Both of these are discussed more extensively in subsequent sections of this chapter.

TYPES OF SYSTEMS

In discussing the impact of EDP systems on auditing methods, it is necessary to distinguish between different levels of complexity. In some instances the systems are so complex that the entire audit approach must be changed, whereas in others there is no significant change in any aspect of the audit. Four basic types of systems are discussed in this section: small systems, common systems, sophisticated systems, and unique systems. The characteristics and the audit implications of each type of system are briefly considered.

Small Systems

The primary function performed by a small computer system is the *sorting and manipulation* of input data and the *printing* of output reports. Transactions are easily traced in this type of system, and there is no loss of the audit trail. In a typical example of this type of system, shipping data, including the prices of the products, are keypunched and processed through the system along with accounts receivable detailed subsidiary ledgers. The output is a multicopy sales invoice for each sale, updated detailed subsidiary ledgers, and a sales journal.

The audit of this type of system is likely to require little training and background in EDP. Although it is unacceptable to completely ignore the computer installations because some of the controls involve EDP, for the most part this type of system can be viewed in the same manner as a manual system.

Common Systems

Common systems are characterized by the *batch processing mode*, the existence of *one central processing unit*, and the extensive use of *master files on magnetic tape* in processing. In this type of system the processing is usually restricted to calculations, extensions, summarizations, and similar activities. Typically, there is some loss of audit trail, but it is not significant. An example is the processing of shipping data where the only input is the customer number, the product number shipped, and the quantity shipped. The computer can automatically perform a credit check, price and extend the sales invoice, and update the accounts receivable master file of accounts receivable. Frequently, sales forecasts and production records can be simultaneously updated. Typically, the only loss of printed audit trail is the accounts receivable subsidiary ledger, but in some cases the detailed listing of sales invoices in the sales journal is also not available. However, this information is normally available in machine-readable form.

The audit of a common system can be performed by auditors with limited specialized training in EDP auditing. Because of the extent of a printed audit trail, the auditor has the option of performing some of the audit tests with or without the use of the computer. The decision can be made primarily on the basis of the auditor's experience and personal preference. Even though an audit trail exists, an active involvement in evaluating the EDP system is essential, since there are many opportunities for incompatible functions or other inadequate controls. Inasmuch as common systems represent the bulk of systems in use today, most of the discussion in this chapter is limited to this type.

Sophisticated Systems

In a sophisticated system, transactions are typically *initiated within the computer*, there is *extensive processing of data*, and there is *a substantial loss of audit trail*. Most of the *output is in machine-readable language*, aside from exceptions and control totals. An example is the input of shipping documents by the shipping department on remote or on-line teletype. All information in this system is processed by the computer and maintained in machine readable form.

Heavy reliance must be placed on internal control in the audit of a sophisticated system, and the system requires extensive testing with the use of the computer. Since many of these tests require EDP skills beyond the knowledge of most auditors, the auditor often must call upon *EDP specialists* within the CPA firm for assistance. Careful advance planning is an absolute necessity in auditing this type of system because many of the decisions about the documents and records the auditor will need and the approach the auditor intends to use in testing must be made before data are processed.

Unique Systems

Unique systems include such features as *highly complex processing*, a *network of processors and input and output devices*, and *on-line, real-time input* with inquiry from many points in the system covering widespread geographical locations. There is an *extensive loss of audit trail* and *automatic self-balancing*. The only *reporting is by exception*, and a common output is the actual finalized financial statement balances.

This highly complex computer operation requires extensive use of *high-level computer audit specialists*. Since this type of system presents a great opportunity for employee or management fraud, it must be carefully evaluated and controlled. In most instances where unique systems are employed, the auditor is involved with the client on a continuous basis. Computer processes and systems changes are often evaluated as they take place rather than subsequent to their installation. Also, extensive assistance is obtained from client EDP personnel and internal auditors.

AREAS OF ENGAGEMENT CONCERN

When a computer is used in the processing of financial data, five different areas of concern must be carefully considered as a part of the planning process before the bulk of the audit field work is begun: evaluate internal accounting control, evaluate going-concern exposure, determine desirability of using computer-assisted audit techniques, evaluate potential for fraud, and make operating recommendations. Each area is introduced at this point, and the most important areas (evaluate internal accounting control and determine the desirability of using computer-assisted techniques) are subsequently discussed in more detail in the remainder of the chapter.

Evaluate Internal Accounting Control. As with all parts of the system, those involving computer processing must be described, understood, and evaluated as a basis for determining which audit procedures should be performed and which internal controls are to be relied upon.

Evaluate Going-Concern Exposure. In some industries the electronic data processing system plays such an integral role in a company's operations that a failure of the system could put the company out of business. In this type of situation the auditor must be particularly concerned with backup capabilities, recovery plans, and insurance. If these do not exist, the auditor must consider the need for disclosure and the possibility of qualifying his report as to the going-concern basis of the entity.

Determine Desirability of Using Computer-Assisted Audit Techniques. Whether or not the auditor relies on and tests computer controls, it is often advantageous to use the computer as an audit tool. Significantly more information is often available in computer files than in related output reports. The major basis for deciding upon the extent to use the computer is the access to machine-readable information and cost.

Evaluate Potential for Fraud. Although the professional literature, engagement letters, and letters of representation state that auditors' responsibility for fraud is limited, the auditor cannot ignore those situations where material fraud appears likely. Since the computer provides a vehicle through which the size of a defalcation can compound almost instantaneously, auditors must be particularly alert to those weaknesses in the client's EDP system that may provide opportunity for fraud, and make recommendations for their elimination. If the potential for material fraud is significant, expanded testing is necessary.

Make Operating Recommendations. Client expectations are much greater for the auditor making meaningful recommendations about operating efficiency in the computer area than for manual systems because many managements lack expertise in this area and rely upon the auditor to protect them.

INTERNAL CONTROLS IN AN EDP SYSTEM

The objectives of internal control do not change with the introduction of EDP, but the nature of certain of the basic elements may be somewhat different. The emphasis in this section is on the differences rather than on the similarities. The basic elements developed in Chapter 7 are repeated here as a starting point for the discussion of internal control in an EDP system:

- Competent, trustworthy personnel with clear lines of authority and responsibility.
- Adequate separation of duties.
- Proper procedures for authorization.
- Adequate documents and records.
- Proper procedures for record keeping.
- Physical control over assets and records.
- Independent checks on performance.

The types of controls in an EDP system can be conveniently classified into *general controls* and *application controls*. A general control relates to all parts of the EDP system and must therefore be evaluated early in the audit. Application controls, on the other hand, apply to a specific use of the system, such as for the processing of sales or cash receipts, and must be evaluated specifically for every audit area in which the client uses the computer. The following summary of the subparts of these two categories forms the basis for the subsequent discussion.

GENERAL CONTROLS:

- The plan of organization and operation of the EDP activity.
- The procedures for documenting, reviewing, testing, and approving systems and programs and changes therein.
- Controls built into the equipment by the manufacturer (commonly referred to as "hardware controls").
- Controls over access to equipment and data files.

APPLICATION CONTROLS:

- Input controls
- Processing controls
- Output controls[1]

Plan of Organization

In a computer system it is not practical to segregate the recording function in a manner that produces the automatic cross-checks traditionally available in a manual system. In a manual system it is desirable to have one person record accounting information in the journals while a different person records the same data in the related subsidiary ledger, but in most EDP systems the functions of recording the journals, the subsidiary ledgers, and the general ledger are performed simultaneously by the computer. Since no organizational checks are available for EDP systems, different kinds of controls are needed over input, processing, and output to compensate for the inability to segregate the recording functions.

[1]Adapted from Section 321 of SASs.

Even though segregation of the recording function is impractical, it is possible to have *segregation of duties within EDP* to reduce the likelihood of errors. The most important data-processing responsibilities that should be segregated are the following:

Systems Analyst.   The systems analyst is responsible for the general design of the system. He sets the objectives of the overall system and the specific design of particular applications.

Programmer.   Based upon the individual objectives specified by the systems analyst, the programmer develops special flowcharts for the application, prepares computer instructions, tests the program, and documents the results. It is important that the programmer not have access to input data or computer operation, since his understanding of the program can easily be used for his personal benefit.

Computer Operator.   The computer operator is responsible for running data through the system in conjunction with the computer program. The operator follows the instructions set forth in the *program run book* which has been developed by the programmer.

Ideally, the operator should be prevented from having sufficient knowledge of the program to modify it immediately before or during its use. In several cases of recorded fraud, the operator had covered an embezzlement by temporarily changing the original program.

Librarian.   The librarian is responsible for maintaining the computer programs, transactions files, and other important computer records. The librarian provides a means of important physical control over these records and releases them only to authorized personnel.

Data Control Group.   The function of the data control group is to test the effectiveness and efficiency of all aspects of the system. This includes the adequacy of various types of controls, the quality of the input, and the reasonableness of the output. Inasmuch as control group personnel operate much like internal auditors, the importance of their independence is obvious.

Naturally, the extent of separation of duties depends heavily upon the size of the organization. In many small companies it is not practical to segregate the duties to the extent suggested. In these cases the audit evidence may require modification.

Procedures for Documenting, Reviewing, Testing, and Approving Systems and Programs and Changes Therein

The purpose of this general control area is to ensure that the client is adequately *controlling the computer programs* and other aspects of the system at all times. In concept these procedures are similar to those in a manual system.

The primary evidence the auditor reviews in this area is the *documentation standards manual*, which typically includes the systems documentation, the program documentation, and the run book documentation. The *systems documentation* sets forth the general objectives of an application and is used for broad planning. It includes the form of the input and output, testing procedures, authorizations, and similar items. The *program documentation* is the basis for developing the computer program and is much more specific. It should include the provisions for reviewing, testing, operating, and changing the computer program. The *run book documentation* is the basis for developing the operating instructions. It includes a description of the input, the detailed operating instructions, and a description of the output.

The documentation standards manual must be carefully reviewed by the auditor well in advance of the actual audit. It is the primary basis for the initial evaluation of the detailed procedures for any computer operation. In most instances an EDP audit specialist is needed to assist the regular auditor.

Hardware Controls

Hardware controls are built into the equipment by the manufacturer to *detect equipment failure*. There are a considerable number of possible specific hardware controls available in EDP systems.

From an internal control point of view, the independent auditor is *less* concerned about the adequacy of the hardware controls in the system than he is about the organization's methods of handling the errors that the computer identifies. The hardware controls are usually carefully designed by the manufacturer to adequately discover and report all machine failures. It is obvious, however, that unless the client's organization has made specific provision for handling machine errors, the output data will remain uncorrected.

Controls over Access to Equipment and Data Files

The auditor is interested in the client's means of *safeguarding the EDP records and files* to ensure that there is an adequate audit trail for the auditor's evidence accumulation needs and to permit advising the client about the potential loss of records that are important to the client's accounting and operating requirements.

The *physical safeguards* over records and files that are important in an EDP system are not significantly different from those that should exist in a manual accounting system. However, the compactness of EDP records and the possibility of erasing a large amount of information on some storage media make such records more vulnerable to accidental or intentional destruction, and thus it is essential that fire and security protection be provided by the use of adequate vaults and off-premises storage.

File protection rings are a useful safeguard against the erasure of information stored on magnetic tape. The presence *or* absence of the file protection ring permits the reading of information, but it cannot be erased when the ring is removed. Similarly, *internal and external file labels*, which are discussed in more detail shortly, are a means of protecting the information in files.

Input Controls

Input controls have to do with the application of a specific operation performed by EDP. They are of major importance in EDP systems, since the quality of the output depends upon the quality of the input. An *input error* is generally defined as any error in the data up to the time it is entered into the computer in machine readable form. The error can result from improper authorization, conversion into a machine readable form, lost data, added data, and other types of errors common to manual systems. The following are a few examples of input controls.

Keypunch Verifying. Having different operators check part or all of the original keypunching is a means of controlling errors from this source. The procedure consists of inserting the punched card into a *verifier* and rekeying data from the original documents. If the results do not match, the card is rejected. Since the operators are generally instructed to keypunch the information exactly as it is stated on the original documents, this control is useful only for detecting keypunching errors.

Check Digit. A check digit is a number that is a part of an *identification number*. It is used as a means of determining whether a recorded identification number is correct. As a highly oversimplified example of check digits, assume that sales personnel identification numbers range from 1 to 9000. For the salesperson with the identification number 3624, the number 15 (the summation of the four digits is the check digit in this example) could be added to the number for a new identification number of 362415. After this is done for each salesperson, the computer can easily be programmed to determine whether the sum of the first four digits of each identification number equals the last two digits. This is a useful control for detecting keypunching, machine, or programming errors. It is unnecessary to *keypunch-verify* identification numbers if check digits are used.

Control Totals. Control totals are used to determine whether all the data that were put into the system were processed. Generally, the purpose of a control total is to make certain that no data are lost in handling or processing, but in some cases it is used to verify that the dollar amount is correct. A count or summation of a batch of input must be completed before the input goes into the system. After the data are processed the control total is compared with the final output. As an example, a batch of sales invoice documents might be footed before they are given to keypunching and then, after information has been processed by the computer, the total can be compared with the output. In many cases the final comparison of the control total with the output total is performed by the computer.

Transmittal Controls and Route Slips. Both of these are forms used by organizations to help ensure that all batches of data are entirely processed. The *transmittal control* form is used to log the receipt of data, the date they are processed, and the release of the data. This control device is useful both for determining which data have been received but not processed and for isolating where unprocessed data are located. The *route slip* is attached to the file of data to inform the processing center of the proper path of processing and to provide a record of the actual processing performed.

Processing Controls

Processing controls are meant to check for reliability throughout a particular EDP application. The purpose is to test whether all transactions are recorded and processed properly and to be sure that no transactions are added. For the most part, these controls are programmed into the system as a part of designing a particular application. A few of these controls are listed next.

Tests for Valid Data. Data validity tests are performed to aid in determining whether inputs and outputs that should be included do in fact appear, as well as whether the information in question is correct. For example, it is possible to test each field to make sure that all fields actually have data. Similarly, a salesperson's employee number can be compared with a master list to determine whether he sells the type of product included in the sales transaction being processed.

Crossfooting Tests. These are similar to those normally found in a manual accounting system. Individual categories are totaled independently by the computer and are then compared to make sure that they are equal to other related totals. Examples include crossfooting the individual categories in the sales journal or the payroll journal. If the totals are not equal, an error message is printed out.

Reasonableness Tests. These tests identify a total or transaction that exceeds some predesignated reasonable limit. One example of a reasonableness test consists of checking whether the recorded payroll hours worked by an employee who is paid on a weekly basis exceed a specified number, such as 70 hours. Other examples are reasonableness tests of each office employee's salary for the month, the maximum and minimum number of units of merchandise sold to a retail customer, and the maximum and minimum supplies expense for a given month. These controls are useful for controlling all kinds of large errors, including keypunch or program errors, loss of documents, and machine failures. Clearly, adequate reasonableness checks are important to the auditor as a means of preventing material errors.

File Label Controls. To ensure that the proper transaction or master file is used with the program being run, file labels that identify the file and summarize its contents are customarily used. An *internal file label* has the relevant information in machine language at both the beginning and the end of the file. The information at the beginning typically includes the file name, its identification number, and the reel number in a multi-reel file. At the end of the file there is usually the record count and the applicable control totals, as well as an indication that the record is the last item in the file. *External file labels* in a readable form aid operators, librarians, and other users to correctly identify the files. When magnetic tape or disks are used, the external label is attached directly to the tape reel or disk, whereas in a punched card file the information is normally written on the top of the file of cards.

Output Controls

Control over the reliability of output of an EDP system depends primarily on the *reliability of the input* and the *processing*. In addition, it is desirable to have a final review in the data processing department to check for obvious output errors such as incomplete output, control totals that do not reconcile, and missing information. It is also desirable to secure final *reasonableness tests* as a means of avoiding material errors. The *users* of the output are another potential source of control over errors in the output when they use the data for their information needs. It is important that provisions be made for formal feedback from the users to the data processing center to help make certain that the cause of the errors is corrected.

An *error listing* is a common means of communicating errors that have been discovered in a data processing system. The system can be programmed to automatically report errors discovered during the processing of data (e.g., invalid data, control data differences, internal file label errors, and hardware malfunctions). Similarly, the procedures manual should require a manually prepared error listing whenever input or keypunch errors occur.

The error listing represents an essential method of controlling and evaluating the system for both the auditor and the client. The client should use the error listing as a means of making certain that all errors are corrected; but even more important, it should be used as a means of correcting the cause and thus preventing future errors. Similarly, the auditor learns from the error listing the kinds of errors that are occurring in the system, as well as the corrective measures the client has taken to eliminate the cause.

EVALUATING INTERNAL CONTROL
IN AN EDP SYSTEM

The objective of the view of internal control in a EDP system is the same as for a manual one: to aid in determining, on the basis of the adequacy of existing controls, the audit evidence that should be accumulated. Similarly, the technique of internal control evaluation for both EDP and non-EDP systems is to obtain information about the client's prescribed system, to evaluate its strengths and weaknesses, and to ascertain that the system is actually operating in accordance with the plan.

In obtaining information about the client's prescribed system and evaluating the system for strengths and weaknesses, the auditor is concerned with determining the existence and adequacy of the EDP controls that were enumerated in the preceding pages. Of course, it is also necessary to evaluate the non-EDP controls discussed earlier in the book, such as the separation of the custody over assets from the recording function.

It is common to start the internal control evaluation of an EDP system by obtaining preliminary information from three major sources: *flowcharts*, *EDP questionnaires*, and a study of the *error listings* generated by the system. The flowcharts and questionnaires have counterparts in non-EDP systems, but an error listing is unique to EDP systems. In most cases it is desirable to use all three approaches in evaluating internal control because they offer different types of information. The flowchart emphasizes the organization of the company and the flow of information throughout the system, whereas the internal control questionnaire emphasizes specific controls without relating individual controls to one another. The error listing supports both these approaches by showing the actual errors that were reported by the EDP system. Ultimately, the auditor must use the information obtained to determine the most important strengths and weaknesses in the internal control system.

After the auditor obtains a preliminary understanding of the EDP system, he is in a position to decide upon the degree to which he plans to rely upon its controls. In doing this, he must also consider the related non-EDP controls and the total system affecting each application. Where controls in one segment, such as the EDP controls, are weak, he may determine that controls in the other segments are compensating, and vice versa. Whenever the auditor feels that the total system cannot be relied upon, he will, of course, expand the substantive portion of the audit. This approach to internal control evaluation is the same as that discussed in Chapters 7 through 11.

If the auditor decides the system is potentially reliable, it is necessary to proceed with the evaluation by obtaining an in-depth understanding of the system. The procedures should include observations and interviewing of personnel, the performance of compliance tests, and investigating exceptions to prescribed controls and procedures.

As in manual systems, the auditor may decide not to rely upon the EDP controls even if they are adequate. This approach is followed if he believes the cost of an exhaustive study and test of the controls will exceed the reduction in the cost of the other procedures. When the auditor decides not to test the controls, they cannot be relied upon.

AUDITING AROUND THE COMPUTER

When the auditor relies completely on the non-EDP segment of a system, it is commonly referred to as auditing around the computer. Under this approach the auditor reviews internal control and performs tests of transactions and account balance verification procedures in the same manner as in non-EDP systems; there is no attempt to test the client's EDP controls or to use the computer to perform audit procedures.

To audit around the computer, the auditor must have access to sufficient source documents and a detailed listing of output in a readable form. This is possible only when all the following conditions are met:

- The source documents are available in a nonmachine language.
- The documents are filed in a manner that makes it possible to locate them for auditing purposes.
- The output is listed in sufficient detail to enable the auditor to trace individual transactions from the source documents to the output and vice versa.

If any of these conditions does not exist, the auditor will have to rely upon computer-oriented controls and possibly use the computer for carrying out his procedures. Auditing around the computer is an acceptable and often desirable approach when the informational needs of the client's organization require it to maintain the necessary source documents and detailed output.

Complete reliance on manual controls, use of traditional techniques, and failure of the auditor to use the computer in carrying out audit procedures where the conditions allow it does not imply that he ignores the EDP installation. He continues to have a responsibility for a thorough review of the system of internal control to determine the weaknesses in the system as an aid in deciding on the appropriate audit procedures and the sample size necessary for each procedure. This includes both manual and EDP segments.

AUDITING WITH THE USE OF THE COMPUTER

There are two distinct ways in which the auditor uses the computer to perform audit procedures: (1) processing the auditor's test data on the client's computer system as a part of the review of internal control and (2) testing the records maintained by the computer as a means of verifying the client's financial statements.

Test Data Approach

The objective of the use of the test data approach is to determine whether the client's computer programs can correctly handle valid and invalid transactions as they arise. To fulfill this objective, the auditor develops different types of transactions that are processed under his own control using the client's computer programs on the client's EDP equipment. The auditor's test data must include both *valid and invalid transactions* in order to determine whether the client's computer programs will react properly to different kinds of data. Since the auditor has complete knowledge of the errors that exist in the test data, it is possible for him to check whether the client's system has properly processed the input. The auditor does this by examining the error listing and the details of the output resulting from the test data.

Test data are helpful in reviewing the client's system of processing data and its control over errors, but several difficulties must be overcome before this approach can be used. The major concerns are as follows:

The Test Data Must Include All Relevant Conditions That the Auditor Desires to Test. The test data should provide for a test of the adequacy of all the controls discussed previously that are applicable to the client's program under review. Because considerable competence is required in developing data to test for all the relevant types of error that could occur, the assistance of an EDP specialist is generally required.

The Program Tested by the Auditor's Test Data Must Be the Same Program That Is Used throughout the Year by the Client. One approach the auditor can take to ensure that this condition is met is to run the test data on a surprise basis, possibly at random points throughout the year. This approach is both costly and time-consuming. A more realistic method is to rely on the client's system of internal control over the use of the program and changes in the program.

In Some Cases the Test Data Must Be Eliminated from the Client's Records. The elimination of the test data is necessary if the program being tested is for the updating of a master file such as the accounts receivable trial balance. It would not be proper to permanently include fictitious test transactions in a master file. There are feasible methods of eliminating the test data, but they generally require the assistance of an EDP specialist.

Auditor's Computer Program Approach

The second approach to auditing with the computer is for the auditor to run his own program on a controlled basis in order to verify the client's data recorded in a machine language. The auditor's computer program and the test data approach are complementary rather than mutually exclusive, in the same manner as are tests of transactions and direct balance verification. When the auditor uses test data he is evaluating the ability of the client's system to handle different types of transactions, whereas in the auditor's computer program approach the output of the system is being tested for correctness.

The auditor can potentially perform many different kinds of tests and other functions with a computer program if the client's data are in a machine language. These include:

Verifying Extensions and Footings. A computer program can be used to verify the accuracy of the client's computations by calculating the information independently. Examples include recalculating sales discounts taken and employees' net pay computations, footing an aging, and totaling the client's accounts receivable trial balance.

Examining Records for Quality, Completeness, Consistency, and Correctness.

In auditing a manual system, the auditor re-examines the accounting records for propriety as a matter of routine because they are visible and any inconsistencies or inaccuracies can be observed without difficulty. When auditing computerized records, the auditor's program can be instructed to scan all records for propriety in terms of specified criteria and print out the exceptions. Examples include reviewing accounts receivable balances for amounts over the credit limit and reviewing payroll files for terminated employees.

Comparing Data on Separate Files.

Where records on separate files should contain compatible information, a program can be used to determine if the information agrees or to make other comparisons. For instance, changes in accounts receivable balances between two dates can be compared with details of sales and cash receipts on transaction files, and payroll details can be compared with personnel records.

Summarizing or Resequencing Data and Performing Analyses.

Computer programs can be developed to change the format and aggregate data in a variety of ways. The ability to change the form of data allows the auditor to mechanically prepare analyses used in audit procedures and to simulate the client's data-processing systems to determine the reasonableness of recorded information. Examples include verifying accounts receivable aging, preparing general ledger trial balances, summarizing inventory turnover statistics for obsolescence analysis, and resequencing inventory items by location to facilitate physical observations.

Comparing Data Obtained through Other Audit Procedures with Company Records.

Audit evidence gathered manually can be converted to machine-readable form (i.e., keypunched) and compared with other machine-readable data. Examples include comparing confirmation responses with the subsidiary records and comparing creditor statements with accounts payable files.

Selecting Audit Samples.

The computer can be programmed to select samples from any machine-readable data in several different ways, including at random. It is also possible to use more than one criterion for sample selection, such as a 100 percent sample of high-dollar accounts receivable and random sampling of all other receivables.

Printing Confirmation Requests. After a sample has been selected, the auditor can have the data printed on confirmation request forms. This is a useful time-saving device for the preparation of confirmations.

The most serious problem in the use of computer programs for testing client data is to obtain a suitable program at a reasonable cost. Three approaches are available to auditors in selecting a computer program:

Use the Client's Program. This is an acceptable and economical alternative when the client already has a program that the auditor can use, such as for extensions of inventory and footing of totals. When this approach is followed, it is important to test the client's program for reliability before it is used.

Use a Program Written by the Auditor for the Specific Audit. This approach is applicable when the client's programs are not available and when a generalized program is not feasible because of such problems as high processing cost or inaccessibility. A computer program written by the auditor fits the audit application for which it is being developed, but it has the disadvantage of high program development cost.

Use a Generalized Program. A generalized audit program is one developed by a CPA firm or other organization which can be used on different audits for most of the seven types of applications listed previously. The generalized program consists of a series of computer programs which together perform various data processing functions. These functions for the most part can be described as data manipulations. Generalized programs are a recent development in auditing that has greatly increased the potential use of the computer for handling tasks. They have two important advantages. First, generalized programs are developed in such a manner that most of the audit staff can be quickly trained to use the program even though they have little formal EDP education. Second, generalized programs have a wide range of application, which can be made with a single program without having to incur the cost or inconvenience of developing an individualized program. The major disadvantages of generalized computer programs are the high initial cost of their development and their relatively inefficient processing speed.

The decision whether to use test data or auditor computer programs or to audit without the use of a computer must be made by the auditor on the basis of his professional experience. Sometimes the auditor is forced to use the computer to perform procedures due to the inaccessibility of source documents and detailed listing of output. Even if records are accessible, it may be desirable to perform tests with the computer if sufficient competent evidence can be accumulated at a reduced cost.

GENERALIZED AUDIT PROGRAM

Since generalized audit programs (GAPs) are extensively used by CPA firms, it is important that students of auditing understand them. These programs are first explained in general terms and followed by an illustration of how they could be used.

Figure 13-1 illustrates the GAP process for any application. The steps are as follows:

Objective Setting. The purpose of the test must be carefully specified in advance to achieve the desired results. The objective can be to foot a data file, select a random sample, or perform one or more of the other tasks previously described.

Application Design. The second step consists of three parts:

- Identify and describe the client's data files and the pertinent information that might be accessed. This is necessary to extract data from the client's files.
- Design the most useful format and contents of the auditor's GAP reports.
- Develop a logical approach to extract and manipulate the data obtained from the client's records. This is done by the auditor with the use of a simple programming language.

Coding. The results of the application design are then coded on worksheets by the auditor in the simple GAP language. These are instructions telling the GAP what to do with the client's files to meet the audit objectives specified.

Keypunching. The coded worksheets are keypunched, verified by the CPA's employees, and submitted to the computer, along with the GAP and the client's data files.

Processing. The processing phase consists of two stages. In the first stage, the GAP directs the computer to read the data file and to extract pertinent information. It is important to understand that all further processing takes place on the extracted information. The client's data file is no longer used and is removed from the process, thus ensuring that it will not be inadvertently changed or destroyed. Should it be necessary for the GAP to produce an intermediate output file, it is referred to as a work file. The second stage involves the functions required to produce the GAP reports. At the completion of the processing, the client's data files are returned to the client and the GAP file is returned to the CPA's office. Frequently, the GAP coding instructions are retained for possible use on subsequent audits. The GAP reports are used for their intended audit purpose and retained in the working papers as documentation.

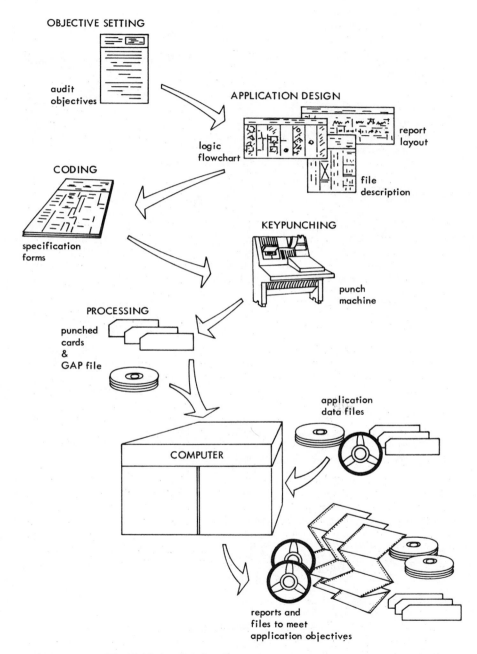

OBJECTIVE SETTING

audit objectives

APPLICATION DESIGN

logic flowchart

report layout

file description

CODING

specification forms

KEYPUNCHING

punch machine

PROCESSING

punched cards & GAP file

COMPUTER

application data files

reports and files to meet application objectives

FIGURE 13–1 The GAP Application Process

Illustration of the Use of a Generalized Audit Program for Accounts Receivable

The following is an illustration of a GAP application presented in terms of the steps given above.

Objective Setting

- Foot and crossfoot the accounts receivable master file and print the total and any crossfoot exceptions.
- Determine if any balances are in excess of their credit limit and print a report of all exceptions.
- Prepare and print an aging summary.
- Randomly select accounts and print confirmations as follows:
  a. Positive confirmation of all accounts over $10,000 or over 90 days old.
  b. Positive confirmation of 25 percent of all accounts between $1,000 and $10,000 not over 90 days old.
  c. Negative confirmation of 5 percent of all others.
- Print a control listing of accounts selected for confirmation.
- Select 5 percent of all accounts to trace to source documents, for a test of aging.
- Select and print a list of accounts for collectibility follow-up which are "for special handling."

Application Design. The client maintains accounts receivable on both a master file and a name and address file. The following is a list of the contents, noting whether the information was used in the application:

Accounts Receivable Master File

Element No.	Description of Contents	Used	Not Used
1	Division	X	—
2	Customer number	X	—
3	Credit limit	X	—
4	Sales personnel code	—	X
5	Cash discount percent	—	X
6	Date of last payment	X	—
7	Date of last purchase	X	—
8	Balance due	X	—
	Aging of balance due:		
9	Current	X	—
10	30 days	X	—
11	60 days	X	—
12	90 days	X	—
13	6 months	X	—
14	1 year	X	—

Name and Address File

Element No.	Description of Contents	Used	Not Used
1	Division	X	—
2	Customer number	X	—
3	Customer name	X	—
4	Street address	X	—
5	City and state	X	—
6	Zip code	X	—
7	Shipping location code	—	X
8	Customer type	—	X
9	Risk-rating code	X	—
	1 = no risk		
	2 = normal handling		
	3 = approval required when balance over 60 days		
	4 = special handling required for each purchase		

Coding. The objectives of this application were met by coding the various GAP functions to process the client's data files as follows:

1. The accounts receivable master file was read and the designated information was extracted. This was followed by extracting the name, address, and risk information from the name and address file.
2. The extracted information was next subjected to the following selection criteria:
   a. Add the aging fields within each record and subtract total from balance due field. Place any difference in an aging overflow field and code the record for Report No. 1.
   b. Foot aging and balance due fields for all records. The GAP prints such totals automatically.
   c. Compare the balance due field with the credit limit field. If the balance exceeds the limit, code the record for Report No. 2.
   d. Compare balance due with $10,000. If greater than $10,000, code the record for positive confirmation and Report No. 3.
   e. Compare aging fields 90 days, 6 months, and 1 year with zero. If greater than zero, code the record for positive confirmation and Report No. 3.
   f. Compare balance due with $1,000. If greater than $1,000 and not previously coded for positive confirmation, select 25 percent at random and code for positive confirmation and Report No. 3.
   g. Compare balance due with $1,000. If less than $1,000 and not coded for positive confirmation, select 5 percent at random and code for negative confirmation and Report No. 4.
   h. Select 5 percent of all accounts at random and code for Report No. 5.
   i. Code any records with a risk rating equal to 4 and not selected for confirmation to Report No. 6.

Keypunching and Processing. After the codes were punched, they were processed with the GAP and the accounts receivable master file and the name and address file.

Reports. The following reports were printed:

- Report No. 1—all accounts where aging does not crossfoot (if any).
- Report No. 2—all accounts where balance is in excess of credit limit (if any).
- Report No. 3—accounts selected for positive confirmation and collectibility follow-up.
- Report No. 4—accounts selected for negative confirmation.
- Report No. 5—accounts for test of aging, showing all aging details, including dates of last payment and purchase.
- Report No. 6—additional high-risk accounts selected for collectibility follow-up.

In addition, positive and negative confirmations were printed.

AUDIT OF COMPUTER SERVICE CENTERS

Many clients now have their data processed at an independent computer service center rather than having their own computer. This is a logical approach for a business with an excessive volume of transactions for a manual system but inadequate volume to justify the cost of owning a computer.

In a computer service center operation, the client submits input data, and the service center processes the data for a fee and returns it to the client along with the agreed-upon output. Generally, the service center is responsible for designing the computer system and providing adequate controls to ensure that the processing is reliable.

The difficulty the independent auditor faces when a computer service center is used is in determining the adequacy of the service center's controls. The auditor cannot automatically assume the controls are adequate simply because it is an independent enterprise. If the client's service center application involves the processing of significant financial data, the auditor must consider the need to evaluate and test the service center's controls.

The extent of the review and testing of the service center should be based upon the same criteria the auditor follows in evaluating a client's own system. The depth of the review depends upon the complexity of the system and the extent to which the auditor intends to rely upon the system to reduce other audit tests. If the auditor concludes that active involvement with the service center is the only feasible way to conduct the audit, it may be necessary to perform an extensive review of the system, test the system by the use of test data and other compliance tests, and use the computer to perform tests of the type discussed in the preceding section. Extensive testing of this nature is unlikely in most audits, however, because most service center applications are reasonably simple. On the other hand, some review of the service center is usually done.

In recent years it has become increasingly common to have *one* independent auditor examine and test the system of internal control of the service center for the use of *all* customers and their independent auditors. The purpose of these independent reviews is to provide customers with a reasonable level of assurance of the adequacy of the service center's system and to eliminate the need for redundant audits by customers' auditors. If the service center has many customers and each customer requires a review of the service center records by its own independent auditor, the inconvenience to the service center can be substantial. When the service center's independent CPA firm completes the audit of the controls and records, a special report is issued indicating the scope of the audit and the conclusions. It is then the responsibility of the customer's auditor to decide upon the extent to which he wants to rely on the service center's audit report.

REVIEW QUESTIONS

13-1. Define what is meant by an audit trail and explain how the client's introduction of EDP can alter it. How does this change affect the auditor?

13-2. List the four types of EDP systems in the order of their complexity. What are the distinguishing characteristics of each of these systems?

13-3. Evaluate the following statement: "As EDP systems become more complex, the role of the traditional auditor declines. It is desirable that auditors involved with EDP systems either become competent in specialized computer concepts or use computer audit specialists on the engagement."

13-4. In what ways is the potential for fraud greater in a highly complex EDP system than in a manual system?

13-5. List five specific internal controls that are equally applicable in a manual or an EDP system.

13-6. In what ways does the ideal segregation of duties for an EDP system differ from those found in a typical non-EDP system? List the major functions that should be segregated in an EDP system and explain why they should be segregated.

13-7. Distinguish between hardware controls and programmed controls and explain the purpose of each.

13-8. Distinguish between a file protection ring and a file label control and explain the purpose of each.

13-9. Explain why input controls are essential in an EDP system. Give three examples of input controls.

13-10. What is meant by processing controls? Give several examples of the type of errors they are meant to prevent.

13-11. Compare the methodology of evaluating a system of internal control in an EDP and a manual system.

13–12. Explain what is meant by auditing around the computer. Under what circumstances is it acceptable to follow this approach?

13–13. Explain what is meant by the test data approach to auditing with the computer. What are the major difficulties in using this approach?

13–14. List seven kinds of tests or other functions commonly performed by auditors' computer programs and give one specific example of each use.

13–15. Explain what is meant by a generalized audit program and discuss its importance as an audit tool.

15–16. Explain why it is unacceptable for an auditor to assume that an independent computer service center is providing reliable accounting information to an audit client. What can the auditor do to test the service center's system?

DISCUSSION QUESTIONS AND PROBLEMS

13–17. Select the best answer choice for the following:
The detection and correction of errors in the processing of data should be the responsibility primarily of
a. the data processing manager.
b. the machine operator.
c. an independent internal control group.
d. the independent public accountant.   (AICPA adapted)

13–18. The audit of the financial statements of a client that utilizes the services of a computer for accounting functions compels the CPA to understand the operation of his client's EDP system.

Required:

a. The first requirement of an effective system of internal control is a satisfactory plan of organization. List the characteristics of a satisfactory plan of organization for an EDP department, including the relationship between the department and the rest of the organization.

b. An effective system of internal control also requires an effective system of records control of operations and transactions (source data and its flow) and of classification of data within the accounts. For an EDP system, these controls include input controls, processing controls, and output controls. List the characteristics of a satisfactory system of input controls. (Confine your comments to a batch-controlled system employing punched cards and to the steps that occur prior to the processing of the input cards in the computer.)   (AICPA adapted)

13–19. When auditing an electronic data processing (EDP) accounting system, the independent auditor should have a general familiarity with the effects of the use of EDP on the various characteristics of accounting control and on the auditor's study and evaluation of such control. The independent auditor must be aware of those control procedures that are commonly referred to as "general" controls and those that are commonly referred to as "application" controls. General controls relate to all EDP activities and application controls relate to specific accounting tasks.

Required:

a. What are the general controls that should exist in EDP-based accounting systems?

b. What are the purposes of each of the following categories of application controls?

   (1) Input controls.
   (2) Processing controls.
   (3) Output controls.

(AICPA adapted)

13–20. George Beemster, CPA, is examining the financial statements of the Louisville Sales Corporation, which recently installed an off-line electronic computer. The following comments have been extracted from Mr. Beemster's notes on computer operations and the processing and control of shipping notices and customer invoices:

> To minimize inconvenience Louisville converted without changing its existing data-processing system, which utilized tabulating equipment. The computer company supervised the conversion and has provided training to all computer department employees (except keypunch operators) in systems design, operations, and programming.
>
> Each computer run is assigned to a specific employee, who is responsible for making program changes, running the program, and answering questions. This procedure has the advantage of eliminating the need for records of computer operations because each employee is responsible for his own computer runs.
>
> At least one computer department employee remains in the computer room during office hours, and only computer department employees have keys to the computer room.
>
> System documentation consists of those materials furnished by the computer company—a set of record formats and program listings. These and the tape library are kept in a corner of the computer department.
>
> The company considered the desirability of programmed controls but decided to retain the manual controls from its existing system.
>
> Company products are shipped directly from public warehouses, which forward shipping notices to general accounting. There a billing clerk enters the price of the item and accounts for the numerical sequence of shipping notices from each warehouse. The billing clerk also prepares daily adding machine tapes ("control tapes") of the units shipped and the unit prices.
>
> Shipping notices and control tapes are forwarded to the computer department for keypunching and processing. Extensions are made on the computer. Output consists of invoices (in six copies) and the daily sales register. The daily sales register shows the aggregate totals of units shipped and unit prices which the computer operator compares with the control tapes.

All copies of the invoice are returned to the billing clerk. The clerk mails three copies to the customer, forwards one copy to the warehouse, maintains one copy in a numerical file, and retains one copy in an open invoice file that serves as a detail accounts receivable record.

Required:

Describe weaknesses in internal control over information and data flows and the procedures for processing shipping notices and customer invoices, and recommend improvements in these controls and processing procedures. Organize your answer as follows:

Weakness	*Recommended Improvement*

(AICPA adapted)

13–21. You have been engaged by Central Savings and Loan Association to examine its financial statements for the year ended December 31.

In January of the current year the association installed an on-line real-time computer system. Each teller in the association's main office and seven branch offices has an on-line input-output terminal. Customers' mortgage payments and savings account deposits and withdrawals are recorded in the accounts by the computer from data input by the teller at the time of the transaction. The teller keys the proper account by account number and enters the information in the terminal keyboard to record the transaction. The accounting department at the main office has both punched card and typewriter input-output devices. The computer is housed at the main office.

In addition to servicing its own mortgage loans, the association acts as a mortgage servicing agency for three life insurance companies. In this latter activity the association maintains mortgage records and serves as the collection and escrow agent for the mortgagees (the insurance companies), who pay a fee to the association for these services.

You would expect the association to have certain internal controls in effect because an on-line real-time computer system is employed. List the internal controls that should be in effect solely because this system is employed, classifying them as

a. Those controls pertaining to input of information

b. All other types of computer controls   (AICPA adapted)

13–22. Bill Goatly, CPA, has examined the financial statements of the Frey Manufacturing Company for several years and is making preliminary plans for the audit for the year ended June 30. During this examination, Goatly plans to use a set of generalized audit programs. Frey's EDP manager has agreed to prepare special tapes of data from company records for the CPA's use with the GAPs.

The following information is applicable to Goatly's examination of Frey's accounts payable and related procedures:

a. The formats of pertinent tapes are given below.

b. The following monthly runs are prepared:
   (1) Cash disbursements by check number.
   (2) Outstanding payables.
   (3) Purchase journals arranged (1) by account charged and (2) by vendor.

c. Vouchers and supporting invoices, receiving reports, and purchase order copies are filed by vendor code. Purchase orders and checks are filed numerically.

d. Company records are maintained on magnetic tapes. All tapes are stored in a restricted area within the computer room. A grandfather-father-son policy is followed for retaining and safeguarding tape files.

Required:

a. Explain the grandfather-father-son policy. Describe how files could be reconstructed when this policy is used.

b. Discuss whether company policies for retaining and safeguarding the tape files provide adequate protection against losses of data.

c. Describe the controls that the CPA should maintain over
   (1) preparing the special tape.
   (2) processing the special tape with the GAPs.

d. Prepare a schedule for the EDP manager outlining the data that should be included on the special tape for the CPA's examination of accounts payable and related procedures. This schedule should show
   (1) the client tape from which the item should be extracted.
   (2) the name of the item of data. (AICPA adapted)

13–23. The Meyers Pharmaceutical Company has the following system for billing and recording accounts receivable:

a. An incoming customer's purchase order is received in the order department by a clerk who prepares a prenumbered company sales order form on which is inserted the pertinent information, such as the customer's name and address, customer's account number, and quantity and items ordered. After the sales order form has been prepared, the customer's purchase order is stapled to it.

b. The sales order form is then passed to the credit department for credit approval. Rough approximations of the billing values of the orders are made in the credit department for those accounts on which credit limitations are imposed. After investigation, approval of credit is noted on the form.

c. Next the sales order form is passed to the billing department where a clerk types the customer's invoice on a billing machine that crossmultiplies the number of items and the unit price, then adds the automatically extended amounts for the total amount of the invoice. The billing clerk determines the unit prices for the items from a list of billing prices.

The billing machine has registers that automatically accumulate daily totals of customer account numbers and invoice amounts to provide "hash" totals and control amounts. These totals, which are inserted in a daily record book, serve as predetermined batch totals for verification of computer inputs. The billing is done on prenumbered, continuous, carbon-interleaved forms having the following designations:

(1) "Customer's copy."
(2) "Sales department copy" for information purposes.
(3) "File copy."
(4) "Shipping department copy," which serves as a shipping order.

Bills of lading are also prepared as carbon copy by-products of the invoicing procedure.

d. The shipping department copy of the invoice and the bills of lading are then sent to the shipping department. After the order has been shipped, copies of the bill of lading are returned to the billing department. The shipping department copy of the invoice is filed in the shipping department.

e. In the billing department one copy of the bill of lading is attached to the customer's copy of the invoice and both are mailed to the customer. The other copy of the bill of lading, together with the sales order form, is then stapled to the invoice file copy and filed in invoice numerical order.

f. A keypunch machine is connected to the billing machine so that punched cards are created during the preparation of the invoices. The punched cards then become the means by which the sales data are transmitted to a computer. The punched cards are fed to the computer in batches. One day's accumulation of cards makes up a batch. After the punched cards have been processed by the computer, they are placed in files and held for about two years.

Required:

List the procedures that a CPA would employ in his examination of his selected audit samples of the company's

a. typed invoices, including the source documents.
b. punched cards.

(*Note:* The listed procedures should be limited to the verification of the sales data being fed into the computer. Do not carry the procedures beyond the point at which the cards are ready to be fed to the computer.)

(AICPA adapted)

13-24. You are conducting an audit of sales for the James Department Store, a retail chain store with a computerized sales system in which computerized cash registers are integrated directly with accounts receivable, sales, perpetual inventory records, and sales commission expense. At the time of sale the salesclerks keypunch the following information directly into the cash register:

- Product number.
- Quantity sold.
- Unit selling price.
- Store code number.
- Salesclerk number.

- Date of sale.
- Cash sale or credit sale.
- Customer account number for all credit sales.

The total amount of the sale, including sales tax, is automatically computed by the system and indicated on the cash register's visual display. The only printed information for cash sales is the cash register receipt, which is given to the customer. For credit sales, a credit slip is prepared and one copy is retained by the clerk and submitted daily to the accounting department.

A summary of sales is printed out daily in the accounting department. The summary includes daily and monthly totals by salesclerks for each store as well as totals for each of ninety-three categories of merchandise by store. Perpetual inventory and accounts receivable records are updated daily on magnetic tape, but supporting records are limited primarily to machine-readable records.

Required:

a. What major problems does the auditor face in verifying sales and accounts receivable?

b. How can the concept of test data be employed in this audit? Explain the difficulties the auditor would have to overcome in using test data.

c. How can a GAP be employed in this audit? List several tests that can be conducted using this approach.

d. The client is interested in installing several controls to automatically signal cash register operators when they have made an error. List four programmed controls the auditor could recommend to reduce the likelihood of these types of errors.

e. The client would also like to reduce the time it takes to keypunch the information into the cash register. Suggest several ways this could be accomplished, considering the information now being manually keypunched.

13–25. In the audit of Greenline Manufacturing Company for the year ended 12-31-X8, Roberta Bond, CPA, concluded that the lack of an audit trail for the property, plant, and equipment accounts precluded auditing that area in the traditional manner. As a result, the decision was made to use a generalized audit program in the verification of certain aspects of the accounts. The generalized audit program includes the following specific objectives:

a. Foot the file and print totals by major property category for cost of all assets, cost of current additions, and accumulated and current depreciation for both book and tax purposes.

b. Prepare a listing of all additions over $5,000 for vouching and inspection.

c. Prepare a listing of all disposals for detailed verification.

d. Verify the calculations of depreciation expenses for both book and tax purposes.

The permanent asset master files for 12-31-X7 were saved by the client and include the same information as the 12-31-X8 files. Their contents are as follows:

Element No.	Description of Contents
1	Asset number
2	Description
3	Type code
4	Location code
5	Year of acquisition
6	Cost
7	Accum. deprec.—beginning book
8	Depreciation—YTD book
9	Useful life
10	Tax depreciation method
11	Accum. deprec.—beginning tax
12	Depreciation—YTD tax

(*Note:* All fixed assets use the straight-line method for book depreciation. Tax depreciation may be straight-line, double-declining-balance, or sum-of-the-years' digits.)

Required:

a. Explain in detail how the information on the 12-31-X7 and 12-31-X8 master files should be used to fulfill the four audit objectives.

b. List the reports that will be generated by the GAP.

c. Explain what additional verification is necessary on each of these reports to satisfy the auditor that property, plant, and equipment is fairly stated.

13–26. A CPA's client, Boos & Baumkirchner, Inc., is a medium-sized manufacturer of products for the leisure time activities market (camping equipment, scuba gear, bows and arrows, etc.). During the past year, a computer system was installed, and inventory records of finished goods and parts were converted to computer processing. The inventory master file is maintained on a disc. Each record of the file contains the following information:

- Item or part number.
- Description.
- Size.
- Unit of measure code.
- Quantity on hand.
- Cost per unit.
- Total value of inventory on hand at cost.
- Date of last sale or usage.
- Quantity used or sold this year.
- Economic order quantity.
- Code number of major vendor.
- Code number of secondary vendor.

In preparation for year-end inventory the client has two identical sets of preprinted inventory count cards. One set is for the client's inventory counts and the other is for the CPA's use to make audit test counts. The following information has been keypunched into the cards and interpreted on their face:

- Item or part number.
- Description.
- Size.
- Unit-of-measure code.

In taking the year-end inventory, the client's personnel will write the actual counted quantity on the face of each card. When all counts are complete, the counted quantity will be keypunched into the cards. The cards will be processed against the disc file, and quantity-on-hand figures will be adjusted to reflect the actual count. A computer listing will be prepared to show any missing inventory count cards and all quantity adjustments of more than $100 in value. These items will be investigated by client personnel, and all required adjustments will be made. When adjustments have been completed, the final year-end balances will be computed and posted to the general ledger.

The CPA has available a general-purpose computer audit software package that will run on the client's computer and can process both card and disk files.

Required:

a. In general and without regard to the facts above, discuss the nature of general-purpose computer audit software packages and list the various types and uses of such packages.
b. List and describe at least five ways a general purpose computer audit software package can be used to assist in all aspects of the audit of the inventory of Boos & Baumkirchner, Inc. (For example, the package can be used to read the disk inventory master file and list items and parts with a high unit cost or total value. Such items can be included in the test counts to increase the dollar coverage of the audit verification.)

(AICPA)

13–27. An auditor is conducting an examination of the financial statements of a wholesale cosmetics distributor with an inventory consisting of thousands of individual items. The distributor keeps its inventory in its own distribution center and in two public warehouses. An inventory computer file is maintained on a computer disk and at the end of each business day the file is updated. Each record of the inventory file contains the following data:

- Item number.
- Location of item.
- Description of item.
- Quantity on hand.
- Cost per item.
- Date of last purchase.
- Date of last sale.
- Quantity sold during year.

The auditor is planning to observe the distributor's physical count of inventories as of a given date. The auditor will have available a computer tape of the data on the inventory file on the date of the physical count and a general-purpose computer software package.

Required:

The auditor is planning to perform basic inventory auditing procedures. Identify the basic inventory auditing procedures and describe how the use of the general-purpose software package and the tape of the inventory file data might be helpful to the auditor in performing such auditing procedures.

Organize your answer as follows:

Basic inventory auditing procedure	*How general-purpose computer software package and tape of the inventory file data might be helpful*
1. Observe the physical count, making and recording test counts where applicable.	Determining which items are to be test-counted by selecting a random sample of a representative number of items from the inventory file as of the date of the physical count.

(AICPA)

14

AUDIT
OF THE PAYROLL
AND PERSONNEL CYCLE

The payroll and personnel cycle involves the employment and payment of all employees, regardless of classification or method of determining compensation. The employees include executives on straight salary plus bonus, office workers on monthly salary with or without overtime, salespeople on a commission basis, and factory and unionized personnel paid on an hourly basis. The cycle is important for several reasons. First, the salaries, wages, employer taxes, and other employer costs are a major expense in all companies. Second, labor is such an important consideration in the valuation of inventory in manufacturing and construction companies that the improper classification and allocation of labor can result in a material misstatement of net income. Finally, payroll is an area where occasionally large amounts of company resources are wasted because of inefficiency or are stolen through fraud.

As with the sales and collection cycle, the audit of the payroll and personnel cycle includes analytical review procedures, the evaluation of internal controls and tests of transactions, and direct tests of financial balances. Accordingly, the first part of this chapter deals with the nature of the cycle, including documents and records, and the primary functions and internal controls. The second part discusses analytical review procedures. The third part includes tests of transactions for the cycle related to key internal controls. Finally, the fourth part of the chapter focuses on the verification of the related liability and expense accounts with direct tests. These accounts include all salaries and wages expense accounts, employer payroll taxes and fringe benefits, and the liability for accrued wages, payroll taxes, and similar items connected with payroll.

The way in which accounting information flows through the various accounts in the payroll and personnel cycle is illustrated by T-accounts in Figure 14-1. In most systems the accrued wages and salaries account is used only at the end of an accounting period. Throughout the period, expenses are charged when the employees are actually paid rather than when the labor costs are incurred. The accruals for labor are recorded by adjusting entries at the end of the period for any earned but unpaid labor costs.

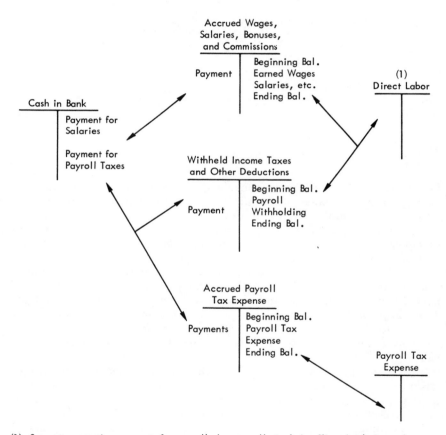

(1) Separate operating accounts for payroll also normally include officers' salaries and and bonuses, office salaries, sales salaries, and commissions and indirect manufacturing labor. These accounts have the same relationship to accrued wages and withheld taxes and other deductions that is shown for direct labor.

FIGURE 14-1 Accounts in the Payroll and Personnel Cycle

NATURE OF THE PAYROLL
AND PERSONNEL CYCLE

The payroll and personnel cycle begins with the hiring of personnel and ends with the payment to the employees for the services performed and to the government and other institutions for the withheld and accrued payroll taxes and benefits. In between, the cycle involves obtaining services from the employees consistent with the objectives of the company and accounting for the services in a proper manner. An overview flowchart of the payroll and personnel cycle for a typical small manufacturing company is shown in Figure 14-2.

Documents and Records

Various documents and records are of major importance in supporting the record flow used in the cycle:

Personnel Records. Records that include such data as the date of employment, personnel investigations, rates of pay, authorized deductions, performance evaluations, and termination of employment.

Deduction Authorization Form. A form authorizing payroll deductions, including the number of exemptions for witholding of income taxes, U.S. savings bonds, and community fund.

Rate Authorization Form. A form authorizing the rate of pay. The source of the information is a labor contract, authorization by management, or, in the case of officers, authorization from the board of directors.

Time Card. A document indicating the time the employee started and stopped working each day and the number of hours the employee worked. For many employees, the time card is prepared automatically by the use of time clocks. Time cards are usually submitted weekly.

Job Time Ticket. A document indicating particular jobs on which a factory employee worked during a given time period. This form is used only where an employee works on different jobs or in different departments.

Payroll Check. A check written to the employee for services performed. The amount of the check is the gross pay less taxes and other deductions withheld. After the check is cashed and returned to the company from the bank, it is referred to as a canceled check.

Payroll Journal. A journal for recording payroll checks. It typically indicates gross pay, withholdings, and net pay. The journal is normally totaled and posted to the general ledger monthly.

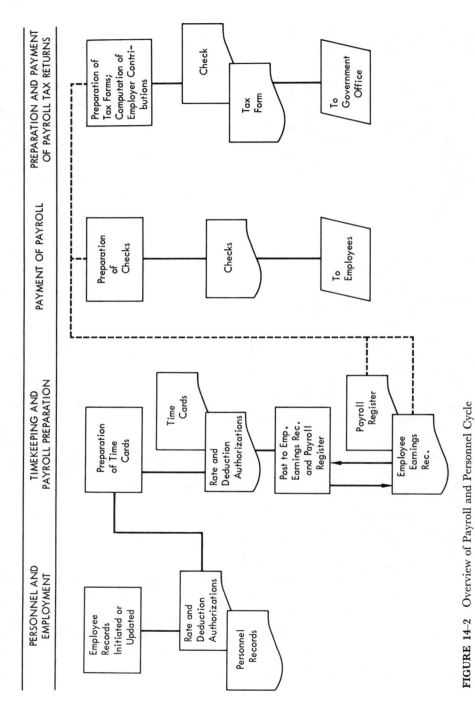

FIGURE 14-2 Overview of Payroll and Personnel Cycle

Labor Distribution. A record summarizing the accounts in the general ledger that should be debited for payroll charges. The total on the labor distribution equals the total gross payroll in the payroll journal.

Earnings Record. A record maintained for each employee indicating the gross pay for each payment period, deductions from gross pay, net pay, check number, and date.

W-2. A form issued for each employee summarizing the earnings record for the calendar year. The information includes gross pay, income taxes withehld, and FICA withheld. The same information is also submitted to the Internal Revenue Service and the State Commission of Income Taxation.

Payroll Tax Returns. Tax forms submitted to local, state, and federal units of government for the payment of withheld taxes and the employer's tax. The nature and due date of the forms vary depending on the type of taxes. For example, federal withholding and social security payments are due monthly, and state unemployment taxes are due quarterly.

Functions in the Cycle and Internal Controls

Typically, four functions are accomplished through the payroll and personnel cycle. They are:

- Personnel and employment.
- Timekeeping and payroll preparation.
- Payment of payroll.
- Preparation of payroll tax returns and payment of taxes.

These functions are now examined in detail with regard to a typical manufacturing company where employees are required to maintain a record of the job on which they are working. The emphasis in this discussion is on the use of certain internal controls to prevent errors in providing data and to ensure the safety of assets.

Personnel and Employment. The personnel department plays the role of providing an independent source for interviewing and hiring qualified personnel. The department is also an independent source of records for the internal verification of wage information.

From an audit point of view, the most important internal controls in personnel involve the formal method of informing the timekeeping and payroll preparation personnel of the authorization of new employees, the authorization of initial and periodic changes in pay rates, and the termination date of employees no longer working for the company. As a part of these controls, segregation of duties is particularly important. No individual with access to time cards, payroll records, or checks should also be permitted access to personnel records. A second important control is the adequate investigation of the competence and trustworthiness of new employees. Frequently, an investigation of previous employment can uncover an unsatisfactory background.

Timekeeping and Payroll Preparation. This function is of major importance in the audit of payroll because it directly affects payroll expense for the period. It includes the preparation of time cards by employees, the summarization and calculation of gross pay, deductions, and net pay, the preparation of payroll checks, and the preparation of payroll records. There must be adequate controls to prevent errors in each of these activities.

Adequate control over the time on the time cards includes the use of a time clock or other method of making certain that employees are paid for the number of hours they worked. There should also be controls to prevent anyone from checking in for several employees or submitting a fictitious time card.

The summarization and calculation of the payroll can be controlled by well-defined policies for the payroll department, separation of duties to provide automatic cross-checks, reconciliation of payroll hours with independent production records, and independent internal verification of all important data. For example, payroll policies should require a competent independent person to recalculate actual hours worked, review for the proper approval of all overtime, examine time cards for erasures and alterations, and recheck pay rates and calculations.

Controls over the preparation of checks include preventing anyone who is responsible for preparing the checks from also having responsibility for summarizing the records or signing or distributing the checks. In addition, the checks should be prenumbered and recorded in the payroll journal on a timely basis.

When manufacturing labor affects inventory valuation, special emphasis should be put on controls to make sure labor is distributed to proper account classifications. There must also be an adequate system of recording job time tickets and other relevant payroll information in the cost accounting records. Independent internal verification of this information is an essential control.

Payment of Payroll. The actual signing and distribution of the checks must be properly handled to prevent their theft. The controls should include limiting the authorization for signing the checks to a responsible employee who does not have access to timekeeping or the preparation of the payroll, the distribution of payroll by someone who is not involved in the other payroll functions, and the immediate return of unclaimed checks for redeposit. If a check-signing machine is used to replace a manual signature, the same controls are required; in addition, the check-signing machine must be carefully controlled.

Most companies use an *imprest payroll account* to prevent the payment of unrecorded payroll transactions. An imprest payroll account is a separate payroll account in which a small balance is maintained. A check for the exact amount of each net payroll is transferred from the general account to the imprest account immediately before the distribution of the payroll. The advantages of an imprest account are that it limits the client's exposure to payroll fraud, allows the delegation of payroll check-signing duties, separates routine payroll expenditures from irregular expenditures, and facilitates cash management. It also simplifies the reconciliation of the payroll bank account if it is done at the low point in the payment cycle.

Preparation of Payroll Tax Returns and Payment of Taxes. The careful and timely preparation of all payroll tax returns is necessary to avoid penalties and criminal charges against the company. The most important control in the preparation of these returns is a well-defined set of policies that carefully indicate when each form must be filed. The independent verification by a competent individual is also an important control to prevent errors and potential liability for taxes and penalties.

ANALYTICAL REVIEW PROCEDURES

The use of analytical review procedures is as important in the payroll and personnel cycle as it is in every other cycle. The following types of analytical tests performed for the balance sheet and income statement accounts in the payroll and personnel cycle are useful for uncovering areas where additional investigation is desirable:

- Compare the payroll expense account balance with those of previous years. Ideally, the previous years' balances should be adjusted for pay rate increases and increases in volume.
- Compare direct labor ÷ sales with industry standards and those of previous years.
- Compare commission expense ÷ sales with industry standards and those of previous years.
- Compare payroll tax expenses ÷ salaries and wages with those of previous years. This comparison is not meaningful unless previous years' balances are adjusted for changes in the tax rate. It is also desirable to exclude officers' salaries from the calculation.
- Compare accrued payroll taxes accounts with those of previous years.

TESTS OF TRANSACTIONS

Tests of transactions procedures are the *most important* means of verifying account balances in the payroll and personnel cycle. The emphasis on tests of transactions is due to the lack of independent third-party evidence, such as confirmation, for verifying accrued wages, withheld income taxes, accrued payroll taxes, and other balance sheet accounts. Furthermore, in most audits the amounts in the balance sheet accounts are small and can be verified with relative ease if the auditor is confident that the journals and payroll tax returns are properly prepared.

Even though the tests of transactions are the most important part of testing payroll, many auditors spend little time in this area. In many audits there is a minimal risk of material misstatements even though payroll is frequently a significant part of total expenses. There are three reasons for this: employees are likely to complain to management if they are underpaid, all payroll transactions are typically uniform and uncomplicated, and payroll transactions are extensively audited by federal and state governments for income-tax withholding, social security, and unemployment taxes.

Under certain circumstances auditors may extend their procedures considerably in the audit of payroll: (1) when payroll significantly affects the valuation of inventory and (2) when the auditor is concerned about the possibility of material fraudulent payroll transactions because of a weak system of internal control.

Relationship between Payroll and Inventory Valuation

In audits where the payroll is a significant portion of inventory, such as frequently occurs for manufacturing and construction companies, the improper account classification of payroll can significantly affect asset valuation for accounts such as work in process, finished goods, or construction in process. For example, the overhead charged to inventory at the balance sheet can be overstated if the salaries of administrative personnel are inadvertently or intentionally charged to indirect manufacturing overhead. Similarly, the valuation of inventory is affected if the direct labor cost of individual employees is improperly charged to the wrong job or process. When some jobs are billed on a cost-plus basis, revenue and the valuation of inventory are both affected by charging labor to incorrect jobs.

When labor is a material factor in inventory valuation, there should be special emphasis on testing the internal controls over proper classification of payroll transactions. Consistency from period to period, which is essential for classification, can be tested by reviewing the chart of accounts and procedures manuals. It is also desirable to trace job tickets or other evidence of an employee's having worked on a particular job or process to the accounting records that affect inventory valuation. For example, if each employee must account for all of his time on a weekly basis by assigning it to individual job numbers, a useful test is to trace the recorded hours of several employees for a week to the related job-cost records to make sure each has been properly recorded. It may also be desirable to trace from the job-cost records to employee summaries as a test for nonexistent payroll charges being included in inventory.

Tests for Fictitious Payroll

Although the auditor is not ordinarily responsible for the detection of fraud, he must extend his audit procedures when internal controls over payroll are inadequate. There are several ways employees can significantly defraud a company in the payroll area, but in this section the discussion is limited to tests for the two most common types of fictitious employees and fraudulent hours.

Fictitious Employees. The issuance of payroll checks for individuals who do not work for the company frequently results from the continuance of an employee's check after his employment has been terminated. Usually the person committing the fraudulent act is a payroll clerk, foreman, fellow employee, or perhaps the former employee himself. For example, under some systems a foreman could clock in daily for an employee and approve the time card at the end of the time period. If the foreman also distributes paychecks, considerable opportunity for fraud exists.

Certain procedures can be performed on canceled checks as a means of detecting fraud. A procedure used on virtually every payroll audit is to compare the names on canceled checks with time cards and with other records for authorized signatures and reasonableness of the endorsements. It is also common to scan endorsements on canceled checks for unusual or recurring second endorsements as an indication of a possible fictitious check. The examination of checks that are recorded as voided is also desirable to make sure they have not been fraudulently used.

A test for invalid employees is to trace selected transactions recorded in the payroll journal to the personnel department to determine whether the employees were actually employed during the payroll period. The endorsement on the canceled check written out to an employee can be compared with the authorized signature on the employee's withholding authorization forms.

A procedure that tests for proper handling of terminated employees is to select several files for employees that were terminated in the current year from the personnel records to determine whether each former employee received his termination pay in accordance with company policy. Continuing payments to terminated employees is tested by examining the payroll records in the subsequent period to ascertain that the employee is no longer being paid. Naturally, this procedure is not effective if the personnel department is not informed of terminations.

In some cases the auditor may request a surprise payroll payoff. This is a procedure in which each employee must pick up and sign for his check in the presence of a supervisor and the auditor. Any checks that have not been claimed must be subject to an extensive investigation to determine whether an unclaimed check is fraudulent. Surprise payoff is frequently expensive and in some cases may even cause problems with a labor union, but it may be the only likely means of detecting a fraud.

Fraudulent Hours. Because of the lack of available evidence, it is usually difficult for an auditor to discover if an employee records more time on his time card than he actually worked. One procedure is to reconcile the total hours paid according to the payroll records with an independent record of the hours worked, such as those often maintained by production control. Similarly, it may be possible to observe an employee clocking in more than one time card under a buddy approach. However, it is ordinarily easier for the client to prevent this type of fraud by adequate controls than for the auditor to detect it.

Internal Controls, Compliance Tests, and Substantive Tests

Following the same approach that was used in Chapter 9 for tests of sales and cash transactions, the internal controls, compliance tests, and substantive tests for each of the internal control and audit objectives are summarized in Figure 14-3. Again, the reader should recognize that:

- The internal controls will vary from company to company; therefore, the auditor must evaluate the strengths and weaknesses of each system on the basis of the existing controls.
- Controls the auditor intends to rely upon for reducing substantive tests must be tested with compliance tests.
- The substantive tests will vary depending upon the quality of the internal controls and the other considerations of the audit, such as the effect of payroll on inventory.
- The tests of transactions are not actually performed in the order given in Figure 14–3. The compliance and substantive tests are combined into dual-purpose tests and where appropriate are performed in as convenient a manner as possible.

The purpose of the controls and the meaning and methodology of audit tests that can potentially be used for payroll should be apparent from the descriptions in Figure 14-3. An extended discussion of these procedures is therefore not necessary.

Other Considerations

Three aspects of the payroll and personnel cycle and the related tests of transactions that were not included in the preceding summary also require consideration: preparation of payroll tax forms, payment of the payroll taxes withheld and other withholdings on a timely basis, and reimbursement of the payroll imprest account.

Preparation of Payroll Tax Forms. The auditor should review the preparation of at least one of each type of payroll tax form the client is responsible for filing as a part of testing the system. There is a potential liability for

FIGURE 14-3

Summary of Tests of Payroll Transactions

Internal Control and Audit Objective	Key Internal Controls	Common Compliance Tests	Common Substantive Tests
Payroll transactions as recorded in the payroll journal are reasonable.	• Payroll transactions are periodically reviewed by an independent person for reasonableness.	• Inquiry of independent person and examination of reports and recommendations prepared by reviewer.	• Review the payroll journal, general ledger, and payroll earnings records for large or unusual amounts.
Recorded payroll payments are for work actually performed by nonfictitious employees.	• Time cards are approved by foremen. • Time clock is used to record time. • Adequate personnel file. • Separation of duties between personnel, timekeeping, and payroll disbursements.	• Examine the cards for indication of approvals. • Examine time cards. • Review personnel policies. • Review organization chart, discuss with employees, and observe duties being performed.	• Compare canceled checks with payroll journal for name, amount, and date. • Examine canceled checks for proper endorsement. • Compare canceled checks with personnel records.
Payroll transactions are properly authorized.	Specific or general approval is important at five points: • Authorization to work. • Hours worked, especially overtime. • Wage rate, salary, or commission rate. • Withholdings, including amounts for insurance and payroll savings. • Issuance of check.	• Examine personnel files. • Examine time cards for indication of approval. • Examine payroll records for indication of internal verification. • Examine authorizations in personnel file. • Examine payroll records for indication of approval.	• Compare time card with independent record of hours worked.
Existing payroll transactions are recorded.	• Payroll checks are prenumbered and accounted for. • Independent preparation of bank reconciliation.	• Account for a sequence of payroll checks. • Discuss with employees and observe reconciliation.	• Reconcile the disbursements in the payroll journal with the disbursements on the payroll bank statement. • Prove the bank reconciliation.

FIGURE 14-3 (cont.)

Internal Control and Audit Objective	Key Internal Controls	Common Compliance Tests	Common Substantive Tests
Recorded payroll transactions are for the amount of time actually worked and at the proper pay rate; withholdings are properly calculated.	• Internal verification of calculations and amounts.	• Examine indication of internal verification.	• Recompute hours worked from time cards. • Compare pay rates with union contract approval by board of directors of other source. • Recompute gross pay. • Check withholdings by reference to tax tables and authorization forms in personnel file. • Recompute net pay. • Compare canceled check with payroll journal for amount.
Payroll transactions are properly classified.	• Adequate chart of accounts. • Internal verification of classification.	• Review chart of accounts. • Examine indication of internal verification.	• Compare classification with chart of accounts or procedures manual. • Review time card for employee department and job ticket for job assignment, and trace through to labor distribution.
Payroll transactions are recorded on a timely basis.	• Procedures require recording transactions as soon as possible after the payroll is paid. • Internal verification.	• Examine procedures manual. • Observe when recording takes place.	• Compare date of recorded check in the payroll journal with date on canceled checks and time cards. • Compare date on check with date the check cleared the bank.
Payroll transactions are properly included in the employee earnings record; they are properly summarized.	• Internal verification.	• Examine indication of internal verification.	• Test clerical accuracy, e.g., foot the payroll journal and trace postings to general ledger and employee earnings record.

unpaid taxes, penalty, and interest if the client fails to properly prepare the tax forms. The payroll tax forms are for such taxes as federal income and FICA withholding, state and city income withholdings, and federal and state unemployment.

A detailed reconciliation of the information on the tax forms and the payroll records may be necessary when the auditor believes that there is a reasonable chance the tax returns may be improperly prepared. Indications of potential errors in the returns include the payment of penalties and interest in the past for improper payments, new personnel in the payroll department who are responsible for the preparation of the returns, the lack of internal verification of the information, and the existence of serious liquidity problems for the client.

Payment of the Payroll Taxes Withheld and Other Withholdings on a Timely Basis. It is desirable to test whether the client has fulfilled its legal obligation in submitting payments for all payroll withholdings as a part of the payroll tests even though the payments are usually made from general cash disbursements. The withholdings of concern in these tests are such items as taxes, union dues, insurance, and payroll savings. The auditor must first determine the client's requirements for submitting the payments. The requirements are determined by reference to such sources as tax laws, union contracts, and agreements with employees. After the auditor knows the requirements, it is easy to determine whether the client has paid the proper amount on a timely basis by comparing the subsequent payment with the payroll records.

Reimbursement of the Payroll Imprest Account. The periodic payment from the general cash account to the payroll account for net payroll is usually such a large amount that it should be tested for at least one payroll period. The major audit concern is the adequacy of the internal controls for making sure the check is prepared for the proper amount and deposited before payroll checks are handed out. The auditor should ascertain whether the amount of the canceled check paid from the general cash account equals the net payroll for the payroll period.

Analysis of Errors and Drawing Conclusions

Most payroll systems, in order to adequately control cash disbursed and to minimize employee complaints and dissatisfaction, are highly structured and well controlled. It is very common to use electronic data processing techniques to prepare all journals and payroll checks. In-house systems are often used, as are commercial outside service center systems. For factory and office employees, there are usually a large number of relatively homogeneous, small amount transactions. There are fewer executive payroll transactions, but they are also ordinarily consistent in timing, content, and amount. Thus, auditors seldom expect to find errors in testing payroll transactions. Occasionally, compliance errors occur, but most monetary errors are corrected by internal verification controls or in response to employee complaints. However, there are specific types of errors that give the auditor particular concern in auditing payroll transactions:

- Classification errors in charging labor to inventory and job cost accounts. As previously indicated, these can result in misstated earnings.
- Computational errors where electronic data processing is used. Recall that one of the primary characteristics of the computer is processing consistency. If a calculation error is made for one item, it is probably also made on every other similar item.
- Any errors that indicate possible fraud, particularly relating to the executive payroll.

Generally, the tests of transactions performed in the payroll cycle will utilize *attributes sampling* under a plan that assumes a zero error rate. Sample size should be large enough to give the auditor a reasonable chance of finding at least one error if an intolerable quantity of errors exist.

If classification errors are found through this procedure, the sample selected for attributes will often be used to then make a *variables estimate* of the total monetary error involved. Sample expansion is usually necessary, however, to achieve a precise enough estimate to conclude whether the total error is material in amount.

If a computational or possible fraud type error is found, specific investigation will be required to determine the facts that allowed such error to occur. Generally, further sampling and estimation are not done; rather, a *judgmental* approach based on the circumstances is taken.

If no errors are found, or if errors found are not alarming or unexpected, the auditor will conclude that the internal controls can be relied upon as planned and he will proceed with the direct tests of the affected accounts without modification.

DIRECT TESTS OF FINANCIAL BALANCES

Audit of Liability Accounts

The verification of the liability accounts associated with payroll, often termed *accrued payroll expenses*, ordinarily is straightforward if the system of internal control is operating effectively. When the auditor is satisfied that payroll transactions are being properly recorded in the payroll journal and the related payroll tax forms are being accurately prepared and promptly paid, the tests should not be time-consuming.

The two major objectives in testing payroll-related liabilities are: accruals in the trial balance are properly valued and transactions in the payroll and personnel cycle are recorded in the proper period. The primary concern in both objectives is to make sure there are no understated or omitted accruals. The major liability accounts in the payroll and personnel cycle are now discussed.

Amounts Withheld from Employees' Pay. Payroll taxes withheld, but not yet disbursed, can be tested by comparing the balance with the payroll journal, the payroll tax form prepared in the subsequent period, and the subsequent period cash disbursements. Other withheld items such as union dues, savings bonds, and insurance can be verified in the same manner. If the system is operating effectively, cutoff and valuation can easily be tested at the same time by these procedures.

Accrued Salaries and Wages. The accrual for salaries and wages arises whenever employees are not paid for the last few days or hours of earned wages until the subsequent period. Salaried personnel usually receive all of their pay except overtime on the last day of the month, but frequently several days of wages for hourly employees are unpaid at the end of the year.

The correct cutoff and valuation of accrued salaries and wages depends on company policy, which should be followed consistently from year to year. Some companies calculate the exact hours of pay that were earned in the current period and paid in the subsequent period, whereas others compute an approximate proportion. For example, if the subsequent payroll results from three days' employment during the current year and two days' employment during the subsequent year, the use of 60 percent of the subsequent period's gross pay as the accrual is an example of an approximation.

Once the auditor has determined the company's policy for accruing wages and knows it is consistent with that of previous years, the appropriate audit procedure to test for cutoff and valuation is to recalculate the client's accrual. The most likely error of any significance in the balance is the failure to include the proper number of days of earned but unpaid wages.

Accrued Commissions. The same concepts used in verifying accrued salaries and wages are applicable to accrued commissions, but the accrual is often more difficult to verify because companies frequently have several different types of agreements with salespeople and other commission employees. For example, some salespeople might be paid a commission every month and earn no salary, while others will get a monthly salary plus a commission paid quarterly. In some cases the commission varies for different products and may not be paid until several months after the end of the year. In verifying accrued commissions, it is necessary to first determine the nature of the commission agreement and then test the calculations based on the agreement. It is important to compare the method of accruing commissions with previous years for purposes of consistency. If the amounts are material, it is also common to confirm the amount that is due directly with the employees.

Accrued Bonuses. In many companies the year-end unpaid bonuses to officers and employees are such a major item that the failure to record them would result in a material misstatement. The verification of the recorded accrual can usually be accomplished by comparing it with the amount authorized in the minutes of the board of directors.

Accrued Vacation Pay, Sick Pay, or Other Benefits. The consistent accrual of these liabilities relative to those of the preceding year is the most important consideration in evaluating the fairness of the amounts. The company policy for recording the liability must first be determined, followed by the recalculation of the recorded amounts.

Accrued Payroll Taxes. Payroll taxes such as FICA and state and federal unemployment taxes can be verified by examining tax forms prepared in the subsequent period to determine the amount that should have been recorded as a liability at the balance sheet date.

Audit of Expense Accounts

Several accounts in the income statement are affected by payroll transactions. The most important include officers' salaries and bonuses, office salaries, sales salaries and commissions, and direct manufacturing labor. There is frequently a further breakdown of costs by division, product, or branch. Fringe benefits such as medical insurance may also be included in the expenses.

There should be relatively little additional testing of the income statement accounts in most audits beyond the analytical review procedures, tests of transactions, and related tests of liability accounts, which have already been discussed. Extensive additional testing should only be necessary when there are weaknesses in the system of internal control, significant errors are discovered in the liability tests, or major unexplained variances are found in the analytical tests. Nevertheless, some income statement accounts are often tested in the personnel and payroll cycle. These include:

Officers' Compensation. It is common to verify whether the total compensation of officers is the amount authorized by the board of directors because their salaries and bonuses must be included in the SEC's 10-K report and the federal income-tax return. Verification of officers' compensation is also warranted because some individuals may be in a position to pay themselves more than the authorized amount. The usual audit test is to obtain the authorized salary of each officer from the minutes of the board of directors and compare it with the related earnings record.

Commissions. Commission expense can be verified with relative ease if the commission rate is the same for each type of sale and the necessary sales information is available in the accounting records. The total commission expense can be verified by multiplying the commission rate for each type of sale by the amount of sales in that category. If the desired information is not available, it may be necessary to test the annual or monthly commission payments for selected salespeople and trace those into the total commission payments. When the auditor believes it is necessary to perform these tests, they are normally done in conjunction with tests of accrued liabilities.

Payroll Tax Expense. Payroll tax expense for the year can be tested by first reconciling the total payroll on each payroll tax form with the total payroll for the entire year. Total payroll taxes can then be recomputed by multiplying the appropriate rate by the taxable payroll. The calculation is frequently time-consuming because the tax is usually applicable on only a portion of the payroll and the rate may change part way through the year if the taxpayer's financial statements are not on a calendar year basis. The calculation is not worth the effort expended to obtain the information on most audits. When the auditor believes the test is necessary, it is ordinarily done in conjunction with tests of payroll tax accruals.

Total Payroll. A closely related test to the one for payroll taxes is the reconciliation of total payroll expense in the general ledger with the payroll tax returns and the W-2s. The objectives of the test are to determine whether payroll transactions were charged to a nonpayroll account or not recorded in the payroll journal at all. The audit objectives are certainly relevant, but it is questionable whether the procedure is useful in uncovering the type of error for which it was intended. Since the payroll tax records are usually prepared directly from the payroll journal, the errors, if any, are likely to be in both records. The procedure may be worthwhile in rare situations, but it is usually not necessary to perform it. Tests of transactions are a better means of uncovering these two types of errors in most audits.

REVIEW QUESTIONS

14–1. Explain the relationship between the payroll and personnel cycle and inventory valuation.

14–2. List five compliance tests that can be performed for the payroll cycle and state the purpose of each control being tested.

14–3. Explain why the percentage of total audit time in the cycle devoted to performing tests of transactions is usually far greater for the payroll and personnel cycle than for the sales and collection cycle.

14–4. Evaluate the following comment by an auditor: "My job is to determine whether the payroll records are fairly stated in accordance with generally accepted accounting principles, not to find out whether they are following proper hiring and termination procedures. When I conduct an audit of payroll I keep out of the personnel department and stick to the time cards, journals, and payroll checks. I don't care whom they hire and whom they fire, as long as they properly pay the one they have."

14–5. Distinguish between the following payroll audit procedures and state the purpose of each: (1) trace a random sample of prenumbered time cards to the related payroll checks in the payroll register and compare the hours worked with the hours paid, and (2) trace a random sample of payroll checks from the payroll register to the related time cards and compare the hours worked with the hours paid. Which of these two procedures is typically more important in the audit of payroll? Why?

14–6. In auditing payroll withholding and payroll tax expense, explain why emphasis should normally be on evaluating the adequacy of the payroll tax return preparation procedures rather than the payroll tax liability. If the preparation procedures are inadequate, explain the impact this will have on the remainder of the audit.

14–7. List several analytical tests for the payroll and personnel cycle and explain the type of error that might be indicated when there is a significant deviation in the comparison of the current year with previous years' results for each of the tests.

14–8. Explain the circumstances under which an auditor should perform audit tests primarily designed to uncover fraud in the payroll and personnel cycle. List five audit procedures that are primarily for the detection of fraud and state the type of fraud the procedure is meant to uncover.

14–9. Distinguish between an employee's earnings record, a W-2, and a payroll tax return. Explain the purpose of each.

14–10. List the supporting documents and records the auditor will examine in a typical payroll audit where the primary objective is to detect fraud.

14–11. List the five types of authorizations in the payroll and personnel cycle and state the type of error that is enhanced when each authorization is lacking.

14–12. Explain why it is common to verify total officers' compensation even when the test of transactions results in payroll are excellent. What audit procedures can be used to verify officers' compensation?

14–13. Explain what is meant by an imprest payroll account. What is its purpose as a control over payroll?

14–14. List several audit procedures the auditor can use to determine whether recorded payroll transactions are recorded at the proper amount.

14–15. Explain how attributes sampling can be used to test the payroll and personnel cycle.

DISCUSSION QUESTIONS AND PROBLEMS

14–16. For each of the following questions, select the best response.
  a. A factory foreman at Steblecki Corporation discharged an hourly worker but did *not* notify the payroll department. The foreman then forged the worker's signature on time cards and work tickets and, when giving out the checks, diverted the payroll checks drawn from the discharged worker

to his own use. The most effective procedure for preventing this activity is to

(1) require written authorization for all employees added to or removed from the payroll.

(2) have a paymaster who has *no* other payroll responsibility distribute the payroll checks.

(3) have someone other than persons who prepare or distribute the payroll obtain custody of unclaimed payroll checks.

(4) from time to time, rotate persons distributing the payroll.

b. The CPA reviews Pyzi's payroll procedures. An example of an internal control weakness is to assign to a department supervisor the responsibility for

(1) distributing payroll checks to subordinate employees.

(2) reviewing and approving time reports for subordinates.

(3) interviewing applicants for subordinate positions prior to hiring by the personnel department.

(4) initiating requests for salary adjustments for subordinate employees.

c. From the standpoint of good procedural control, distributing payroll checks to employees is best handled by the

(1) accounting department.

(2) personnel department.

(3) treasurer's department.

(4) employee's departmental supervisor.

d. To minimize the opportunity for fraud, unclaimed salary checks should be

(1) deposited in a special bank account.

(2) kept in the payroll department.

(3) left with the employee's supervisor.

(4) held for the employee in the personnel department.

(AICPA adapted)

14-17. Items a through i are selected questions typically found in internal control questionnaires used by auditors in evaluating controls in the payroll and personnel cycle. In using the questionnaire for a particular client, a yes response to a question indicates a possible strength in the system, whereas a no indicates a potential weakness.

a. Does an appropriate official authorize initial rates of pay and any subsequent change in rate?

b. Are written termination notices required that document reasons for termination?

c. Are formal records such as time clocks used for keeping time?

d. Is approval by a department head or foreman required for all time cards before they are submitted for payment?

e. Does anyone verify pay rates, overtime hours, and computations of gross payroll before payroll checks are prepared?

f. Does an adequate system exist for identifying jobs or products, such as work orders, job numbers, or some similar identification provided to employees to ensure proper coding of time records?

g. Are employees paid by checks prepared by persons independent of time-keeping?

h. Are employees required to show identification to receive paychecks?

i. Is a continuing record maintained of all unclaimed wages?

Required:

a. For each of the questions above, state the internal control objective(s) being fulfilled if the control is in effect.

b. For each control, list a compliance procedure to test its effectiveness.

c. For each of the questions above, identify the nature of the potential financial error(s) if the control is not in effect.

d. For each of the potential errors in part c, list a substantive audit procedure for determining whether a material error exists.

14–18. Following are some of the tests of transaction procedures frequently performed in the payroll and personnel cycle (each procedure is to be done on a sample basis).

a. Reconcile the monthly payroll total for direct manufacturing labor with labor cost distribution.

b. Examine the time card for the approval of a foreman.

c. Recompute hours on the time card and compare the total with the total hours for which the employee has been paid.

d. Compare the employee name, date, check number, and amounts on canceled checks with the payroll journal.

e. Trace the hours from the employee time cards to job tickets to make sure the total reconciles, and trace each job ticket to the job-cost record.

f. Account for a sequence of payroll checks in the payroll journal.

g. Select employees from the personnel file who have been terminated and determine whether their termination pay was in accordance with the union contract. As part of this procedure, examine two subsequent periods to determine whether the terminated employee is still being paid.

Required:

a. Identify whether each of the procedures is primarily a compliance or a substantive test.

b. State the purpose(s) of each of the procedures.

14–19. You are reviewing audit work papers containing a narrative description of the Tenney Corporation's factory payroll system. A portion of that narrative follows:

> Factory employees punch time clock cards each day when entering or leaving the shop. At the end of each week the timekeeping department collects the time cards and prepared duplicate batch-control slips by department showing total hours and number of employees. The time cards and original batch-control slips are sent to the payroll accounting section. The second copies of the batch-control slips are filed by date.
>
> In the payroll accounting section, payroll transaction cards are keypunched from the information on the time cards, and a batch total

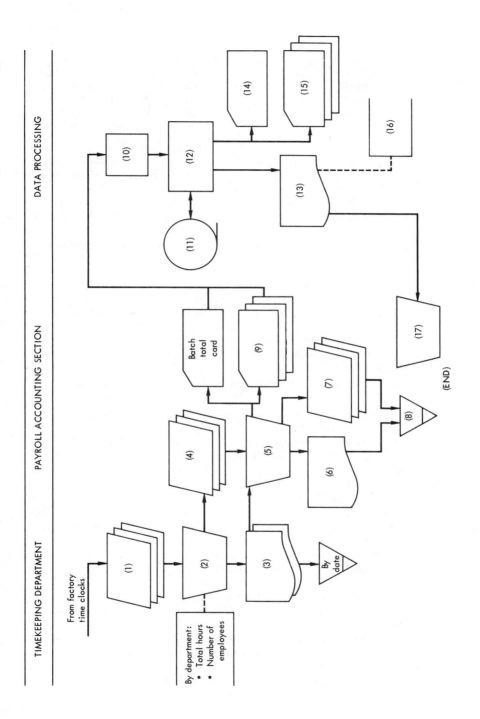

TIMEKEEPING DEPARTMENT   PAYROLL ACCOUNTING SECTION   DATA PROCESSING

From factory time clocks

By department:
• Total hours
• Number of employees

Batch total card

By date

(END)

card for each batch is keypunched from the batch-control slip. The time cards and batch-control slips are then filed by batch for possible reference. The payroll transaction cards and batch total card are sent to data processing where they are sorted by employee number within batch. Each batch is edited by a computer program which checks the validity of employee number against a master employee tape file and the total hours and number of employees against the batch total card. A detail printout by batch and employee number is produced which indicates batches that do not balance and invalid employee numbers. This printout is returned to payroll accounting to resolve all differences.

In searching for documentation you found a flowchart of the payroll system which included all appropriate symbols (American National Standards Institute, Inc.) but was only partially labeled. The portion of this flowchart described by the foregoing narrative appears on the preceding page.

Required:

a. Number your answers 1 through 17. Next to the corresponding number of your answer, supply the appropriate labeling (document name, process description, or file order) applicable to each numbered symbol on the flowchart.

b. Flowcharts are one of the aids an auditor may use to determine and evaluate a client's internal control system. List advantages of using flowcharts in this context.

c. List several internal control strengths in the client's payroll system.

(AICPA adapted)

14–20. The following errors or omissions are included in the accounting records of Lathen Manufacturing Company.

a. Direct labor was unintentionally charged to job 620 instead of job 602 by the payroll clerk when he posted the labor distribution sheets. Job 602 was completed and the costs were expensed in the current year, whereas job 620 was included in work in process.

b. Joe Block and Frank Demery take turns "punching in" for each other every few days. The absent employee comes in at noon and tells his foreman that he had car trouble or some other problem. The foreman does not know the employee is getting paid for the time.

c. The foreman submits a fictitious time card for a former employee each week and delivers the related payroll check to his house on the way home from work. They split the amount of the paycheck.

d. Employees frequently overlook recording their hours worked on job-cost tickets as required by the system. Many of the client's contracts are on a cost-plus basis.

e. The payroll clerk prepares a check to the same fictitious person every week, records the amount in the payroll journal, and submits it along with all other payroll checks for signature. When the checks are returned to him for distribution, he takes the check and deposits it in a special bank account bearing that person's name.

f. In withholding payroll taxes from employees, the payroll clerk deducts $.50 extra federal income taxes from several employees each week and credits the amount to his own employee earnings record.

g. The payroll clerk frequently forgets to record one or two checks in the payroll journal.

Required:

a. For each error, state a control that should have prevented the error from occurring on a continuing basis.

b. For each error, state a substantive audit procedure that could uncover the error.

14–21. In comparing total payroll tax expense with the preceding year, Merlin Brendin, CPA, observed a significant increase relative to the preceding year, even though the total number of employees had only increased from 175 to 195. To investigate the difference, he selected a large sample of payroll disbursement transactions and carefully tested the withholdings for each employee in the sample by referring to federal and state tax withholding schedules. In his test he found no exceptions; therefore, he concluded that payroll tax expense was fairly stated.

Required:

a. Evaluate Brendin's approach to testing payroll tax expense.

b. Discuss a more suitable approach for determining whether payroll tax expense was properly stated in the current year.

14–22. As part of the audit of McGree Plumbing and Heating, you have responsibility for testing the payroll and personnel cycle. Payroll is the largest single expense in the client's trial balance, and hourly wages make up most of the payroll total. A unique aspect of its business is the extensive overtime incurred by employees on some days. It is common for employees to work only three or four days during the week but to work long hours while they are on the job. McGree's management has found that this actually saves money, in spite of the large amount of overtime, because the union contract requires payment for all travel time. Since many of the employees' jobs require long travel times and extensive startup costs, this policy is supported by both McGree and the employees.

You have already carefully evaluated and tested the payroll system and concluded that it contains no significant weaknesses. Your tests included tests of the time cards, withholdings, pay rates, the filing of all required tax returns, payroll checks, and all other aspects of payroll.

As part of the year-end tests of payroll, you are responsible for verifying all accrued payroll as well as accrued withheld payroll taxes. The accrued factory payroll includes the last six working days of the current year. The client has calculated accrued wages by taking 60 percent of the subsequent period's gross payroll and has recorded it as an adjusting entry to be reversed in the subsequent period.

Required:

List all audit procedures you would follow in verifying accrued payroll, withheld payroll taxes, and accrued payroll taxes.

14–23. You have been retained by the Ratliff Construction Company to verify the payroll expenses charged to Ratliff by a subcontractor retained on a series of cost-plus contracts over a two-year period. The management of Ratliff believes the subcontractor may have charged excessive costs to several jobs in the past few months and wants you to examine the subcontractor's records. Ratliff's contract permits the review and audit of all subcontractors' records as long as the cost is borne by Ratliff.

In examining the subcontractor's system, you observe that all charges to Ratliff are based on daily prenumbered job sheets prepared by each employee. Each day the employee fills out a job sheet that includes the employee's number, the jobs worked on, the hours worked for each job, and the date. At the end of each week the job sheets become the basis for preparing the payroll record. After the payroll is prepared, a copy is made of the daily job sheets as a basis for accumulating the total hours worked for any job. A copy of the employee's job sheets is inserted in a job folder for each project he worked on during the day. If he worked on more than one job, multiple copies of the job sheet are prepared and the hours for each job are circled before they are inserted. At the completion of a project, the total hours included in the job folder are totaled and multiplied by a standard labor rate. This becomes the basis for billing the prime contractor. The standard labor rate is the average of the union rate for all employees.

In reviewing the system, you observe that the subcontractor provides services for several prime contractors under several different types of arrangements. In some cases the company also acts as a prime contractor.

Required:

a. List the audit procedures you would perform in the verification of payroll in this situation and state the reason for performing each procedure.
b. What kind of audit report would you issue to Ratliff?

14–24. In the audit of Larnet Manufacturing Company, the auditor concluded that the system of internal control was inadequate because of the lack of segregation of duties. As a result, the decision was made to have a surprise payroll payoff one month before the client's balance sheet date. Since the auditor had never been involved in a payroll payoff, she did not know how to proceed.

Required:

a. What is the purpose of a surprise payroll payoff?
b. What other audit procedures can the auditor perform that may fulfill the same objectives?
c. Discuss the control procedures the auditor should require the client to observe when the surprise payroll payoff is taking place.

d. At the completion of the payroll payoff, there are frequently several unclaimed checks. What procedures should be followed for these?

14–25. The Kowal Manufacturing Company employs about 50 production workers and has the following payroll procedures:

The factory foreman interviews applicants and on the basis of the interview either hires or rejects the applicants. When the applicant is hired he prepares a W-4 form (Employee's Withholding Exemption Certificate) and gives it to the foreman. The foreman writes the hourly rate of pay for the new employee in the corner of the W-4 form and then gives the form to a payroll clerk as notice that the worker has been employed. The foreman verbally advises the payroll department of rate adjustments.

A supply of blank time cards is kept in a box near the entrance to the factory. Each worker takes a time card on Monday morning, fills in his name, and notes in pencil on the time card his daily arrival and departure times. At the end of the week the workers drop the time cards in a box near the door to the factory.

The completed time cards are taken from the box on Monday morning by a payroll clerk. Two payroll clerks divide the cards alphabetically between them, one taking the A to L section of the payroll and the other taking the M to Z section. Each clerk is fully responsible for her section of the payroll. She computes the gross pay, deductions, and net pay, posts the details to the employee's earnings records, and prepares and numbers the payroll checks. Employees are automatically removed from the payroll when they fail to turn in a time card.

The payroll checks are manually signed by the chief accountant and given to the foreman. The foreman distributes the checks to the workers in the factory and arranges for the delivery of the checks to the workers who are absent. The payroll bank account is reconciled by the chief accountant, who also prepares the various quarterly and annual payroll tax reports.

Required:

a. List the most serious weaknesses in the system of internal control and state the errors that are likely to result from the weaknesses. In your audit of Kowal's payroll, what will you emphasize in your audit tests? Explain.

b. List your suggestions for improving the Kowal Manufacturing Company's system of internal control for the factory hiring practices and payroll procedures.
(AICPA adapted)

14–26. During the first-year audit of Jones Wholesale Stationery you observe that commissions amount to almost 25 percent of total sales, which is somewhat higher than in previous years. Further investigation reveals that the industry typically has larger sales commissions than Jones and that there is significant variation in rates depending on the product sold.

At the time a sale is made, the salesperson records his commission rate and the total amount of the commissions on the office copy of the sales invoice. When sales are recorded in the sales journal, the debit to sales commission expense and credit to accrued sales commission are also recorded. As part of recording the sales and sales commission expense, the accounts receivable clerk verifies the prices, quantities, commission rates, and all calculations on the sales invoices. When the sale is posted to the customer accounts receivable subsidiary ledger, the sales commission is posted to a salesperson's commission ledger. On the fifteenth day after the end of the month the salesperson is paid for the preceding month's sales commissions.

Required:

a. Develop an audit program to verify sales commission expense, assuming that no audit tests have been conducted in any audit area to this point.

b. Develop an audit program to verify accrued sales commissions at the end of the year, assuming that the tests you designed in part a resulted in no significant errors.

14-27. During your audit of the accounts of the Gelard Manufacturing Corporation, your assistant tells you that he has found errors in the computation of the wages of factory workers and he wants you to verify his work.

Your assistant has extracted from the union contract the following description of the systems for computing wages in various departments of the company. The contract provides that the minimum wage for a worker is his base rate, which is also paid for any "downtime," time when the worker's machine is under repair or he is without work. The standard work week is 40 hours. The union contract also provides that workers be paid 150 percent of base rates for overtime production. The company is engaged in interstate commerce.

1. *Straight piecework.* The worker is paid at the rate of $.20 per piece produced.

2. *Percentage bonus plan.* Standard quantities of production per hour are established by the engineering department. The worker's average hourly production, determined from his total hours worked and his production, is divided by the standard quantity of production to determine his efficiency ratio. The efficiency ratio is then applied to his base rate to determined his hourly earnings for the period.

3. *Emerson Efficiency System.* A minimum wage is paid for production up to $66\frac{2}{3}$ percent of standard output or "efficiency." When the worker's production exceeds $66\frac{2}{3}$ percent of the standard output, he is paid at a bonus rate. The bonus rate is determined from the following table:

Efficiency (%)	Bonus (%)
Up to $66\frac{2}{3}$	0
$66\frac{2}{3}$–79	10
80–99	20
100–125	45

Your assistant has prepared the following schedule of information pertaining to certain workers for a weekly payroll selected for examination:

Worker	Wage Incentive Plan	Total Hours	Down-time Hours	Units Pro-duced	Stan-dard Units	Base Rate	Gross Wages per Books
Long	Straight piecework	40	5	400	—	$1.80	$ 82.00
Loro	Straight piecework	46	—	455*	—	1.80	91.00
Huck	Straight piecework	44	4	420†	—	1.80	84.00
Nini	Percentage bonus plan	40	—	250	200	2.20	120.00
Boro	Percentage bonus plan	40	—	180	200	1.90	67.00
Wiss	Emerson	40	—	240	300	2.10	92.00
Alan	Emerson	40	2	590	600‡	2.00	118.00

*Includes 45 pieces produced during the 6 overtime hours.
†Includes 50 pieces produced during the 4 overtime hours. The overtime, which was brought about by the "downtime," was necessary to meet a production deadline.
‡Standard units for 40 hours of production.

Required:

a. Prepare a schedule comparing each individual's gross wages per books and his gross wages per your calculation. Computations of workers' wages should be in good form and labeled with the workers' names.

b. All the errors described above, as well as others, were found in a weekly payroll selected for examination. The total number of errors was substantial. Discuss the courses of action you can take.

14-28. You are engaged in auditing the financial statements of Henry Brown, a large independent contractor. All employees are paid in cash because Brown believes this arrangement reduces clerical expenses and is preferred by his employees.

During the audit you find in the petty cash fund approximately $200, of which $185 is stated to be unclaimed wages. Further investigation reveals that Brown has installed the procedure of putting any unclaimed wages in the petty cash fund so that the cash can be used for disbursements. When the claimant to the wages appears, he is paid from the petty cash fund. Brown contends that this procedure reduces the number of checks drawn to replenish the petty cash fund and centers the responsibility for all cash on hand in one person inasmuch as the petty cash custodian distributes the pay envelopes.

Required:

a. Does Brown's system provide proper internal control of unclaimed wages? Explain fully.

b. Because Brown insists on paying salaries in cash, what procedures would you recommend to provide better internal control over unclaimed wages?

(AICPA adapted)

14-29. In many companies, labor costs represent a substantial percentage of total dollars expended in any one accounting period. One of the auditor's primary means of verifying payroll transactions is by a detailed payroll test.

You are making an annual examination of the Joplin Company, a medium-sized manufacturing company. You have selected a number of hourly employees for a detailed payroll test. The following worksheet outline has been prepared.

Column Number	Column Heading
1	Employee number
2	Employee name
3	Job classification
	Hours worked
4	Straight time
5	Premium time
6	Hourly rate
7	Gross earnings
	Deductions
8	FICA withheld
9	FIT withheld
10	Union dues
11	Hospitalization
12	Amount of check
13	Check number
14	Account number charged
15	Description of account

Required:

a. What factors should the auditor consider in selecting his sample of employees to be included in any payroll test?

b. Using the column numbers above as a reference, state the principal way(s) that the information in each column would be verified.

c. In addition to the payroll test, the auditor employs a number of other audit procedures in the verification of payroll transactions. List five additional procedures that may be employed.   (AICPA adapted)

14–30. The Generous Loan Company has 100 branch loan offices. Each office has a manager and four or five subordinates who are employed by the manager. Branch managers prepare the weekly payroll, including their own salaries, and pay employees from cash on hand. The employee signs the payroll sheet signifying receipt of his salary. Hours worked by hourly personnel are inserted in the payroll sheet from time cards prepared by the employees and approved by the manager.

The weekly payroll sheets are sent to the home office along with other accounting statements and reports. The home office compiles employee earnings records and prepares all federal and state salary reports from the weekly payroll sheets.

Salaries are established by home office job-evaluation schedules. Salary adjustments, promotions, and transfers of full-time employees are approved by a home office salary committee based upon the recommendations of branch managers and area supervisors. Branch managers advise the salary committee of new full-time employees and terminations. Part-time and temporary employees are hired without referral to the salary committee.

Required:

a. Based upon your review of the payroll system, how might funds for payroll be diverted?

b. Prepare a payroll audit program to be used in the home office to audit the branch office payrolls of the Generous Loan Company.

(AICPA adapted)

15

AUDIT
OF THE ACQUISITION
AND PAYMENT CYCLE

The third major transaction cycle discussed in this text is the acquisition of and payment for goods and services from outsiders. The acquisition of goods and services includes such items as the purchase of raw materials, equipment, supplies, utilities, repairs and maintenance, and research and development. The cycle does not include the acquisition and payment of employees' services or the internal transfers and allocations of costs within the organization. The former are a part of the payroll and personnel function, and the latter are audited as a part of the verification of individual assets or liabilities. The acquisition and payment cycle also excludes the acquisition and repayment of capital (interest-bearing debt and owner's equity), which are considered separately in Chapter 18.

The audit of the acquisition and payment cycle is studied in Chapters 15 and 16. In this chapter the basic format for discussing internal control cycles introduced in Chapter 9 and used again in Chapter 14 is repeated. The first part of the chapter deals with the nature of the acquisition and payment cycle, including documents and records, and primary functions and internal controls. The second part discusses tests of transactions for the cycle related to key internal controls. The third and final part covers direct tests of accounts payable, the major balance sheet account in the cycle. This last part gives special emphasis to the relationship between the tests of transactions and the direct tests performed. In Chapter 16 several other important balance sheet accounts which are a part of the acquisition and payment cycle are examined. These are manufacturing equipment, prepaid insurance, and accrued property taxes. The chapter also takes up direct tests of the income statement accounts included in the acquisition and payment cycle.

The large number and different types of accounts included in the acquisition and payment cycle distinguishes it from the other two previously studied cycles. For example, here are a few of the account titles the auditor is concerned with in a typical manufacturing company besides those indicated above:

- Raw material inventory
- Office supplies
- Rent
- Legal expense
- Fines and penalties
- Leasehold improvements
- Repairs and maintenance
- Insurance expense
- Officers' travel
- Accrued personal property taxes
- Retirement benefits
- Utilities

The way the accounting information flows through the various accounts in the acquisition and payment cycle is illustrated by T-accounts in Figure 15-1. To keep the illustration manageable, only the control accounts are shown for the three major categories of expenses used by most companies. For each control account, examples of the subsidiary expense accounts are also given.

Figure 15-1 shows that every transaction is either debited or credited to accounts payable. Because many companies make some purchases directly by check or through petty cash, the overview is an oversimplification. We assume that cash transactions are processed in the same manner as all others.

NATURE OF THE ACQUISITION AND PAYMENT CYCLE

The acquisition and payment cycle involves the decisions and processes necessary for obtaining the goods and services for operating a business. The cycle typically begins with the initiation of a purchase requisition by an authorized employee who needs the goods or services and ends with the payment for the benefits received. Although the discussion that follows deals with a small manufacturing company that makes tangible products for sale to third parties, the same principles apply to a service company, a government unit, or any other type of organization.

The *functions* and *flow of documents* for the acquisition and payment cycle of a typical manufacturing company are illustrated in Figure 15-2. The overview flowchart is meant to show how the information in Figure 15-1

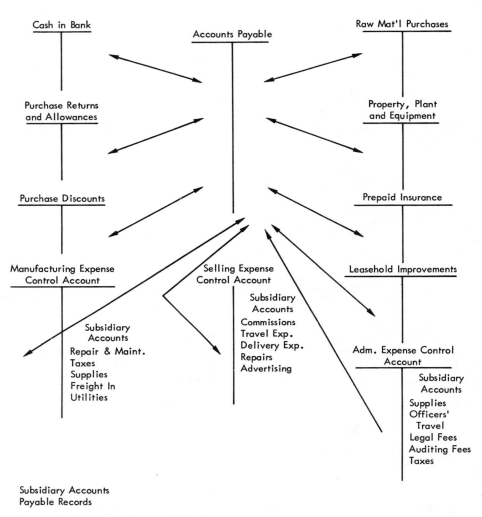

Cash in Bank

Accounts Payable

Raw Mat'l Purchases

Purchase Returns
and Allowances

Property, Plant
and Equipment

Purchase Discounts

Prepaid Insurance

Manufacturing Expense
Control Account

Selling Expense
Control Account

Leasehold Improvements

Subsidiary
Accounts
Repair & Maint.
Taxes
Supplies
Freight In
Utilities

Subsidiary
Accounts
Commissions
Travel Exp.
Delivery Exp.
Repairs
Advertising

Adm. Expense Control
Account

Subsidiary
Accounts
Supplies
Officers'
Travel
Legal Fees
Auditing Fees
Taxes

Subsidiary Accounts
Payable Records

Includes beginning balance, acquisitions,
payments, and the ending balance for each
customer. The total of all customer
balances equals the total in the accounts
payable control account.

FIGURE 15–1 Accounts in the Acquisition and Payment Cycle

is generated by a system. Many of the controls ordinarily integrated into a
system are not included at this point.

Documents and Records

To support the record flow in the acquisition and payment cycle, several
important documents and records are used:

502

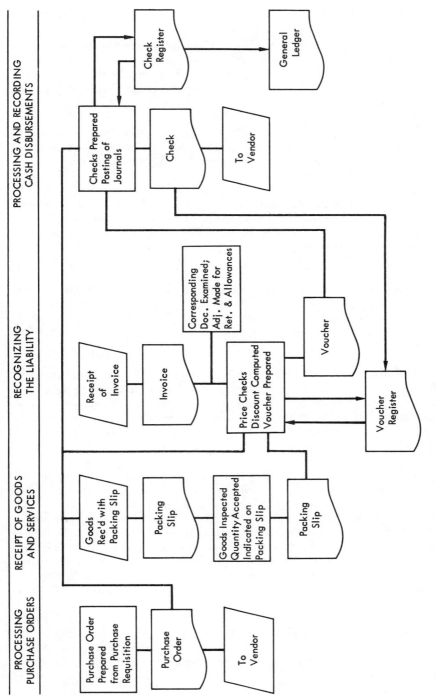

FIGURE 15-2 Flowchart of the Acquisition and Payment Cycle

503

Purchase Requisition. A request for goods and services by an authorized employee. It may take the form of a request for such acquisitions as materials by a foreman or the storeroom supervisor, outside repairs by office or factory personnel, or insurance by the vice-president in charge of property and equipment.

Purchase Order. A document recording the description, quantity, and related information for goods and services the company intends to purchase. This document is frequently used to indicate authorization to procure goods and services.

Receiving Report. A document prepared at the time tangible goods are received which indicates the description of goods, the quantity received, the date received, and other relevant data. The receipt of goods and services in the normal course of business represents the date clients normally recognize the liability for an acquisition.

Vendor's Invoice. A document that indicates such things as the description and quantity of goods and services received, the price including freight, the cash discount terms, and the date of the billing. It is an essential document because it specifies the amount of money owed to the vendor for an acquisition.

Voucher. A document frequently used by organizations to establish a formal means of recording and controlling acquisitions. Vouchers are the basis not only for recording acquisitions in the voucher register or purchase journal but also for making cash disbursements. Typically, the original copy of the voucher has a copy of the vendor's invoice, receiving report, and purchase order attached.

Voucher Register. A journal for recording the vouchers for the acquisition of goods and services. It usually includes several classifications for the most significant types of acquisitions, such as the purchase of inventory, repairs and maintenance, and supplies. There is also a column for miscellaneous debits and credits, and of course there must be a column for the credit to accounts payable. Individual transactions can be recorded in the voucher register, or several vouchers can be combined and recorded in summary form. When a voucher register is not used, the journal for recording acquisition transactions remains substantially unchanged, but it is called an *accounts payable journal* or *purchase journal*.

Check. The means of paying for the acquisition when payment is due. After the check is signed by an authorized person, it is an asset. When cashed by the vendor and cleared by the client's bank, it is referred to as a canceled check.

Cash Disbursements Journal. A journal for recording disbursements by check. It indicates the total cash paid, the debit to accounts payable at the amount for which the transaction being paid was recorded in the voucher register, the discounts taken, and other debits and credits. The daily entries in the cash disbursements journal are supported by canceled checks.

Accounts Payable Subsidiary Ledger. A subsidiary ledger for recording the individual acquisitions, cash disbursements, and total balance due to each vendor. The total from the individual ledgers equals the total balance in accounts payable. Many companies do not maintain a formal accounts payable subsidiary ledger. These companies ordinarily pay on the basis of individual vouchers; therefore, the total of the unpaid vouchers equals the total accounts payable.

Vendor's Statement. A statement prepared monthly by the vendor indicating the beginning balance, acquisitions, payments to the vendor, and ending balance. These balances and activities are the vendor's representations of the transactions for the period and not the client's. Hence, except for disputed amounts and timing differences, the client's accounts payable subsidiary ledger should be the same as the vendor's statement.

Functions in the Cycle and Internal Controls

A discussion of the primary functions in the acquisition and payment cycle will clarify what the auditor is trying to accomplish in the audit of the cycle. Four functions are involved:

- Processing purchase orders
- Receipt of goods and services
- Recognizing the liability
- Processing and recording cash disbursements

These functions are discussed in the order of their occurrence in a typical transaction cycle (see Figure 15-2). The emphasis is on the most important controls used to prevent errors in processing data and to ensure safety of assets.

Processing Purchase Orders. The request for goods or services by the client's personnel is the starting point for the cycle. The exact form of the request and the required approval depends upon the nature of the goods and services and the company policy.

Proper *authorization* for acquisitions is an essential part of this function because it ensures that the goods and services purchased are for authorized company purposes and it avoids the purchase of excessive or unnecessary items. Most companies permit general authorization for the purchase of regular operating needs such as inventory at one level and acquisitions of capital assets or similar items at another. For example, purchases of permanent assets in excess of a specified dollar limit may require board of director action; items purchased relatively infrequently, such as insurance policies and long-term service contracts, are approved by certain officers; supplies and services costing less than a designated amount are approved by foremen and department heads; and some types of raw materials and supplies are reordered automatically whenever they fall to a predetermined level. After the acquisition has been approved, there must be an *initiation of an order* to purchase the goods or services. An order is issued to a vendor for a specified item at a certain price to be delivered at or by a designated time. The order is usually in writing and is a legal document that is an offer to buy. For most routine items, a purchase order is used to indicate the offer.

It is common for companies to establish purchasing departments to ensure an adequate quality of goods and services at a minimum price. For good internal control, the purchasing department should not be responsible for authorizing the acquisition or receiving of the goods. All purchase orders should be prenumbered and should include sufficient columns and spaces to minimize the likelihood of unintentional omissions on the form when goods are ordered.

Receipt of Goods and Services. The receipt by the company of goods or services from the vendor is a critical point in the cycle because it is the point at which most companies first recognize the associated liability on their records. When goods are received, adequate control requires examination for description, quantity, timely arrival, and condition.

Most companies have the receiving department initiate a receiving report as evidence of the receipt and examination of the goods. One copy is normally sent to the storeroom and another to the accounts payable department for their information needs. To prevent theft and misuse, it is important that the goods be *physically controlled* from the time of their receipt until they are disposed of. The personnel in the receiving department should be independent of the storeroom personnel and the accounting department. Finally, the accounting records should transfer responsibility for the goods as they are transferred from receiving to storage and from storage to manufacturing.

Recognizing the Liability. The proper recognition of the liability for the receipt of goods and services requires *accurate and prompt* recording. The initial recording has a significant effect on the recorded financial statements and the actual cash disbursement; therefore, great care must be taken to include only valid company acquisitions at the correct amount.

The accounts payable department typically has the responsibility for verifying the propriety of acquisitions and for recording them in the voucher register or accounts payable journal. When the accounts payable department receives a vendor's invoice, a comparison should be made of the descriptions, prices, quantities, terms, and freight on the invoice with the information on the purchase order and, where applicable, the receiving report. Typically, extensions and footings are verified, and account distribution is entered on the invoice. If a voucher system is used, the documents are assigned a voucher number. Next, the acquisition transaction is recorded in the voucher register as a liability and an expense or asset, and the amount is posted in the accounts payable subsidiary record.

An important control in the accounts payable department is to require that those personnel who record disbursements of cash *do not have access* to cash, marketable securities, and other assets, Adequate documents and records, proper procedures for record keeping, and independent checks on performance are also necessary controls in the accounts payable function.

Processing and Recording Cash Disbursements. For most companies, the vouchers are held by the accounts payable department until the time of payment. Payment is usually made by check in a multicopy format, with the original going to the payee, one copy filed with the voucher, and another filed alphabetically by payee. In most cases individual checks are recorded in the cash disbursements journal, but sometimes a numerical file of check copies is maintained which serves as a cash disbursements journal.

The most important controls in the cash disbursements function include the signing of checks by an individual with proper authority, separation of responsibilities for signing the checks and performing the accounts payable function, and careful examination of the supporting documentation by the check signer at the time the check is signed.

The checks should be prenumbered and printed on special paper that makes it difficult to alter the name or amount. Care should be taken to physically control blank, voided, and signed checks before they are mailed. It is also important to have a method of canceling the supporting documents to prevent their reuse as support for another check at a later time. A common method is to write the check number on the supporting documents.

TESTS OF TRANSACTIONS

The most time-consuming accounts to verify by direct tests of financial balances in a typical audit are accounts receivable, inventory, permanent assets, accounts payable, and expense accounts. Of these five accounts, four are directly related to the acquisition and payment cycle. The net time savings can be dramatic if the auditor can reduce the direct tests in the accounts by spending time verifying the effectiveness of the acquisition system by tests of transactions. It should not be surprising, therefore, that tests of transactions for the acquisition and payment cycle receive a considerable amount of attention in well-conducted audits, especially when the client has effective controls.

The tests of transactions for the acquisition and payment cycle are divided into the two broad areas of *tests of acquisitions* and *tests of payments*. The acquisition tests concern three of the four functions discussed earlier in the chapter: processing purchase orders, receipt of goods and services, and recognizing the liability. The tests of payments concern the fourth function, processing and recording cash disbursements. The eight objectives previously used for other cycles provide the frame of reference for discussing the audit procedures for these two areas.

Tests for Verifying Acquisitions

Key internal controls, common compliance tests, and common substantive tests for each of the internal control and audit objectives are included in Figure 15-3. An assumption underlying the internal controls and audit procedures is the existence of a separate purchase journal for recording all acquisitions.

For each objective, the auditor must go through the same process of logic that has been discussed in previous chapters. First he must understand the system to determine which controls exist. After the auditor is aware of all existing controls for the objective, he can make a preliminary evaluation of the strengths and weaknesses of the system. At this point he must make a decision as to which strengths (controls) he intends to rely on to reduce substantive tests. These controls must be tested for compliance and evaluated for effectiveness. The substantive tests can be determined for the objective largely on the basis of this evaluation. After the auditor has developed the audit procedures for each of the objectives, the procedures can be combined into an audit program that can be efficiently performed.

In studying the summary in Figure 15-3, it is important to relate internal controls to audit objectives, compliance tests to internal controls, and substantive tests to audit objectives and strengths and weaknesses in the system. It should be kept in mind that a set of procedures for a particular audit engagement will vary with the internal controls and other circumstances.

Four of the eight audit objectives for acquisitions deserve special attention. A discussion of each of these four essential objectives follows:

Recorded Acquisitions Are for Goods and Services Received, Consistent with the Best Interests of the Client (Validity). If the auditor is satisfied that the controls are adequate for this objective, tests for improper and invalid transactions can be greatly reduced. Adequate controls are likely to prevent the client from including as a business expense or asset those transactions that primarily benefit management or other employees rather than the entity being audited. In some instances improper transactions are obvious, such as the acquisition of unauthorized personal items by employees or the actual embezzlement of cash by recording a fraudulent purchase in the voucher register. In other instances the propriety of a transaction is more difficult to evaluate, such as the payment of officers' memberships to country clubs, expense-paid vacations to foreign countries for members of management and their families, and management-approved illegal payments to officials of foreign countries. If the controls over improper or invalid transactions are inadequate, extensive examination of supporting documentation is necessary.

FIGURE 15–3

Summary of Tests of Acquisitions

Internal Control and Audit Objectives	Key Internal Controls	Common Compliance Tests	Common Substantive Tests
Acquisition transactions as recorded are reasonable.	• Acquisition transactions are periodically reviewed by an independent person for reasonableness.	• Inquiry of independent person and examination of reports and recommendations prepared by reviewer.	• Review the purchases journal, general ledger, and accounts payable subsidiary records for large or unusual amounts.
Recorded acquisitions are for goods and services received, consistent with the best interests of the client (validity).	• Existence of purchase requisition, purchase order, receiving report, and vendor's invoice attached to the voucher.	• Examine documents in voucher for existence.	• Examine underlying documents for reasonableness and authenticity (vendor's invoices, receiving reports, purchase orders, and requisitions).
	• Approval of acquisitions at the proper level.	• Examine indication of approval.	• Trace inventory purchases to perpetual records.
	• Cancelation of documents to prevent their reuse.	• Examine indication of cancelation.	• Examine permanent assets acquired.
	• Internal verification of vendor's invoices, receiving reports, purchase orders, and purchase requisitions.	• Examine indication of internal verification.	
Acquisition transactions are authorized.	• Approval of acquisitions at the proper level.	• Examine indication of approval.	• Examine supporting documentation for propriety.
Existing acquisition transactions are recorded.	• Purchase orders are prenumbered and accounted for.	• Account for a sequence of purchase orders.	• Trace from a file of receiving reports to the purchases journal.
	• Receiving reports are prenumbered and accounted for.	• Account for a sequence of receiving reports.	• Trace from a file of vouchers to the purchases journal.
	• Vouchers are prenumbered and accounted for.	• Account for a sequence of vouchers.	

FIGURE 15-3 (cont.)

Internal Control and Audit Objectives	Key Internal Controls	Common Compliance Tests	Common Substantive Tests
Recorded acquisition transactions are correctly valued.	• Internal verification of calculations and amounts.	• Examine indication of internal verification.	• Compare recorded transactions in the purchases journal with the vendor's invoice, receiving report, and other supporting documentation. • Recompute the clerical accuracy on vendor's invoices, including discounts and freight.
Acquisition transactions are properly classified.	• Adequate chart of accounts. • Internal verification of classification.	• Examine procedures manual and chart of accounts. • Examine indication of internal verification.	• Compare classification with chart of accounts by reference to vendor's invoices.
Acquisitions are recorded on a timely basis.	• Procedures require recording transactions as soon as possible after the goods and services have been received. • Internal verification.	• Examine procedures manual and observe whether unrecorded vendor's invoices exist. • Examine indication of internal verification.	• Compare dates of receiving reports and vendor's invoices with dates in the purchase journal.
Acquisition transactions are properly included in the accounts payable and inventory subsidiaries; they are properly summarized.	• Internal verification.	• Examine indication of internal verification.	• Test clerical accuracy, e.g., footing journals and tracing postings to general ledger and accounts payable and inventory subsidiaries.

Existing Acquisitions Are Recorded.   Failure to record the acquisition of goods and services received directly affects the balance in accounts payable. The auditor can rely on the system and thereby reduce the direct tests of accounts payable if he is confident that all acquisitions are recorded on a timely and accurate basis. Since the audit of accounts payable generally takes a considerable amount of audit time, the reliance on existing controls can significantly reduce audit costs.

When a client uses a perpetual inventory system, the tests of inventory can also be significantly reduced if the auditor believes the perpetuals are reliable. The controls over the acquisitions included in the perpetuals are normally tested as a part of the tests of transactions for acquisitions, and the controls over this objective play a key role in the audit. The inclusion of both quantity and unit costs in the inventory perpetual records permits a reduction in the tests of the physical count and the unit costs of inventory if the controls are operating effectively.

Acquisitions Are Correctly Valued.   Since the valuation of many asset, liability, and expense accounts depends on the correct recording of transactions in the purchase journal, the extent of direct tests of many balance sheet and expense accounts depends on the auditor's evaluation of the effectiveness of the internal controls over the correct valuation of acquisition transactions. For example, if the auditor believes the permanent assets are correctly valued in the books of original entry, it is acceptable to vouch fewer current period acquisitions than if the controls are inadequate.

Acquisitions Are Correctly Classified.   The auditor can reduce the direct tests of certain individual accounts if he believes the system is adequate to provide reasonable assurance of correct classification in the purchase journal. Although all accounts are affected to some degree by effective controls over classification, the two areas most affected are current period acquisitions of permanent assets and all expense accounts arising from the voucher register, such as repairs and maintenance, utilities, and advertising. Since vouching of current period permanent asset acquisitions for valuation and classification and verifying the classification of expense accounts are relatively time-consuming audit procedures, the saving in audit time can be significant.

Audit Procedures for Verifying Cash Disbursements

The basic format used for acquisitions is also used in Figure 15-4 for the internal controls and tests of transaction procedures for cash disbursements. The assumption underlying these controls and audit procedures is the existence of a separate cash disbursements and purchase journal. The comments previously made about the methodology and process for developing audit procedures for acquisitions apply equally to cash disbursements.

Once the auditor has decided on procedures, the acquisition and cash disbursements tests are typically performed concurrently. For example,

FIGURE 15-4

Summary of Tests of Cash Disbursements

Internal Control and Audit Objectives	Key Internal Controls	Common Compliance Tests	Common Substantive Tests
Cash disbursement transactions are recorded are reasonable.	• Cash disbursement transactions are periodically reviewed by an independent person for reasonableness.	• Inquiry of independent person and examination of reports and recommendations prepared by reviewer.	• Compare classification with chart of accounts by reference to vendor's invoices.
Recorded cash disbursements are for goods and services actually received.	• Adequate segregation of duties between accounts payable and custody of signed checks. • Examination of supporting documentation before signing of checks by an authorized person. • Internal verification.	• Discuss with personnel and observe activities. • Discuss with personnel and observe activities. • Examine indication of internal verification.	• Trace the canceled check to the related purchases journal entry and examine for payee name and amount. • Examine canceled check for authorized signature, proper endorsement, and cancellation by the bank.
Recorded cash disbursement transactions are properly authorized.	• Approval of payment on supporting documents at the time checks are signed.	• Examine indication of approval.	• Examine supporting documents as a part of the tests of acquisitions.
Existing cash disbursement transactions are recorded.	• Checks are prenumbered and accounted for. • A bank reconciliation is prepared monthly by an employee independent of recording cash disbursements or custody of assets.	• Account for a sequence of checks. • Examine bank reconciliations and observe their preparation.	• Reconcile recorded cash disbursements with the cash disbursements on the bank statement (proof of cash disbursements).

FIGURE 15-4 (cont.)

Internal Control and Audit Objectives	Key Internal Controls	Common Compliance Tests	Common Substantive Tests
Recorded cash disbursement transactions are properly valued.	• Internal verification of calculations and amounts. • Monthly preparation of a bank reconciliation by an independent person.	• Examine indication of approval. • Examine bank reconciliations and observe their preparation.	• Compare canceled checks with the related purchase journal and cash disbursements journal entries. • Recompute cash discounts. • Prepare a proof of cash disbursements.
Cash disbursement transactions are properly classified.	• Adequate chart of accounts. • Internal verification of classification.	• Examine procedures manual and chart of accounts. • Examine indication of internal verification.	• Compare classification with chart of accounts by reference to vendor's invoices and purchase journal.
Cash disbursements are recorded on a timely basis.	• Procedures require recording of transactions as soon as possible after the check has been signed. • Internal verification.	• Examine procedures manual and observe whether unrecorded checks exist. • Examine indication of internal verification.	• Compare dates on canceled checks with the cash disbursements journal.
			• Compare dates on canceled checks with the bank cancelation date.
Cash disbursement transactions are properly included in the accounts payable subsidiary; they are properly summarized.	• Internal verification.	• Examine indication of internal verification.	• Test clerical accuracy, e.g., footing journals and tracing postings to general ledger and accounts payable subsidiary.

for a transaction selected for examination from the purchase journal, the vendor's invoice and the receiving report are examined at the same time as the related canceled check. Thus, the verification is speeded up without reducing the effectiveness of the tests.

Attributes Sampling for Tests of Acquisition and Payment Transactions

Because of the importance of tests of transactions for acquisitions and payments, the use of attributes sampling is common in this audit area. The approach to using attributes sampling for tests of acquisitions and payments is basically the same as for the tests of sales transactions discussed in Chapter 10. It should be noted, however, with particular reference to the most essential objectives presented earlier, that most of the important attributes in the acquisition and payment cycle have a direct monetary effect on the accounts. Further, many of the types of errors that might be found represent a misstatement of earnings and are of significant concern to the auditor. For example, there may be inventory cutoff errors, or direct misrecording of an expense amount. Because of this, the desired upper precision limit selected by the auditor in tests of many of the attributes in this cycle is relatively low. Since the amounts of individual transactions in the cycle cover a wide range, it is also common to segregate very large and unusual items and test them on a 100 percent basis.

ACCOUNTS PAYABLE

Accounts payable are *unpaid obligations* for goods and services received in the ordinary course of business. It is sometimes difficult to distinguish between accounts payable and accrued liabilities, but it is useful to define a liability as an accounts payable if the total amount of the obligation is *known and owed at the balance sheet date*. The accounts payable account therefore includes obligations for the acquisition of raw materials, equipment, utilities, repairs, and many other types of goods and services that were received before the end of the year. The great majority of accounts payable can also be recognized by the existence of vendor's invoices for the obligation. Accounts payable should also be distinguished from interest-bearing obligations. If an obligation includes the payment of interest, it should properly be recorded as a note payable, contract payable, mortgage payable, or bond.

Internal Controls

The effect of the client's internal controls in the acquisition and payment cycle on accounts payable tests can be illustrated by two examples. In the first example, assume the client has a highly effective system of recording and paying for acquisitions. The receipt of goods is promptly documented by prenumbered receiving reports; prenumbered vouchers are promptly and efficiently prepared and recorded in the voucher register and the accounts payable subsidiary ledger. Payments are also made promptly when due, and the disbursements are immediately recorded in the cash disbursements journal and the accounts payable subsidiary records. On a monthly basis, individual accounts payable subsidiary records are reconciled with vendors' statements, and the total is compared with the general ledger by an independent person. Under these circumstances, the verification of accounts payable should require little audit effort once the auditor concludes that the system is operating effectively. In the second example, assume the client defers recording acquisitions until cash disbursements are made, receiving reports are not used, and, because of a weak cash position, bills are frequently paid several months after their due date. When an auditor faces such a situation, there is a high likelihood of an understatement of accounts payable; therefore, under these circumstances, extensive direct tests are necessary to determine whether accounts payable is properly stated at the balance sheet date.

The most important controls over accounts payable have already been discussed as a part of the acquisition and payment cycle. In addition to those controls, it is important to have a monthly reconciliation of vendors' statements with recorded liabilities and subsidiary records with the general ledger. This should be done by an independent person.

Overall Audit Objectives

The overall audit objective in the audit of accounts payable is to determine whether accounts payable is fairly stated and properly disclosed. Eight of the nine detailed objectives discussed in Chapter 6 are applicable to accounts payable (liabilities cannot be owned).

The auditor should recognize the difference in emphasis between the audit of liabilities and the audit of assets. When assets are being verified, attention is focused on making certain that the balance in the account is not overstated. The validity of recorded assets is constantly questioned and verified by confirmation, physical examination, and examination of supporting documents. The auditor should certainly not ignore the possibility of assets being understated, but the fact remains that the auditor is more concerned about the possibility of overstatement than understatement. The opposite approach is taken in verifying liability balances; that is, the main focus is on the discovery of understated or omitted liabilities.

The difference in emphasis in auditing assets and liabilities results directly from the *legal liability of CPAs*. If equity investors, creditors, and other users determine subsequent to the issuance of the audited financial statements that owner's equity was materially overstated, a lawsuit against the CPA firm is fairly likely. Since an overstatement of owner's equity can arise either from an overstatement of assets or from an understatement of liabilities, it is natural for CPAs to emphasize those two types of misstatements. The probability of a successful lawsuit against a CPA for failing to discover an understatement of owner's equity is far less likely.

Nevertheless, the auditing profession must avoid too much emphasis on protecting users from overstatements of owner's equity at the expense of ignoring understatements. If assets are consistently understated and liabilities are consistently overstated for large numbers of audited companies, the decision-making value of financial statement information is likely to decline. Therefore, even though it is natural for auditors to emphasize the possibility of overstating assets and understating liabilities, the uncovering of the opposite types of misstatements is also a significant responsibility.

Audit Tests of Accounts Payable

The same detailed audit objectives, with minor modifications, that were used as a frame of reference for verifying accounts receivable in Chapter 11 are also applicable to liabilities. The most obvious difference in verifying liabilities is the nonapplicability of the ownership objective. Ownership is an important part of verifying assets, but not of verifying liabilities. The second difference was discussed above: in auditing liabilities, the emphasis is on the search for understatements rather than for overstatements.

The usual starting point for tests of accounts payable is a *list* of accounts payable provided to the auditor by the client. That list is the frame of reference in the audit program.

Figure 15-5 includes the detailed objectives and common internal controls for accounts payable. The actual audit procedures will vary considerably depending on the materiality of accounts payable, the nature and effectiveness of the system of internal control, and the other factors discussed in Chapter 4.

Out-of-Period Liabilities Test

Because of the emphasis on understatements in liability accounts, out-of-period liability tests are important for accounts payable. The extent of tests to uncover unrecorded accounts payable, which is frequently referred to as the *search for unrecorded accounts payable*, depends heavily on the reliability of the system of internal control and the materiality of the potential balance in the account. The same audit procedures to uncover unrecorded payables are also applicable to the valuation objective. The audit procedures that follow are typical tests:

Examine Underlying Documentation for Subsequent Cash Disbursements. The purpose of this audit procedure is to uncover payments made in the subsequent accounting period that represent liabilities at the balance sheet date. The supporting documentation is examined to determine whether a

FIGURE 15–5

Summary of Direct Tests of Balances—Accounts Payable

Audit Objectives	Common Direct Tests of Balances Procedures	Comments

The account balance and details of accounts payable and related asset and expense accounts are reasonable.	• Compare related expense account balances to prior years.
	• Review list of accounts payable for unusual, nonvendor, and interest-bearing payables.
	• Compare individual accounts payable to previous years
	• Calculate ratios such as:
	   Purchases ÷ accounts payable
	   Accounts payable ÷ current liabilities
		• Comparisons of expenses with prior years is more likely to reveal errors in accounts payable than are analytical tests of accounts payable.

Accounts payable in the accounts payable list agree with related subsidiary amounts, and the total is correctly added and agrees with the general ledger.	• Foot the accounts payable list. • Trace the total to the general ledger. • Trace individual problems to subsidiary ledger for vendor's names and amounts.	• All pages need not ordinarily be footed. • Unless controls are weak, tracing to subsidiaries should be limited.
Accounts payable in the accounts payable list are valid.	• Trace from accounts payable list to vendor's invoices and statements. • Confirm accounts payable, emphasizing large and unusual amounts.	• Ordinarily receives little attention because the primary concern is with understatements.
Existing accounts payable are in the accounts payable list.	• Perform out-of-period liability tests—see discussion.	• These are essential audit tests for accounts payable.
Accounts payable in the accounts payable list are properly valued.	• Perform same procedures as those used for out-of-period liability tests.	• Ordinarily, the auditor is more concerned with understatements than with overstatements. • The emphasis in these procedures for valuation is understatement rather than omission.
Accounts payable in the accounts payable list are properly classified.	• Review the list and subsidiary records for related parties, notes or other interest-bearing liabilities, long-term payables, and debit balances. • Discussions with the client.	• Knowledge of the client's business is essential for these tests.
Transactions in the acquisitions and payment cycle are recorded in the proper period.	• Perform out-of-period liability tests—see discussion. • Performed detailed tests as a part of physical observation of inventory—see discussion. • Test for inventory in transit—see discussion.	• These are essential audit tests for accounts payable. These are referred to as cutoff tests.
Accounts in the acquisition and payment cycle are properly disclosed.	• Review statements to make sure material related parties, long-term, and interest-bearing liabilities are segregated.	• Ordinarily not a problem.

payment was for a current period obligation. For example, if inventory was received prior to the balance sheet date, it will be so indicated on the receiving report. Frequently, documentation for payments made in the subsequent period are examined for several weeks, especially when the client does not pay its bills on a timely basis. Any payment that is for a current period obligation should be traced to the accounts payable list to make sure it has been included as a liability.

Examine Underlying Documentation for Bills That Still Have Not Been Paid Several Weeks after the End of the Year. This procedure is carried out in the same manner as the preceding one and serves the same purpose. The only difference is that it is done for unpaid obligations near the end of the examination rather than for obligations that have already been paid. For example, in an audit with a March 31 year-end, if the auditor examines the supporting documentation for checks paid until June 28, bills that are still unpaid at that date should be examined to determine whether they are obligations of the year ended March 31.

Trace Vendors' Statements That Show a Balance Due to the Accounts Payable List. If the client maintains a file of vendors' statements, any statement indicating a balance due can be traced to the listing to make sure it is included as an account payable.

Send Confirmations to Vendors with Which the Client Does Business. Although the use of confirmations for accounts payable is less common than for accounts receivable, it is often used to test for vendors omitted from the accounts payable list, omitted transactions, and misstated account balances. The sending of confirmations to active vendors for which a balance has not been included in the accounts payable list is a useful means of searching for omitted amounts. This type of confirmation is commonly referred to as *zero balance confirmation*. Additional discussion of confirmation of accounts payable is deferred until the end of the chapter.

Trace Receiving Reports Issued before Year-End to Related Vendors' Invoices. All merchandise received before the end of the accounting period, indicated by the issuance of a receiving report, should be included as accounts payable. By tracing receiving reports issued at and before year-end to vendors' invoices and making sure they are included in accounts payable, the auditor is testing for unrecorded obligations.

Cutoff Tests

The five audit steps discussed under the section on out-of-period liabilities are concerned with ascertaining that accounts payable obligations are recorded in the proper period. This is a problem of cutoff. Since these procedures have already been discussed, only two aspects of cutoff are enlarged upon here: the examination of receiving reports and the determination of the amount of inventory in transit.

Relationship of Cutoff
to Physical Observation of Inventory

In determining that the accounts payable cutoff is correct, *it is essential that the cutoff tests be coordinated with the physical observation of inventory.* For example, assume that an inventory acquisition for $40,000 is received late in the afternoon of December 31, after the physical inventory is completed. If the acquisition is included in accounts payable and purchases, but excluded from inventory, the result is an understatement of net earnings of $40,000. On the other hand, if the acquisition is excluded from both inventory and accounts payable, there is an error in the balance sheet, but the income statement is correct. The only way the auditor will know which type of error has occurred is to coordinate cutoff tests with the observation of inventory.

The cutoff information for purchases should be obtained *during the physical observation* of the inventory. At this time the auditor should review the procedures in the receiving department to determine that all inventory received was counted, and he should record in his working papers the last receiving report number of inventory included in the physical count. During the year-end field work, the auditor should then test the accounting records for cutoff. He should trace receiving report numbers to the accounts payable records to verify that they are correctly included or excluded from accounts payable. For example, assume that the last receiving report number representing inventory included in the physical count was 3167. The auditor should record this document number and subsequently trace it and several preceding numbers to their related vendor's invoice and to the accounts payable list or the accounts payable subsidiary records to determine that they are all included. Similarly, accounts payable for purchases recorded on receiving reports numbered larger than 3167 should be excluded from accounts payable.

When the client's physical inventory takes place before the last day of the year, it is still necessary to perform an accounts payable cutoff at the time of the physical count in the manner described in the preceding paragraph. In addition, the auditor must verify whether all acquisitions taking place between the physical count and the end of the year were added to the physical inventory and accounts payable. For example, if the client takes the physical count on December 27 for a December 31 year-end, the cutoff information is taken as of December 27. During the year-end field work, the auditor must first test to determine whether the cutoff was accurate as of December 27. After he is satisfied that the December 27 cutoff is accurate, the auditor must test whether all inventory received subsequent to the physical count, but before the balance sheet date, was added to inventory and accounts payable by the client.

Inventory in Transit. A distinction in accounts payable must be made between acquisitions of inventory that are on an *FOB destination* basis and those that are made *FOB origin.* Title passes to the buyer when it is received for inventory that is purchased on an FOB destination basis. Therefore, only inventory received prior to the balance sheet date should be included in inventory and accounts payable at year-end. When inventory is purchased on an FOB origin basis, the inventory and related accounts payable must be recorded in the current period if shipment occurred before the balance sheet date.

Determining whether inventory has been purchased on an FOB destination or origin basis is done by examining vendors' invoices. The auditor should examine invoices for merchandise received shortly after year-end to determine if they were on an FOB origin basis. For those that were, and where the shipment dates were prior to the balance sheet date, the inventory and related accounts payable must be recorded in the current period if the amounts are material.

Reliability of Vendors' Statements, Vendors' Invoices, and Confirmations

In deciding upon the appropriate evidence to accumulate for verifying accounts payable, it is essential that the auditor understand the relative reliability of the three primary types of evidence ordinarily used: vendors' invoices, vendors' statements, and confirmations.

Distinction between Vendors' Invoices and Vendors' Statements. In verifying the valuation of an account balance, the auditor should make a major distinction between vendors' invoices and vendors' statements. In examining vendors' invoices and related supporting documents, such as receiving reports and purchase orders, the auditor gets highly reliable *evidence of the valuation of individual transactions.* A vendor's statement is not as desirable as invoices for verifying individual transactions because a statement only includes the total amount of the transaction. The units acquired, price, freight, and other data are not included. On the other hand, a statement has the advantage of including the ending balance according to the vendor's records. Which of these two documents is better for verifying the correct balance in accounts payable? *The vendor's statement is superior for verifying accounts payable* because it includes the ending balance. The auditor could compare existing vendors' invoices with the client's list and still not uncover missing ones, which is the primary concern in accounts payable. Which of these two documents is better for testing acquisitions in tests of transactions? *The vendor's invoice is superior for verifying tests of transactions* because the auditor is verifying individual transactions and the invoice shows the details of the acquisitions.

Difference between Vendors' Statements and Confirmations. The most important distinction between a vendor's statement and a confirmation of accounts payable is the source of the information. A vendor's statement has been prepared by an independent third party, but it is in the hands of the client at the time the auditor examines it. This provides the client with an opportunity to alter a vendor's statement or not make particular statements available to the auditor. A confirmation of accounts payable, which normally is a request for an itemized statement sent directly to the CPA's office, provides the same information as the statement, but the information can be regarded as more reliable. In addition, confirmations of accounts payable frequently include a request for information about notes and acceptances payable as well as consigned inventory that is owned by the vendor but stored on the client's premises. An illustration of a typical accounts payable confirmation request is given in Figure 15-6.

Because of the availability of vendors' statements and vendors' invoices, which are both relatively reliable evidence because they originate from a third party, the *confirmation of accounts payable is less common than confirmation of accounts receivable.* If the client has an adequate system of internal control and vendors' statements are available for examination, confirmations are normally not sent. On the other hand, when the client's system is weak, when statements are not available, or when the auditor questions the client's integrity, it is desirable to send confirmation requests to vendors. The number of confirmations sent should depend upon the quality of the controls, the materiality of accounts payable, and the number of accounts outstanding. Because of the emphasis on understatements of liability accounts, the sample should include large accounts, active accounts, accounts with a zero balance, and a representative sample of all others.

In most instances where accounts payable are confirmed, it is done shortly after the balance sheet date. However, if the system of internal control is strong, it may be possible to confirm accounts payable at an interim date as a test of the quality of the system. Then if the confirmation indicates that the controls are ineffective, it is possible to design other audit procedures to test accounts payable at year-end.

When vendors' statements are examined or confirmations are received, there must be a *reconciliation* of the statement or confirmation with the accounts payable list. Frequently, differences are caused by inventory in transit, checks mailed by the client but not received by the vendor at the statement date, and delays in processing the accounting records. The reconciliation is of the same general nature as that discussed in Chapter 11 for accounts receivable. The documents typically used to reconcile the balances on the accounts payable list with the confirmation or vendor's statement include receiving reports, vendor's invoices, and canceled checks.

Sample Size

Sample sizes for accounts payable tests vary considerably depending on such factors as the materiality of accounts payable, number of accounts out-

Roger Mead, Inc.

January 15, 1981

Jones Sales, Inc.
2116 Stewart Street
Waynewill, Kentucky 36021

Gentlemen:

Our auditors, Murry and Rogers, CPAs, are making an examination of
our financial statements. For this purpose, please furnish them
with the following information as of December 31, 1980.

(1) Itemized statements of our accounts payable to
     you showing all unpaid items;

(2) A complete list of any notes and acceptances
     payable to you (including any which have been
     discounted) showing the original date, dates due,
     original amount, unpaid balance, collateral and
     endorsers; and

(3) An itemized list of your merchandise consigned
     to us.

Your prompt attention to this request will be appreciated. An
envelope is enclosed for your reply.

Yours truly,

Phil Geriovini

Phil Geriovini, President

FIGURE 15-6 Accounts Payable Confirmation Request

standing, system of internal control, and results of the prior year. When a client's system is weak, which is not uncommon for accounts payable, almost all population items must be verified. In other situations, minimal testing is needed.

Statistical sampling is less commonly used for the audit of accounts payable than for accounts receivable. The reason is the greater difficulty of defining the population and determining the population size in accounts payable. Since the emphasis is on omitted accounts payable, it is essential that the population include all potential payables. Defining the population to include all potential payables often makes the population size unmanageable.

Two examples where variables sampling could practically be used to test for account payables are:

- The auditor is satisfied that all vendor's names are included in the accounts payable list even though some may be at the wrong amount. The population is defined as all vendors on the list. The emphases on the tests are validity, valuation, and classification.
- The auditor is satisfied that all accounts payable at the balance sheet date have been paid subsequent to year end. The population is defined as all disbursements subsequent to year-end.

REVIEW QUESTIONS

15–1. List five asset accounts, three liability accounts, and 10 expense accounts included in the acquisition and payment cycle for a typical manufacturing company.

15–2. List one possible internal control for each of the eight internal control objectives for cash disbursements. For each internal control, list a compliance procedure to test the effectiveness of the control.

15–3. List one possible control for each of the eight internal control objectives for acquisitions. For each control, list a compliance procedure to test the effectiveness of the control.

15–4. Evaluate the following statement by an auditor concerning tests of acquisitions and payments: "In selecting the acquisitions and disbursements sample for testing, the best approach is to select a random month and test every transaction for the period. Using this approach enables me to thoroughly understand the system because I have examined everything that happened during the period. As a part of the monthly test, I also test the beginning and ending bank reconciliations and prepare a proof of cash for the month. At the completion of these tests I feel I can evaluate the effectiveness of the system."

15–5. What is the importance of cash discounts to the client and how can the auditor verify whether they are being taken in accordance with company policy?

15–6. What are the similarities and differences in the objectives of the following two procedures: (1) select a random sample of receiving reports and trace them to related vendors' invoices and purchase journal entries, comparing the vendor's name, type of material and quantity purchased, and total amount of the acquisition; and (2) select a random sample of purchases journal entries and trace them to related vendors' invoices and receiving reports, comparing the vendor's name, type of material and quantity purchased, and total amount of the acquisition.

15–7. If an audit client does not have prenumbered checks, what type of error has a greater chance of occurring? Under the circumstances, what audit procedure can the auditor use to compensate for the weakness?

15–8. What is meant by a voucher and a voucher register? Explain how their use can improve an organization's internal controls.

15–9. Explain why most auditors consider the receipt of goods and services the most important point in the acquisition and payment cycle.

15–10. Explain the relationship between tests of the acquisition and payment cycle and tests of inventory. Give specific examples of how these two types of tests affect each other.

15–11. Explain the relationship between tests of the acquisition and payment cycle and tests of accounts payable. Give specific examples of how these two types of tests affect each other.

15–12. The CPA examines all unrecorded invoices on hand as of February 29, 19X8, the last day of field work. Which of the following errors is most likely to be uncovered by this procedure? Explain.
   a. Accounts payable are overstated at December 31, 19X7.
   b. Accounts payable are understated at December 31, 19X7.
   c. Operating expenses are overstated for the twelve months ended December 31, 19X7.
   d. Operating expenses are overstated for the two months ended February 29, 19X8.   (AICPA adapted)

15–13. Explain why it is common for auditors to send confirmation requests to vendors with "zero balances" on the client's accounts payable listing, but uncommon to follow the same approach in verifying accounts receivable.

15–14. Distinguish between a vendor's invoice and a vendor's statement. Which document should ideally be used as evidence in auditing acquisition transactions and which for directly verifying accounts payable balances? Why?

15–15. It is less common to confirm accounts payable at an interim date than accounts receivable. Explain why.

15–16. In testing the cutoff of accounts payable at the balance sheet date, explain why it is important that auditors coordinate their tests with the physical observation of inventory. What can the auditor do during the physical inventory to enhance the likelihood of an accurate cutoff?

15–17. Distinguish between FOB destination and FOB origin. What procedures should the auditor follow concerning acquisitions of inventory on a FOB origin basis near year-end?

DISCUSSION QUESTIONS AND PROBLEMS

15–18. For each of the following questions, select the one best response.

a. In comparing the confirmation of accounts payable with suppliers and confirmation of accounts receivable with debtors, the true statement is that

(1) confirmation of accounts payable with suppliers is a more widely accepted auditing procedure than is confirmation of accounts receivable with debtors.

(2) statistical sampling techniques are more widely accepted in the confirmation of accounts payable than in the confirmation of accounts receivable.

(3) as compared with the confirmation of accounts payable, the confirmation of accounts receivable will tend to emphasize accounts with zero balances at balance sheet date.

(4) it is less likely that the confirmation request sent to the supplier will show the amount owed him than that the request sent to the debtor will show the amount due from him.

b. As part of his search for unrecorded liabilities, a CPA examines invoices and accounts payable vouchers. In general this examination may be limited to

(1) unpaid accounts payable vouchers and unvouchered invoices on hand at the balance sheet date.

(2) accounts payable vouchers prepared during the subsequent period and unvouchered invoices received through the last day of field work whose dollar values exceed reasonable amounts.

(3) invoices received through the last day of field work (whether or not accounts payable vouchers have been prepared) but must include all invoices of any amount received during this period.

(4) a reasonable period following the balance sheet date, normally the same period used for the cutoff bank statement. (AICPA adapted)

15–19. Questions a through h are typically found in questionnaires used by auditors in evaluating internal controls in the acquisition and payment cycle. In using the questionnaire for a particular client, a yes response to a question indicates a possible strength in the system, whereas a no indicates a potential weakness.

a. Is the purchasing function performed by personnel who are independent of the receiving and shipping functions and the payables and disbursing functions?

b. Are all vendor's invoices routed directly to accounting from the mailroom?

c. Are all vouchers prenumbered and the numerical sequence checked by a person independent of voucher preparation?

d. Are all extensions, footings, discounts, and freight terms on vendors' invoices checked for accuracy?

e. Does a responsible employee review and approve the invoice account distribution before it is recorded in the purchases journal?

f. Are checks recorded in the cash disbursements journal as they are prepared?

g. Are all supporting documents properly canceled at the time the checks are signed?

h. Is the custody of checks after signature and before mailing handled by an employee independent of all payable, disbursing, cash, and general ledger functions?

Required:

a. For each of the questions above, state the internal control objective(s) being fulfilled if the control is in effect.

b. For each internal control, list a compliance procedure to test its effectiveness.

c. For each of the questions above, identify the nature of the potential financial error(s) if the control is not in effect.

d. For each of the potential errors in part c, list a substantive audit procedure that can be used to determine whether a material error exists.

15–20. Following are some of the tests of transactions procedures frequently performed in the acquisition and payment cycle. Each procedure is to be done on a sample basis.

a. Trace transactions recorded in the purchases journal to supporting documentation, comparing the vendor's name, total dollar amounts, and authorization for purchase.

b. Account for a sequence of receiving reports and trace selected ones to related vendors' invoices and purchases journal entries.

c. Review vouchers and supporting documents for clerical accuracy, propriety of account distribution, and reasonableness of expenditure in relation to the nature of the client's operations.

d. Examine documents in support of vouchers to make sure each voucher has an approved vendor's invoice, receiving report, and purchase order attached.

e. Foot the cash disbursements journal, trace postings of the total to the general ledger, and trace postings of individual purchases to the accounts payable subsidiary ledger.

f. Account for a numerical sequence of checks in the cash disbursements journal and examine all voided or spoiled checks for proper cancellation.

g. Prepare a proof of cash disbursements for an interim month.

h. Compare dates on canceled checks with dates on the cash disbursements journal and the bank cancellation date.

Required:

   a. State whether each of the procedures above is primarily a compliance or a substantive test.

   b. State the purpose(s) of each of the procedures.

15–21. The following errors or omissions are included in the accounting records of Westgate Manufacturing Company.

   a. Telephone expense (account 2112) was unintentionally charged to repairs and maintenance (account 2121).

   b. Purchases of raw materials are frequently not recorded until several weeks after the goods are received due to the failure of the receiving personnel to forward receiving reports to accounting. When pressure from a vendor's credit department is put on Westgate's accounting department, it searches for the receiving report, records the transactions in the purchases journal, and pays the bill.

   c. The accounts payable clerk prepares a monthly check to Story Supply Company for the amount of an invoice owed and submits the unsigned check to the treasurer for payment along with related supporting documents which have already been approved. When he receives the signed check from the treasurer, he records it as a debit to accounts payable and deposits the check in a personal bank account for a company named Story Company. A few days later he records the invoice in the purchases journal again, resubmits the documents and a new check to the treasurer, and sends the check to the vendor after it has been signed.

   d. The amount of a check in the cash disbursements journal is recorded as $4,612.87 instead of $6,412.87.

   e. The accounts payable clerk intentionally excluded from the cash disbursements journal seven larger checks written and mailed on December 26 to prevent cash in the bank from having a negative balance on the general ledger. They were recorded on January 2 of the subsequent year.

   f. Each month a fictitious receiving report is submitted to accounting by an employee in the receiving department. A few days later he sends Westgate an invoice for the quantity of goods ordered from a small company he owns and operates in the evening. A check is prepared, and the amount is paid when the receiving report and the vendor's invoice are matched by the accounts payable clerk.

Required:

   a. For each error, state a control that should have prevented the error from occurring on a continuing basis.

   b. For each error, state a substantive audit procedure that could uncover the error.

15–22. In testing cash disbursements for the Jay Klein Company, you have carefully reviewed the accounting system and evaluated the controls. The controls are reasonably good in the system, and no unusual audit problems have arisen in previous years.

Although there are not many personnel in the accounting department, there is a reasonable separation of duties in the organization. There is a separate purchasing agent who has responsibility for ordering goods and a separate receiving department for counting the goods when they are received and preparing receiving reports. There is a separation of duties between cash disbursements and accounts payable, and all information is recorded in the two journals independently. The controller reviews all supporting documents before signing the checks, and he immediately mails the check to the vendor. Check copies are used for subsequent recording.

All aspects of the system seem satisfactory to you, and you perform minimum tests of 75 transactions as a means of evaluating the system. In your tests you discover the following exceptions:

a. Two items in the purchases journal have been misclassified.
b. Three invoices had not been initialed by the controller, but there were no dollar errors evident in the transactions.
c. Five receiving reports were recorded at least two weeks later in the purchases journal than their date on the receiving report.
d. One invoice had been paid twice. The second payment was supported by a duplicate copy of the invoice. Both copies of the invoice had been marked "Paid."
e. One check amount in the cash disbursements journal was for $100 less than the amount stated on the vendor's invoice.
f. One voided check was missing.
g. Two receiving reports were missing from the voucher jacket for the invoice. One vendor's invoice had an extension error, and the invoice had been initialed that the amount had been checked.

Required:

a. What is the audit importance of each of these errors?
b. What follow-up procedures would you use to determine more about the nature of each error?
c. How would each of these errors affect the balance of your audit? Be specific.
d. How should each of the errors have been prevented by the client?

15–23. You are the staff accountant testing the combined purchases and cash disbursements journal for a small audit client. The system is regarded as reasonably good, considering the number of personnel.

The in-charge auditor has decided that a sample of 80 items should be sufficient for this audit because of the excellent controls. He gives you the following instructions:

a. All transactions selected must exceed $100.
b. At least 50 of the transactions must be for purchases of raw material because these transactions are typically material.
c. It is not acceptable to include the same vendor in the sample more than once.

    d. All vendors' invoices that cannot be located must be replaced with a new sample item.

    e. Both checks and supporting documents are to be examined for the same transactions.

    f. The sample must be random, after modifications for the above instructions.

Required:

    a. Evaluate each of these instructions for testing cash disbursements transactions.

    b. Explain the difficulties of applying each of these instructions to attributes sampling.

15–24. During your audit of the Pientak Corporation for 19X7 you find that the corporation plans to install the following purchase order draft system for paying vendors.

    a. The corporation will issue a draft in the form of a blank check attached to the purchase order for purchases. The purchase order draft (POD) form will combine a purchase order (upper half of form) with a blank check (lower half of form), and the two documents will be prenumbered with the same number and perforated so that the check can be easily detached.

    b. The purchasing department will be responsible for the issuance, and the PODs will be valid for a period of 90 days from the date of issuance. Each of eight buyers will maintain a supply of PODs. The supply will be replenished as needed.

    c. The cashier's department will maintain a log of the numbers of the PODs given to each buyer. Unissued PODs will be kept in a safe in the cashier's office. The POD form will consist of five parts, which will be distributed as follows:

        (1) Copy 1 will be the purchase order and will be mailed to the vendor.

        (2) Copy 2 will be sent to the receiving department.

        (3) Copy 3 will be sent to the bookkeeping department.

        (4) Copy 4 will be filed numerically in the purchasing department.

        (5) Copy 5 will be kept by the buyer for follow-up purposes.

    d. When the purchase order is issued, the buyer will enter the quantity, unit price, extended amount, and the total estimated amount of the order on the upper half of the POD form. The check will be made out in the vendor's name, dated and signed by the buyer. The original of the five-part form will then be mailed to the vendor.

    e. The vendor will enter his invoice number, quantity, unit price, and total amount of goods to be shipped in the space provided on the check. When the goods are shipped, the vendor will enter the total amount of the shipment on the face of the check and present the completed check to the bank for payment. No partially filled orders will be accepted. Vendors who deliver a quantity less than that ordered must receive a new purchase order for additional quantities to be delivered.

f. The bank will honor the check if it has not matured, stamp it "Paid," and charge the amount to the corporation's general cash account. The bank will send the paid checks to the cashier's department daily. After reviewing the paid checks, the cashier's department will prepare an adding machine tape of the amounts and enter the total each day in the cash disbursements journal, debiting accounts payable. The paid checks will then be sent to the purchasing department.

g. When the goods are received, the receiving department will compare the quantity of items received with copy 2 of the POD, indicate the date the goods are received, initial copy 2, and route it to the purchasing department. The purchasing department will match the receiving department's copy 2 with the paid POD received from the cashier's department and enter the account distribution on the description section of the check. The extensions of unit prices multiplied by quantities entered by the vendor will be checked and the receiving department's copy 2 attached to the paid check and the documents sent to the bookkeeping department.

h. The bookkeeping department will charge the appropriate assets or expense accounts at the time the paid checks are recorded in the accounts payable register. The checks, together with the related receiving reports, will then be filed by vendor.

Required:

a. The treasurer of the corporation requests your aid in preparing a memorandum informing the bank of the new "POD" procedures. List the instructions that you would recommend be given to the bank regarding POD bank account and the payment of "POD" checks.

b. The internal control procedures within the corporation with regard to purchases in general are excellent. Suggest additional internal control measures needed for the use of purchase order drafts and verifications of paid and unpaid PODs. (AICPA adapted)

15-25. Each year near the balance sheet date when the president of Bargon Construction, Inc., takes a three-week vacation to Hawaii, he signs several checks to pay major bills during the period he is absent. Jack Morgan, head bookkeeper for the company, uses this practice to his advantage. Morgan makes out a check to himself for the amount of a large vendor's invoice, and since there is no purchases journal, he records the amount in the cash disbursements journal as a purchase to the supplier listed on the invoice. He holds the check until several weeks into the subsequent period to make sure the auditors do not get an opportunity to examine the canceled check. Shortly after the first of the year when the president returns, Morgan resubmits the invoice for payment and again records the check in the cash disbursements journal. At that point, he marks the invoice "paid" and files it with all other paid invoices. Morgan has been following this practice successfully for several years and feels confident that he has developed a foolproof method.

Required:

a. What is the auditor's responsibility for discovering this type of embezzlement?

b. What weaknesses exist in the client's system of internal control?

c. What audit procedures are likely to uncover the fraud?

15–26. On January 11, 19X7, at the beginning of your annual audit of the Grover Manufacturing Company's financial statements for the year ended December 31, 19X6, the company president confides in you that an employee is living on a scale in excess of that which his salary would support.

The employee has been a buyer in the purchasing department for six years and has charge of purchasing all general materials and supplies. He is authorized to sign purchase orders for amounts up to $200. Purchase orders in excess of $200 require the countersignature of the general purchasing agent.

The president understands that the usual examination of financial statements is not designed, and cannot be relied upon, to disclose fraud or conflicts of interest, although their discovery may result. The president authorizes you, however, to expand your regular audit procedures and to apply additional audit procedures to determine whether there is any evidence that the buyer has been misappropriating company funds or has been engaged in activities that were a conflict of interest.

Required:

a. List the audit procedures that you would apply to the company records and documents in an attempt to

(1) discover evidence within the purchasing department of defalcations being committed by the buyer. Give the purpose of each audit procedure.

(2) provide leads as to possible collusion between the buyer and the suppliers. Give the purpose of each audit procedure.

b. Assume that your investigation disclosed that some suppliers have been charging the Grover Manufacturing Company in excess of their usual prices and apparently have been making kickbacks to the buyer. The excess charges are material in amount. What effect, if any, would the defalcation have upon (1) the financial statements that were prepared before the defalcation was uncovered and (2) your auditor's report? Discuss.

(AICPA adapted)

15–27. You were in the final stages of your examination of the financial statements of Ozine Corporation for the year ended December 31, 19X7, when you were consulted by the corporation's president who believes there is no point to your examining the 19X8 voucher register and testing data in support of 19X8 entries. He stated that (a) bills pertaining to 19X7 which were received too late to be included in the December voucher register were recorded as of the year-end by the corporation by journal entry, (b) the internal auditor made tests after the year-end, and (c) he would furnish you with a letter certifying that there were no unrecorded liabilities.

Required:

a. Should a CPA's test for unrecorded liabilities be affected by the fact that the client made a journal entry to record 19X7 bills which were received late? Explain.

b. Should a CPA's test for unrecorded liabilities be affected by the fact that a letter is obtained in which a responsible management official certifies that to the best of his knowledge all liabilities have been recorded? Explain.

c. Should a CPA's test for unrecorded liabilities be eliminated or reduced because of the internal audit tests? Explain.

d. Assume that the corporation, which handled some government contracts, had no internal auditor but that an auditor for a federal agency spent three weeks auditing the records and was just completing his work at this time. How would the CPA's unrecorded liability test be affected by the work of the auditor for a federal agency?

e. What sources in addition to the 19X8 voucher register should the CPA consider to locate possible unrecorded liabilities? (AICPA adapted)

15–28. Because of the small size of the company and the limited number of accounting personnel, the Dry Goods Wholesale Company initially records all acquisitions of goods and services at the time cash disbursements are made. At the end of each quarter when financial statements for internal purposes are prepared, accounts payable are recorded by adjusting journal entries. The entries are reversed at the beginning of the subsequent period. Except for the lack of a purchases journal, the controls over acquisitions are excellent for a small company. (There are adequate prenumbered documents for all acquisitions, proper approvals, and adequate internal verification wherever possible.)

Before the auditor arrives for the year-end audit, the bookkeeper prepares adjusting entries to record the accounts payable as of the balance sheet date. A list of all outstanding balances is prepared, by vendor, on an accounts payable listing and is given to the auditor. All vendors' invoices supporting the list are retained in a separate file for the auditor's use.

In the current year, the accounts payable balance has increased dramatically because of a severe cash shortage. (The cash shortage apparently arose from expansion of inventory and facilities rather than lack of sales.) Many accounts have remained unpaid for several months and the client is getting pressure from several vendors to pay the bills. Since the company had a relatively profitable year, management is anxious to complete the audit as early as possible so that the audited statements can be used to obtain a large bank loan.

Required:

a. Explain how the lack of a purchases journal will affect the auditor's tests of transactions for acquisitions and payments.

b. What should the auditor use as a sampling unit in performing tests of acquisitions?

    c. Assuming there are no errors discovered in the auditor's tests of transactions for acquisitions and payments, how will the existing system affect the verification of accounts payable?

    d. Discuss the reasonableness of the client's request for an early completion of the audit and the implications of the request from the auditor's point of view.

    e. List the audit procedures that should be performed in the year-end audit of accounts payable.

    f. State your opinion as to whether it is possible to conduct an adequate audit in these circumstances.

15–29. The Moss Company manufactures household appliances that are sold through independent franchised retail dealers. The electric motors in the appliances are guaranteed for five years from the date of sale of the appliances to the consumer. Under the guaranty defective motors are replaced by the dealers without charge.

    Inventories of replacement motors are kept in the dealers' stores and are carried at cost in the Moss Company's records. When the dealer replaces a defective motor, he notifies the factory and returns the defective motor to the factory for reconditioning. After the defective motor is received by the factory, the dealer's account is credited with an agreed fee for the replacement service.

    When the appliance is brought to the dealer after the guaranty period has elapsed, the dealer charges the owner for installing the new motor. The dealer notifies the factory of the installation and returns the replaced motor for reconditioning. The motor installed is then charged to the dealer's account at a price in excess of its inventory value. In this instance, to encourage the return of replaced motors, the dealer's account is credited with a nominal value for the returned motor.

    Dealers submit quarterly inventory reports of the motors on hand. The reports are later verified by factory salesmen. Dealers are billed for inventory shortages determined by comparison of the dealers' inventory reports with the factory's perpetual records of the dealers' inventories. The dealers order additional motors as they need them. One motor is used for all appiances in a given year, but the motors are changed in basic design each model year.

    The Moss Company has established an account, estimated liability for product guaranties, in connection with the guaranties. An amount representing the estimated guaranty cost prorated per sales unit is credited to the estimated liability account for each appliance sold, and the debit is charged to a provision account. The estimated liability account is debited for the service fees credited to the dealers' accounts and for the inventory cost of motors installed under the guaranties.

    The engineering department keeps statistical records of the number of units of each model sold in each year and the replacements that were made. The effect of improvements in design and construction is under continuous study by the engineering department, and the estimated guaranty cost per unit is adjusted annually on the basis of experience and improvements in design. Experience shows that, for a given motor model, the number of guaranties made good varies widely from year to year during the guaranty period, but the total number of guaranties to be made good can be reliably predicted.

Required:

a. Prepare an audit program to satisfy yourself as to the propriety of transactions recorded in the estimated liability for product guaranties account for the year ended December 31, 19X8.
b. Prepare the worksheet format that would be used to test the adequacy of the balance in the estimated liability for product guaranties account. The worksheet column headings should describe clearly the data to be inserted in the columns.   (AICPA adapted)

15–30. Mincin, CPA, is the auditor of the Raleigh Corporation. Mincin is considering the audit work to be performed in the accounts payable area for the current year's engagement.

The prior year's working papers show that confirmation requests were mailed to 100 of Raleigh's 1,000 suppliers. The selected suppliers were based on Mincin's sample that was designed to select accounts with large dollar balances. A substantial number of hours were spent by Raleigh and Mincin resolving relatively minor differences between the confirmation replies and Raleigh's accounting records. Alternative audit procedures were used for those suppliers who did not respond to the confirmation requests.

Required:

a. Identify the accounts payable audit objectives that Mincin must consider in determining the audit procedures to be followed.
b. Identify situations when Mincin should use accounts payable confirmations and discuss whether Mincin is required to use them.
c. Discuss why the use of large dollar balances as the basis for selecting accounts payable for confirmation might not be the most efficient approach and indicate what more efficient procedures could be followed when selecting accounts payable for confirmation.   (AICPA adapted)

15–31. As part of the 6-30-X8 audit of accounts payable of Milner Products Company, the auditor sent 22 confirmations of accounts payable to vendors in the form of requests for statements. Four of the statements were not returned by the vendors, and five vendors reported balances different from the amounts recorded on Milner's accounts payable subsidiary ledgers. The auditor made duplicate copies of the five vendors' statements to maintain control of the independent information and turned the originals over to the client's accounts payable clerk to reconcile the differences. Two days later the clerk returned the five statements to the auditor with the following information on a working paper:

Statement 1	Balance per vendor's statement	$ 6,618.01
	Payment by Milner 6-30-X8	(4,601.01)
	Balance per subsidiary ledger	$ 2,017.00
Statement 2	Balance per vendor's statement	$ 9,618.93
	Invoices not received by Milner	(2,733.18)
	Payment by Milner 6-15-X8	(1,000.00)
	Balance per subsidiary ledger	$ 6,885.75
Statement 3	Balance per vendor's statement	$26,251.80
	Balance per subsidiary ledger	20,516.11
	Difference cannot be located due to the vendor's failure to provide details of its account balance	$ 5,735.69
Statement 4	Balance per vendor's statement	$ 6,170.15
	Credit memo issued by vendor on 7-15-X8	2,360.15
	Balance per subsidiary ledger	$ 3,810.00
Statement 5	Balance per vendor's statement	$ 8,619.21
	Payment by Milner 7-3-X8	(3,000.00)
	Unlocated difference not followed up due to minor amount	215.06
	Balance per subsidiary ledger	$ 5,834.27

Required:

a. Evaluate the acceptability of having the client perform the reconciliations, assuming the auditor intends to perform adequate additional tests.
b. Describe the additional tests that should be performed for each of the five statements that included differences.
c. What audit procedures should be performed for the nonresponses to the confirmation requests?

15–32. In confirming accounts payable at 12-31-X8, the following procedures are suggested to you for a client that has an excellent system of internal control and a history of prompt payment of all current liabilities.
a. Obtain a list of accounts payable at December 31, 19X8, from the client and
  (1) Foot the list.
  (2) Compare the total with the balance shown in the general ledger.
  (3) Compare the amounts shown on the list with the balances in the accounts payable subsidiary ledger.
b. Selection of accounts to confirm.
  (1) Select each account with a balance payable in excess of $2,000.
  (2) Select a random sample of 50 other accounts over $100.
  (3) Indicate the accounts to be confirmed on the accounts payable list, make a copy of the list, and give it to the accounts payable clerk along with instructions to type the vendor's name, address, and balance due on confirmations.
c. Compare the confirmations with the subsidiary ledger.

    d. Have the client's controller sign each confirmation.

    e. Have the accounts payable clerk insert the confirmations and return envelopes addressed to the CPA firm in the client's envelopes. The envelopes are also to be stamped and sealed by the clerk. This should all be done under the auditor's control.

    f. Mail the confirmations.

Required:

Evaluate the procedures for confirming accounts payable.

15–33. The physical inventory for Ajak Manufacturing was taken on December 30, 19X8, rather than December 31 because the client had to operate the plant for a special order the last day of the year. At the time of the client's physical count, you observed that purchases represented by receiving report number 2631 and all preceding ones were included in the physical count, whereas inventory represented by succeeding numbers was excluded. On the evening of December 31, you stopped by the plant and noted that inventory represented by receiving report numbers 2632 through 2634 was received subsequent to the physical count, but prior to the end of the year. You later noted that the final inventory on the financial statements contained only those items included in the physical count. In testing accounts payable at December 31, 19X8, you obtain a schedule from the client to aid you in testing the adequacy of the cutoff. The schedule includes the following information that you have not yet resolved:

			Information on the Vendor's Invoice		
Receiving Report Number	*Amount of Vendor's Invoice*	*Amount Presently Included in or Excluded from Accounts Payable**	*Invoice Date*	*Shipping Date*	*FOB Origin or Destination*
2631	$2,619.26	Included	12-30-X8	12-30-X8	Origin
2632	3,709.16	Excluded	12-26-X8	12-15-X8	Destination
2633	5,182.31	Included	12-31-X8	12-26-X8	Origin
2634	6,403.00	Excluded	12-16-X8	12-27-X8	Destination
2635	8,484.91	Included	12-28-X8	12-31-X8	Origin
2636	5,916.20	Excluded	1- 3-X9	12-31-X8	Destination
2637	7,515.50	Excluded	1- 5-X9	12-26-X8	Origin
2638	2,407.87	Excluded	12-31-X8	1- 3-X9	Origin

**All entries to record inventory purchases are recorded by the client as a debit to purchases and a credit to accounts payable.*

Required:

a. Explain the relationship between inventory and accounts payable cutoff.

b. For each of the receiving reports, state the error in inventory or accounts payable if any exists and prepare an adjusting entry to correct the financial statements if an error exists.

c. Which of the errors in part b are most important? Explain.

15-34. You are provided with the following description of the accounting and internal control procedures relating to materials purchases by the Johnson Machinery Company, a medium-sized firm that builds special machinery to order.

Materials purchase requisitions are first approved by the plant foreman, who then sends them to the purchasing department. A prenumbered purchase order is prepared in triplicate by one of several department employees. Employees account for all purchase order numbers. The original copy is sent to the vendor. The receiving department is sent the second copy to use for a receiving report. The third copy is kept on file in the purchasing department along with the requisition.

Delivered materials are immediately sent to the storeroom. The receiving report, which is a copy of the purchase order, is sent to the purchasing department. A copy of the receiving report is sent to the storeroom. Materials are issued to factory employees subsequent to a verbal request by one of the foremen.

When the mailroom clerk receives vendors' invoices, he forwards them to the purchasing department employee who placed the order. The invoice is compared with the purchase order on file for price and terms by the employee. The invoice quantity is compared with the receiving department's report. After checking footings, extensions, and discounts, the employee indicates approval for payment by initialing the invoice. The invoice is then forwarded to the accounting department (voucher section) where it is coded for account distribution, assigned a voucher number, recorded in the voucher register, and filed by payment date due. The purchase order and receiving report are filed in the purchasing department.

On payment dates the voucher section requisitions prenumbered checks from the cashier. They are prepared, except for signature, and then returned to the cashier, who puts them through the check-signing machine. After accounting for the sequence of numbers, the cashier sends the checks to the bookkeeper, who makes entries in the cash disbursements journal. The checks are then forwarded to the voucher section where payment dates are entered in the voucher register. The checks are placed in envelopes and sent to the mailroom. The vouchers are subsequently filed in numerical order. At the end of each month an adding machine tape of unpaid invoices is prepared by a voucher clerk, and the total is compared with the general ledger balance. Any differences disclosed are investigated.

Required:

a. Prepare a flowchart for the acquisition and the payment system for Johnson Machinery Company.

b. List the controls in existence for each of the seven internal control objectives for acquisitions.

c. For each control in part b, list one compliance procedure for verifying its effectiveness.

d. List the most important weaknesses in the acquisition and payment system.

e. Design an audit program to test the system of internal control. The program should include, but not be limited to, the compliance tests from part c and procedures to compensate for the weaknesses in part d.

16

THE ACQUISITION AND PAYMENT CYCLE— VERIFICATION OF SELECTED ACCOUNTS

An important characteristic of the acquisition and payment cycle is the large number of accounts involved. These include the following:

Cash in the bank	Rent payable
Inventory	Accrued professional fees
Supplies	Accrued property taxes
Leases and leasehold improvements	Income taxes payable
Land	Rent expense
Buildings	Property taxes
Manufacturing equipment	Income taxes expense
Organization costs	Professional fees
Patents, trademarks, and copyrights	Cost of goods sold
Commercial franchises	Supplies
Prepaid rent	Fines and penalties
Prepaid taxes	Insurance expense
Prepaid insurance	Retirement benefits
Accounts payable	Utilities

Since the audit procedures for many of these accounts are basically similar, an understanding of the appropriate methodology for each account can be obtained by studying the following selected account balances:

- Cash in the bank—affected by all transaction cycles (Chapter 19).
- Inventory—represents tangible assets and is typically used up in one year (Chapter 17).
- Prepaid insurance—represents prepaid expenses (Chapter 16).

- Manufacturing equipment—represents long-lived tangible assets (Chapter 16).
- Accounts payable—represents specific liabilities where the amount and the date of the future payment date are known (Chapter 15).
- Accrued property taxes—represents estimated liabilities (Chapter 16).
- Operations accounts—included are several methods of verifying all accounts in this category (Chapter 16).

AUDIT OF MANUFACTURING EQUIPMENT

Property, plant, and equipment are assets that have expected lives of more than one year, are used in the business, and are not acquired for resale. The intention to use the assets as a part of the operation of the client's business and their expected life of more than one year are the significant characteristics that distinguish these assets from inventory, prepaid expenses, and investments.

Property, plant, and equipment can be classified as follows:

- Land and land improvements
- Buildings and building improvements
- Manufacturing equipment
- Furniture and fixtures
- Autos and trucks
- Leasehold improvements
- Construction of property, plant, and equipment in process

In this section the audit of *manufacturing equipment* is discussed as an illustration of an appropriate approach to the audit of all of the accounts in property, plant, and equipment. When there are significant differences in the verification of other types of property, plant, or equipment, these are briefly examined.

Overview of the Accounts

The accounts commonly used for manufacturing equipment are illustrated in Figure 16-1. The relationship of manufacturing equipment to the acquisition and the payment cycle is apparent by examining the debits to the asset account. Since the source of debits in the asset account is the purchases journal, the current period's additions to manufacturing equipment have already been partially verified as part of the tests of the acquisition and payment cycle.

Audit Objectives

The objectives when auditing manufacturing equipment and the related depreciation and accumulated depreciation accounts are to determine whether:

- Additions represent actual property installed or constructed that has been properly capitalized.
- Costs and related depreciation for all significant retirements, abandonments, and disposals of property have been properly recorded.
- The balances in the property accounts, including the amounts carried forward from the preceding year, are properly stated.
- Depreciation has been accurately computed using a method that is acceptable and consistent with previous periods.
- The balances in accumulated depreciation accounts are reasonable, considering expected useful lives of property units and possible net salvage values.

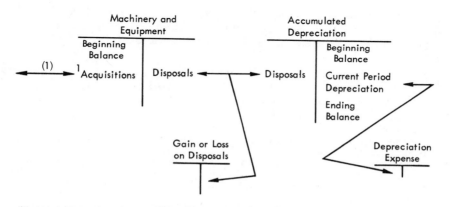

(1) Acquisitions of machinery and equipment arise from the acquisition and payment cycle. See Figure 15-1.

FIGURE 16-1   Machinery and Equipment T-Accounts

An Approach to Auditing Manufacturing Equipment

Manufacturing equipment is normally audited differently from current asset accounts for three reasons: there are usually fewer current period acquisitions of manufacturing equipment, the amount of any given acquisition is often material, and the equipment is likely to be kept and maintained in the accounting records for several years. Because of these differences, the emphasis in auditing manufacturing equipment is on the verification of current period acquisitions rather than on the balance in the account carried forward from the preceding year. In addition, the expected life of assets over one year requires depreciation and accumulated depreciation accounts which is verified as a part of the audit of the assets.

Although the approach to verifying manufacturing equipment is dissimilar from that used for current assets, several other accounts are verified in much the same manner. These include patents, copyrights, catalog costs, and all property, plant, and equipment accounts.

In the audit of manufacturing equipment, it is helpful to separate the tests into the following categories:

- Analytical review procedures
- Verification of current-year acquisitions
- Verification of current-year disposals
- Verification of the ending balance in the asset account
- Verification of depreciation expense
- Verification of the ending balance in accumulated depreciation

Analytical Review Procedures

As in all audit areas, the nature of the analytical review procedures depends upon the nature of the client's operations, but the following are illustrative of the type of ratio and trend analysis frequently performed.

Ratio or Trend	*Use As It Relates to Manufacturing Equipment*
• Depreciation expense ÷ gross manufacturing equipment cost	Possibility of a material error in computing depreciation
• Accumulated depreciation ÷ gross manufacturing equipment cost	Possibility of an error in accumulated depreciation
• Monthly or annual comparison of repairs and maintenance, supplies expense, small tools expense, and similar accounts with previous years	Indication of expensing of a capital item or the increasing deterioration of the quality of the equipment
• Gross manufacturing equipment cost ÷ some measure of production	Possibility of idle equipment or equipment that has been disposed of

Verification of Current-Year Acquisitions

The proper recording of current-year additions is important because of the long-term effect the assets have on the financial statements. The failure to capitalize a permanent asset, or the recording of an acquisition at the improper amount, affects the balance sheet until the firm disposes of the asset. The income statement is affected until the asset is fully depreciated.

Because of the importance of current-period acquisitions in the audit of manufacturing equipment, eight of the nine objectives for direct tests of balances are used as a frame of reference. (Disclosure is discussed in connection with the verification of ending balances.)

The audit objectives and common audit tests are shown in Figure 16-2. As in all other audit areas, the actual audit tests and sample size depend heavily upon materiality, the system of internal control, and the results of prior-year tests. Materiality is of special importance for verifying current-year additions. They vary from immaterial amounts in some years to a large number of significant purchases in others. Valuation and classification are usually the major objectives for this part of the audit.

FIGURE 16–2

Summary of Direct Tests of Balances—Manufacturing Equipment Additions

Audit Objectives	Common Direct Tests of Balances Procedures	Comments
Current-year acquisitions as listed are reasonable.	• Compare to prior-year additions. • Evaluate whether each material acquisition is reasonable considering the company's business. • Evaluate total acquisitions considering business changes and economic conditions.	• Requires a good knowledge of the client's business.
Current-year acquisitions in the acquisitions schedule agree with related subsidiary ledger amounts, and the total agrees with the general ledger.	• Foot the acquisitions schedule. • Trace the total to the general ledger. • Trace the individual acquisitions to the subsidiary ledger for amounts and descriptions.	• These tests should be limited unless controls are weak. • All increases in the general ledger balance for the year should reconcile to the schedule.
Current-year acquisitions as listed are valid.	• Examine vendor's invoices and receiving reports. • Physically examine assets.	• It is uncommon to physically examine additions unless controls are weak or amounts are material.
Existing acquisitions are listed.	• Examine vendor's invoices of closely related accounts such as repairs and maintenance to uncover items that should be manufacturing equipment. • Review lease and rental agreements.	• This objective is one of the most important ones for manufacturing equipment.
Current-year acquisitions as listed are owned.	• Examine vendor's invoices.	• Ordinarily no problem for equipment. Property deeds, abstracts, and tax bills are frequently examined for land or major buildings.
Current-year acquisitions as listed are properly valued.	• Examine vendor's invoices. • Recalculation of investment credit.	• Extent depends on effectiveness of system.
Current-year acquisitions as listed are properly classified.	• Examine vendor's invoices in manufacturing equipment account to uncover items that should be classified as office equipment, part of the buildings, or repairs. • Examine vendor's invoices of closely related accounts such as repairs to uncover items that should be manufacturing equipment. • Examine rent and lease expense for capitalizable leases.	• The objective is closely related to tests for omissions. It is done in conjunction with that objective and tests for valuation.
Current-year acquisitions are recorded in the proper period.	• Review transactions near the balance sheet date for proper period.	• Usually done as a part of accounts payable cutoff tests.
Accounts in the acquisition and payment cycle are properly disclosed.	• None.	• Done as a part of tests of year-end balances.

The starting point for the verification of current-year acquisitions is normally a schedule obtained from the client of all purchases recorded in the general ledger during the year. A typical schedule lists each addition separately and includes the date of the acquisition, vendor, description, notation of new or used, life of the asset for depreciation purposes, depreciation method, cost, and investment credit.

As a part of examining Figure 16-2, it is important to recognize the importance of examining vendors' invoices and related documents in verifying acquisitions of manufacturing equipment. That subject is discussed in the next section.

Examination of Supporting Documentation for Acquisitions

The most common audit test to verify additions is examination of vendors' invoices and receiving reports (vouching). Additional vouching besides what is done as a part of the tests of transactions is frequently considered necessary to verify the current-period additions because of the complexity of many equipment transactions and the materiality of the amounts. It should ordinarily be unnecessary to examine supporting documentation for each addition, but it is normal to verify large and unusual transactions for the entire year as well as a representative sample of typical additions. The extent of the verification depends upon the auditor's willingness to rely on the client's internal controls over acquisitions and the materiality of the additions.

Tests for acquisitions are accomplished by comparing the charges on vendors' invoices with recorded amounts. The auditor must be aware of the client's capitalization policies to determine whether acquisitions are valued in accordance with generally accepted accounting principles and are treated consistently with those of the preceding year. For example, many clients automatically expense items that are less than a certain amount, such as $100. The auditor should be alert for the possibility of material transportation and installation costs, as well as the trade-in of existing equipment.

The auditor must also test by recalculation the client's calculations of the investment credit taken on qualified additions as a part of the valuation objective. The proper credit against the federal income tax for an acquisition depends on the federal tax laws governing the investment credit for the particular year under audit, the nature of the asset, its length of life, and whether the asset was acquired new as compared to used.

In conjunction with testing current-period additions for existence and valuation, the auditor should also review recorded transactions for proper classification. In some cases, amounts recorded as manufacturing equipment should be classified as office equipment or as a part of the building. There is also the possibility that the client has improperly capitalized repairs, rents, or similar expenses.

The inclusion of transactions that should properly be recorded as assets in repairs and maintenance expense, lease expense, supplies, small tools, and similar accounts is a common client error. The error results from lack of understanding of generally accepted accounting principles and some clients' desire to avoid income taxes. The likelihood of these types of misclassifications should be evaluated in conjunction with the review of the controls in the acquisition and payment cycle. If the auditor concludes that they are highly likely, it may be necessary to vouch the larger amounts debited to the expense accounts. It is a common practice to do this as a regular part of the audit of the property, plant, and equipment accounts.

Verification of Current-Year Disposals

Controls over Disposals.   The most important control over the disposal of manufacturing equipment is the existence of a formal system to inform management of the sale, trade-in, abandonment, or theft of recorded machinery and equipment. If the client fails to record disposals, the original cost of the manufacturing equipment account will be overstated indefinitely, and the net book value will be overstated until the asset is fully depreciated. Another important control to protect assets from unauthorized disposal is a provision for authorization for the sale or other disposal of manufacturing equipment. Finally, there should be adequate internal verification of recorded disposals to make sure assets are correctly removed from the accounting records.

Audit Tests for Disposal.   The two major objectives in the verification of the sale, trade-in, or abandonment of manufacturing equipment are: *existing disposals are recorded*, and *recorded disposals are properly valued.*

The starting point for verifying disposals is the client's schedule of recorded disposals. The schedule typically includes the date the asset was disposed of, the name of the person or firm acquiring the asset, the selling price, the original cost of the asset, the acquisition date, the accumulated depreciation of the asset, and the investment credit recapture, if any. Mechanical accuracy tests of the schedule are necessary, including footing the schedule, tracing the totals on the schedule to the recorded disposals in the general ledger, and tracing the cost and accumulated depreciation of the disposals to the manufacturing equipment subsidiary ledgers.

Because the failure to record disposals of manufacturing equipment no longer used in the business can significantly affect the financial statements, *the search for unrecorded disposals is essential.* The nature and adequacy of the controls over disposals affect the extent of the search. The following procedures are frequently used for verifying disposals:

- Review whether newly acquired assets replace existing assets.
- Analyze gains on the disposal of assets and miscellaneous income for receipts from the disposal of assets.
- Review plant modifications and changes in product line, taxes, or insurance coverage for indications of deletions of equipment.
- Make inquiries of management and production personnel about the possibility of the disposal of assets.

When an asset is sold or disposed of without having been traded in for a replacement asset, the *valuation* of the transaction can be verified by examining the related sales invoice and subsidiary property records. The auditor should compare the cost and accumulated depreciation in the subsidiary records with the recorded entry in the general journal and recompute the gain or loss on the disposal of the asset for comparison with the accounting records.

Two areas deserve special attention in the valuation objective. The first is the *trade-in of an asset for a replacement*. When trade-ins occur, the auditor should be sure the new asset is properly capitalized and the replaced asset properly eliminated from the records, considering the book value of the asset traded in and the additional cost of the new asset. The second area of special concern is the disposal of assets affected by the *investment credit recapture provisions*. Since the recapture affects the current year's income-tax expense and liability, the auditor must evaluate its significance. An understanding of the recapture provisions for the year the asset was acquired is necessary before the calculation can be made.

Verification of the Ending Balance in the Asset Account

Controls over Existing Assets. The nature of the physical and accounting controls over existing assets determines whether it is necessary to verify manufacturing equipment acquired in prior years. Important controls include the use of a subsidiary ledger for individual fixed assets, adequate physical controls over assets that are easily movable (such as tools and vehicles), assignment of identification numbers to each plant asset, and periodic physical count of fixed assets and their reconciliation by accounting personnel. A formal system for informing the accounting department of all disposals of permanent assets is also an important control over the balance of assets carried forward into the current year.

Audit Tests

Usually, the auditor does not obtain a listing from the client of all assets included in the ending balance of manufacturing equipment. Instead, audit tests are determined on the basis of the subsidiary ledgers.

Typically, the first audit step concerns the mechanical accuracy objective: manufacturing equipment as listed in the subsidiary ledgers agrees with the general ledger. The objective is satisfied by adding the individual subsidiary amounts to arrive at the ending total in the general ledger.

After reviewing the controls over existing assets and their related records, the auditor must decide whether it is necessary to verify the existence (validity) of individual items of manufacturing equipment included in the subsidiary ledger. If the auditor believes there is a high likelihood of significant missing permanent assets that are still recorded on the accounting records, an appropriate procedure is to select a sample from the subsidiary records and examine the actual assets. In rare cases the auditor may believe it is necessary that the client take a complete physical inventory of fixed assets to make sure they actually exist. If a physical inventory is taken, the auditor normally observes the physical count.

Ordinarily, it is unnecessary to test the valuation of fixed assets recorded in prior periods because presumably they were verified in previous audits at the time they were acquired. But the auditor should be aware that companies may occasionally have on hand manufacturing equipment that is no longer used in operations. If the amounts are material, the auditor should evaluate whether they should be written down to net realizable value or at least be disclosed separately as "nonoperating equipment."

A major consideration in verifying the ending balance in permanent assets is the possibility of existing *legal encumbrances* (disclosure objective). A number of methods are available to determine if manufacturing equipment is encumbered. These include reading the terms of loan and credit agreements and mailing loan confirmation requests to banks and other lending institutions. Information with respect to encumbered assets may also be obtained through discussions with the client or confirmations with legal counsel. In addition, it is desirable to obtain information on possible liens by sending a "Request for Information under the Uniform Commercial Code" to the secretary of state or other appropriate officials of the state in which the company operates.

The *proper disclosure* of manufacturing equipment in the financial statements must be carefully evaluated to make sure generally accepted accounting principles are followed. Manufacturing equipment should include the gross cost and should ordinarly be separated from other permanent assets. Leased property should also be disclosed separately, and all liens on property must be included in the footnotes.

Verification of Depreciation Expense

Depreciation expense is one of the few expense accounts that is not verified as a part of tests of transactions. The recorded amounts are determined by *internal allocations* rather than by exchange transactions with outside parties. When depreciation expense is material, more direct tests of balance verification are required than for an account that has already been verified through tests of transactions.

The most important objective for depreciation expense is proper valuation.

Two major concerns are involved in the valuation objective: determining whether the client is following *a consistent depreciation policy* from period to period and whether the client's *calculations are accurate*. In determining whether the client is following a consistent depreciation policy there are five considerations: the useful life of current period acquisitions, the method of depreciation, the estimated salvage value, and the policy of depreciating assets in the year of acquisition and disposition. The client's policies can be

determined by having discussions with the client and comparing the re-
ponses with the information in the auditor's permanent files.

In deciding on the reasonableness of the useful lives assigned to newly
acquired assets, the auditor must consider a number of factors: the actual
physical life of the asset, the expected life (taking into account obsolescence
or the company's normal policy of upgrading equipment), and established
company policies on trading in equipment. Occasionally, changing circumstances may necessitate a revaluation of the useful life of an asset and a change
in the lives for depreciation purposes. When this occurs, a change in
accounting estimate rather than a change in accounting principle is involved.
The impact of this change on depreciation must be carefully evaluated.

A useful method of testing depreciation is to make a calculation of its
overall reasonableness. The calculation is made by multiplying the undepre-
ciated fixed assets by the depreciation rate for the year. In making these
calculations, the auditor must of course make adjustments for current-year
additions and disposals, assets with different lengths of life, and assets with
different methods of depreciation. The calculations can be made fairly
easily if the CPA firm includes in the permanent file a breakdown of the fixed
assets by method of depreciation and length of asset life. If the overall
calculations are reasonably close to the client's totals and the system of internal control is adequate, detailed testing can be minimized.

In many audits it is also desirable to check the mechanical accuracy
of depreciation calculations. This is done by recomputing depreciation
expense for selected assets to determine whether the client is following a
proper and consistent depreciation policy. To be relevant, the detailed
calculations should be tied into the total depreciation calculations by footing
the depreciation expense on individual subsidiary accounts and reconciling
the total with the general ledger. If the client maintains its depreciation and
amortization records on data-processing equipment, it may be desirable to
consider using the computer in testing the calculations.

Verification of the Ending Balance
in Accumulated Depreciation

The debits to accumulated depreciation are normally tested as a part of the
audit of disposals of assets, whereas the credits are verified as a part of depreciation expense. If the auditor traces selected transactions to the accumulated
depreciation records in the subsidiary permanent asset ledger as a part of
these tests, little additional testing should be required.

Two objectives are usually emphasized in the audit of accumulated
depreciation:

- Accumulated depreciation as stated in the subsidiary ledgers agrees with the
  general ledger. This objective can be satisfied by footing the accumulated
  depreciation for each asset and tracing the total to the general ledger.
- Accumulated depreciation in the subsidiary ledgers is properly valued.

In some cases the life of manufacturing equipment may be significantly reduced because of such changes as reductions in customer demands for products, unexpected physical deterioration, or a modification in operations. Because of these possibilities, it is necessary to evaluate the adequacy of the allowances for accumulated depreciation each year to make sure the net book value exceeds the realizable value of the assets.

AUDIT OF PREPAID INSURANCE

Prepaid expenses, deferred charges, and intangibles are assets that vary in life from several months to several years. Their inclusion as assets results more from the concept of matching expenses with revenues than from their resale or liquidation value. The following are examples:

Prepaid rent	Organization costs
Prepaid taxes	Patents
Prepaid insurance	Trademarks
Deferred charges	Copyrights

Audit Objectives

The objectives in the verification of the prepaid expenses, deferred charges, and intangibles are much the same as for other asset accounts. The nine detailed objectives are also applicable to these accounts.

One typical difference between these assets and others, such as accounts receivable and inventory, is the immateriality of the former in many audits. Frequently, analytical review procedures are sufficient for prepaids, deferred charges, and intangibles.

In this section the audit of prepaid insurance is discussed as an account representative of this group because (1) it is found in most audits—virtually every company has some type of insurance; (2) it is typical of the problems frequently encountered in the audit of this class of accounts; and (3) the auditor's responsibility for the review of insurance coverage is an additional consideration not encountered in the other accounts in this category.

Overview of the Accounts

The accounts typically used for prepaid insurance are illustrated in Figure 16-3. The relationship between prepaid insurance and the acquisition and payment cycle is apparent in examining the debits to the asset account. Since the source of the debits in the asset account is the purchase journal, the payments of insurance premiums have already been partially tested as part of the tests of acquisition and payment transactions.

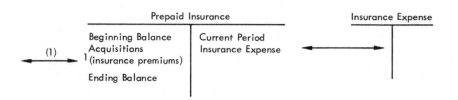

(1) Acquisitions of insurance premiums arise from the acquisitions and payment cycle. This can be observed by examining Figure 15-1.

FIGURE 16–3 Prepaid Insurance T-Accounts

Internal Controls

The internal controls for prepaid insurance and insurance expense can be conveniently divided into three categories: controls over the acquisition and recording of insurance, controls over the insurance register, and controls over the charge-off of insurance expense.

Controls over the acquisition and recording of insurance are a part of the acquisition and payment cycle. The controls should include proper authorization for new insurance policies and payment of insurance premiums consistent with those discussed in that cycle.

A record of insurance policies in force and the due date of each policy (*insurance register*) is an essential control to make sure the company has adequate insurance at all times. The control of the insurance register should include a provision for periodic review of the adequacy of the insurance coverage by an independent qualified person.

The detailed records of the information in the prepaid insurance schedule should be verified by someone independent of the person preparing them after they have been completed. A closely related control is the use of monthly "standard journal entries" for insurance expense. If a significant entry is required to adjust the balance in prepaid insurance at the end of the year, it indicates a potential error in the recording of the acquisition of insurance throughout the year or in the calculation of the year-end balance in prepaid insurance.

Audit Tests of Prepaid Insurance

Throughout the audit of prepaid insurance and insurance expense the auditor should keep in mind that the amount in insurance expense is a residual based upon the beginning balance in prepaid insurance, the payment of premiums during the year, and the ending balance. The only verification that is ordinarily necessary of the balance in the expense account is an analytical review and a brief test to be sure the charges to insurance expense arose from credits to prepaid insurance. Since the payments of premiums are tested as part of the tests of transactions and analytical review, the emphasis in the direct tests of insurance is on prepaid insurance.

In the audit of prepaid insurance, a schedule is obtained from the client or prepared by the auditor which includes each insurance policy in force, policy number, insurance coverage for each policy, premium amount, premium period, insurance expense for the year, and prepaid insurance at the end of the year. An example of a schedule obtained from the client for the auditor's working papers is given in Figure 16-4. The auditor's tests of prepaid insurance are normally indicated on the schedule.

The Policies, Prepaid Amounts, and Insurance Expense in the Prepaid Schedule Are Reasonable.

A major consideration the auditor should keep in mind throughout the audit of prepaid insurance is the frequent *immateriality* of the beginning and ending balances. Furthermore, few transactions are debited and credited to the balance during the year, most of the transactions are small, and the transactions are usually simple to understand. Therefore, the auditor can generally spend practically no time verifying the balance. When he plans not to verify the balance in detail, the analytical review becomes increasingly important as a means of identifying potentially significant errors. The following are commonly performed analytical tests of prepaid insurance and insurance expense:

- Compare total prepaid insurance and insurance expense with previous years as a test of reasonableness.
- Compute the ratio of prepaid insurance to insurance expense and compare it with previous years.
- Compare the individual insurance policies and their coverage on the schedule obtained from the client with the preceding year's schedule as a test of the elimination of certain policies or a change in insurance coverage.
- Compare the computed prepaid insurance balance on a policy-by-policy basis for the current year with that of the preceding year as a test of an error in calculation.
- Review the *insurance coverage* listed on the prepaid insurance schedule with an appropriate client official or insurance broker for adequacy of coverage. The auditor cannot be an expert on insurance matters, but his understanding of accounting and the valuation of assets is certainly important in making certain a company is not underinsured.

For many audits, no additional tests need be performed beyond the review for overall reasonableness unless the tests indicate a high likelihood of a significant error or the internal control is considered inadequate. The remaining audit procedures should be performed only when there is a special reason for doing so. The discussion of these tests is organized around the audit objectives for performing direct tests of asset balances. For convenience of discussion, certain objectives are combined and the order in which they are discussed is different than that previously used.

Insurance Policies in the Prepaid Schedule Are Valid and Existing Policies Are Listed.

The verification of validity and tests for omissions of the insurance policies in force can be tested in one of two ways: by referring to supporting documentation or by obtaining a confirmation of insurance infor-

ABC Company, Inc.
Prepaid Insurance

Schedule **F-2** Date
Prepared by *Client/JL* 1/20
Approved by *JL* 1/25

12/31/8x

Insurer	Policy Number	Coverage	Term	
Ever-ready Casualty Co.	IBB-79016 ②	Auto liability, collision, comprehensive, uninsured motorist – covers all autos owned and leased by the company.	6/1/8w-8x 6/1/8w-8y	
Everystate Insurance	74-48-914 ②	Multi-peril – Headquarters and plant, including contents.	3/15/8w-8x 3/15/8w-8y	① ①
Standard Surety Co.	1973 016 ②	Blanket Position Bond – $25,000	7/1/8w-8x	
Commercial Bonding Co.	717-639 ②	Commercial Blanket Bond – $100,000	7/1/8x-8y	

Reconciliation to Insurance Expense (General) Account:

Dependable Insurance	DIC-9161 ②	Personal property-Sales offices	1/1/8x-12/31/8x	

Insurance expense

① Policy term is 3 years, expiring 3/14/8z; premium shown is annual portion. Annual premium is estimated, subject to annual review and adjustment. Premium is payable in monthly instalments under terms of contract. (See work paper section CC, Contracts Payable.)

② Reviewed and briefed policies; details of coverage in permanent file. Blanket Position Bond replaced by Commercial Blanket Bond on expiration.

③ Annual premium adjustment; traced to invoice and voucher.

④ Charged directly to expense; traced to invoice and voucher, premium paid 1/14/8x. Policy renewed 1/1/8y, premium paid 1/20/8y.

FIGURE 16-4 Schedule of Prepaid Insurance

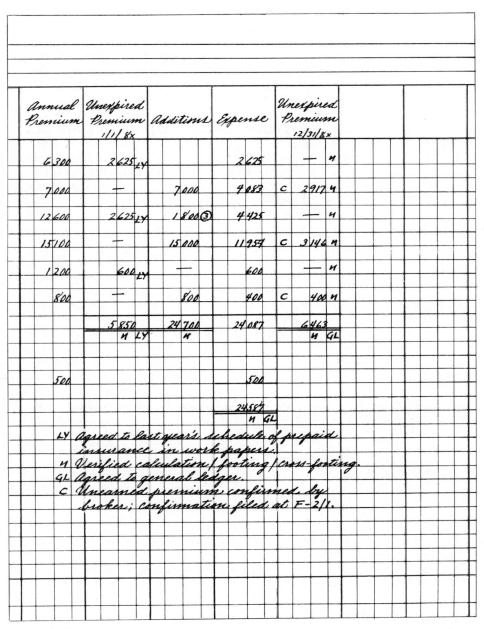

Annual Premium	Unexpired Premium 1/1/8x	Additions	Expense	Unexpired Premium 12/31/8x			
6 300	2 625 LY		2 625	— ⁿ			
7 000	—	7 000	4 083	c 2 917 ⁿ			
12 600	2 625 LY	1 800 ③	4 425	— ⁿ			
15 100	—	15 000	11 954	c 3 146 ⁿ			
1 200	600 LY	—	600	— ⁿ			
800	—	800	400	c 400 ⁿ			
	5 850 ⁿ LY	24 700 ⁿ	24 087	6 463 ⁿ GL			
500			500				
			24 587 ⁿ GL				

LY Agreed to last year's schedule of prepaid insurance in work papers.
ⁿ Verified calculation / footing / cross-footing.
GL Agreed to general ledger.
c Unearned premium confirmed by broker; confirmation filed at F-2/1.

FIGURE 16–4 (cont.)

mation from the company's insurance agent. The first approach entails examining insurance invoices and policies in force. If these tests are performed, they should be done on a limited test basis. The sending of a confirmation to the client's insurance agent is a preferable approach because it is usually less time-consuming than vouching tests, and it provides 100 percent confirmation. The use of confirmations for this purpose has grown rapidly in the past few years.

Insurance Policies in the Prepaid Schedule Are Owned.   The party who will receive the benefit if an insurance claim is filed is considered the owner. Ordinarily, the recipient named in the policy is the client, but when there are mortgages or other liens, the insurance claim may be payable to a creditor. The review of insurance policies for claimants other than the client is an excellent test of unrecorded liabilities and pledged assets.

Prepaid Amounts on the Schedule Are Properly Valued and the Total Is Correctly Added and Agrees with the General Ledger.   The valuation of prepaid insurance involves verifying the total amount of the insurance premium, the length of the policy period, and the allocation of the premium to unexpired insurance. The amount of the premium for a given policy and its time period can be verified simultaneously by examining the premium invoice or the confirmation from an insurance agent. Once these two have been verified, the client's calculations of unexpired insurance can be tested by recalculation. The schedule of prepaid insurance can then be footed and the totals traced to the general ledger to complete the mechanical accuracy tests.

The Related Expense to Prepaid Insurance Is Properly Classified.   The proper classification of debits to different insurance expense accounts should be reviewed as a test of the income statement. In some cases the appropriate expense account is obvious because of the type of insurance (such as insurance on a piece of equipment), but in other cases allocations are necessary. For example, fire insurance on the building may require allocation to several accounts, including manufacturing overhead. Consistency with previous years is the major consideration in evaluating classification.

Insurance Transactions Are Recorded in the Proper Period.   Cutoff for insurance expense is normally not a significant problem because of the small number of policies and the immateriality of the amount. If the cutoff is checked at all, it is reviewed as a part of accounts payable cutoff tests.

Prepaid Insurance Is Properly Disclosed.   In most audits, prepaid insurance is combined with other prepaid expenses and included as a current asset. The amount is usually small and is not a significant consideration to statement users.

AUDIT OF ACCRUED PROPERTY TAXES

Accrued liabilities are estimated unpaid obligations for services or benefits that have been received prior to the balance sheet date. Many accrued liabilities represent future obligations for unpaid services resulting from the passage of time but are not payable at the balance sheet date. For example, the benefits of property rental accrue throughout the year; therefore, at the balance sheet date a certain portion of the total rent cost that has not been paid should be accrued. If the balance sheet date and the termination of the rent agreement take place on the same date, any unpaid rent is more appropriately called rent payable than an accrued liability.

A second type of accrual is made up of those in which the amount of the obligation must be estimated due to the uncertainty of the amount due. An illustration is the obligation for federal income taxes when there is a reasonable likelihood that the amount reported on the tax return will be changed after an audit has been conducted by the Internal Revenue Service. The following are common accrued liabilities, including payroll-related accruals which were discussed as a part of Chapter 14:

Accrued officer bonuses	Accrued payroll taxes
Accrued commissions	Accrued pension costs
Accrued income taxes	Accrued professional fees
Accrued interest	Accrued rent
Accrued payroll	Accrued warranty costs

The verification of accrued expenses varies depending upon the nature of the accrual and the circumstances of the client. For most audits, accruals take little audit time, but in some instances accounts such as accrued income taxes, warranty costs, and pension costs are material and require considerable audit effort. To illustrate the audit of accruals, accrued property taxes are discussed in this section.

Overview of the Accounts

The accounts typically used by companies for accrued property taxes are illustrated in Figure 16-5. The relationship between the accrued property taxes and the acquisition and payment cycle is the same as for prepaid insurance and is apparent from examining the debits to the liability account. Since the source of the debits is the purchase journal, the payments of the property taxes have already been partially tested as a part of the test of the acquisition and payment cycle.

As for insurance expense, the balance in property tax expense is a residual amount that results from the beginning and ending balances in accrued property taxes and the payments of property taxes. Therefore, the emphasis in the tests should be on the property tax liability and property tax payments.

Accrued Property Taxes		Property Tax Expense
Acquisitions (Property taxes)	Beg. Balance Current Period Property Tax Expense	
	Ending Balance	

(1) Acquisitions of property taxes arise from the acquisition and payment cycle. This can be observed by examining Figure 15-1.

FIGURE 16-5 Accrued Property Taxes T-Accounts

In verifying accrued property taxes all nine objectives except ownership are relevant. But two objectives are of special significance:

- Existing properties for which accrual of taxes is appropriate are in the accrual schedule. The failure to include properties that taxes should be accrued for would understate the liability.
- Accrued property taxes is properly valued. The greatest concern in valuation is the consistent treatment of the accrual from year to year.

The primary methods of testing for the inclusion of all accruals are (1) to perform the accrual tests in conjunction with the audit of current year property tax payments and (2) to compare the accruals with those of previous years. In most audits there are few property tax payments, but each payment is often material and therefore it is common to verify each one.

First, the auditor should obtain a schedule of property tax payments from the client and compare each payment with the preceding year's schedule to determine whether all payments have been included in the client-prepared schedule. It is also necessary to examine the permanent asset working papers for major additions and disposals of assets which may affect the property taxes accrual. If the client is expanding its operations, all property affected by local property tax regulations should be included in the schedule even if the first tax payment has not yet been made.

After the auditor is satisfied that all taxable property has been included in the client-prepared schedule, it is necessary to evaluate the reasonableness of the total amount of property taxes on each property being used as a basis to estimate the accrual. In some instances the total amount has already been set by the taxing authority, and it is possible to verify the total by comparing the amount in the schedule with the tax bill in the client's possession. In other instances the preceding year's total payments must be adjusted for the expected increase in property tax rates.

The auditor can verify the accrued property tax by recomputing the portion of the total tax applicable to the current year for each piece of property. The most important consideration in making this calculation is to use the same portion of each tax payment as the accrual that was used in the preceding year unless justifiable conditions exist for a change. After the accrual and property tax expense for each piece of property have been recomputed, the totals should be added and compared with the general ledger. In many cases property taxes are charged to more than one expense account. When this happens the auditor should test for proper classification by evaluating whether the proper amount was charged to each account.

A typical working paper showing the property tax expense, the accrued property taxes, and the audit procedures used to verify the balances is illustrated in Figure 16-6.

AUDIT OF OPERATIONS

Objectives

The audit of operations is meant to determine whether the income and expense accounts in the financial statements are fairly presented in accordance with generally accepted accounting principles. The auditor must be satisfied that each of the income and expense totals included in the income statement as well as net earnings is not materially misstated.

In conducting audit tests of the financial statements, the auditor must always be aware of the importance of the income statement to users of the statements. It is clear that many users rely more heavily on the income statement than the balance sheet for making decisions. Equity investors, long-term creditors, union representatives, and frequently even short-term creditors are more interested in the ability of a firm to generate profit than in the liquidity value or book value of the individual assets.

Considering the purposes of the statement of earnings, the following two concepts are essential in the audit of operations:

- The matching of periodic income and expense is necessary for a proper determination of operating results.
- The consistent application of accounting principles for different periods is necessary for comparability.

These two concepts must be applied to the recording of individual transactions and to the combining of accounts in the general ledger for statement presentation.

Approach to Auditing Operations

The audit of operations cannot be regarded as a separate part of the total audit process. A misstatement of an income statement account will most often equally affect a balance sheet account, and vice-versa. The audit of operations is so intertwined with the other parts of the audit that it is necessary to interrelate different aspects of testing operations with the different types of

ABC Company, Inc.
Property Tax Worksheet

Schedule	I-6	Date
Prepared by	PR	1/15
Approved by	GS	1/20

12/31/8x

Tax Bill No.	Area Code	Assessing Authority	Property	Assessed Value (1)	Total Tax (2)	Date		Period Covered
						Lien Payable (3)	Paid (4)	
		West Coast Facilities						
526391	51	King County	Westside Warehouse	400000	16000	Jan 1, 198x		198x
						Apr. 30, 1984		
						Oct. 31, 1984		
526392	51	King County	Headquarters Bldg.	250000	10000	Jan 1, 198w		198w
						Apr. 30, 198x		
						Oct. 31, 198x		
						Jan 1, 198x		198x
		Mid-West Facility						
17923	A	Minor County	Manufacturing Plant	2000000	23000	Jul. 1, 198w	Jul. 1, 198w-8x	
					25000	Jul. 1, 198x	Jul. 1, 198x-84	
						Dec. 31, 198x		

(1) Assessed valuation is defined by the laws of both states as 50% of "true and fair value."

(2) Millage rates:
  King County .0400 ($40 per $1000)
  Minor County .0115 ($11.50 per $1000) for 198w-8x
        .0125 ($12.50 per $1000) for 198x-84

(3) Laws of both states establish the lien date to be the same as the assessment date; assessment date for the West Coast state is statutorily defined as January 1, and for the Midwest state as July 1.

(4) Taxes are payable as follows:
  West Coast state — one half no later than April 30 and the balance no later than October 31, for the preceding calendar year.
  Midwest state — payable in full not later than December 31 following assessment date.

FIGURE 16-6 Schedule for Property Taxes

Beginning Balance	Prepaid Additions (6)	Expense	Ending Balance	Beginning Balance	Accrued Additions (6)	Payments	Ending Balance
—0—	16,000 ✓	16,000 ∧	—0— ⤬	(5) —0—	16,000 ✓	—0—	16,000 ⤬
				10,000			
						5,000 T	
						5,000 T	—0— ⤬
—0—	10,000 ✓	10,000 ∧	—0— ⤬	—0—	10,000 ✓		10,000 ⤬
11,500		11,500 ∧	—0— ⤬	—0—			—0— ⤬
	25,000 ✓	12,500 ∧	12,500 ⤬	—0—	25,000 ✓		
						25,000 T	—0— ⤬
11,500	51,000	50,000	12,500 ⤬	10,000	51,000	35,000	26,000 ⤬
⌐ LY	⌐	⌐	⌐	⌐ LY	⌐	⌐	⌐

(5) Warehouse certified complete and accepted Dec. 22, 198w, inspected and valued by County in March 198x. Per state law (note 3), assessment date and lien date statutorily set at Jan. 1, 198x.

(6) Liability and deferred charge are recorded by company on the lien date. The deferred charge is amortized monthly, and the liability account relieved when instalments are paid.

LY Agreed to last year's workpapers.
✓ Agreed to county tax due notice (identified in left column).
∧ Agreed to amortization schedule and traced to standard journal entry.
T Traced to cancelled check and validated receipt.
∧,⤬ Footed, cross-footed.

FIGURE 16–6 (cont.)

tests previously discussed. A brief description of these tests serves as a review of material covered in other chapters, but more important, it shows the interrelationship of different parts of the audit with operations testing. The parts of the audit directly affecting operations are as follows:

- Analytical review procedures
- Tests of transactions
- Review of transactions with affiliates and interplant accounts
- Analysis of account balances
- Direct tests of balance sheet accounts
- Tests of allocations

The emphasis in this section is on the operations accounts directly related to the acquisition and payment cycle, but the same basic concepts apply to the operations accounts in all other cycles.

Analytical Review Procedures

Analytical review procedures (tests) were first discussed in Chapter 4 as a general concept and have been referred to in subsequent chapters as a part of particular audit areas. Analytical tests should be thought of as a part of the test of the fairness of the presentation of both balance sheet and income statement accounts. A few analytical tests and their effect upon operations in the acquisition and payment cycle are shown in Figure 16-7.

FIGURE 16–7

Analytical Test	*Purpose in Relation to Operations*
• Comparison of individual expenses with those of previous years	A possible overstatement or understatement of a balance
• Comparison of individual asset and liability balances with those of previous years	A possible overstatement or understatement of a balance sheet account which would also affect an income statement account (e.g., a misstatement of inventory affects costs of goods sold)
• Comparison of individual expenses with budgets	A possible misstatement of income statement accounts
• Comparison of gross margin percent ratio with that of previous years	A possible misstatement of sales or cost of goods sold
• Comparison of inventory turnover ratio with that of previous years	A possible misstatement of cost of goods sold
• Comparison of prepaid insurance expense with that of previous years	A possible misstatement of insurance expense
• Comparison of commission expense ÷ sales with that of previous years	A possible misstatement of commission expense
• Comparison of individual manufacturing expenses ÷ total manufacturing expenses with those of previous years	A possible misstatement of individual manufacturing expenses

Tests of Transactions

Compliance tests of internal controls and substantive tests of individual transactions both have the effect of simultaneously verifying balance sheet and operations accounts. For example, when an auditor concludes that the controls are adequate to provide reasonable assurance that transactions in the voucher register are valid, properly valued, correctly classified, and recorded in a timely manner, evidence exists as to the correctness of individual balance sheet accounts such as accounts payable and fixed assets, and income statement accounts such as advertising and repairs. On the other hand, inadequate controls and errors discovered through tests of transactions are an indication of the likelihood of misstatements in both the income statement and the balance sheet.

The evaluation of internal control and the related tests of transactions are the most important means of verifying many of the operations accounts in each of the transaction cycles. For example, if the auditor concludes after adequate tests that the system of internal control over acquisitions is reliable, the only additional verfication of operating accounts such as utilities, advertising, and purchases should be cutoff tests. On the other hand, certain income and expense accounts are not verified at all by tests of transactions and others must be tested more extensively by other means. These are discussed as we proceed.

Review of Transactions with Affiliates and Interplant Accounts

The examination of underlying documents as a part of the tests of transactions is primarily designed to verify transactions with third parties, but transactions taking place with affiliates and subdivisions within the client's organization are closely related. The possibility of improper recording and disclosing of transactions between closely interdependent entities was discussed in Chapter 6 as a part of discussing the requirements of auditing and disclosing related party transactions (Section 335 of SASs).

When a client deals with related parties, SASs (Section 335) requires the auditor to determine the amount of the transactions, and whether the transactions have been recorded at an amount equal to the value of a similar exchange between independent, unrelated third parties. The auditor must also make sure that the nature of the relationship and the amount of the transactions are properly disclosed.

In some cases the relationship between related parties is so close that an affiliate must be considered a part of the same entity. For example, when interplant transactions take place, they must be eliminated when the combined statements are prepared if the amounts are material. If the affiliate is not part of the same entity, the proper valuation of purchases of inventory, services acquired from related parties, and other exchange transactions must be carefully evaluated for propriety and reasonableness. Obviously, related party transactions must be audited more extensively than those with third parties.

Analysis of Account Balances

For some accounts the amounts included in the operations accounts must be analyzed even though the three previously mentioned tests have been performed. The meaning and methodology of analysis of accounts will be described first, followed by a discussion of those occasions when expense account analysis is appropriate.

Expense account analysis is the examination of underlying documentation of the individual transactions and amounts making up the total of a particular expense account. The underlying documents are of the same nature as those used for examining transactions as a part of tests of acquisitions transactions and include such documents as invoices, receiving reports, purchase orders, and contracts.

Thus, expense accounts analysis is closely related to tests of transactions. The major difference between the two is the degree of concentration on an individual account. Since the test of transactions is meant to test the effectiveness of the overall system, it constitutes a general review that usually includes the verification of many different accounts. The analysis of expense and other operations accounts consists of the examination of the transactions in particular accounts to determine the propriety, classification, valuation, and other specific information about each account analyzed.

Cutoff tests, which are typically thought of as direct tests of balance sheet accounts, simultaneously affect both the income statement and the balance sheet. An example is when the auditor verifies the cutoff of sales as a part of the audit of accounts receivable. It does not matter whether cutoff tests are regarded as tests of operations or tests of the balance sheet—they affect both. The only reason for performing cutoff tests as a part of verifying balance sheet accounts is convenience.

Also, in many instances the expense account analysis as discussed above takes place as a part of the verification of the related asset. For example, it is common to analyze repairs and maintenance as a part of verifying fixed assets, rent expense as a part of verifying prepaid or accrued rent, and insurance expense as a part of testing prepaid insurance.

Tests of Allocations

Several expense accounts that have not yet been discussed are those arising from the internal allocation of accounting data. These include expenses such as depreciation, depletion, and the amortization of copyrights and catalog costs. The allocation of manufacturing overhead between inventory and cost of goods sold is an example of a different type of allocation that affects the expenses. Naturally, these accounts must be tested in some way during the course of the audit.

ABC Company, Inc.
General and Administrative Expenses

12/31/8x

Acct. 913 – Legal Expense

Paid to	For	Date	Amount
② Alexander J. Schweppe	Retainer – 12 months @ $500	Monthly ①	6000 ✓
" "	ABC vs. Casson – patent infringement suit	Apr. 14 / Aug. 9	2800 ✓ / 3109 ✓
② Smith, Todd & Ball	Consultation re: inquiry from Consumer Protection Bureau, State Attorney General's office	June 6 / July 18	200 ✓ / 200 ✓
③ L. Marvin Hall	Assistance in collecting overdue receivable from Star Mfg.	Nov. 10	105 ✓
			12414 G.L. ⌐

① Per minutes of meeting of Board of Directors 1/10/8x Schweppe reappointed general counsel, with retainer.
② Attorney's letters requested { Received 1/23/8x: all matters listed are covered therein; letters filed in General Section of workpapers.
③ Attorney's letter not requested. Per phone conversation with Mr. Hall, 1/21/8x, he rarely represents the company, and his services have been limited to collection problems. The Star Mfg. matter was closed in October 198x and he has not been involved in any other matters related to the company since that time.

✓ Examined statements and vouchers.
⌐ Footed.
GL Agreed to general ledger.

FIGURE 16–8 Expense Analysis for Legal Expense

Allocations are important because they determine whether a particular expenditure is an asset or a current period expense. If the client fails to follow generally accepted accounting principles or fails to calculate the allocation properly, the financial statements can be materially misstated. The allocation of many expenses such as the depreciation of fixed assets and the amortization of copyrights is required because the life of the asset is greater than one year. The original cost of the asset is verified at the time of acquisition, but the charge-off takes place over several years. Other types of allocations directly affecting the financial statements arise because the life of a short-lived asset does not expire on the balance sheet date. Examples include prepaid rent and insurance. Finally, the allocation of costs between current period manufacturing expenses and inventory is required by generally accepted accounting principles as a means of reflecting all the costs of making a product.

In testing the allocation of expenditures such as prepaid insurance and manufacturing overhead, the two most important considerations are adherence to generally accepted accounting principles and consistency with the preceding period. The two most important audit procedures for allocations are tests for overall reasonableness and recalculation of the client's results. The most common way to perform these tests is as a part of the audit of the related asset or liability accounts. For example, depreciation expense is usually verified as part of the audit of property, plant, and equipment; the amortization of patents is tested as part of verifying new patents or the disposal of existing ones; and the allocations between inventory and cost of goods sold are verified as part of the audit of inventory.

REVIEW QUESTIONS

16–1. Explain the relationship between the tests of the system for the acquisition and payment cycle and those for the verification of property, plant, and equipment. Which aspects of property, plant, and equipment are directly affected by the tests of the system and which are not?

16–2. Explain why the emphasis in auditing property, plant, and equipment is on the current period acquisitions and disposals rather than on the balance in the account carried forward from the preceding year. Under what circumstances will the emphasis be on the balances carried forward?

16–3. What is the relationship between the audit of property accounts and the audit of repair and maintenance accounts? Explain how the auditor organizes the audit to take this relationship into consideration.

16–4. List and briefly state the purpose of all audit procedures that might reasonably be applied by an auditor to determine that all property and equipment retirements have been recorded on the books.

16–5. In auditing depreciation expense, what major considerations should the auditor keep in mind? Explain how each of these can be verified.

16–6. Explain the relationship between the tests of the system for the acquisition and payment cycle and those for the verification of prepaid insurance.

16–7. Explain why the audit of prepaid insurance should ordinarily take a relatively small amount of audit time if the client's system of internal control is effective.

16–8. Distinguish between the evaluation of the adequacy of insurance coverage and the verification of prepaid insurance. Explain which of these is more important in a typical audit.

16–9. What are the similarities and differences in verifying prepaid insurance and patents?

16–10. Explain the relationship between rent payable and the tests of the system for the acquisition and payment cycle. Which aspects of rent payable are not verified as a part of the tests of transactions?

16–11. How should the emphasis differ in verifying income taxes payable and accrued warranty expense?

16–12. In verifying accounts payable it is common to restrict the audit sample to a small portion of the population items, whereas in auditing accrued property taxes it is common to verify all transactions for the year. Explain the reason for the difference.

16–13. Which documents will be used to verify prepaid property taxes and the related expense accounts?

16–14. List three expense accounts that are tested as part of the acquisition and payment cycle or the payroll and personnel cycle. List three expense accounts that are not directly verified as a part of either of these cycles.

16–15. What is meant by the analysis of expense accounts? Explain how expense account analysis relates to the tests of transactions that the auditor has already completed for the acquisition and payment cycle.

16–16. How would the approach for verifying repair expense differ from that used to audit depreciation expense? Why would the approach be different?

16–17. List the factors that should affect the auditor's decision as to whether or not to analyze a particular account balance. Considering these factors, list four expense accounts that are commonly analyzed in audit engagements.

16–18. Explain how cost of goods sold for a wholesale company could in part be verified by each of the following types of tests:
   a. Analytical tests.
   b. Tests of transactions.
   c. Review of transactions with affiliates.
   d. Analysis of account balances.
   e. Direct tests of balance sheet accounts.
   f. Tests of allocations.

DISCUSSION QUESTIONS AND PROBLEMS

16–19. For each of the following errors in property, plant, and equipment accounts, state an internal control the client could install to prevent the error from occurring and a substantive audit procedure the auditor could use to discover the error.

a. The asset lives used to depreciate equipment are less than reasonable expected useful lives.

b. Capitalizable assets are routinely expensed as repairs and maintenance, perishable tools, or supplies expense.

c. Construction equipment that is abandoned or traded for replacement equipment is not removed from the accounting records.

d. Depreciation expense for manufacturing operations is charged to administrative expenses.

e. Tools necessary for the maintenance of equipment are stolen by company employees for their personal use.

f. Acquisitions of property are recorded at an improper amount.

g. A loan against existing equipment is not recorded in the accounting records. The cash receipts from the loan never reached the company because they were used for the down payment on a piece of equipment now being used as an operating asset. The equipment is also not recorded in the records.

16–20. The following types of internal controls are commonly employed by organizations for property, plant, and equipment:

a. Individual detailed subsidiary ledgers are maintained for each fixed asset.

b. Written policies exist and are known by accounting personnel to differentiate between capitalizable additions, freight, installation costs, replacements, and maintenance expenditures.

c. Purchases of permanent assets in excess of $20,000 are approved by the board of directors.

d. Wherever practical, equipment is labeled with metal tags and is inventoried on a systematic basis.

e. Depreciation charges for individual assets are calculated for each asset, recorded in individual subsidiary ledgers, and verified periodically by an independent clerk.

Required:

a. State the purpose of each of the internal controls listed above. Your answer should be in the form of the type of error that is likely to be reduced because of the control.

b. For each control, list one compliance procedure the auditor can use to test for the existence of the control.

c. List one substantive procedure for testing whether the control is actually preventing errors in property, plant, and equipment.

16–21. In connection with a recurring examination of the financial statements of the Louis Manufacturing Company for the year ended December 31, 19X8, you have been assigned the audit of the manufacturing equipment, manufacturing equipment–accumulated depreciation, and repairs of manufacturing equipment accounts. Your review of Louis's policies and procedures has disclosed the following pertinent information:

a. The manufacturing equipment account includes the net invoice price plus related freight and installation costs for all of the equipment in Louis's manufacturing plant.

    b. The manufacturing equipment and accumulated depreciation accounts are supported by a subsidiary ledger which shows the cost and accumulated depreciation for each piece of equipment.

    c. An annual budget for capital expenditures of $1,000 or more is prepared by the budget committee and approved by the board of directors. Capital expenditures over $1,000 which are not included in this budget must be approved by the board of directors, and variations of 20 percent or more must be explained to the board. Approval by the supervisor of production is required for capital expenditures under $1,000.

    d. Company employees handle installation, removal, repair, and rebuilding of the machinery. Work orders are prepared for these activities and are subject to the same budgetary control as other expenditures. Work orders are not required for external expenditures.

Required:

    a. Cite the major objectives of your audit of the manufacturing equipment, manufacturing equipment–accumulated depreciation, and repairs of manufacturing equipment accounts. Do not include in this listing the auditing procedures designed to accomplish these objectives.

    b. Prepare the portion of your audit program applicable to the review of 19X8 additions to the manufacturing equipment account.   (AICPA adapted)

16–22. In connection with the annual examination of Johnson Corp., a manufacturer of janitorial supplies, you have been assigned to audit the fixed assets. The company maintains a detailed property ledger for all fixed assets. You prepared an audit program for the balances of property, plant, and equipment but have yet to prepare one for accumulated depreciation and depreciation expense.

Required:

    Prepare a separate comprehensive audit program for the accumulated depreciation and depreciation expense accounts.   (AICPA adapted)

16–23. Hardware Manufacturing Company, a closely held corporation, has operated since 19X4 but has not had its financial statements audited. The company now plans to issue additional capital stock expected to be sold to outsiders and wishes to engage you to examine its 19X8 transactions and render an opinion on the financial statements for the year ended December 31, 19X8.

    The company has expanded from one plant to three plants and has frequently acquired, modified, and disposed of all types of equipment. Fixed assets have a net book value of 70 percent of total assets and consist of land and buildings, diversified machinery and equipment, and furniture and fixtures. Some property was acquired by donation from stockholders. Depreciation was recorded by several methods using various estimated lives.

Required:

    a. May you confine your examination solely to 19X8 transactions as requested by this prospective client whose financial statements have not previously been examined? Why?

  b. Prepare an audit program for the January 1, 19X8, opening balances of the
     land, building, and equipment and accumulated depreciation accounts of
     Hardware Manufacturing Company. You need not include tests of 19X8
     transactions in your program.   (AICPA adapted)

16–24. The following program has been prepared for the audit of prepaid real estate
     taxes of a client that pays taxes on 25 different pieces of property, some of
     which have been acquired in the current year.
  a. Obtain a schedule of prepaid taxes from the client and tie the total to the
     general ledger.
  b. Compare the charges for annual tax payments with property tax assessment
     bills.
  c. Recompute prepaid amounts for all payments on the basis of the portion
     of the year expired.

  Required:

  a. State the purpose of each procedure.
  b. Evaluate the adequacy of the audit program.

16–25. You have just commenced your examination of the financial statements of
     Vickey Corporation for the year ended December 31, 19X6. Analyses of the
     company's prepaid insurance and insurance expense accounts are shown on
     page 569.
       Your examination also disclosed the following information.
  a. Only one policy of those prepaid at January 1, 19X6, remained in force
     on December 31, and it will expire on March 31, 19X7. The policy was
     a 24-month policy and the total premium was $600.
  b. Cash value of the life insurance policy on the life of the president increased
     from $1,110 to $1,660 during 19X6. The corporation is the beneficiary on
     the policy.
  c. The corporation signed a note payable to an insurance company for the
     balance due on the fire insurance policy which was effective as of April 1.
     The note called for nine additional $1,000 semiannual payments plus
     interest at 6 percent per annum on the unpaid balance (also paid semi-
     annually).
  d. An accrual dated December 31, 19X5, for $170 for insurance payable was
     included among accrued liabilities.
  e. Included in miscellaneous income was a credit dated April 10 for $100 for
     a 4 percent dividend on the renewal of the automobile collision insurance
     policy. The insurance company is a mutual company. Also included in
     miscellaneous income was a credit dated November 2 for $350 for a check
     from the same insurance company for a claim filed October 19.
  f. An invoice dated November 15 for $1,560 for employee fidelity bonds
     from November 15, 19X6, to November 15, 19X7, was not paid or
     recorded.
  g. An invoice dated January 13, 19X7, for $2,800 for the 19X7 workmen's
     compensation policy was not recorded. The net amount of the invoice was
     $2,660 after a credit of $140 from the payroll audit for the year ended
     December 31, 19X6.

Vickey Corporation
Worksheet for Distribution of Insurance
for Year Ended December 31, 19X6

Date (19X6)		Prepaid Insurance	Folio	Amount Debit	Amount Credit
January	1	Balance forward		$ 5,550	
	10	Premium on president's policy	CD	1,240	
	14	Deposit on workmen's compensation policy for 19X6	CD	2,750	
	31	Monthly amortization	JE		$ 410
April	1	Down payment on fire policy (April 1, 19X6, to April 1, 19X9)	CD	1,000	
		Total		$10,540	$ 410

Insurance Expense

January	10	Trip insurance on officers (inspection tour of dealers in December 19X5)	CD	$ 170	
	31	Monthly amortization	JE	410	
February	21	Balance on workmen's compensation policy (per payroll audit for policy year ending December 31, 19X5)	CD	250	
April	10	Automobile collision policy (policy year April 1, 19X6 to April 1, 19X7)	CD	2,500	
June	10	Increase in fire policy (May 1, 19X6 to April 1, 19X9)	CD	590	
August	10	Fleet public liability and property damage policy (September 1, 19X6, to September 1, 19X7)	CD	3,780	
	17	Check from insurance company for reduction in auto collision rate for entire policy year	CR		$ 120
October	1	Fire policy payment	CD	1,300	
	19	Cost of repair to automobile damaged in a collision	CD	400	
		Total		$ 9,400	$ 120

Required:

Prepare a worksheet to properly distribute all amounts related to insurance for 19X6. The books have not been closed for the year. The worksheet should provide columns to show the distribution to prepaid insurance, to insurance expense, and to other accounts. The names of other accounts affected should be indicated. Formal journal entries are not required.

(AICPA adapted)

16–26. You have assigned your assistant to the examination of the Cap Sales Company's fire insurance policies. All routine audit procedures with regard to the fire insurance register have been completed (i.e., vouching, footing, examination of canceled checks, computation of insurance expense and prepayment, tracing of expense charges to appropriate expense accounts, etc.). Your assistant has never examined fire insurance policies and asks for detailed instructions.

Required:

a. In addition to examining the policies for the amounts of insurance and premium and for effective and expiration dates, to what other details should your assistant give particular attention as he examines the policies? Give the reasons for examining each detail. (Confine your comments to fire insurance policies covering buildings, their contents, and inventories.)

b. After reviewing your assistant's working papers, you concur in his conclusion that the insurance coverage against loss by fire is inadequate and that if loss occurs the company may have insufficient assets to liquidate its debts. After a discussion with you, management refuses to increase the amount of insurance coverage.
   (1) What mention will you make of this condition and contingency in your short-form report? Why?
   (2) What effect will this condition and contingency have upon your opinion? Give the reasons for your position.   (AICPA adapted)

16–27. As part of the audit of different audit areas, it is important to be alert for the possibility of unrecorded liabilities. For each of the following audit areas or accounts, describe a liability that could be uncovered and the audit procedures that could uncover it.
   a. Minutes of the board of directors' meetings.
   b. Land and buildings.
   c. Rent expense.
   d. Interest expense.
   e. Cash surrender value of life insurance.
   f. Cash in the bank.
   g. Officers' travel and entertainment expense.

16–28. In connection with his examination of the financial statements of the Thames Corporation, a CPA is reviewing the federal income taxes payable account.

Required:

a. Discuss reasons why the CPA should review federal income tax returns for prior years and the reports of internal revenue agents.
b. What information will these reviews provide? (Do not discuss specific tax return items.)   (AICPA adapted)

16–29. With the approval of its board of directors, the Thames Corporation made a sizable payment for advertising during the year being audited. The corporation deducted the full amount in its federal income tax return. The controller acknowledges that this deduction probably will be disallowed because it relates to political matters. He has not provided for this disallowance in his federal income tax provision and refuses to do so because he fears that this will cause the revenue agent to believe that the deduction is not valid. What is the CPA's responsibility in this situation? Explain.   (AICPA adapted)

16–30. While you are having lunch with a banker friend, you become involved in explaining to him how your firm conducts an audit in a typical engagement. Much to your surprise, your friend is interested and is able to converse intelligently in discussing your philosophy of emphasizing the review and evaluation of internal control, analytical tests, tests of the system, and direct tests of balance sheet accounts. At the completion of your discussion, he says, "That all sounds great except for a couple of things. The point of view we take these days at our bank is the importance of a continual earnings stream. You seem to be emphasizing fraud detection and a fairly stated balance sheet. We would rather see you put more emphasis than you apparently do on the income statement."

Required:

How would you respond to your friend's comments?

16–31. You are examining the financial statements of a moderate-sized manufacturing corporation in connection with the preparation of financial statements to be issued with an unqualified opinion. There is some internal control, but the office and bookkeeping staff comprises only three persons. You have tested a random sample of acquisition transactions in detail and found no significant exceptions.

Required:

Submit a detailed audit program setting forth the steps you consider necessary in connection with the following expense accounts (the total of one year's charges in each account is set forth opposite each item):

Advertising	$60,000
Rent	8,000
Salesmen's commissions	39,000
Insurance	4,000

(AICPA adapted)

16–33. State what documents or evidence the auditor would examine in the verification of each of the following.
   a. Advertising expense, where advertising is placed through an agency.
   b. Advertising expense, where advertising is placed directly in newspapers by the client.
   c. Royalty expense.
   d. Repair expense.   (AICPA adapted)

16–34. Brian Day, a staff assistant, has been asked to analyze interest and legal expense as a part of the first-year audit of Rosow Manufacturing Company. In searching for a model to follow, Brian looked at other completed working papers in the current audit file and concluded that the closest thing to what he was looking for was a working paper for repair and maintenance expense account analysis. Following the approach used in analyzing repairs and maintenance, all interest and legal expenses in excess of $500 were scheduled and verified by examining supporting documentation.

Required:

a. Evaluate Brian's approach to verifying interest and legal expense.

b. Suggest a better approach to verifying these two account balances.

16–35. In performing tests of the acquisition and payment cycle for the Orlando Manufacturing Company, the staff assistant did a careful and complete job. Since the controls were evaluated as excellent before the testing began and were determined to be operating effectively on the basis of the lack of errors in the tests of the system, the decision was made to significantly reduce the tests of expense account analysis. The audit senior decided to reduce but not eliminate the acquisition-related expense account analysis for repair expense, legal and other professional, miscellaneous, and utilities expense on the grounds that they should always be verified more extensively than normal accounts. The decision was also made to eliminate any account analysis for the purchase of raw materials, depreciation expense, supplies expense, insurance expense, and the current period additions to fixed assets.

Required:

a. List other considerations in the audit besides the effectiveness of the system of internal control that should affect the auditor's decision as to which accounts to analyze.

b. Assuming no significant problems were identified on the basis of the other considerations in part a, evaluate the auditor's decision of reducing but not eliminating expense account analysis for each account involved. Justify your conclusions.

c. Assuming no significant problems were identified on the basis of the other considerations in part a, evaluate the auditor's decision to eliminate expense account analysis for each account involved. Justify your conclusions.

AUDIT
OF THE INVENTORY
AND WAREHOUSING CYCLE

Inventory takes many different forms, depending upon the nature of the operations of the business. For companies engaged in the retail or wholesale business, the most important inventory is merchandise on hand available for sale. The inventory for hospitals includes food, drugs, and medical supplies. A manufacturing company has raw materials, purchased parts, and supplies for use in production, goods in the process of being manufactured, and finished goods available for sale. We have selected manufacturing company inventories for presentation in this text. However, most of the principles discussed apply to other types of businesses as well.

For the reasons given below, the audit of inventories is often the most complex and time-consuming part of the audit:

- Inventory is generally a major item on the balance sheet, and it is often the largest item making up the accounts included in working capital.
- The inventory is in different locations, which makes the physical control and counting of the inventory difficult. Companies must have their inventory accessible for the efficient manufacture and sale of the product, but this dispersal creates significant audit problems.
- The diversity of the items in inventories creates difficulties for the auditor. Such items as jewels, chemicals, and electronic parts present problems of observation and valuation.
- The valuation of inventory is also difficult due to such factors as obsolescence and the need to allocate manufacturing costs to inventory.
- There are several acceptable inventory valuation methods, but any given client must apply a method consistent from year to year. Moreover, an organization may prefer to use different valuation methods for different parts of the inventory.

573

The physical flow of goods and the flow of costs in the inventory and warehousing cycle are shown in Figure 17-1 for a manufacturing company. The direct tie-in of the inventory and warehousing cycle to the acquisition and payment cycle and to the payroll and personnel cycle can be seen by examining the debits to the raw materials, direct labor, and manufacturing overhead T-accounts. The direct tie-in to the sales and collection cycle occurs at the point where finished goods are relieved (credited) and a charge is made to cost of goods sold. This close relationship to other transaction cycles in the organization is a basic characteristic of the audit of the inventory and warehousing cycle.

NATURE OF THE INVENTORY AND WAREHOUSING CYCLE

Functions in the Cycle and Internal Controls

The inventory and warehousing cycle can be thought of as comprising two separate but closely related systems, one involving the actual *physical flow of goods*, and the other the *related costs*. As inventories move through the company, there must be adequate controls on both their physical movement and their related costs. A brief examination of the six functions making up the inventory and warehousing cycle will help in understanding these controls and the audit evidence needed to test their effectiveness.

Processing Purchase Orders.   *Purchase requisitions* are used to request the purchasing department to place orders for inventory items. Requisitions may be initiated by stockroom personnel when inventory reaches a predetermined level, orders may be placed for the materials required to produce a particular customer order, or orders may be initiated on the basis of a periodic inventory count by a responsible person. Regardless of the method followed, the controls over purchase requisitions and the related purchase orders are evaluated and tested as part of the acquisition and payment cycle.

Receipt of New Materials   The receiving of the ordered materials is also part of the acquisition and payment cycle. Material received should be inspected for quantity and quality. The receiving department produces a *receiving report* which becomes a part of the necessary documentation before payment is made. After inspection, the material is sent to the storeroom and the receiving documents are typically sent to purchasing, the storeroom, and accounts payable.

Storage of Raw Materials.   When material is received, it is stored in the stockroom until needed for production. Materials are issued out of stock to production upon presentation of a properly approved material requisition, work order, or similar document which indicates the type and quantity of

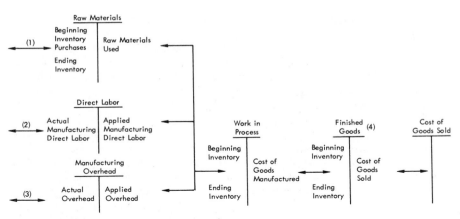

(1) Purchases arise from the acquisition and payment cycle.
(2) Actual costs arise from the payroll and personnel cycle.
(3) Actual costs arise from the acquisition and payment cycle, the payroll and personnel cycle, and the allocation of costs.
(4) Transfers to cost of goods sold arise from the sales and collection cycle.

FIGURE 17–1 Flow of Inventory and Costs in the Inventory and Warehousing Cycle

material needed. This requisition document is used to post perpetual inventory records and to make book transfers from the raw materials to work in process accounts.

Processing the Goods. The processing portion of the inventory and warehousing cycle varies greatly from company to company. The determination of the items and quantities to be produced is generally based on specific orders from customers, sales forecasts, predetermined finished goods inventory levels, and economic production runs. Frequently a separate production control department is responsible for the determination of the type and quantities of production. Within the various production departments, provision must be made to account for the quantities produced, control of scrap, quality controls, and physical protection of the material in process. The production department must generate production and scrap reports so that accounting can reflect the movement of materials in the books and determine accurate costs of production.

In any company involved in manufacturing, an adequate *cost accounting system* is an important part of the processing of goods function. A cost system is necessary to indicate the relative profitability of the various products for management planning and control and to value inventories for financial statement purposes. There are basically two types of cost systems, although many variations and combinations of these systems are employed: *job cost* and *process cost*. The main difference is whether costs are accumulated by individual jobs when material is issued and labor costs incurred (job cost), or whether they are accumulated by particular processes, with unit costs for each process assigned to the products passing through the process (process cost).

Cost system records consist of ledgers, worksheets, and reports which accumulate material, labor, and overhead costs by job or process as the costs are incurred. When jobs or products are completed, the related costs are transferred from work in process to finished goods on the basis of production department reports.

Storage of Finished Goods. As finished goods are completed by the production department, they are placed in the stockroom awaiting shipment. In companies with goods internal controls, finished goods are kept under physical control in a separate limited access area. The control of finished goods is often considered part of the sales and collection cycle.

Shipment. Shipping of completed goods is an integral part of the sales and collection cycle. Any shipment or transfer of finished goods must be authorized by a properly approved shipping document. The controls for shipment have already been studied in previous chapters.

Summary. The physical movement and related documentation in a basic inventory and warehousing cycle is shown in Figure 17-2. The figure reemphasizes the important point that the recording of costs and movement of inventory as shown in the books must correspond to the physical movements and processes.

Parts of the Audit of the Inventory and Warehousing Cycle

The overall objective in the audit of the inventory and warehousing cycle is to determine that raw materials, work in process, finished goods inventory, and cost of goods sold are fairly stated on the financial statements. The basic inventory and warehousing cycle can be divided into five distinct parts:

Acquisition of Raw Materials, Labor, and Overhead Costs and Recording the Amounts in the Accounting Records. This part of the inventory and warehousing cycle includes the first three functions in Figure 17-2: processing of purchase orders, receipt of new materials, and storage of raw materials. The controls over these three functions are evaluated and tested as a part of performing compliance and substantive tests of transactions in the acquisition and payment cycle and the payroll and personnel cycle. At the completion of the acquisition and payment cycle, the auditor should be satisfied that acquisitions of raw materials and manufacturing costs are correctly stated. Similarly, when labor is a significant part of inventory, the payroll and personnel cycle tests should verify the proper accounting for these costs.

FIGURE 17-2

Basic Inventory and Warehousing Cycle

	Processing of Purchase Orders	Receipt of New Materials	Storage of Raw Materials*	Processing the Goods*	Storage of Finished Goods*	Shipment
Flow of material and goods	1. Purchase requested by production department 2. Order placed by purchasing department	1. Goods received and inspected by separate receiving department	1. Goods placed in stockroom	1. Material placed in production 2. Direct labor incurred in production 3. Overhead costs incurred	1. Finished goods transferred from production to stockroom	1. Goods removed from stockroom and shipped

Related documentation	1. Production department issues purchase requisition
	
	2. Purchasing department issues purchase order and sends copy to:
	  a. Vendor
	  b. Receiving department
	  c. Production department
	  d. Accounting
		1. Receiving department sends receiving reports and inspection reports to:
		  a. Perpetual inventory
		  b. Purchasing
		  c. Stockroom
		  d. Accounting
		
		2. Accounting matches receiving reports, purchase orders, and invoices and records purchase
			1. Quantities compared with receiving report (receiving report may be sent to accounting at this point in some systems)
			
			2. Entries made in perpetual inventory records
				1. Material requisitions recorded by
				  a. Perpetual inventory
				  b. Cost accounting
				  c. General accounting
				
				2. Labor and overhead cost distributed to applicable jobs or processes in cost records and in total in the general ledger
					1. Production reports sent to:
					  a. Perpetual inventory
					  b. Cost accounting
					
					2. Costs transferred from work in process to finished goods account
						1. Shipping documents sent to:
						  a. Perpetual records
						  b. Accounting
						
						2. Cost of sales entry made based on quantities shipped

*Inventory counts are taken and compared with perpetual and book amounts at any stage of the cycle, being certain that cutoff for recording documents corresponds to the physical location of the items. A count must ordinarily be taken at least once a year.

577

Internal Transfers of Assets and Costs. Internal transfers include the fourth and fifth functions in Figure 17-2: processing the goods and storage of finished goods. These two activities are not related to any other transaction cycles and therefore must be evaluated and tested as part of the inventory and warehousing cycle. The accounting records concerned with these functions are referred to as the *cost accounting records.*

Shipment of Goods and Recording the Revenue and Costs. The recording of shipments and related costs, which is the last function in Figure 17-2, is part of the sales and collection cycle. Thus, the controls over the function are evaluated and tested as a part of auditing the sales and collection cycle. The tests of the system should include procedures to verify the accuracy of the perpetual inventory records.

Physical Observation of Inventory. Observing the client taking a physical inventory count is necessary to determine whether recorded inventory actually exists at the balance sheet date and is properly counted by the client. Inventory is the first audit area in the text where physical examination is an essential type of evidence used to verify the balance in an account. Physical observation is studied in this chapter.

Inventory Pricing and Compilation. The costs used to value the physical inventory must be tested to determine whether the client has correctly followed an inventory method that is in accordance with generally accepted accounting principles and is consistent with previous years. The audit procedures used to verify these costs are referred to as *price tests.* In addition, the auditor must verify whether the physical counts were correctly summarized, the inventory quantities and prices were correctly extended, and the extended inventory was correctly footed. These tests are called *compilation tests.*

The first and third parts of the audit of the inventory and warehousing cycle have already been studied in connection with the other cycles. The importance of the tests of these other cycles should be kept in mind throughout the remaining sections of this chapter.

AUDIT OF COST ACCOUNTING

The cost accounting systems of different companies vary more than most other systems because of the wide variety of items of inventory and the level of sophistication desired by management. For example, a company that manufactures an entire line of farm machines will have a completely different kind of cost system than a steel fabricating shop that makes and installs custom-made metal cabinets. It should also not be surprising that small companies whose owners are actively involved in the manufacturing process will need less sophisticated records than will large multiproduct companies.

Controls over the Cost Accounting Department

Cost accounting controls are those controls that are related to the physical inventory and the consequent costs from the point where raw materials are requisitioned to the point where the manufactured product is completed and transferred to storage. It is convenient to divide these controls into two broad categories: the physical control over raw materials, work in process, and finished goods inventory, and the controls over the related costs.

Almost all companies need physical control over their assets to prevent loss from misuse and theft. The use of physically segregated, limited access storage areas for raw material, work in process, and finished goods is one major control to protect assets. In some instances the assignment of custody of inventory to specific responsible individuals may be necessary to protect the assets. Approved prenumbered documents for authorizing movement of inventory also protect the assets from improper use. Copies of these documents should be sent directly to accounting by the persons issuing them, bypassing people with custodial responsibilities. An example of an effective document of this type is an approved material requisition for obtaining raw material from the storeroom.

Perpetual inventory records maintained by persons who do not have custody of or access to assets is another useful cost accounting control. Perpetual inventory records are important for a number of reasons: they provide a record of items on hand, which is used to initiate production or purchase of additional materials or goods; they provide a record of the use of raw materials and the sale of finished goods, which can be reviewed for obsolete or slow-moving items; and they provide a record that can be used to pinpoint responsibility for custody as a part of the investigation of differences between physical counts and the amount shown on the records.

Another important control in cost accounting is the existence of an adequate system that integrates production and accounting records for the purpose of obtaining accurate costs for all products. The existence of adequate cost records is important to management as an aid in pricing, controlling costs, and costing inventory.

Tests of the Cost Accounting System

In auditing the cost accounting system, the auditor is concerned with four aspects: physical controls over inventory, documents and records for transferring inventory, perpetual records, and unit cost records.

Physical Controls. The auditor's tests of the adequacy of the physical controls over raw materials, work in process, and finished goods must be restricted to observation and inquiry. For example, the auditor can examine the raw materials storage area to determine whether the inventory is protected from theft and misuse by the existence of a locked storeroom. The existence of an adequate storeroom with a competent custodian in charge also ordinarily results in the orderly storage of inventory. If the auditor concludes that the physical controls are so inadequate that the inventory will be difficult to count, he should expand his observation of physical inventory tests to make sure that an adequate count is carried out.

Documents and Records for Transferring Inventory. The auditor's primary concerns in verifying the transfer of inventory from one location to another are that the recorded transfers are valid, the transfers that have actually taken place are recorded, and the quantity, description, and date of all recorded transfers are accurate. As in all other systems, it is necessary to understand the client's accounting system for recording transfers before relevant tests can be performed. Once the system is understood, the tests can easily be performed by examining documents and records. For example, a procedure to test the validity and accuracy of the transfer of goods from the raw material storeroom to the manufacturing assembly line is to account for a sequence of raw material requisitions, examine the requisitions for proper approval, and compare the quantity, description, and date with the information on the raw material perpetual records. Similarly, completed production records can be compared with the perpetual records to be sure all manufactured goods were physically delivered to the finished goods storeroom.

Perpetual Records. The existence of adequate perpetual inventory records has a major effect on the *timing and extent* of the auditor's physical examination of inventory. For one thing, when there are reliable perpetual records it is frequently possible to test the physical inventory prior to the balance sheet date. An interim physical inventory can result in significant cost savings for both the client and the auditor, and it enables the client to get the audited statements earlier. Perpetual records also enable the auditor to reduce the extent of the tests of physical inventory because reliance can be put on this control.

Tests of the perpetual records for the purpose of reducing the tests of physical inventory or changing their timing are done through the use of documentation. Documents to verify the purchase of raw materials can be examined at the time the auditor is verifying acquisitions as part of the tests of the acquisition and payment cycle. Documents supporting the reduction of raw material inventory for use in production and the increase in the quantity of finished goods inventory when goods have been manufactured are examined as part of the tests of the cost accounting documents and records in the manner discussed in the preceding section. Support for the reduction in the finished goods inventory through the sale of goods to customers is ordinarily tested as part of the sales and collection cycle. Usually, it is relatively easy to test the accuracy of the perpetual records after the auditor determines how the system is designed and decides to what degree he intends to rely on the system.

Unit Cost Records. Obtaining accurate cost data for raw materials, direct labor, and manufacturing overhead is an essential part of the cost accounting system. An adequate cost system must be integrated with production and accounting records in order to produce accurate costs of all products. The cost accounting system is pertinent to the auditor in that the valuation of ending inventory depends upon the proper design and use of the system.

In testing the inventory cost records, the auditor must first develop an understanding of how the system operates. This is frequently somewhat time-consuming because the flow of costs is usually integrated with other systems, and it may not be obvious how the system provides for the internal transfers of raw materials and for direct labor and manufacturing overhead as production is carried out.

Once the auditor understands how the system operates, the approach to internal verification involves the same concepts that were discussed in the verification of sales and purchase transactions. Whenever possible, it is desirable to test the cost accounting records as a part of the acquisition, payroll, and sales tests to avoid testing the records more than once. For example, when the auditor is testing purchase transactions as a part of the acquisition and payment cycle, it is desirable to trace the units and unit costs of raw materials to the perpetual records and the total cost to the cost accounting records. Similarly, when payroll cost data are maintained for different jobs, it is desirable to trace from the payroll summary directly to the job cost record as a part of testing the payroll and personnel cycle.

A major difficulty in the verification of inventory cost records is determining the reasonableness of cost allocations. For example, the assignment of manufacturing overhead costs to individual products entails certain assumptions that can significantly affect the unit costs of inventory and therefore the fairness of the inventory valuation. In evaluating these allocations, the auditor must consider the reasonableness of both the numerator and the denominator that result in the unit costs. For example, in testing overhead applied to inventory on the basis of direct labor dollars, the overhead rate should approximate total actual manufacturing overhead divided by total actual direct labor dollars. Since total manufacturing overhead is tested as part of the tests of the acquisition and payment cycle and direct labor is tested as part of the payroll and personnel cycle, determining the reasonableness of the rate is not difficult. On the other hand, if manufacturing overhead is applied on the basis of machine hours, the auditor must verify the reasonableness of the machine hours by separate tests of the client's machine records. A major consideration in evaluating the reasonableness of all cost allocations, including manufacturing overhead, is consistency with previous years.

PHYSICAL OBSERVATION OF INVENTORY

Prior to the late 1930s auditors generally avoided responsibility for determining either the physical existence or the accuracy of the count of inventories. The audit evidence for the inventory quantities was usually restricted to obtaining a certification from management as to the correctness of the stated amount. In 1938 the discovery of major fraud in the McKesson & Robbins Company caused a reappraisal by the accounting profession of its responsibilities relating to inventory. In brief, the financial statements for McKesson & Robbins at December 31, 1937, which were "certified to" by a major accounting firm, reported total consolidated assets of $87 million. Of this amount, approximately $19 million was subsequently determined to be fictitious: $10 million in inventory and $9 million in receivables. Due primarily to their adherence to generally accepted auditing practice of that period, the auditing firm was not held directly at fault in the inventory area. However, it was noted that if certain procedures, such as observation of the physical inventory, had been carried out, the fraud would probably have been detected. SAS 1 (Section 331.09) states the following requirement exists for inventory observation as a result of the McKesson & Robbins fraud:

> . . . it is ordinarily necessary for the independent auditor to be present at the time of count, and, by suitable observation, tests, and inquiries, satisfy himself respecting the effectiveness of the methods of inventory-taking and the measure of reliance which may be placed upon the client's representations about the quantities and physical condition of the inventories.

An essential point in the SAS 1 requirement is the distinction between the observation of the physical inventory and the responsibility for taking it. The client has responsibility for setting up the procedures for taking an accurate physical inventory and actually making and recording the counts. The auditor's responsibility is to evaluate and observe the client's physical procedures and draw conclusions about the adequacy of the physical inventory.

The requirement of physical examination of inventory is not applicable in the case of *inventory in a public warehouse*. The AICPA position on inventory stored in a public warehouse is summarized as follows in SAS 1 (Section 331.14):

> In the case of inventories which in the ordinary course of business are in the hands of public warehouses or other outside custodians, direct confirmation in writing from the custodians is acceptable provided that, where the amount involved represents a significant proportion of the current assets or the total assets, supplemental inquiries are made to satisfy the independent auditor as to the bona fides of the situation.[1]

The Committee on Auditing Standards recommends that the supplemental inquiries include the following steps, to the extent that the auditor considers them necessary in the circumstances:

- Discussion with the owner as to the owner's control procedures in investigating the warehouseman, and tests of related evidential matter.

[1]SAS 1, p. 62.

- Review of the owner's control procedures concerning performance of the warehouseman, and tests of related evidential matter.
- Observation of physical counts of the goods, wherever practicable and reasonable.
- Where warehouse receipts have been pledged as collateral, confirmation (on a test basis, where appropriate) from lenders as to pertinent details of the pledged receipts.[2]

Controls over the Physical Count of Inventory

Regardless of the client's inventory record-keeping method, there must be a periodic physical count of the inventory items on hand. The client can take the physical count at or near the balance sheet date, at a preliminary date, or on a cycle basis throughout the year. The last two approaches are appropriate only if an adequate perpetual inventory system exists.

In connection with the client's physical count of inventory, adequate control procedures include proper instructions for the physical count, supervision by responsible personnel, independent internal verification of the counts, independent reconciliations of the physical counts with perpetual records, and adequate control over count tags or sheets.

An important aspect of the auditor's evaluation of the client's physical inventory control procedures is complete familiarity with them before the inventory begins. This is obviously necessary to evaluate the effectiveness of the client's procedures, but it also enables the auditor to make constructive suggestions beforehand. If the inventory instructions do not provide adequate controls, the auditor must spend more time making sure the physical count is accurate.

Audit Decisions in Physical Observation of Inventory

The auditor's decisions in the physical observation of inventory are of the same general nature as in any other audit area: selection of audit procedures, timing, determination of sample size, and selection of the items for testing. The selection of the audit procedures is discussed throughout the section; the other three decisions are discussed briefly at this time.

Timing. The auditor decides whether the physical count can be taken prior to year-end primarily on the basis of the accuracy of the perpetual inventory records. When an interim physical count is permitted, the auditor observes it at that time and also tests the perpetual records for transactions from the date of the count to year-end. In instances where the perpetual records are highly reliable, it may be unnecessary for the client to count the inventory every year. Instead, the auditor can test the perpetual records to the actual inventory on a sample basis at a convenient time. When there are

[2]*Ibid.*

no perpetual records and the inventory is material, a complete physical inventory must be taken by the client near the end of the accounting period and tested by the auditor at the same time.

Sample Size. Sample size in physical observation is usually impossible to specify in terms of the number of items because the emphasis during the tests is on observing the client's procedures rather than on selecting particular items for testing. A convenient way to think of sample size in physical observation is in terms of the total number of hours spent on the observation rather than the number of inventory items counted. The most important determinants of the amount of time needed to test the inventory are the quality of the controls over the physical counts, the reliability of the perpetual records, the total dollar amount and the type of inventory, the number of different significant inventory locations, and the nature and extent of errors discovered in previous years. In some situations inventory is such a significant item that dozens of auditors are necessary to observe the physical count, whereas in other situations one person can complete the observation in a short time.

Selection of Items. The selection of the particular items for testing is an important part of the audit decision in inventory observation. Care should be taken to observe the counting of the most significant items and a representative sample of typical inventory items, to inquire about items that are likely to be obsolete or damaged, and to discuss with management the reasons for excluding any material items.

Physical Observation Tests

The same detailed objectives that have been used in previous sections for direct tests of balances provide the frame of reference for discussing the physical observation tests. However, before the detailed objectives are discussed, some comments that apply to all of the objectives are appropriate.

The most important part of the observation of inventory is determining whether the physical count is being taken in accordance with the client's instructions. To do this effectively, *it is essential that auditor be present* while the physical count is taking place. When the client's employees are not following the inventory instructions, the auditor must either contact the supervisor to correct the problem or modify the physical observation procedures. For example, if the procedures require one team to count the inventory and a second team to recount it as a test of accuracy, the auditor should inform management if he observes both teams counting together.

Obtaining an adequate understanding of the client's business is even more important in physical observation of inventory than for most aspects of the audit because inventory varies so significantly for different companies. A proper understanding of the client's business and its industry enables the auditor to ask about and discuss such problems as inventory valuation, potential obsolescence, and existence of consignment inventory intermingled with owned inventory. A useful starting point for the auditor to familiarize himself with the client's inventory is a tour of the client's facilities, including receiving, storage, production, planning, and record-keeping areas. The tour should be led by a supervisor who can answer questions about production, especially about any changes in the past year.

Common audit procedures for physical observation are shown in Figure 17-3. The order of the objectives is changed from those in previous chapters for convenience. The assumption throughout is that the client records inventory on prenumbered tags on the balance sheet date.

AUDIT OF PRICING AND COMPILATION

An important part of the audit of inventory is to perform all of the procedures necessary to make certain the physical counts were properly priced and compiled. *Pricing* includes all the tests of the client's unit prices to determine whether they are correct. *Compilation* includes all the tests of the summarization of the physical counts, the extension of price times quantity, footing the inventory summary, and tracing the totals to the general ledger.

Controls over Pricing and Compilation

The existence of an adequate cost system that is integrated with production and accounting records is the most important control for ensuring that reasonable costs are used for valuing ending inventory. A closely related control is the use of a *standard cost system* that indicates variances in material, labor, and overhead costs and can be used to evaluate the production system. When standard costs are used, procedures must be designed to keep the standards updated for changes in production processes and costs. The review of unit costs for reasonableness by someone independent of the department responsible for developing the costs is also a useful control over valuation.

A control designed to prevent the overstatement of inventory through the inclusion of obsolete inventory is a formal system of review and reporting of obsolete, slow-moving, damaged, and overstated inventory items. The review should be done by a competent employee by reviewing perpetual records for inventory turnover and holding discussions with engineering or production personnel.

Compilation controls are needed to provide a means of ensuring that the physical counts are properly summarized, priced at the same amount as the unit records, correctly extended and totaled, and included in the general ledger at the proper amount. Important compilation controls are adequate documents and records for taking the physical count and proper internal verification. If the physical inventory is taken on prenumbered tags and carefully reviewed before the personnel are released from the physical exami-

FIGURE 17–3

Summary of Audit Tests for Physical Inventory Observation

Audit Objectives	Common Inventory Observation Procedures	Comments
Inventory as recorded on tags is valid (actually exists).	• Select a random sample of tag numbers and identify the tag with that number attached to the actual inventory. • Observe whether movement of inventory takes place during the count.	• The purpose is to uncover the inclusion of nonexistent items as inventory.
Existing inventory is counted and tagged.	• Examine inventory to make sure it is tagged. • Observe whether movement of inventory takes place during the count. • Inquire as to inventory in other locations.	• Special concern should be directed to omission of large sections of inventory.
Inventory as recorded on tags is owned.	• Inquiry as to consignment or customer inventory included on client's premises. • Be alert for inventory that is set aside or specially marked as indications of nonownership.	
Inventory is counted accurately and excludes unusable items (valuation).	• Recount client's counts to make sure the recorded counts are accurate on the tags (also check descriptions and unit of count, such as dozen or gross). • Compare physical counts with perpetual records. • Record client's counts for subsequent testing. • Test for obsolete inventory by inquiry of factory employees and management, and alertness for items that are damaged, rust- or dust-covered, or located in inappropriate places.	• Recording client counts in the working papers on *inventory count sheets* is done for two reasons: to obtain documentation that an adequate physical examination was made, and to test for the possibility that the client might change the recorded counts after the auditor leaves the premises.
Inventory is classified correctly on the tags.	• Examine inventory descriptions on the tags and compare to the actual inventory for raw material, work in process, and finish goods. • Evaluate whether the percent of completion recorded on the tags for work in process is reasonable.	• These tests would be done as a part of the first procedure in the valuation objective.
Information is obtained to make sure sales and inventory purchases are recorded in the proper period (cutoff).	• Record in the working papers for subsequent follow-up the last shipping document number used at year-end. Make sure the inventory for that item was excluded from the physical count. • Review shipping area for inventory set aside for shipment, but not counted.	• Obtaining proper cutoff information for sales and purchases is an essential part of inventory observation. The appropriate tests during the field work were discussed for sales in

FIGURE 17-3 (cont.)

Audit Objectives	Common Inventory Observation Procedures	Comments
	• Record in the working papers for subsequent follow-up the last receiving report number used at year-end. Make sure the inventory for that item was included in the physical count. • Review receiving area for inventory that should be included in the physical count.	Chapter 9 and purchases in Chapter 15.
Tags are accounted for to make sure none are missing (mechanical accuracy).	• Account for all used and unused tags to make sure none are lost or intentionally omitted. • Record the tag number for those used and unused for subsequent follow-up.	• These tests should be done at the completion of the physical count.
The inventory as included on the tags is reasonable.	• Follow-up all exceptions to make sure they are resolved. • Compare the larger items to the counts in the previous year and the perpetual records. • Tour the facilities to make sure inventory at all locations has been counted and properly tagged.	• These tests should be done near the completion of the physical count.
Inventory is adequately disclosed.		• Disclosure tests cannot be done until the inventory is completed, priced, extended, and totaled.

nation of inventory, there should be little risk of error in summarizing the tags. The most important control over accurate determination of prices, extensions, and footings is internal verification by a competent independent person.

Pricing and Compilation Procedures

The nine detailed objectives for direct tests of balances are also useful in discussing pricing and compilation procedures. The objectives and related tests are shown in Figure 17-4, except for the cutoff objective. The order followed is again changed for convenience. Physical observation, which was previously discussed, is a major source of cutoff information for sales and purchases. The tests of the accounting records for cutoff are done as a part of sales (sales and collection cycle) and purchases (acquisition and payment cycle).

FIGURE 17–4

Summary of Direct Tests of Balances—
Inventory Pricing and Compilation

Audit Objectives	Common Direct Tests of Balances Procedures	Comments
The inventory balance, details listed on the inventory listing schedule, and related account balances are reasonable.	• See Figure 17–5 for illustrative analytical review procedures.	• Several of these analytical tests have been discussed in other chapters.
Inventory in the inventory listing schedule agrees with the physical inventory counts, the extensions are correct, and the total is correctly added and agrees with the general ledger.	• Perform compilation tests (see validity, existence, and valuation objectives). • Extend the quantity times the price on selected items. • Foot the inventory listing schedules for raw materials, work in process, and finished goods. • Trace the totals to the general ledger.	• Unless controls are weak, extending and footing tests should be limited.
Inventory in the inventory listing schedule are valid.	• Trace inventory listed in the schedule to inventory tags and auditor's recorded counts for existence and description.	• These three objectives and the compilation portion of valuation place reliance on the physical inventory observation.
Existing inventory items are included in the inventory listing schedule.	• Account for unused tag numbers shown in the auditor's working papers to make sure no tags have been added. • Trace from inventory tags the inventory listing schedules and make sure inventory on tags are included. • Account for unused tag numbers to make sure none have been deleted.	• The tag numbers and counts verified as a part of physical inventory observation are traced to the inventory listing schedule as a part of these tests. The extent of the tests depends on the internal controls, materiality, and inventory population size.
Inventory items in the inventory listing schedule are properly valued.	• Trace inventory listed in the schedule to inventory tags and auditor's recorded counts for quantity and description. • Perform price tests of inventory. For a discussion of price tests, see text material on page 590.	
Inventory items in the inventory listing schedule are properly classified.	• Compare the classification into raw materials, work in process, and finished goods by comparing the descriptions on inventory tags and auditor's recorded test counts to the inventory listing schedule.	

FIGURE 17–4 (cont.)

Common Direct Tests
of Balances Procedures

Audit Objectives	Common Direct Tests of Balances Procedures	Comments
Inventory items in the inventory listing schedule are owned.	• Trace inventory tags identified as nonowned during the physical observation to the inventory listing schedule to make sure these have not been included. • Review contracts with suppliers and customers and inquire of management for the possibility of the inclusion of consigned or other nonowned inventory, or the exclusion of owned inventory that is not included.	• Most ownership tests are as a part of physical observation.
Inventory and related accounts in the inventory and warehousing cycle are properly disclosed.	• Examine financial statements for proper disclosure, including: Separate disclosure of raw materials, work in process, and finished goods. Proper description of the inventory costing method. Description of pledged inventory. Inclusion of significant sales and purchase commitments.	• Pledging of inventory and sales and purchase commitments are usually uncovered as a part of other audit tests.

The frame of reference for applying the objectives is a listing of inventory obtained from the client that includes each inventory item description, quantity unit price, and extended value. The inventory listing is in inventory item description order with raw material, work in process, and finished goods separated. The total equals the general ledger balance.

FIGURE 17–5

Illustrative Analytical Review Procedures
for Inventory and Warehousing

Analytical Review Procedure	Indication of Error in Inventory
• Comparison of gross margin percentage with previous years	• Possible overstatement or understatement of inventory
• Comparison of inventory turnover (costs of goods sold ÷ average inventory) with previous years	• Possible obsolescence of inventory
• Comparison of unit costs of inventory with previous years	• Possible significant overstatement or understatement of unit costs
• Comparison of extended inventory value with previous year	• Possible significant error in compilation, unit costs, or extensions
• Comparison of current year manufacturing costs with previous years (variable costs should be adjusted for changes in volume)	• Possible misstatement of unit costs of inventory, especially direct labor and manufacturing overhead

Valuation of Inventory

The proper valuation (pricing) of inventory is often one of the most important and time-consuming parts of the audit. In performing pricing tests, three things about the client's method of pricing are of the utmost importance: the method must be in accordance with generally accepted accounting principles, the application of the method must be consistent from year to year, and the lower of cost or market must be considered. Because the method of verifying the pricing of inventory depends upon whether items are purchased or manufactured, these two categories are discussed separately.

Pricing Purchased Inventory. The primary types of inventory included in this category are raw materials, purchased parts, and supplies.

As a first step in verifying the valuation of purchased inventory, it is necessary to clearly establish whether LIFO, FIFO, weighted average, or some other valuation method is being used. It is also necessary to determine which costs should be included in the valuation of a particular item of inventory. For example, the auditor must find out whether freight, storage, discounts, and other costs are included in the cost and compare the findings with the preceding year's audit working papers to make sure the methods are consistent.

In selecting specific inventory items for pricing, emphasis should be put on the larger dollar amounts and on products that are known to have wide fluctuations in price, but a representative sample of all types of inventory and departments should be included as well. Stratified variables sampling is commonly used in these tests.

The auditor should list the inventory items he intends to verify for pricing and request the client to locate the appropriate vendors' invoices for him. It is important that sufficient invoices be examined to account for the entire quantity of inventory for the particular item being tested, especially for the FIFO valuation method. Examining sufficient invoices is useful to uncover situations where clients value their inventory on the basis of the most recent invoice only and in some cases to discover obsolete inventory. As an illustration, assume that the client's valuation of a particular inventory is $12.00 per unit for 1,000 units, using FIFO. The auditor should examine the most recent invoices for acquisitions of that inventory item made in the year under audit until the valuation of all of the 1,000 units is accounted for. If the most recent acquisition of the inventory item was for 700 units at $12.00 per unit and the immediately preceding acquisition was for 600 units at $11.30 per unit, the inventory item in question is overstated by $210.00 (300 × $.70).

When the client has perpetual inventory records that include unit costs of acquisitions, it is usually desirable to test the pricing by tracing the unit costs to the perpetual records rather than to vendors' invoices. In most cases the effect is to significantly reduce the cost of verifying inventory valuation. Naturally, when the perpetual records are used to verify unit costs, it is essential to test the unit costs on the perpetual records to vendors' invoices as a part of the tests of the acquisition and payment cycle.

590

Lower of cost or market must also be considered in pricing inventory. The most recent cost of an inventory item as indicated on a vendor's invoice of the subsequent period is a useful way to test for the market replacement cost, but it is also necessary to consider the sales value of the inventory item and the possible effect of rapid fluctuation of prices. As part of evaluating the lower of cost or market, it is also necessary to consider the possibility of obsolescence.

Pricing Manufactured Inventory. The auditor must consider the cost of raw materials, direct labor, and manufacturing overhead in pricing work in process and finished goods. The need to verify each of these has the effect of making the audit of work in process and finished goods inventory more complex than the audit of purchased inventory. Nevertheless, such considerations as selecting the items to be tested, testing for the lower of cost or market, and evaluating the possibility of obsolescence also apply.

It is necessary to consider both the unit cost of the raw materials and the number of units required to manufacture a unit of output in pricing raw materials in manufactured products. The unit cost can be verified in the same manner as that used for other purchased inventory—by examining vendor's invoices or perpetual records. Then it is necessary to examine engineering specifications, inspect the finished product, or find a similar method to determine the number of units it takes to manufacture a particular product.

Similarly, the hourly costs of direct labor and the number of hours it takes to manufacture a unit of output must be verified while testing direct labor. Hourly labor costs can be verified by comparison with labor payroll or union contracts. The number of hours needed to manufacture the product can be determined from engineering specifications or similar sources.

The proper manufacturing overhead in work in process and finished goods is dependent upon the approach being used by the client. It is necessary to evaluate the method being used for consistency and reasonableness and to recompute the costs to determine whether the overhead is correct. For example, if the rate is based on direct labor dollars, the auditor can divide the total manufacturing overhead by the total direct labor dollars to determine the actual overhead rate. This rate can then be compared with the overhead rate used by the client to determine unit costs.

When the client has a *standard cost system*, an efficient and useful method of determining valuation is by the review and analysis of variances. If the variances in material, labor, and manufacturing overhead are small, it is evidence of reliable cost records.

AN INTEGRATION OF THE TESTS

The most difficult part of understanding the audit of the inventory and warehousing cycle is to grasp the interrelationship of the many different tests the auditor makes to evaluate whether inventory and cost of goods sold are fairly stated. The following summary endeavors to aid the reader in perceiving the audit of the inventory and warehousing cycle as a series of integrated tests. The summary is depicted graphically in Figure 17-6.

OBJECTIVE: Determine whether there is a fair presentation on the financial statements of raw materials, work in process, finished goods, and cost of goods sold.

INTERRELATED TESTS:

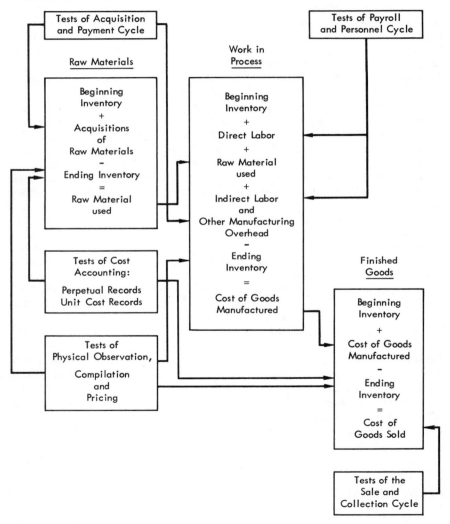

FIGURE 17-6   Interrelationship of Various Tests in Auditing Inventory and Cost of Goods Sold

Tests of the Acquisition and Payment Cycle. Whenever the auditor verifies acquisitions as part of the tests of the acquisition and payment cycle, evidence is being obtained about the accuracy of raw materials purchased and all manufacturing overhead costs except labor. These acquisition costs either flow directly into cost of goods sold or become the most significant part of the ending inventory of raw material, work in process, and finished goods. In audits involving perpetual inventory systems, it is common to test these as a part of tests of transactions procedures in the acquisition and payment cycle. Similarly, if manufacturing costs are assigned to individual jobs or processes, they are usually tested as a part of the same cycle.

Tests of the Payroll and Personnel Cycle. When the auditor verifies labor costs, the same comments apply as for acquisitions. In most cases the cost accounting records for direct and indirect labor costs can be tested as part of the audit of the payroll and personnel cycle if there is adequate advance planning.

Tests of the Sales and Collection Cycle. Although there is a less close relationship between the sales and collection and the inventory and warehousing cycles than the two previously discussed, the relationship is still important. Most of the audit testing in the storage of finished goods as well as the shipment and recording of sales takes place when the sales and collection cycle is tested. In addition, if a standard cost system is used, it may be possible to test the standard cost of goods sold at the same time that sales tests are performed.

Tests of Cost Accounting. Tests of cost accounting are meant to verify the controls affecting inventory that were not verified as part of the three previously discussed cycles. Tests are made of the physical controls, transfers of raw material costs to work in process, transfers of costs of completed goods to finished goods, perpetual records, and unit cost records.

Physical Inventory, Compilation, and Pricing. In most audits the underlying assumption in testing the inventory and warehousing cycle is that cost of goods sold is a residual of beginning inventory plus acquisitions of raw materials, direct labor, and other manufacturing costs minus ending inventory. When the audit of inventory and cost of goods sold is approached with this idea in mind, the importance of ending inventory becomes obvious. Physical inventory, compilation, and pricing are each equally important in the audit because an error in any one results in misstated inventory and cost of goods sold.

In testing the physical inventory, it is possible to rely heavily upon the perpetual records if they have been tested as a part of one or more of the previously discussed tests. In fact, if the perpetual records are considered reliable, the auditor can observe and test the physical count at some time during the year and rely upon the perpetuals to keep adequate records of the quantities.

When testing the unit costs, it is also possible to rely, to some degree, on the tests of the cost records made during the tests of transaction cycles. The existence of standard cost records is also useful for the purpose of comparison with the actual unit costs. If the standard costs are used to represent historical cost, they must be tested for reliability.

REVIEW QUESTIONS

17–1. Give the reasons why inventory is often the most difficult and time-consuming part of many audit engagements.

17–2. Explain the relationship between the acquisition and payment cycle and the inventory and warehousing cycle in the audit of a manufacturing company. List several audit procedures in the acquisition and payment cycle that support your explanation.

17–3. State what is meant by cost accounting records and explain their importance in the conduct of an audit.

17–4. Many auditors assert that certain audit tests can be significantly reduced for clients with adequate perpetual records that include both units and cost data. What are the most important tests of the perpetual records the auditor must make before he can rely on them to reduce other audit tests? Assuming the perpetuals are determined to be effective, which tests can be reduced?

17–5. Before the physical examination, the auditor obtains a copy of the client's inventory instructions and reviews them with the controller. In evaluating the adequacy of inventory procedures for a small manufacturing company these deficiencies are identified: Shipping operations will not be completely halted during the physical examination and there will be no independent verification of the original inventory count by a second counting team. Evaluate the importance of each of these deficiencies and state the effect of each one on the auditor's observation of inventory.

17–6. At the completion of an inventory observation, the controller requested the auditor to give him a copy of all recorded test counts to facilitate the correction of all discrepancies between the client's and the auditor's counts. Should the auditor comply with the request? Why?

17–7. What major audit procedures are involved in testing for the ownership of inventory during the observation of the physical counts and as a part of subsequent valuation tests?

17–8. In the verification of the amount of the inventory, one of the CPA's concerns is that slow-moving and obsolete items be identified. List the auditing procedures that the CPA could employ to determine whether slow-moving or obsolete items have been included in inventory.

17–9. During the taking of physical inventory, the controller intentionally withheld several inventory tags from the employees responsible for the physical count. After the auditor left the client's premises at the completion of the inventory observation, the controller recorded nonexistent inventory on the tags and thereby significantly overstated earnings. How could the auditor have uncovered the misstatement, assuming there are no perpetual records?

17–10. Explain why a proper cutoff of purchases and sales is heavily dependent on the physical inventory observation. What information should be obtained during the physical count to make sure cutoff is accurate?

17–11. Define what is meant by compilation tests. List several examples of audit procedures to verify compilation.

17–12. List the major overall reasonableness tests for inventory. For each test, explain the type of error that could be identified.

17–13. Included in the 12-31-X7 inventory of the Wholeridge Supply Company are 2,600 deluxe ring binders in the amount of $5,902. An examination of the most recent purchases of binders showed the following costs: 1-26-X8, 2,300 at $2.42 each; 12-6-X7, 1,900 at $2.28 each; 11-26-X7, 2,400 at $2.07 each. What is the error in valuation of the 12-31-X7 inventory for deluxe ring binders assuming FIFO inventory valuation? What would your answer be if the 1-26-X8 purchase was for 2,300 binders at $2.12 each?

17–14. The Ruswell Manufacturing Company applied manufacturing overhead to inventory at 12-31-X7 on the basis of $3.47 per direct labor hour. Explain how you would evaluate the reasonableness of total direct labor hours and manufacturing overhead in the ending inventory of finished goods.

17–15. Each employee for the Gedding Manufacturing Co., a firm using a job-cost system, must reconcile his total hours worked with the hours worked on individual jobs by the use of a "Job Time Sheet" at the time weekly payroll time cards are prepared. The Job Time Sheet is then stapled to the time card. Explain how you could test the direct labor dollars included in inventory as a part of the payroll and personnel tests.

17–16. Assuming that the auditor properly documents receiving report numbers as a part of the physical inventory observation procedures, explain how he should verify the proper cutoff of purchases, including tests for the possibility of raw materials in transit, later in the audit.

DISCUSSION QUESTIONS AND PROBLEMS

17–17. For each of the following independent questions concerned with inventory controls, select the best response.
   a. In a company whose materials and supplies include a great number of items, a fundamental deficiency in control requirements would be indicated if
   (1) perpetual inventory records were not maintained for items of small value.
   (2) the storekeeping function were to be combined with production and record keeping.
   (3) the cycle basis for physical inventory taking were to be used.
   (4) minor supply items were to be expensed when purchased.

b. For control purposes, the quantities of materials ordered may be omitted from the copy of the purchase order which is
   (1) forwarded to the accounting department.
   (2) retained in the purchasing department's files.
   (3) returned to the requisitioner.
   (4) forwarded to the receiving department.

c. Freije Refrigeration Co. has an inventory of raw materials and parts consisting of thousands of different items which are of small value individually but significant in total. A fundamental control requirement of Freije's inventory system is that
   (1) perpetual inventory records be maintained for all inventory items.
   (2) the taking of physical inventories be conducted on a cycle basis rather than at year-end.
   (3) the storekeeping function not be combined with the production and inventory record-keeping functions.
   (4) materials requisitions be approved by an officer of the company.

d. A CPA observes his client's physical inventory count on December 31, 19X1. There are eight inventory-taking teams, and a tag system is used. The CPA's observation normally may be expected to result in detection of which of the following inventory errors:
   (1) The inventory takers forget to count all the items in one room of the warehouse.
   (2) An error is made in the count of one inventory item.
   (3) Some of the items included in the inventory had been received on consignment.
   (4) The inventory omits items on consignment to wholesalers.

(AICPA adapted)

17–18. Items a through h are selected questions typically found in questionnaires used by auditors in evaluating internal controls in the inventory and warehousing cycle. In using the questionnaire for a particular client, a yes response to a question indicates a possible strength in the system, whereas a no indicates a potential weakness.

a. Does the receiving department prepare prenumbered receiving reports and account for the numbers periodically for all inventory received, showing the description and quantity of materials?

b. Is all inventory stored under the control of a custodian in areas where access is limited?

c. Are all shipments to customers authorized by prenumbered shipping orders?

d. Are detailed perpetual inventory records maintained for raw materials inventory?

e. Are physical inventory counts made by someone other than storekeepers and those responsible for maintaining perpetual records?

f. Is a standard cost system in effect for raw materials, direct labor, and manufacturing overhead?

g. Is there a stated policy with specific criteria for writing off obsolete or slow-moving goods?

h. Is the clerical accuracy of the final inventory compilation checked by a person independent of those responsible for preparing it?

Required:
a. For each of the questions above, state the purpose of the control.
b. For each control, list a compliance procedure to test its effectiveness.
c. For each of the questions above, identify the nature of the potential financial error(s) if the control is not in effect.
d. For each of the potential errors in part c, list a substantive audit procedure to determine whether a material error exists.

17–19. Following are audit procedures frequently performed in the inventory and warehousing cycle for a manufacturing company.
a. Compare the client's count of physical inventory at an interim date with the perpetual records.
b. Trace the auditor's test counts recorded in the working papers to the final inventory compilation and compare the tag number, description, and quantity.
c. Compare the unit price on the final inventory summary with vendor's invoices.
d. Read the client's physical inventory instructions and observe whether they are being followed by those responsible for counting the inventory.
e. Account for a sequence of raw material requisitions and examine each requisition for an authorized approval.
f. Trace the recorded additions on the finished goods perpetual records to the records for completed production.
g. Account for a sequence of inventory tags and trace each tag to the physical inventory to make sure it actually exists.

Required:
a. Identify whether each of the procedures is primarily a compliance or substantive test.
b. State the purpose(s) of each of the procedures.

17–20. The following errors or omissions are included in the inventory and related records of Westbox Manufacturing Company.
a. An inventory item was priced at $12 each instead of at the correct cost of $12 per dozen.
b. In taking the physical inventory, the last shipments for the day were excluded from inventory and were not included as a sale until the subsequent year.
c. The clerk in charge of the perpetual inventory records altered the quantity on an inventory tag to cover up the shortage of inventory caused by its theft during the year.
d. Several inventory tags were lost after the auditor left the premises and were not included in the final inventory summary.
e. In recording raw material purchases, the improper unit price was included in the perpetual records. Therefore, the inventory valuation was misstated because the physical inventory was priced by referring to the perpetual records.

f. During the physical count, several obsolete inventory items were included.

g. Because of a significant increase in volume during the current year and excellent control over manufacturing overhead costs, the manufacturing overhead rate applied to inventory was far greater than actual cost.

Required:

a. For each error, state a control that should have prevented the error from occurring.

b. For each error, state a substantive audit procedure that could be used to uncover the error.

17–21. The client's cost system is often the focal point in the CPA's examination of the financial statements of a manufacturing company.

Required:

a. For what purposes does the CPA review the cost system?

b. The Summerfield Manufacturing Company employs standard costs in its cost accounting system. List the audit procedures that you would apply to satisfy yourself that Summerfield's cost standards and related variance amounts are acceptable and have not distorted the financial statements. (Confine your audit procedures to those applicable to *materials*.)

(AICPA adapted)

17–22. Often an important aspect of a CPA's examination of financial statements is his observation of the taking of the physical inventory.

Required:

a. What are the general objectives or purposes of the CPA's observation of the taking of the physical inventory? (Do not discuss the procedures or techniques involved in making the observation.)

b. For what purposes does the CPA make and record test counts of inventory quantities during his observation of the taking of the physical inventory? Discuss.

c. A number of companies employ outside service companies who specialize in counting, pricing, extending, and footing inventories. These service companies usually furnish a certificate attesting to the value of the inventory.

Assuming that the service company took the inventory on the balance sheet date:

(1) How much reliance, if any, can the CPA place on the inventory certificate of outside specialists? Discuss.

(2) What effect, if any, would the inventory certificate of outside specialists have upon the type of report the CPA would render? Discuss.

(3) What reference, if any, would the CPA make to the certificate of outside specialists in his short-form report? (AICPA adapted)

17–23. Your audit client, Household Appliances, Inc., operates a retail store in the center of town. Because of lack of storage space, Household keeps inventory that is not on display in a public warehouse outside of town. The warehouseman receives inventory from suppliers and, on request from your client by a shipping advice or telephone call, delivers merchandise to customers or to the retail outlet.

The accounts are maintained at the retail store by a bookkeeper. Each month the warehouseman sends to the bookkeeper a quantity report indicating opening balance, receipts, deliveries, and ending balance. The bookkeeper compares book quantities on hand at month-end with the warehouseman's report and adjusts his books to agree with the report. No physical counts of the merchandise at the warehouse were made by your client during the year.

You are now preparing for your examination of the current year's financial statements in this recurring engagement. Last year you rendered an unqualified opinion.

Required:

a. Prepare an audit program for the observation of the physical inventory of Household Appliances, Inc.
   (1) at the retail outlet.
   (2) at the warehouse.
b. As part of your examination, would you verify inventory quantities at the warehouse by means of
   (1) a warehouse confirmation? Why?
   (2) test counts of inventory at the warehouse? Why?
c. Since the bookkeeper adjusts books to quantities shown on the warehouseman's report each month, what significance would you attach to the year-end adjustments if they were substantial? Discuss.   (AICPA adapted)

17-24. Ace Corporation does not conduct a complete annual physical count of purchased parts and supplies in its principal warehouse but uses statistical sampling instead to estimate the year-end inventory. Ace maintains a perpetual inventory record of parts and supplies and believes that statistical sampling is highly effective in determining inventory values and is sufficiently reliable to make a physical count of each item of inventory unnecessary.

Required:

a. Identify the audit procedures that should be used by the independent auditor that change or are in addition to normal required audit procedures when a client utilizes statistical sampling to determine inventory value and does not conduct a 100 percent annual physical count of inventory items.
b. List at least 10 normal audit procedures that should be performed **to verify physical quantities** whenever a client conducts a periodic physical count of all or part of its inventory.   (AICPA adapted)

17-25. You encountered the following situations during the December 31, 19X7, physical inventory of Latner Shoe Distributor Company.
   a. Latner maintains a large portion of the shoe merchandise in 10 warehouses throughout the eastern United States. This ensures swift delivery service for its chain of stores. You are assigned alone to the Boston warehouse to observe the physical inventory process. During the inventory count, several express trucks pulled in for loading. Although infrequent, express ship-

ments must be attended to immediately. As a result, the employees who were counting the inventory stopped to assist in loading the express trucks. What should you do?

b. (1) In one storeroom of 10,000 items, you have test-counted about 200 items of high value and a few items of low value. You found no errors. You also note that the employees are diligently following the inventory instructions.

Do you think you have tested enough items? Explain.

(2) What would you do if you counted 150 items and found a substantial number of counting errors?

c. In observing an inventory of liquid shoe polish, you note that a particular lot is five years old. From inspection of some bottles in an open box, you find that the liquid has solidified in most of the bottles. What action should you take?

d. During your observation of the inventory count in the main warehouse, you found that most of the prenumbered tags that had been incorrectly filled out are being destroyed and thrown away. What is the significance of this procedure and what action should you take?

17-26. During the month of April, you are engaged to examine the balance sheet of a new client as of March 31. The client manufactures steel castings and forgings. A physical count of all inventories is made at the end of each quarter of the fiscal year, and the company adjusts its inventory book amounts to reflect the physical counts. As you were not engaged at the time of the physical inventory on March 31, you request that the company make another physical inventory count at the end of April in order that you may observe and make test counts. The client agrees and another inventory is taken on April 30 which you witness.

Inventories of raw materials, work in process, and finished goods totaled $125,000 at March 31. Total current assets amounted to $188,000, total current liabilities were $186,000, and total assets were $450,000.

The company maintains perpetual inventory records of raw materials and supplies but has no job-cost system or perpetual records of work in process or finished goods. Production records are kept in the plant showing the tons of castings poured each day, and sales records reflect the tons of castings and forgings sold daily to various customers of the company.

Required:

What audit procedures would you use to satisfy yourself as to the *quantities* on hand at the balance sheet date? (AICPA adapted)

17-27. In connection with his examination of the financial statements of Knutson Products Co., an assembler of home appliances, for the year ended May 31, 19X7, Ray Abel, CPA, is reviewing with Knutson's controller the plans for a physical inventory at the company warehouse on May 31, 19X7.

Finished appliances, unassembled parts, and supplies are stored in the warehouse, which is attached to Knutson's assembly plant. The plant will operate during the count. On May 30 the warehouse will deliver to the plant the estimated quantities of unassembled parts and supplies required for May 31 production, but there may be emergency requisitions on May 31. During the count the warehouse will continue to receive parts and supplies and to ship finished appliances. However, appliances completed on May 31 will be held in the plant until after the physical inventory.

Required:

What procedures should the company establish to ensure that the inventory count includes all items that should be included and that nothing is counted twice? (AICPA adapted)

17–28. Line-Rite Manufacturing Company, Inc., is a moderate-sized company manufacturing equipment for use in laying pipe lines. The company has prospered in the past, gradually expanding to its present size. Recognizing a need to develop new products if its growth is to continue, the company created an engineering research and development section. During 19X7, at a cost of $70,000, this section designed, patented, and successfully tested a new machine which greatly accelerates the laying of small-sized lines.

In order to adequately finance the manufacture, promotion, and sale of this new product, it has become necessary to expand the company's plant and to enlarge inventories. Required financing to accomplish this has resulted in the company engaging you in April 19X7 to examine its financial statements as of September 30, 19X7, the end of the current fiscal year. This is the company's initial audit.

In the course of your preliminary audit work you obtain the following information.

a. The nature of the inventory and related manufacturing processes do not lend themselves well to taking a complete physical inventory at year-end or at any other given date. The company has an inventory team which counts all inventory items on a cycle basis throughout the year. Perpetual inventory records, maintained by the accounting department, are adjusted to reflect the quantities on hand as determined by these counts. At year-end an inventory summary is prepared from the perpetual inventory records. The quantities in this summary are subsequently valued in developing the final inventory balances.

b. The company carries a substantial parts inventory which is used to service equipment sold to customers. Certain parts are also used in current production. The company considers any part to be obsolete only if it shows no usage or sales activity for two consecutive years. Parts falling into this category are reserved for fully. A reserve of $10,000 exists at present.

Your tests indicate that obsolescence in inventories might approximate $50,000. As part of your audit you must deal with each of the foregoing matters.

Required:

a. With respect to inventories, define the overall problem involved in this first audit.

b. Outline a program for testing inventory quantities.

c. Enumerate and discuss the principal problems involved in inventory obsolescence for the company, assuming the amount involved was significant with respect to the company's financial position. (AICPA adapted)

17–29. You are assigned to the December 31, 19X6, audit of Sea Gull Airframes, Inc. The company designs and manufactures aircraft superstructures and airframe components. You observed the physical inventory at December 31 and are satisfied it was properly taken. The inventory at December 31, 19X6, has been priced, extended, and totaled by the client and is made up of about 5,000 inventory items with a total valuation of $8,275,000. In performing inventory price tests you have decided to stratify your tests, and you conclude that you should have two strata: items with a total value over $5,000 and those with a value of less than $5,000. The book values are as follows:

	No. of Items	Total Value
More than $5,000	500	$4,150,000
Less than $5,000	4,500	4,125,000
	5,000	$8,275,000

In performing your pricing and extension tests, you have decided to test about 50 inventory items in detail. You selected 40 of the over $5,000 items and 10 of those under $5,000 at random from the population. You find all items to be correct except for some of the items A through G below which you believe may be in error. You have tested the following items, to this point, exclusive of A through G.

	No. of Items	Total Value
More than $5,000	36	$360,000
Less than $5,000	7	2,600

Sea Gull Airframes uses a periodic inventory system and values its inventory at lower of FIFO cost or market. You were able to locate all invoices needed for your examination. The seven inventory items in the sample you believe may be in error, along with the relevant data for determining the proper valuation, are shown below.

Inventory Items That Are Possibly in Error
(Amounts Are as Stated on Client's Inventory)

Description	Quantity	Price	Total
A. L37 Spars	3,000 meters	$8.00/meter	$24,000
B. B68 Metal formers	10,000 inches	1.20/foot	12,000
C. R01 Metal ribs	1,500 yards	10.00/yard	15,000
D. St26 Struts	1,000 feet	8.00/foot	8,000
E. Industrial hand drills	45 units	20.00 each	900
F. L803 Steel leaf springs	40 pairs	69.00 each	276
G. V16 Fasteners	5.50 dozen	10.00/dozen	55

Voucher Number	Voucher Date	Date Paid	Terms	Receiving Report Date	Invoice Description
7-68	8-01-X1	8-21-X1	Net FOB dest.	8-01-X1	77 V16 fasteners at $10 per dozen
11-81	10-16-X6	11-15-X6	Net FOB dest.	10-18-X6	1,100 yards R01 metal ribs at $9.50 per yard; 2,000 feet St26 struts at $8.20 per foot
12-06	12-08-X6	12-30-X6	2/10, n/30 FOB S.P.	12-10-X6	180 L803 steel leaf springs at $69 each
12-09	12-10-X6	12-18-X6	Net FOB dest.	12-11-X6	45 industrial hand drills at $20 each; guaranteed for four years
12-18	12-27-X6	12-27-X6	2/10, n/30 FOB S.P.	12-21-X6	4,200 meters L37 spars at $8 per meter
12-23	12-24-X6	1-03-X7	2/10, n/30 FOB dest.	12-26-X6	12,800 inches B68 metal formers at $1.20 per foot
12-61	12-29-X6	1-08-X7	Net FOB dest.	12-29-X6	1,000 yards R01 metal ribs at $10 per yard; 800 feet St26 struts at $8 per foot
12-81	12-31-X6	1-20-X7	Net FOB dest.	1-06-X7	2,000 meters L37 spars at $7.50 per meter; 2,000 yards R01 metal ribs at $10 per yard

In addition, you noted a freight bill for voucher 12-23 in the amount of $200. This bill was entered in the freight-in account. Virtually all of the freight was for the metal formers.

This is the first time Sea Gull Airframes has been audited by your firm.

Required:

Review all information and determine the inventory errors of the seven items in question. State any assumptions you consider necessary to determine the amount of the errors.

17–30. The following calculations were made as of 12-31-X7 from the records of the Aladdin Products Supply Company, a wholesale distributor of cleaning supplies.

	19X7	19X6	19X5	19X4
Gross margin as percent of sales	26.4%	22.8%	22.7%	22.4%
Inventory turnover	56.1 days	47.9 days	48.3 days	47.1 days

Required:

List several logical causes of the changes in the two ratios. What should the auditor do to determine the actual cause of the changes?

17–31. In an annual audit at December 31, 19X7, you find the following transactions near the closing date:

a. Merchandise costing $1,822 was received on January 3, 19X8, and the related purchase invoice recorded January 5. The invoice showed the shipment was made on December 29, 19X7, *FOB destination*.

b. Merchandise costing $625 was received on December 28, 19X7, and the invoice was not recorded. You located it in the hands of the purchasing agent; it was marked *on consignment*.

c. A packing case containing products costing $816 was standing in the shipping room when the physical inventory was taken. It was not included in the inventory because it was marked *Hold for shipping instructions*. Your investigation revealed that the customer's order was dated Dec. 18, 19X7, but that the case was shipped and the customer billed on January 10, 19X8. The product was a stock item of your client.

d. Merchandise received on January 6, 19X8, costing $720 was entered in the purchase register on January 7, 19X8. The invoice showed shipment was made FOB supplier's warehouse on December 31, 19X7. Since it was not on hand at December 31, it was not included in inventory.

e. A special machine, fabricated to order for a customer, was finished and in the shipping room on December 31, 19X7. The customer was billed on that date and the machine excluded from inventory, although it was shipped on January 4, 19X8.

Assume that each of the amounts is material.

Required:

a. State whether the merchandise should be included in the client's inventory.

b. Give your reason for your decision on each item above.

(AICPA adapted)

17–32. A processor of frozen foods carries an inventory of finished products consisting of 50 different types of items valued at approximately $2 million. About $750,000 of this value represents stock produced by the company and billed to customers prior to the audit date. This stock is being held for the customers at a monthly rental charge until they request shipment, and is not separated from the company's inventory.

The company maintains separate perpetual ledgers at the plant office for both stock owned and stock being held for customers. The cost department also maintains a perpetual record of stock owned. The above perpetual records reflect quantities only.

The company does not take a complete physical inventory at any time during the year, since the temperature in the cold storage facilities is too low to allow one to spend more than 15 minutes inside at a time. It is not considered practical to move items outside or to defreeze the cold storage facilities for the purpose of taking a physical inventory. As a result, it is impractical to test-count quantities to the extent of completely verifying specific items. The company considers as its inventory valuation at year-end the aggregate of the quantities reflected by the perpetual record of stock owned, maintained at the plant office, priced at the lower of cost or market.

Required:

a. What are the two principal problems facing the auditor in the audit of the inventory? Discuss briefly.
b. Outline the audit steps that you would take to enable you to render an unqualified opinion with respect to the inventory. (You may omit consideration of a verification of unit prices and clerical accuracy.)

(AICPA adapted)

17–33. As a part of your clerical tests of inventory for Martin Manufacturing, you have tested about 20 percent of the dollar items and have found the following exceptions:

a. *Extension errors:*

Description	Quantity	Price	Extension as Recorded
Wood	465 board feet	$ .12/board feet	$ 5.58
Metal-cutting tools	29 units	30.00 each	670.00
Cutting fluid	16 barrels	40.00/barrel	529.00
Sandpaper	300 sheets	.95/hundred	258.00

b. *Differences located in comparing last year's costs with the current year's costs on the client's inventory lists:*

Description	Quantity	This Year's Cost	Preceding Year's Cost
TA-114 Precision-cutting torches	12 units	$500.00 each	Unable to locate
Aluminum scrap	4,500 pounds	5.00/ton	$65.00/ton
Lubricating oil	400 gallons	6.00/gallon	4.50/barrel

c. *Test counts that you were unable to find when tracing from the test counts to the final inventory compilation:*

Tag No.	Quantity	Current-Year Cost	Description
2958	15 tons	$75/ton	Cold-rolled bars
0026	2,000 feet	2.25/foot	4″ aluminum stripping

d. *Page total, footing errors:*

Page No.	Client Total	Correct Total
14	$1,375.12	$1,375.08
82	8,721.18	8,521.18

Required:

a. State the amount of the actual error in each of the four tests. For any item where the amount of the error cannot be determined from the information given, state the considerations that would affect your estimate of the error.

b. As a result of your findings, what would you do about clerical accuracy tests of the inventory in the current year?

c. What changes, if any, would you suggest in internal controls and procedures for Martin Manufacturing during the compilation of next year's inventory to prevent each type of error?

17–34. You have been engaged for the audit of the Y company for the year ended December 31, 19X7. The Y Company is engaged in the wholesale chemical business and makes all sales at 25 percent over cost.

Shown below are portions of the client's sales and purchases accounts for the calendar year 19X7.

Sales

Date	Reference	Amount	Date	Reference	Amount
12-31	Closing entry	$699,860	Balance forward		$658,320
			12-27	*SI#965	5,195
			12-28	SI#966	19,270
			12-28	SI#967	1,302
			12-31	SI#969	5,841
			12-31	SI#970	7,922
			12-31	SI#971	2,010
		$699,860			$699,860

Purchases

Date	Reference	Amount	Date	Reference	Amount
Balance forward		$360,300	12-31	Closing entry	$385,346
12-28	†RR#1059	3,100			
12-30	RR#1061	8,965			
12-31	RR#1062	4,861			
12-31	RR#1063	8,120			
		$385,346			$385,346

*SI, sales invoice.
†RR, receiving report.

You observed the physical inventory of goods in the warehouse on December 31, 19X7, and were satisfied that it was properly taken.

When performing a sales and purchases cutoff test, you found that at December 31, 19X7, the last receiving report that had been used was No. 1063 and that no shipments had been made on any sales invoices with numbers larger than No. 968. You also obtained the following additional information.

a. Included in the warehouse physical inventory at December 31, 19X7, were chemicals which had been purchased and received on receiving report No. 1060 but for which an invoice was not received until 19X8. Cost was $2,183.

b. In the warehouse at December 31, 19X7, were goods that had been sold and paid for by the customer but which were not shipped out until 19X8. They were all sold on sales invoice No. 965 and were not inventoried.

c. On the evening of December 31, 19X7, there were two cars on the Y Company siding:
   (1) Car AR38162 was unloaded on January 2, 19X8, and received on receiving report No. 1063. The freight was paid by the vendor.
   (2) Car BAE74123 was loaded and sealed on December 31, 19X7, and was switched off the company's siding on January 2, 19X8. The sales price was $12,700 and the freight was paid by the customer. This order was sold on sales invoice No. 968.

d. Temporarily stranded at December 31, 19X7, on a railroad siding were two cars of chemicals en route to the Z Pulp and Paper Co. They were sold on sales invoice No. 966 and the terms were FOB destination.

e. En route to the Y Co. on December 31, 19X7, was a truckload of material which was received on receiving report No. 1064. The material was shipped FOB destination and freight of $75 was paid by the Y Co. However, the freight was deducted from the purchase price of $975.

f. Included in the physical inventory were chemicals exposed to rain in transit and deemed unsalable. Their invoice cost was $1,250, and freight charges of $350 had been paid on the chemicals.

Required:

a. Compute the adjustments that should be made to the client's physical inventory at December 31, 19X7.

b. Prepare the auditor's worksheet adjusting entries which are required as of December 31, 19X7.   (AICPA adapted)

18

AUDIT OF THE
CAPITAL ACQUISITION
AND REPAYMENT CYCLE

The final transaction cycle discussed in this text relates to the acquisition of capital resources in the form of interest-bearing debt and owner's equity and the repayment of the capital. The capital acquisition and repayment cycle also includes the payment of interest and dividends. The following are the major accounts in the cycle:

Notes payable	Paid-in capital in excess of par
Contracts payable	Donated capital
Mortgages payable	Retained earnings
Bonds payable	Appropriations of retained earnings
Interest expense	Treasury stock
Accrued interest	Dividends declared
Cash in the bank	Dividends payable
Capital stock—common	Proprietorship—capital account
Capital stock—preferred	Partnership—capital account

Four characteristics of the capital acquisition and repayment cycle significantly influence the audit of these accounts.

- *Relatively few transactions affect the account balances, but each transaction is often highly material in amount.* For example, bonds are infrequently issued by most companies, but the amount of a bond issue is normally large. Due to their size it is common to verify each transaction taking place in the cycle for the entire year as a part of verifying the balance sheet accounts. It is not unusual to see audit working papers that include the beginning balance of every account in the capital acquisition and repayment cycle and documentation of every transaction that occurred during the year.

- *The exclusion of a single transaction could be material in itself.* Considering the impact of understatements of liabilities and owner's equity, which was discussed in Chapter 15, omission is a major audit concern.
- *There is a legal relationship between the client entity and the holder of the stock, bond, or similar ownership document.* In the audit of the transactions and amounts in the cycle, the auditor must take great care in making sure that the significant legal requirements affecting the financial statements have been properly fulfilled and adequately disclosed in the statements.
- *There is a direct relationship between the interest and dividends accounts and debt and equity.* In the audit of interest-bearing debt, it is desirable to simultaneously verify the related interest expense and interest payable. This similarly holds true for owner's equity, dividends declared, and dividends payable.

The audit procedures for many of the accounts in the capital acquisition and repayment cycle can best be understood by selecting representative accounts for study. Therefore, this chapter discusses (1) the audit of notes payable and the related interest expense and interest payable to illustrate interest-bearing capital, and (2) common stock, paid-in capital in excess of par, retained earnings, and dividends.

NOTES PAYABLE

A *note payable* is a legal obligation to a creditor, which may be unsecured or secured by assets. Typically, a note is issued for a period of time somewhere between one month and one year, but there are also long-term notes of over a year. Notes are issued for many different purposes, and the pledged property includes a wide variety of assets, such as securities, inventory, and permanent assets. The principal and interest payments on the notes must be made in accordance with the terms of the loan agreement. For short-term loans a principal and interest payment is usually required only when the loan becomes due, but for loans over ninety days the note usually calls for monthly or quarterly interest payments.

Overview of the Accounts

The accounts used for notes payable and related interest are shown in Figure 18-1. It is common to include tests of principal and interest payments as a part of the audit of the acquisition and payment cycle because the payments are recorded in the cash disbursements journal. But due to their relative infrequency, in many cases no capital transactions are included in the tests of transactions sample. Therefore, it is also normal to test these transactions as a part of the capital acquisition and repayment cycle.

Audit Objectives

The objectives of the auditor's examination of notes payable are to determine whether:

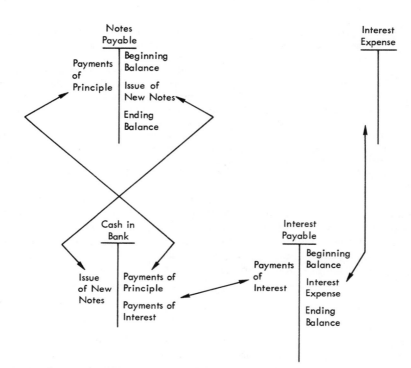

FIGURE 18–1 Notes Payable and the Related Interest Accounts

- Internal controls over notes payable are adequate.
- Transactions for principal- and interest-involving notes are properly authorized and recorded as defined by the eight tests of transactions objectives.
- The liability for notes payable and the related interest expense and accrued liability are properly stated as defined by eight of the nine direct tests of balances objectives (ownership is not applicable).

Internal Controls

There are four important controls over notes payable:

- Proper authorization for the issue of new notes. Responsibility for the issuance of new notes should be vested in the board of directors or high-level management personnel. Generally, two signatures of properly authorized officials are required for all loan agreements. The amount of the loan, the interest rate, the repayment terms, and the particular assets pledged are all part of the approved agreement. Whenever notes are renewed, it is important that they be subject to the same authorization procedures as those for the issuance of new notes.
- Adequate controls over the repayment of principle and interest. The periodic payments of interest and principal should be controlled as a part of the acqui-

610

sition and payment cycle. At the time the note was issued, the accounting department should have received a copy of the note in the same manner in which it receives vendors' invoices and receiving reports. The accounts payable department should automatically issue checks for the notes when they become due, again in the same manner in which it prepares checks for acquisitions of goods and services. The copy of the note is the supporting documentation for payment.

- Proper documents and records. Proper documents and records include the maintenance of subsidiary records and the maintenance of control over blank and paid notes by a responsible person. Paid notes should be canceled and retained under the custody of an authorized official.
- Periodic independent verification. Periodically, the detailed note records should be reconciled with the general ledger and compared with the noteholders' records by an employee who is not responsible for maintaining the detailed records. At the same time, an independent person should recompute the interest expense on notes to test the accuracy and propriety of the record keeping.

Tests of Transactions

Tests of notes payable transactions involve the issue of notes and the repayment of principal and interest. The audit tests are a part of transactions tests for cash receipts (Chapter 9) and cash disbursements (Chapter 15). Additional transaction tests are often performed as a part of direct tests of balances because of the materiality of individual transactions.

Notes payable and related interest tests of transactions should emphasize testing the four important internal controls discussed in the previous section. In addition, the receipt and payment of proper amounts (valuation) is emphasized.

Direct Tests of Balances

The normal starting point for the audit of notes payable is a *schedule of notes payable and accrued interest* obtained from the client. A typical schedule is shown in Figure 18-2. The usual schedule includes detailed information of all transactions that took place during the entire year for principal and interest, the beginning and ending balances for notes and interest payable, and descriptive information about the notes, such as the due date of each note, the interest rate, and the assets pledged as collateral.

When there are numerous transactions involving notes during the year, it may not be practical to obtain a schedule of the type shown in Figure 18-2. In that stituation the auditor is likely to request that the client prepare a schedule of only those notes with unpaid balances at the end of the year. This would show a description of each note, its ending balance, and the interest payable at the end of the year, including the collateral and interest rate.

The objectives and common audit procedures are summarized in

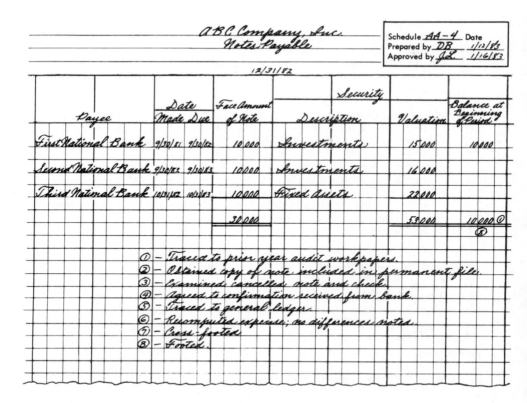

FIGURE 18-2 Schedule of Notes Payable and Accrued Interest

Figure 18-3. The schedule of notes payable is the frame of reference for the procedures. Again the amount of testing depends heavily upon materiality of notes payable and the effectiveness of the system of internal control.

The three most important objectives in notes payable are:

- Existing notes payable are included.
- Notes payable in the schedule are properly valued.
- Notes payable are properly disclosed.

The first two objectives are important because an error could be material if even one note is omitted or misstated. Disclosure is important because generally accepted accounting principles require that the footnotes adequately describe the terms of notes payable outstanding and the assets pledged as collateral for the loans. If there are significant restrictions on the

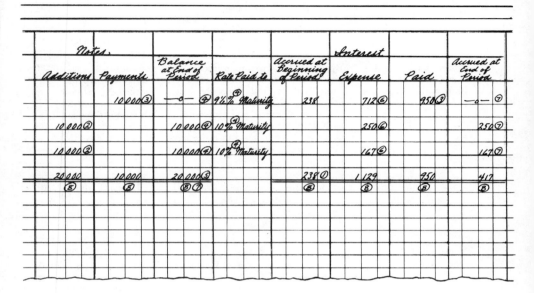

Notes					Interest			
Additions	Payments	Balance at End of Period	Rate	Paid to	Accrued at Beginning of Period	Expense	Paid	Accrued at End of Period
	10,000③	—0— ④	9½% ④	Maturity ④	238	712⑥	950③	—0— ⑦
10,000②		10,000④	10% ④	Maturity ④		250⑥		250⑦
10,000②		10,000④	10% ④	Maturity ④		167⑥		167⑦
20,000	10,000	20,000③			238①	1,129	950	417
⑤	②	⑤⑦			④	⑧	⑤	⑧

FIGURE 18-2 (cont.)

activities of the company required by the loans, such as compensating balance provisions or restrictions on the payment of dividends, these must also be disclosed in the footnotes.

OWNER'S EQUITY

A major distinction must be made in the audit of owner's equity between *publicly and closely held corporations*. In most closely held corporations there are few if any transactions during the year for capital stock accounts and there are typically only a few shareholders. The only transactions entered in the entire owner's equity section are likely to be the change in owner's equity for the annual earnings or loss and the declaration of dividends. The amount of time spent verifying owner's equity is frequently minimal for closely held corporations even though the auditor must test the existing corporate records.

For publicly held corporations the verification of owner's equity is more complex due to the larger numbers of shareholders and frequent changes in the individuals holding the stock. In this section the appropriate tests for verifying capital stock—common, paid-in capital in excess of par, retained earnings, and the related dividends in a publicly held corporation

FIGURE 18-3

Summary of Direct Tests of Balances—
Notes Payable, Interest Expense, and Accrued Interest

Audit Objectives	Common Direct Tests of Balances Procedures	Comments
Notes payable, accrued interest payable, and interest expense are reasonable.	• Recalculate approximate interest expense on the basis of average interest rates and overall monthly notes payable. • Compare individual notes outstanding with the prior year. • Compare total balance in notes payable, interest expense, and in accrued interest.	• Additional tests of interest expense and accrued interest are often unnecessary if analytical review procedures do not indicate potential errors.
Notes payable in the notes payable schedule agree with the client's notes payable register or subsidiary ledger.	• Foot the notes payable list for notes payable and accrued interest. • Trace the totals to the general ledger. • Trace the individual notes payable to the subsidiary ledger.	• Frequently, these are done on a 100 percent basis because of the small population size.
Notes payable in the schedule are valid.	• Confirm notes payable. • Examine duplicate copy of notes for authorization. • Examine corporate minutes for loan approval.	• The validity objective is not as important as the inclusion of existing notes or valuation.
Existing notes payable are included in the notes payable schedule.	• Examine notes paid after year-end to determine whether they were liabilities at the balance sheet date. • Obtain a *standard bank confirmation* which includes specific reference to the existence of notes payable from all banks with which the client does business. (Bank confirmations are discussed more fully in Chapter 19.) • Review the *bank reconciliation* for new notes credited directly to the bank account by the bank. On the bank reconciliation such a note should be indicated as a "reconciling item." Bank reconciliations are also discussed more fully in Chapter 19. • Obtain confirmations from creditors who have held notes from the client in the past and are not currently included in the notes payable schedule. This is the same concept as a "zero balance" confirmation in accounts payable. • Obtain a standard confirmation for secured notes under the Uniform Commercial Code. Figure 18-4 is an example of this type of confirmation.	• This objective is important for uncovering both errors and irregularities. The first three of these procedures are done on most audits. The others are frequently done only when internal controls are weak.

FIGURE 18-3 (cont.)

Audit Objectives	Common Direct Tests of Balances Procedures	Comments
	• Analyze interest expense to uncover a payment to a creditor who is not included in the notes payable schedule. This procedure is automatically done if the schedule is similar to the one in Figure 18-2 because all interest payments are reconciled with the general ledger. • Examine paid notes for cancelation to make sure they are not still outstanding. They should be maintained in the client's files. • Review the minutes of the board of directors for authorized but unrecorded notes.	
Notes payable and accrued interest on the schedule are properly valued.	• Examine duplicate copies of notes for principle and interest rates. • Confirm notes payable, interest rates, and last date for which interest has been paid with holders of notes. • Recalculate accrued interest.	• In some cases it may be necessary to calculate, using present-value techniques, the imputed interest rates or the principal amount of the note. An example is when equipment is purchased for a note.
Notes payable in the schedule are properly classified.	• Examine due dates on duplicate copies of notes to determine whether all or part of the notes are a noncurrent liability. • Review notes to determine whether any are related party notes or accounts payable.	
Notes payable are included in the proper period.	• Examine duplicate copies of notes to determine whether notes were dated on or before the balance sheet date.	• Notes should be included as current-period liabilities when dated on or before the balance sheet date.
Notes payable, interest expense, and accrued interest are properly disclosed.	• Examine duplicate copies of notes. • Confirm notes payable. • Examine notes, minutes, and bank confirmations for restrictions. • Examine balance sheet for proper disclosure of noncurrent portions, related parties, assets pledged as security for notes, and restrictions resulting from notes payable.	• Proper statement presentation, including footnote disclosure, is an important consideration for notes payable.

Uniform Commercial Code - REQUEST FOR INFORMATION OR COPIES - Form UCC 11

JULIUS BLUMBERG, INC. 80 EXCHANGE PLACE, N.Y.C. 10004

IMPORTANT - Read instructions on back before filling out form

REQUEST FOR COPIES OR INFORMATION. Present in DUPLICATE to Filing Officer.

1 Debtor (Last Name First) and Address	Party requesting information or copies: (Name and Address)	For Filing Officer, Date, Time, No.-Filing Office

☐ INFORMATION REQUEST: ☐ COPY REQUEST:

Filing officer please furnish certificate showing if there is on file under the code as of_____, 19___at_____ ___M., any presently effective financing statement filed pursuant to the UCC naming the above named debtor and any statement of assignment thereof, and if there is, giving the date and hour of filing of each such statement and the name(s) and address(es) of each secured party(ies) therein. Enclosed is uniform fee of $3.00.

Filing officer please furnish exact copies of each page of financing statements and statements of assignment listed below, at the rate of $1.00 each, which are on file with your office. Enclosed is $_____fee for copies requested. In case any of said statements contain more than one page the undersigned agrees to pay the sum of $1.00 for each additional page payable in advance.

Date_____ _____(Signature of Requesting Party)_____

File No.	Date and Hour of Filing	Name(s) and Address(es) of Secured Party(ies) and Assignees, if any

CERTIFICATE: The undersigned filing officer hereby certifies that:

☐ the above listing is a record of all presently effective financing statements and statements of assignment which name the above debtor and which are on file in my office as of _____, 19___at_____ ___M.

☐ the attached_____pages are true and exact copies of all available financing statements or statements of assignment listed in above request

COPY 1   Date   Signature of Filing Officer

9/65 STANDARD FORM NEW YORK STATE FORM UCC-11   APPROVED BY SECRETARY OF STATE OF NEW YORK

FIGURE 18-4 Standard Confirmation Under the Uniform Commercial Code

are discussed. The other accounts in owner's equity are verified in much the same way as these.

Overview of the Accounts

An overview of the specific owner's equity accounts discussed in this section is given in Figure 18-5.

Audit Objectives

The objectives of the auditor's examination of owner's equity are to determine whether

- Internal controls over capital stock and related dividends are adequate.
- Owner's equity transactions are recorded properly as defined by the eight tests of transactions objectives.
- Owner's equity balances are properly stated and disclosed as defined by the direct tests of balances objectives (ownership is not applicable).

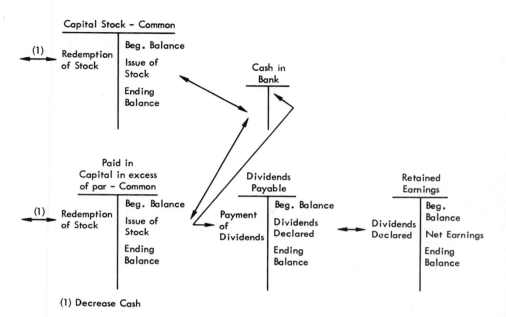

FIGURE 18–5   Owner's Equity and Dividends Accounts

Internal Controls

Several important internal controls are of concern to the independent auditor in owner's equity: proper authorization of transactions, proper record keeping, adequate segregation of duties between maintaining owner's equity records and handling cash and stock certificates, and the use of an independent registrar and stock transfer agent.

Proper Authorization of Transactions. Since each owner's equity transaction is typically material, many of these transactions must be approved by the board of directors. The following types of owner's equity transactions usually require specific authorization:

Issuance of Capital Stock. The authorization includes the type of the equity to issue (such as preferred or common stock), number of shares to issue, par value of the stock, privileged condition for any stock other than common, and date of the issue.

Repurchase of Capital Stock. The repurchase of common or preferred shares, the timing of the repurchase, and the amount to pay for the shares should all be approved by the board of directors.

Declaration of Dividends. The board of directors should authorize the form of the dividends (such as cash or stock), the amount of the dividend per share, and the record and payment dates of the dividends.

Proper Record Keeping and Segregation of Duties.

When a company maintains its own records of stock transactions and outstanding stock, the controls must be adequate to make sure that the actual owners of the stock are recognized in the corporate records, the correct amount of dividends is paid to the stockholders owning the stock as of the dividend record date, and the potential for employee fraud is minimized. The proper assignment of personnel and adequate record-keeping procedures are useful controls for these purposes.

The most important procedures for preventing errors in owner's equity are (1) well-defined policies for preparing stock certificates and recording capital stock transactions, and (2) independent internal verification of information in the records. The client must be certain when issuing and recording capital stock that both the state laws governing corporations and the requirements in the corporate charter are being complied with. For example, the par value of the stock, the number of shares the company is authorized to issue, and the existence of state taxes on the issue of capital stock all affect issuance and recording.

A control over capital stock used by most companies is the maintenance of stock certificate books and a shareholder's ledger. A *capital stock book* is a record of the issuance and repurchase of capital stock for the life of the corporation. The record for a particular sales transaction includes such information as the certificate number, the number of shares issued, the name of the person to whom it was issued, and the issue date. When shares are repurchased, the capital stock book should include the canceled certificates and the date of their cancellation. A *shareholder's ledger* is the record of the outstanding shares at any point in time. The ledger acts as a check on the accuracy of the capital stock book and the balances in the general ledger and is used as the basis for the payment of dividends.

The disbursement of cash for the payment of dividends should be controlled in much the same manner as has been described in Chapter 14 for the preparation and payment of payroll. Dividend checks should be prepared from the capital stock book by someone who is not responsible for maintaining the capital stock records. After the checks are prepared, it is desirable to have an independent verification of the stockholders' names and the amount of the checks and a reconciliation of the total amount of the dividend checks with the total dividends authorized in the minutes. The use of a separate *imprest dividend account* is desirable to prevent the payment of a larger amount of dividends than was authorized.

Independent Registrar and Stock Transfer Agent.

Any company whose stock is listed on a securities exchange is required to engage an *independent registrar* as a control to prevent the improper issue of stock certificates.

The responsibility of an independent registrar is to make sure that stock is issued by a corporation in accordance with the capital stock provisions in the corporate charter and the authorization of the board of directors. The registrar is responsible for signing all newly issued stock certificates and making sure old certificates are received and canceled before a replacement certificate is issued when there is a change in the ownership of the stock.

Most large corporations also employ the services of a *stock transfer agent* for the purpose of maintaining the stockholder records, including records documenting transfers of stock ownership. The employment of a transfer agent not only serves as a control over the stock records by putting them in the hands of an independent organization, but reduces the cost of record keeping by the use of a specialist. Many companies also have the transfer agent disburse cash dividends to shareholders, thereby further improving internal controls.

Audit Tests of Capital Stock and Paid-in Capital in Excess of Par

There are four primary concerns in auditing capital stock and paid-in capital in excess of par:

- Existing capital stock transactions are recorded.
- Recorded capital stock transactions are authorized and properly valued.
- Capital stock is properly valued.
- Capital stock is properly disclosed.

The first two concerns involve tests of transactions, and the last two, direct tests of balances.

Existing Capital Stock Transactions Are Recorded. This objective is easily satisfied when a registrar or transfer agent is used. The auditor can confirm with them whether any capital stock transactions occurred and the valuation of existing transactions. Review of the minutes of the board of directors, especially near the balance sheet date, and examination of client-held stock record books are also useful to uncover issues and repurchases of capital stock.

Recorded Capital Stock Transactions Are Authorized and Properly Valued. The issuance of new capital stock for cash, the merger with another company through an exchange of stock, donated shares, and the purchase of treasury shares each require extensive auditing. Regardless of the controls in existence, it is normal practice to verify all capital stock transactions 100 percent because of their materiality and permanence in the records.

Authorization can ordinarily be tested by examining the minutes of the board of directors.

The correct valuation of capital stock transactions for cash can be readily verified by confirming the amount with the transfer agent and tracing the amount of the recorded capital stock transactions to cash receipts. (In the case of treasury stock the amounts are traced to the cash disbursements journal.) In addition, the auditor must verify whether the correct amounts were credited to capital stock and paid-in capital in excess of par by referring to the corporate charter to determine the par or stated value of the capital stock.

When capital stock transactions are for stock dividends, acquisition of property for stock, mergers, or similar noncash transactions, the verification of valuation may be considerably more difficult. For these types of transactions the auditor must be certain that the client has correctly computed the amount of the capital stock issue in accordance with generally accepted accounting principles. For example, in the audit of a major merger transaction the auditor has to evaluate whether the transaction is a purchase or a pooling of interests. Frequently considerable research is necessary to determine which accounting treatment is correct for the existing circumstances. After the auditor reaches a conclusion as to which method is appropriate, it is necessary to verify that the amounts were correctly computed.

Capital Stock Is Properly Valued. The ending balance in the capital account is verified by first determining the number of shares outstanding at the balance sheet date. A confirmation from the transfer agent is the simplest way to obtain this information. When no transfer agent exists, the auditor must rely on examining the stock records and accounting for all shares outstanding in the stock certificate books, examining all canceled certificates, and accounting for blank certificates. After the auditor is satisfied that the number of shares outstanding is correct, the recorded par value in the capital account can be verified by multiplying the number of shares by the par value of the stock. The ending balance in the capital in excess of par account is a residual amount. It is audited by verifying the amount of recorded transactions during the year and adding them to or subtracting them from the beginning balance in the account.

A major consideration in the valuation of capital stock is verifying whether the number of shares used in the calculation of earnings per share is accurate. It is easy to determine the correct number of shares to use in the calculation when there is only one class of stock and a small number of capital stock transactions. The problem becomes much more complex when there are convertible securities, stock options, or stock warrants outstanding. A thorough understanding of APB 15 is important before the number of primary and fully diluted shares can be verified.

Capital Stock Is Properly Disclosed. The most important sources of information for determining proper disclosure are the corporate charter, the minutes, and the auditor's analysis of capital stock transactions. The auditor should determine that there is a proper description of each class of stock, including such information as the number of shares issued and outstanding and any special rights of an individual class. The proper disclosure of stock options, stock warrants, and convertible securities should also be verified by examining legal documents or other evidence of the provisions of these agreements.

Audit Tests for Cash Dividends and Dividends Payable

The emphasis in the audit of dividends is on the transactions rather than the ending balance. The exception is when there are dividends payable.

The eight internal control objectives for transactions are relevant for dividends. But typically dividends are audited on a 100 percent basis and cause few audit problems. The following are the most important objectives, including those concerning dividends payable.

- Recorded dividends are authorized.
- Existing dividends are recorded.
- Dividends are properly valued.
- Dividends as paid to stockholders are valid.
- Dividends payable are recorded.
- Dividends payable are properly valued.

Authorization can be checked by examining the board of directors' minutes for the amount of the dividend per share and the dividend date. When the auditor examines the board of directors' minutes for dividends declared, he should be alert to the possibility of unrecorded dividends declared, particularly shortly before the balance sheet date. A closely related audit procedure is to review the permanent audit working paper file to determine if there are restrictions on the payment of dividends in bond indenture agreements or preferred stock provisions.

Valuation of a dividend declaration can be audited by recomputing the amount on the basis of the dividend per share and the number of shares outstanding. If the client uses a transfer agent to disburse dividends, the total can be traced to a cash disbursement entry to the agent and also confirmed.

When the client keeps its own dividend records and pays the dividends itself, the auditor can verify the total amount of the dividend by recalculation and reference to cash disbursed. In addition, it is necessary to verify whether the payment was made to the stockholders who owned the stock as of the dividend record date. The auditor can test this by selecting a sample of recorded dividend payments and tracing the payee's name on the canceled check to the dividend records to make sure the payee was entitled to the dividend. At the same time, the amount and the authenticity of the dividend check can be verified.

Tests of dividends payable should be done in conjunction with declared dividends. Any unpaid dividend should be included as a liability.

Audit Tests for Retained Earnings

The only transactions involving retained earnings for most companies are net earnings for the year and dividends declared. But there may also be corrections of prior period earnings, prior period adjustments charged or credited directly to retained earnings, and the setting up or elimination of appropriations of retained earnings.

The starting point for the audit of retained earnings is an analysis of retained earnings for the entire year. The audit schedule showing the analysis, which is usually a part of the permanent file, includes a description of every transaction affecting the account.

The audit of the credit to retained earnings for net income for the year (or the debit for a loss) is accomplished by simply tracing the entry in retained earnings to the net earnings figure on the income statement. The performance of this procedure must of course take place fairly late in the audit after all adjusting entries affecting net earnings have been completed.

An important consideration in auditing debits and credits to retained earnings other than net earnings and dividends is determining whether the transactions should actually have been included. For example, prior period adjustments can be included in retained earnings only if they satisfy the requirements of APB Opinions and the Financial Accounting Standards Board Statements.

After the auditor is satisfied that the recorded transactions are appropriately classified as retained earnings transactions, the next step is to decide whether they are properly valued. The audit evidence necessary to determine proper valuation depends on the nature of the transactions. If there is a requirement for an appropriation of retained earnings for a bond sinking fund, the correct amount of the appropriation can be determined by examining the bond indenture agreement. If there is a major loss charged to retained earnings because of a material nonrecurring abandonment of a plant, the evidence needed to determine the amount of the loss could include significant numbers of documents and records of the plant.

Another important consideration in the audit of retained earnings is evaluating whether there are any transactions that should have been included but were not. If a stock dividend was declared, for instance, the market value of the securities issued should be capitalized by a debit to retained earnings and a credit to capital stock. Similarly, if the financial statements include appropriations of retained earnings, the auditor should evaluate whether it is still necessary to have the appropriation as of the balance sheet date. As an example, an appropriation of retained earnings for a bond sinking fund should be eliminated by crediting retained earnings after the bond has been paid off.

The primary concern in determining whether retained earnings is correctly disclosed on the balance sheet is the existence of any restrictions on the payment of dividends. Frequently, agreements with bankers, stockholders, and other creditors prohibit or limit the amount of dividends the client can pay. These restrictions must be disclosed in the footnotes to the financial statements.

REVIEW QUESTIONS

18–1. List four examples of interest-bearing liability accounts commonly found in balance sheets. What characteristics do these liabilities have in common? How do they differ?

18–2. Why are liability accounts included in the capital acquisition and repayment cycle audited differently from accounts payable?

18–3. It is common practice to audit the balance in notes payable in conjunction with the audit of interest expense and interest payable. Explain the advantages of this approach.

18–4. Which controls should the auditor be most concerned about in the audit of notes payable? Explain the importance of each of these controls.

18–5. Which overall reasonableness test is the most important in verifying notes payable? Which types of errors can the auditor uncover by the use of this test?

18–6. Why is it more important to search for unrecorded notes payable than for unrecorded notes receivable? List several audit procedures the auditor can use to uncover unrecorded notes payable.

18–7. What is the primary purpose of analyzing interest expense? Given this purpose, what primary considerations should the auditor keep in mind when doing the analysis?

18–8. Distinguish between the audit of transactions and direct tests of balances for liability accounts in the capital acquisition and repayment cycle.

18–9. List four types of restrictions long-term creditors often put on companies when granting them a loan. How can the auditor find out about each of these restrictions?

18–10. Describe what is meant by an imputed interest rate. How does an auditor determine whether the client's imputed rate is reasonable? What should be done in the audit of notes payable after the auditor is satisfied that the rate is reasonable?

18–11. What are the primary objectives in the audit of owner's equity accounts?

18–12. Evaluate the following statement: "The corporate charter and the bylaws of a company are legal documents; therefore, they should not be examined by the auditors. If the auditor wants information about these documents, an attorney should be consulted."

18–13. What are the major internal controls over owner's equity?

18–14. How does the audit of owner's equity for a closely held corporation differ from that for a publicly held corporation? In what respects are there no significant differences?

18–15. Describe the duties of a stock registrar and a transfer agent. How does the use of their services affect the effectiveness of the client's internal controls?

18–16. What kinds of information can be confirmed with a transfer agent?

18–17. Evaluate the following statement: "The most important audit procedure to verify dividends for the year is a comparison of a random sample of canceled dividend checks with a dividend list that has been prepared by management as of the dividend record date."

18-18. If a transfer agent disburses dividends for a client, explain how the audit of dividends declared and paid is affected. What audit procedures are necessary to verify dividends paid when a transfer agent is used?

18-19. What should be the major emphasis in auditing the retained earnings account? Explain your answer.

18-20. Explain the relationship between the audit of owner's equity and the calculations of earnings per share. What are the main auditing considerations in verifying the earnings-per-share figure?

DISCUSSION QUESTIONS AND PROBLEMS

18-21. Items a through f are questions typically found in a standard internal control questionnaire used by auditors in evaluating internal controls for notes payable. In using the questionnaire for a particular client, a yes response indicates a possible strength in the system, whereas a no indicates a potential weakness.

a. Are liabilities for notes payable incurred only after written authorization by a proper company official?

b. Is a subsidiary ledger of notes payable maintained?

c. Is the individual who maintains the notes payable subsidiary records someone other than the person who approves the issue of new notes or handles cash?

d. Are paid notes canceled and retained in the company files?

e. Is a periodic reconciliation made of the subsidiary records with the actual notes outstanding by an individual who does not maintain the subsidiary records?

f. Are interest expense and accrued interest recomputed periodically by an individual who does not record interest transactions?

Required:

a. For each of the questions above, state the purpose of the control.

b. For each of the questions above, identify the type of financial statement error that could occur if the control were not in effect.

c. For each of the potential errors in part b, list an audit procedure the auditor can use to determine whether a material error exists.

18-22. The following are frequently performed audit procedures for the verification of bonds payable that were issued in previous years.

a. Obtain a copy of the bond indenture agreement and review its important provisions.

b. Determine that each of the bond indenture provisions has been met.

c. Analyze the general ledger account for bonds payable, interest expense, and unamortized bond discount or premium.

d. Test the client's calculations of interest expense, unamortized bond discount or premium, accrued interest, and bonds payable.

e. Obtain a confirmation from the bondholder.

f. Determine that each of the bond indenture provisions has been met.

Required:

a. State the purpose of each of the six audit procedures listed previously.

b. List the provisions for which the auditor should be alert in examining the bond indenture agreement.

c. For each provision listed in part b, explain how the auditor can determine whether its terms have been met.

d. Explain how the auditor should verify the unamortized bond discount or premium.

e. List the information that should be requested in the confirmation of bonds payable with the bondholder.

18–23. In making an audit of a corporation that has a bond issue outstanding, the trust indenture is reviewed and a confirmation as to the issue is obtained from the trustee.

Required:

List eight matters of importance to the auditor that might be found either in the indenture or in the confirmation obtained from the trustee. Explain briefly the reason for the auditor's interest in each of the items.

(AICPA adapted)

18–24. The Fox Company is a medium-sized industrial client that has been audited by your CPA firm for several years. The only interest-bearing debt owed by Fox Company is $200,000 in long-term notes payable held by the bank. The notes were issued three years previously and will mature in six more years. Fox Company is highly profitable, has no pressing needs for additional financing, and has excellent internal controls over the recording of loan transactions and related interest costs.

Required:

a. Describe the auditing that you think would be necessary for notes payable and related interest accounts in these circumstances.

b. How would your answer differ if Fox Company was unprofitable, had a need for additional financing, and had weak internal controls?

18–25. The ending general ledger balance of $186,000 in notes payable for the Sterling Manufacturing Company is made up of 28 notes to eight different payees. The notes vary in duration anywhere from 30 days to two years, and in amount from $1,000 to $10,000. In some cases the notes were issued for cash loans; in other cases the notes were issued directly to vendors for the purchase of inventory or equipment. The use of relatively short-term financing is necessary because all existing properties are pledged for mortgages. Nevertheless, there is still a serious cash shortage.

Record-keeping procedures for notes payable are not good, considering the large number of loan transactions. There is no notes payable subsidiary ledger or independent verification of ending balances; however, the notes payable records are maintained by a secretary who does not have access to cash.

The audit has been done by the same CPA firm for several years. In the current year the following procedures were performed to verify notes payable:

a. Obtain a listing of notes payable from the client, foot the notes payable balances on the list, and trace the total to the general ledger.

b. Examine duplicate copies of notes for all outstanding notes included on the listing. Compare the name of the lender, amount, and due date on the duplicate copy with the listing.

c. Obtain a confirmation from lenders for all listed notes payable. The confirmation should include the due date of the loan, the amount, and the interest payable at the balance sheet date.

d. Recompute accrued interest on the listing for all notes. The information for determining the correct accrued interest is to be obtained from the duplicate copy of the note. Foot the accrued interest amounts and trace the balance to the general ledger.

Required:

a. What should be the emphasis in the verification of notes payable in this situation? Explain.

b. State the purpose of each of the four audit procedures listed.

c. Evaluate whether each of the four audit procedures was necessary. Evaluate the sample size for each procedure.

d. List other audit procedures that should be performed in the audit of notes payable in these circumstances.

18–26. The Milfred Company is a medium-sized, closely held company that has been an audit client of Gordon and Coopers, CPAs, for several years. In the current year the senior on the audit, Rick Smith, CPA, compares interest expense with the amount in the preceding year and observes that the total has increased from $16,300 to $21,000. To Smith the increase seems large, especially since the company has not expanded in recent years.

Smith decides to discuss this matter with the controller and is told that the increase is a result of higher interest rates and a greater number of loans outstanding. The controller informs Smith that short-term interest rates were 12 percent for the first six months and 15 percent thereafter. He also tells him that on May 29 the secured loan from the First National Bank for the building was refinanced and the interest rate went from 7.3 percent to 9.7 percent.

The balances in the loan accounts as stated in the general ledger are as follows:

| | *Short-Term Loans* | | | | *Long-Term Secured Loan* | | |
	Dr.	Cr.	Balance		Dr.	Cr.	Balance
1-1-X7			$47,500	1-1-X7			$138,500
Jan.	$20,000	$31,700	59,200	Jan.	$427		138,073
Feb.	20,000	31,400	70,600	Feb.	435		137,638
Mar.	20,000	20,200	70,800	Mar.	444		137,194
Apr.	20,000	10,400	61,200	Apr.	454		136,740
May	20,000	2,500	43,700	May	465	$80,000	216,275
June	20,000	—	23,700	June	367		215,908
July	23,700	—	0	July	371		215,537
Aug.	—	—	0	Aug.	376		215,161
Sept.	—	12,700	12,700	Sept.	382		214,779
Oct.	20,000	33,700	26,400	Oct.	390		214,389
Nov.	20,000	29,200	35,600	Nov.	398		213,991
Dec.	20,000	40,600	56,200	Dec.	407		213,584

Required:

a. Why should the auditor be concerned about an increase in interest expense?

b. Perform overall reasonableness tests of interest expense to determine whether the interest expense of $21,000 is reasonable.

c. What additional verification is appropriate in this situation?

18–27. The following covenants are extracted from the indenture of a bond issue. The indenture provides that failure to comply with its terms in any respect automatically advances the due date of the loan to the date of noncompliance (the regular date is 20 years hence). Give any audit steps or reporting requirements you feel should be taken or recognized in connection with each one of the following.

a. "The debtor company shall endeavor to maintain a working capital ratio of 2 to 1 at all times, and, in any fiscal year following a failure to maintain said ratio, the company shall restrict compensation of officers to a total of $100,000. Officers for this purpose shall include Chairman of the Board of Directors, President, all vice-presidents, Secretary, and Treasurer."

b. "The debtor company shall keep all property which is security for this debt insured against loss by fire to the extent of 100 percent of its actual value. Policies of insurance comprising this protection shall be filed with the trustee."

c. "The debtor company shall pay all taxes legally assessed against property which is security for this debt within the time provided by law for payment without penalty, and shall deposit receipted tax bills or equally acceptable evidence of payment of same with the trustee."

d. "A sinking fund shall be deposited with the trustee by semiannual payments of $300,000, from which the trustee shall, in his discretion, purchase bonds of this issue." (AICPA adapted)

18–28. You were engaged to examine the financial statements of Ronlyn Corporation for the year ended June 30, 19X7.

On May 1, 19X7, the corporation borrowed $500,000 from the Second National Bank to finance plant expansion. The long-term note agreement provided for the annual payment of principal and interest over five years. The existing plant was pledged as security for the loan.

Due to unexpected difficulties in acquiring the building site, the plant expansion had not begun at June 30, 19X7. To make use of the borrowed funds, management decided to invest in stocks and bonds, and on May 16, 19X7, the $500,000 was invested in securities.

Required:

a. What are the audit objectives in the examination of long-term debt?

b. Prepare an audit program for the examination of the long-term note agreement between Ronlyn and Second National Bank.

(AICPA adapted)

18–29. The Redford Corporation took out a 20-year mortgage on 6-15-X8 for $2,600,000 and pledged its only manufacturing building and the land on which the building stands as collateral. Each month subsequent to the issue of the mortgage a monthly payment of $20,000 was paid to the mortgagor. You are in charge of the current year audit for Redford, which has a balance sheet date of December 31, 19X8. The client has been audited previously by your CPA firm, but this is the first time Redford Corporation has had a mortgage.

Required:

a. Explain why it is desirable to prepare a working paper for the permanent file for the mortgage. What type of information should be included in the working paper?
b. Explain why the audit of mortgage payable, interest expense, and interest payable should all be done together.
c. List the audit procedures that should ordinarily be performed to verify the issue of the mortgage, the balance in the mortgage and interest payable at 12-31-X8, and the balance in interest expense for the year 19X8.

18–30. Items a through f are common questions found in internal control questionnaires used by auditors in evaluating internal controls for owner's equity. In using the questionnaire for a particular client, a yes response indicates a possible strength in the system, whereas a no indicates a potential weakness.

a. Does the company use the services of an independent registrar or transfer agent?
b. Are issues and retirements of stock authorized by the board of directors?
c. If an independent registrar and transfer agent are not used:
   (1) Are unissued certificates properly controlled?
   (2) Are canceled certificates mutilated to prevent their reuse?
d. Are subsidiary ledgers and stock certificate books periodically reconciled with the general ledger by an independent person?
e. Is an independent transfer agent used for disbursing dividends? If not, is an imprest dividend account maintained?
f. Are all entries in the owner's equity accounts authorized at the proper level in the organization?

Required:

a. For each of the questions above, state the purpose of the control.
b. For each of the questions above, identify the type of potential financial statement errors if the control is not in effect.
c. For each of the potential errors in part b, list an audit procedure the auditor can use to determine whether a material error exists.

18–31. The following audit procedures are frequently performed by auditors in the verification of owner's equity:

a. Review the articles of incorporation and bylaws for provisions relating to owner's equity.
b. Review the minutes of the board of directors for the year for approvals related to owner's equity.
c. Analyze all owner's equity accounts for the year and document the nature of any recorded change in each account.

    d. Account for all certificate numbers in the capital stock book for all shares outstanding.

    e. Examine the stock certificate book for any stock that was canceled.

    f. Recompute earnings per share.

    g. Review debt provisions and senior securities with respect to liquidation preferences, dividends in arrears, and restrictions on the payment of dividends or the issue of stock.

Required:

    a. State the purpose of each of these seven audit procedures.

    b. List the type of errors the auditors could uncover by the use of each audit procedure.

18–32. You are engaged in the audit of a corporation whose records have not previously been audited by you. The corporation has both an independent transfer agent and a register for its capital stock. The transfer agent maintains the record of stockholders and the registrar checks that there is no overissue of stock. Signatures of both are required to validate certificates.

    It has been proposed that confirmations be obtained from both the transfer agent and the registrar as to the stock outstanding at the balance sheet date. If such confirmations agree with the books, no additional work is to be performed as to capital stock.

    If you agree that obtaining the confirmations as suggested would be sufficient in this case, give the justification for your position. If you do not agree, state specifically all additional steps you would take and explain your reasons for taking them. (AICPA adapted)

18–33. The Rico Corporation is a medium-sized wholesaler of grocery products with 4,000 shares of stock outstanding to approximately 25 stockholders. Because of the age of several retired stockholders and the success of the company, management has decided to pay dividends six times a year. The amount of the bimonthly dividend per share varies depending upon the profits, but it is ordinarily between $5 and $7 per share. The chief accountant, who is also a stockholder, prepares the dividend checks, records the checks in the dividend journal, and reconciles the bank account. Important controls include manual check signing by the president and the use of an imprest dividend bank account.

    The auditor verifies the dividends by maintaining a schedule of the total shares of stock issued and outstanding in the permanent working papers. The total amount of stock outstanding is multiplied by the dividends per share authorized in the minutes to arrive at the current total dividend. This total is compared with the deposit that has been made to the imprest dividend account. Since the transfer of stock is infrequent, it is possible to verify dividends paid for the entire year in a comparatively short time.

Required:

    a. Evaluate the usefulness of the approach followed by the auditor in verifying dividends in this situation. Your evaluation should include both the strengths and the weaknesses of the approach.

b. List other audit procedures that should be performed in verifying dividends in this situation. Explain the purpose of each procedure.

18–34. Holmes Company has decided to declare a 10 percent stock dividend in the current year rather than having a cash dividend. There are 160,000 shares outstanding to approximately two thousand stockholders as of the date of the dividend. The stock was selling for $38 per share on the date the dividend was declared, but it had dropped to $26 as of the balance sheet date. The par value of the stock is $20 per share. The company does not employ the services of a transfer agent.

Required:

a. What is the proper accounting treatment of the stock dividend?
b. What audit procedures should be used to verify the stock dividend? Describe the purpose of each procedure.

18–35. In 1956 Jack Harrigan and his brothers started a small manufacturing company as a sideline to their regular occupations. What began as a small informal partnership eventually became a successful business, and when the sons of two of the original partners entered the firm, the need to formalize the relationship became obvious to everyone concerned. After lengthy discussions among themselves and with attorneys and CPAs, the decision was made to enter into a clearly defined partnership agreement rather than to incorporate. The partnership agreement was completed in 1971.

The firm has continued to operate successfully without internal difficulties since that time. Great care is taken by the firm to keep the affairs of the partnership entity and those of the individual partners completely separate. For example, if a personal transaction of a partner is paid by the partnership, his capital account is charged.

Your firm has audited the partnership entity for several years, and the individuals involved have concluded that the system of internal control is excellent. No unusual difficulties have been encountered in any year.

Required:

a. How does the fact that the business is a partnership rather than a corporation affect the audit of the capital acquisition and repayment cycle? (Be specific.)
b. How do the tests of transactions for each of the cycles other than the capital acquisition and repayment cycle differ when the client is a partnership rather than a corporation?
c. How do the direct tests of balances for each of the cycles other than the capital acquisition and repayment cycle differ when the client is a partnership rather than a corporation?

18–36. You are a CPA engaged in an examination of the financial statements of Pate Corporation for the year ended December 31, 19X9. The financial statements and records of Pate Corporation have not been audited by a CPA in prior years.

The stockholders' equity section of Pate Corporation's balance sheet at December 31, 19X9, follows:

Stockholders' equity:

Capital stock—10,000 shares of $10 par value authorized; 5,000 shares issued and outstanding	$ 50,000
Capital contributed in excess of par value of capital stock	32,580
Retained earnings	47,320
Total stockholders' equity	$129,900

Pate Corporation was founded in 19X1. The corporation has ten stockholders and serves as its own registrar and transfer agent. There are no capital stock subscription contracts in effect.

Required:

a. Prepare the detailed audit program for the examination of the three accounts comprising the stockholders' equity section of Pate Corporation's balance sheet. (Do not include in the audit program the verification of the results of the current year's operations.)

b. After every other figure on the balance sheet has been audited by the CPA, it might appear that the retained earnings figure is a balancing figure and requires no further verification. Why does the CPA verify retained earnings as he does the other figures on the balance sheet? Discuss.

(AICPA adapted)

18–37. You were engaged on May 1, 19X7, by a committee of stockholders to perform a special audit as of December 31, 19X6, of the stockholders' equity of the Major Corporation, whose stock is actively traded on a stock exchange. The group of stockholders who engaged you believe that the information contained in the stockholders' equity section of the published annual report for the year ended December 31, 19X6, is not correct. If your examination confirms their suspicions, they intend to use the report in a proxy fight.

Management agrees to permit your audit but refuses to permit any direct confirmation with stockholders. To secure cooperation in the audit, the committee of stockholders has agreed to this limitation and you have been instructed to limit your audit in this respect. You have been instructed also to exclude the audit of revenue and expense accounts for the year.

Required:

a. Prepare a general audit program for the usual examination of the stockholders' equity section of a corporation's balance sheet, assuming no limitation on the scope of your examination. Exclude the audit of revenue and expense accounts.

b. Describe any special auditing procedures you would undertake in view of the limitations and other special circumstances of your examination of the Major Corporation's stockholders' equity accounts.   (AICPA adapted)

19

AUDIT
OF CASH BALANCES

The audit of cash balances is the last area studied in this text because the evidence accumulated for cash balances depends heavily on the results of the tests in all the various transaction cycles. For example, if the review and evaluation of internal control and audit tests of the acquisition and payment cycle lead the auditor to believe the controls over cash disbursements are excellent, it is appropriate to reduce the tests of the ending balance in cash. On the other hand, if the tests indicate the client's controls are inadequate, extensive year-end testing may be necessary.

TYPES OF CASH ACCOUNTS

It is important to understand the various types of cash accounts because the auditing approach differs between them. The following are the major types of cash accounts:

General Cash Account. The general account is the focal point of cash for most organizations because virtually all cash receipts and disbursements flow through the general cash account at some time. The disbursements for the acquisition and payment cycle are normally paid from this account, and the receipts of cash in the sales and collection fund are deposited in the account. In addition, the deposits and disbursements for all other cash accounts are normally made through the general account. Most small companies have only one bank account—the general cash account.

Imprest Payroll Account. As a means of improving control, many companies establish a separate imprest bank account for making payroll payments to employees. In an imprest payroll account, a fixed balance, such as $1,000, is maintained in a separate bank account. Immediately before each pay period one check is drawn on the general cash account to deposit the total amount of the net payroll in the payroll account. After all payroll checks have cleared the imprest payroll account, the bank account should have a $1,000 balance. The only deposits into the account are of the weekly and semimonthly payroll, and the only disbursements are paychecks to employees. For companies with many employees, the use of an imprest payroll account can improve internal controls and also reduce the time needed to reconcile bank accounts.

Branch Bank Account. For a company operating in multiple locations, it is frequently desirable to have a separate bank balance at each location. Branch bank accounts are useful for building public relations in local communities and permitting the centralization of operations at the branch level.

In some companies the deposits and disbursements for each branch are made to a particular bank account, and the excess cash is periodically sent to the main office general bank account. The branch account in this instance is much like a general account, but at the branch level.

A somewhat different type of branch account consists of one bank account for receipts and a separate one for disbursements. All receipts are deposited in the branch bank, and the total is transferred to the general account periodically. The disbursement account is set up on an *imprest basis*, but in a different manner than an imprest payroll account. A fixed balance is maintained in the imprest account, and the authorized branch personnel use these funds for disbursements at their own discretion as long as the payments are consistent with company policy. When the cash balance has been depleted, an accounting is made to the home office and a reimbursement is made to the branch account from the general account *after* the expenditures have been approved. The advantages of using an imprest branch bank account are the resulting controls over receipts and disbursements.

Imprest Petty Cash Fund. A petty cash fund is actually not a bank account, but it is sufficiently similar to cash on deposit to merit inclusion. It is used for small cash purchases which can be paid more conveniently and quickly by cash than by check, or for the convenience of employees in cashing personal or payroll checks. An imprest cash account is set up on the same basis as an imprest branch bank account, but the expenditures are normally for a much smaller amount. Typical expenses include minor office supplies, stamps, and small contributions to local charities. Usually a petty cash account does not exceed $500 and may not be reimbursed more than once or twice each month.

Savings Accounts. Excess cash accumulated during certain parts of the operating cycle which will be needed in the reasonably near future is usually deposited in certificates of deposit or interest-bearing savings accounts. This money is not meant for use in the business until it is transferred back to the general cash account.

This chapter focuses on three types of accounts: the general cash account, the imprest payroll bank account, and the imprest petty cash fund. The others are similar to these and need not be discussed.

RELATIONSHIP BETWEEN CASH IN THE BANK AND THE TRANSACTION CYCLES

A brief discussion of the relationship between cash in the bank and the other transaction cycles serves a dual function: it clearly shows the importance of the tests of various transaction cycles to the audit of cash and it aids in further understanding the integration of the different transaction cycles. Figure 19-1 illustrates the relationship of the various transaction cycles, the focal point being the general cash account.

An examination of Figure 19-1 indicates why the general cash account is considered significant in almost all audits even when the ending balance is immaterial. The amount of cash *flowing* into and out of the cash account is frequently larger than for any other account in the financial statements. Furthermore, the susceptibility of cash to defalcation is greater than for other types of assets because most other assets must be converted to cash to make them usable.

An important distinction in the audit of cash should be made between verifying the client's reconciliation of the balance on the bank statement to the balance in the general ledger and verifying whether recorded cash in the general ledger correctly reflects all cash transactions that took place during the year. It is relatively easy to verify the client's reconciliation of the balance in the bank account to the general ledger, which is the primary subject of this chapter, but a significant part of the total audit of a company involves verifying whether cash transactions are properly recorded. For example, the following errors will each ultimately result in the improper payment of cash or the failure to receive cash, but none of them will normally be discovered as a part of the audit of the bank reconciliation:

- Failure to bill a customer.
- Billing a customer at a lower price than called for by company policy.
- A defalcation of cash by interception of collections from customers before they are recorded. The account is charged off as a bad debt.
- Duplicate payment of a vendor's invoice.
- Improper payments of officers' personal expenditures.
- Payment for raw materials that were not received.
- Payment to an employee for more hours than he worked.
- Payment of interest to a related party for an amount in excess of the going rate.

If these errors are to be uncovered in the audit, their discovery must come about through the tests of the systems that were discussed in the preceding chapters. The first three errors should be discovered as part of the audit of the sales and collection cycle; the next three errors should ordinarily be discovered as part of the acquisition and payment cycle; and the discovery of the last two errors should result from the payroll and personnel cycle and the capital acquisition and repayment cycle, respectively.

Entirely different types of errors are normally discovered as a part of the tests of a bank reconciliation. For example:

- Failure to include a check that has not cleared the bank on the outstanding check list, even though it has been recorded in the cash disbursements journal.
- Cash received by the client subsequent to the balance sheet date but recorded as cash receipts in the current year.
- Deposits recorded in the cash book near the end of the year, deposited in the bank, and included in the bank reconciliation as a deposit in transit.
- The existence of payments on notes payable that were debited directly to the bank balance by the bank but were not entered in the client's records.

The appropriate methods for discovering the preceding errors by testing the client's bank reconciliation will become apparent as we proceed. At this point it is important only that the reader distinguish between tests of transactions that are related to the cash account and tests that determine whether the book balance reconciles to the bank balance.

AUDIT OF THE GENERAL CASH ACCOUNT

The Auditor's Objectives

In testing the year-end balance in the general cash account, the auditor must accumulate sufficient evidence to evaluate whether cash, as stated on the balance sheet, is fairly stated and properly disclosed in accordance with seven of the nine detailed objectives used for all direct tests of balances. Ownership of general cash and its classification on the balance sheet are not a problem.

Internal Controls

The controls over the year-end cash balances in the general account can be divided into two categories: *controls over the transaction cycles* affecting the recording of cash receipts and disbursements, and *independent bank reconciliations*.

The controls affecting the recording of cash transactions have been discussed in preceding chapters. For example, in the acquisition and payment

FIGURE 19-1 Relationship between Cash in the Bank and the Transaction Cycles

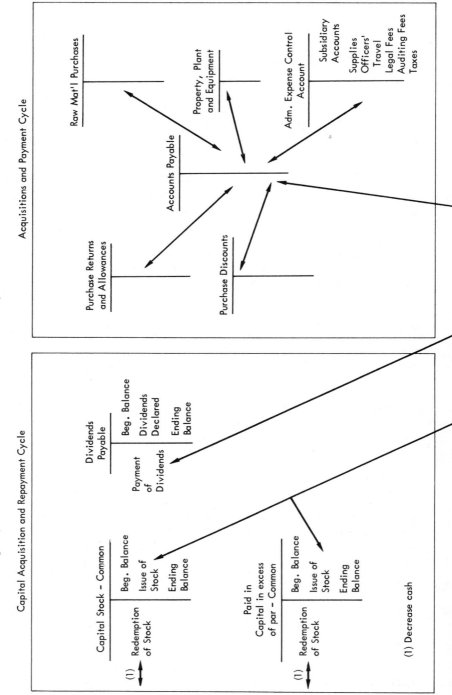

Acquisitions and Payment Cycle

Capital Acquisition and Repayment Cycle

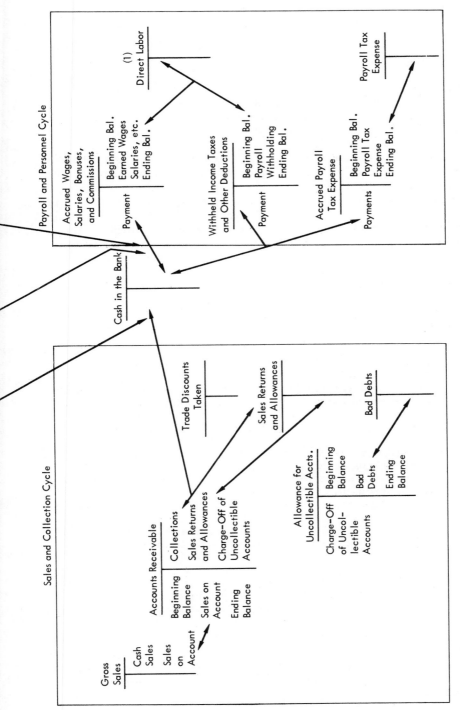

FIGURE 19-1 (cont.)

cycle, major controls include the adequate segregation of duties between check signing and the accounts payable function, the signing of checks only by a properly authorized person, the use of prenumbered checks that are printed on special paper, adequate control of blank and voided checks, careful review of supporting documentation by the check signer before checks are signed, and adequate internal verification. If the controls affecting cash-related transactions are adequate, it is possible to reduce the audit tests for the year-end bank reconciliation.

Monthly reconciliation of the general bank account on a timely basis by someone independent of the handling or recording of cash receipts and disbursements is an essential control over the cash balance. The reconciliation is important to make sure the books reflect the same cash balance as the actual amount of cash in the bank after consideration of reconciling items; but even more important, the *independent* reconciliation provides a unique opportunity for an internal verification of cash receipts and disbursements transactions. If the bank statements are received unopened by the reconciler and physical control is maintained over the statements until the reconciliations are complete, the canceled checks, duplicate deposit slips, and other documents included in the statement can be examined by him without concern for the possibility of alteration, deletions, or additions. A careful bank reconciliation by competent client personnel includes the following:

- Comparison of canceled checks with the cash disbursements journal for date, payee, and amount.
- Examination of canceled checks for signature, endorsement, and cancellation.
- Comparison of deposits in the bank with recorded cash receipts for date, customer, and amount.
- Accounting for the numerical sequence of checks, and the investigation of missing ones.
- Reconciliation of all items causing a difference between the book and bank balance and the verification of their propriety.
- Reconciliation of total debits on the bank statement with the totals in the cash disbursements journal.
- Reconciliation of total credits on the bank statement with the totals in the cash receipts journal.
- Review of month-end interbank transfers for propriety and proper recording.
- Periodic follow-up on outstanding checks and stop-payment notices.

The first four of these internal procedures are directly related to the tests of transactions that were discussed in previous chapters. The last five procedures are directly related to the reconciliation of the book and bank balance and are discussed in greater detail later.

Because of the importance of monthly reconciliation of bank accounts, another common control for many companies is to have a responsible employee review the monthly reconciliation as soon as possible after its completion. This review function is often performed by an internal auditor if the organization has such a function.

A major consideration the auditor must keep in mind in auditing the general cash balance is the possibility of fraud. The auditor must extend his audit procedures in the audit of year-end cash to determine the possibility of a material fraud when there are inadequate internal controls, especially the improper segregation of duties between the handling of cash and the recording of cash transactions in the journals. The study of cash in the following section assumes the existence of adequate controls over cash; therefore, fraud detection is not emphasized. At the completion of the study of typical audit procedures for the reconciliation of year-end cash, procedures designed primarily for the detection of fraud are examined. The starting point for the verification of the balance in the general bank account is to obtain a bank reconciliation from the client for inclusion in the auditor's working papers. Figure 19-2 depicts a bank reconciliation after adjustments. Notice that the bottom figure in the working paper is the adjusted balance in the general ledger.

In discussing the verification of year-end cash, seven of the nine detailed objectives that have been used in studying the audit of other asset balances are again used. There is no discussion of the ownership and classification objectives, since they are not significant for cash in the bank.

The frame of reference for the audit tests is the bank reconciliation. The objectives and common direct tests of balances are shown in Figure 19-3. As in all other audit areas, the actual audit procedures depend upon the considerations discussed in previous chapters. Also, because of their close relationship in the audit of year-end cash, the validity of recorded cash in the bank, valuation, and inclusion of existing cash are combined. These three objectives are the most important ones for cash and therefore receive the greatest attention.

The following three procedures are discussed more thoroughly because of their importance and greater complexity.

Receipt of a Bank Confirmation. The direct receipt of a bank confirmation from every bank with which the client does business is necessary for every audit, except when there are an unusually large number of inactive accounts. If the bank does not respond to a confirmation request, the auditor must send a second request or ask the client to telephone the bank. As a convenience to auditors as well as to bankers who are requested to fill out bank confirmations, the AICPA has approved the use of a *standard bank confirmation* form. Figure 19-4 depicts a completed standard bank confirmation.

The importance of bank confirmations in the audit extends beyond the verification of the actual cash balance. Because of the multiple services offered by banks, the standard bank confirmation includes space for information of interest to the auditor besides specific information relating to the general cash account bank balance, such as

ABC Company, Inc.
Bank Reconciliation
12/31/8x

Schedule A-2   Date
Prepared by DED   1/10/8x
Approved by SW   1/18/8x

Acct. 101—General account, First National Bank

Balance per Bank		109 713	A-2/1
Add:			
Deposits in transit ①			
12/30	10 017		
12/31	11 100	21 117	
Deduct:			
Outstanding checks ①			
# 7 993 12/16	3 068		
8 007 12/16	9 765		
8 012 12/23	11 916		
8 013 12/23	14 717		
8 029 12/24	37 998		
8 038 12/30	10 000	⟨87 462⟩	
Other reconciling items: Bank error			
Deposit to Payroll account credited			
to General account by bank, in error		⟨15 200⟩	A-3
Balance per books, adjusted		28 168	T/B
Balance per books, before adjustments		32 584	A-1
Adjustments:			
Unrecorded bank service charge	216		A-3
Non-sufficient funds check			
returned by bank, not			
collectible from customer	4 200	4 416	C-3/1
Balance per books, adjusted		28 168	A-1
① Cut-off bank statement procedures completed by			1/10/8x
		DED	1/10/8x
② Cut-off bank statement enclosures returned to			
client, acknowledged by		M. Smith	1/12/8x

FIGURE 19–2   Working Paper for a Bank Reconciliation

640

FIGURE 19–3

Summary of Direct Tests of Balances
General Cash in Bank

Audit Objectives	Common Direct Tests of Balances Procedures	Comments
Cash in the bank as stated on the bank reconciliation is reasonable.	• Compare the ending balance, deposits in transit, outstanding checks, and other reconciling items to the prior-year reconciliation. • Compare ending balance in cash to previous months.	• Frequently, the bank reconciliation is tested on a 100 percent basis; therefore, overall reasonableness tests are less important than for many areas.
Cash in the bank as stated on the reconciliation foots correctly and agrees with the general ledger.	• Foot the outstanding check list and deposits in transit. • Prove the bank reconciliation as to additions and subtractions, including all reconciling items. • Trace the book balance on the reconciliation to the general ledger.	• These tests are done entirely on the bank reconciliation, with no reference to documents or other records except the general ledger.
Cash in the bank as stated on the reconciliation is valid. Cash in the bank as stated on the reconciliation is correctly valued. Existing cash in the bank is included.	(See extended discussion for each of these.) • Receipt and tests of a bank reconciliation. • Receipt and tests of a cutoff bank statement. • Tests of the bank reconciliation. • Extended tests of the bank reconciliation. • Proof of cash. • Tests for kiting.	• These are the three most important objectives for cash in the bank. • The procedures are combined because of their close interdependence. • There is extended discussion for each procedure. • The last three procedures should only be done when there are internal control weaknesses.
Cash receipts and cash disbursements transactions are recorded in the proper period.	Cash receipts: • Count the cash on hand on the first day of the year and subsequently trace to deposits in transit and the cash receipts journal. • Trace deposits in transit to subsequent period bank statement (cutoff bank statement). Cash disbursements: • Record the last check number used on the last day of the year and subsequently trace to the outstanding checks and the cash disbursements journal. • Trace outstanding checks to subsequent period bank statement.	• When cash receipts received after year-end are included in the journal, a better cash position than actually exists is shown. It is called "holding open" the cash receipts journal. Holding open the cash disbursements journal reduces accounts payable and usually overstates the current ratio. • The first procedure listed for receipts and disbursement cutoff

FIGURE 19–3 (cont.)

Audit Objectives	Common Direct Tests of Balances Procedures	Comments
		tests requires the auditor's presence on the client's premise at the end of the last day of the year.
Cash in the bank is properly disclosed.	• Examine minutes, loan agreements, and the bank confirmation for restrictions on the use of cash and compensating balances. • Review financial statements to make sure (a) material savings accounts and certificates of deposit are disclosed separately from cash in the bank; (b) cash restricted to certain uses and compensating balances are adequately disclosed; and (c) bank overdrafts are included as current liabilities.	• An example of a restriction on the use of cash is cash deposited with a trustee for the payment of mortgage interest and taxes on the proceeds of a construction mortgage. A compensating balance is the client's agreement with a bank to maintain a specified minimum in its checking account.

- The balances in all bank accounts.
- Restrictions on withdrawals. An example of a restriction is the bank's requirement of a compensating balance in the checking account.
- The interest rate on interest-bearing accounts.
- Information on liabilities to the bank for notes, mortgages, or other debt, including the amount of the loan, the date of the loan, its due date, interest rate, and the existence of collateral.
- Contingent liabilities, open letters of credit, and similar items requiring disclosure in the financial statements.

After the bank confirmation has been received, the balance in the bank account confirmed by the bank should be traced to the amount stated on the bank reconciliation. Similarly, all other information on the reconciliation should be traced to the relevant audit working papers. In any case where the information is not in agreement, an investigation must be made of the difference.

Receipt of a Cutoff Bank Statement. A cutoff bank statement is a partial period bank statement and the related canceled checks, duplicate deposit slips, and other documents included in bank statements, which is mailed by the bank directly to the CPA firm's office. The purpose of the cutoff bank statement is to verify the reconciling items on the client's year-end bank reconciliation with evidence that is inaccessible to the client. To fulfill this purpose, the auditor requests the client to have the bank send the

ORIGINAL
To be mailed to accountant

December 23, 19 8X

Dear Sirs:

Your completion of the following report will be sincerely appreciated. **IF THE ANSWER TO ANY ITEM IS "NONE", PLEASE SO STATE.** Kindly mail it in the enclosed stamped, addressed envelope direct to the accountant named below.

Report from

Yours truly, ABC Company, Inc.
(ACCOUNT NAME PER BANK RECORDS)

(Bank) First National Bank

By _G. L. Moore_
Authorized Signature

123 Financial Street

Bank customer should check here if confirmation of bank balance only (item 1) is desired. ☐

Middletown

NOTE — If the space provided is inadequate, please enter totals hereon and attach a statement giving full details as called for by the columnar headings below.

Accountant   Smart & Allen
New York, New York

Dear Sirs:

1. At the close of business on December 31, 19 8X our records showed the following balance(s) to the credit of the above named customer. In the event that we could readily ascertain whether there were any balances to the credit of the customer not designated in this request, the appropriate information is given below.

AMOUNT	ACCOUNT NAME	ACCOUNT NUMBER	Subject to Withdrawal by Check?	Interest Bearing? Give Rate
$ 109,713.11	General account	19751-974	Yes	No
1,000.00	Payroll account	19751-989	Yes	No

2. The customer was directly liable to us in respect of loans, acceptances, etc., at the close of business on that date in the total amount of $ 300,000, as follows:

AMOUNT	Date of Loan or Discount	Due Date	INTEREST Rate	INTEREST Paid To	DESCRIPTION OF LIABILITY, COLLATERAL, SECURITY INTERESTS, LIENS, ENDORSERS, ETC.
$ 150,000	12/9/8X	1/9/8Y	10	N/A	General Security Agreement
90,000	12/16/8X	1/16/8Y	10		
60,000	12/23/8X	1/23/8Y	10		

3. The customer was contingently liable as endorser of notes discounted and/or as guarantor at the close of business of that date in the total amount of $ None, as below:

AMOUNT	NAME OF MAKER	DATE OF NOTICE	DUE DATE	REMARKS
$				

4. Other direct or contingent liabilities, open letters of credit, and relative collateral, were

None

5. Security agreements under the Uniform Commercial Code or any other agreements providing for restrictions, not noted above, were as follows (if officially recorded, indicate date and office in which filed):

UCC filing, Secretary of State, 1/12/8Y, Capital City

Yours truly, (Bank) First National Bank

Date   January 10, 19 8Y

By _Margaret Davis_, V.P.
Authorized Signature

If the space provided is inadequate, please enter totals hereon and attach a statement giving full details as called for by the above columnar headings.

FIGURE 19-4 Standard Bank Confirmation

statement for seven to ten days subsequent to the balance sheet date directly to the auditor.

Many auditors prove the subsequent period bank statement if a cutoff statement is not received directly from the bank. They perform the proof in the month subsequent to the balance sheet date by (1) footing all the canceled checks, debit memos, deposits, and credit memos; (2) checking to see that the bank statement balances when the footed totals are used; and (3) reviewing the items included in the footings to make sure they were canceled by the bank in the proper period and do not include any erasures or alterations. The purpose of this proof is to test whether the client's employees have omitted, added, or altered any of the documents accompanying the statement. It is obviously a test for intentional errors.

Tests of the Bank Reconciliation. The reason for testing the bank reconciliation is to verify whether the client's recorded bank balance is the same amount as the actual cash in the bank except for deposits in transit, outstanding checks, and other reconciling items. In testing the reconciliation, the cutoff bank statement provides the information for conducting the tests. Several major procedures are involved:

- Trace the balance on the cutoff statement to the balance per bank on the bank reconciliation; a reconciliation cannot take place until these two are the same.
- Trace checks included with the cutoff bank statement to the list of outstanding checks on the bank reconciliation and to the cash disbursements journal. All checks that cleared the bank after the balance sheet date which were included in the cash disbursements journal should also be included on the outstanding check list. If a check was included in the cash disbursements journal, it should be included as an outstanding check if it did not clear before the balance sheet date. Similarly, if a check cleared the bank prior to the balance sheet date, it should not be on the bank reconciliation.
- Investigate all significant checks included on the outstanding check list that have not cleared the bank on the cutoff statement. The first step in the investigation should be to trace the amount of any items not clearing to the cash disbursements journal. The reason for the check not being cashed should be discussed with the client, and if the auditor is concerned about the possibility of fraud, the vendor's accounts payable balance should be confirmed to determine whether the vendor has recognized the receipt of the cash in his records. In addition, the canceled check should be examined prior to the last day of the audit if it becomes available.
- Trace the deposits in transit to the subsequent bank statement. All cash receipts not deposited in the bank at the end of the year should be traced to the cutoff bank statement to make sure they were deposited shortly after the beginning of the new year.
- Account for other reconciling items on the bank statement and bank reconciliation. These include such items as bank service charges, bank errors and corrections, and unrecorded note transactions debited or credited directly to the bank account by the bank. These reconciling items should be carefully investigated to be sure they have been treated properly by the client.

It is frequently necessary for the auditor to extend his year-end audit procedures to test more extensively for the possibility of material fraud when the client's internal controls are weak. Many fraudulent activities are difficult if not impossible to uncover; nevertheless, the auditor is responsible for making a reasonable effort to detect fraud when he has reason to believe it may exist. The following procedures for uncovering fraud are discussed in this section: extended tests of the bank reconciliation, proofs of cash, and tests for kiting.

Extended Tests of the Bank Reconciliation. When the auditor believes the year-end bank reconciliation may be intentionally misstated, it is appropriate to perform extended tests of the year-end bank reconciliation. The purpose of the extended procedures is to verify whether all transactions included in the journals for the last month of the year were correctly included in or excluded from the bank reconciliation and to verify whether all items in the bank reconciliation were correctly included. Let us assume that the system of internal control is weak and the client's year-end is December 31. A common approach is to start with the bank reconciliation for November and compare all reconciling items with canceled checks and other documents in the December bank statement. In addition, all remaining canceled checks and deposit slips in the December bank statement should be compared with the December cash disbursements and receipts journals. All uncleared items in the November bank reconciliation and the December cash disbursements and receipts journals should be included in the client's December 31 bank reconciliation. Similarly, all reconciling items in the December 31 bank reconciliation should be items from the November bank reconciliation and December's journals that have not yet cleared the bank.

In addition to the tests just described, the auditor must also carry out procedures subsequent to the end of the year with the use of the bank cutoff statement. These tests would be performed in the same manner as previously discussed.

Proofs of Cash. Auditors frequently prepare a proof of cash when the client's internal controls over cash are not considered adequate. A proof of cash includes the following:

- A reconciliation of the balance on the bank statement with the general ledger balance at the beginning of the proof-of-cash period.
- A reconciliation of cash receipts deposited with the cash receipts journal for a period of time.
- A reconciliation of canceled checks clearing the bank with the cash disbursements journal for a period of time.
- A reconciliation of the balance on the bank statement with the general ledger balance at the end of the proof-of-cash period.

A proof of cash of this nature is commonly referred to as a four-column proof of cash—one column is used for each of the types of information listed above. A proof of cash can be performed for one or more interim months, the entire year, or the last month of the year. Figure 19-5 depicts a four-column proof of cash for an interim month.

The auditor uses a proof of cash to determine the following:

- Whether all recorded cash receipts were deposited.
- Whether all deposits in the bank were recorded in the accounting records.
- Whether all recorded cash disbursements were paid by the bank.
- Whether all amounts that were paid by the bank were recorded.

The concern in an interim-month proof of cash is not with adjusting account balances: it is with reconciling the amounts per books and bank.

When the auditor does a proof of cash, he is combining tests of transactions and direct tests of balances. For example, the proof of the cash receipts is a test of recorded transactions, whereas the bank reconciliation is a test of the balance in cash at a point in time. The proof of cash is an excellent method of comparing recorded cash receipts and disbursements with the bank account and with the bank reconciliation. On the other hand, the auditor must recognize that the proof of cash disbursements is not useful for discovering checks written for an improper amount, invalid checks, or other errors where the dollar amount appearing on the cash disbursements records is incorrect. Similarly, the proof of cash receipts is not useful for uncovering the theft of cash receipts or the recording and deposit of an improper amount of cash.

Tests for Kiting. Embezzlers occasionally cover a defalcation of cash by a practice known as *kiting:* transferring money from one bank to another and improperly recording the transaction. Near the balance sheet date a check is drawn on one bank account and immediately deposited in a second account for credit before the end of the accounting period. In making this transfer, the embezzler is careful to make sure the check is deposited at a late enough date so that it does not clear the first bank until after the end of the period. Assuming the bank transfer is not recorded until after the balance sheet date, the amount of the transfer is recorded as an asset in both banks. Although there are other ways of perpetrating this fraud, each involves the basic device of increasing the bank balance to cover a shortage by the use of bank transfers.

A useful approach to testing for kiting, as well as for unintentional errors in recording bank transfers, is to list all bank transfers made a few days before and after the balance sheet date and trace each one to the accounting records for proper recording. For example, if a bank transfer is recorded in the current period as a disbursement, the auditor should examine the bank cancellation date on the check to see when it cleared. If the check cleared after the balance sheet date, it should be included as an outstanding check. Similarly, transfers deposited in the bank near the end of the year or

ABC Company, Inc.
Year-end Proof of Cash

Schedule _____ Date
Prepared by _JG_ 7/15/8x
Approved by _RP_ 7/17/8x

6/30/8x

Acct. 101 – General account, First National Bank

		5/31/8x	Receipts	Disbursements	6/30/8x
Balance per Bank	①	121,782.12	627,895.20	631,111.96	118,565.36
Deposits in transit –					
5/31	②	21,720.00	‹21,720.00›		
6/30	②		16,592.36		16,592.36
Outstanding checks –					
5/31	③	‹36,396.50›		‹36,396.50›	
6/30	③			14,800.10	‹14,800.10›
NSF checks –	④		‹4,560.00›	‹4,560.00›	
To allow for effect of a cash disbursement recorded as a credit item in Cash Receipts Journal			8,500.00	8,500.00	
Balance per books, adjusted		107,105.62	626,707.56	613,455.56	120,357.62
Balance per books, unadjusted		107,105.62	626,707.56	614,957.04	118,856.14
Bank debit memos	⑤			120.00	‹120.00›
Payroll checks erroneously entered in General Disbursements Journal	⑥			‹1,621.48›	1,621.48
Balance per books, adjusted		107,105.62	626,707.56	613,455.56	120,357.62

① Per 6/30/8x bank statement
② Detailed listing filed below; traced to subsequent bank statements.
③ Outstanding-check list filed below; examined cancelled checks.
④ Detailed listing filed below; all NSF items were redeposited and had cleared as of 7/15/8x.
⑤ Safety deposit rentals; traced to recording via journal entry. Requested list of contents of safety deposit boxes.
⑥ Traced to journal entry correcting error.

FIGURE 19-5 Interim Proof of Cash

included as deposits in transit can be traced to the cash receipts or disbursements journal to make sure they have been recorded in the journals in the proper period. For example, if a transfer was received by the bank and included as a deposit in transit on the bank reconciliation, kiting has probably occurred.

Even though audit tests of bank transfers are usually fraud-oriented, they are often performed on audits where there are numerous bank transfers, regardless of the system of internal control. When there are numerous intercompany transfers, it is difficult to be sure each one is correctly handled unless a schedule of transfers near the end of the year is prepared and each transfer is traced to the accounting records and bank statements. In addition to the possibility of kiting, inaccurate handling of transfers could result in a misclassification between cash and accounts payable. The materiality of transfers and the relative ease of performing the tests make many auditors believe they should always be performed.

Summary. In designing audit procedures for uncovering fraud, careful consideration should be given to the nature of the weaknesses in the system of internal control, the type of fraud that is likely to result from the weaknesses, the potential materiality of the fraud, and the audit procedures that are most effective in uncovering the error. When the auditor is specifically testing for fraud, he should keep in mind that audit procedures other than direct tests of cash balances can also be useful. Examples of procedures that may uncover fraud in the cash receipts area include the confirmation of accounts receivable, tests for lapping, reviewing the general ledger entries in the cash account for unusual items, tracing from customer orders to sales and subsequent cash receipts, and examining approvals and supporting documentation for bad debts and sales returns and allowances. Similar tests can be used for testing for the possibility of fraudulent cash disbursements.

AUDIT OF THE PAYROLL BANK ACCOUNT

Tests of the payroll bank reconciliation should take only a few minutes if there is an imprest payroll account and an independent reconciliation of the bank account such as that described for the general account. Typically, the only reconciling items are outstanding checks, and for most audits the great majority clear shortly after the checks are issued. In testing the payroll bank account balances, it is necessary to obtain a bank reconciliation, a bank confirmation, and a cutoff bank statement. The reconciliation procedures are performed in the same manner as those described for general cash. Naturally, extended procedures are necessary if the controls are inadequate or if the bank account does not reconcile with the general ledger imprest cash balance.

The discussion in the preceding paragraph should not be interpreted as implying that the audit of payroll is unimportant. A review of Chapter 13 should remind the reader that the most important audit procedures for verifying payroll are tests of transactions, which are designed to test the controls. The most likely payroll errors will be discovered by those procedures rather than by checking the imprest bank balance.

AUDIT OF PETTY CASH

Petty cash is a unique account because it is frequently immaterial in amount, yet it is verified on most audits. The account is verified primarily because of the potential for defalcation and the client's expectation of an audit review even when the amount is immaterial.

Internal Controls over Petty Cash

The most important control over petty cash is the use of an imprest fund that is the responsibility of *one individual*. In addition, petty cash funds should not be mingled with other receipts, and the fund should be kept separate from all other activities. There should also be limits on the amount of any expenditure from petty cash, as well as the total amount of the fund. The type of expenditure that can be made from petty cash transactions should be well defined by company policy.

Whenever a disbursement is made from petty cash, adequate controls require a responsible official's approval on a prenumbered petty cash form. The total of the actual cash and checks in the fund plus the total unreimbursed petty cash forms that represent actual expenditures should equal the total amount of the petty cash fund stated in the general ledger. Periodically, surprise counts and a reconciliation of the petty cash fund should be made by the internal auditor or other responsible official.

When the petty cash balance runs low, a check payable to the petty cash custodian should be made out on the general cash account for the reimbursement of petty cash. The check should be for the exact amount of the prenumbered vouchers that are submitted as evidence of actual expenditures. These vouchers should be verified by the accounts payable clerk and canceled to prevent their reuse.

Audit Tests for Petty Cash

The emphasis in verifying petty cash should be on testing petty cash transactions rather than the ending balance in the account. Even if the amount of the petty cash fund is small, there is potential for numerous improper transactions if the fund is frequently reimbursed.

An important part of testing petty cash is to first determine the client's procedures for handling petty cash by discussing the system with the custodian and examining the documentation of a few transactions. As a part of developing an understanding of the system, it is necessary to evaluate its strengths and weaknesses. Even though most petty cash systems are not complex, it is often desirable to use a flowchart and an internal control questionnaire, primarily for documentation in subsequent audits.

The tests of the system depend on the number and size of the petty cash reimbursements and the strengths and weaknesses of the system. When there are excellent controls and few reimbursement payments during the year, it is common for auditors not to test any further for reasons of immateriality. When the auditor decides to test petty cash, the two most common procedures are to count the petty cash balance and to carry out detailed tests of one or two reimbursement transactions. In such a case the primary procedures should include footing the petty cash vouchers supporting the amount of the reimbursement, accounting for a sequence of petty cash vouchers, examining the petty cash vouchers for authorization and cancellation, and examining the attached documentation for reasonableness. Typical supporting documentation includes cash register tapes, invoices, and receipts.

The petty cash tests can ordinarily be performed at any time during the year, but as a matter of convenience they are typically done on an interim date. If the balance in the petty cash fund is considered material, which is rarely the case, it should be counted at the end of the year. Unreimbursed expenditures should be examined as a part of the count to determine whether the amount of unrecorded expenses is material.

REVIEW QUESTIONS

19–1. Explain the relationship between internal control evaluation and tests of transactions for cash receipts, and the direct tests of cash balances.

19–2. Explain the relationship between internal control evaluation and tests of transactions for cash disbursements, and the direct tests of cash balances. Give one example where the conclusions reached about the controls in cash disbursements would affect the tests of cash balances.

19–3. Why is the monthly reconciliation of bank accounts by an independent person an important internal control over cash balances? Which individuals would generally not be considered independent for this responsibility?

19–4. Evaluate the effectiveness and state the shortcomings of the preparation of a bank reconciliation by the controller in the manner described in the following statement: "When I reconcile the bank account the first thing I do is to sort the checks in numerical order and find which numbers are missing. Next I determine the amount of the uncleared checks by reference to the cash disbursements journal. If the bank reconciles at that point, I am all finished with the reconciliation. If it does not, I search for deposits in transit, checks from the beginning outstanding check list that still have not cleared, other reconciling items, and bank errors until it reconciles. In most instances I can do the reconciliation in twenty minutes."

19–5. How do bank confirmations differ from positive confirmations of accounts receivable? Distinguish between them in terms of the nature of the information confirmed, the sample size, and the appropriate action when the confirmation is not returned after the second request. Explain the rationale for the differences between these two types of confirmation.

19–6. Evaluate the necessity of following the practice described by an auditor: "In confirming bank accounts I insist upon a response from every bank the client has done business with in the past two years, even though the account may be closed at the balance sheet date."

19–7. Describe what is meant by a cutoff bank statement and state its purpose.

19–8. Why are auditors usually less concerned about the client's cash receipts cutoff than the cutoff for sales? Explain the procedure involved in testing for the cutoff for cash receipts.

19–9. What is meant by an imprest bank account for a branch operation? Explain the purpose of using this type of bank account.

19–10. Explain the purpose of a four-column proof of cash. List two types of errors it is meant to uncover.

19–11. When the auditor fails to obtain a cutoff bank statement, it is common to "prove" the entire statement for the month subsequent to the balance sheet date. How is this done and what is its purpose?

19–12. Distinguish between *lapping* and *kiting*. Describe audit procedures that can be used to uncover each of them.

19–13. Assume that a client with excellent internal controls uses an imprest payroll bank account. Explain why the verification of the payroll bank reconciliation ordinarily takes less time than the tests of the general bank account even if the number of checks exceeds those written on the general account.

19–14. Distinguish between the verification of petty cash reimbursements and the verification of the balance in the fund. Explain how each of these is done. Which is more important?

19–15. Why is there a greater emphasis on the detection of fraud in direct tests of cash balances than for other balance sheet accounts? Give two specific examples that demonstrate how this emphasis affects the auditor's evidence accumulation in auditing year-end cash.

19–16. Explain why, in verifying bank reconciliations, most auditors emphasize the possibility of a nonexistent deposit in transit being included in the reconciliation and an outstanding check being omitted rather than the omission of a deposit in transit and the inclusion of nonexistent outstanding check.

DISCUSSION QUESTIONS AND PROBLEMS

19–17. Select the best response for each of the following multiple-choice questions:
   a. On December 31, 19X7, a company erroneously prepared an accounts payable voucher (Dr. cash, Cr. accounts payable) for a transfer of funds between banks. A check for the transfer was drawn January 3, 19X8. This error resulted in overstatements of cash and accounts payable at December 31, 19X7. Of the following procedures, the least effective in disclosing this error is review of the

      (1) December 31, 19X7, bank reconciliations for the two banks.

      (2) December 19X7 check register.

      (3) support for accounts payable at December 31, 19X7.

      (4) schedule of interbank transfers.

   b. A CPA obtains a January 10 cutoff bank statement for his client directly from the bank. Very few of the outstanding checks listed on his client's December 31 bank reconciliation cleared during the cutoff period. A probable cause for this is that the client

      (1) is engaged in kiting.

      (2) is engaged in lapping.

      (3) transmitted the checks to the payees after year-end.

      (4) has overstated its year-end bank balance.

   c. The cashier of Baker Company covered a shortage in his cash working fund with cash obtained on December 31 from a local bank by cashing an unrecorded check drawn on the company's New York bank. The auditor would discover this manipulation by

      (1) preparing independent bank reconciliations as of December 31.

      (2) counting the cash working fund at the close of business on December 31.

      (3) investigating items returned with the bank cutoff statements.

      (4) confirming the December 31 bank balances.   (AICPA adapted)

19–18. Following are errors an auditor might expect to find in the client's year-end cash balance (assume the balance sheet date is June 30).

   a. A check was omitted from the outstanding check list on the June 30 bank reconciliation. It cleared the bank July 7.

   b. A check was omitted from the outstanding check list on the bank reconciliation. It cleared the bank September 6.

   c. Cash receipts collected on accounts receivable from July 1 to July 5 were included as June 29 and 30 cash receipts.

   d. A loan from the bank on June 26 was credited directly to the client's bank account. The loan was not entered as of June 30.

   e. A check that was dated June 26 and disbursed in June was not recorded in the cash disbursements journal, but it was included as an outstanding check on June 30.

   f. A bank transfer recorded in the accounting records on July 1 was included as a deposit in transit on June 30.

   g. The outstanding checks on the June 30 bank reconciliation were underfooted by $2,000.

Required:

   a. Assuming that each of these errors was intentional, state the most likely motivation of the person responsible for making the error.

   b. What internal control procedure could be instituted for each of these errors to reduce the likelihood of occurrence?

   c. List an audit procedure the auditor could use to discover each error.

19–19. Following are errors an auditor might expect to find through tests of transactions or by direct tests of cash balances:

a. The bookkeeper failed to record checks in the cash disbursements journal that were written and mailed during the first month of the year.

b. The bookkeeper failed to record or deposit a material amount of cash receipts during the last month of the year. Cash is prelisted by the president's secretary.

c. The cash disbursements journal was held open for two days after the end of the year.

d. A check was paid to a vendor for a carload of raw materials that was never received by the client.

e. A discount on a purchase was not taken even though the check was mailed before the discount period had expired.

f. Cash receipts for the last two days of the year were recorded in the cash receipts journal for the subsequent period and listed as deposits in transit on the bank reconciliation.

g. A check written during the last month of the year to a vendor was recorded in the cash disbursements journal twice to cover an existing fraud. The check cleared the bank and did not appear on the bank reconciliation.

Required:

a. List an audit procedure to uncover each of the preceding errors.

b. For each procedure in part a, state whether it is a direct test of cash balances or a test of transactions.

19–20. Explain the objective(s) of each of the following audit procedures concerned with direct tests of general cash balances.

a. Compare the bank cancellation date with the date on the canceled check for checks dated on or shortly before the balance sheet date.

b. Trace deposits in transit on the bank reconciliation to the cutoff bank statement and the current year cash receipts journal.

c. Obtain a standard bank confirmation from each bank with which the client does business.

d. Compare the balance on the bank reconciliation obtained from the client with the bank confirmation.

e. Compare the checks returned along with the cutoff bank statement with the list of outstanding checks on the bank reconciliation.

f. List the check number, payee, and amount of all material checks not returned with the cutoff bank statement.

g. Review minutes of the board of directors, loan agreements, and bank confirmations for interest-bearing deposits, restrictions on the withdrawal of cash, and compensating balance agreements.

h. Prepare a four-column proof of cash.

19–21. When you arrive at your client's office on January, 11, 19X7, to begin the December 31, 19X6, audit, you discover that the client had been drawing checks as creditors' invoices became due but not necessarily mailing them. Because of a working capital shortage, some checks may have been held for two or three weeks.

The client informs you that unmailed checks totaling $27,600 were on hand at December 31, 19X6. He states that these December-dated checks had been entered in the cash disbursements book and charged to the respective creditors' accounts in December because the checks were prenumbered. Heavy collections permitted him to mail the checks before your arrival.

The client wants to adjust the cash balance and accounts payable at December 31 by $27,600 because the cash account had a credit balance. He objects to submitting to his bank your audit report showing an overdraft of cash.

Required:

a. Prepare an audit program indicating the procedures you would use to satisfy yourself of the accuracy of the cash balance on the client's statements.

b. Discuss the acceptability of reversing the indicated amount of outstanding checks. (AICPA adapted)

19–22. William Green recently acquired the financial controlling interest of Importers and Wholesalers, Inc., importers and distributors of cutlery. In his review of the duties of employees, Green became aware of loose practices in the operation of the petty cash fund. You have been engaged as the company's CPA, and Green's first request is that you suggest a system of sound practices for operation of the petty cash fund. In addition to Green, who is the company president, the company has twenty employees, including four corporate officers. The petty cash fund has a working balance of about $200, and about $500 is expended by the fund each month.

Required:

Prepare a letter to Green containing your recommendations for good internal control procedures for operation of the petty cash fund. (Where the effect of the control procedure is not evident, give the reason for the procedure.) (AICPA adapted)

19–23. Discuss briefly what you regard as the more important deficiencies in the system of internal control in the following situation, and in addition include what you consider to be a proper remedy for each deficiency.

The cashier of the Easy Company intercepted customer A's check payable to the company in the amount of $500 and deposited it in a bank account which was part of the company petty cash fund, of which he was custodian. He then drew a $500 check on the petty cash fund bank account payable to himself, signed it, and cashed it. At the end of the month while processing the monthly statements to customers, he was able to change the statement to customer A so as to show that A had received credit for the $500 check that had been intercepted. Ten days later he made an entry in the cash received book which purported to record receipt of a remittance of $500 from customer A, thus restoring A's account to its proper balance, but overstating cash in bank. He covered the overstatement by omitting from the list of outstanding checks in the bank reconcilement, two checks, the aggregate amount of which was $500. (AICPA adapted)

19–24. The Patrick Company had poor internal control over its cash transactions. Facts about its cash position at November 30, 19X8, were as follows:

The cash books showed a balance of $18,901.62, which included undeposited receipts. A credit of $100 on the bank's records did not appear on the books of the company. The balance per bank statement was $15,550. Outstanding checks were: No. 62 for $116.25, No. 183 for $150.00, No. 284 for $253.25, No. 8621 for $190.71, No. 8623 for $206.80, and No. 8632 for $145.28.

The cashier abstracted all undeposited receipts in excess of $3,794.41 and prepared the following reconciliation:

Balance, per books, November 30, 19X8		$18,901.62
Add: Outstanding checks:		
8621	$190.71	
8623	206.80	
8632	145.28	442.79
		$19,344.41
Less: Undeposited receipts		3,794.41
Balance per bank, November 30, 19X8		$15,550.00
Deduct: Unrecorded credit...................		100.00
True cash, November 30, 19X8		$15,450.00

Required:

a. Prepare a supporting schedule showing how much the cashier abstracted.
b. How did he attempt to conceal his theft?
c. Taking only the information given, name two specific features of internal control which were apparently missing. (AICPA adapted)

19–25. On an audit with a September 30 balance sheet date, the auditor obtained the October bank statement from the client on November 26 during his year-end field work. In comparing the September checks clearing the bank in October with the year-end outstanding check list, the auditor observed that a check for $4,206 had not cleared. The auditor traced the check number and amount to the October 31 bank reconciliation to make sure it was included, and examined supporting documentation to test the propriety for the payment. The auditor concluded that the bank reconciliation was correct.

What had actually happened, however, was a defalcation by the bookkeeper. He forged a check to himself late in September for the amount owed on a purchase of merchandise. On October 2 he deposited the check in his personal account. He removed the canceled check from the bank statement when he received the checks from the bank for reconciliation. Since the bookkeeper knew the auditor would trace the uncleared check to the subsequent reconciliation, he included the check number and amount but reduced other outstanding checks from November by a corresponding amount. In late October the bookkeeper submitted a check for signature that was made out to the same vendor and included the invoice in the amount of $4,206 as support for the disbursement.

Required:

a. What weaknesses in the controls should have alerted the auditor to the possibility of fraud?

b. List four ways the auditor could have uncovered this defalcation.

19–26. In his examination of cash, the CPA is watchful for signs of kiting.

Required:

a. Define *kiting*.

b. List the CPA's audit procedures that would uncover kiting.

(AICPA adapted)

19–27. In the audit of the Regional Transport Company, a large branch that maintains its own bank account, cash is periodically transferred to the central account in Cedar Rapids. On the branch account's records, bank transfers are recorded as a debit to the home office clearing account and a credit to the branch bank account. Similarly, the home office account is recorded as a debit to the central bank account and a credit to the branch office clearing account. Gordon Light is the head bookkeeper for both the home office and the branch bank accounts. Since he also reconciles the bank account, the senior auditor, Cindy Marintette, is concerned about the weakness in the system of internal control.

As a part of the year-end audit of bank transfers, Marintette asks you to schedule the transfers for the last few days in 19X7 and the first few days of 19X8. You prepare the following list:

Amount of Transfer	Date Recorded in the Home Office Cash Receipts Journal	Date Recorded in the Branch Office Cash Disbursements Journal	Date Deposited in the Home Office Bank Account	Date Cleared the Branch Bank Account
$12,000	12-27-X7	12-29-X7	12-26-X7	12-27-X7
26,000	12-28-X7	1- 2-X8	12-28-X7	12-29-X7
14,000	1- 2-X8	12-30-X7	12-28-X7	12-29-X7
11,000	12-26-X7	12-26-X7	12-28-X7	1- 3-X8
15,000	1- 2-X8	1- 2-X8	12-28-X7	12-31-X7
28,000	1- 7-X8	1- 5-X8	12-28-X7	1- 3-X8
37,000	1- 4-X8	1- 6-X8	1- 3-X8	1- 5-X8

Required:

a. In verifying each bank transfer, state the appropriate audit procedures you should perform.

b. Prepare any adjusting entries required in the home office records.

c. Prepare any adjusting entries required in the branch bank records.

d. State how each bank transfer should be included in the 12-31-X7 bank reconciliation for the home office account before your adjustments in part b.

e. State how each bank transfer should be included in the 12-31-X7 bank reconciliation of the branch bank account before your adjustments in part c.

19–28. A surprise count of the Y Company's imprest petty cash fund, carried on the books at $5,000, was made on November 10, 19X7.

The company acts as agent for an express company in the issuance and sale of money orders. Blank money orders are held by the cashier for issuance upon payment of the designated amounts by employees. Settlement with the express company is made weekly with its representative who calls at the Y Company office. At that time he collects for orders issued, accounts for unissued orders, and leaves additional blank money orders serially numbered.

The count of the items presented by the cashier as composing the fund was as follows:

Currency (bills and coin)		$2,200
Cashed checks		500
Vouchers (made out in pencil and signed by recipient)		740
N.S.F. checks (dated June 10 and 15, 19X7)		260
Copy of petty cash receipt vouchers:		
Return of expense advance	$200	
Sale of money orders (#C1015–1021)	100	300
Blank money orders—claimed to have been purchased for $100 each from the Express Company (C1022–1027)		600

At the time of the count there was also on hand the following:

Unissued money orders C1028–1037
Unclaimed wage envelopes (sealed and amounts not shown)

The following day the custodian of the fund produced vouchers aggregating $400 and explained that these vouchers had been temporarily misplaced the previous day. They were for wage advances to employees.

Required:

a. Show the proper composition of the fund at November 10, 19X7.
b. State the audit procedures necessary for the verification of the items in the fund.

19–29. In connection with your audit of the ABC Company at December 31, 19X7, you were given a bank reconciliation by a company employee which shows:

Balance per bank	$15,267
Deposits in transit	18,928
	$34,195
Checks outstanding	21,378
Balance per books	$12,817

As part of your verification you obtain the bank statement and canceled checks from the bank on January 15, 19X8. Checks issued from January 1 to January

15, 19X8, per the books were $11,241. Checks returned by the bank on January 15 amounted to $29,219. Of the checks outstanding December 31, $4,800 were not returned by the bank with the January 15 statement, and of those issued per the books in January 19X8, $3,600 were not returned.

Required:

a. Prepare a schedule showing the foregoing data in proper form.

b. Suggest four possible explanations for the condition existing here and state what your action would be in each case, including any necessary journal entries.   (AICPA adapted)

19–30. Toyco, a retail toy chain, honors two bank credit cards and makes daily deposits of credit card sales in two credit card bank accounts (Bank A and Bank B). Each day Toyco batches its credit card sales slips, bank deposit slips, and authorized sales return documents, and keypunches cards for processing by its electronic data processing department. Each week detailed computer printouts of the general ledger credit card cash accounts are prepared. Credit card banks have been instructed to make an automatic weekly transfer of cash to Toyco's general bank account. The credit card banks charge back deposits that include sales to holders of stolen or expired cards.

The auditor conducting the examination of the 1981 Toyco financial statements has obtained the following copies of the detailed general ledger cash account printouts, a summary of the bank statements and the manually prepared bank reconciliations, all for the week ended December 31, 1981.

Toyco
Detailed General Ledger Credit Card Cash Account Printouts
for the Week Ended December 31, 1981

	Bank A Dr. or (Cr.)	Bank B Dr. or (Cr.)
Beginning balance —December 24, 1981	$12,100	$ 4,200
Deposits		
—December 27, 1981	2,500	5,000
—December 28, 1981	3,000	7,000
—December 29, 1981	0	5,400
—December 30, 1981	1,900	4,000
—December 31, 1981	2,200	6,000
Cash transfer —December 27, 1981	(10,700)	0
Chargebacks —Expired cards	(300)	(1,600)
Invalid deposits (physically deposited in wrong account)	(1,400)	(1,000)
Redeposit of invalid deposits	1,000	1,400
Sales returns for week ending December 31, 1981	(600)	(1,200)
Ending balance —December 31, 1981	$ 9,700	$29,200

Toyco
Summary of the Bank Statements
for the Week Ended December 31, 1981

	Bank A	Bank B
	(*Charges*) *or Credits*	
Beginning balance		
—December 24, 1981	$10,000	$ 0
Deposits dated		
—December 24, 1981	2,100	4,200
—December 27, 1981	2,500	5,000
—December 28, 1981	3,000	7,000
—December 29, 1981	2,000	5,500
—December 30, 1981	1,900	4,000
Cash transfers to general bank account		
—December 27, 1981	(10,700)	0
—December 31, 1981	0	(22,600)
Chargebacks		
—Stolen cards	(100)	0
—Expired cards	(300)	(1,600)
Invalid deposits	(1,400)	(1,000)
Bank service charges	0	(500)
Bank charge (unexplained)	(400)	0
Ending balance		
—December 31, 1981	$ 8,600	$ 0

Toyco
Bank Reconciliations
for the Week Ended December 31, 1981

Code No.	Bank A	Bank B
	Add or (*Deduct*)	
1. Balance per bank statement		
—December 31, 1981	$8,600	$ 0
2. Deposits in transit		
—December 31, 1981	2,200	6,000
3. Redeposit of invalid deposits —(physically deposited in wrong account)	1,000	1,400
4. Difference in deposits of December 29, 1981	(2,000)	(100)
5. Unexplained bank charge	400	0
6. Bank cash transfer not yet recorded	0	22,600
7. Bank service charges	0	500
8. Chargebacks not recorded —stolen cards	100	0
9. Sales returns recorded but not reported to the bank	(600)	(1,200)
10. Balance per general ledger —December 31, 1981	$9,700	$29,200

Required:

a. Based on a review of the December 31, 1981, bank reconciliations and the related information available in the printouts and the summary of bank statements, describe what action(s) the auditor should take to obtain audit satisfaction **for each item** on the bank reconciliations.

b. Assume that all amounts are material and all computations are accurate.

c. Organize your answer sheet as follows, using the appropriate code number **for each item** on the bank reconciliations:

Code No.	Action(s) to Be Taken by the Auditor to Obtain Audit Satisfaction
1.	

(AICPA adapted)

19–31. In connection with an audit you are given the following worksheet:

Bank Reconciliation
December 31, 19X7

Balance per ledger 12-31-X7		$17,174.86
Add:		
Collections received on the last day of December and charged to "cash in bank" on books but not deposited		2,662.25
Debit memo for customer's check returned unpaid (check is on hand but no entry has been made on the books)		200.00
Debit memo for bank service charge for December		5.50
		$20,142.61
Deduct:		
Checks drawn but not paid by bank (see detailed list below)	$2,267.75	
Credit memo for proceeds of a note receivable which had been left at the bank for collection but which has not been recorded as collected	400.00	
Check for an account payable entered on books as $240.90 but drawn and paid by bank as $419.00	178.10	2,945.85
Computed balance		$17,196.76
Unlocated difference................................		200.00
Balance per bank (checked to confirmation)............		$16,996.76

Checks Drawn but Not Paid by Bank

No.	Amount
573	$ 67.27
724	9.90
903	456.67
907	305.50
911	482.75
913	550.00
914	366.76
916	10.00
917	218.90
	$2,267.75

Required:

a. Prepare a corrected reconciliation.

b. Prepare journal entries for items that should be adjusted prior to closing
the books. (AICPA adapted)

19–32. Glatfelt Rural Electric Power Cooperative issues books of sight drafts to
the foremen of its 10 field crews. The foremen use the drafts to pay the
expenses of the field crews when they are on line duty requiring overnight
stays.

The drafts are prenumbered and, as is clearly printed on the drafts, are
limited to expenditures of $300 or less. The foremen prepare the drafts in
duplicate and send the duplicates, accompanied by expense reports substantiating the drafts, to the general office.

The draft duplicates are accumulated at the general office and a
voucher is prepared when there are two or three draft duplicates on hand.
The voucher is the authority for issuing a company check for deposit in an
imprest fund of $5,000 maintained at a local bank to meet the drafts as they
are presented for payment. The cooperative maintains a separate general
ledger account for the imprest fund.

The audit of the voucher register and cash disbursements disclosed the
following information pertaining to sight drafts and the reimbursement of
the imprest fund:

a. Voucher 10524 dated 12-31-X7, paid by check 10524 dated 12-31-X7, for
the following drafts:

Draft No.	*Date*	*Crew No.*	*Explanation*	*Amount*
6001	12-24-X7	3	Expenses, 12-22–12-24	$160
2372	12-28-X7	6	Expenses, 12-26–12-28	310
5304	12-30-X7	7	Cash advance to foreman	260
			Voucher total	$730

b. Voucher 10531 dated 12-31-X7, paid by check 10531 dated 1-3-X8, for
the following drafts:

Draft No.	*Date*	*Crew No.*	*Explanation*	*Amount*
4060	12-29-X7	1	Expenses, 12-27–12-29	$150
1816	1-3-X8	4	Expenses, 1-1–1-3	560
			Voucher total	$710

c. Voucher 23 dated 1-8-X8, paid by check 23 dated 1-8-X8, for the following
drafts:

Draft No.	*Date*	*Crew No.*	*Explanation*	*Amount*
1000	12-31-X7	9	Expenses, 12-28–12-31	$270
2918	1-3-X8	10	Expenses, 12-28–12-31	190
4061	1-7-X8	1	Expenses, 1-4–1-6	210
			Voucher total	$670

d. All of the vouchers listed above were charged to Travel Expense.

e. Examination of the imprest fund's bank statement for December, the January cutoff bank statement, and accompanying drafts presented for payment disclosed the following information:

(1) Reimbursement check 10524 was not credited on the December bank statement.

(2) The bank honored draft 2372 at the established maximum authorized amount.

(3) Original 19X7 drafts drawn by foremen but not presented to the client's bank for payment by 12-31-X7 totaled $1,600. This total included all 19X7 drafts itemized above except 4060 and 2372, which were deducted by the bank in December.

(4) December bank service charges listed on the December bank statement but not recorded by the client amounted to $80.

(5) The balance per the bank statement at December 31, 19X7 was $5,650.

Required:

a. Prepare the auditor's adjusting journal entry to correct the books at December 31, 19X7. (The books have not been closed.) A supporting working paper analyzing the required adjustments should be prepared in good form.

b. Prepare a reconciliation of the balance per bank statement and the financial statement figure for the imprest cash account. The first figure in your reconciliation should be the balance per bank statement.

(AICPA adapted)

19–33. The following information was obtained in an audit of the cash account of Tuck Company as of December 31, 19X7. Assume that the CPA has satisfied himself as to the validity of the cash book, the bank statements, and the returned checks, except as noted.

a. The bookkeeper's bank reconciliation at November 30, 19X7.

Balance per bank statement			$ 19,400
Add deposit in transit			1,100
Total			$ 20,500
Less outstanding checks			
	#2540	$140	
	1501	750	
	1503	480	
	1504	800	
	1505	30	2,300
Balance per books			$ 18,200

b. A summary of the bank statement for December 19X7.

Balance bought forward	$ 19,400
Deposits	148,700
	$168,100
Charges	132,500
Balance, December 31, 19X7	$ 35,600

c. A summary of the cash book for December 19X7 before adjustments.

Balance brought forward	$ 18,200
Receipts	149,690
	$167,890
Disbursements	124,885
Balance, December 31, 19X7.....................	$ 43,005

d. Included with canceled checks returned with the December bank statement were the following:

Number	Date of Check	Amount of Check	
1501	November 28, 19X7	$ 75	This check was in payment of an invoice for $750 and was recorded in the cash book as $750.
1503	November 28, 19X7	$ 580	This check was in payment of an invoice for $580 and was recorded in the cash book as $580.
1523	December 5, 19X7	$ 150	Examination of this check revealed that it was unsigned. A discussion with the client disclosed that it had been mailed inadvertently before it was signed. The check was endorsed and deposited by the payee and processed by the bank even though it was a legal nullity. The check was recorded in the cash disbursements.
1528	December 12, 19X7	$ 800	This check replaced 1504 that was returned by the payee because it was mutilated. Check 1504 was not canceled on the books.
——	December 19, 19X7	$ 200	This was a counter check drawn at the bank by the president of the company as a cash advance for travel expense. The president overlooked informing the bookkeeper about the check.
——	December 20, 19X7	$ 300	The drawer of this check was the Tucker Company.
1535	December 20, 19X7	$ 350	This check had been labeled N.S.F. and returned to the payee because the bank had erroneously believed that the check was drawn by the Luck Company. Subsequently the payee was advised to redeposit the check.
1575	January 5, 19X8	$10,000	This check was given to the payee on December 30, 19X7, as a postdated check with the understanding that it would not be deposited until January 5. The check was not recorded on the books in December.

e. The Tuck Company discounted its own 60-day note for $9,000 with the bank on December 1, 19X7. The discount rate was 6 percent. The bookkeeper recorded the proceeds as a cash receipt at the face value of the note.

f. The bookkeeper records customers' dishonored checks as a reduction of cash receipts. When the dishonored checks are redeposited they are recorded as a regular cash receipt. Two N.S.F. checks for $180 and $220 were returned by the bank during December. The $180 check was redeposited, but the $220 check was still on hand at December 31.

Cancellations of Tuck Company checks are recorded by a reduction of cash disbursements.

g. December bank charges were $20. In addition a $10 service charge was made in December for the collection of a foreign draft in November. These charges were not recorded on the books.

h. Check 2540 listed in the November outstanding checks was drawn in 19X5. Since the payee cannot be located, the president of Tuck Company agreed to the CPA's suggestion that the check be written back into the accounts by a journal entry.

i. Outstanding checks at December 31, 19X7, totaled $4,000, excluding checks 2540 and 1504.

j. The cutoff bank statement disclosed that the bank had recorded a deposit of $2,400 on January 2, 19X8. The bookkeeper had recorded this deposit on the books on December 31, 19X7, and then mailed the deposit to the bank.

Required:

Prepare a four-column proof of cash of the cash receipts and cash disbursements recorded on the bank statement and on the company's books for the month of December 19X7. The reconciliation should agree with the cash figure that will appear in the company's financial statements.

(AICPA adapted)

20

COMPLETING
THE AUDIT

After the auditor has completed the tests in specific audit areas, it is necessary to summarize the results and perform additional testing of a more general nature. Summarization and general tests are an essential part of the audit because an overall evaluation of the combined results is performed during this phase. The following subjects are covered in discussing completion of the audit:

- Review for contingent liabilities and commitments.
- Post-balance sheet review.
- Subsequent discovery of facts existing at the date of the auditor's report.
- Summarizing and drawing conclusions.
- Review for financial statement disclosures.
- Unaudited replacement cost information.
- Management representation letters.
- Working paper review.
- Management letters.

REVIEW FOR CONTINGENT LIABILITIES
AND COMMITMENTS

A *contingent liability* is a potential future obligation to an outside party for an unknown amount resulting from activities that have already taken place. The most important characteristic of a contingent liability is the uncertainty of the amount: if the amount were known, it would be included in the financial statements as an actual liability rather than a contingency.

The proper disclosure in the financial statements of material contingencies is through footnotes. A *footnote* should describe the nature of the contingency to the extent it is known and the opinion of legal counsel or management as to the expected outcome. The following is an illustration of a footnote related to pending litigation:

> As of December 31, 1981, the company is a defendant in several lawsuits related to product liability. The aggregate amount of damages claimed is $10,000,000 in excess of product liability insurance coverage. Management and legal counsel believe that the company's liability for such excess, if any, should not be material in amount.

Certain contingent liabilities are of considerable concern to the auditor:

- Pending litigation for patent infringement, product liability, or other actions.
- Income-tax disputes.
- Product warranties.
- Notes receivable discounted.
- Guarantees of obligations of others.
- Unused balances in outstanding letters of credit.

Many of these potential obligations are ordinarily verified as an integral part of various segments of the engagement rather than at a point in time near the end of the audit. For example, unused balances in outstanding letters of credit may be tested as a part of confirming bank balances and loans from banks. Similarly, income-tax disputes can be checked as a part of analyzing income tax expense, reviewing the general correspondence file, and examining revenue agent reports. Even if the contingencies are verified separately, it is common to perform the tests well before the last few days of completing the engagement to ensure their proper verification. The tests of contingent liabilities near the end of the engagement are more of a review than an initial search.

General Audit Procedures

The appropriate audit procedures for testing contingencies are less well defined than the procedures that have already been discussed in other audit areas because the primary objective at the initial stage of the tests is to determine the *existence* of contingencies. As the reader knows from the study of other audit areas, it is more difficult to discover unrecorded transactions or events than to properly verify recorded information. Once the auditor is aware that contingencies exist, the evaluation of their materiality and the disclosure required can ordinarily be satisfactorily resolved.

The following are some audit procedures commonly used to search for contingent liabilities. The list is not all-inclusive, and each procedure is not necessarily performed on each audit.

- Inquire of management (orally and in writing) regarding the possibility of unrecorded contingencies. In these inquiries the auditor must be specific in describing the different kinds of contingencies that may require disclosure. Naturally, inquiries of management are not useful in uncovering the intentional failure to disclose existing contingencies, but if management has overlooked a particular type of contingency or does not fully comprehend accounting disclosure requirements, the inquiry can be fruitful. At the completion of the audit, management is typically asked to make a written statement that it is aware of no undisclosed contingent liabilities as a part of the letter of representation.
- Review current and previous years' internal revenue agent reports of income-tax settlements. The reports may indicate areas where disagreement over unsettled years are likely to arise. If a review has been in progress for a long time, there is an increased likelihood of an existing tax dispute.
- Review the minutes of directors' and stockholders' meetings for indications of lawsuits or other contingencies.
- Analyze legal expense for the period under audit and review invoices and statements from legal counsel for indications of contingent liabilities, especially lawsuits and pending tax assessments.
- Obtain a confirmation from all major attorneys performing legal services for the client as to the status of pending litigation or other contingent liabilities. This procedure is discussed in more depth shortly.
- Review existing working papers for any information that may indicate a potential contingency. For example, bank confirmations may indicate notes receivable discounted or guarantees of loans.
- Obtain letters of credit in force as of the balance sheet date and obtain a confirmation of the used and unused balance.

Confirmation from Client's Legal Counsel

A major procedure auditors rely upon for discovering contingencies is a *letter of confirmation from the client's legal counsel* informing the auditor of pending litigation or any other information involving legal counsel that is relevant to financial statement disclosure. If a contingent liability actually exists, the auditor should also obtain the attorney's professional opinion of the expected outcome of the lawsuit and the likely amount of the liability, including court costs.

As a matter of tradition, many CPA firms analyze legal expense for the entire year and have the client send a standard attorney's letter to every attorney the client has been involved with in the current or preceding year, plus any attorney the firm occasionally engaged. In some cases this involves a large number of attorneys, including some who deal in aspects of law that are far removed from potential lawsuits.

Attorneys in recent years have become reluctant to provide certain information to auditors because of their own exposure to legal liability for providing incorrect or confidential information. The nature of the refusal of attorneys to provide auditors with complete information about contingent liabilities falls into two categories: the refusal to respond due to a lack of knowledge about matters involving contingent liabilities and the refusal to disclose information that the attorney regards as confidential between himself and his client. As an example of the latter situation, the attorney might be aware of a violation of a patent agreement which could result in a significant loss to the client if it were known (unasserted claim). The inclusion of the information in a footnote could actually cause the lawsuit and therefore be damaging to the client.

When the nature of the attorney's legal practice does not involve contingent liabilities, his refusal to respond causes no audit problems. It is certainly reasonable for attorneys to refuse to make statements about contingent liabilities when they are not involved with lawsuits or similar aspects of the practice of law that directly affect the financial statements.

A serious audit problem does arise, however, when an attorney refuses to provide information that is within his jurisdiction and may directly affect the fair presentation of financial statements. If an attorney refuses to provide the auditor with information about material existing lawsuits (asserted claim) or unasserted claims, *the audit opinion would have to be modified to reflect the lack of available evidence.* This requirement (SAS 12; Section 337) has the effect of requiring management to give its attorneys permission to provide contingent liability information to auditors and to encourage attorneys to cooperate with auditors in obtaining information about contingencies.

The standard letter of confirmation from the client's attorney, which should be prepared on the client's letterhead and signed by one of the company's officials, should include the following:

- A list, prepared by management, of material pending, threatened litigation, claims, or assessments with which the attorney has had significant involvement. An alternative is for the letter to request the attorney to prepare the list.
- A list, prepared by management, of likely material unasserted claims and assertions with which the attorney has had significant involvement.
- A request that the attorney furnish information or comment about the progress of each listed claim or assessment, the legal action the client intends to take, the likelihood of an unfavorable outcome, and an estimate of the amount or range of the potential loss.
- A request for the identification of any unlisted pending or threatened legal actions or a statement that the client's list was complete.
- A statement by the client informing the attorney of his responsibility to inform management whenever in the attorney's judgment there is a legal matter requiring disclosure in the financial statements. The letter of inquiry should also request that the attorney confirm directly to the auditor that he understands this responsibility.
- A request that the attorney identify and describe the nature of any reasons for any limitations in this response.

An example of a typical standard letter that is now sent by the client to the attorney for return directly to the CPA's office is shown in Figure 20-1.

```
              Banergee Building Co.
                 409 Lane Drive
              Buffalo, New York 10126

                                      1-26-82

Bailwick & Bettle, Attorneys
11216 - 5th Street N E
New York, New York 10023

Gentlemen:

          Our auditors, Clarrett & Co., CPAs (1133 Broadway, New York,

New York 10019), are making an examination of our financial state-

ments for the fiscal year ended 12-31-81.  In connection with their

examination, we have prepared, and furnished to them, a description

and evaluation of certain contingencies, including those attached,

involving matters with respect to which you have been engaged and

to which you have devoted substantive attention on behalf of the

Company in the form of legal consultation or representation.  For

the purpose of your response to this letter, we believe that as to

each contingency an amount in excess of $10,000 would be material,

and in total, $50,000.  However, determination of materiality with

respect to the overall financial statements cannot be made until our

auditors complete their examination.  Your response should include

matters that existed at 12-31-81 and during the period from that

date to the date of the completion of their examination, which is

anticipated to be on or about 2-13-82.

          Please provide to our auditors the following information:

(1) such explanation, if any, you consider necessary to supplement

the listed judgments rendered or settlements made involving the

Company from the beginning of this fiscal year through the date of

your reply.
```

FIGURE 20–1 Typical Attorney's Letter

(2) such explanation, if any, that you consider necessary to supplement the listing of pending or threatened litigation, including an explanation of those matters as to which your views may differ from those stated and an identification of the omission of any pending or threatened litigation, claim, and assessment or a statement that the list of such matters is complete.

(3) such explanation, if any, you consider necessary to supplement the attached information concerning unasserted claims and assessments, including an explanation of those matters as to which your views may differ from those stated.

We understand that whenever, in the course of performing legal services for us with respect to a matter recognized to involve an unasserted possible claim or assessment that may call for financial statement disclosure, if you have formed a professional conclusion that we should disclose or consider disclosure concerning such possible claim or assessment, as a matter of professional responsibility to us, you will so advise us and will consult with us concerning the question of such disclosure and the applicable requirements of Statement of Financial Accounting Standards No. 5. Please specifically confirm to our auditors that our understanding is correct.

Please specifically identify the nature of and reasons for any limitation on your response.

Yours very truly,

Banergee Building Co.

Clark Jones

Clark Jones, Pres.

FIGURE 20–1 (cont.)

Notice in the first paragraph of the letter that the attorney is requested to communicate about contingencies up to approximately *the date of the auditor's report.*

Evaluation of Known Contingent Liabilities

The auditor must evaluate the significance of the potential liability and the nature of the disclosure that is necessary in the financial statements if he concludes that there are contingent liabilities. The potential liability is sufficiently well known in some instances to be included in the statements as an actual liability. In other instances, disclosure may be unnecessary if the contingency is highly remote or immaterial. Frequently, the CPA firm obtains a separate evaluation of the potential liability from its own legal counsel rather than rely on management or management's attorneys. The client's attorney is an advocate for the client and frequently loses perspective in evaluating the likelihood of losing the case and the amount of the potential judgment.

Commitments

Closely related to contingent liabilities are commitments to purchase raw materials or to lease facilities at a certain price, agreements to sell merchandise at a fixed price, bonus plans, profit-sharing and pension plans, royalty agreements, and similar items. In a commitment the most important characteristic is the *agreement to commit the firm to a set of fixed conditions* in the future regardless of what happens to profits or the economy as a whole. In a free economy presumably the entity agrees to commitments as a means of bettering its own interests, but they may turn out to be less or more advantageous than originally anticipated. All commitments are ordinarily either described together in a separate footnote or combined with a footnote related to contingencies.

The search for unknown commitments is usually performed as a part of the audit of each audit area. For example, in verifying sales transactions the auditor should be alert for sales commitments. Similarly, commitments for the purchase of raw materials or equipment can be identified as a part of the audit of each of these accounts. The auditor should also be aware of the possibility of commitments as he is reading contracts and correspondence files, and inquiries should be made of management.

POST-BALANCE SHEET REVIEW

The auditor has a responsibility to review transactions and events occurring after the balance sheet date to determine whether anything occurred that might affect the valuation or disclosure of the statements being audited. The auditing procedures employed to verify these transactions and events are commonly referred to as the review of *subsequent events* or *post-balance sheet review.*

The auditor's responsibility for reviewing for subsequent events is normally limited to the period beginning with the balance sheet date and ending with the date of the auditor's report. Since the date of the auditor's report corresponds to the completion of the important auditing procedures in the client's office, the subsequent events review should be completed near the end of the engagement. (When the auditor's name is associated with a registration statement under the Securities Act of 1933, his responsibility for reviewing subsequent events extends beyond the date of the auditor's report to the date the registration becomes effective.)

Types of Subsequent Events

Two types of subsequent events require consideration by management and evaluation by the auditor: those that have a direct effect on the financial statements and require adjustment and those that have no direct effect on the financial statements but for which disclosure is advisable.

Those That Have a Direct Effect on the Financial Statements and Require Adjustment. These events or transactions provide additional information to management in determining the valuation of account balances as of the balance sheet date and to auditors in verifying the balances. For example, if the auditor is having difficulty in determining the correct valuation of inventory because of obsolescence, the sale of raw material inventory as scrap in the subsequent period should be used as a means of determining the correct valuation of the inventory as of the balance sheet date. The scrap value of the inventory would be entered in the accounting records as the carrying value of the inventory at the balance sheet date.

Such subsequent period events as the following require an adjustment of account balances in the current year's financial statements if the amounts are material:

- The declaration of bankruptcy due to deteriorating financial condition of a customer with an outstanding accounts receivable balance.
- The settlement of a litigation at an amount different from the amount recorded on the books.
- The disposal of equipment not being used in operations at a price below the current book value.
- The sale of investments at a price below recorded cost.

Whenever subsequent events are used to evaluate the amounts included in the statements, care must be taken to distinguish between conditions that existed at the balance sheet date and those that came into being after the end of the year. The subsequent information should not be incorporated directly into the statements if the conditions causing the change in valuation did not take place until subsequent to the year-end. For example, the sale of scrap in the subsequent period would not be relevant in the valuation of inventory for obsolescence if the obsolescence took place after the end of the year.

Those That Have No Direct Effect on the Financial Statements but for Which Disclosure Is Advisable. Subsequent events of this type provide evidence of conditions that did not exist at the date of the balance sheet being reported on but are so significant that they require disclosure even though they do not require adjustment. Ordinarily, these subsequent events can be adequately disclosed by the use of footnotes, but occasionally such an event may be so significant as to require *supplementing the historical statements* with statements that include the effect of the event as if it had occurred on the balance sheet date.

Following are examples of events or transactions occurring in the subsequent period that may require disclosure rather than an adjustment in the financial statements:

- A decline in market value of securities held for temporary investment or resale.
- The issuance of bonds or equity securities.
- The settlement of litigation where the event that caused the lawsuit took place subsequent to the balance sheet date.
- A decline in market value of inventory as a consequence of governmental action barring further sale of a product.
- An uninsured loss of inventories as a result of fire.

Audit Tests

The audit procedures for the post-balance sheet review can be conveniently divided into two categories: procedures normally integrated as a part of the verification of year-end account balances, and those performed specifically for the purpose of discovering events or transactions that must be recognized in the current period.

The first category includes cutoff and valuation tests which are done as a part of the direct tests of financial balances. For example, subsequent period sales and purchases transactions are examined to determine whether the cutoff is accurate. Similarly, many valuation tests involving subsequent events are also performed as a part of the verification of account balances. As an example, it is common to test the collectibility of accounts receivable by reviewing subsequent period cash receipts. It is also a normal audit procedure to compare the subsequent period purchase price of inventory with the recorded cost as a test of lower of cost or market valuation. The procedures for cutoff and valuation have been discussed sufficiently in preceding chapters and are not repeated here.

The second category tests are performed specifically for the purpose of obtaining information that must be incorporated into the current year's account balances or disclosed by a footnote.

These tests include the following:

Inquire of Management. The nature of the inquiries varies from client to client, but they normally include inquiries about the existence of potential contingent liabilities or commitments, significant changes in the asset or capital structure of the company, the current status of items that were not completely resolved at the balance sheet date, and the existence of unusual adjustments made subsequent to the balance sheet date.

The inquiries of management about subsequent events must be held with the proper client personnel to obtain meaningful answers. For example, discussing tax or union matters with the accounts receivable supervisor would not be appropriate. Most inquiries should be held with the controller, the vice-presidents, and the president, depending on the information desired.

Correspond with Attorneys. Correspondence with attorneys, which was previously discussed, takes place as a part of the search for contingent liabilities. In obtaining confirmation letters from attorneys, the auditor must remember his responsibility for testing for subsequent events up to the date of the audit report. A common approach is to request the attorney to date and mail the attorney's letter as of the expected completion date for the field work.

Review Internal Statements Prepared Subsequent to the Balance Sheet Date. The emphasis in the review should be on changes in the business relative to the current year's results for the same period, particularly on major changes in the business or environment in which the client is operating. The statements should be discussed with management to determine whether they are prepared on the same basis as the current period statements, and there should be inquiries about significant changes in the operating results.

Review Records of Original Entry Prepared Subsequent to the Balance Sheet Date. Journals and ledgers should be reviewed to determine the existence and nature of any transaction related to the current year. If the journals are not kept up to date, the documents relating to the journals should be reviewed.

Examine Minutes Issued Subsequent to the Balance Sheet Date. The minutes of stockholders' and directors' meetings subsequent to the balance sheet date must be examined for important subsequent events affecting the current-period financial statements.

Obtain a Letter of Representation. The letter of representation written by the client to the auditor formalizes statements the client has made about different matters throughout the audit, including discussions about subsequent events.

Important Considerations in Post-Balance Sheet Reviews

Three major considerations should be kept in mind throughout the review for subsequent events: the nature and intensity should vary, depending on the conditions existing at the time of the review; the auditor must be familiar with the client and the industry; and careful follow-up and analysis is required in inquiries of management.

The post-balance sheet review must be conducted by an auditor who has been actively involved in the entire audit and understands the circumstances of the engagement. The importance of the performance of the review by an adequately experienced auditor was clearly shown in the 1968 case of *Escott* v. *Bar Chris Construction Corporation*, which revolved around inadequate disclosure of subsequent events. The case was discussed in Chapter 2. It was disclosed in the case that the staff person—an audit senior—used a written audit program and spent over 20 hours performing the subsequent audit review but failed to discover any of the material subsequent events. It was his first year as senior on an engagement, he was not a CPA, and he had had no previous experience in the industry. A major problem in the review was the senior's inability to recognize the symptoms of the deteriorating financial condition of the client.

Whenever the auditor discusses post-balance sheet events with management, there must be a careful follow-up to determine whether management's responses to questions are reasonable. For example, one of the criticisms of the audit in the *Bar Chris* case was that the senior on the engagement appeared to ask many of the right questions, but he neither looked at nor asked for any supporting documentation to verify the reasonableness of management's responses.

SUBSEQUENT DISCOVERY OF FACTS EXISTING AT THE DATE OF THE AUDITOR'S REPORT

If the auditor becomes aware *after the audited financial statements have been released* that some information included in the statements is materially misleading, he has an obligation to make certain that users who are relying on the financial statements are informed about the misstatements.[1] The most likely case in which the auditor is faced with this problem occurs when the financial statements are determined to include a material error subsequent to the issuance of an unqualified report. There are many possible causes of misstated statements, among them the inclusion of fictitious sales, the failure to write off obsolete inventory, or the omission of an essential footnote. Regardless of whether the failure to discover the error was the fault of the auditor, his responsibility remains the same.

The most desirable approach to follow when the auditor discovers the statements are misleading is to request that the client issue an immediate

[1]The discussion in this section is more closely related to audit reports, which is the subject of Chapter 21, than it is to completing the audit. However, many students of auditing confuse the examination of subsequent period events as a part of post-balance sheet review with the subsequent discovery of facts existing at the balance sheet date. The latter is studied at this point to eliminate the confusion.

revision of the financial statements containing an explanation of the reasons for the revision. If a subsequent period's financial statements were completed before the revised statements could be issued, it is acceptable to disclose to users that new statements were completed before the revised statements could be issued and disclose the misstatements in the current statements. Whenever it is pertinent, the client should inform the Securities and Exchange Commission and other regulatory agencies of the misleading financial statements. The auditor has the responsibility for making certain that the client has taken the appropriate steps in informing users of the misleading statements.

If the client refuses to cooperate in disclosing the misstated information, the auditor must inform the board of directors of this fact. The auditor must also notify the regulatory agencies having jurisdiction over the client and each person who, to his knowledge, relies on the financial statements that the statements are no longer trustworthy. If the stock is publicly held, it is acceptable to request the Securities and Exchange Commission and the stock exchange to notify the stockholders.

It is important to understand that the subsequent discovery of facts requiring the recall or reissuance of financial statements *does not arise from developments occurring after the date of the auditor's report.* For example, if an account receivable is believed to be collectible after an adequate review of the facts at the date of the audit report, but the customer subsequently files bankruptcy, a revision of the financial statements is not required. The statements must be recalled or reissued only when information that would indicate that the statements were not fairly presented *already existed at the audit report date.*

In the previous section it was shown that the responsibility for post-balance sheet review begins as of the balance sheet date and ends on the date of the completion of the field work. Any pertinent information discovered as a part of the review can be incorporated in the financial statements before they are issued. On the other hand, the auditor has no responsibility to search for subsequent facts of the nature discussed in this section, but if he discovers that issued financial statements are improperly stated, he must take action to correct them. The auditor's responsibility for reporting on improperly issued financial statements does not start until the date of the audit report. Typically, an existing material error is found as a part of the subsequent year's audit, or it may be reported to the auditor by the client.

SUMMARIZING AND DRAWING CONCLUSIONS

At the completion of the application of all the specific audit procedures for each of the audit areas, it is necessary to integrate the results into *one overall conclusion.* Ultimately, the auditor must decide whether sufficient audit evidence has been accumulated to warrant the conclusion that the financial statements are stated in accordance with generally accepted accounting principles, applied on a basis consistent with those of the preceding year. There are two important aspects of this conclusion. The first is *determining whether sufficient evidence has been obtained,* and the second is *deciding whether the existing evidence supports the auditor's opinion* that the statements are fairly stated.

Evaluating Whether Sufficient Evidence Has Been Obtained

The final summarization of the adequacy of the evidence is a review by the auditor of the entire audit to determine whether all important aspects of the engagement have been adequately tested considering the circumstances of the engagement. A major step in this process is reviewing the audit program to make sure that all parts have been accurately completed and documented. An important part of the review is to decide whether the audit program is adequate considering the problem areas that were discovered as the audit progressed. For example, if errors were discovered as a part of the tests of the sales system, the initial plans for the direct tests of accounts receivable may have been insufficient and should have been revised.

As an aid in drawing final conclusions about the adequacy of the audit evidence, auditors frequently use *completing the engagement checklists.* These are reminders of aspects of the audit frequently overlooked. An illustration of part of a completing the engagement checklist is given in Figure 20-2.

If the auditor concludes that he has *not* obtained sufficient evidence to draw a conclusion about the fairness of the client's representations, there are two choices: additional evidence must be obtained, or either a qualified opinion or a disclaimer of opinion must be issued.

Evaluating Whether the Existing Evidence Supports the Auditor's Opinion

An important part of evaluating whether the financial statements are fairly stated is summarizing the errors uncovered in the audit. Whenever the auditor uncovers errors that are in themselves material, the trial balance should be adjusted to correct the statements. It may be difficult to determine the appropriate amount of the adjustment because the true value of the error is unknown; nevertheless, it is the auditor's responsibility to decide on the required adjustment. In addition to the material errors, there are often a large number of immaterial errors discovered which are not adjusted at the time they are found. It is necessary to combine individually immaterial errors to evaluate whether the combined amount is material. The auditor can keep track of the errors and combine them in several different ways, but many auditors use a convenient method known as an *unadjusted error worksheet* or *summary of possible adjustments.* It is relatively easy to evaluate the overall significance of several immaterial errors with this type of working paper. An example of a summary of possible adjustments is given in Figure 20-3.

FIGURE 20–2

Completing the Engagement Checklist

	Yes	No
1. *Examination of prior year's working papers*		
a. Were last year's working papers and review notes examined for areas of emphasis in the current year audit?	____	____
b. Was the permanent file reviewed for items that affect the current year?	____	____
2. *Internal control evaluation*		
a. Has internal control been adequately reviewed?	____	____
b. Is the scope of the audit adequate in light of the weaknesses in the system?	____	____
c. Have all major weaknesses been included in a management letter?	____	____
3. *General documents*		
a. Were all current year minutes and resolutions reviewed, abstracted, and followed up?	____	____
b. Has the permanent file been updated?	____	____
c. Have all major contracts and agreements been reviewed and abstracted or copied to ascertain that the client complies with all existing legal requirements?	____	____

If the auditor believes that he *has* sufficient evidence, but it does not warrant a conclusion of fairly presented financial statements, the auditor again has two choices. The statements must be revised to the auditor's satisfaction, or either a qualified opinion or an adverse opinion must be issued. Notice that the options are different than in the case where insufficient evidence was obtained.

REVIEW FOR FINANCIAL STATEMENT DISCLOSURES

A major consideration in completing the audit is to determine whether the disclosures in the financial statements are adequate. Throughout the audit the emphasis in most examinations is on verifying the accuracy of the balances in the general ledger by testing the most important accounts on the auditor's trial balance. Another important task is to make sure the account balances on the trial balance are correctly aggregated and disclosed on the financial statements. Naturally, adequate disclosure includes consideration of all of the statements, including related footnotes.

The auditor actually prepares the financial statements from the trial balance in many small audits and submits them to the client for approval. Performing this function may seem to imply that the client has been relieved of responsibility for the fair representation in the statements, but that is not the case. The auditor acts in the role of adviser when he prepares the financial statements, but *management retains the final responsibility for approving the issuance of the statements.*

Workpaper Source					Total Amount	Current Assets
B-32 C-4	Unreimbursed petty cash vouchers				480	⟨480⟩
C-4	Possible underprovision in allowance for doubtful accounts				4000	⟨4000⟩
C-8	Accounts receivable/Sales cutoff errors				600	600
D-2	Difference between physical inventory and book figures				5200	5200
H-7/2	Unrecorded liabilities				4650	2000
V-10	Repairs expense items which should be capitalized				900	
	Totals					3,320

ABC Company, Inc.
Summary of Possible Adjustments

12/31/8x

Schedule **A-3** Date
Prepared by **PR** 1/28
Approved by **GS** 1/31

Conclusion:

The net effects of the above items are as follows:

Working capital $ ⟨2,440⟩
Total assets 6,070
Net income ⟨610⟩

None of these aggregate effects or of the individual items has a material effect on the financial statements in total or with respect to the components they pertain to. On this basis, adjustment of any or all of the items is passed.

Paul Roberts
1/28

FIGURE 20–3   Unadjusted Error Worksheet

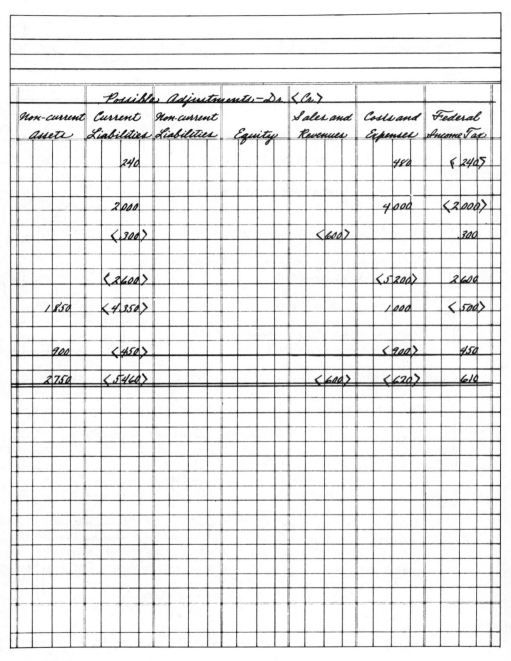

FIGURE 20–3 (cont.)

The review for the adequacy of disclosure in the financial statements at the completion of the audit is not the only time the auditor is interested in proper disclosure. Unless he is constantly alert for disclosure problems, it is impossible to adequately perform the final disclosure review. For example, as part of the examination of accounts receivable, the auditor must be aware of the need to separate notes receivable and amounts due from affiliates from trade accounts due from customers. Similarly, there must be a segregation between current and noncurrent receivables and a disclosure of the factoring or discounting of notes receivable if such is the case. An important part of verifying all account balances is determining whether generally accepted accounting principles were properly applied on a basis consistent with that of the preceding year. The auditor must carefully document this information in the working papers to facilitate the final review.

As part of the final review for financial statement disclosure, many CPA firms require the completion of a *financial statement disclosure checklist* for every engagement. These questionnaires are designed to remind the auditor of common disclosure problems encountered on audits and also to facilitate the final review of the entire audit by a partner. An illustration of a partial financial statement disclosure checklist is given in Figure 20-4. Naturally, it is not sufficient to rely on a checklist as a replacement for the auditor's own knowledge of generally accepted accounting principles. In any given audit, some aspects of the engagement require a much deeper level of expertise about accounting than can be obtained from such a checklist.

UNAUDITED REPLACEMENT COST INFORMATION

Rule 3.17 of SEC Regulation S-X requires the inclusion of replacement cost information in a *footnote or separate section of the statements* for certain capital-intensive companies. These disclosures are intended to make the financial statements more informative during periods of inflation.

The replacement cost information *is not audited*, but certain procedures are suggested by SAS 18 (Section 730) to test the reasonableness of the disclosures. These procedures are likely to be done as a part of completing the engagement. The suggested procedures all include inquiries of management rather than procedures such as confirmation and documentation. The following are examples of suggested inquiries of management:

- Inquire whether the replacement cost information has been prepared and disclosed in accordance with SEC requirements.
- Inquire about the methods selected to calculate replacement cost information, the reasons for using these methods, and the procedures used to compile the data.
- Inquire about reasons for changing disclosure methods if there has been a change in method.

The auditor need not substantiate the responses to inquiries of manage-

FIGURE 20–4

Financial Statement Disclosure Checklist with
References to Authoritative Accounting Literature

Property, Plant, and Equipment

1. Are the following disclosures included in the financial statements or notes (APB 12, para. 5):
   a. Balances of major classes of depreciable assets (i.e., land, building, equipment, etc.) at the balance sheet date?
   b. Allowances for depreciation, by class or in total, at the balance sheet date?
   c. General description of depreciation methods for major classes of PP&E? (APB 22, para. 13)
   d. Total amount of depreciation charged to expense for each income statement presented?
   e. Basis of valuation? (SAS 1, para. 430.02)
2. Are carrying amounts of property mortgaged and encumbered by indebtedness disclosed? (FASB 5, para. 18)
3. Are details of sale and leaseback transactions during the period disclosed? (FASB 13, para. 32–34)
4. Is the carrying amount of property not a part of operating plant (i.e., idle, or held for investment or sale) segregated?
5. Has consideration been given to disclosure of fully depreciated capital assets still in use and capital assets not presently in use?

ment about replacement cost information with audit evidence. No comment or modification in the auditor's standard report is required if the responses to the inquiries of management appear consistent with the statement disclosures and if the statements clearly indicate the replacement cost information is unaudited.

If the auditor believes there are inconsistencies between responses to inquiries and the disclosures, additional action is required. Either additional inquiries are needed, or a modification of the standard auditor's report is required. A modification of the auditor's report is also required if the client is unwilling or unable to respond to the auditor's inquiries.

MANAGEMENT REPRESENTATION LETTER

SAS 19 (Section 333) *requires the auditor* to obtain a *letter of representation,* which documents management's most important oral representations during the audit. The management representation letter is prepared on the client's letterhead, addressed to the CPA firm, and signed by high-level corporate officials, usually the president and controller.

The letter should be dated as of the auditor's report date to make sure there are representations related to post-balance sheet review. The letter implies that it has originated with the client, but it is common practice for the auditor to prepare the letter and request the client to type it on the company's letterhead and sign it. Refusal by a client to prepare and sign the letter would require a qualified opinion or disclaimer of opinion.

There are two purposes of letters of representation:

- *To impress upon management its responsibility for the representations in the financial statements.* For example, if the letter of representation includes a reference to pledged assets and contingent liabilities, honest management may be reminded of its unintentional failure to adequately disclose the information. To fulfill this objective, the letter of representation should be sufficiently detailed to act as a reminder to management.
- *To document the responses from management to inquiries about various aspects of the audit.* This provides written documentation of client representations in the event of disagreement or a lawsuit between the auditor and client.

SAS 19 (Section 333.04) suggests 20 specific matters that should be included, when applicable, in a management representation letter. A few of these matters are:

- Management's acknowledgment of its responsibility for the fair presentation in the financial statements of financial position, results of operations, and changes in financial position in conformity with generally accepted accounting principles or other comprehensive basis of accounting.
- Availability of all financial records and related data.
- Completeness and availability of all minutes of meetings of stockholders, directors, and committees of directors.
- Information concerning related party transactions and related amounts receivable or payable.
- Plans or intentions that may affect the carrying value or classification of assets or liabilities.
- Disclosure of compensating balance or other arrangements involving restrictions on cash balances, and disclosure of a line of credit or similar arrangements.

A representation letter is a written statement from a nonindependent source and therefore *cannot be regarded as reliable evidence.* The letter does provide minimal evidence of having asked management certain questions, but its primary purpose is psychological and to protect the auditor from potential claims by management that it was unaware of its responsibility.

WORKING PAPER REVIEW

There are three primary reasons why it is essential that the working papers be thoroughly reviewed by another member of the audit firm at the completion of the audit:

To Evaluate the Performance of Inexperienced Personnel. A considerable portion of most audits is performed by audit personnel with less than four or five years' experience. These people may have sufficient technical training to conduct an adequate audit, but their lack of experience affects their ability to make sound professional judgments in complex situations.

To Make Sure That the Audit Meets the CPA Firm's Standard of Performance. Within any organization the performance quality of individuals varies considerably, but careful review by top-level personnel in the firm assists in maintaining a uniform quality of auditing.

To Counteract the Bias That Frequently Enters into the Auditor's Judgment. Auditors may attempt to remain objective throughout the audit, but it is easy to lose proper perspective on a long audit when there are complex problems to solve.

Except for a final "independent review" which will be discussed shortly, the review of the working papers must be conducted by someone who is knowledgeable about the client and the unique circumstances in the audit. It is not possible for an auditor to evaluate whether a particular audit is adequate without extensive knowledge of the client. As a result, the initial review of the working papers prepared by any given auditor is normally done by his immediate supervisor. For example, the least experienced auditor's work is ordinarily reviewed by the audit senior; the senior's immediate superior, who is normally a supervisor or manager, carefully reviews the senior's work and also reviews the papers of the inexperienced auditor less thoroughly; finally, the partner assigned to the audit must ultimately review all working papers, but he reviews those prepared by the supervisor or manager more thoroughly than the others.

There are several considerations the auditor should keep in mind in reviewing working papers. These considerations are dealt with as separate topics in the following discussion, but they are ordinarily performed simultaneously by the reviewer.

Mechanical Accuracy. Certain aspects of the working papers are of a mechanical nature; nevertheless, they must be reviewed by someone before the audit is completed. These include the proper identification of all working papers, the date each working paper was prepared, and the initials of the preparer. Similarly, auditor calculations must be accurate, balances on the working papers must tie out to the trial balance when appropriate, and all adjusting entries must be posted.

Adequacy of Individual Working Papers. The reviewer should evaluate whether each working paper in the file fulfills the purpose for which it was intended. This part of the review can be especially useful as a means of training assistants in the proper preparation of working papers in accordance with the CPA firm's policy.

Adequacy of Evidence. The most important and time-consuming part of the review is evaluating the adequacy of the evidence and the reasonableness of the conclusions. Each major audit area must be reviewed to determine whether sufficient competent evidence was accumulated considering the circumstances of the engagement. The reviewer must evaluate the adequacy of the audit procedures, the sample sizes, the selection of the particular items for testing, and the timing of the procedures for each of the major segments of the audit. As part of this evaluation, consideration should be given to areas where there was excessive auditing or improper emphasis as well as instances where insufficient testing was done.

Reasonableness of the Conclusions. One of the important concepts emphasized throughout the text is the need to draw conclusions about the population on the basis of the sample. A major responsibility of the reviewer is to evaluate whether the conclusions were reasonable considering the information obtained in the sample.

Financial Statement Disclosures. The reviewer must evaluate the adequacy of the financial statements based upon the information included in the working papers. The review should be along the same lines as those performed by the auditor making the original decision as to the acceptability of the client's disclosures.

Legal Defensibility. At the completion of the audit, the working papers are the auditor's documentation of the evidence accumulated and the conclusions reached. If the auditor is ever called upon to defend the quality of the audit, the working papers become primary evidence for both the prosecution and the defense. The best defense against a lawsuit is a well-conducted audit with adequate documentation. At the same time, the reviewer must always be aware of the possibility of the working papers' being used as legal evidence of an inadequate audit. Good reviewers make sure there are no unanswered questions, ambiguous conclusions, inconsistent evaluations, or other incriminating evidence in the working papers.

Independent Review

At the completion of larger audits, it is common to have the entire set of working papers reviewed by a completely independent reviewer who has had no experience on the engagement. This reviewer frequently takes an adversary position to make sure the conduct of the audit was adequate. The audit team must be able to justify the evidence they have accumulated and the conclusions they reached on the basis of the unique circumstances of the engagement.

MANAGEMENT LETTERS

The purpose of a management letter (letter of recommendations) is to inform the client of the CPA's recommendations for improving the client's business (Figure 20-5). The recommendations range from suggestions for the improvement of the system of internal control to suggestions for more efficient operations. The combination of the auditor's experience in various businesses

ABLE AND BAKER, CPAS
New York, New York

March 3, 198y

BOARD OF DIRECTORS
ABC FINANCIAL INDUSTRIES, INC.
   and SUBSIDIARIES
NEW YORK, NEW YORK

In connection with our examination of the consolidated financial statements of ABC Financial Industries, Inc. and Subsidiaries for the year ending
December 31, 198x, we reviewed the companies' accounting procedures and system
of internal control. While we believe the existing controls and procedures to
be adequate in most respects, we noted the following areas in which we believe
more effective internal control or increased efficiency is necessary. We recognize that certain of the recommendations may have been adopted prior to
issuance of this letter.

GENERAL

The following recommendations will have little impact unless implemented
as part of a sustained program for developing the overall financial potential
of the organization. ABC Financial has reached a size and complexity that
demands the full attention of a financially oriented person, and we strongly
urge consideration be given to employing such an individual.

DATA PROCESSING AND SYSTEMS INTEGRATION

Systems design and program changes over the past two to three years have
been made principally on a patchwork basis, with the result that newly implemented systems have not been fully integrated with existing systems, and program
documentation has not been updated for all changes.

Thus, it is possible for the same information to be processed differently
through two systems, or for data to be processed through one part of a system
and not another with the result that general or control records are not in agreement with subsidiary records.

Documentation of many of the systems reviewed had not been updated during
the last two years, and included references to programs no longer in use or
files no longer maintained.

A thorough review of the data processing function should be undertaken,
first, to define the systems and procedures as they now stand, including all
reports produced and their distribution; second, to identify and prioritize
needed revisions to the existing systems; and third, to integrate the systems
and procedures to provide accurate data to the operations and production
departments.

CONTRACTS RECEIVABLE

A significant portion of the business of the corporations centers around
the installment contracts receivable from customers. We believe there are a
number of methods in which the contracts and related procedures may be improved.

FIGURE 20-5 Management Letter

Controls over the initiation, processing, recording and follow-up on customer contracts have been generally lax and heavy reliance has been placed on the individual abilities of company personnel rather than a more formal business management system.

There is at present no effective means of assuring that all contract sales by the individual sales offices are reported to the finance subsidiary, or for ensuring prompt and thorough follow-up on such sales.

The following points should be considered as a framework for providing strength in this area:

1. Complete centralization of contract responsibility in the finance subsidiary.

2. Use of prenumbered contract forms, all of which must be accounted for.

3. Use of prenumbered receipt forms, accounted for in the same manner as contract forms.

4. Establishment of a requirement that all contracts be recorded and ultimate disposition noted in the records. This should be accomplished by adoption of a policy defining follow-up procedures and standard disposition methods.

5. Design, implementation, and enforcement of filing procedures which would provide adequate support for customer receivables.

Contract form –

Collection personnel are at times hesitant to attempt enforcement of the present contract and have adopted the policy of terminating collection action when a delinquent patron invites or threatens legal action. It therefore appears that a new contract form should be drafted with legal assistance to assure an enforceable agreement.

Collection agencies –

Contracts turned over to collection agencies during the past year appear to be providing little return to the companies, and in fact may work to their detriment. It appears that one or two persons against whom the collection agency has attempted to file suit or garnishment proceedings have been able to substantiate payment to a sales office for the alleged delinquency. Inasmuch as accounting procedures in effect at the time of processing these early contracts were somewhat lax, it would be difficult to defend against such claims. We recommend that you consider abandoning collection efforts on these contracts in light of the minimal return being received and the possibility that such action could result in unfavorable publicity.

We further recommend that definite policies be established with regard to conditions under which contracts will be turned over to collection agencies.

FIGURE 20–5 (cont.)

Sales policies and techniques –

Sales and collection data which we accumulated during our review indicated
that the largest portion of uncollectible contracts arose from sales having
one or more of the following characteristics:

1. Contract amount significantly larger than normal.

2. Contract payment period significantly longer than normal.

3. Down payment significantly lower than normal.

We believe sales personnel should concentrate on what might be considered
a "normal" sale, avoiding programs of excessive terms or nominal down payments.
The policy of encouraging accelerated cash payments should be continued.

The second major factor contributing to uncollectible contract balances
is dissatisfaction on the part of the customer shortly after receipt of the
merchandise. Collection personnel have encountered resistance from patrons
to whom salespeople had apparently promised results other than those contained in the written agreement. We believe these problems could be minimized through establishment and enforcement of sales guidelines to avoid
issuance of implied guarantees beyond those in the service agreement.

To assist in achieving the goals outlined above, we believe the present
commission and bonus policies should be modified to include collections as a
factor to provide an incentive for obtaining acceptable credit risks and
down payments within established guidelines.

CASH RECEIPTS

The present system provides no assurance that all receipts are being deposited to company accounts. The use of "deposit only" type bank accounts in
proximity to each sales office is a significant strength in this area, but
should be augmented through the use of prenumbered receipt forms and strict
enforcement of the requirement that receipts be deposited daily.

We noted also that the sales offices maintain records of customer payments paralleling those kept by the finance subsidiary. Comparison of these
dual records revealed a number of discrepancies, and we believe there is little
justification for maintaining both. Ostensibly, such records are kept at the
sales office in order that services to persons delinquent in their accounts
can be restricted; however, it appears that this could be achieved through
periodic notification to the sales offices by the finance company, thus remov-
ing the accounting functions from the sales offices.

At the home office, control over receipts could be strengthened by more
systematic review and control of bank deposit tickets.

CASH DISBURSEMENTS

It is sometimes the practice of corporate officers to carry a supply of
checks on a corporation general bank account for use on an as-needed basis,
with the result that these checks often remain unaccounted for over long periods.
Use of an executive checking account on an imprest basis should be considered,
if this practice is necessary.

FIGURE 20–5 (cont.)

688

Other procedures to be considered in the area of cash disbursements are the timely review of outstanding checks for removal of old or improper items; annotation of general ledger account distribution on paid invoices; and establishment of a log for control of transfers from the numerous deposit-only accounts and efficient utilization of funds in these accounts.

The list of authorized signers supplied by various banks includes two former employees. The list should be updated and the banks notified to preclude unauthorized access to cash.

PAYROLL

Controls over payroll disbursements appear to be generally adequate, except that preparation and distribution of payroll for the newly-opened Texas sales offices is performed by the same individual. This procedure could be strengthened by either requiring signature of the manager and the employee on the individual time slip, or sending the checks from the home office directly to the sales office managers for distribution.

We recommend that policies on commissions be formalized and that computations for each employee be made a part of the payroll record; current practice places the determination in the hands of the area supervisor, with little or no documentation available for support.

FACILITIES AND EQUIPMENT

At present, leasehold improvements and equipment are identified only by the vendor from whom acquired and, to a limited extent, by location. Major equipment items should be identified by location and information provided with respect to costs, dates of acquisition, and estimated lives.

We noted that the companies have an exclusive manufacturing agreement with a major equipment supplier. The document evidencing this agreement appears quite informal and we suggest that the situation be reviewed with your attorney to determine the advisability of redrafting the agreement.

OPERATING RESULTS, REPORTING, AND PLANNING

In light of the multistate expansion of operations, we believe that consideration should be given to centralization of common procedures for increased control and efficiency. This would involve the centralization of the financing and contract handling functions in the finance subsidiary and the development of standardized accounting techniques and documents for submission to the central accounting office.

In order to provide meaningful management operating reports, corporate expenses should be identified and recorded as direct charges to the appropriate sales offices, as costs of operations, or as general, administrative, and selling expenses. Sales and performance data should be accumulated, analyzed and applied in a comprehensive approach to management which includes cash forecasting and profit planning.

FIGURE 20-5 (cont.)

It is suggested that a series of operating reports be designed and implemented at the earliest possible date to permit effective management control. The specific nature of the reports will be dictated by the requirements of management, but, at a minimum, should measure actual against planned performance for:

1. Weekly – Gross sales for each location.

2. Biweekly – Collections and cash receipts for each location.

3. Monthly – Complete operating statements for each location.

4. Quarterly – Consolidated corporate financial statements.

OTHER

With regard to the newly formed finance company, we noted a tendency on the part of the collection personnel to exaggerate,their intended actions in the event payments were not forthcoming, to make threats of collection which may not be enforceable, and in general, to make any statements to the patrons which they believed would exact payment from them. In light of the questions raised about the present contract, and the unfavorable publicity which could result from official or semiofficial investigation, we believe that every attempt should be made to ensure that the actions of collection personnel are within their authority and do nothing to discredit the organization.

We further noted the practice adopted by the collectors of requesting that patrons remit delinquent payments by special delivery to the attention of the individual collectors, and that such payments are often routed, unopened, directly to these collectors. This could result in a serious breach of controls regarding the handling of cash, and we recommend that all incoming mail be opened by an employee not associated with the collection or recordkeeping functions.

We would be pleased to discuss the above comments and recommendations further with you and to assist in their implementation.

Able and Baker
Certified Public Accountants

FIGURE 20–5 (cont.)

690

and a thorough understanding gained in conducting the audit put the auditor in a unique position to provide management with assistance.

A management letter must be distinguished from a required communication of internal control. The latter is required by SAS 20 (Section 323) whenever there are material internal control weaknesses. The latter must follow a prescribed format and be sent in accordance with SAS requirements. A management letter is optional and is intended to help the client operate its business more effectively. Auditors write management letters for two reasons: to make for better relationships between the CPA firm and management, and to suggest additional tax and management services the CPA firm can provide.

There are no standard formats or approaches for writing management letters. Each letter should be developed to meet the style of the auditor and the needs of the client, consistent with the CPA firm's concept of management letters.

REVIEW QUESTIONS

20–1. Distinguish between a contingent liability and an actual liability and give three examples of each.

20–2. In the audit of the James Mobley Company, you are concerned about the possibility of contingent liabilities resulting in income-tax disputes. Discuss the procedures you could use for an extensive investigation in this area.

20–3. Explain why the analysis of legal expense is an essential part of every audit engagement.

20–4. During the audit of the Merril Manufacturing Company, Ralph Pyson, CPA, has become aware of four lawsuits against the client by having discussions with the client, reading corporate minutes, and reviewing correspondence files. How should Pyson determine the materiality of the lawsuits and the proper disclosure in the financial statements?

20–5. Distinguish between an asserted and an unasserted claim. Explain why a client's attorney may not reveal an unasserted claim.

20–6. Describe the action that an auditor should take if an attorney refuses to provide information that is within his jurisdiction and may directly affect the fair presentation of the financial statements.

20–7. Distinguish between the two general types of subsequent events and explain how they differ. Give two examples of each type.

20–8. In obtaining confirmations from attorneys, Bill Malano attempts to obtain the confirmation request as early as possible after the balance sheet date. This approach enables him to make sure he has a signed letter from every attorney and to properly investigate any exceptions. It also eliminates the problem of having a lot of unresolved loose ends near the end of the audit. Evaluate Malano's approach.

20–9. Explain why an auditor would be interested in a client's future commitments to purchase raw materials at a fixed price.

20–10. What major considerations should the auditor take into account in determining how extensive the post-balance sheet review should be?

20–11. Distinguish between the subsequent events occurring between the balance sheet date and the date of the auditor's report, and the subsequent discovery of facts existing at the date of the auditor's report. Give two examples of each and explain the appropriate action by the auditor in each instance.

20–12. Miles Lawson, CPA, believes the final summarization is the easiest part of the audit if careful planning is followed throughout the engagement. He makes sure each segment of the audit is completed before he goes on to the next. When the last segment of the engagement is completed, he is finished with the audit. He believes this may take a little longer on each part of the audit, but he makes up for it by not having to do the final summarization. Evaluate Lawson's approach.

20–13. Compare and contrast the accumulation of audit evidence and the evaluation of the adequacy of the disclosures in financial statements. Give three examples where adequate disclosure could depend heavily upon the accumulation of evidence and three others where audit evidence does not normally significantly affect the adequacy of the disclosure.

20–14. State the auditor's responsibility for replacement cost information that is included in the financial statements.

20–15. Distinguish between a management representation letter and a management letter and state the primary purpose of each. List five items that might be included in the contents of each letter.

20–16. List the primary things the reviewer should consider in the review of working papers and explain the importance of each.

20–17. Distinguish between regular working paper review and independent review and state the purpose of each. Give two examples of important potential findings in each of these two types of review.

DISCUSSION QUESTIONS AND PROBLEMS

20–18. Select the best response for each of the multiple-choice questions.

    a. The audit step most likely to reveal the existence of contingent liabilities is

      (1) a review of vouchers paid during the month following the year-end.

      (2) accounts payable confirmations.

      (3) an inquiry directed to legal counsel.

      (4) mortgage-note confirmation.

    b. A principal purpose of a letter of representation from management is to

      (1) serve as an introduction to company personnel and an authorization to examine the records.

      (2) discharge the auditor from legal liability for his examination.

      (3) confirm in writing management's approval of limitations on the scope of the audit.

      (4) remind management of its primary responsibility for financial statements.

    c. Three months subsequent to the date of his report, a CPA becomes aware of facts that existed at the date of his report and affect the reliability of the financial statements of a client whose securities are widely held. If the client refuses to make appropriate disclosure, the CPA should notify

      (1) regulatory agencies having jurisdiction over the client.

      (2) all stockholders.

      (3) all present and potential investors in the company.

      (4) stockholders and the financial press.

    d. An example of an event occurring in the period of the auditor's field work subsequent to the end of the year being audited which normally would not require disclosure in the financial statements or auditor's report would be

      (1) decreased sales volume resulting from a general business recession.

      (2) serious damage to the company's plant from a widespread flood.

      (3) issuance of a widely advertised capital stock issue with restrictive covenants.

      (4) settlement of a large liability for considerably less than the amount recorded.

    e. Assuming that none of the following has been disclosed in the financial statements, the most appropriate item for footnote disclosure is the

      (1) collection of all receivables subsequent to year-end.

      (2) revision of an employees' pension plan.

      (3) retirement of the president of the company and election of a new president.

      (4) a material decrease in the advertising budget for the coming year and its anticipated effect upon income.

20–19. You are making an annual examination for the purpose of rendering an opinion regarding the financial statements for use in an annual report to stockholders. Answer the following questions concerning events subsequent to the date of the financial statements.

    a. What auditing procedures should normally be followed in order to obtain knowledge of subsequent happenings?

    b. What is the period with which the auditor is normally concerned with regard to post-balance sheet events?

    c. Give five different examples of events or transactions that might occur in the subsequent period.

    d. What is the auditor's general responsibility, if any, for reporting such events or transactions?

    e. In your report, how would you deal with each of the examples you listed in part c? (AICPA adapted)

20–20. The following unrelated events occurred after the balance sheet date but before the audit report was prepared:

    a. The granting of a retroactive pay increase.

    b. Determination by the federal government of additional income tax due for a prior year.

    c. Filing of an antitrust suit by the federal government.

d. Declaration of a stock dividend.

e. Sale of a fixed asset at a substantial profit.

Required:

a. Explain how each of the items might have come to the auditor's attention.

b. Discuss the auditor's responsibility to recognize each of these in connection with his report.   (AICPA adapted)

20–21. During an audit engagement Harper, CPA, has satisfactorily completed an examination of accounts payable and other liabilities and now plans to determine whether there are any loss contingencies arising from litigation, claims, or assessments.

Required:

What are the audit procedures that Harper should follow with respect to the existence of loss contingencies arising from litigation, claims, and assessments? Do not discuss reporting requirements.   (AICPA adapted)

20–22. The philosophy of George Hatton, CPA, is to intensively audit transactions taking place during the current audit period, but to ignore subsequent transactions. He believes each year should stand on its own and be audited in the year in which the transactions take place. According to Hatton, "if a transaction recorded in the subsequent period is audited in the current period, it is verified twice—once this year and again in next year's audit. That is a duplication of effort and a waste of time."

Required:

a. Explain the fallacy in Hatton's argument.

b. Give six specific examples of information obtained by examining subsequent events that are essential to the current period audit.

20–23. In analyzing legal expense for the Boastman Bottle Company, Bart Little, CPA, observes that the company has paid legal fees to three different law firms during the current year. In accordance with his CPA firm's normal operating practice, Little requests standard confirmation letters as of the balance sheet date from each of the three law firms.

On the last day of field work, Little notes that one of the confirmations has not yet been received. The second confirmation request contains a statement to the effect that the law firm deals exclusively in registering patents and refuses to comment on any lawsuits or other legal affairs of the client. The third attorney's letter states that there is an outstanding unpaid bill due from the client and recognizes the existence of a potentially material lawsuit against the client but refuses to comment further to protect the legal rights of the client.

Required:

a. Evaluate Little's approach to sending the confirmations and his follow-up on the responses.

b. What should Little do about each of the confirmations?

20–24. In an examination of the Marco Corporation as at 12-31-X7, the following situations exist. No entries in respect thereto have been made in the accounting records.

 a. The Marco Corporation has guaranteed the payment of interest on the 10-year, first-mortgage bonds of the Newart Company, an affiliate. Outstanding bonds of the Newart Company amount to $150,000 with interest payable at 5 percent per annum, due June 1 and December 1 of each year. The bonds were issued by the Newart Company on December 1, 19X5, and all interest payments have been met by that company with the exception of the payment due December 1, 19X7. The Marco Corporation states that it will pay the defaulted interest to the bondholders on January 15, 19X8.

 b. During the year 19X7 the Marco Corporation was named as a defendant in a suit for damages by the Dalton Company for breach of contract. An adverse decision to the Marco Corporation was rendered and the Dalton Company was awarded $40,000 damages. At the time of the audit, the case was under appeal to a higher court.

 c. On December 23, 19X7, the Marco Corporation declared a common stock dividend of 1,000 shares, par $100,000, of its common stock, payable February 2, 19X8, to the common stockholders of record December 30, 19X7.

Required:

 a. Define *contingent liability.*

 b. Describe the audit procedures you would use to learn about each of the situations above.

 c. Describe the nature of the adjusting entries or disclosure, if any, you would make for each of these situations. (AICPA adapted)

20–25. The field work for the 6-30-X7 audit of Tracy Brewing Company was finished 8-19-X7, and the completed financial statements, accompanied by the signed audit reports, were mailed 9-6-X7. In each of the highly material independent events (a through i), state the appropriate action (1 through 4) for the situation and justify your response. The alternative actions are as follows:

(1) Adjust the 6-30-X7 financial statements.

(2) Disclose the information in a footnote in the 6-30-X7 financial statements.

(3) Request the client to recall the 6-30-X7 statements for revision.

(4) No action is required.

The events are as follows:

 a. On 12-14-X7 the auditor discovered that a debtor of Tracy Brewing went bankrupt on 10-2-X7. The sale had taken place 4-15-X7, but the amount appeared collectible at 6-30-X7 and 8-19-X7.

 b. On 8-15-X7 the auditor discovered that a debtor of Tracy Brewing went bankrupt on 8-1-X7. The most recent sale had taken place 4-2-X6, and no cash receipts had been received since that date.

c. On 12-14-X7 the auditor discovered that a debtor of Tracy Brewing went bankrupt on 7-15-X7 due to declining financial health. The sale had taken place 1-15-X7.

d. On 8-6-X7 the auditor discovered that a debtor of Tracy Brewing went bankrupt on 7-30-X7. The cause of the bankruptcy was an unexpected loss of a major lawsuit on 7-15-X7 resulting from a product deficiency suit by a different customer.

e. On 8-6-X7 the auditor discovered that a debtor of Tracy Brewing went bankrupt on 7-30-X7 for a sale that took place 7-3-X7. The cause of the bankruptcy was a major uninsured fire on 7-20-X7.

f. On 5-31-X7 the auditor discovered an uninsured lawsuit against Tracy Brewing which had originated on 2-28-X7.

g. On 7-20-X7 Tracy Brewing settled a lawsuit out of court which had originated in 19X4 and is currently listed as a contingent liability.

h. On 9-14-X7 Tracy Brewing lost a court case which had originated in 19X6 for an amount equal to the lawsuit. The 6-30-X7 footnotes state that in the opinion of legal counsel there will be a favorable settlement.

i. On 7-20-X7 a lawsuit was filed against Tracy Brewing for a patent infringement action which allegedly took place in early 19X7. In the opinion of legal counsel there is danger of a significant loss to the client.

20–26. In connection with his examination of Flowmeter, Inc., for the year ended December 31, 19X7, Hirsh, CPA, is aware that certain events and transactions that took place after December 31, 19X7, but before he issues his report dated February 28, 19X8, may affect the company's financial statements.

The following material events or transactions have come to his attention:

a. On January 3, 19X8, Flowmeter, Inc., received a shipment of raw materials from Canada. The materials had been ordered in October 19X7 and shipped FOB shipping point in November 19X7.

b. On January 15, 19X8, the company settled and paid a personal injury claim of a former employee as the result of an accident which occurred in March 19X7. The company had not previously recorded a liability for the claim.

c. On January 25, 19X8, the company agreed to purchase for cash the outstanding stock of Porter Electrical Co. The acquisition is likely to double the sales volume of Flowmeter, Inc.

d. On February 1, 19X8, a plant owned by Flowmeter, Inc., was damaged by a flood resulting in an uninsured loss of inventory.

e. On February 5, 19X8, Flowmeter, Inc., issued and sold to the general public $2 million in convertible bonds.

Required:

For each of the events or transactions described above, indicate the audit procedures that should have brought the item to the attention of the auditor, and the form of disclosure required in the financial statements including the reasons for such disclosures.

Arrange your answer in the following format:

Item No.	Audit Procedures	Required Disclosure and Reasons

(AICPA adapted)

20-27. Mel Adams, CPA, is a partner in a medium-sized CPA firm and takes an active part in the conduct of every audit he supervises. He follows the practice of reviewing all working papers of subordinates as soon as it is convenient, rather than waiting until the end of the audit. When the audit is nearly finished, Adams reviews the working papers again to make sure he hasn't missed anything significant. Since he makes most of the major decisions on the audit, there is rarely anything that requires further investigation. When he completes the review, he prepares a pencil draft of the financial statements, gets them approved by management, and has them typed and assembled in his firm's office. No other partner reviews the working papers because Adams is responsible for signing the audit reports.

Required:

   a. Evaluate the practice of reviewing the working papers of subordinates on a continuing basis rather than when the audit is completed.
   b. Is it acceptable for Adams to prepare the financial statements rather than make the client assume the responsibility?
   c. Evaluate the practice of not having a review of the working papers by another partner in the firm.

20-28. Ron Morgan, CPA, has prepared a letter of representation for the president and controller to sign. It contains references to the following items:
   a. Inventory is fairly stated at the lower of cost or market and includes no obsolete items.
   b. All actual and contingent liabilities are properly included in the statements.
   c. All subsequent events of relevance to the financial statements have been disclosed.

Required:

   a. Why is it desirable to have a letter of representation from the client concerning the above matters when the audit evidence accumulated during the course of the engagement is meant to verify the same information?
   b. To what extent is the letter of representation useful as audit evidence? Explain.
   c. List several other types of information commonly included in a letter of representation.

20-29. In a management letter to the Cline Wholesale Company, Jerry Schwartz, CPA, informed management of its weak system in the control of inventory. He elaborated on how the system could result in a significant misstatement of inventory by the failure to recognize the existence of obsolete items. In addition, Schwartz made specific recommendations on how to improve the system and save clerical time by installing a computer system for the company's perpetual records. Management accepted the recommendations and installed the system under Schwartz's direction. For several months the system worked beautifully, but unforeseen problems developed when a master file was erased. The cost of reproducing and processing the inventory records to correct the error was significant, and management decided to scrap the entire project. The company sued Schwartz for failure to use adequate professional judgment in making the recommendations.

Required:

a. What is Schwartz's legal and professional responsibility in the issuance of management letters?

b. Discuss the major considerations that will determine whether he is liable in this situation.

20–30. Lancaster Electronics produces electronic components for sale to manufacturers of radios, television sets, and phonographic systems. In connection with his examination of Lancaster's financial statements for the year ended December 31, 19X7, Don Olds, CPA, completed field work two weeks ago. Mr. Olds is now evaluating the significance of the following items prior to preparing his auditor's report. Except as noted, none of these items have been disclosed in the financial statements or footnotes.

1. Recently Lancaster interrupted its policy of paying cash dividends quarterly to its stockholders. Dividends were paid regularly through 19X6, discontinued for all of 19X7 in order to finance equipment for the company's new plant, and resumed in the first quarter of 19X8. In the annual report dividend policy is to be discussed in the president's letter to stockholders.

2. A 10-year loan agreement, which the company entered into three years ago, provides that dividend payments may not exceed net income earned after taxes subsequent to the date of the agreement. The balance of retained earnings at the date of the loan agreement was $298,000. From that date through December 31, 19X7, net income after taxes has totaled $360,000 and cash dividends have totaled $130,000. Based upon these data the staff auditor assigned to this review concluded that there was no retained earnings restriction at December 31, 19X7.

3. The company's new manufacturing plant building, which cost $600,000 and has an estimated life of 25 years, is leased from the Sixth National Bank at an annual rental of $100,000. The company is obligated to pay property taxes, insurance, and maintenance. At the conclusion of its ten-year noncancelable lease, the company has the option of purchasing the property for $1. In Lancaster's income statement the rental payment is reported on a separate line.

4. A major electronics firm has introduced a line of products that will compete directly with Lancaster's primary line, now being produced in the specially designed new plant. Because of manufacturing innovations, the

competitor's line will be of comparable quality but priced 50 percent below Lancaster's line. The competitor announced its new line during the week following completion of field work. Mr. Olds read the announcement in the newspaper and discussed the situation by telephone with Lancaster executives. Lancaster will meet the lower prices which are high enough to cover variable manufacturing and selling expenses but will permit recovery of only a portion of fixed costs.

Required:

For each of items 1 to 4, discuss the additional disclosure in the financial statements and footnotes required for the fair presentation of financial statements. (AICPA adapted)

20–31. In connection with your examination of the financial statements of Olars Mfg. Corporation for the year ended December 31, 19X6, your post-balance sheet date review disclosed the following items:

a. January 3, 19X7: The state government approved a plan for the construction of an express highway. The plan will result in the appropriation of a portion of the land area owned by Olars Mfg. Corporation. Construction will begin in late 19X7. No estimate of the condemnation award is available.

b. January 4, 19X7: The funds for a $25,000 loan to the corporation made by Mr. Olars on July 15, 19X6, were obtained by him by a loan on his personal life insurance policy. The loan was recorded in the account "loan from officers." Mr. Olars's source of the funds was not disclosed in the company records. The corporation pays the premiums on the life insurance policy, and Mrs. Olars, wife of the president, is the beneficiary of the policy.

c. January 7, 19X7: The mineral content of a shipment of ore enroute on December 31, 19X6, was determined to be 72 percent. The shipment was recorded at year-end at an estimated content of 50 percent by a debit to raw material inventory and a credit to accounts payable in the amount of $20,600. The final liability to the vendor is based on the actual mineral content of the shipment.

d. January 15, 19X7: Culminating a series of personal disagreements between Mr. Olars, the president, and his brother-in-law, the treasurer, the latter resigned, effective immediately, under an agreement whereby the corporation would purchase his 10 percent stock ownership at book value as of December 31, 19X6. Payment is to be made in two equal amounts in cash on April 1 and October 1, 19X7. In December the treasurer had obtained a divorce from his wife, who was Mr. Olars's sister.

e. January 31, 19X7: As a result of reduced sales, production was curtailed in mid-January and some workers were laid off. On February 5, 19X7, all the remaining workers went on strike. To date the strike is unsettled.

f. February 10, 19X7: A contract was signed whereby Mammoth Enterprises purchased from Olars Mfg. Corporation all of the latter's fixed assets (including rights to receive the proceeds of any property condemnation), inventories, and the right to conduct business under the name "Olars

Mfg. Division." The effective date of the transfer will be March 1, 19X7. The sale price was $500,000 subject to adjustment following the taking of a physical inventory. Important factors contributing to the decision to enter into the contract were the policy of the board of directors of Mammoth Industries to diversify the firm's activities and the report of a survey conducted by an independent market appraisal firm which revealed a declining market for Olars products.

Required:

Assume that the items described above came to your attention prior to completion of your audit work on February 15, 19X7, and that you will render a shortform report. For *each* item:

a. Give the audit procedures, if any, that would have brought the item to your attention. Indicate other sources of information that may have revealed the item.

b. Discuss the disclosure that you would recommend for the item, listing all details that you would suggest should be disclosed. Indicate those items or details, if any, that should not be disclosed. Give your reasons for recommending or not recommending disclosure of the items or details.

(AICPA adapted)

20–32. You have completed your audit of Carter Corporation and its consolidated subsidiaries for the year ended December 31, 19X7, and were satisfied with the results of your examination. You have examined the financial statements of Carter Corporation for the past three years. The corporation is now preparing its annual report to shareholders. The report will include the consolidated financial statements of Carter Corporation and its subsidiaries and your short-form auditor's report. During your audit the following matters came to your attention:

a. The Internal Revenue Service is currently examining the corporation's 19X5 federal income tax return and is questioning the amount of a deduction claimed by the corporation's domestic subsidiary for a loss sustained in 19X5. The examination is still in process, and any additional tax liability is indeterminable at this time. The corporation's tax counsel believes that there will be no substantial additional tax liability.

b. A vice-president who is also a stockholder resigned on December 31, 19X7, after an argument with the president. The vice-president is soliciting proxies from stockholders and expects to obtain sufficient proxies to gain control of the board of directors so that a new president will be appointed. The president plans to have a footnote prepared which would include information of the pending proxy fight, management's accomplishments over the years, and an appeal by management for the support of stockholders.

Required:

Prepare the footnotes, if any, that you would suggest for the two items listed above. (AICPA adapted)

21

SHORT-FORM
AUDITOR'S REPORTS

An audit report informs financial statement users of the extent to which the auditor has performed his evidence accumulation responsibilities and the results of his findings. Earlier it was established that management, rather than the auditor, has the basic responsibility for the fairness of the representations in the financial statements. If the auditor believes the statements are not fairly stated in accordance with generally accepted accounting principles, and the client refuses to make revisions, the audit report informs users that the statements are not fairly stated. Similarly, if for any reason the auditor is unable to satisfy himself that the statements are fairly stated, the report informs users that the auditor lacks knowledge about the fairness of the financial statement presentation.

The only information about the audit that is normally available to statement users comes through the audit report, and therefore the wording must clearly communicate the auditor's message. Due to the need for unambiguous statements about the work performed and the results found, the profession has developed standard audit reports for different circumstances and well-defined rules for determining the appropriate type of report.

The basic requirements for issuing audit reports are derived from the Generally Accepted Standards of Reporting. They are included on page 15 in Chapter 1. The last standard is especially important because it requires an expression of opinion about the overall financial statements or a specific statement that an overall opinion is not possible, along with the reasons for not expressing an opinion. The standard also requires a clear-cut statement by the auditor of the nature of the examination and the degree to which the auditor limits his responsibility.

STANDARD UNQUALIFIED OPINION

A standard short-form audit report can be issued when certain conditions have been met. An example of the short-form report is included in Chapter 1 on page 19. An explanation of the five parts of the short-form report is also included in Chapter 1 (p. 19). It is suggested that the section on short-form reports be reread at this time. In subsequent discussion, mention of a *standard scope paragraph* refers to the first paragraph in the short-form report and a *standard opinion* refers to the second paragraph. For purposes of convenience, the address, signature of the CPA firm, and date of the audit report are deleted from examples of short-form reports in the remainder of this chapter.

Requirements of the Standard Short-Form Report

The standard short-form report can be issued only under the following circumstances:

- Sufficient evidence has been accumulated, and the auditor has conducted the engagement in a manner that enables him to conclude that the three standards of field work have been met.
- The three general standards have been followed in all respects on the engagement.
- The financial statements are presented in accordance with generally accepted accounting principles which are applied on a basis consistent with that of the preceding period.
- There are no unusual uncertainties concerning future developments which cannot be reasonably estimated or satisfactorily resolved.

Modifications in the Wording of the Unqualified Opinion

In certain situations an unqualified opinion is issued, but the wording deviates from the standard unqualified opinion. It is important to distinguish between these reports and the qualified opinions discussed later in the chapter. The *unqualified opinion with modified wording* meets the criteria of a complete audit with satisfactory results and financial statements that are fairly presented, but the auditor feels it is important to provide additional information. In a *qualified opinion* the auditor either has not performed a satisfactory audit or is not satisfied that the financial statements are fairly presented.

The following are the most important causes of a modification in the wording of the unqualified short-form report containing an unqualified opinion:

Reports Involving the Use of Other Auditors. When the CPA relies upon a different CPA firm to perform part of the audit, which is common when the client has several widespread branches or subdivisions, the principal CPA firm can follow one of three alternatives:

Make No Reference in the Audit Report. When no reference is made, a standard unqualified opinion is given unless other circumstances require a departure. This approach is typically followed when the other auditor examined an immaterial portion of the statement, the other auditor is well known or closely supervised by the principal auditor or the principal auditor has thoroughly reviewed the other auditor's work. The other auditor is still responsible for his own report and work in the event of a lawsuit or SEC action.

Make Reference in the Report (Modified Wording Report). This type of report is referred to as a shared opinion or report. A shared unqualified opinion is appropriate when it is impractical to review the work of the other auditor or when the portion of the financial statements audited by the other CPA is material in relation to the total. The following is an example of the relevant portion of a shared opinion that should not be construed as a qualification:

(SCOPE PARAGRAPH—UNQUALIFIED SHARED)

We have examined the consolidated balance sheets of Big Company, Inc., and subsidiaries as of December 31, 1982 and 1981, and the related consolidated statements of earnings, retained earnings and changes in financial position for the years then ended. Our examination was. . . . We did not examine the financial statements of Little Company, which statements reflect total assets and revenues constituting approximately 20% and 30%, respectively, of the related consolidated totals for 1982 and 1981. These statements were examined by other auditors whose report thereon has been furnished to us and our opinion expressed herein insofar as it relates to the amounts included for Little Company is based solely upon the report of the other auditors.

(OPINION PARAGRAPH—UNQUALIFIED SHARED)

In our opinion, based on our examination and the report of other auditors referred to above, the aforementioned consolidated financial statements present fairly. . . .

Qualify the Opinion. The principal auditor may conclude that a qualified opinion is required. A qualified opinion or disclaimer depending on materiality is required if the principal auditor is not willing to assume any responsibility for the work of the other auditor.

Reports on Less Than a Full Set of Statements. The auditor is frequently asked to report on one basic financial statement and not the others. A common example is a report on the balance sheet only. For this type of examination, it is acceptable to issue an unqualified opinion on the statement if the auditor has unrestricted access to all the information he needs and conducts the audit in accordance with generally accepted auditing standards.

Departures from a Promulgated Accounting Principle with Which the Auditor Agrees. Rule 203 of the AICPA Code of Professional Ethics states that in unusual situations a departure from a published accounting principle promulgated by a body designated by the AICPA to establish accounting principles may not require a qualified or adverse opinion. However, to justify an unqualified opinion, the auditor must be satisfied and must state in the audit report that to have adhered to the published position would have produced a misleading result in that particular situation.

Comments to Emphasize Certain Points. Under certain circumstances the CPA may wish to emphasize specific matters regarding the financial statements even though he intends to express an unqualified opinion. Normally, such explanatory information should be included in a separate middle paragraph in the report. The following are examples of explanatory information the auditor may feel should be expressed:

- The existence of significant related party transactions.
- Important events occurring subsequent to the balance sheet date.
- The description of accounting matters affecting the comparability of the financial statements with those of the preceding year.

CONDITIONS REQUIRING A DEPARTURE FROM AN UNQUALIFIED OPINION

A major responsibility of the auditor is to recognize when an unqualified report is no longer applicable. The conditions that require a departure for an unqualified report were introduced in Chapter 1. They are restated at this point and studied in more detail shortly.

- The scope of the auditor's examination has been significantly restricted by the client.
- The auditor has been unable to perform significant audit procedures or obtain essential information because of conditions beyond either the client's or the auditor's control.
- The financial statements have not been prepared in accordance with generally accepted accounting principles.
- The accounting principles used in the financial statements have not been consistently applied.
- There are unusual uncertainties affecting the financial statements which cannot be reasonably estimated at the date of the auditor's report.

- The auditor is not independent with respect to the entity that is being audited.

Materiality and Audit Opinions

Figure 1-3 on page 24 shows the relationship between materiality and the auditor's opinion. The relationship between materiality and the conditions requiring a departure is an important part of audit reporting and requires additional study.

In concept the application of materiality to types of opinions as shown in Figure 1-3 is straightforward. In application the problem is difficult because deciding upon the actual materiality of a departure for the first five of the six conditions is a difficult judgment. (The independence condition is not affected by materiality.)

The common definition of materiality as it applies to accounting and therefore to audit reporting is: *a misstatement in the financial statements can be considered material if knowledge of the misstatement would affect a decision of a reasonably intelligent user of the statements.*

If the auditor believes the actual or potential misstatement due to scope limitations (conditions 1 and 2), accounting departures (conditions 3 and 4), or uncertainties (condition 5) would not affect the decision of any potential decision makers, an unqualified opinion is appropriate. An adverse opinion or a disclaimer of opinion is needed when users' decisions may be greatly affected by an actual or potential misstatement. In between the two extremes of an unqualified opinion and a disclaimer or adverse opinion, a qualified opinion is appropriate.

The total dollar error in the accounts involved is usually the greatest concern in measuring materiality. As discussed in Chapter 20, the auditor must combine all unadjusted errors and evaluate whether there may be individually immaterial errors that significantly affect the statements when combined with others. The magnitude of these errors must be compared to some measurement base before a decision can be made about the relative materiality of individual or combined errors. Common bases include net earnings, total assets, current assets, and working capital. Similarily, the magnitude of the potential errors in areas where there are scope limitations is important in determining whether an unqualified, qualified, or disclaimer of opinion is required for conditions 1 and 2.

Several other aspects of materiality must also be considered in evaluating the appropriate type of opinion to issue.

Expected Use of the Statements. Different users of financial statements have different interests in the financial position and results of operations. For example, if the auditor knew a client planned to sell the business for a multiple of current year's earnings, a lower standard of materiality is likely to be used than if the business was expected to continue with the same owners. The auditor knows that:

- Outside shareholders are most likely to be interested in net income and conditions affecting a company's ability to pay dividends or to generate cash for reinvestment.
- Short-term creditors, on the other hand, are most likely to be interested in the liquidity of a company's net assets and the coverage of its debt.

To the degree the likely users are known or predictable, the expected use of the statements may affect the auditor's opinion. The auditor should always recognize the possibility of unexpected users relying on the statements, but when the auditor knows some users are relying on the statements, special care should be taken to satisfy their needs. This concept is much like level of assurance, discussed in Chapter 4.

Measurability. The dollar error of some misstatements cannot be accurately measured. For example, a client's unwillingness to disclose an existing lawsuit or the acquisition of a new company subsequent to the balance sheet date are difficult, if not impossible, to measure in terms of dollar errors. The materiality question the auditor must evaluate in such a situation is the impact on statement users of the failure to make the disclosure.

Uncertainty of Outcome. In some cases it is nearly impossible to determine the dollar magnitude of a misstatement. For example, when there is a large lawsuit against a client, it may be unnecessary to require disclosure if the likelihood of success is remote. Similarly, there is nearly always some possibility of material obsolete inventory. But if the likelihood is small, an unqualified opinion is appropriate. Naturally, the evaluation of uncertainty of outcome is a professional judgment.

Nature of the Item. The decision of a user may also be affected by the kind of error in the statement. The following are a few items that may affect user's decision and therefore the auditor's opinion in a different way than most errors:

- Transactions involve related parties.
- Transactions are illegal or fraudulent.
- An item may materially affect some future period even though it is immaterial when only the current period is considered.
- An item has a "psychic" effect (e.g., small profit versus small loss or cash balance versus overdraft).
- An item may be important in terms of possible consequences arising from contractual obligations (e.g., the impact of failure to comply with a debt restriction may result in a material loan being called).

The Scope of the Auditor's Examination Has Been Restricted by the Client

When clients impose restrictions on the auditor's scope, a qualified opinion, or a disclaimer of opinion, should be issued unless the restrictions are minor. Due to the potential effect of client restrictions on the independence of auditors, the AICPA has encouraged the use of a disclaimer of opinion whenever the materiality is in question.

Two common restrictions imposed on the auditor's scope are the observation of physical inventory and the confirmation of accounts receivable, but other restrictions may also occur. Reasons for a client restricting the auditor's scope may be to save audit fees and, in the case of confirming receivables, prevent possible conflicts between the client and customer when amounts differ. The auditor's concern is that the client may be concealing a misstatement.

A qualified or disclaimer of opinion resulting from client restriction ordinarily requires a middle paragraph. An example of a disclaimer for a client restriction in the previous year where no such restriction exists in the current year follows:

SCOPE PARAGRAPH

We have examined the balance sheet of X Company as of September 30, 19X2, and the related statements of income and retained earnings and changes in financial position for the year then ended. Our examination was made in accordance with generally accepted auditing standards, and accordingly included such tests of the accounting records and such other auditing procedures as we considered necessary in the circumstances, except as stated in the following paragraph.

MIDDLE PARAGRAPH

Because we were not engaged as auditors until after September 30, 19X1, we were not present to observe the physical inventory taken at that date and we have not satisfied ourselves by means of other procedures concerning inventory quantities. The amount of the inventory at September 30, 19X1, enters materially into the determination of the results of operations and changes in financial position for the year ended September 30, 19X2. Therefore, we do not express an opinion on the accompanying statements of income and retained earnings and changes in financial position for the year ended September 30, 19X2.

OPINION PARAGRAPH

In our opinion, the accompanying balance sheet presents fairly the financial position of X Company at September 30, 19X2, in conformity with generally accepted accounting principles applied on a basis consistent with that of the preceding year.

The Scope of the Auditor's Examination Has Been Restricted by Conditions

A scope qualification and, depending on the materiality, either an opinion qualification or a disclaimer of opinion is necessary whenever conditions beyond the client's or the auditor's control prevent the auditor from performing procedures that he considers necessary. For example, if the auditor is unable to examine the client's recorded minutes because they are lost, it is necessary to issue a disclaimer of opinion, since the minutes often include vital information that cannot be found elsewhere. When the auditor cannot perform procedures he considers desirable, but he is able to satisfy himself with alternative procedures that the information being verified is fairly stated, an unqualified report is acceptable.

The most common case in which the auditor cannot carry out important procedures occurs when the engagement is agreed upon after the client's balance sheet date. The confirmation of accounts receivable, the physical examination of inventory, and other important procedures may not be possible under these circumstances.

For example, the following report would be appropriate for a company where the amounts were material but not pervasive if the auditor had not been on hand to observe inventory and could not satisfy himself by alternative procedures:

(Scope Paragraph—Qualified)

We have examined the balance sheet of X Company as of December 31, 19X2, and the related statements of income and retained earnings for the year then ended. Our examination was made in accordance with generally accepted auditing standards, and accordingly included such tests of the accounting records and such other auditing procedures as we considered necessary in the circumstances, except as stated in the following paragraph.

(Middle Paragraph)

We did not observe the taking of physical inventories as of December 31, 19X2, since this date was prior to our initial engagement as auditors for the company. The company's records do not permit adequate retroactive tests of inventory quantities.

(Opinion Paragraph—Qualified)

In our opinion, except for the effect of such adjustments, if any, as might have been disclosed had we been able to observe the physical inventory taken as of December 31, 19X2, or to make retroactive tests, the statements present fairly. . . .

When the amounts are so material that a disclaimer of opinion is required, the scope and middle paragraphs could remain the same, but the opinion paragraph might be as follows:

(Opinion Paragraph—Disclaimer)

Because the inventories referred to in the preceding paragraphs enter materially into the determination of financial position and the results of operations, we are unable to express an opinion on the accompanying financial statements taken as a whole.

In the previous example, the auditor can issue an unqualified audit report even if it is not practical for him to be on hand during the count if he performs the necessary alternative procedures. These must ordinarily include tests of the client's perpetual records and examination of enough physical counts of the inventory at a different date to satisfy the auditor that the inventory was fairly stated at the balance sheet date.

The Financial Statements Have Not Been Prepared in Conformity with Generally Accepted Accounting Principles

When the auditor knows that the financial statements may be misleading because they were not prepared in accordance with generally accepted accounting principles, he must issue a qualified or an adverse opinion, depending on the materiality of the item in question. The opinion must clearly state the nature of the deviation from the accepted principles and the amount of the misstatement, if it is known. An example of a qualified opinion for the failure to capitalize leases follows:

(SCOPE PARAGRAPH—UNQUALIFIED)
(MIDDLE PARAGRAPH)

> The Company has excluded from property and debt in the accompanying balance sheet certain lease obligations, which in our opinion should be capitalized in order to conform with generally accepted accounting principles. If these lease obligations were capitalized, property would be increased by $4,750,000, long-term debt by $4,200,000, and retained earnings by $550,000 as of December 31, 19X2, and net income and earnings per share would be increased by $450,000 and $47, respectively, for the year then ended.

(OPINION PARAGRAPH—QUALIFIED)

> In our opinion, except for the effects of not capitalizing certain lease obligations, as discussed in the preceding paragraph, the financial statements present fairly. . . .

When the amounts are so material that an adverse opinion is required, the scope would still be unqualified, the middle paragraph could remain the same, but the opinion paragraph might be as follows:

(OPINION PARAGRAPH—ADVERSE)

> In our opinion, because of the effects of the matters discussed in the preceding paragraph, the financial statements referred to above do not present fairly, in conformity with generally accepted accounting principles, the financial position of Billet Company as of December 31, 19X2, or the results of its operations and changes in its financial position for the year then ended.

When the client fails to include information that is necessary for the fair presentation of financial statements in the body of the statements or in the related footnotes, it is the responsibility of the auditor to present the information in the audit report and issue a qualified or an adverse opinion. It is common to put this type of qualification in a middle paragraph and to refer to the middle paragraph in the opinion paragraph. An example of an audit report in which the auditor considered the financial statement disclosure inadequate follows:

(SCOPE PARAGRAPH—UNQUALIFIED)

(MIDDLE PARAGRAPH)

On January 15, 19X3, the Company issued debentures in the amount of $3,600,000 for the purpose of financing plant expansion. The debenture agreement restricts the payment of future cash dividends to earnings after December 31, 19X2.

(OPINION PARAGRAPH—QUALIFIED)

In our opinion, the accompanying financial statements, except for the omission of the information in the preceding paragraph, present fairly. . . .

Definition of Generally Accepted Accounting Principles. Determining whether statements are in accordance with generally accepted accounting principles can be a difficult judgment problem. Ethics Rule 203 permits a departure from Accounting Research Bulletins, Accounting Principles Board Opinions, and FASB Statements when the auditors believe that adherence to these would result in misleading statements:

Rule 203—Accounting Principles. A member shall not express an opinion that financial statements are presented in conformity with generally accepted accounting principles if such statements contain any departure from an accounting principle promulgated by the body designated by Council to establish such principles which has a material effect on the statements taken as a whole, unless the member can demonstrate that due to unusual circumstances the financial statements would otherwise have been misleading. In such cases his report must describe the departure, the approximate effects thereof, if practicable, and the reasons why compliance with the principle would result in a misleading statement.

When the auditor decides that adherence to generally accepted accounting principles would result in misleading statements, there should be a complete explanation in a middle paragraph. The middle paragraph should fully explain the departure and the reason why generally accepted accounting principles would have resulted in misleading statements. The opinion paragraph should then be unqualified except for the reference to the middle paragraph when generally accepted principles are mentioned.

Restatement of Prior-Year Statements. The client must, in some circumstances, restate prior-year statements included in the current year's comparative statements to reflect the presently used accounting principles.

The following circumstances require the restatement of prior year's statements:

- A change in the reporting entity.
- A change from the LIFO method of inventory costing to another method.
- A change in the method of accounting for long-term construction contracts.
- A change to or from the full-cost method of accounting used in the extractive industries.

The purpose of the restatement is to enhance comparability. Even though the prior-year statements have been restated, a qualification of the following nature is required in the first year in which the change in principles took place. The following is an illustration of the appropriate report for a change in accounting principles with restatement.

(SCOPE PARAGRAPH—UNQUALIFIED)
(OPINION PARAGRAPH—QUALIFIED)

. . . applied on a consistent basis after restatement for the change, with which we concur, in the method of accounting for long-term construction contracts as described in Note X to the financial statements.

The Accounting Pinciples Used in the Financial Statements Have Not Been Consistently Applied

Whenever there is a change in accounting principles that has a material effect on the current year's statements or is expected to have a material effect in future years, it is necessary to report the change in the opinion *even if the change has been fully disclosed in the financial statements.* Assuming that the accounting principle used in the current period's financial statements is generally accepted, it is sufficient to issue a qualified opinion. For example, if the client changed from the accelerated to the straight-line method of computing depreciation, the following wording is appropriate:

(SCOPE PARAGRAPH—UNQUALIFIED)
(OPINION PARAGRAPH—QUALIFIED)

. . . in conformity with generally accepted accounting principles applied on a basis consistent with that of the preceding year, except for the change (in which we concur) in depreciation methods as described in Note 6 to the financial statements.

If there were no footnotes in the financial statements explaining the nature of the above-mentioned change and the effect on the financial statements, the information must be included directly in the report rather than by reference to the footnotes. The inclusion of the auditor's expression of approval in the opinion is optional.

Omission of Statement of Changes in Financial Position.   The failure
to include a statement of changes in financial position is specifically addressed
in the SAS (Section 545). When the statement is omitted, the following
report is required:

(SCOPE PARAGRAPH—UNQUALIFIED)

(MIDDLE PARAGRAPH)

> The company declined to present a statement of changes in financial
> position for the year ended December 31, 19X2. Presentation of such statement
> summarizing the company's financing and investing activities and other
> changes in its financial position is required by Opinion No. 19 of the Accounting
> Principles Board.

(OPINION PARAGRAPH—QUALIFIED)

> In our opinion, except that the omission of a statement of changes in
> financial position results in an incomplete presentation as explained in the
> preceding paragraph, the aforementioned financial statements present fairly
> the financial position of X Company.

Change to a Method Lacking General Acceptance.   The auditor is
required to issue either a qualified or an adverse opinion, depending on the
materiality of the effect on the financial statements, when there is a change
from a generally accepted accounting principle to one that lacks general
acceptance. The reason for an adverse opinion in such a case is due to the
failure to follow generally accepted accounting principles, not the consistency exception.

The auditor must be able to distinguish between changes that affect
consistency and those that may affect comparability but do not affect consistency. The following are changes that affect consistency and therefore
require a qualified report if they are material:

- Changes in accounting principles, such as a change from LIFO to FIFO
  inventory valuation.
- Changes in reporting entities, such as the inclusion of an additional company
  in combined financial statements.
- Corrections of errors in principle by changing from an accounting principle
  that is not generally acceptable to one that is generally acceptable, including
  correction of the resulting error.

Consistency Exceptions versus Comparability.   Changes that do not
affect consistency and therefore need not be included in the audit report as
a consistency exception include the following:

- Changes in an estimate, such as a decrease in the life of an asset for depreciation purposes.
- Error corrections not involving principles, such as a previous year's mathematical error.
- Variations in format and presentation of financial information.

- Changes because of substantially different transactions or events, such as new endeavors in research and development or the sale of a subsidiary.

If those items that do not require a consistency exception because of their nature materially affect the comparability of financial statements, disclosure is required in the footnotes. A qualification for inadequate disclosure may be required if the client refuses to disclose the items properly.

Use of Middle Paragraph. Ordinarily, a middle paragraph is not necessary for consistency exceptions. Exceptions usually can be adequately explained in the opinion paragraph. The following are three exceptions to the general rule:

- There was a change to a principle not conforming to generally accepted accounting principles.
- Management has not provided reasonable justification for the change in accounting principles.
- It is the first examination by the CPA firm and because of inadequate records it is impractical to determine whether principles have been consistently used.

Unusual Uncertainties Affecting the Financial Statements

A number of estimates are customarily made by management in the preparation of financial statements, including the useful lives of the depreciable assets, the collectibility of receivables, and the realizability of inventory and other assets. There is usually enough evidence so that these items are susceptible to reasonable estimation. Sometimes, however, the auditor encounters a situation in which the outcome of a matter cannot be reasonably estimated at the time the statements are being issued. These matters are defined as *"uncertainties."* Examples of such uncertainties include:

- Recoverability of a deferred cost.
- Income tax or litigation contingencies (collectible or payable).
- Realizability of a significant receivable.
- Continued availability of required financing.

There are also less specific situations in which the ability of the company to continue to operate as a *going concern* is open to question. For example, the existence of one or more of the following factors raises the question of uncertainty about the ability of a company to continue to operate:

- The company's controls over operations are inadequate.
- There are significant recurring operating losses.
- The company has been unable to pay its debt obligations as they come due.
- Serious shortages of liquidity are evidenced by the current liabilities exceeding the current assets.

The appropriate type of opinion to issue when either specific or general uncertainties exist depends on the materiality of the items in question. An unqualified opinion is appropriate if the uncertainty is immaterial. A qualified opinion, with the use of a "subject to" qualification, should be issued in those middle-ground situations where the financial statements are overshadowed by a material uncertainty. When the potential effect of the uncertainty is so pervasive that a subsequent adverse resolution of the uncertainty would require a radical change in the financial statements, the CPA firm *may issue a disclaimer but is not required to do so if a qualified opinion is issued and the uncertainty is adequately explained in a footnote.* Although SASs do not require a disclaimer of opinion when highly material uncertainties exist, many CPA firms follow the policy of requiring them in extreme cases.

An illustration of a "subject to" opinion when there is an uncertainty due to existing litigation follows:

(SCOPE PARAGRAPH—UNQUALIFIED)
(MIDDLE PARAGRAPH)

As discussed in Note 3 to the financial statements, the Company is defendant in a lawsuit alleging infringement of certain patent rights and claiming royalties and punitive damages. The Company has filed a counter action, and preliminary hearings and discovery proceedings on both actions are in progress. Company officers and counsel believe the Company has a good chance of prevailing, but the ultimate outcome of the lawsuits cannot presently be determined, and no provision for any liability that may result has been made in the financial statements.

(OPINION PARAGRAPH—QUALIFIED)

In our opinion, subject to the effects of such adjustments, if any, as might have been required had the outcome of the uncertainty referred to in the preceding paragraph been known, the financial statements referred to above present fairly. . . .

The following is an illustration of a disclaimer that is considered necessary because the validity of the going concern assumption is questionable and there are material uncertainties:

(SCOPE PARAGRAPH—UNQUALIFIED)
(MIDDLE PARAGRAPH)

The Company has sustained substantial losses from operations and, as described in the notes to the financial statements, the operations of the Company have been substantially reduced. The future of the Company as an operating business will depend upon its ability to operate profitably and the availability of such financing as may be required. It is not possible to determine the effect on the 19X2 financial statements referred to above because of the possible consequences of the following matters:

(a) The adequacy of the allowance for obsolescence of $2,000,000 on the plant, property, and equipment. (Note 6)
(b) The uncertainties arising from the contingent liabilities described in the notes to the financial statements.

(Opinion Paragraph—Disclaimer)

Because it is impossible to determine the future operational activity of the Company and the effect of the material uncertainties referred to in the previous paragraphs, we are unable to and do not express an opinion on the accompanying consolidated financial statements for the year ended December 31, 19X2.

The Auditor Is Not Independent

If the auditor has not fulfilled the independence requirements specified by the Code of Professional Ethics, a disclaimer of opinion is required even though all the audit procedures considered necessary in the circumstances were performed. The following report is recommended when the auditor is not independent:

We are not independent with respect to XYZ Company, and the accompanying balance sheet as of December 31, 19X2, and the related statements of income and retained earnings and the statement of changes in financial position for the year then ended were not audited by us. Accordingly, we do not express an opinion on them.

The lack of independence overrides any other scope limitations. Therefore, no other reason for disclaiming an opinion should be cited. There should be no mention of the performance of any audit procedures in the report. An interesting requirement is that each page of the statements must be marked unaudited even if a complete audit was done.

EXISTENCE OF MORE THAN ONE CONDITION REQUIRING EXCEPTION

Frequently, auditors encounter situations involving more than one of the conditions requiring modification of the unqualified report. In these circumstances, the auditor should qualify his opinion for each condition unless the less significant exception has the effect of neutralizing the more serious exception. For example, if there is a scope limitation and a situation where the auditor was not independent, the scope limitation should not be revealed. In the following situations more than one exception should be included in the report:

- The auditor is not independent and the auditor knows the company has not followed generally accepted accounting principles.
- The auditor issues a qualified opinion because of a scope limitation and the knowledge of a contingent liability concerning litigation that may cause bankruptcy if an adverse ruling is given.
- The statements are unaudited and the auditor knows they do not conform to generally accepted accounting principles.

- There is a deviation in the statements' preparation in accordance with generally accepted accounting principles and another accounting principle was applied on a basis that was not consistent with that of the preceding year.

REPORTING ON "OTHER INFORMATION"

For certain types of documents the auditor is responsible under Section 550 of SAS 8 to determine whether information in other parts of a document containing audited financial statements is inconsistent with the financial statements. For example, the auditor must read the annual report to shareholders before it is issued to determine whether statements made in the president's letter are at variance with the audited statements. Possible inconsistencies would be the incorrect earnings per share in the president's letter or a statement that sales increased 20 percent when they actually increased 10 percent. The need for this requirement of financial reports arises because the auditor is responsible for auditing only the financial statements, not the entire annual report. Yet a significant inconsistency between the statements and the other information could raise questions as to the accuracy of the statements.

The following types of documents are covered by Section 550 when they include audited financial statements:

- Annual reports issued to stockholders.
- Annual reports filed with the SEC under the 1934 SEC Act (information required under the 1933 Act is specifically excluded from Section 550).
- Annual reports of charitable organizations distributed to the public.
- Other documents where the client wants the auditor to devote attention to them.

The auditor's only responsibility is to *read the information* in the document and evaluate whether it is inconsistent with information in the audited statements, or materially misleading. The client should be requested to change the information if there is a material inconsistency. If the client refuses, a paragraph in the audit report explaining the inconsistency is a likely course of action. Other actions could be to withhold the report or withdraw from the engagement.

A more difficult problem arises when the auditor believes information related to the financial statements may be materially incorrect, but not inconsistent with statement information. An example is the statement in the annual report that the company leads the industry in research and development as a percent of sales. In such a situation the matter should be discussed with management and perhaps outsiders who may have knowledge of such matters. Information of this type need not be audited. Furthermore, the meaning of materially misstated as used in Section 550 is not clearly defined and allows considerable leeway in judgment for the auditor.

SEGMENT INFORMATION

FASB statement 14 requires an entity to include disaggregated information in its financial statements about different industries, foreign operations, and its major customers. This information is called segment information. For most companies, FASB 14 requires showing separately in the statements such information as revenue, gross profit, capital expenditures, and identifiable assets for each major industry. The failure to include the information is a violation of generally accepted accounting principles.

The Financial Accounting Standards Board responded to criticisms that FASB 14 caused hardships to smaller companies. FASB statement 21 was issued in 1978 requiring segment information *only for companies with publicly held stock*. (FASB 21 also eliminated the requirement for reporting earnings per share for non-publicly held companies).

Section 435 of the SAS 21 (segment information) sets forth auditing requirements relating to the FASB 14 disclosures. It only pertains to companies with publicly held stock.

Procedures. The audit procedures needed to verify segment information depend heavily upon the materiality of the segments and the clients internal accounting control. Section 435 emphasizes that segments should be audited in the context of the overall financial statements rather than independently. The following are procedures that are likely to be applicable.

- Test underlying accounting records as a part of normal audit procedures to determine whether the entity's revenue, operating expenses, and identifiable assets are appropriately classified among segments.
- Inquire of management concerning its methods of determining segment information, and evaluate the reasonableness of those methods.
- Inquire as to the bases of accounting for sales or transfers between segments and test them.
- Test the disaggregation of the entity's financial statements into segment information by the use of analytical review procedures.
- Inquire as to the methods of allocation, evaluate whether the methods are reasonable, and test the allocations.
- Determine whether the segment information has been presented consistently from period to period.

Reporting Requirements. The requirements for segment reports are much like those for any other part of the statements. The auditor's report does not refer to the segment information or procedures performed, unless one of the conditions identified at the beginning of the chapter exists. The following are the most likely qualifications related to segment information:

- Segment information is materially misstated. A qualified or adverse opinion is required for failure to follow generally accepted accounting principles.
- Segment information the auditor considers necessary to disclose is omitted. A qualified or adverse opinion is required for lack of adequate disclosure.

- There is a material inconsistency in the method of presenting segment information. A qualified opinion is required for lack of consistency.
- The auditor is unable to reach a conclusion as to the fair presentation of segment information. The most likely case where this occurs is when management believes that disclosing segment information is not required and has made no provision for segment data in its record keeping. A qualified opinion as to scope and opinion is appropriate when the amounts are material.

NEGATIVE ASSURANCES

It is inappropriate to include in the audit report any additional comments that counterbalance the auditor's opinion. For example, the use of such terminology as "However, nothing came to our attention that would lead us to question the fairness of the presentations" as a part of a disclaimer of opinion is inappropriate and a violation of the standards of reporting. Statements of this kind, which are referred to as *negative assurances*, tend to confuse readers about the nature of the auditor's examination and the degree of responsibility he is assuming.

The use of negative assurances in certain unaudited financial statements is considered appropriate. These are considered in Chapter 22.

REVIEW QUESTIONS

21-1. Explain why auditor's reports are important to users of financial statements.

21-2. List the five parts of an unqualified audit report and explain the meaning of each part. How do the parts compare with those found in a qualified report?

21-3. What four circumstances are required in order that an unqualified opinion can be issued?

21-4. Distinguish between an unqualified report with modified wording and a qualified report. Give examples of when modified wording may be used in an unqualified opinion.

21-5. What kinds of reports can a CPA issue if another CPA has performed part of the audit and has concluded that the financial statements are fairly presented? When should each be issued?

21-6. List the six conditions requiring a departure from an unqualified opinion and give one specific example of each of those conditions.

21-7. Define materiality as it is used in audit reporting. What conditions will affect the auditor's determination of materiality?

21-8. Distinguish between an opinion qualified as to scope only and one with a scope and opinion qualification.

21-9. How does the auditor's opinion differ between scope limitations caused by client restrictions and limitations resulting from conditions beyond the client's control? Under which of these two would the auditor be most likely to issue a disclaimer of opinion? Explain.

21-10. What type of opinion should an auditor issue when the financial statements are not in accordance with generally accepted accounting principles because such adherence would result in misleading statements?

21-11. The client has restated the prior-year statements due to a change from LIFO to FIFO. How should this be reflected in the auditor's report?

21-12. Distinguish between an "except for" and a "subject to" qualified opinion and give one specific example of each.

21-13. Distinguish between a qualified opinion, an adverse opinion, and a disclaimer of opinion and explain the circumstances under which each is appropriate.

21-14. Discuss why the AICPA has such strict requirements on audit opinions when the auditor is not independent.

21-15. Distinguish between changes that affect consistency and those that may affect comparability but do not affect consistency. Give an example of each.

21-16. When an auditor discovers more than one condition that requires modification of the unqualified report, what should his report include?

21-17. Discuss the auditor's responsibility, under Section 550 of the SAS, for reporting on "other information." Give three examples of "other information."

DISCUSSION QUESTIONS AND PROBLEMS

21-18. Select the best response for each of the following questions.
    a. Parnell, CPA, accepted the audit engagement of Treacy Manufacturing, Inc. During the audit, Parnell became aware that he did not have the competence required for the engagement. What should he do?
        (1) Disclaim an opinion.
        (2) Issue a "subject to" opinion.
        (3) Suggest that Treacy engage another CPA to perform the audit.
        (4) Rely on the competence of client personnel.
    b. The date of the CPA's opinion on the financial statements of his client should be the date of the
        (1) closing of the client's books.
        (2) receipt of the client's letter of representation.
        (3) completion of all important audit procedures.
        (4) submittal of the report to the client.
    c. When an auditor issues a qualified opinion because of an uncertainty, the reader of the auditor's report should conclude that
        (1) the auditor was not able to form an opinion on the financial statements taken as a whole.
        (2) the uncertainty occurred after the balance sheet date but prior to the audit report date.
        (3) there were no audit procedures possibly available to the auditor by which he could obtain satisfaction concerning the uncertainty.
        (4) the ability of the company to continue as a "going concern" is questionable.   (AICPA adapted)

21–19. Select the best response for each of the following.
   a. A CPA will issue an adverse auditor's opinion if
      (1) the scope of his examination is limited by the client.
      (2) his exception to the fairness of presentation is so material that an "except for" opinion is not justified.
      (3) he did not perform sufficient auditing procedures to form an opinion on the financial statements taken as a whole.
      (4) such major uncertainties exist concerning the company's future that a "subject to" opinion is not justified.
   b. An auditor will express an "except for" opinion if
      (1) the client refuses to provide for a probable federal income tax deficiency that is material.
      (2) the degree of uncertainty associated with the client company's future makes a "subject to" opinion inappropriate.
      (3) he did not perform procedures sufficient to form an opinion on the consistency of application of generally accepted accounting principles.
      (4) he is basing his opinion in part upon work done by another auditor.
   c. John Greenbaum, CPA, provides bookkeeping services to Santa Fe Products Company. He also is a director of Santa Fe and performs limited auditing procedures in connection with his preparation of Santa Fe's financial statements. Greenbaum's report accompanying these financial statements should include a
      (1) detailed description of the limited auditing procedures performed.
      (2) complete description of the relationships with Santa Fe that imperil Greenbaum's independence.
      (3) disclaimer of opinion and a statement that financial statements are unaudited on each page of the financial statements.
      (4) qualified opinion because of his lack of independence together with such assurance as his limited auditing procedures can provide.
   d. A CPA was unable to observe the physical inventory that his client conducted on the balance sheet date. The CPA satisfied himself as to inventory quantities by other procedures. These procedures included making some physical counts of the inventory a week later and applying appropriate tests to intervening transactions. In his report on the financial statements, the CPA
      (1) must disclose the modification of the scope of his examination and express a qualified opinion.
      (2) must disclose the modification of the scope of his examination but may express an unqualified opinion.
      (3) may omit reference to any modification of the scope of his examination and express an unqualified opinion.
      (4) may omit reference to modification of the scope of his examination only if he describes the circumstances in an explanatory paragraph or his opinion paragraph.
   e. In forming his opinion concerning the consolidated financial statements of Juno Corporation, a CPA relies upon another auditor's examination

of the financial statements of Hera, Inc., a wholly owned subsidiary whose operations constitute 30 percent of Juno's consolidated total. Hera's auditor expresses an unqualified opinion on that company's financial statements.

The CPA examining Juno Corporation may be expected to express an unqualified opinion but refer to the report by the other auditor if

(1) he concludes, based upon a review of the other auditor's professional standing and qualifications, that he is willing to assume the same responsibility as though he had performed the audit of Hera's financial statements himself.

(2) he is satisfied with the audit scope for the subsidiary, based upon his review of the audit program, but his inquiries disclose that the other auditor is not independent or lacks professional standing.

(3) he is satisfied with the other auditor's professional standing but concludes, based upon a review of the audit program, that the audit scope for the examination of Hera's financial statements was inadequate.

(4) he is satisfied with the other auditor's professional reputation and audit scope but is unwilling to assume responsibility for the other auditor's work to the same extent as though he had performed the work himself.

f. If a principal auditor decides that he will refer in his report to the examination of another auditor, he is required to disclose the

(1) name of the other auditor.

(2) nature of his inquiry into the other auditor's professional standing and extent of his review of the other auditor's work.

(3) portion of the financial statements examined by the other auditor.

(4) reasons why he is unwilling to assume responsibility for the other auditor's work.

g. A CPA conducting his first examination of the financial statements of Apollo Corporation is considering the propriety of reducing his work by consulting with the predecessor auditor and reviewing the predecessor's working papers. This procedure is

(1) acceptable.

(2) required if the new auditor is to render an unqualified opinion.

(3) acceptable only if the CPA refers in his report to his reliance upon the predecessor auditor's work.

(4) unacceptable because the CPA should bring an independent viewpoint to a new engagement.

h. An auditor's unqualified short-form report

(1) implies only that items disclosed in the financial statements and footnotes are properly presented and takes no position on the adequacy of disclosure.

(2) implies that disclosure is adequate in the financial statements and footnotes.

(3) explicitly states that disclosure is adequate in the financial statements and footnotes.

(4) explicitly states that all material items have been disclosed in conformity with generally accepted accounting principles.

(AICPA adapted)

21–20. The auditor's report must contain an expression of opinion or a statement to the effect that an opinion cannot be expressed. Four types of opinions that meet these requirements are generally known as:

a. An unqualified opinion.

b. A qualified opinion.

c. An adverse opinion.

d. A disclaimer of opinion.

Required:

For each of the following situations, indicate which type of opinion you would render and give your reasons. Select the *best* answer choice and mark only one answer for each item.

Unless there is an implication to the contrary in the situation as stated, you may assume that the examination was made in accordance with generally accepted auditing standards, that the financial statements present fairly the financial position and results of operations in conformity with generally accepted accounting principles applied on a consistent basis, and that the statements include adequate informative disclosure necessary not to be misleading.

a. During the course of his examination, the CPA suspects that a material amount of the assets of his client, Ash Corporation, has been misappropriated through fraud. The corporation refuses to allow the auditor to expand the scope of his examination sufficiently to confirm these suspicions.

b. The CPA is examining the Chestnut Corporation's financial statements for the first time. Former financial statements carry the unqualified opinion of a CPA who is unknown to the CPA currently conducting the examination. The CPA believes the balance sheet presents fairly the corporation's financial position, but the CPA was not authorized to test the activity of previous periods and is unwilling to assume any responsibility for the work performed by the prior CPA.

c. The CPA was engaged to examine the Fig Wholesale Corporation's financial statements after the close of the corporation's fiscal year. On the completion of his examination, the CPA is satisfied that the corporation's financial statements are presented fairly except that he is not satisfied that the Fig Wholesale Corporation's inventory is fairly stated on the balance sheet date. The amount of the inventory is material.

d. On the basis of an examination made in accordance with generally accepted auditing standards, the independent auditor formed the opinion that the financial statements present fairly the financial position and results of operations in conformity with generally accepted accounting principles applied on a consistent basis and that the statements include all informative disclosures necessary to make the statements not misleading.

e. The CPA has examined Ginkgo Corporation's financial statements for many years. During the year just ended a service bureau was employed to process the corporation's financial data by computer. The CPA knows very little about computers and does not wish to conduct the audit for the year just ended. The CPA and the president of the corporation are old friends, however, and the president persuaded the CPA that he should not withdraw from the engagement. After glancing at the records and comparing the current year's statements with those of previous years, the CPA believes that the statements prepared by the service bureau are stated fairly.

f. Subsequent to the close of Holly Corporation's fiscal year, a major debtor was declared bankrupt because of a deteriorating financial condition. The debtor had confirmed the full amount due to Holly Corporation at the balance sheet date. Since the account was confirmed at the balance sheet date, Holly Corporation refuses to disclose any information in relation to this subsequent event.

g. A satisfactory audit is performed of the Wholesale Hardware Company, and in the opinion of the auditors, the financial statements are fairly presented. On the last day of the field work, the audit partners discover that the auditor in charge of the engagement has a substantial investment in the client's stock.

h. Linden Corporation has material investments in stocks of subsidiary companies. Stocks of the subsidiary companies are not actively traded on the market, and the CPA's engagement does not extend to any subsidiary company. The CPA is able to satisfy himself that all investments are carried at orginal cost, and he has no reason to suspect that the amounts are not stated fairly. (AICPA adapted)

21–21. For each of the following, state the appropriate type of audit report to issue (unqualified, qualified, disclaimer, or adverse).

a. Subsequent to the close of Holly Corporation's fiscal year, a major debtor was declared bankrupt due to a series of events. The receivable is significantly material in relation to the financial statements, and recovery is doubtful. The debtor had confirmed the full amount due to Holly Corporation at the balance sheet date. Since the account was good at the balance sheet date, Holly Corporation refuses to disclose any information in relation to this subsequent event. The CPA believes that all accounts were stated fairly at the balance sheet date.

b. Kapok Corporation is a substantial user of electronic data-processing equipment and has employed an outside service bureau to process data in years past. During the current year Kapok adopted the policy of leasing all hardware and expects to continue this arrangement in the future. This change in policy is adequately disclosed in footnotes to Kapok's financial statements, but uncertainty prohibits either Kapok or the CPA from assessing the impact of this change upon future operations.

c. The president of Lowe, Inc., would not allow the auditor to confirm the receivable balance from one of its major customers. The amount of the receivable is material in relation to Lowe's financial statements. The auditor was unable to satisfy himself as to the receivable balance by alternative procedures.

d. Sempier Corporation issued financial statements that purported to present its financial position and results of operations but omitted the related statement of changes in financial position (the omission is not sanctioned by APB 19). (AICPA adapted)

21–22. As part of his examination of the financial statements of the Marlborough Corporation for the year ended March 31, 19X7, Mario Romito, CPA, is reviewing the balance sheet presentation of a $1,200,000 advance to Franklin Olds, Marlborough's president. The advance, which represents 50 percent of current assets and 10 percent of total assets, was made during the year ended March 31, 19X7. It has been described in the balance sheet as "miscellaneous accounts receivable" and classified as a current asset.

Mr. Olds informs the CPA that he has used the proceeds of the advance to purchase 35,000 shares of Marlborough's common stock in order to forestall a takeover raid on the company. He is reluctant to have his association with the advance described in the financial statements because he does not have voting control and fears that this "will just give the raiders ammunition."

Mr. Olds offers the following four-point program as an alternative to further disclosure:

1. Have the advance approved by the board of directors. (This can be done expeditiously because a majority of the board members are officers of the company.)
2. Prepare a demand note payable to the company with interest of 7.5 percent (the average bank rate paid by the company).
3. Furnish an endorsement of the stock to the company as collateral for the loan. (During the year under audit, despite the fact that earnings did not increase, the market price of Marlborough common rose from $20 to $40 per share. The stock has maintained its $40-per-share market price subsequent to year-end.)
4. Obtain a written opinion from the company attorney supporting the legality of the company's advance and the use of the proceeds.

Required:

a. Discuss the proper balance sheet classification of the advance to Mr. Olds and other appropriate disclosures in the financial statements and footnotes. (Ignore SEC regulations and requirements, tax effects, creditors' restrictions on stock repurchase, and the presentation of common stock dividends and interest income.)
b. Discuss each point of Mr. Olds's four-point program as to whether it is desirable and as to whether it is an alternative to further disclosure.
c. If Mr. Olds refuses to permit further disclosure, what is the effect on the auditor's report? Discuss.
d. In his discussion with the CPA, Mr. Olds warns that the raiders, if successful, will probably appoint new auditors. What consideration should the CPA give to this factor? Explain. (AICPA adapted)

21–23. You are engaged in the examination of the financial statements of Rapid, Inc., and its recently acquired subsidiary, Slow Corporation. In acquiring

Slow Corporation during 19X7, Rapid exchanged a large number of its shares of common stock for 90 percent of the outstanding common stock of Slow Corporation in a transaction that was accounted for as a pooling of interests. Rapid is now preparing its annual report to shareholders and proposes to include in the report combined financial statements for the year ended December 31, 19X7, with a footnote describing its exchange of stock for that of Slow Corporation.

Rapid also proposes to include in its report the financial statements of the preceding year as they appeared in Rapid's 19X6 annual report along with a five-year financial summary from Rapid's prior annual reports, all of which have been accompanied by your unqualified auditor's opinion.

Required:

a. Discuss the objectives or purposes of the standard of reporting that requires the auditor's report to state whether generally accepted accounting principles have been consistently observed over the past two periods.

b. Describe the treatment in the auditor's report of interperiod changes having a material effect on the financial statements arising from
   (1) a change to an alternative generally accepted accounting principle.
   (2) changed conditions that necessitate accounting changes but do not involve changes in the accounting principles employed.
   (3) changed conditions unrelated to accounting.

c. (1) Would the financial reporting treatment proposed by Rapid for the 19X7 annual report be on a consistent basis? Discuss.
   (2) Describe the auditor's report that should accompany the financial statements as proposed by Rapid for inclusion in the annual report.

(AICPA adapted)

21–24. Charles Burke, CPA, has completed field work for his examination of the Willingham Corporation for the year ended December 31, 19X7, and is now in the process of determining whether to modify his report. Two independent, unrelated situations have arisen.

(1) In September 19X7 a lawsuit was filed against Willingham to have the court order it to install pollution-control equipment in one of its older plants. Willingham's legal counsel has informed Burke that it is not possible to forecast the outcome of this litigation; however, Willingham's management has informed Burke that the cost of the pollution-control equipment is not economically feasible and that the plant will be closed if the case is lost. In addition, Burke has been told by management that the plant and its production equipment would have only minimal resale value and that the production that would be lost could not be recovered at other plants.

(2) During 19X7 Willingham purchased a franchise amounting to 20 percent of its assets for the exclusive right to produce and sell a newly patented product in the northeastern United States. There has been no production in marketable quantities of the product anywhere to date. Neither the franchisor nor any franchisee has conducted any market research with respect to the product.

Required:

In deciding the type-of-report modification, if any, Burkes should take into account such considerations as the following:

- Relative magnitude.
- Uncertainty of outcome.
- Likelihood of error.
- Expertise of the auditor.
- Pervasive impact on the financial statements.
- Inherent importance of the item.

Discuss Burke's type of report decision for each situation in terms of the foregoing and other appropriate considerations. Assume that each situation is adequately disclosed in the notes to the financial statements. Each situation should be considered independently. In discussing each situation, ignore the other. It is not necessary for you to decide the type of report that should be issued.   (AICPA adapted)

21-25. Following are three independent, unrelated auditor's reports. The corporation being reported on, in each case, is profit oriented and publishes general-purpose financial statements for distribution to owners, creditors, potential investors, and the general public. Each of the three reports contains deficiencies.

AUDITOR'S REPORT I

We have examined the consolidated balance sheet of Belasco Corporation and subsidiaries as of December 31, 19X7, and the related consolidated statements of income and retained earnings and changes in financial position for the year then ended. Our examination was made in accordance with generally accepted auditing standards and therefore included such tests of the accounting records and such other auditing procedures as we considered necessary in the circumstances. We did not examine the financial statements of Seidel Company, a major consolidated subsidiary. These statements were examined by other auditors whose reports thereon have been furnished to us, and our opinion expressed herein, insofar as it relates to Seidel Company, is based solely upon the reports of the other auditors.

In our opinion, except for the reports of the other auditors, the accompanying consolidated balance sheet and consolidated statements of income and retained earnings and changes in financial position present fairly the financial position of Belasco Corporation and subsidiaries at December 31, 19X7 and the results of its operations and the changes in its financial position for the year then ended, in conformity with generally accepted accounting principles applied on a basis consistent with that of the preceding year.

AUDITOR'S REPORT II

The accompanying balance sheet of Jones Corporation as of December 31, 19X7, and the related statements of income and retained earnings and changes in financial position for the year then ended, were not audited by us; however, we confirmed cash in the bank and performed a general review of the statements.

During our engagement, nothing came to our attention to indicate that the aforementioned financial statements do not present fairly the financial position of Jones Corporation at December 31, 19X7, and the results of its operations and the changes in its financial position for the year then ended, in conformity with generally accepted accounting principles applied on a basis consistent with that of the preceding year; however, we do not express an opinion on them.

AUDITOR'S REPORT III

I made my examination in accordance with generally accepted auditing standards. However, I am not independent with respect to Mavis Corporation because my wife owns 5 percent of the outstanding common stock of the company. The accompanying balance sheet as of December 31, 19X7, and the related statements of income and retained earnings and changes in financial position for the year then ended were not audited by me; accordingly, I do not express an opinion on them.

Required:

For each auditor's report, describe the reporting deficiencies, explain the reasons therefor, and briefly discuss how the report should be corrected. Each report should be considered separately. When discussing one report, ignore the other two. Do not discuss the addressee, signatures, and date. Also do not rewrite any of the auditor's reports. Organize your answer sheet as follows:

Report No.	*Deficiency*	*Reason*	*Correction*

(AICPA adapted)

21–26. About two years ago you were engaged to conduct an annual audit of Pierson Company. This was shortly after the majority stockholders assumed control of the company and discharged the president and several other corporate officers. A new president canceled a wholesaler's contract to distribute Pierson Company products. The wholesaler is a Pierson Company minority stockholder and was one of the discharged officers. Shortly after you commenced your initial audit, several lawsuits were filed against Pierson Company by the wholesaler. Pierson Company filed countersuits.

None of the suits has been decided. The principal litigation is over the canceled contract, and the other suits are claims against the company for salary, bonus, and pension fund contributions. Pierson Company is the plaintiff in suits totaling approximately $300,000 and defendant in suits totaling approximately $2 million. Both amounts are material in relation to net income and total assets. Pierson's legal counsel believes that the outcome of the suits is uncertain and that all the suits are likely to be "tied up in court" for an extended time.

You were instructed by the board of directors each year to issue an audit report only if it contained an unqualified opinion. Pierson Company refuses to provide for an unfavorable settlement in the financial statements because legal counsel advised the board of directors that such a provision in the financial statements could be used against Pierson by the opposition in court. The pending litigation was fully disclosed in a footnote to the financial statements, however.

You did not issue a report on the completion of your audit one year ago, and you have now completed your second annual audit. The scope of your audits was not restricted in any way, and you would render unqualified opinions if there were no pending litigations. You have attended all meetings of the stockholders and the directors and have answered all questions addressed to you at these meetings. You were promptly paid for all work completed to the current date. The board of directors of Pierson Company invited you to deliver to them an audit report containing an unqualified opinion or to attend the annual meeting of the stockholders one week hence to answer questions concerning the results of your audit if you are unwilling to render an unqualified opinion.

Required:

a. Discuss the issues raised by the fact that the CPA attended the stockholders' and directors' meetings and answered all questions addressed to him. Do not consider the propriety of his failure to issue a written audit report.

b. Should a CPA issue his audit report promptly after he has completed his examination? Why?

c. Write the auditor's opinion you would render on Pierson Company's financial statements for the year just ended.   (AICPA adapted)

21–27. You are completing an examination of the financial statements of the Hilty Manufacturing Corporation for the year ended December 19X7. Hilty's financial statements have not been examined previously. Hilty's controller has given you the following draft of proposed footnotes to the financial statements.

The Hilty Manufacturing Corporation

Notes to Financial Statements

Year Ended December 31, 19X7

Note 1. Because we were not engaged as auditors until after December 31, 19X7, we were unable to observe the taking of the ending physical inventory. We satisfied ourselves as to the balance of physical inventory at December 28, 19X7, by alternative procedures.

Note 2. With the approval of the Commissioner of Internal Revenue, the company changed its method of accounting for inventories from the first-in, first-out method to the last-in, first-out method on January 1, 19X7. In the opinion of the company the effects of this change on the pricing of inventories and cost of goods manufactured were not material in the current year but are expected to be material in future years.

Note 3. The investment property was recorded at cost until October 19X7, when it was written up to its appraisal value. The company plans to sell the property in 19X8, and an independent real estate agent in the area has indicated that the appraisal price can be realized. Pending completion of the sale, the amount of the expected gain on the sale has been recorded in a deferred credit account.

Note 4. The stock dividend described in our May 24, 19X7, letter to stockholders has been recorded as a 105-for-100 stock split. Accordingly, there were no changes in the stockholders' equity account balances from this transaction.

Note 5. For many years the company has maintained a pension plan for certain employees. Prior to the current year pension expense was recognized as payments were made to retired employees. There was no change in the plan in the current year, but upon the recommendation of its auditor, the company provided $64,000, based upon an actuarial estimate, for pensions to be paid in the future to current employees.

Required:

For each of Notes 1 through 5, discuss
a. the adequacy and needed revisions, if any, of the financial statements or the note.
b. the necessary disclosure in or opinion modification of the auditor's report, assuming the revisions mentioned in part a have been made.

(AICPA adapted)

21–28. You are newly engaged by the James Company, a New England manufacturer with a sales office and warehouse located in a western state. The James Company audit must be made at the peak of your busy season when you will not have a senior auditor available for travel to the western outlet. Furthermore, the James Company is reluctant to bear the travel expenses of an out-of-town auditor.

Required:

a. Under what conditions would you, the principal auditor, be willing to accept full responsibility for the work of another auditor?
b. What would be your requirements with respect to the integrity of the other auditor? To whom would you direct inquiries about the other auditor?
c. What reference, if any, would you make to the other auditor in your report if you were
   (1) assuming full responsibility for his work?
   (2) not assuming responsibility for his work? (AICPA adapted)

21–29. The following draft of an auditor's report has been submitted for review:

> To: Eric Jones, Chief Accountant
>   Sunshine Manufacturing Co.
>
> We have examined the balance sheet of the Sunshine Manufacturing Co. for the year ended August 31, 19X7, and the related statements of income and retained earnings. Our examination included such tests of the accounting records and such other auditing procedures as we considered necessary in the circumstances except that, in accordance with your instructions, we did not count the buyers' cash working fund.
>
> In our opinion, subject to the limitation on our examination discussed above, the accompanying balance sheet and statements of income and earned surplus present fairly the financial position of the Sunshine Manufacturing Co. at August 31, 19X7, and the results of its operations for the year then ended.
>
> Frank George & Co.
August 31, 19X7
>
> It has been determined that
> a. except for the omission of the count of the buyers' cash working fund, there were no scope restrictions placed on the auditor's examination.
> b. Sunshine Manufacturing has been in continuous operation since 1942, but its financial statements have not previously been audited.

Required:

a. Assuming that Frank George & Co. was able to perform alternative auditing procedures to satisfactorily substantiate the buyers' cash working fund and purchases through the fund, identify and discuss the deficiencies in the auditor's report.
b. Assuming that Frank George & Co. was unable to satisfactorily substantiate the buyers' cash working fund and purchases through the fund by alternative auditing procedures, discuss the appropriateness of the opinion qualification proposed by Frank George & Co.'s report.
c. Discuss the potential consequences to the CPA of issuing a substandard report or failing to adhere in his examination to generally accepted auditing standards.   (AICPA adapted)

21–30. The financial statements of the Modern Manufacturing Company for the fiscal year ended September 30, 19X7, are presented below. The president of the company has requested you to make this year's examination and render a short-form audit report on the statements. The report would be addressed to the board of directors, and no restrictions would be placed on the scope of your audit work.

During the course of the audit you learn that inventories of finished products and work in process are stated at material cost alone, without including either labor or manufacturing overhead; that this practice has been followed for both tax and financial accounting purposes since the inception of the company in 1946; and that the elements of cost in the inventories should have been as follows for the beginning and end of the fiscal period:

	Finished Goods September 30 19X7	Finished Goods September 30 19X6	Work in Process September 30 19X7	Work in Process September 30 19X6
Materials	$88,000	$75,000	$34,000	$31,000
Labor	55,000	52,000	16,000	14,000
Overhead	28,000	24,000	17,000	16,000
	$171,000	$151,000	$67,000	$61,000

Except for the company's inventory methods, the statements are found to be acceptable in all respects.

Through an examination of the previous auditor's working papers, you have been able to satisfy yourself as to the correctness of the physical count and materials cost of the opening inventory.

Required:

Prepare an audit report addressed to the board of directors, such as is justified in the circumstances set forth above. Do not submit financial statements or notes to financial statements. (AICPA adapted)

21–31. You have been engaged by the board of directors of the Products Company, a medium-sized manufacturer, to examine its balance sheets as of December 31, 19X6, and the related statement of income and retained earnings for the year then ended. You have made a similar examination for the preceding year. At the conclusion of your examination you will be expected to issue a short-form report relating to the financial statements.

In conducting your examination you encounter the following situations:

Modern Manufacturing Company
Balance Sheet
December 31, 19X7

Assets		*Liabilities and Stockholders' Equity*	
Current assets		Current liabilities	
Cash	$12,000	Trade accounts payable	$29,000
Accounts receivable (net)	22,000	Salaries and wages	5,500
Inventories, at material cost		Taxes, other than taxes on	
(first-in, first-out) or mar-		income	8,000
ket, whichever lower	146,000	Taxes on income	13,000
Prepaid expenses	6,000		
Total current assets	$186,000	Total current liabilities	$55,500
Property, plant, and equip-		Stockholders' equity	
ment (net)	158,000	Common stock, par value	
		$100 a share, authorized,	
		issued and outstanding	
		2,000 shares	200,000
		Retained earnings	88,500
	$344,000		$344,000

Modern Manufacturing Company
Statement of Income and Retained Earnings
Year Ended December 31, 19X7

Net sales of manufactured product	$750,000
Cost of materials, including freight	300,000
Gross profit on sales	$450,000
Operating expenses	385,000
Earnings from operations	$ 65,000
Other deductions, less other income	22,000
Earnings before taxes on income	$ 43,000
Taxes on income (federal $12,000, state $1,000)	13,000
Net earnings	$ 30,000
Retained earnings—December 30, 19X6	58,500
Retained earnings—December 30, 19X7	$ 88,500

a. In response to a request for positive confirmation of its outstanding balance, one of the company's customers, a large mail-order concern whose balance represents almost one-half of total accounts receivable and 20 percent of total current assets, replies that its records are not maintained in a manner permitting confirmation.

b. It is the company's practice to store most of its finished goods in public warehouses from which shipments to customers are made. At December 31, 19X6, the date of the examination of inventory quantities, the inventory in these warehouses is substantial in relation to the company's total assets. One warehouse alone, which is located in a distant city and which is operated by a company not known to you, holds one-third of the company's finished goods.

c. The company has advised you that it is the defendant in litigation brought by a competitor for patent infringement. Counsel for the company advises that the amount of the damages sought by the competitor is in excess of the company's net worth. Counsel also states that in his opinion judgment will be in favor of your client.

d. For the entire year under examination, the company, in accordance with your recommendation made last year, charged its expenditures for computer development costs to current expenses. Previously such expenditures, which were material in amount in relation to the company's operations, had been recorded as deferred charges. The amounts so recorded in previous years are being amortized over five-year periods.

Required:

Considering the specific facts in these four situations, and assuming that any additional audit procedures you recommend will result in substantiating the facts as presented, you are to *state* and *justify fully* for each situation.

a. The additional audit procedures, if any, that should be followed.

b. The disclosures, if any, that should be made in the financial statements or in footnotes thereto.

c. The qualifications, comments, or references, if any, you should include in the short-form report in addition to the items in part b.

(AICPA adatped)

21–32. For each of the following independent situations, state the nature of the appropriate qualification in the audit report.

a. Subsequent to the date of the financial statements as part of his post-balance sheet date audit procedures, a CPA learned of heavy damage to one of a client's two plants due to a recent fire; the loss will not be reimbursed by insurance. The newspapers described the event in detail. The financial statements and appended notes as prepared by the client did not disclose the loss caused by the fire.

b. A CPA is engaged in the examination of the financial statements of a large manufacturing company with branch offices in many widely separated cities. The CPA was not able to count the substantial undeposited cash receipts at the close of business on the last day of the fiscal year at all branch offices.

As an alternative to this auditing procedure used to verify the accurate cutoff of cash receipts, the CPA observed that deposits in transit as shown on the year-end bank reconciliation appeared as credits on the bank statement on the first business day of the new year. He was satisfied as to the cutoff of cash receipts by the use of the alternative procedure.

c. On January 2, 19X7, the Retail Auto Parts Company received a notice from its primary supplier that effective immediately all wholesale prices would be increased 10 percent. On the basis of the notice, Retail Auto Parts revalued its December 31, 19X6, inventory to reflect the higher costs. The inventory constituted a material proportion of total assets; however, the effect of the revaluation was material to current assets but not to total assets or net income. The increase in valuation is adequately disclosed in the footnotes.

d. During 19X7 the research staff of Scientific Research Corporation devoted its entire efforts toward developing a new pollution-control device. All costs that could be attributed directly to the project involving the pollution-control device were accounted for as deferred charges and classified on the balance sheet at December 31, 19X7, as a noncurrent asset. In the course of his audit of the corporation's 19X7 financial statements, Anthony, CPA, found persuasive evidence that the research conducted to date would probably result in a marketable product. The deferred research charges are significantly material in relationship to both income and total assets.

e. For the past five years a CPA has audited the financial statements of a manufacturing company. During this period, the examination scope was limited by the client as to the observation of the annual physical inventory. Since the CPA considered the inventories to be of material amount and he was not able to satisfy himself by other auditing procedures, he was not able to express an unqualified opinion on the financial statements in each of the five years.

The CPA was allowed to observe physical inventories for the current year ended December 31, 19X7, because the client's banker would no longer accept the audit reports. In the interest of economy, the client requested the CPA to not extend his audit procedures to the inventory as of January 1, 19X7.

f. During the course of his examination of the financial statements of a corporation for the purpose of expressing an opinion on the statements, a CPA is refused permission to inspect the minute books. The corporation secretary instead offers to give the CPA a certified copy of all resolutions and actions relating to accounting matters.

g. A CPA has completed his examination of the financial statements of a bus company for the year ended December 31, 19X7. Prior to 19X7 the company had been depreciating its buses over a 10-year period. During 19X7 the company determined that a more realistic estimated life for its buses was 12 years and computed the 19X7 depreciation on the basis of the revised estimate. The CPA has satisfied himself that the 12-year life is reasonable.

The company has adequately disclosed the change in estimated useful lives of its buses and the effect of the change on 19X7 income in a note to the financial statements. (AICPA adapted)

21–33. Following are the financial statements of the Young Manufacturing Corporation and the auditor's report of their examination for the year ended January 31, 19X7. The examination was conducted by John Smith, an individual practitioner who has examined the corporation's financial statements and has reported on them for many years.

Young Manufacturing Corporation
Statements of Condition
January 31, 19X7 and 19X6

	19X7	19X6
Assets		
Current assets:		
Cash	$ 43,822	$ 51,862
Accounts receivable, pledged—less allowances for doubtful accounts of $3,800 in 19X7 and $3,000 in 19X6 (see note)	65,298	46,922
Inventories, pledged—at average cost, not in excess of replacement cost	148,910	118,264
Other current assets	6,280	5,192
Total current assets	$264,310	$222,240
Fixed assets:		
Land—at cost	38,900	62,300
Buildings—at cost, less accumulated depreciation of $50,800 in 19X7 and $53,400 in 19X6	174,400	150,200
Machinery and equipment—at cost, less accumulated depreciation of $30,500 in 19X7 and $25,640 in 19X6	98,540	78,560
Total fixed assets	$311,840	$291,060
Total assets	$576,150	$513,300

	19X7	19X6
Liabilities and Stockholders' Equity		
Current liabilities:		
Accounts payable	$ 27,926	$ 48,161
Other liabilities	68,743	64,513
Current portion of long-term mortgage payable	3,600	3,600
Income taxes payable	46,840	30,866
Total current liabilities	$147,109	$147,140
Long-term liabilities:		
Mortgage payable	90,400	94,000
Total liabilities	$237,509	$241,140
Stockholders' equity:		
Capital stock, par value $100, 1,000 shares authorized, issued and outstanding	$100,000	$100,000
Retained earnings	238,641	172,160
Total stockholders' equity	$338,641	$272,160
Total liabilities and stocholders' equity	$576,150	$513,300

Young Manufacturing Corporation
Income Statements
for the Years Ended January 31, 19X7 and 19X6

	19X7	19X6
Income:		
Sales	$884,932	$682,131
Other income	3,872	2,851
Total	$888,804	$684,982
Costs and expenses:		
Cost of goods sold	$463,570	$353,842
Selling expenses	241,698	201,986
Administrative expenses	72,154	66,582
Provision for income taxes	45,876	19,940
Other expenses	12,582	13,649
Total	$835,880	$655,999
Net income	$ 52,924	$ 28,983

TO: Mr. Paul Young, President   March 31, 19X7
    Young Manufacturing Corporation

    I have examined the balance sheet of the Young Manufacturing Corporation and the related statements of income and retained earnings.

    These statements present fairly the financial position and results of operations in conformity with generally accepted principles of accounting applied on a consistent basis. My examination was made in accordance with generally accepted auditing standards, and accordingly included such tests of the accounting records and such other auditing procedures as I considered necessary in the circumstances.

                      (Signed) John Smith

Required:

List and discuss the deficiencies of the auditor's report prepared by John Smith. Your discussion should include justifications that the matters you cited are deficiencies. (Do not check the addition of the statements. Assume that the addition is correct.)   (AICPA adapted)

21–34. Upon completion of all field work on September 23, 19X5, the following short-form report was rendered by Timothy Ross to the directors of The Rancho Corporation.

To the Directors of
The Rancho Corporation:

We have examined the balance sheet and the related statement of income and retained earnings of The Rancho Corporation as of July 31, 19X5. In accordance with your instructions, a complete audit was conducted.

In many respects, this was an unusual year for The Rancho Corporation. The weakening of the economy in the early part of the year and the strike of plant employees in the summer of 19X5 led to a decline in sales and net income. After making several tests of sales records, nothing came to our attention that would indicate that sales have not been properly recorded.

In our opinion, with the explanation given above, and with the exception of some minor errors that are considered immaterial, the aforementioned financial statements present fairly the financial position of The Rancho Corporation at July 31, 19X5, and the results of its operations for the year then ended, in conformity with pronouncements of the Accounting Principles Board and the Financial Accounting Standards Board applied consistently throughout the period.

Timothy Ross, CPA
September 23, 19X5

Required:

List and explain deficiencies and omissions in the auditor's report. The type of opinion (unqualified, qualified, adverse, or disclaimer) is of no consequence and need not be discussed.   (AICPA adapted)

22

UNAUDITED
AND OTHER REPORTS

In addition to being involved with short-form reports for companies follow-ing generally accepted accounting principles, CPAs commonly deal with situations requiring other kinds of reports. These other kinds of reports are the subject of this chapter. The following topics are included:

- Specified elements, accounts, or items.
- Other comprehensive basis of accounting.
- Debt compliance letters.
- Long-form report.
- Forecasts.
- Compilation and review.
- Review of interim financial information.

The first three topics all concern audits of specific aspects of financial state-ments or audits of statements that do not purport to follow generally accepted accounting principles. The last four topics deal with financial information or statements where the CPA is involved with the client but some or all of the information has not been audited.

SPECIFIED ELEMENTS, ACCOUNTS, OR ITEMS

Frequently, auditors are asked to issue reports on particular aspects of finan-cial statements. A common example is a special report on sales of a retail store in a shopping center to be used as a basis for rental payments. Other common examples are reports on royalties, profit participation, and provision for income taxes.

There are two primary differences in the audits and reports of specified elements and those prepared as a part of ordinary audits.

- Materiality is defined in terms of the element, account, or items involved rather than in relation to the overall statements. The effect is to ordinarily require more evidence than would be needed if the item being verified were just one of many parts of the statements. For example, if the sales account is being reported separately, a smaller error would be considered material than when sales is just one account of many being reported on as a part of a regular audit.
- The first standard of reporting does not apply because the statements are not in accordance with generally accepted accounting principles.

The following illustrates a report for royalties, which is a specified account:

> We have examined the schedule of royalties applicable to engine production of the Q Division of XYZ Corporation for the year ended December 31, 19X2, under the terms of a license agreement dated May 14, 19X0, between ABC Company and XYZ Corporation. Our examination was made in accordance with generally accepted auditing standards and, accordingly, included such tests of the accounting records and such other auditing procedures as we considered necessary in the circumstances.
>
> We have been informed that, under XYZ Corporation's interpretation of the agreement referred to above, royalties were based on the number of engines produced after giving effect to a reduction for production retirements that were scrapped, but without a reduction for field returns that were scrapped, even though the field returns were replaced with new engines without charge to customers. This treatment is consistent with that followed in prior years.
>
> In our opinion, the schedule of royalties referred to above presents fairly the number of engines produced by the Q Division of XYZ Corporation during the year ended December 31, 19X2, and the amount of royalties applicable thereto under the license agreement referred to above, on the basis indicated in the preceding paragraph.

Several characteristics required of reports on specified elements are included in the report:

- The specified account is identified.
- The report states whether the examination was made in accordance with generally accepted auditing standards.
- The basis on which the specified account is presented and the agreements specifying the basis are described.
- There is reference to consistency of the basis with prior years.
- An opinion is given as to the fair presentation of the account on the basis indicated.

A common added complication arises when the scope of the audit of the specified items is limited. In such a situation the second and third standards of field work do not apply (internal control evaluation and sufficient competent evidence). Nevertheless, it is acceptable to conduct such an examination and issue a report if all parties have a clear understanding of the procedures to be performed, the report is to go only to the parties of the agreement, and regular financial statements of the entity do not accompany the report. Care must be followed in preparing the report to specify the nature of the engagement, the procedures performed, and the results found.

OTHER COMPREHENSIVE BASES OF ACCOUNTING

Auditors frequently do audits of statements other than ones prepared in accordance with generally accepted accounting principles. Generally accepted auditing standards apply to these audits, but the reporting requirements differ somewhat from those described in Chapter 21. The following are common examples of a basis other than generally accepted accounting principles:

Cash Basis. Only cash receipts and disbursements are recorded. There are no accruals.

Modified Cash Basis. The cash basis is followed except for certain items, such as recording fixed assets and depreciation.

Basis Used to Comply with the Requirements of a Regulatory Agency. Common examples include the uniform system of accounts required of railroads, utilities, and some insurance companies.

Income-Tax Basis. The same measurement rules used for filing the tax returns are often used for financial statement preparation, even though this is not in accordance with generally accepted accounting principles.

A concern in reporting on a comprehensive basis is to make sure the statements clearly indicate that they are on a basis other than generally accepted accounting principles. If the statements imply that generally accepted accounting principles are followed, the reporting requirements of Chapter 21 apply. Consequently, terms such as balance sheet and statement of operations must be avoided by the client. Instead, a title such as "statement of assets and liabilities arising from cash transactions" would be appropriate for a cash basis statement.

The reporting requirements for these comprehensive bases of accounting include the following:

A Scope Paragraph. This paragraph is equivalent to a report on statements that follow generally accepted accounting principles. The statements are identified and the paragraph states that the examination was made in accordance with generally accepted auditing standards.

A Middle Paragraph Stating the Accounting Basis.   The paragraph should include a description of the accounting basis or a reference to a footnote explaining the basis and a statement that generally accepted accounting principles are not followed.

An Opinion Paragraph.   This paragraph is also equivalent to a report on statements that follow generally accepted accounting principles. The auditor must express an opinion on the statement's fair presentation on the basis of accounting followed. There must also be a reference to consistency.

The following is a common example of a report prepared on the entities' income-tax basis:

> We have examined the statement of assets, liabilities, and capital—income tax basis of ABC Partnership as of December 31, 19X2, and the related statements of revenue and expenses—income tax basis and of changes in partners' capital accounts—income tax basis for the year then ended. Our examination was made in accordance with generally accepted auditing standards and, accordingly, included such tests of the accounting records and such other auditing procedures as we considered necessary in the circumstances.
>
> As described in Note X, the Partnership's policy is to prepare its financial statements on the accounting basis used for income tax purposes; consequently, certain revenue and the related assets are recognized when received rather than when earned, and certain expenses are recognized when paid rather than when the obligation is incurred. Accordingly, the accompanying financial statements are not intended to present financial position and results of operations in conformity with generally accepted accounting principles.
>
> In our opinion, the financial statements referred to above present fairly the assets, liabilities, and capital of ABC Partnership as of December 31, 19X2, and its revenue and expenses and changes in its partners' capital accounts for the year then ended, on the basis of accounting described in Note X, which basis has been applied in a manner consistent with that of the preceding year.

DEBT COMPLIANCE LETTERS

Clients occasionally enter into contracts that require them to provide the lender with a report from a CPA as to the existence or nonexistence of some condition. For example, borrowing arrangements may require maintenance of a certain dollar amount of working capital at specified points in time and an independent accountant's report as to the compliance with the requirement.

Three aspects of debt compliance letters are important for the auditor to observe:

- The report should be limited to compliance matters the auditor is qualified to evaluate. Some of the provisions of a debt compliance letter the auditor is normally in a position to verify are whether principal and interest payments were made when they were due, whether the proper limitations were maintained on dividends, working capital, and debt ratios, and whether the accounting records were adequate for conducting an ordinary audit. On the other hand, determining whether the client has properly restricted its business activity to the requirements of an agreement or evaluating if it has title to pledged property are legal questions that the CPA is not qualified to answer. Furthermore, the Code of Professional Ethics prohibits the auditor from practicing as an attorney in these circumstances.

- The auditor should provide a debt compliance letter only for a client where an audit was done of its overall financial statements. A debt compliance letter on a matter such as the existence of a current ratio of 2.5 or better would be difficult to do without having conducted a complete audit.
- *Negative assurance* should be provided in the auditor's report as a *separate report* or as a *separate paragraph* in the report on financial statements. Instead of a positive statement of compliance, negative assurance states that "nothing came to the auditor's attention that would lead the auditor to believe there was noncompliance."

Following is an example of a report including a limitation of the scope of the compliance review and negative assurance.

We have examined the consolidated financial statements of the XYZ Company and subsidiaries as of December 31, 19X2, and have reported thereon in a separate audit report dated March 17, 19X3.

In connection therewith, we have reviewed Section 1 and 8 of the Note Agreement between the ABC Insurance Company and XYZ Company dated October 15, 19X0. In making such examination, as independent accountants, we obtained no knowledge of the existence of any condition or event that in our opinion constituted a default under the terms of Section 1 or 8 of the aforementioned note agreement. The purpose and scope of our examination was such that it would not necessarily disclose all defaults, if any, which may exist with respect to the Note Agreement with ABC Insurance Company.

LONG-FORM REPORTS

A typical long-form report includes the financial statements associated with a short-form report plus additional information likely to be useful to management and other statement users. The profession has intentionally refrained from defining or restricting the appropriate supplementary information included so as to enable auditors to individualize each long-form report to meet the needs of statement users. But several standard types of information are commonly included in the additional information section of a long-form report:

- Detailed comparative statements supporting the control totals on the primary financial statements for accounts such as cost of goods sold, operating expenses, and miscellaneous assets.
- Statistical data for past years in the form of ratios and trends.
- A schedule of insurance coverage.
- Specific comments on the changes that have taken place in the statements.

It is important that the auditor clearly distinguish between his responsibility for the primary financial statements and his responsibility for additional information. Usually, the auditor has not performed a sufficiently detailed audit to justify an opinion on the additional information, but in some instances he may be confident that the information is fairly presented. The profession's reporting standards require the auditor to make a clear statement about the degree of responsibility he is taking for the additional information.

When long-form reports are issued to some users and only the basic financial statements on the same audit are issued to others, the auditor should exercise special care to assure himself that the long-form report does not include information that might support a claim that there is inadequate disclosure in the short-form report. For example, if the supplementary comments contain exceptions, reservations, or material disclosures not appearing in the short-form report, there is a basis for potential legal claims against the auditor for inadequate disclosure from those users who have received only the short-form report.

FORECASTS

Rule 201 of the AICPA Code of Professional Ethics specifically prohibits opinions on the accuracy of forecasts of any kind, but forecasts may be prepared and presented to the client. Whenever the CPA assists in preparing forecasts, the underlying assumptions should be specifically stated and a disclaimer of opinion such as the following must be attached to the forecast:

> Since projections are based on assumptions about circumstances and events that have not yet taken place, they are subject to the variations that may arise as future operations actually occur. Accordingly, we cannot give assurance that the projected results will actually be attained.

COMPILATION AND REVIEW

Background

Many CPAs are involved with clients that do not have audits. Some likely reasons a company may believe an audit is unnecessary is the active involvement of the owners in the business, lack of significant debt, and absence of regulations requiring the company to have an audit. Common examples are smaller companies and professional organizations such as partnerships of physicians and attorneys.

These same organizations often want to engage a CPA to provide tax services and assist in the preparation of accurate financial information without an audit. Providing these services is a significant part of the practice of many smaller CPA firms. When a CPA provides any services involving financial statements, certain requirements exist.

Accounting services provided to clients without audit where financial statements resulted have traditionally been called unaudited financial statements. Reporting and minimum standards of performance for unaudited financial statements were under the authority of the Auditing Standards Board until 1979. During the late 1960s and 1970s considerable controversy surrounded unaudited financial statements, for two reasons. First, there was a significant number of lawsuits against CPAs for unaudited financial statements. Second, there was considerable disagreement as to the "unaudited procedures" needed when a CPA firm was involved with unaudited financial statements.

In 1977 the AICPA established a new committee to develop standards for unaudited financial statements. The committee, which has authority equivalent to the Auditing Standards Board, is called the Accounting and Review Services Committee.

Effective for periods ending after June 30, 1979, the traditional unaudited financial statement requirements are no longer in effect. From that date unaudited financial statements are called *compilation of financial statements* or *review of financial statements*. The new requirements are determined by the document, "Statement on Standards for Accounting Review Services No. 1" (SSARS No. 1), which concerns the *Compilation and Review of Financial Statements*.

The statement does not pertain to such things as preparing a working trial balance for a client, assisting in adjusting the client's accounts, preparing tax returns, or providing various manual or automated bookkeeping or data-processing services *unless the output is financial statements.*

Levels of Assurance.   SSARS No. 1 recognizes three different levels of assurance for different types of engagements. A level of assurance as used in SSARS No. 1 refers to how much credence the user should be willing to place on the statement. This corresponds to the discussion of levels of assurance in Chapter 4.

As we have already studied, even an audit does not guarantee the accuracy of statements and does not therefore provide 100 percent assurance. Compilations provide little if any assurance and reviews provide limited assurance. These are indicated in Figure 22-1.

FIGURE 22-1

Levels of Assurance for Compilation, Review, and Audits

Report on	*Report on*	*Audit*
Compilation	*Review*	*Report-Opinion*

0   100%

Little or	Limited	High
no assurance	assurance	assurance

Levels of Assurance

Compilation

Compilation services are intended to enable a CPA firm to compete with bookkeeping firms. It is common for smaller CPA firms to own a small computer and provide bookkeeping services, monthly or quarterly financial statements, and tax services for smaller clients.

Compilation is defined in SSARS No. 1 as presenting in the form of financial statements information that is the representation of management without undertaking to express any assurance on the statements.

One of three forms of compilation can be provided to clients:

Compilation with Full Disclosure. Compilation of this type requires disclosures in accordance with generally accepted accounting principles, the same as for audited financial statements. The following report is appropriate in such circumstances:

> The accompanying balance sheet of XYZ Company as of December 31, 19X2, and the related statements of income, retained earnings, and changes in financial position for the year then ended have been compiled by us.
>
> A compilation is limited to presenting in the form of financial statements information that is the representation of management. We have not audited or reviewed the accompanying financial statements and, accordingly, do not express an opinion or any other form of assurance on them.

Compilation That Omits Substantially All Disclosures. This type of compilation is acceptable if *the report indicates the lack of disclosures* and the absence of disclosures is not, to the CPA's knowledge, undertaken with the intent to mislead users. This type of statement is expected to be used primarily for management's purposes only, but affects all statements prepared to be shown to external users.

The following report is appropriate where the accountant compiles statements where disclosures are not included.

> The accompanying balance sheet of XYZ Company as of December 31, 19X2, and the related statements of income and retained earnings for the year then ended have been compiled by us.
>
> A compilation is limited to presenting in the form of financial statements information that is the representation of management. We have not audited or reviewed the accompanying financial statements and, accordingly, do not express an opinion or any other form of assurance on them.
>
> Management has elected to omit substantially all of the disclosures and the statement of changes in financial position required by generally accepted accounting principles. If the omitted disclosures were included in the financial statements, they might influence the user's conclusions about the company's financial position, results of operations, and changes in financial position. Accordingly, these financial statements are not designed for those who are not informed about such matters.

Compilation without Independence. A CPA firm can issue a compilation report even if it is not independent with respect to the client, as defined by the Code of Ethics. The following should be included when the accountant lacks independence as a separate last paragraph in either of the two previously discussed reports: "We are not independent with respect to XYZ Company."

For any of the three reports, the following two things are also required:

- The date of the accountant's report is the date of completion of the compilation.
- Each page of the financial statements compiled by the accountant should state "See Accountant's Compilation Report."

Requirements for Compilation. Compilation does not mean that the accountant has no responsibilities. The accountant is always responsible for exercising due care in performing all duties. Several things are required by SSARS No. 1 for compilation. The preparer of the statements must:

- Know something about the accounting principles and practices of the client's industry. He can study AICPA industry guides or other sources to obtain industry knowledge.
- Know the client, the nature of its business transactions, accounting records and employees, and the basis, form, and content of the financial statements.
- Make inquiries to determine if the client's information is satisfactory.
- Read the compiled financial statements and be alert for any obvious omissions or errors in arithmetic and generally accepted accounting principles.
- Disclose in the report any omissions or departures from generally accepted accounting principles of which the accountant is aware. This requirement does not apply to all disclosures for compilation that omits substantially all disclosures.

The accountant does not have to make other inquiries or perform other procedures to verify information supplied by the entity. But if he becomes aware that the statements are not fairly presented, the accountant should obtain additional information. If the client refuses to provide the information, the accountant should withdraw from the compilation engagement.

Review

Review is defined by SSARS No. 1 as:

> Performing inquiry and analytical procedures that provide the accountant with a reasonable basis for expressing limited assurance that should be made to the statements in order for them to be in conformity with generally accepted accounting principles or, if applicable, with another comprehensive basis of accounting.

Form of Report. There is only one form of review—review of financial statements with full disclosure. The following report is appropriate when the accountant has made a proper review of the accounting records and the financial statements and has concluded that they appear reasonable.

We have reviewed the accompanying balance sheet of XYZ Company as of December 31, 19X2, and the related statements of income, retained earnings, and changes in financial position for the year then ended, in accordance with standards established by the American Institute of Certified Public Accountants. All information included in these financial statements is the representation of the management of XYZ Company.

A review consists principally of inquiries of company personnel and analytical procedures applied to financial data. It is substantially less in scope than an examination in accordance with generally accepted auditing standards, the objective of which is the expression of an opinion regarding the financial statements taken as a whole. Accordingly, we do not express such an opinion.

Based on our review, we are not aware of any material modifications that should be made to the accompanying financial statements in order for them to be in conformity with generally accepted accounting principles.

For the review report, the following are also required:

- The date of the accountant's report is the date of completion of the accountant's inquiry and analytical procedures.
- Each page of the financial statements reviewed by the accountant states "See Accountant's Review Report."

Procedures Suggested for Reviews. Reviews imply a level of assurance somewhere between compilation and an audit. A review does not include a study and evaluation of internal control, tests of accounting records, or independent confirmation or physical examination. The emphasis in reviews is in four broad categories:

- Obtain knowledge of the accounting principles and practices of the client's industry. The level of knowledge for reviews should be somewhat higher than that for compilation.
- Obtain knowledge of the client. The information should be about the nature of the client's business transactions, its accounting records and employees, and the basis, form, and content of the financial statements. The level of knowledge should be higher than for compilation.
- Make inquiries of management. The objective of these inquiries is to determine whether the financial statements are fairly presented assuming that management does not intend to deceive the accountant. Inquiry is the most important of the review procedures. The following are illustrative inquiries:
    1. Inquire as to the company's procedures for recording, classifying, and summarizing transactions, and disclosing information in the statements.
    2. Inquire into actions taken at meetings of stockholders and board of directors.
    3. Inquire of persons having responsibility for financial and accounting matters concerning whether the financial statements have been prepared in conformity with generally accepted accounting principles consistently applied.

4. Perform analytical review procedures. The analytical procedures are meant to identify relationships and individual items that appear to be unusual. The appropriate analytical procedures are no different from the ones already studied in Chapter 6 and in those chapters dealing with direct tests of balances.

Failure to Follow GAAP. The only time that material departure for failure to follow generally accepted accounting principles is acceptable is for compilation without complete disclosure. In all other cases a modification of the report is needed if statements do not follow generally accepted accounting principles, including adequate disclosure. The accountant is not required to determine the *effect of a departure* if management has not done so, but that fact must also be disclosed in the report. For example, the use of replacement cost rather than FIFO for inventory valuation would have to be disclosed, but the effect of the departure on net earnings does not require disclosure.

The disclosure must be made in a separate paragraph in the report for either compilation or review. The following are examples of suggested wording:

(SEPARATE PARAGRAPH)

As disclosed in Note X to the financial statements, generally accepted accounting principles require that land be stated at cost. Management has informed us that the company has stated its land at appraised value and that, if generally accepted accounting principles had been followed, the land account and stockholders' equity would have been decreased by $500,000.

or

(SEPARATE PARAGRAPH)

A statement of changes in financial position for the year ended December 31, 19X2, has not been presented. Generally accepted accounting principles require that such a statement be presented when financial statements purport to present financial position and results of operations.

REVIEW OF INTERIM FINANCIAL INFORMATION

Reviews of interim financial information are done to help management of publicly held companies meet their reporting responsibilities to regulatory agencies. The Securities and Exchange Commission requires quarterly financial information as a part of quarterly 10-Q reports. The statements do not have to be audited and the CPA firm's name need not be associated with the quarterly statements. But, *the SEC requires a footnote in the annual audited financial statements*, disclosing quarterly sales, gross profit, income, and earnings per share for the past two years. Typically, the footnote in the annual statements is labeled *unaudited.*

At a minimum the CPA firm must perform review procedures, as defined by SAS 24, of the footnote in the annual statements disclosing the quarterly information. There is no requirement that the review procedures be done on a quarterly basis. The review can be done as a part of the annual audit.

The disadvantage of doing the review procedures at the time of the annual audit is that potential discrepancies may arise between the quarterly information in the annual statement's footnote and the quarterly 10-Qs. Management therefore frequently asks auditors to do quarterly reviews of financial statements to maximize the likelihood of consistency between the 10-Q reports and the footnotes to the annual statements.

SAS 24 Reviews versus SSARS No. 1

The requirements of reviews of interim information for publicly held companies are set forth by SAS 24. Even though they are issued by the Auditing Standards Board, the requirements are more closely related to unaudited review requirements of SSARS No. 1 than to audit requirements.

Like reviews under SSARS No. 1, an SAS 24 review does not provide a basis for expressing an audit opinion. Internal control is not evaluated, and ordinarily there are no tests of the accounting records or independent confirmations or physical examinations.

The objective of an SAS 24 review is to provide the accountant with a basis for *reporting to the board of directors on significant accounting matters that he finds through inquiry and analytical review.* Two differences between the two types of reports are who the report goes to and the time periods covered by the reports. SSARS No. 1 reviews can be addressed to management, stockholders, or any other group and they can be for monthly, quarterly, or annual statements. SAS 24 reviews are addressed to the board of directors and are for quarterly statements.

Review Procedures. The following are some of the procedures recommended in SAS 24 as a part of interim reviews:

- Inquire about the accounting system for recording, classifying, and summarizing information.
- Inquire about any changes in the accounting system.
- Perform analytical review procedures.
- Read the interim financial information to see whether it conforms to generally accepted accounting principles.
- Inquire of officers of changes in accounting principles, changes in business activities, and events subsequent to the balance sheet date.
- Obtain a letter of representation.

These procedures are similar to those for SSARS No. 1 reviews except for two aspects. SAS 24 reviews require a letter of representations from management and there is a responsibility to inquire about changes in the accounting system.

Another less obvious difference is in the level of knowledge the accountant has about the client's accounting system and business. Because an annual audit is done for companies that have limited reviews, the accountant is already knowledgeable about such things as the client's accounting and reporting practices, the system of internal accounting control, and specialized industry problems. Finally, the accountant will also have a good idea whether the quarterly statements were accurate after the annual audit is complete. This information will be useful in determining the review procedures in subsequent years. The combination of these factors probably implies that an SAS 24 review results in a higher level of assurance than SSARS No. 1 reviews.

Reporting

The standard report for interim financial statements where there has been a review is recommended in SAS 24:

> We have made a review of the consolidated balance sheet of Rainer Company and consolidated subsidiaries as of September 30, 19X1, and the related statements of earnings, retained earnings, and financial position for the three-month and nine-month periods then ended, in accordance with standards established by the American Institute of Certified Public Accountants.
>
> A review of interim financial information consists principally of obtaining an understanding of the system for the preparation of interim financial information, applying analytical review procedures to financial data, and making inquiries of persons responsible for financial and accounting matters. It is substantially less in scope than an examination in accordance with generally accepted auditing standards, the objective of which is the expression of an opinion regarding the financial statements taken as a whole. Accordingly, we do not express such an opinion.
>
> Based on our review, we are not aware of any material modifications that should be made to the accompanying financial statements for them to be in conformity with generally accepted accounting principles.

The following comments refer to this report:

- The standards referred to in the first paragraph are those established in SAS 24.
- The middle paragraph defines in more specific terms than does a standard unqualified opinion the nature of the work performed.
- The middle paragraph states that an audit was not done and an opinion is not expressed.
- The final paragraph includes a *negative* assurance that "we are not aware of any material modifications. . . ."

The auditor must include the previously described review report with the quarterly statements if the client represents to the SEC that a review has been performed. Otherwise, no one else besides the board of directors need receive the report.

When interim information is included as a footnote in the annual audited statements and labeled unaudited, it is unnecessary for the auditor to include a separate report. If the auditor has done the review procedures and if the information is fairly presented, the standard audit report is sufficient.

REVIEW QUESTIONS

22–1. Give two examples of special reports that a CPA may be asked to issue on specified elements, accounts, or items. Explain why these reports would be requested.

22–2. How does materiality differ in the audits and reports of specified elements as compared to those prepared as a part of an ordinary audit? Why?

22–3. List five characteristics required of reports on specific elements.

22–4. State the reporting requirements for statements prepared on a basis other than generally accepted accounting principles.

22–5. The Absco Corporation has requested that Herb Germany, CPA, provide a report to the Northern State Bank as to the existence or nonexistence of certain loan conditions. The conditions that are required to be reported on are the working capital ratio, dividends paid on preferred stock, aging of accounts receivable, and the competency of management. This is Herb's first experience with Absco. Should Herb accept this engagement? Substantiate your answer.

22–6. What is a "negative assurance?" Why is it used in a debt compliance letter?

22–7. Explain how a long-form report differs from a short-form report.

22–8. Under what circumstances can an auditor be involved with forecast financial statements? What two specific items should be included in the auditor's report on forecast financial statements?

22–9. Distinguish between compilation and review of financial statements. What is the level of assurance for each?

22–10. List and distinguish the three forms of compilation that a CPA can provide to clients.

22–11. List five things that are required of an auditor by SSARS No. 1 for compilation.

22–12. What steps should an auditor take if during a compilation engagement he becomes aware that the financial statements are misleading?

22–13. What procedures should the auditor use to obtain the information necessary to give the level of assurance required of reviews of financial statements?

22–14. What should the auditor do if during a review of financial statements he discovers that generally accepted accounting principles are not being followed?

22–15. What are the differences between the two types of reports covered by SSARS No. 1 and SAS 24?

22–16. Explain why a review of interim financial statements may provide a higher level of assurance than do SSARS No. 1 reviews.

22–17. Explain the difference between a disclaimer of opinion and a disclaimer for unaudited financial statements. Under what circumstances might the auditor have a difficult time deciding which one is appropriate?

DISCUSSION QUESTIONS AND PROBLEMS

22–18. Select the best response for the following.

The CPA who regularly examines Viola Corporation's financial statements has been asked to prepare projected income statements for the next five years. If the statements are to be based upon the corporation's operating assumptions and are for internal use only, the CPA should

(1) reject the engagement because the statements are to be based upon assumptions.

(2) reject the engagement because the statements are for internal use.

(3) accept the engagement provided full disclosure is made of the assumptions used and the extent of the CPA's responsibility.

(4) accept the engagement provided Viola certifies in writing that its statements are for internal use only.

22–19. The following multiple-choice questions concern the compilation and review of financial statements. Each has one best correct response.

a. A CPA has been engaged to perform review sessions for a client. Identify which of the following is a correct statement.

(1) The CPA must perform the basic audit procedures necessary to determine that the statements are in conformity with generally accepted accounting principles.

(2) The financial statements are primarily representations of the CPA.

(3) The CPA may prepare the statements from the books but may not assist in adjusting and closing the books.

(4) The CPA is performing an accounting service rather than an audit of the financial statements. (AICPA adapted)

b. It is acceptable for a CPA to be associated with financial statements when he is not independent with respect to the client and still issue a substantially unmodified report for which of the following:

(1) Audits of companies following generally accepted accounting principles.

(2) Audits of companies on a compliance basis of accounting other than generally accepted accounting principles.

(3) Compilation of financial statements following generally accepted accounting principles.

(4) Review of financial statements following generally accepted accounting principles.

    c. A CPA is performing review services for a small, closely held manufacturing company. As a part of the follow-up of a significant decrease in the gross margin for the current year, the CPA discovers that there are no supporting documents for $40,000 of disbursements. The chief financial officer assures her that the disbursements are proper. What should the CPA do?

      (1) Include the unsupported disbursements without further work in the statements on the grounds that she is not doing an audit.

      (2) Modify the review opinion or withdraw from the engagement unless the unsupported disbursements are satisfactorily explained.

      (3) Exclude the unsupported disbursements from the statements.

      (4) Obtain a written representation from the chief financial officer that the disbursements are proper and should be included in the current financial statements.

    d. Which of the following best describes the responsibility of the CPA when he performs compilation services for a company?

      (1) He must understand the client's business and accounting methods, and read the financial statements for reasonableness.

      (2) He has only to satisfy himself that the financial statements were prepared in conformity with generally accepted accounting principles.

      (3) He should make a proper study and evaluation of the existing internal control as a basis for reliance thereon.

      (4) He is relieved of any responsibility to third parties.

    e. Frank, CPA, performed compilation services omitting substantially all disclosures for a client and issued the appropriate report. Three months after the statements were issued, the client informed Frank that the statements had been given to a bank for a secured loan. Which of the following is appropriate under these circumstances?

      (1) Frank must revise the statements to include appropriate footnotes and attach a revised disclaimer of opinion.

      (2) The client may give the statements to the banker as long as Frank's disclaimer of opinion accompanies the statements.

      (3) The client should retype the statements on plain paper and send them to the banker without Frank's report.

      (4) The client may let the banker review the statements and take notes, but should not give the banker a copy of the statements.

22–20. The following multiple-choice questions concern special reports issued by auditors. Select the best response.

    a. Which of the generally accepted auditing standards of reporting would *not* normally apply to special reports such as cash basis statements?

      (1) First standard.

      (2) Second standard.

      (3) Third standard.

      (4) Fourth standard.

    b. An auditor is reporting on cash basis financial statements. These statements are best referred to in his opinion by which one of the following descriptions?

    (1) Cash receipts and disbursements and the assets and liabilities arising from cash transactions.

    (2) Financial position and results of operations arising from cash transactions.

    (3) Balance sheet and income statement resulting from cash transactions.

    (4) Cash balance sheet and the source and application of funds.

c. An auditor's report would be designated as a special report when it is issued in connection with which of the following?

    (1) Financial statements for an interim period which are subjected to a limited review.

    (2) Financial statements prepared in accordance with a comprehensive basis of accounting other than generally accepted accounting principles.

    (3) Financial statements that purport to be in accordance with generally accepted accounting principles but do **not** include a presentation of the statement of changes in financial position.

    (4) Financial statements that are unaudited and are prepared from a client's accounting records.   (AICPA adapted)

22–21. The following multiple-choice questions concern long-form auditors' reports. Select the best response.

a. Which of the following best describes the difference between a long-form auditor's report and the standard short-form report?

    (1) The long-form report may contain a more detailed description of the scope of the auditor's examination.

    (2) The long-form report's use permits the auditor to explain exceptions or reservations in a way that does not require an opinion qualification.

    (3) The auditor may make factual representations with a degree of certainty that would not be appropriate in a short-form report.

    (4) The long-form report's use is limited to special situations such as cash-basis statements, modified accrual basis statements, or not-for-profit organization statements.

b. Ansman, CPA, has been requested by a client, Rainco Corp., to prepare a long-form report for this year's audit engagement. Which of the following is the *best* reason for Rainco's requesting a long-form report?

    (1) To provide for a piecemeal opinion because certain items are not in accordance with generally accepted accounting principles.

    (2) To provide Rainco's creditors a greater degree of assurance as to the financial soundness of the company.

    (3) To provide Rainco's management with information to supplement and analyze the basic financial statements.

    (4) To provide the documentation required by the Securities and Exchange Commission in anticipation of a public offering of Rainco's stock.

c. Ansman, CPA, has been requested by a client, Rainco Corp., to prepare a long-form report for this year's audit engagement. In issuing a long-form report, Ansman must be certain to

    (1) issue a standard short-form report on the same engagement.

    (2) include a description of the scope of the examination in more detail than the description in the usual short-form report.

    (3) state the source of any statistical data and that such data have not been subjected to the same auditing procedures as the basic financial statements.

    (4) maintain a clear-cut distinction between the management's representations and the auditor's representations.

d. A long-form report generally includes the basic financial statements but would not include

    (1) exceptions or reservations to the standard (short-form) report.

    (2) details of items in basic financial statements.

    (3) statistical data.

    (4) explanatory comments.

e. Which of the following best describes the difference between a long-form auditor's report and the standard short-form report?

    (1) The long-term report may contain a more detailed description of the scope of the auditor's examination.

    (2) The long-form report's use permits the auditor to explain exceptions or reservations in a way that does not require an opinion qualification.

    (3) The auditor may make factual representations with a degree of certainty that would not be appropriate in a short-form report.

    (4) The long-form report's use is limited to special situations, such as cash basis statements, modified accrual basis statements, or not-for-profit organization statements. (AICPA adapted)

22–22. Select the best response for each of the following multiple-choice questions.

a. A CPA's report accompanying a cash forecast or other type of projection should

    (1) not be issued in any form because it would be in violation of the AICPA *Code of Professional Ethics.*

    (2) disclaim any opinion as to the forecast's achievability.

    (3) be prepared only if the client is a not-for-profit organization.

    (4) be a qualified short-form audit report if the business concern is operated for a profit.

b. An auditor should not render a report on

    (1) the achievability of forecasts.

    (2) client internal control.

    (3) management performance.

    (4) quarterly financial information.

c. A footnote to a company's financial statements includes an indication that the company's auditor performed certain procedures regarding the company's unaudited replacement cost information. The footnote does **not** indicate whether the auditor expresses an opinion on the replacement cost information. Which of the following is appropriate in these circumstances?

    (1) The auditor's report on the audited financial statements should be expanded to include a disclaimer of opinion on the replacement cost information.

    (2) A separate report on the unaudited replacement cost information should be rendered and should include a disclaimer of opinion on the replacement cost information.

    (3) The auditor's report on the audited financial statements should be qualified because of the replacement cost information.

    (4) A separate report on the replacement cost information should be rendered and should indicate whether the information is fairly presented in relation to the basic financial statements.

  d. A report based on a limited review of interim financial statements would include all of the following elements except

    (1) a statement that an examination was performed in accordance with generally accepted auditing standards.

    (2) a description of the procedures performed or a reference to the procedures described in an engagement letter.

    (3) a statement that a limited review would not necessarily disclose all matters of significance.

    (4) an identification of the interim financial information reviewed.

  e. If, as a result of a limited review of interim financial information, a CPA concludes that such information does not conform with generally accepted accounting principles, the CPA should

    (1) insist that the management conform the information with generally accepted accounting principles and if this is not done, resign from the engagement.

    (2) adjust the financial information so that it conforms with generally accepted accounting principles.

    (3) prepare a qualified report that makes reference to the lack of conformity with generally accepted accounting principles.

    (4) advise the board of directors of the respects in which the information does not conform with generally accepted accounting principles.

  f. A CPA has a financial interest in a corporation and is associated with that corporation's unaudited financial statements. Under such circumstances the CPA's report should state that the CPA is *not* independent with respect to the corporation and should include

    (1) a statement that the financial statements were unaudited and accordingly the CPA does *not* express an opinion on the financial statements.

    (2) a description of the reasons for the CPA's lack of independence and a disclaimer of opinion on the financial statements.

    (3) a statement that each page of the financial statements is "unaudited" and a qualified opinion on the financial statements.

    (4) a description of the reasons for the CPA's lack of independence and a qualified opinion on the financial statements.   (AICPA adapted)

22–23. Carl Monson, the owner of Major Products Manufacturing Company, a small successful long-time audit client of your firm, has requested you to work with them in preparing three-year forecasted information for the year ended 12-31-8X and the two subsequent years. Carl informs you he intends to use the forecasts, together with the audited financial statements, to seek additional financing to expand their businesses. Carl has little experience in formal forecast preparation and counts on you to assist him in any way possible. He wants the most supportive opinion possible from your firm to add to the credibility of the forecasts. He informs you he is willing to do anything necessary to help you prepare the forecast.

First, he wants projections of sales and revenues and earnings from the existing business, which he believes could continue to be financed from existing capital.

Second, he intends to buy a company in a closely related business that is currently operating unsuccessfully. Carl states that he wants to sell some of the operating assets of the business and replace them with others. He believes that the company can then be made highly successful. He has made an offer on the new business, subject to obtaining of proper financing. He also informs you he has an offer on the assets he intends to sell.

Required:

a. Explain circumstances under which it would be and would not be acceptable to accept the engagement.
b. Why is it important that Monson understand the nature of your reporting requirements before the engagement proceeds?
c. What information will Monson have to provide you before you can complete the forecasted statements? Be as specific as possible.
d. Discuss, in as specific terms as possible, the nature of the report you will issue with the forecasts, assuming that you are able to properly complete them.

22–24. As a part of the audit of Ren Gold Manufacturing Company, management requests both a short-form and a long-form report. Management stated intent is to use the short-form report for bankers, other creditors, and the two owners who are not involved in management. The long-form report is to be used by management. Management requests the inclusion of specific information but asks that no audit work be done beyond what is needed for the short-form report. The following is requested:

a. A schedule of insurance in force.
b. The auditor's feelings about the adequacy of the insurance coverage.
c. A five-year summary of the most important company ratios. The appropriate ratios are to be determined at the auditor's discretion.
d. A schedule of notes payable accompanied by interest rates, collateral, and a payment schedule.
e. An aged trial balance of accounts receivable and an evaluation of the adequacy of the allowance for uncollectible accounts.
f. A summary of fixed asset additions and investment credit taken on each class of additions.
g. Material weaknesses in internal control and recommendations to improve the accounting system.

Required:

a. What is the difference between a long-form and a short-form report?
b. What are the purposes of long-form reports?

c. For the previously listed items (1 through 7), state which could appropriately be included in a long-form report. Give reasons for your answer.

d. Identify three other items that may appropriately be included in a long-form report.

e. Assume that an unqualified opinion is appropriate for the short-form report, that no testing was done beyond that required for the short-form report, and that only information appropriate for a long-form report is included in the supplemental information. Write the appropriate audit report.

22–25. You have conducted an audit for the California Society of Licensed Appraisers, who are on a cash basis of accounting. Following is a statement of cash receipts and disbursements.

California Society of Licensed Appraisors Statement
of Cash Receipts and Disbursements and Marketable Securities
Year Ended August 31, 198X

Receipts, net of directly related disbursements		
Dues	$258,211	
Less dues remitted to national headquarters	47,637	
Net dues received		$210,574
Contributions		66,431
Sale of U.S. bonds		12,600
Interest received		635
Net receipts from special projects		1,900
		$292,140
Disbursements, net of directly related receipts		
Salaries, including employees' share of payroll taxes		$127,430
Employer's share of payroll taxes		8,261
Convention expense		91,416
Directors' meals and drinks		1,147
Quarterly publication	$ 87,428	
Less advertising receipts	37,500	
Net publication disbursements		49,928
Other		617
		$278,799
Increase in cash during year		$ 13,340
Cash balance, beginning		26,450
Cash balance, ending		$ 39,790
Marketable securities, at end of year, U.S. bonds, at cost		
(market $27,200)		$ 26,800

Required:

a. Assuming that an audit has been performed and the results are fairly stated, prepare the auditor's report.

b. Assuming that review services have been performed, modify the financial statements as needed and prepare the accountant's report.

22–26. You have been requested by the management of J. L. Lockwood Co. to issue a debt compliance letter as a part of the audit of Taylor Fruit Farms, Inc. J. L. Lockwood Co. is a supplier of irrigation equipment. Much of the equipment, including that to supplied Taylor, is sold on a secured contract basis. Taylor Fruit Farms is an audit client of yours, but Lockwood is not. In addition to the present equipment, Lockwood informs you they are evaluating whether they should sell another $500,000 of equipment to Taylor Fruit Farms.

You have been requested to send them a debt compliance letter concerning the following matters:

a. The current ratio has exceeded 2.0 in each quarter of the unaudited statements prepared by management and the annual audited statements.
b. Total owner's equity is more than $800,000.
c. The company has not violated any of the legal requirements of California fruit-growing regulations.
d. Management is competent and has made reasonable business decisions in the past three years.
e. Management owns an option to buy additional fruitland adjacent to their present property.

Required:

a. Define the purpose of a debt compliance letter.
b. Why is it necessary to conduct an audit of a company before it is acceptable to issue a debt compliance letter?
c. For which of the five requested items is it acceptable for a CPA firm to issue a debt compliance letter? Give reasons for your answer.

22–27. Independent certified public accountants customarily issue two types of auditor's reports in connection with an examination of financial statements: a so-called short-form auditor's report in connection with financial statements intended for publication, and a so-called long-form auditor's report for the purposes of management and other parties.

Required:

a. Outline in *general terms* the kinds of materials that are commonly included in a long-form report other than those commonly included in a short-form report.
b. Does the auditor assume the same degree of responsibility for other data in the long-form report that he assumes for individual items in the customary basic financial statements (balance sheet and statements of income, retained income, and capital)? State the reasons for your answer.

(AICPA adapted)

22–28. Evaluate the following comments about compiled financial statements: "When a CPA associates his name with compiled financial statements, his only responsibility is to the client and that is limited to the proper summarization and presentation on the financial statements of information provided by the client. The opinion clearly states that the auditor has not conducted an audit and does not express an opinion on this fair presentation. If a user of the statement relies on compiled financial statements, he does so at his own risk and should never be able to hold the CPA responsible for inadequate performance. The user should interpret the financial statements as if they had been prepared by management."

22–29. You are doing review services and the related tax work for Regency Tools, Inc., a tool and die company with $2,000,000 in sales. Inventory is recorded at $125,000. Prior-year unaudited statements, presented by the company without assistance from a CPA firm, disclose that the inventory is based on "historical cost estimated by management." You determine four facts.

1. The company has been growing steadily for the past five years.
2. The unit cost of the typical material used by Regency Tools has increased dramatically for several years.
3. The inventory cost has been approximately $125,000 for five years.
4. Management intends to use a value of $125,000 again for 19X1.

When you discuss with management the need to get a physical count and an accurate inventory, the response is negative. Management is concerned about the property-tax impact and the income-tax effect of a more realistic inventory. They have never been audited and have followed this practice for years. You are convinced, based upon inquiry and ratio analysis, that a conservative evaluation would be $500,000 at historical cost.

Required:

a. What are the generally accepted accounting principle requirements for valuation and disclosure of inventory for unaudited financial statements?
b. Identify the potential legal and professional problems that you face in this situation.
c. What procedures would you normally follow for review services when the inventory is a material amount? Be as specific as possible.
d. How should you resolve the problem in this situation? Identify alternatives and evaluate the costs and benefits of each alternative.

22–30. SSARS No. 1 provides illustrative review procedures for accountants to use as a guideline for conducting reviews. The introduction to the illustrative inquiries states:

> The inquiries to be made in a review of financial statements are a matter of the accountant's judgment. In determining his inquiries, an accountant may consider (a) the nature and materiality of the items, (b) the likelihood of misstatement, (c) knowledge obtained during current and previous engagements, (d) the stated qualifications of the entity's accounting personnel, (e) the extent to which a particular item is affected by management's judgment, and (f) inadequacies in the entity's underlying financial data. The following list of inquiries is for illustrative purposes only. The inquiries do not necessarily apply to every engagement, nor are they meant to be all-inclusive.

The inquiry procedures included in SSARS No. 1 for the sales and collection cycle are:

Revenue

a. Are revenues from the sale of major products and services recognized in the appropriate period?

Receivables

a. Has an adequate allowance been made for doubtful accounts?
b. Have receivables considered uncollectible been written off?
c. If appropriate, has interest been reflected?
d. Has a proper cutoff of sales transactions been made?
e. Are there any receivables from employees and related parties?
f. Are any receivables pledged, discounted, or factored?
g. Have receivables been properly classified between current and non-current?

Required:

a. What other information about accounts receivable and revenue, besides item a for revenue and items a through g for receivables, would the accountant have to obtain?
b. Compare the illustrative procedures for review services and those commonly performed for audits. What are the major differences?
c. Who should the accountant make the inquiries of in a small closely held company?
d. Under what circumstances would procedures beyond those illustrated likely be performed? (Be specific.)
e. Compare the level of achieved assurance for review services and audits. Is the achieved level much higher for audits, somewhat higher, or approximately the same? Give reasons for your answer.

22-31. Bengston, CPA, is conducting the ordinary audit of Pollution Control Devices, Inc. In addition, a supplemental negative assurance report is required to a major mortgage holder. The supplemental report concerns indenture agreements to keep the client from defaulting on the mortgage. Total assets are $14 million and the mortgage is for $4 million. The major provisions of the indenture are:

a. The current ratio must be maintained above 2.3 to 1.
b. The debt/equity ratio must be maintained below 3.0.
c. Net earnings after taxes must exceed dividends paid by at least $1,000,000.

Required:

a. Write the appropriate supplemental report if all three indenture agreements had been satisfied.
b. How would the supplemental report change if net earnings after taxes was $1,010,000 and dividends paid was $60,000?
c. Assume the same situation as in part b and also assume that the client refuses to modify its financial statements or disclose the violation of the indenture agreement on the grounds that the amount is immaterial. What is the nature of the appropriate auditor's report?

d. What is the nature of the appropriate supplemental report if all the indenture agreements have been satisfied but there is a lawsuit against the company which has resulted in a subject to opinion due to contingencies for the regular audit report?

22-32. Quality CPA Review is the franchisor of a national CPA review course for candidates taking the CPA exam. Quality CPA Review is responsible for providing all materials, including cassettes and video material, doing all national and local advertising, and giving assistance in effectively organizing and operating local franchises. The fee to the participant is $500 for the full course if all parts of the exam are taken. There are lower rates for candidates taking selected parts of the exam. Quality CPA Review gets 50 percent of the total fee.

The materials for the review course are purchased by Quality CPA Review from Ronny Johnson, CPA, a highly qualified writer of CPA review materials. Quality CPA Review receives one copy of those materials from Ronnie and reproduces them for candidates. Quality CPA Review must pay Ronnie a $60 royalty for each full set of materials used and 12 percent of the participant fee for partial candidates. The contract between Johnson and Quality CPA Review requires an audited report to be provided by Quality CPA Review on royalties due to Johnson. Recorded gross fees for the 198X review course are $1,500,000.

Even before the audit is started, there is a dispute between Quality CPA Review and Johnson. Quality CPA Review does not intend to pay royalties on certain materials. Johnson disagrees with that conclusion but the contract does not specify anything about it. The following are the disputed sales on which Quality CPA Review refuses to pay royalties:

a. Materials sent to instructors for promotion	$31,000
b. Uncollected fees due to bad debts	6,000
c. Candidates who paid no fee because they performed administrative duties during the course	16,000
d. Refunds to customers who were dissatisfied with the course	22,000
Total	$75,000

Required:

a. Assume that you are engaged to do the ordinary audit of Quality CPA Review and the special audit of royalties for Johnson. What additional audit testing beyond the normal tests of royalties is required because of the special audit?

b. Assuming that the financial statements of Quality CPA Review are found to be fairly stated, except for the unresolved dispute between Johnson and Quality CPA Review, write the appropriate audit report.

c. Write the special report for total royalties to Johnson, assuming that the information as stated in the case is all correct and the dispute is not resolved.

22-33. Jones, CPA, has completed the audit of Sarack Lumber Supply Co. and has issued a standard unqualified report. In addition to a report on the overall financial statements, the company also needs a special audited report on three specific accounts: sales, net fixed assets, and inventory valued at FIFO. The report is to be issued to Sarack's lessor, who bases annual rentals on these three accounts. Jones was not aware of the need for the special report until after the overall audit was completed.

Required:

a. Explain why Jones is unlikely to be able to issue the special audit report without additional audit tests.

b. What additional tests are likely to be needed before the special report can be issued?

c. Assuming that Jones is able to satisfy all the requirements needed to issue the special report, write the report. Make any necessary assumptions.

INDEX

A

Accounting, separation of duties within, 217–20
Accounting principles, 56, 710
Accounting services, 11
Accounts payable, 514–23
Accounts payable subsidiary ledger, 505
Accounts receivable, 300–301, 369–401
Accounts receivable subsidiary ledgers, 283
Acquisition and payment cycle, 500–572
  functions in, 505–7
  integrated tests of, 593
  tests of transactions, 507–14
  verification of selected accounts in, 539–72
Acquisitions, tests for, 508–11
Adjusting entries in working papers, 124–25
Adverse opinions (report), 21
Advertising, 61–62
Aged trial balance, 372–76
Allocations, tests of, 562–64

Alpha risk, 415–16
American Institute of Certified Public Accountants (AICPA)
  auditing pronouncements of, 13–18
  Auditing Standards Board, 13, 29
  code of ethics, 39–76
  Commission on Auditors' Responsibilities, 28–29
  Division of CPA Firms, 29–30
  functions, 13–14
  Generally Accepted Auditing Standards, 14–15, 17–18
  peer review in, 30
  Private Companies Practice Section, 29
  publications of, 14
  Public Oversight Board, 30
  SEC Practice Section, 29–30
Analysis schedules, 126–27
Analytical tests, 257
  as audit evidence, 120
  for CPA audit, 110
  of financial balances, 371–78
  function of, 187–96

U

Ultramares Corporation v. *Touche,* 83
Uncollectible accounts, 300
Uncollectible accounts authorization
    forms, 283
Uncollectible accounts receivable, 285
Unit cost records, 580–81
United States v. *Simon,* 93–95
Unqualified opinions, 702–4
    departures from, 20, 704–16

V

Vacation pay, accrued, 486
Validity tests, 300, 508
Variables sampling, 402–38
Vendors' invoices, 504, 520
Vendors' statements, 505, 521
Verification, 3, 545–49
Voucher registers, 504
Vouchers, 504

Vouching, *see* Documentation

W

W–2 Form, 475
Wage and price controls, 184
Walk-through test, 232
Weaknesses
    defined, 236
    required communication of material,
        237
    six-step method to deal with, 237
Working paper review, 683–85
Working papers, 120–29
    review of previous, 181
Working trial balance, 124

Y

Year-end cash, audit of, 639–44